1,001

DELICIOUS
RECIPES
FOR PEOPLE WITH
DIABETES

EDITED BY

SUE SPITLER
LINDA EUGENE R.D., C.D.E., WITH
LINDA YOAKAM R.D., M.S.

**SURREY
BOOKS**

CHICAGO

Second edition

Surrey Books is an imprint of Agate Publishing, Inc.
Art direction, book design, and typesetting: Joan Sommers Design, Chicago
Nutritional analyses: Linda R. Yoakam, R.D., M.S.
Printed in Canada

Library of Congress Cataloging-in-Publication data:
    1,001 delicious recipes for people with diabetes / edited by Sue Spitler and Linda Euguene with Linda Yoakam, R.D., M.S.—2nd ed.
    p. cm.
    ISBN-13: 978-1-57284-086-7 (pbk.)
    ISBN-10: 1-57284-086-2 (pbk.)
    1. Diabetes—Diet therapy—Recipes. I. Spitler, Sue. II. Eugene, Linda. III. Yoakam, Linda R. IV. Title: One thousand one delicious recipes for people with diabetes. V. Title: One thousand and one delicious recipes for people with diabetes.

RC662.A16 2007
641.5'6314—dc22

                                                                        2006102117

10 9 8 7 6 5 4 3 2

Agate and Surrey books are available in bulk at discount prices. For more information, go to agatepublishing.com.

CONTENTS

ACKNOWLEDGMENTS

Heartfelt thanks go to Perrin Davis and editorial assistant Caroline Olson for their enthusiasm, patience, and amazing computer, editing, and indexing skills. Also a thank you goes to my associate Pat Molden, a tireless proofreader on this project. Linda Yoakam's nutritional calculations and counsel were greatly appreciated. And kudos to publisher Doug Seibold for his support in making this important new edition possible!

FOREWORD

A T THE UNIVERSITY OF CHICAGO, we are doing extensive research on diabetes mellitus, with the goal of finding a cure for a disease that affects about 16 million people in the U.S. That is nearly a 40 percent increase in the past decade. Almost all of these patients (90 percent) have a form of the disease called Type 2 that is often tied to obesity and resistance to insulin (whereas in Type 1, the cause is the absence of insulin).

Until we find a cure for Type 2 diabetes, we will continue to counsel our patients that they can reduce symptoms dramatically by losing weight, which they can do by adopting an easy-to-follow meal plan that is low in saturated fats and simple carbohydrates* and by becoming moderately active. That's it: diet and exercise.

And now we have proof. In 2002, the Diabetes Prevention Program results were announced. This multi-center National Institutes of Health-sponsored trial was ended a year early because the result showed beyond a doubt that lifestyle modification—moderate weight loss and exercise—can actually prevent the onset of diabetes mellitus in at-risk adults, young and old, from a wide variety of ethnic groups.

Diabetes is a complex disease involving insulin production and blood sugar levels, but to the person who has it, it has a great deal to do with food—what is all right to eat and what is not. Working with your doctor or diabetes educator, you will learn how your body processes food, and the two of you will work as a team to develop a diet and exercise program suited to your needs so you can stay in control.

---

* See *Report of the Dietary Guidelines Committee on the Dietary Guidelines for Americans, 2000* (U. S. Dept. of Agriculture, Agricultural Research Service, Washington, D.C., 2000).

Here is where *1,001 Delicious Recipes for People with Diabetes* can be very helpful. The editors—culinary expert Sue Spitler, registered dietitian Linda Yoakam, and certified diabetes educator Linda Eugene, with whom I worked at the University of Chicago—have chosen recipes that are easy to make, good to eat, and fit easily into a diabetic meal plan. They have tested and selected hundreds and hundreds of good tasting, healthy recipes, including desserts, that will meet your needs as well as those of a non-diabetic spouse and active children.

Until we find a cure for diabetes, there is hope, and plenty of good eating.

— Louis H. Philipson, MD, PhD
Section of Endocrinology, Department of Medicine
University of Chicago, Chicago, Illinois

INTRODUCTION

CONTRARY TO POPULAR MYTH, there is no "diabetes diet," according to the Mayo Clinic newsletter. In fact, medical and nutritional professionals have transformed the diabetes diets of years past into contemporary meal planning that includes just about any food you like as long as nutrition, balance, and moderation are given careful attention. No longer are foods labeled as "good," "bad," or "forbidden," and a diagnosis of diabetes today does not mean a life sentence of bland, boring, and unappetizing meals.

1,001 Delicious Recipes for People with Diabetes is the perfect cookbook for you, with its array of delicious recipes from appetizers to desserts. Each recipe is accompanied with the nutritional data you need to stay within your meal-planning goals.

Even though people with diabetes do not have to give up favorite dishes and the treats they like, including sweets and snacks, it is important to plan meals carefully, both for nutritional quality and quantity. It is even more important for those with diabetes than for the general population to choose foods that are low fat, limited in carbohydrates, low salt, high fiber, and rich in vitamins and minerals. Limiting calorie intake, of course, is essential, because even though you can eat moderate portions of just about anything, weight gain can be a serious threat to controlling diabetes.

BALANCING YOUR DIET

For people with diabetes, controlling carbohydrate intake can be of major importance since carbohydrates dramatically spike glucose levels. Carbohydrates are found in foods with natural or added sugar such as breads, crackers, cereals, potatoes, fresh fruits and juices, milk, refined sugar, jams, and jellies. Many other foods contain carbohydrates in combination with proteins and fats; some examples are cakes, ice cream, doughnuts, pizza, potato chips, and soups.

A healthy and nutritious meal plan should include a variety of foods from all 6 food groups in the new My Pyramid nutrition plan from the U.S. Department of Agriculture: bread or starch, fruit, milk, vegetables, meat, and fat. Despite their glucose-raising effects, carbohydrates, which are found in all of the food groups except meat and fat, are not discouraged in the diets of people with diabetes. Although specific nutrition goals that reflect blood glucose targets and other medical aims should be discussed with your doctor or registered dietitian, the following guidelines for daily allowances of carbohydrate, protein, and fat can form the basis of a balanced meal plan.

Calories per Day	50% Carbohydrates	20% Protein	30% Fat
1500	188 gm	75 gm	50 gm
1800	225 gm	90 gm	60 gm
2000	250 gm	100 gm	66 gm
2200	275 gm	110 gm	73 gm

Knowing your carbohydrate, protein, and fat limits will help you choose recipes that meet these goals, and you can continue to eat most of your favorite foods. If you look at the nutrition data we have supplied with every recipe in *1,001 Delicious Recipes for People with Diabetes*, you will be surprised at what a wide variety of recipes you can enjoy while staying within your target nutrient range. Note, too, that meal-plan consistency is very important. To keep blood sugar at a consistent level, try to eat the same quantity of food and the same proportions of carbohydrate, protein, and fat each day.

THE "EXCHANGE" SYSTEM VS. COUNTING CARBOS

A variety of meal-planning strategies can be used to control your diabetes. Keep in mind that there is no single meal plan that is appropriate for everyone. Individualizing your meal plan is the key to successful control of blood glucose levels. Also remember that according to the American Diabetes Association and the American Dietetic Association, meal planning for diabetes is really little more than establishing a healthy way of eating. People with diabetes today eat the same foods as people without diabetes.

Two popular meal-planning strategies are in wide use among people with diabetes. One is the "exchange" system, wherein foods are divided into six basic food groups according to the nutrients they contain. Foods in the same group with similar nutrients can be exchanged, or substituted for one another, to meet the daily-allowed quantity of that particular food group. A registered dietitian can best assist people in deciding how many exchanges, or servings, of which foods should be allowed at each meal. However, until meeting with a registered dietitian, the following meal plan can serve as a guide. To use the exchange list method, simply compare the number of exchanges recommended in the chart below with the number contained in each recipe.

Breakfast	A.M. Snack	Lunch	P.M. Snack	Dinner	Bedtime
2 bread	1 bread	3 meat	1 fruit	3 bread	2 bread
1 fruit		2 bread		3 meat	1 meat
1 milk		1 fruit		2 vegetable	
1 meat		1 vegetable		1 fat	
1 fat		1 milk			
		1 fat			

Another method of meal planning for people with diabetes is to count the number of carbohydrate grams eaten. This number is given for each recipe in the book to help a person using this method stay within daily prescribed limits and still enjoy a wide variety of foods. Of course, for a balanced diet, one needs more than just carbohydrates, so we have included suggested quantities of other nutrients in this hypothetical meal plan.

Breakfast	A.M. Snack	Lunch	P.M. Snack	Dinner	Bedtime
60 gm carbo.	15 gm carbo.	45 gm carbo.	15 gm carbo.	55 gm carbo.	15 gm carbo.
1 oz. meat		2 oz. meat		3 oz. meat	
1 tsp. fat		½ cup veg.		1 cup veg.	
		1 tsp. fat		1 tsp. fat	

NUTRITIONAL INFORMATION

These delicious and nutritious recipes for people with diabetes were created using the highest quality low-fat ingredients available. Low-fat meats such as skinless chicken breasts, beef eye of round, and pork tenderloin are used instead of higher-fat cuts. Many nutritious fat-free and reduced-fat dairy products are called for such as fat-free milk, fat-free half-and-half, low-fat cheeses, and low-fat sour cream. Egg whites and liquid egg substitute are often used in place of their higher-cholesterol equivalents. Fat-free, reduced-sodium broths are used. A variety of herbs, spices, and seasonings enhance flavors while keeping sodium content down.

Recipes throughout the 15 chapters reflect the highest nutritional standards and follow the guidelines recommended by the United States

Department of Agriculture for the general population as well as for people with diabetes:

Aim for Fitness:
    Aim for a healthy weight.
    Be physically active each day.

Build a Healthy Base:
    Let the My Pyramid nutrition plan guide your food choices.
    Choose a variety of grains daily, especially whole grains.
    Choose a variety of fruits and vegetables daily.
    Keep food safe to eat.

Choose Sensibly:
    Choose a diet that is low in saturated fat and cholesterol and
        moderate in total fat.
    Choose beverages and foods to moderate your intake of sugars.
    Choose and prepare foods with less salt.
    If you drink alcohol, do so in moderation.

In accordance with American Heart Association guidelines, very few recipes in this book exceed 30 percent calories from fat, and almost all adhere to the following nutritional criteria:

Type of Recipe	Maximum Amounts per Serving		
	Calories	Cholesterol (mg)	Sodium (mg)
Soups, First Courses	200	50	600
Main-Dish Soups, Entrées, Salads, Sandwiches	400	100	800
Main-Dish Meals (including pasta, rice, grains)	500	125	800
Main-Dish Eggs, Cheese	400	450	800
Side-Dish Salads, Pasta, Grains, Vegetables	200	50	600
Sauces, Condiments	200	25	600
Breads	200	50	600
Desserts	350	90	600

The specific nutritional data and diabetic exchanges provided for recipes are not infallible. Nutritional analyses are derived using prestigious nutritional software programs, but they are meant as guidelines only. Figures are based on laboratory values of ingredients, so results may vary slightly depending on the brand of ingredient used and the method of preparation. Other factors that can affect the accuracy of nutritional data include variability in sizes, weights, and measures of fruits, vegetables, and other foods. There is also a possible 20 percent error factor in the nutritional labeling of prepared foods.

Exchange values are averages. If the carbohydrate content of a day's intake is estimated using the exchanges shown, there may be a significant difference between the estimate and the actual values consumed.

Ingredients noted as "optional," "to taste," or "as garnish" are not included in the nutritional data. When alternate choices or amounts of ingredients are given, the ingredient or amount listed first has been used for analysis. Similarly, data is based on the first, or fewer, number of servings where a range is shown.

Other factors that can affect the accuracy of nutritional data include variability in sizes, weights, and measures of fruits, vegetables, and other foods. There is also a possible 20 percent error factor in the nutritional labeling of prepared foods.

NEW IN THIS EDITION

The Vegetarian Entree chapter is new to this edition. Recipes are coded as follows so you can quickly tell if they are vegan, lacto-ovo vegetarian, lacto-vegetarian, or ovo-vegetarian.

V (vegan)—Recipes contain only plant-based food, with no dairy products or eggs.

LO (lacto-ovo vegetarian)—Recipes contain dairy products and eggs.

L (lacto vegetarian)—Recipes contain dairy products, but no eggs.

O (ovo vegetarian)—Recipes contain eggs, but no dairy products.

Also new to this edition is the designation of over 550 recipes that can be prepared in 45 minutes or less! We know busy lifestyles allow precious little cooking time for many of us, so recipes are designed to get you in and out of the kitchen as quickly and effortlessly as possible. For easy identification, these recipes will have this symbol **45**. If the recipe requires baking, refrigeration, or freezing in addition to the actual preparation time, the symbols ⬤, for baking, and ❄, for refrigeration/ freezing, will also appear.

To prepare the designated recipes in 45 minutes, you'll want to assemble ingredients and equipment and read through the recipe to plan your preparation strategy. For example, you'll want to begin cooking pasta first and prepare other ingredients while the pasta is cooking. Or, start pizza dough and proceed with the recipe while the dough is rising. To aid in strategy planning, many recipes will include a 45 Minute Preparation Tip, which is located at the end of the recipe.

ENJOY YOURSELF

Even though you have diabetes, you can see how, with a little knowledge and effort, you can eat delicious food, enjoy meals with friends, and take steps to keep your glucose under control. Now you have our "1,001" best wishes for happy and healthy dining, to which we say, bon appétit!

—Sue Spitler, Linda Eugene, R.D., C.D.E., and
Linda R. Yoakam, M.S, RD, LD

INGREDIENT INFORMATION

THE INGREDIENTS in this book are readily available in supermarkets and health food stores. Following is helpful information on some of the ingredients we've used, with explanations of those you may not be very familiar with.

Artificial Sweeteners — Recipes have been tested with Equal® for Recipes and Splenda, as indicated in the recipes. If substituting another brand, follow directions on the package. Some experimentation may be necessary as various sweeteners perform differently, especially in baking.

Bead Molasses — Used mostly in Asian recipes, bead molasses is very dark and thick with an intense flavor. Like other molasses products, it is refined from the concentrated juice of sun-ripened sugar cane. It is readily available in the Asian sections of supermarkets; other molasses products can be substituted.

Butter — Butter is suggested as an alternate for margarine for its lower trans-fat content and improved flavor, except in Vegan recipes in the Vegetarian Entree chapter.

Cream Cheese — The block-type of reduced-fat and fat-free cream cheese is usually specified in the recipes in this book; the tub type is much softer in texture and does not always work the same in recipes. If substituting fat-free cream cheese in your favorite recipes for dips, use the block type and add any liquid ingredients gradually, as the cream cheese thins much more quickly than full-fat or reduced-fat cream cheese. Fat-free cream cheese can be used to make cake glaze but not frosting, as it thins with the addition of powdered sugar and cannot be thickened.

Cooking Sprays — Vegetable and olive oil cooking sprays are used to greatly reduce the amounts of oil or fat needed in recipes. When a recipe calls for "sautéing in a lightly greased skillet," spray the skillet lightly with cooking spray or wipe the pan with a lightly oiled paper towel.

Fillo Pastry — These paper-thin pastry sheets are found in the freezer section of supermarkets or in Mediterranean groceries; store them in the freezer. Before using, thaw the entire package of fillo overnight in the refrigerator, or for several hours at room temperature. After removing fillo from the package, always cover the unused sheets with a damp cloth to keep them soft, as they become dry and brittle very quickly. Unused fillo can be rolled or folded, sealed in plastic wrap, and refrozen.

Herbs and Spices — In most recipes, dried or ground forms are called for, but where no such designation is made, fresh or whole items are intended. Fresh herbs may be substituted by using two to three times as much as indicated for the dried or ground version.

Margarine — Use an all-vegetable product. Use regular rather than diet margarine, and be sure to shop for one of the new trans fat-free varieties.

Olive Oil — As we have kept the use of oil to a minimum, we prefer using virgin olive oil to take advantage of its more intense flavor. Canola oil can be substituted, if desired.

Pasta, Grains, and Beans — When a dried and uncooked ingredient is called for, the ingredient will read: "8 ounces spaghetti, cooked." When a cooked ingredient is called for, the ingredient will read: "12 ounces cooked spaghetti." When dry pasta or rice noodles are called for, they are always egg-free and can be used in vegan dishes. Fresh pasta or refrigerated pasta such as ravioli, tortellini, wontons, and some flat noodles do contain eggs and can be used in lacto-ovo and ovo vegetarian recipes.

Roasted Garlic — See Roasted Garlic and Three-Cheese Spread, Step 1 (p. 10) for directions on roasting garlic. We suggest roasting several heads at a time to keep extra on hand for your favorite recipes. Roasted garlic can be refrigerated, wrapped in plastic wrap, for up to 2 weeks. Purchased chopped roasted garlic can be used for convenience, but the flavor is less robust.

Sesame Oil — We have specified Asian sesame oil in recipes, as this dark oil has an intense sesame flavor; it can be purchased in ethnic sections of supermarkets. There is also a light-colored sesame oil that can be found in the vegetable oil section of the supermarket; it can be substituted, but the sesame flavor is extremely subtle. Store at room temperature.

Shortening — The manufacturing process of shortening usually creates trans fats; shop carefully for one of the new trans fat-free brands.

Tahini Paste — This flavorful paste is made with ground toasted sesame seeds and is used in Greek hummus and other Mediterranean dishes.

See our recipes for Black Bean Hummus and Sun-Dried Tomato Hummus (pp. 574, 2). Store tahini in the refrigerator.

Tamari Soy Sauce — This highly flavored soy sauce is naturally brewed and is made without sugar. It is available in regular or low-sodium brands in Asian sections of supermarkets. Other soy sauce products can be substituted. Store in the refrigerator.

Tempeh — A nutritious cultured product made from cooked soybeans, tempeh has its origins in Indonesia. The soybean mixture is pressed into cakes, sometimes being combined with grains and/or other ingredients, and has a texture that is firmer, or "meatier," than tofu. Like tofu, it readily absorbs flavors from soy sauce or marinades. Because of its firm texture, tempeh is great for grilling. Purchased in the produce section of supermarkets, tempeh can be stored in the refrigerator or freezer.

Textured Vegetable Protein (TVP) — This versatile product made from soy flour can be added as a meat substitute to recipes such as chili, Meatless Sloppy Joes (see p. 265), or Hash Brown Loaf with Eggs (see p. 265). Textured vegetable protein is dry and comes in either granular or chunk form; it must be reconstituted with water, vegetable broth, or liquid before using in recipes like loaves and patties. Like tofu and tempeh, textured vegetable protein takes on the flavor of whatever it is cooked with. Purchase in supermarkets or health food stores and store in an airtight package at room temperature.

Tofu, or Bean Curd — Originating in China, tofu is made by coagulating soy milk, which is the liquid remaining from cooked ground soy beans. Pressed into cakes, tofu is made in a variety of textures—soft or silken, firm, and extra-firm. It is also available seasoned and in baked and smoked forms. Soft tofu has a very fine, delicate texture and is perfect for dips, sauces, soups, and dressings; the firmer textures are better for cooking, stir-frying, broiling, and baking. As tofu is extremely mild in flavor, it is generally marinated in soy sauce or other marinades before cooking. Tofu is extremely nutritious, but it is not low in fat, ranging between 40 and 45 percent calories from fat. We call for lower fat light tofu in most recipes. Purchase tofu in the produce section of supermarkets; it is most commonly packaged in liquid in plastic tubs. Once opened, tofu has a several-day limited storage time in the refrigerator; it should be stored covered in water, and the water should be changed daily. Tofu can also be frozen; it changes to an amber color in the freezer and when thawed is firmer in texture and somewhat crumbly.

Vegetarian Protein Products — A number of interesting and flavorful vegetarian protein products are available in the freezer section of the supermarket. Many are seasoned to resemble the flavor of beef sausage, and chicken. They come in various forms, such as patties, links, strips, and crumbles. Usually soy-based, these products may also contain grains, vegetables, nuts, and cheese.

Check your local grocery periodically for new food items. Literally hundreds of fresh, frozen, canned, and packaged new food products find their way to grocery shelves each year. An occasional visit to a gourmet store may garner specialty items to keep in your pantry or freezer for interesting menu additions.

ONE

Appetizers

SUN-DRIED TOMATO HUMMUS

45

❄

Sun-dried tomatoes and herbs embellish this Mediterranean favorite.

8 servings (about ¼ cup each)

1 can (15 ounces) chick peas, rinsed, drained

⅓ cup fat-free yogurt

2–3 tablespoons tahini (sesame seed paste)

3 cloves garlic

4 sun-dried tomato halves (not in oil), finely chopped

1 teaspoon each: dried oregano and mint leaves

2–3 teaspoons lemon juice

Salt and white pepper, to taste

Dippers: pita breads, cut into wedges, or Pita Chips (see p. 574)

Per Serving:
Calories: 73
% of calories from fat: 21
Fat (gm): 1.7
Saturated fat (gm): 0.2
Cholesterol (mg): 0.2
Sodium (mg): 256
Protein (gm): 3.6
Carbohydrate (gm): 11.4

Exchanges:
Milk: 0.0
Vegetable: 0.0
Fruit: 0.0
Bread: 1.0
Meat: 0.0
Fat: 0.0

1. Process chick peas, yogurt, tahini, and garlic in food processor until smooth. Stir in sun-dried tomatoes and herbs; season to taste with lemon juice, salt, and white pepper. Refrigerate 1 to 2 hours for flavors to blend. Serve with dippers (not included in nutritional data).

VARIATION

Parthenon Platter — Make hummus as above and spoon into a 6-inch flattened mound on serving platter. Combine 4 chopped canned artichoke hearts, ½ cup halved grape tomatoes, 6 sliced Greek olives, ⅓ cup crumbled fat-free feta cheese, 2 tablespoons olive oil, and ¾ teaspoon dried Italian seasoning; toss and spoon over hummus. Garnish plate with pepperoncini and serve with Pita Chips (see p. 574).

ROASTED GARLIC AND HERB CANNELLINI DIP

45

Another good-for-you dip that tastes terrific! Italian cannellini beans are white kidney beans that are similar in flavor and appearance to navy or Great Northern beans.

6 servings (about ¼ cup each)

1 can (15 ounces) cannellini or Great Northern beans, rinsed, drained

1 teaspoon minced roasted garlic

1 tablespoon each: olive oil, prepared horseradish

2 tablespoons minced chives

½ teaspoon each: dried oregano and basil leaves

2–3 drops hot pepper sauce

2–3 teaspoons lemon juice

Salt and white pepper, to taste

Dippers: Pita Chips (see p. 574) and assorted vegetables

Per Serving:
Calories: 75
% of calories from fat: 25
Fat (gm): 2.8
Saturated fat (gm): 0.3
Cholesterol (mg): 0
Sodium (mg): 167
Protein (gm): 5.3
Carbohydrate (gm): 13.1

Exchanges:
Milk: 0.0
Vegetable: 0.0
Fruit: 0.0
Bread: 1.0
Meat: 0.0
Fat: 0.5

1. Process beans, garlic, olive oil, and horseradish in food processor until smooth. Mix in chives, herbs, and hot pepper sauce. Season to taste with lemon juice, salt, and white pepper. Refrigerate 1 to 2 hours for flavors to blend. Serve with dippers (not included in nutritional data).

CURRY DIP

45

Raw sweet potato slices and broccoli florets are particularly good with this dip.

12 servings (about 2 tablespoons each)

1½ cups fat-free mayonnaise

½ cup fat-free sour cream

¼ cup thinly sliced green onions

1½–2 teaspoons each: prepared horseradish, curry powder

2–3 teaspoons sugar

2–4 teaspoons lemon juice

Salt and white pepper, to taste

Dippers: assorted vegetable relishes, Pita Chips (see p. 574)

Per Serving:
Calories: 34
% of calories from fat: 1
Fat (gm): 0
Saturated fat (gm): 0
Cholesterol (mg): 0
Sodium (mg): 393
Protein (gm): 0.7
Carbohydrate (gm): 8

Exchanges:
Milk: 0.0
Vegetable: 0.0
Fruit: 0.0
Bread: 0.5
Meat: 0.0
Fat: 0.0

1. Mix mayonnaise, sour cream, green onions, horseradish, curry powder, and sugar. Season to taste with lemon juice, salt, and white pepper. Refrigerate several hours for flavors to blend. Serve with dippers (not included in nutritional data).

BLACK BEAN DIP WITH BAKED TORTILLA CHIPS

45

Nutritious black beans are a great source of folate.

12 servings (about 2 tablespoons each)

½ cup thinly sliced green onions

1–2 cloves garlic, minced

1 can (15 ounces) black beans, rinsed, drained

¾ cup (3 ounces) shredded reduced-fat Cheddar cheese

¼ teaspoon salt

⅓ cup vegetable broth, or water

1–2 tablespoons finely chopped cilantro

Baked Tortilla Chips (recipe follows)

Per Serving:
Calories: 48
% of calories from fat: 21
Fat (gm): 3.8
Saturated fat (gm): 0.5
Cholesterol (mg): 3.8
Sodium (mg): 254
Protein (gm): 4.5
Carbohydrate (gm): 7

Exchanges:
Milk: 0.0
Vegetable: 0.0
Fruit: 0.0
Bread: 0.5
Meat: 0.0
Fat: 0.5

1. Sauté onions and garlic in lightly greased skillet until tender, about 3 minutes.

2. Process black beans, cheese, and salt in food processor or blender until almost smooth, adding enough broth to make desired dipping consistency. Mix in onion mixture and cilantro. Serve with Baked Tortilla Chips.

Baked Tortilla Chips

6 flour or corn tortillas, each cut into 8 wedges
Vegetable cooking spray
Salt, to taste

1. Arrange tortilla strips on cookie sheet; spray lightly with cooking spray and toss. Bake at 375 degrees until browned, about 10 minutes, stirring occasionally.

PINTO BEAN AND AVOCADO DIP

45

Avocado and tomato brighten this well-flavored bean dip. Increase the amount of jalapeño chili if you dare!

12 servings (about 2 tablespoons each)

1 can (15 ounces) pinto beans, rinsed, drained
¾ cup finely chopped onion
2 cloves garlic, minced
½ jalapeño chili, minced
3 tablespoons finely chopped cilantro
1 large tomato, chopped
½ medium avocado, chopped
Salt and pepper, to taste
Baked tortilla chips

Per Serving:
Calories: 50
% of calories from fat: 25
Fat (gm): 1.4
Saturated fat (gm): 0.2
Cholesterol (mg): 0.0
Sodium (mg): 114
Protein (gm): 2.1
Carbohydrate (gm): 7.7

Exchanges:
Milk: 0.0
Vegetable: 0.0
Fruit: 0.0
Bread: 0.5
Meat: 0.0
Fat: 0.5

1. Process beans in food processor or blender until smooth; add onion, garlic, jalapeño chili, and cilantro and process until blended. Mix in tomato and avocado; season to taste with salt and pepper. Refrigerate 1 to 2 hours for flavors to blend. Serve with tortilla chips (not included in nutritional data).

CHILI CON QUESO

45 *Our health-conscious version of this popular dip is made with reduced-fat pasteurized processed cheese for creamy texture and fat-free Cheddar cheese for accented flavor.*

12 servings (about 2 tablespoons each)

5 medium anaheim or 2 medium poblano chilies, seeds and veins discarded, cut into halves
⅓ cup each: chopped onion, tomato
½ teaspoon dried oregano leaves
2 cups (8 ounces) shredded reduced-fat pasteurized processed cheese
1 cup (4 ounces) shredded fat-free Cheddar cheese
2–4 tablespoons fat-free milk
Baked tortilla chips

Per Serving:
Calories: 72
% of calories from fat: 26
Fat (gm): 2.8
Saturated fat (gm): 1.8
Cholesterol (mg): 9.1
Sodium (mg): 412
Protein (gm): 7.4
Carbohydrate (gm): 5.7

Exchanges:
Milk: 0.0
Vegetable: 0.0
Fruit: 0.0;
Bread: 0.5
Meat: 1.0
Fat: 0.0

1. Place chilies, skin sides up, on baking pan. Broil 6 inches from heat source until chilies are browned and soft, 5 to 8 minutes. Cool and cut into strips.

2. Sauté onion, tomato, and oregano in lightly greased skillet until onion is tender, about 5 minutes. Add cheeses and chili strips; cook over low heat until cheeses are melted, stirring in milk for desired consistency. Serve warm with tortilla chips (not included in nutritional data).

SOMBRERO DIP

Use Florida avocados for the Guacamole, as they're lower in fat than the California variety.

6 servings

¼ cup each: chopped poblano chili, onion
½ cup (¼ recipe) cooked, crumbled Chorizo (see p. 140)
4–5 leaves romaine lettuce
1 can (15 ounces) refried beans
½ cup each: prepared medium or hot salsa, chopped romaine lettuce, tomato

Guacamole (recipe follows)
¼ cup (1 ounce) shredded fat-free Cheddar cheese
½ cup fat-free sour cream
1 green onion, thinly sliced
Baked tortilla chips

Per Serving:
Calories: 175
% of calories from fat: 16
Fat (gm): 3.2
Saturated fat (gm): 0.7
Cholesterol (mg): 23.7
Sodium (mg): 214
Protein (gm): 13.3
Carbohydrate (gm): 25

Exchanges:
Milk: 0.0
Vegetable: 2.0
Fruit: 0.0
Bread: 1.0
Meat: 1.0
Fat: 0.0

1. Sauté poblano chili and onion until tender in lightly greased skillet, 3 to 5 minutes; stir in Chorizo.

2. Line a dinner-size serving plate with lettuce; cover with refried beans to within 2 inches of edge of lettuce. Spoon salsa over beans, leaving edge of bean layer showing. Spoon Chorizo mixture over salsa; sprinkle with chopped lettuce and tomato, leaving edge of Chorizo showing. Spoon Guacamole over lettuce and tomato and sprinkle with Cheddar cheese. Spoon sour cream in large dollop on top; sprinkle with green onion. Serve with tortilla chips (not included in nutritional data).

Guacamole
Makes about ⅔ cup

1 medium avocado
½ small onion, finely chopped
1–2 tablespoons finely chopped jalapeño chili, cilantro
Salt and white pepper, to taste

1. Coarsely mash avocado in small bowl; mix in onion, jalapeño chili, and cilantro. Season to taste with salt and pepper.

QUESO FUNDIDO

The flavorful Chorizo recipe can be used to inspire many of your Mexican dishes. Any extra can be frozen for later use.

8 servings

¼ cup chopped red bell pepper

¾ cup (3 ounces) shredded fat-free Cheddar cheese

½ cup (2 ounces) cubed reduced-fat pasteurized processed cheese

¼–⅓ cup fat-free milk

8 corn tortillas, warm

½ cup (¼ recipe) cooked, crumbled Chorizo (see p. 140)

2 tablespoons each: finely chopped green onion, finely chopped cilantro

Per Serving:
Calories: 112
% of calories from fat: 15
Fat (gm): 1.9
Saturated fat (gm): 0.7
Cholesterol (mg): 12.8
Sodium (mg): 274
Protein (gm): 8.7
Carbohydrate (gm): 15.2

Exchanges:
Milk: 0.0
Vegetable: 0.0
Fruit: 0.0
Bread: 1.0
Meat: 1.0
Fat: 0.0

1. Sauté red bell pepper until tender in lightly greased skillet, 2 to 3 minutes. Add cheeses; cook over low heat until melted, stirring in milk for desired consistency. Spoon about 2 tablespoons cheese mixture in the center of each tortilla. Sprinkle with Chorizo, green onion, and cilantro, and roll up.

EGGPLANT CAVIAR

Middle Eastern flavors will tempt you to second helpings!

6 servings (about 2 tablespoons each)

1 large eggplant (1½ pounds)

½ cup chopped tomato

¼ cup finely chopped onion

3 cloves garlic, minced

¼ cup fat-free yogurt

2 teaspoons extra-virgin olive oil

½ teaspoon dried oregano leaves

1–2 tablespoons lemon juice

4 pitted ripe olives, chopped

Salt and pepper, to taste

Dippers: lavosh or pita bread wedges

Per Serving:
Calories: 59
% of calories from fat: 28
Fat (gm): 2.1
Saturated fat (gm): 0.3
Cholesterol (mg): 0.2
Sodium (mg): 19.1
Protein (gm): 1.8
Carbohydrate (gm): 10.1

Exchanges:
Milk: 0.0
Vegetable: 1.5
Fruit: 0.0
Bread: 0.0
Meat: 0.0
Fat: 0.5

1. Pierce eggplant in several places with fork; place in baking pan. Bake at 350 degrees until eggplant is soft, 45 to 50 minutes; cool. Cut eggplant in half; scoop out pulp with spoon. Mix eggplant, tomato, onion, garlic, yogurt, olive oil, and oregano in bowl; season to taste with lemon juice, salt, and pepper. Garnish with olives. Refrigerate 3 to 4 hours for flavors to blend. Serve with dippers (not included in nutritional data).

EGGPLANT MARMALADE

45

A quick kitchen tip—gingerroot does not have to be peeled before using!

12 servings (about 3 tablespoons each)

2 medium eggplant (1¼ pounds each), unpeeled, cubed

⅓ cup coarsely chopped onion

2 tablespoons minced roasted garlic

3 tablespoons each: minced gingerroot, light brown sugar

1½ teaspoons fennel seeds, crushed

2 tablespoons red wine vinegar

2 teaspoons Asian sesame oil

⅓ cup golden raisins

⅓ cup reduced-sodium vegetable broth

2–3 tablespoons toasted pine nuts or slivered almonds

Whole wheat lavosh, or crackers

Per Serving:
Calories: 75
% of calories from fat: 21
Fat (gm): 1.9
Saturated fat (gm): 0.3
Cholesterol (mg): 0
Sodium (mg): 6
Protein (gm): 1.6
Carbohydrate (gm): 14.9

Exchanges:
Milk: 0.0
Vegetable: 2.0
Fruit: 0.5
Bread: 0.0
Meat: 0.0
Fat: 0.0

1. Combine eggplant, onion, garlic, gingerroot, brown sugar, and fennel; toss with vinegar and oil and arrange in single layer on a greased, foil-lined jelly roll pan. Bake at 425 degrees until eggplant is browned and wrinkled, about 1½ hours, stirring every 30 minutes. Stir raisins and broth into mixture; bake until broth is absorbed, 10 to 15 minutes. Stir in pine nuts and cool. Refrigerate overnight for flavors to blend. Serve with lavosh (not included in nutritional data).

ROASTED GARLIC AND THREE-CHEESE SPREAD

For best flavor, make this dip a day in advance.

12 servings (about 2 tablespoons each)

1 small bulb garlic
Olive oil cooking spray
8 ounces fat-free cream cheese, room temperature
1½–2 ounces goat cheese
¼ cup (2 ounces) grated fat-free Parmesan cheese
⅛ teaspoon white pepper
2–4 tablespoons fat-free milk
Dippers: Vegetable relishes and assorted crackers

Per Serving:
Calories: 43
% of calories from fat: 28
Fat (gm): 1.3
Saturated fat (gm): 0.9
Cholesterol (mg): 3.8
Sodium (mg): 142
Protein (gm): 4.7
Carbohydrate (gm): 2.5

Exchanges:
Milk: 0.0
Vegetable: 0.0
Fruit: 0.0
Bread: 0.0
Meat: 0.5
Fat: 0.5

1. Cut off top of garlic bulb to expose cloves. Spray garlic lightly with cooking spray and wrap in aluminum foil; bake at 400 degrees until very tender, 35 to 40 minutes. Cool; gently press cloves to remove from skins. Mash cloves with fork.

2. Mix cheeses, garlic, and white pepper in bowl, adding enough milk to make desired spreading consistency. Refrigerate 2 to 3 hours for flavors to blend. Serve with dippers (not included in nutritional data).

CHUTNEY CHEESE SPREAD

Enjoy these flavors inspired by India. Ginger contributes "heat" as well as flavor to the spread, so adjust according to your taste. Make Pita Chips with curry powder or ground cumin.

8 servings (about 2 tablespoons each)

8 ounces fat-free cream cheese, room temperature
1 cup (4 ounces) shredded reduced-fat
   Cheddar cheese
½ cup chopped mango chutney, divided
¼ cup finely chopped onion
2 tablespoons raisins, chopped
1–2 teaspoons each: finely chopped gingerroot, garlic
½–1 teaspoon curry powder

Per Serving:
Calories: 116
% of calories from fat: 21
Fat (gm): 2.6
Saturated fat (gm): 1.1
Cholesterol (mg): 7.6
Sodium (mg): 367
Protein (gm): 7.4
Carbohydrate (gm): 14.6

Exchanges:
Milk: 0.0
Vegetable: 0.0
Fruit: 1.0
Bread: 0.0
Meat: 0.5
Fat: 0.5

1–2 tablespoons chopped dry-roasted cashews
Thinly sliced green onion tops, as garnish
Pita Chips (see p. 574) or assorted vegetables

1. Mix cheeses, 2 tablespoons chutney, onion, raisins, gingerroot, garlic, and curry powder until blended (do not beat, or fat-free cream cheese will become thin in texture). Refrigerate 1 to 2 hours for flavors to blend.

2. Mound spread on plate; spoon remaining 6 tablespoons chutney over or around spread. Sprinkle with cashews and onion tops; serve with Pita Chips (see p. 574) (not included in nutritional data).

ROASTED ZUCCHINI AND GARLIC SPREAD

45

A great recipe for summer, when garden zucchini are in generous supply.

12 servings (about 2 tablespoons each)

1¼ pounds zucchini, sliced (1-inch)
1 small onion, cut into wedges
2 garlic cloves, peeled
⅓ cup fat-free plain yogurt
2 tablespoons chopped parsley
Lemon juice, to taste
Salt and cayenne pepper, to taste
Dippers: Assorted vegetables and crackers

Per Serving:
Calories: 16
% of calories from fat: 6
Fat (gm): 0.1
Saturated fat (gm): 0.0
Cholesterol (mg): 0.1
Sodium (mg): 11
Protein (gm): 1.1
Carbohydrate (gm): 3.2

Exchanges:
Milk: 0.0
Vegetable: 0.5
Fruit: 0.0
Bread: 0.0
Meat: 0.0
Fat: 0.0

1. Arrange zucchini, onion, and garlic in single layer on a greased, foil-lined pan. Bake at 425 degrees until vegetables are very tender, about 15 to 20 minutes for garlic, 25 to 30 minutes for zucchini and onion. Cool.

2. Process vegetables in food processor until coarsely chopped. Stir in yogurt and parsley; season to taste with lemon juice, salt, and cayenne pepper. Serve with dippers (not included in nutritional data).

BEAN AND VEGETABLE SPREAD

A delicious and nutritious spread for snacking, or to serve as party fare.

12 servings (about 3 tablespoons each)

½ cup each: chopped onion, carrot

2 cloves garlic, minced

2 tablespoons vegetable broth or water

1½ cups cooked dried or canned soybeans

1 cup fat-free sour cream

2 tablespoons minced parsley

1–2 teaspoons lemon juice

Salt and pepper, to taste

Dippers: assorted vegetables or crackers

Per Serving:
Calories: 56
% of calories from fat: 29
Fat (gm): 2
Saturated fat (gm): 0.3
Cholesterol (mg): 0
Sodium (mg): 17
Protein (gm): 5
Carbohydrate (gm): 5.6

Exchanges:
Milk: 0.0
Vegetable: 1.0
Fruit: 0.0
Bread: 0.0
Meat: 0.5
Fat: 0.0

1. Cook onion, carrot, garlic, and broth in small skillet, covered, over medium heat until vegetables are tender and liquid absorbed, 5 to 8 minutes; cool.

2. Process soybeans and sour cream in food processor until smooth. Stir in vegetable mixture and parsley; season to taste with lemon juice, salt, and pepper. Refrigerate several hours for flavors to blend. Serve with dippers (not included in nutritional data).

PINE NUT SPINACH PÂTÉ

Toasted pine nuts provide flavor and texture accents in this unique dip.

12 servings (about 2 tablespoons each)

1 package (10 ounces) frozen chopped spinach,
    thawed, well drained

¼ cup each: coarsely chopped onion, celery

1 clove garlic

2–3 teaspoons lemon juice

1 teaspoon dried dill weed

1–2 tablespoons toasted pine nuts or
    slivered almonds

4 ounces fat-free cream cheese,
    room temperature

Per Serving:
Calories: 19
% of calories from fat: 21
Fat (gm): 0.5
Saturated fat (gm): 0.1
Cholesterol (mg): 0
Sodium (mg): 73
Protein (gm): 2.1
Carbohydrate (gm): 1.9

Exchanges:
Milk: 0.0
Vegetable: 0.5
Fruit: 0.0
Bread: 0.0
Meat: 0.0
Fat: 0.0

Salt and pepper, to taste
Bruschetta (see p. 530)

1. Process spinach, onion, celery, garlic, lemon juice, and dill weed in food processor until almost smooth; add pine nuts and process until coarsely chopped. Stir in cream cheese; season to taste with salt and pepper. Refrigerate several hours for flavors to blend. Serve with Bruschetta (not included in nutritional data).

WILD MUSHROOM PÂTÉ

45

This pâté is most flavorful when made with wild mushrooms, though any type of mushrooms can be used.

8 servings (about 2 tablespoons each)

12 ounces coarsely chopped shiitake or
   portobello mushrooms

½ cup chopped onion

2–4 cloves garlic, minced

¼ cup dry sherry or water

2 tablespoons grated fat-free Parmesan cheese

2–3 teaspoons lemon juice

Salt and pepper, to taste

Crusty bread or crackers

Per Serving:
Calories: 42
% of calories from fat: 2
Fat (gm): 0.1
Saturated fat (gm): 0
Cholesterol (mg): 0
Sodium (mg): 14
Protein (gm): 1.4
Carbohydrate (gm): 8.4

Exchanges:
Milk: 0.0
Vegetable: 1.5
Fruit: 0.0
Bread: 0.0
Meat: 0.0
Fat: 0.0

1. Add mushrooms, onion, garlic, and sherry to lightly greased skillet; cook, covered, over medium heat until mushrooms are wilted, about 5 minutes. Cook, uncovered, over medium heat until vegetables are very tender and all liquid absorbed, 8 to 10 minutes. Cool.

2. Process mushroom mixture and Parmesan cheese in food processor until smooth. Season to taste with lemon juice, salt, and pepper. Refrigerate 2 to 3 hours for flavors to blend. Serve in crock with bread or crackers (not included in nutritional data).

SPRING VEGETABLE TERRINE

45

Spring asparagus and peas are baked in a delicate herb-seasoned egg custard, which is easily unmolded and sliced to serve.

4 servings

½ cup each: thinly sliced green onions, red pepper

2 cloves garlic, minced

1½ pounds asparagus, cut into 1-inch pieces, cooked crisp-tender

1 package (10 ounces) frozen peas, thawed

1 cup fat-free half-and-half

2 tablespoons flour

1 tablespoon margarine or butter

¾ teaspoon dried tarragon leaves

¼ teaspoon ground allspice

½ teaspoon pepper

4 eggs, lightly beaten

Per Serving:
Calories: 224
% of calories from fat: 15
Fat (gm): 3.8
Saturated fat (gm): 0.7
Cholesterol (mg): 0
Sodium (mg): 277
Protein (gm): 16.5
Carbohydrate (gm): 32.4

Exchanges:
Milk: 0.5
Vegetable: 3.0
Fruit: 0.0
Bread: 1.0
Meat: 0.5
Fat: 0.0

1. Sauté green onions, bell pepper, and garlic in lightly greased medium skillet until tender, about 5 minutes. Stir in asparagus and peas; reserve.

2. Whisk half-and-half and flour until smooth in small saucepan. Heat to boiling, whisking until thickened, about 1 minute. Remove from heat and stir in margarine and seasonings. Whisk mixture gradually into eggs; stir in reserved vegetables.

3. Line bottom of 8 x 4-inch loaf pan with parchment paper; spray with cooking spray. Pour vegetable mixture into pan. Bake, uncovered, at 350 degrees 40 minutes, or until sharp knife inserted near center comes out clean. Let stand on wire rack 10 minutes; invert onto serving plate and remove parchment. Cut into thick slices.

MUSHROOMS STUFFED WITH ORZO

45

Enjoy flavor accents of tangy goat cheese and a trio of fresh herbs.

4 servings (3 mushrooms each)

12 large mushrooms, stems removed and chopped
1 tablespoon each: finely chopped shallot, garlic,
    fresh basil leaves
2 teaspoons finely chopped fresh or ½ teaspoon
    dried oregano leaves
½ teaspoon finely chopped fresh or ⅛ teaspoon
    dried thyme leaves
¼ cup (2 ounces) orzo, cooked
1 tablespoon goat cheese or reduced-fat cream cheese

Per Serving:
Calories: 86
% of calories from fat: 24
Fat (gm): 2.6
Saturated fat (gm): 0.6
Cholesterol (mg): 3.4
Sodium (mg): 18
Protein (gm): 5.3
Carbohydrate (gm): 13

Exchanges:
Milk: 0.0
Vegetable: 1.0
Fruit: 0.0
Bread: 0.5
Meat: 0.0
Fat: 0.5

1. Sauté chopped mushroom stems, shallot, garlic and herbs in lightly greased medium skillet until tender, about 6 minutes. Stir in orzo and goat cheese. Spoon filling into mushroom caps and place in 13 x 9-inch baking pan. Bake at 350 degrees, covered with aluminum foil, until mushrooms are tender, about 15 minutes.

STUFFED VEGETABLES

Vegetables can also be stuffed with any of the spread recipes in this chapter.

12 servings (4 pieces each)

12 each: cherry tomatoes, medium mushrooms
    (stems removed)
12 slices (¾-inch thick) each: cucumber, yellow
    summer squash
1 cup Roasted Garlic and Three-Cheese Spread
    (½ recipe) (see p. 10)
Parsley sprigs, ripe olive slices, chopped sun-dried
    tomato, as garnish

Per Serving:
Calories: 55
% of calories from fat: 24
Fat (gm): 1.5
Saturated fat (gm): 0.9
Cholesterol (mg): 3.8
Sodium (mg): 1
Protein (gm): 5.4
Carbohydrate (gm): 5.2

Exchanges:
Milk: 0.0
Vegetable: 0.5
Fruit: 0.0
Bread: 0.0
Meat: 0.5
Fat: 0.5

1. Cut tops off tomatoes and remove seeds. Cut thin slices off bottoms, if necessary for tomatoes to stand up securely. Scoop out centers of cucumber and squash slices with melon baller. Fill vegetables with spread, using pastry bag or small spoon. Top with assorted garnishes.

JICAMA WITH LIME AND CILANTRO

45 *Very simple, and incredibly tasty!*

4 servings

1 medium jicama, peeled, thinly sliced
Salt and lime juice, to taste
1–2 tablespoons finely chopped cilantro

1. Arrange jicama slices on large serving plate and sprinkle lightly with salt, lime juice, and cilantro.

Per Serving:
Calories: 17
% of calories from fat: 2
Fat (gm): 0
Saturated fat (gm): 0
Cholesterol (mg): 0
Sodium (mg): 0
Protein (gm): 0.5
Carbohydrate (gm): 3.8

Exchanges:
Milk: 0.0
Vegetable: 1.0
Fruit: 0.0
Bread: 0.0
Meat: 0.0
Fat: 0.0

TORTELLINI KEBABS WITH MANY-CLOVES GARLIC SAUCE

Serve 3 to 4 skewers each for an entrée, and accompany with broiled tomato halves, a crisp green salad, and Garlic Bread (see p. 531).

8 servings (2 each)

1½ packages (9-ounce size) mushroom
    tortellini, cooked
5 cups assorted whole, cubed and sliced vegetables
    (mushroom caps, cherry tomatoes, bell peppers,
    zucchini, broccoli florets, artichoke hearts, etc.)
Olive oil cooking spray
Many-Cloves Garlic Sauce (recipe follows)

Per Serving:
Calories: 146
% of calories from fat: 26
Fat (gm): 5
Saturated fat (gm): 1.8
Cholesterol (mg): 25.3
Sodium (mg): 171
Protein (gm): 7.4
Carbohydrate (gm): 23.3

Exchanges:
Milk: 0.0
Vegetable: 2.0
Fruit: 0.0
Bread: 1.0
Meat: 0.0
Fat: 0.5

1. Alternate tortellini and vegetables on 16 long skewers and arrange on broiler pan. Spray generously with cooking spray and broil 6 inches from heat source 4 minutes; turn kebabs, spray with cooking spray, and broil 3 to 4 minutes longer. Serve with Many-Cloves Garlic Sauce.

NOTE: Cook firm vegetables such as broccoli and carrots until crisp-tender before using.

Many-Cloves Garlic Sauce
Makes about 2 cups

25 cloves garlic, peeled
1 tablespoon olive oil
1¾ cups fat-free reduced-sodium chicken broth, divided
¼ cup dry white wine or chicken broth
2 tablespoons each: flour, finely chopped parsley
Salt and white pepper, to taste

1. Cook garlic in oil in medium skillet, covered, over medium-low heat until tender, about 10 minutes. Cook, uncovered, over low heat until golden brown, about 10 minutes; mash cloves slightly with a fork.

2. Add 1½ cups broth and wine to skillet and heat to boiling. Mix flour, parsley, and remaining ¼ cup broth and stir into boiling mixture. Boil until thickened, about 1 minute. Season to taste with salt and pepper.

PASTA PIZZA

45 *Pizza flavors on a pasta crust!*

6 servings

4 ounces reduced-fat turkey Italian sausage, casing removed
1 cup sliced mushrooms
½ cup chopped onion
4 sun-dried tomatoes (not in oil), softened, chopped
1 tablespoon each: finely chopped fresh or 1 teaspoon dried oregano and basil leaves
¼ teaspoon each: pepper and salt
6 ounces fettuccine, cooked
1 egg white, beaten
1 tablespoon finely chopped parsley
1½ ounces goat cheese or reduced-fat cream cheese

Per Serving:
Calories: 168
% of calories from fat: 29
Fat (gm): 5.7
Saturated fat (gm): 1.6
Cholesterol (mg): 21.6
Sodium (mg): 281
Protein (gm): 9.1
Carbohydrate (gm): 21.6

Exchanges:
Milk: 0.0
Vegetable: 2.0
Fruit: 0.0
Bread: 1.0
Meat: 0.5
Fat: 0.5

1. Cook sausage in lightly greased medium skillet over medium heat until browned; drain and crumble. Add mushrooms, onion, and tomatoes to skillet and sauté until tender, about 5 minutes. Stir in seasonings. Combine fettuccine, egg white, and parsley; add to lightly greased 10-inch skillet and pat into even layer with pancake turner. Spoon sausage-vegetable mixture over and dot with cheese. Cook over medium heat, covered, 5 minutes. Uncover and cook 5 minutes more or until pasta is lightly browned on bottom. Cut into wedges.

45-MINUTE PREPARATION TIP: Begin cooking the fettuccine before preparing the rest of the recipe.

SPINACH AND CHEESE MINI-QUICHES

The tiny fillo shells, delicious and wonderfully crisp, are available in the frozen food section of supermarkets. You can also make small pastries in mini-muffin cups using a favorite pie pastry.

1½ dozen (1 per serving)

1¼ cups fat-free cottage cheese

¼ cup grated fat-free Parmesan cheese

2 tablespoons each: fat-free milk, flour

½ cup finely chopped fresh spinach

½ teaspoon each: dried oregano and thyme leaves

Salt and white pepper, to taste

2 eggs

1½ dozen frozen mini-fillo shells, thawed

Per Mini-Quiche:
Calories: 48
% of calories from fat: 30
Fat (gm): 1.6
Saturated fat (gm): 0.2
Cholesterol (mg): 23.7
Sodium (mg): 61
Protein (gm): 3.9
Carbohydrate (gm): 4.3

Exchanges:
Milk: 0.0
Vegetable: 0.0
Fruit: 0.0
Bread: 0.5
Meat: 0.0
Fat: 0.5

1. Mix cheeses, milk, flour, spinach, and herbs; season to taste with salt and pepper. Stir in eggs. Spoon mixture into fillo shells on cookie sheet or in mini-muffin tins. Bake at 325 degrees until puffed and beginning to brown on the tops, about 20 minutes.

CHEESE AND SPINACH SQUARES

45

Lots of cheese and spinach in these terrific appetizer squares! For variation, substitute fat-free Swiss or mozzarella cheese for the Cheddar.

12 servings (2 each)

Vegetable cooking spray

1–2 tablespoons unseasoned dry bread crumbs

2 cups fat-free cottage cheese

1½ cups (6 ounces) shredded fat-free Cheddar cheese

2 eggs

6 tablespoons whole wheat flour

l package (10 ounces) frozen chopped spinach, thawed, well drained

¼ cup each: thinly sliced green onions, chopped roasted red bell pepper or pimiento, finely chopped parsley

¼ teaspoon each: black and cayenne pepper

⅛ teaspoon ground nutmeg

Per Serving:
Calories: 81
% of calories from fat: 11
Fat (gm): 1
Saturated fat (gm): 0.3
Cholesterol (mg): 35.5
Sodium (mg): 231
Protein (gm): 11.8
Carbohydrate (gm): 6.7

Exchanges:
Milk: 0.0
Vegetable: 1.0
Fruit: 0.0
Bread: 0.0
Meat: 1.0
Fat: 0.0

1. Spray 13 x 9-inch pan with cooking spray; coat bottom and sides of pan with bread crumbs. Combine cheeses and eggs in bowl; stir in remaining ingredients until blended. Pour into prepared pan and bake at 350 degrees until set and lightly browned, 35 to 40 minutes. Cool 10 minutes before cutting into squares.

BAKED SPINACH BALLS

45

Often laden with butter, these savory treats are rich in flavor.

12 servings (2 each)

2 cups herb-seasoned bread stuffing cubes

¼ cup each: grated fat-free Parmesan cheese,
chopped green onions

2 cloves garlic, minced

⅛ teaspoon ground nutmeg

1 package (10 ounces) frozen chopped spinach,
thawed, well drained

¼–⅓ cup reduced-sodium vegetable broth

2 tablespoons margarine or butter, melted

Salt and pepper, to taste

1 egg, lightly beaten

Per Serving:
Calories: 86
% of calories from fat: 24
Fat (gm): 2.4
Saturated fat (gm): 0.4
Cholesterol (mg): 0
Sodium (mg): 271
Protein (gm): 4.2
Carbohydrate (gm): 13

Exchanges:
Milk: 0.0
Vegetable: 1.0
Fruit: 0.0
Bread: 0.5
Meat: 0.0
Fat: 0.5

1. Combine stuffing cubes, Parmesan cheese, onions, garlic, and
nutmeg in medium bowl. Mix in spinach, broth, and margarine;
season to taste with salt and pepper. Mix in egg. Shape mixture into
24 balls. Bake at 350 degrees on greased jelly roll pan until spinach
balls are browned, about 15 minutes.

MUSHROOM BRUSCHETTA

*Use any desired wild mushrooms and make this filling up to 2 days
in advance.*

12 servings (1 each)

½ cup chopped red bell pepper

2 each: thinly sliced green onions, minced
garlic cloves

2 cups chopped wild mushrooms (portobello,
shiitake, oyster, enoki, etc.)

1½ teaspoons dried basil leaves

2 tablespoons grated fat-free Parmesan cheese

Few drops balsamic vinegar

Salt and pepper, to taste

Per Serving:
Calories: 92
% of calories from fat: 17
Fat (gm): 1.7
Saturated fat (gm): 0.7
Cholesterol (mg): 2.5
Sodium (mg): 194
Protein (gm): 4.4
Carbohydrate (gm): 14.6

Exchanges:
Milk: 0.0
Vegetable: 0.5
Fruit: 0.0
Bread: 1.0
Meat: 0.5
Fat: 0.0

Bruschetta (see p. 530)
¼ cup (2 ounces) shredded reduced-fat mozzarella cheese

1. Sauté bell pepper, onions, and garlic 2 to 3 minutes in lightly greased skillet. Add mushrooms and basil and cook, covered, over medium heat until wilted, about 5 minutes. Uncover and cook until liquid is gone, 8 to 10 minutes. Stir in Parmesan cheese; season to taste with balsamic vinegar, salt, and pepper.

2. Spoon mushroom mixture on Bruschetta and sprinkle with mozzarella cheese; broil 6 inches from heat source until cheese is melted, 1 to 2 minutes.

CURRIED ONION CROUSTADES

The Croustades can be filled with the onion mixture and refrigerated several hours before baking.

8 servings (2 each)

2 cups chopped onions
2 cloves garlic, minced
1 teaspoon curry powder
½ teaspoon ground cumin
2 tablespoons flour
1 cup fat-free half-and-half or fat-free milk
2 tablespoons dried fruit bits
1 tablespoon minced cilantro
Salt, cayenne, and black pepper, to taste
Croustades (see p. 531)
4 teaspoons chopped almonds

Per Serving:
Calories: 125
% of calories from fat: 13
Fat (gm): 1.8
Saturated fat (gm): 0.3
Cholesterol (mg): 0
Sodium (mg): 167
Protein (gm): 4.2
Carbohydrate (gm): 22.3

Exchanges:
Milk: 0.0
Vegetable: 1.0
Fruit: 0.0
Bread: 1.0
Meat: 0.0
Fat: 0.5

1. Sauté onions and garlic in lightly greased skillet 5 minutes; add spices and cook, covered, over low heat until onions are very soft, about 20 minutes. Stir in flour; cook 1 minute longer. Stir half-and-half and fruit into onion mixture; heat to boiling. Reduce heat and simmer, stirring, until thickened. Stir in cilantro; season to taste with salt, cayenne, and black pepper.

2. Place Croustades in baking pan and fill each with slightly rounded tablespoon of onion mixture; sprinkle with almonds. Bake, uncovered, at 425 degrees 10 minutes.

BEEF EMPANADAS

Pork tenderloin or chicken breast can be substituted for the beef in this recipe. The raisins and spices lend a sweet flavor to this traditional Mexican meat filling.

10 servings (3 each)

12 ounces boneless beef eye of round steak,
   fat trimmed
¼ cup finely chopped onion
3 cloves garlic, minced
2 small tomatoes, finely chopped
⅓ cup raisins
2 tablespoons slivered almonds
1 tablespoon cider vinegar
½ teaspoon ground cinnamon
⅛ teaspoon ground cloves
3 tablespoons finely chopped cilantro
Salt and pepper, to taste
Empanada Pastry (recipe follows)
2 tablespoons fat-free milk

Per Serving:
Calories: 159
% of calories from fat: 29
Fat (gm): 5.1
Saturated fat (gm): 1.5
Cholesterol (mg): 16.5
Sodium (mg): 57
Protein (gm): 8.7
Carbohydrate (gm): 19.5

Exchanges:
Milk: 0.0
Vegetable: 0.0
Fruit: 0.0
Bread: 0.5
Meat: 0.5
Fat: 0.0

1. Cut beef into 2-inch cubes and place in saucepan with 2 inches water; heat to boiling. Reduce heat and simmer, covered, until beef is tender, about 15 minutes. Drain, reserving beef and ½ cup broth. Shred beef finely.

2. Sauté onion and garlic in lightly greased medium skillet until tender, about 5 minutes. Add reserved beef and ½ cup broth, tomatoes, raisins, almonds, vinegar, cinnamon, and cloves; cook over medium heat until broth has evaporated but mixture is still moist, about 10 minutes. Stir in cilantro; season to taste with salt and pepper.

3. Roll ½ of the Empanada Pastry on floured surface to ⅛ inch thickness; cut into 3-inch rounds with cookie cutter. Place scant tablespoon meat mixture on each piece pastry. Brush edges of pastry with water; fold in half and crimp edges firmly by hand or with tines of fork. Make cut in top of each pastry with sharp knife. Repeat with remaining pastry and meat mixture. Brush tops of pastries lightly with milk. Bake on greased cookie sheets at 400 degrees until golden, 15 to 20 minutes.

Empanada Pastry

1¼ cups all-purpose flour
1 tablespoon sugar
¼ teaspoon baking powder
⅛ teaspoon salt
3 tablespoons vegetable shortening
1 teaspoon lemon juice or distilled white vinegar
4- tablespoons fat-free milk or water

1. Combine flour, sugar, baking powder, and salt in small bowl; cut in shortening until mixture resembles coarse crumbs. Mix in lemon juice and milk, a tablespoon at a time, to form soft dough. Refrigerate until ready to use.

FIVE-SPICE POTSTICKERS

Purchased wonton wrappers make this recipe simple to prepare. Wonton wrappers can be cut into circles with a 2½-inch cutter, if you like. Assemble wontons up to 1 day in advance; dust lightly with flour and refrigerate, covered, in a single layer on a plate.

12 servings (4 each)

2 cups sliced Chinese or napa cabbage
½ cup shredded carrot
¼ cup each: thinly sliced green onions, celery
1–2 teaspoons minced gingerroot
1 clove garlic, minced
1 tablespoon reduced-sodium tamari soy sauce
¼–½ teaspoon each: hot chili paste, five-spice powder
2 ounces light tofu, cut into small cubes or coarsely crumbled
48 wonton or gyoza wrappers
1 egg white, beaten
Tamari Dipping Sauce (recipe follows)

Per Serving:
Calories: 130
% of calories from fat: 4
Fat (gm): 0.6
Saturated fat (gm): 0.1
Cholesterol (mg): 4
Sodium (mg): 431
Protein (gm): 5.2
Carbohydrate (gm): 25.9

Exchanges:
Milk: 0.0
Vegetable: 2.0
Fruit: 0.0
Bread: 1.0
Meat: 0.0
Fat: 0.0

1. Stir-fry cabbage, carrot, green onions, celery, gingerroot, and garlic in lightly greased wok or large skillet over medium to medium-high heat until cabbage is wilted, 2 to 3 minutes.

Remove from heat; stir in soy sauce, chili paste, and five-spice powder. Add tofu, toss lightly, and cool.

2. Spoon ½ tablespoon filling on wonton wrapper; brush edges of wrapper with egg white. Fold wrapper in half and press edges to seal. Repeat with remaining filling, wrappers, and egg white. Add 6 or 8 wontons to large saucepan of boiling water; simmer, uncovered, until wontons rise to the surface, 2 to 3 minutes. Remove with slotted spoon and drain. Repeat with remaining wontons.

3. Add single layer of wontons to lightly greased wok or large skillet and cook over medium heat until browned on the bottom, 2 to 3 minutes. Spray tops of wontons lightly with cooking spray; turn and cook until browned. Repeat with remaining wontons. Serve hot with Tamari Dipping Sauce.

Tamari Dipping Sauce

12 servings (1 tablespoon each)

½ cup reduced-sodium tamari or soy sauce
2 tablespoons rice wine vinegar
4 teaspoons lemon juice
2 teaspoons honey

1. Mix all ingredients.

CRANBERRY-CHEESE WONTONS

Dried cranberries and gingerroot add a lively accent to these unusual cheese wontons.

12 servings (2 each)

6 ounces fat-free cream cheese, room temperature
3 tablespoons chopped dried cranberries
2 tablespoons each: finely chopped chives, parsley
½–¾ teaspoon minced gingerroot
Salt and white pepper, to taste
24 wonton wrappers
1 egg white, beaten

Per Serving:
Calories: 91
% of calories from fat: 10
Fat (gm): 1
Saturated fat (gm): 0.1
Cholesterol (mg): 2
Sodium (mg): 184
Protein (gm): 3.9
Carbohydrate (gm): 15.8

Exchanges:
Milk: 0.0
Vegetable: 0.0
Fruit: 0.5
Bread: 0.5
Meat: 0.5
Fat: 0.0

Canola or peanut oil, for frying

⅓ cup jalapeño jelly, heated, or Tamari Dipping Sauce (see p. 24)

1. Mix cream cheese, cranberries, chives, parsley, and gingerroot in small bowl; season to taste with salt and white pepper. Spoon ½ tablespoon filling on wonton wrapper; brush edges of wrapper with egg white. Fold wrapper in half and press edges to seal. Repeat with remaining filling, wrappers, and egg white.

2. Heat 2 inches of oil to 375 degrees in large saucepan. Fry wontons, 6 to 8 at a time, until golden, 1 to 2 minutes. Drain on paper toweling. Serve with jalapeño jelly or Tamari Dipping Sauce.

MIXED VEGETABLE EGG ROLLS

The Asian sesame oil in this recipe has a more distinctive sesame flavor than the light-colored domestic brands. Nutritious spinach, alfalfa sprouts, and black beans add a new dimension to these egg rolls.

12 servings (1 each)

1 tablespoon sesame seeds

2–3 teaspoons Asian sesame oil

2 green onions, sliced

1 tablespoon minced gingerroot

2 cloves garlic, minced

2 cups sliced spinach

½ cup each: chopped water chestnuts, shredded carrot, sliced small mushrooms

1 can (15½ ounces) black beans, rinsed, drained

1–1½ teaspoons reduced-sodium tamari soy sauce

Salt and pepper, to taste

2 egg whites

1 cup alfalfa sprouts

12 egg roll wrappers

Peanut, or vegetable, oil

Plum Sauce (recipe follows)

Per Egg Roll:
Calories: 101
% of calories from fat: 12
Fat (gm): 1.6
Saturated fat (gm): 0.2
Cholesterol (mg): 0
Sodium (mg): 342
Protein (gm): 5.8
Carbohydrate (gm): 19

Exchanges:
Milk: 0.0
Vegetable: 1.5
Fruit: 0.0
Bread: 1.0
Meat: 0.0
Fat: 0.0

1. Sauté sesame seeds in Asian sesame oil in large skillet until beginning to brown, 1 to 2 minutes. Add green onions, gingerroot, and garlic; sauté until onions are tender, 1 to 2 minutes. Add spinach, water chestnuts, carrot, and mushrooms; cook, covered, over medium heat until spinach and mushrooms are wilted. Stir in beans and tamari sauce; season to taste with salt and pepper. Cool 5 to 10 minutes; stir in egg whites and alfalfa sprouts.

2. Spoon about ⅓ cup vegetable mixture near corner of 1 egg roll wrapper. Brush edges of wrapper with water. Fold bottom corner of egg roll wrapper up over filling; fold sides in and roll up. Repeat with remaining filling and wrappers.

3. Heat about 2 inches of oil to 375 degrees in deep skillet or large saucepan. Fry egg rolls until golden, 4 to 5 minutes. Drain on paper toweling. Serve hot with Plum Sauce.

Plum Sauce

Makes about 1 cup

¾ cup Oriental plum sauce
2–3 tablespoons each: reduced-sodium tamari soy sauce,
    rice wine vinegar or cider vinegar
1 tablespoon each: grated gingerroot, sliced green onion
1–2 teaspoons light brown sugar, minced garlic

1. Mix all ingredients; refrigerate until ready to serve.

ARTICHOKE-STUFFED APPETIZER BREAD

45

For easy entertaining, assemble this appetizer a day or two in advance. Bread pieces removed from the loaf can be used to make fresh breadcrumbs or croutons.

8 servings (2 each)

8 ounces fat-free cream cheese, room temperature
1 can (14 ounces) artichoke hearts, drained, chopped
½ cup each: chopped red bell pepper, celery
¼ cup chopped pitted green or black, olives
2 teaspoons each: drained capers, minced garlic
½ teaspoon each: dried basil and oregano leaves
1–2 teaspoons white wine vinegar or lemon juice

Per Serving:
Calories: 151
% of calories from fat: 29
Fat (gm): 5.1
Saturated fat (gm): 0.3
Cholesterol (mg): 0
Sodium (mg): 600
Protein (gm): 6.9
Carbohydrate (gm): 20.9

Exchanges:
Milk: 0.0
Vegetable: 1.0
Fruit: 0.0
Bread: 1.0
Meat: 0.0
Fat: 1.0

Salt and white pepper, to taste

1 loaf French bread (8 ounces) (about 15 inches long)

1. Mix cream cheese, artichoke hearts, bell pepper, celery, olives, capers, garlic, and herbs; season to taste with vinegar, salt, and white pepper.

2. Slice bread lengthwise in half. Remove bread from centers of bread halves, using a paring knife or serrated grapefruit spoon, leaving ¾-inch shell of bread. Spoon filling into each bread half; press halves together firmly and wrap in plastic wrap. Refrigerate 2 hours or until serving time. Cut into 16 pieces.

APPLE-CABBAGE STRUDELS

The strudels can be assembled several hours in advance; refrigerate, tightly covered. Spray tops of strudels with cooking spray before baking.

12 servings (2 each)

½ cup thinly sliced onion

2 cloves garlic, minced

3 cups thinly sliced cabbage

⅓ cup apple cider or apple juice

1½ cups peeled, chopped, tart apples

¼ cup dark raisins

1–1½ teaspoons curry powder

Salt and pepper, to taste

8 sheets frozen fillo pastry, thawed

Butter-flavored cooking spray

Per Serving:
Calories: 34
% of calories from fat: 5
Fat (gm): 0.2
Saturated fat (gm): 0
Cholesterol (mg): 0
Sodium (mg): 8
Protein (gm): 0.6
Carbohydrate (gm): 8.5

Exchanges:
Milk: 0.0
Vegetable: 0.0
Fruit: 0.5
Bread: 0.0
Meat: 0.0
Fat: 0.0

1. Sauté onion and garlic in lightly greased skillet until tender, about 5 minutes. Add cabbage and apple cider; cook, covered, over medium heat until cabbage is wilted, about 5 minutes. Stir in apples, raisins, and curry powder; cook, uncovered, until apples are crisp-tender and mixture is almost dry, 5 to 8 minutes. Season to taste with salt and pepper. Cool.

2. Place 1 sheet fillo on clean surface; spray with lightly with butter-flavored cooking spray; top with second sheet of fillo and spray.

Repeat with 3 more sheets of fillo. Spoon half the cabbage mixture evenly along short edge of fillo, leaving a 1-inch space from the edge. Roll up from short edge, tucking ends under. Place seam side down on greased cookie sheet. Repeat with remaining fillo, cooking spray, and cabbage mixture. Spray tops of strudels with cooking spray. Bake at 400 degrees until golden, about 15 minutes. Cool slightly; cut diagonally into 1-inch pieces with serrated knife. Serve warm or at room temperature.

ONION AND BLUE CHEESE FOCACCIA

45

Serve larger portions as a bread with entrée salads.

8 servings

2 cups thinly sliced onions

4 cloves garlic, minced

½ teaspoon dried rosemary leaves

Salt and pepper, to taste

1 focaccia (Italian flat bread) (10 ounces)

¼ cup chopped softened sun-dried tomatoes (not in oil)

2–3 ounces crumbled blue cheese

2 tablespoons grated fat-free Parmesan cheese

Per Serving:
Calories: 146
% of calories from fat: 21
Fat (gm): 3.5
Saturated fat (gm): 1.6
Cholesterol (mg): 5.2
Sodium (mg): 354
Protein (gm): 5.9
Carbohydrate (gm): 23.3

Exchanges:
Milk: 0.0
Vegetable: 2.0
Fruit: 0.0
Bread: 1.0
Meat: 0.0
Fat: 0.5

1. Cook onions and garlic in lightly greased skillet, covered, over medium heat until wilted, about 5 minutes. Cook, uncovered, over low heat until tender and lightly browned, 10 to 15 minutes; stir in rosemary and season with salt and pepper. Arrange onions on bread; sprinkle with sun-dried tomatoes and cheeses. Bake at 350 degrees until bread is hot and cheese melted, about 15 minutes. Cut into 8 wedges.

SWEET ONION TARTE TATIN

You'll win raves when you serve this beautiful upside-down tart! For best flavor, use a sweet onion, such as Vidalia.

6–8 servings

1 tablespoon granulated or light brown sugar

2½ pounds small sweet onions, peeled, halved crosswise

Salt and pepper, to taste

⅓ cup dark or light raisins

1 teaspoon dried thyme leaves

¼ teaspoon ground allspice

1½ cups reduced-sodium vegetable broth

2 teaspoons balsamic vinegar

Tarte Tatin Crust (see p. 30)

Per Serving:
Calories: 291
% of calories from fat: 25
Fat (gm): 8.3
Saturated fat (gm): 1.6
Cholesterol (mg): 0
Sodium (mg): 126
Protein (gm): 5.9
Carbohydrate (gm): 49.8

Exchanges:
Milk: 0.0
Vegetable: 3.0
Fruit: 0.5
Bread: 1.5
Meat: 0.0
Fat: 1.5

1. Heat lightly greased 12-inch skillet with ovenproof handle over medium heat until hot; sprinkle bottom evenly with sugar. Place onion halves, cut sides down, in skillet, fitting in as many as possible. Cut remaining onion halves into pieces, or chop coarsely, and fill in any spaces between onion halves. Sprinkle lightly with salt and pepper; sprinkle with raisins, thyme, and allspice. Cook, uncovered, over medium heat until onions begin to brown on the bottoms, 8 to 10 minutes.

2. Add broth and vinegar to skillet; heat to boiling. Reduce heat and simmer, covered, until onions are tender, 20 to 25 minutes. Heat to boiling; reduce heat and simmer rapidly, uncovered, until liquid is almost gone.

3. Roll pastry for Tarte Tatin Crust on floured surface into 13-inch circle. Ease pastry over onions in skillet, tucking in edges to fit. Bake at 375 degrees until pastry is browned and juices are bubbly, 30 to 35 minutes. Cool in pan on wire rack 10 minutes; place large serving plate over skillet and invert onto plate. Serve warm or room temperature.

Tarte Tatin Crust

1½ cups all-purpose flour
½ teaspoon baking powder
½ teaspoon dried thyme leaves
Pinch salt
4 tablespoons cold margarine or butter cut into pieces
5–6 tablespoons ice water

1. Combine flour, baking powder, thyme, and salt in medium bowl; cut in margarine until mixture resembles coarse crumbs. Add water a tablespoon at a time, mixing lightly with a fork after each addition, until dough just holds together. Refrigerate, covered, at least 30 minutes.

SQUASH AND MUSHROOM GALETTE

The Galette Pastry Dough, made with yeast, is quite special.

4–6 servings

½ cup each: thinly sliced leek, chopped onion, red bell pepper
2 medium portobello mushrooms, sliced
8 cloves garlic, minced
1½ teaspoons dried sage leaves
1 tablespoon olive oil
1½ cups cooked mashed acorn or butternut squash
Salt and pepper, to taste
Galette Pastry Dough (recipe follows)
½ cup (2 ounces) shredded fat-free Cheddar cheese
2 tablespoons grated Parmesan cheese
1 egg white, beaten

Per Serving:
Calories: 339
% of calories from fat: 18
Fat (gm): 7.1
Saturated fat (gm): 1.7
Cholesterol (mg): 58.3
Sodium (mg): 338
Protein (gm): 16.5
Carbohydrate (gm): 54

Exchanges:
Milk: 0.0
Vegetable: 1.0
Fruit: 0.0
Bread: 3.0
Meat: 1.0
Fat: 1.0

1. Sauté leek, onion, bell pepper, mushrooms, garlic, and sage in oil in large skillet until tender, about 5 minutes. Mix in squash; season to taste with salt and pepper.

2. Roll Galette Pastry Dough on lightly floured surface to 14-inch circle; transfer to greased cookie sheet or large pizza pan. Spoon vegetable mixture evenly on dough, leaving 2-inch border around edge. Sprinkle with cheeses. Fold edge of dough over edge of vegetable mixture, pleating to fit; brush dough with egg white. Bake at 400 degrees until crust is golden, about 25 minutes. Cut into wedges; serve warm.

Galette Pastry Dough

1 teaspoon active dry yeast
⅓ cup warm water (115 degrees)
1 egg, beaten
3 tablespoons fat-free sour cream
1½ cups all-purpose flour
¼ teaspoon salt

1. Stir yeast into warm water in medium bowl; let stand 5 minutes. Add egg and sour cream, mixing until smooth. Stir in flour and salt, making a soft dough. Knead dough on lightly floured surface until smooth, about 10 minutes.

VARIATION

Peperonata Galette — Make Peperonata (see p. 485). Roll Galette Pastry Dough as directed in Step 3 above. Spoon peperonata mixture evenly on dough, leaving a 2-inch border around edge; sprinkle with ½ cup (2 ounces) shredded fat-free mozzarella cheese and 1 tablespoon shredded Parmesan cheese. Fold edge of dough over edge of vegetable mixture, pleating to fit. Brush dough with egg white. Bake as above.

CURRIED PINWHEELS

45

Make these easy appetizers up to 2 days in advance and refrigerate until ready to serve.

12 servings (3 each)

6 pieces luncheon-size lavosh (5-inch)

12 ounces fat-free cream cheese, room temperature

2 tablespoons fat-free mayonnaise

1–2 teaspoons spicy brown mustard

1 clove garlic, minced

1–1½ teaspoons curry powder

½ cup finely chopped apple

¼ cup each: finely chopped celery, green onions, dry-roasted peanuts

¾ cup chopped chutney

Per Pinwheel:
Calories: 38
% of calories from fat: 14
Fat (gm): 0.6
Saturated fat (gm): 0.1
Cholesterol (mg): 0
Sodium (mg): 79
Protein (gm): 1.9
Carbohydrate (gm): 6.2

Exchanges:
Milk: 0.0
Vegetable: 0.0
Fruit: 0.5
Bread: 0.0
Meat: 0.0
Fat: 0.0

1. Brush lavosh lightly with water and place between damp kitchen towels until softened enough to roll, about 20 minutes.

2. Mix cream cheese, mayonnaise, mustard, garlic, and curry powder in bowl; spread about 3 tablespoons mixture on each lavosh. Combine remaining ingredients, except chutney, and sprinkle over cheese mixture. Roll lavosh tightly; wrap each roll in plastic wrap and refrigerate at least 4 hours. Cut each roll into 6 pieces; serve with chutney.

SWISS CHEESE AND SPINACH PINWHEELS

45

These fabulous sandwiches can be made in advance and refrigerated up to 2 days—always ready for hungry appetites!

8 servings (2 slices each)

1 large whole wheat lavosh (16 inches diameter)

8 ounces fat-free cream cheese,
    room temperature

1 tablespoon fat-free sour cream

2 tablespoons minced onion

1 teaspoon fennel seeds, crushed

10 slices (7½ ounces) fat-free Swiss cheese

4 cups loosely packed spinach leaves

2 medium tomatoes, thinly sliced

⅓ cup drained, sliced olives

Per Serving:
Calories: 177
% of calories from fat: 29
Fat (gm): 5.8
Saturated fat (gm): 0.9
Cholesterol (mg): 0
Sodium (mg): 782
Protein (gm): 13.4
Carbohydrate (gm): 18.4

Exchanges:
Milk: 0.0
Vegetable: 1.0
Fruit: 0.0
Bread: 1.0
Meat: 1.0
Fat: 0.5

1. Place lavosh between 2 damp clean kitchen towels; let stand until lavosh is softened enough to roll, about 20 minutes.

2. Mix cream cheese, sour cream, onion, and fennel seeds in small bowl; spread on lavosh. Arrange Swiss cheese, spinach, tomatoes, and olives on top. Roll lavosh tightly; wrap in plastic wrap and refrigerate at least 4 hours, but no longer than 2 days. Trim ends and cut into 1-inch slices.

SLICED MUSHROOM PINWHEELS

45

Easy to make and carry, lavosh sandwiches are great for picnics, as well as home dining.

8 servings (2 slices each)

1 large whole wheat lavosh (16 inches diameter)
4 ounces mushrooms
8 ounces fat-free cream cheese,
   room temperature
1 tablespoon fat-free sour cream
1 teaspoon minced garlic
1–2 teaspoons Dijon mustard
1 medium onion, thinly sliced
⅓ cup red bell pepper, thinly sliced
3 tablespoons fat-free Italian salad dressing

Per Serving:
Calories: 122
% of calories from fat: 27
Fat (gm): 3.7
Saturated fat (gm): 0.7
Cholesterol (mg): 0
Sodium (mg): 309
Protein (gm): 6.5
Carbohydrate (gm): 16

Exchanges:
Milk: 0.0
Vegetable: 1.0
Fruit: 0.0
Bread: 1.0
Meat: 0.0
Fat: 0.5

1. Place lavosh between 2 damp clean kitchen towels; let stand until lavosh is softened enough to roll, about 20 minutes.

2. Remove mushroom stems and chop; slice mushroom caps. Mix cream cheese, chopped mushroom stems, sour cream, garlic, and mustard in small bowl; spread mixture on lavosh. Toss sliced mushrooms, onion, and bell pepper with salad dressing; arrange over cheese mixture. Roll lavosh tightly; wrap in plastic wrap and refrigerate at least 4 hours, but no longer than 2 days. Trim ends and cut into 1-inch slices.

TWO

Soups: First Course

and

Entrèe

CREAM OF ARTICHOKE AND MUSHROOM SOUP

45 *Shiitake or cremini mushrooms can be substituted for the portobello mushrooms.*

4 first-course servings (about 1 cup each)

¾ cup chopped portobello mushrooms

2 tablespoons chopped onion

1 tablespoon margarine or butter

1 tablespoon all-purpose flour

3 cups fat-free milk

1 vegetable bouillon cube

1 package (9 ounces) frozen artichoke hearts, thawed, finely chopped

Salt and white pepper, to taste

Paprika, as garnish

Per Serving:
Calories: 135
% of calories from fat: 22
Fat (gm): 3.6
Saturated fat (gm): 0.8
Cholesterol (mg): 3
Sodium (mg): 422
Protein (gm): 9.2
Carbohydrate (gm): 18.9

Exchanges:
Milk: 1.0
Vegetable: 1.0
Fruit: 0.0
Bread: 0.0
Meat: 0.0
Fat: 0.5

1. Sauté mushrooms and onion in margarine in medium saucepan until tender, about 5 minutes. Stir in flour; cook 1 minute. Stir in milk and bouillon cube; heat to boiling. Add artichoke hearts and simmer, uncovered, 5 minutes. Season to taste with salt and white pepper. Sprinkle with paprika.

FLORIDA AVOCADO AND TOMATO CHOWDER

45 *In this easy recipe, colorful ingredients create a kaleidoscope of fresh colors and flavors.*

4 entrée servings

3 cups cubed, peeled potatoes

1 can (14 ounces) reduced-sodium fat-free chicken broth

1 teaspoon dried thyme leaves

8 ounces smoked turkey breast, cubed

1 cup each: whole kernel corn, chopped plum tomatoes, cubed avocado

Juice of 1 lime

3 slices bacon, cooked, crumbled

Salt and pepper, to taste

Per Serving:
Calories: 333
% of calories from fat: 26
Fat (gm): 10.2
Saturated fat (gm): 2.4
Cholesterol (mg): 51.1
Sodium (mg): 765
Protein (gm): 21
Carbohydrate (gm): 44.7

Exchanges:
Milk: 0.0
Vegetable: 2.0
Fruit: 0.0
Bread: 2.0
Meat: 2.0
Fat: 1.5

1. Heat potatoes, broth, and thyme to boiling in medium saucepan; reduce heat and simmer, covered, until potatoes are tender, about 10 minutes. Using slotted spoon, transfer ½ the potatoes to a medium bowl. Process remaining mixture in food processor or blender until smooth; return to saucepan. Add turkey, corn, and reserved potatoes; heat to boiling. Reduce heat and simmer 5 minutes. Stir in tomatoes, avocado, lime juice, and bacon. Season to taste with salt and pepper.

BLACK BEAN SOUP

Dried beans can also be "quick cooked" rather than soaked overnight; see directions in Navy Bean Soup with Ham (p. 384). Or, substitute three cans (15 ounces each) rinsed, drained canned black beans.

4 first-course servings (about 1¼ cups each)

1½ cups dried black beans
1 large onion, chopped
4 cloves garlic, minced
1 teaspoon dried oregano leaves
½ teaspoon dried thyme leaves
1 large tomato, chopped
Salt and pepper, to taste
6 tablespoons fat-free sour cream
Finely chopped oregano or parsley, as garnish

Per Serving:
Calories: 200
% of calories from fat: 4
Fat (gm): 0.9
Saturated fat (gm): 0.2
Cholesterol (mg): 0
Sodium (mg): 20
Protein (gm): 13.8
Carbohydrate (gm): 39

Exchanges:
Milk: 0.0
Vegetable: 1.0
Fruit: 0.0
Bread: 2.0
Meat: 0.5
Fat: 0.0

1. Cover beans with 4 inches water in large saucepan; soak overnight and drain.

2. Sauté onion, garlic and herbs in lightly greased large saucepan until softened, about 4 minutes. Add beans; cover with 2 inches water and heat to boiling. Reduce heat and simmer, covered, until beans are very tender, 1½ to 2 hours, adding tomato during last ½ hour.

3. Process soup in food processor or blender until smooth. Return soup to saucepan; heat over medium heat until hot through, 3 to 4 minutes. Season to taste with salt and pepper. Top servings of soup with dollop of sour cream and sprinkle with oregano.

SHRIMP AND BLACK BEAN SOUP

In Mexico, leaves from the avocado tree are used for seasoning in this favorite Oaxacan soup. We've substituted a bay leaf, which is somewhat stronger in flavor.

6 entrée servings (about 1½ cups each)

2 medium onions, chopped

4 cloves garlic, minced

2 medium tomatoes, cut into wedges

3 cans (14½ ounces each) reduced-sodium fat-free chicken broth, divided

½ cup water

3 cups cooked dried black beans or 2 cans (15 ounces each) black beans, rinsed, drained

1 teaspoon each: dried oregano and thyme leaves, ground cumin

1 bay leaf

8 ounces peeled, deveined shrimp

Salt and pepper, to taste

Finely chopped cilantro, as garnish

Per Serving:
Calories: 190
% of calories from fat: 5
Fat (gm): 1.1
Saturated fat (gm): 0.3
Cholesterol (mg): 58.3
Sodium (mg): 136
Protein (gm): 19.1
Carbohydrate (gm): 27

Exchanges:
Milk: 0.0
Vegetable: 1.0
Fruit: 0.0
Bread: 1.5
Meat: 1.5
Fat: 0.0

1. Sauté onions and garlic in lightly greased medium saucepan until tender, about 5 minutes. Process onion mixture, tomatoes, and 1 can chicken broth in food processor or blender until smooth; return to saucepan. Add remaining 2 cans broth, water, beans, and herbs; heat to boiling. Reduce heat and simmer, uncovered, 10 minutes, adding shrimp during last 5 minutes. Discard bay leaf. Season to taste with salt and pepper; sprinkle with cilantro.

GARBANZO BEAN SOUP

45

Cumin adds a Mexican flavor to this soup; curry powder can be substituted to give an Indian flavor.

4 entrée servings (about 1⅓ cups each)

2 each: finely chopped medium onions, garlic cloves

2 cans (15 ounces each) garbanzo beans, rinsed, drained

2 cans (14½ ounces each) reduced-sodium fat-free chicken broth

1 teaspoon ground cumin

½–¾ teaspoon dried thyme leaves

Salt and pepper, to taste

¼ cup fat-free sour cream

Paprika or chili powder, as garnish

Per Serving:
Calories: 267
% of calories from fat: 15
Fat (gm): 4.6
Saturated fat (gm): 0.6
Cholesterol (mg): 0
Sodium (mg): 627
Protein (gm): 12.4
Carbohydrate (gm): 46.4

1. Sauté onions and garlic in lightly greased large saucepan until tender, about 5 minutes. Add beans, broth, cumin, and thyme and heat to boiling; reduce heat and simmer, covered, 10 minutes. Process soup in food processor or blender until smooth; season to taste with salt and pepper. Top each bowl of soup with a dollop of sour cream and sprinkle with paprika.

Exchanges:
Milk: 0.0
Vegetable: 1.0
Fruit: 0.0
Bread: 3.0
Meat: 0.0
Fat: 0.0

CANNELLINI AND CABBAGE SOUP

45 *Any white bean, such as Great Northern or navy may be substituted for the cannellini.*

8 first-course servings (about 1 cup each)

3 cups thinly sliced or chopped cabbage

1 small onion, coarsely chopped

3 cloves garlic, minced

1 teaspoon crushed caraway seeds

2 cans (14½ ounces each) reduced-sodium chicken broth

1 cup water

1 can (15 ounces) cannellini or Great Northern beans, rinsed, drained

½ cup (4 ounces) mostaccioli (penne), uncooked

Salt and pepper, to taste

Per Serving:
Calories: 107
% of calories from fat: 7
Fat (gm): 1
Saturated fat (gm): 0.1
Cholesterol (mg): 0
Sodium (mg): 175
Protein (gm): 6.9
Carbohydrate (gm): 21.9

Exchanges:
Milk: 0.0
Vegetable: 1.0
Fruit: 0.0
Bread: 1.0
Meat: 0.5
Fat: 0.0

1. Sauté cabbage, onion, garlic, and caraway seeds in lightly greased medium skillet until cabbage begins to wilt, 8 to 10 minutes. Add chicken broth, water, and beans to saucepan; heat to boiling. Stir in pasta; reduce heat and simmer, uncovered, until pasta is al dente, about 15 minutes. Season to taste with salt and pepper.

BEAN-THICKENED SOUP

45 *Pureed beans contribute a hearty texture and subtle flavor to this soup.*

4 first-course servings (about 1⅓ cups each)

2 carrots, sliced

1 small onion, chopped

2 large cloves garlic, minced

1¾ cups vegetable broth

1 can (16 ounces) whole tomatoes, undrained,
    coarsely chopped

1 can (15 ounces) Great Northern beans, rinsed,
    drained, pureed

½ teaspoon each: dried thyme and sage leaves

Salt and pepper, to taste

Per Serving:
Calories: 176
% of calories from fat: 5
Fat (gm): 1
Saturated fat (gm): 0.2
Cholesterol (mg): 0
Sodium (mg): 208
Protein (gm): 9.8
Carbohydrate (gm): 34

Exchanges:
Milk: 0.0
Vegetable: 2.0
Fruit: 0.0
Bread: 1.5
Meat: 0.5
Fat: 0.0

1. Sauté carrots, onion, and garlic in lightly greased large saucepan until onion is tender, about 5 minutes. Stir in broth, tomatoes with liquid, pureed beans, and herbs. Heat to boiling; reduce heat and simmer, covered, until carrots are tender, about 10 minutes. Season to taste with salt and pepper.

WHITE BEAN AND YELLOW SQUASH BEAN CHILI

45 *Add a minced jalapeño chili, if you like your chili hot!*

4 entrée servings (about 1½ cups each)

2 cups chopped onions

1 cup chopped yellow bell pepper

2 teaspoons each: minced garlic, cumin seeds

2- tablespoons olive oil

1 pound lean ground pork

1 medium yellow summer squash, cubed

2 cans (15 ounces each) Great Northern beans,
    rinsed, drained

2 cups reduced-sodium fat-free chicken broth

½ cup dry white wine (optional)

2 teaspoons chili powder

Per Serving:
Calories: 350
% of calories from fat: 23
Fat (gm): 10
Saturated fat (gm): 2.7
Cholesterol (mg): 49.3
Sodium (mg): 719
Protein (gm): 32.7
Carbohydrate (gm): 41.2

Exchanges:
Milk: 0.0
Vegetable: 2.0
Fruit: 0.0
Bread: 2.0
Meat: 3.0
Fat: 0.0

1 teaspoon dried oregano leaves
½ teaspoon ground cinnamon
Salt and pepper, to taste
Chopped tomato and cilantro, as garnish

1. Sauté onions, bell pepper, garlic, and cumin seeds in oil in large saucepan 5 minutes. Add pork and cook over medium heat until browned, about 5 minutes; add remaining ingredients, except salt, pepper, and garnishes and heat to boiling. Reduce heat and simmer, covered, until vegetables are almost tender, about 10 minutes. Simmer, uncovered, until thickened, 5 to 10 minutes. Season to taste with salt and pepper. Sprinkle each bowl of chili with tomato and cilantro.

DILLED BEET SOUP

It's not necessary to peel beets, as the skins slip off easily after cooking.

8 first-course servings (about 1¼ cups each)

12 medium beets, tops trimmed, scrubbed
   (about 3 pounds)
3 cups water
2–3 chicken bouillon cubes
Water
¾–1 cup dry red wine or chicken broth
1½–2 teaspoons dried dill weed
2–3 tablespoons red wine vinegar
Salt and pepper, to taste
Thin lemon slices, as garnish

Per Serving:
Calories: 63
% of calories from fat: 3
Fat (gm): 0.3
Saturated fat (gm): 0
Cholesterol (mg): 0
Sodium (mg): 318
Protein (gm): 1.8
Carbohydrate (gm): 10.6

Exchanges:
Milk: 0.0
Vegetable: 2.0
Fruit: 0.0
Bread: 0.0
Meat: 0.0
Fat: 0.0

1. Heat beets, 3 cups water, and bouillon cubes to boiling in large saucepan; reduce heat and simmer, covered, until beets are tender, 30 to 40 minutes. Drain, reserving cooking liquid. Slip skins off beets and cut into quarters.

2. Add enough water to reserved cooking liquid to make 6 cups. Process beets, wine, reserved cooking liquid, and dill weed in food processor or blender container until smooth. Season to taste with vinegar, salt, and pepper. Serve warm or chilled; garnish each bowl of soup with a lemon slice.

BEET BORSCHT

45   *This delicious soup is flavored in the traditional way with Polish sausage.*

8 first-course servings (about 1¼ cups each)

8 ounces low-fat smoked Polish sausage, sliced
    (½-inch)
2 teaspoons margarine or butter
6 cups reduced-sodium fat-free beef broth
1 small head red cabbage, thinly sliced or shredded
4 medium beets, peeled, julienned
2 carrots, julienned
1 clove garlic, minced
1 bay leaf
2–3 teaspoons sugar
2 tablespoons cider vinegar
Salt and pepper, to taste
Chopped dill weed, as garnish

Per Serving:
Calories: 120
% of calories from fat: 25
Fat (gm): 0.4
Saturated fat (gm): 0.6
Cholesterol (mg): 17.2
Sodium (mg): 437
Protein (gm): 10.9
Carbohydrate (gm): 13.1

Exchanges:
Milk: 0.0
Vegetable: 3.0
Fruit: 0.0
Bread: 0.0
Meat: 1.0
Fat: 0.0

1. Sauté sausage in margarine in Dutch oven until browned, about
5 minutes. Add remaining ingredients, except salt, pepper, and
dill weed; heat to boiling. Reduce heat and simmer, covered, until
vegetables are tender, about 15 minutes. Season to taste with salt
and pepper; sprinkle each bowl of soup with dill weed.

CREAM OF BROCCOLI SOUP

45   *Eat broccoli often—it's high in antioxidants and packed with nutrients.
This soup can be served warm, or chilled.*

6 first-course servings (about 1 cup each)

1 cup chopped onion
3 cloves garlic, minced
2 pounds broccoli, cut into 2-inch pieces
½ teaspoon dried thyme leaves
⅛ teaspoon ground nutmeg
3½ cups reduced-sodium fat-free chicken broth

½ cup fat-free half-and-half or fat-free milk

Salt and white pepper, to taste

6 tablespoons fat-free sour cream

1½ cups Croutons (½ recipe, see p. 532)

(½ recipe, see p. 532)

Per Serving:
Calories: 99
% of calories from fat: 9
Fat (gm): 1.1
Saturated fat (gm): 0.2
Cholesterol (mg): 0
Sodium (mg): 110
Protein (gm): 6.8
Carbohydrate (gm): 17.6

Exchanges:
Milk: 0.0
Vegetable: 2.0
Fruit: 0.0
Bread: 0.5
Meat: 0.0
Fat: 0.0

1. Sauté onion and garlic in lightly greased saucepan until tender, 3 to 5 minutes. Stir in broccoli, thyme, and nutmeg; cook 2 minutes longer. Add broth to saucepan and heat to boiling; reduce heat and simmer, covered, until broccoli is tender, about 10 minutes. Stir in half-and-half.

2. Process soup in food processor or blender until smooth; season to taste with salt and white pepper. Stir 1 tablespoon sour cream into each bowl of soup; sprinkle with Croutons.

VARIATIONS

Dilled Broccoli Soup — Make recipe as above, deleting thyme, nutmeg, and Croutons (see p. 532). Add ⅔ cup loosely packed fresh dill weed to soup when pureeing.

Broccoli-Kale Soup — Make recipe as above, increasing broth to 5 cups, adding ½ teaspoon dried marjoram leaves and deleting the half-and-half, Croutons (see p. 532), and nutmeg. Stir 2 cups lightly packed kale into the soup during the last 5 minutes of cooking time. Process as above, adding more broth as needed for desired consistency.

HERBED BROCCOLI AND PASTA SOUP

45 *A versatile soup, as any vegetable in season and any choice of herb can be substituted for the broccoli and thyme.*

6 first-course servings (about 1 cup each)

3 cans (14½ ounces each) reduced-sodium fat-free chicken broth

4 cloves garlic, minced

2 teaspoons dried thyme leaves

3 cups small broccoli florets

1 cup uncooked fusilli (spirals)

2–3 tablespoons lemon juice

Salt and pepper, to taste

Per Serving:
Calories: 151
% of calories from fat: 7.8
Fat (gm): 1.3
Saturated fat (gm): 0.1
Cholesterol (mg): 0.0
Sodium (mg): 801
Protein (gm): 6.4
Carbohydrate (gm): 29

Exchanges:
Milk: 0.0
Vegetable: 3.0
Fruit: 0.0
Bread: 1.0
Meat: 0.0
Fat: 0.0

1. Heat broth, garlic, and thyme to boiling in medium saucepan. Stir in broccoli and fusilli. Reduce heat and simmer, uncovered, until broccoli is tender and pasta is al dente, about 10 minutes. Season to taste with lemon juice, salt, and pepper.

RUSSIAN CABBAGE SOUP

Use red or green cabbage, fresh or canned beets in this savory soup.

8 first-course servings (about 1½ cups each)

2 medium onions, sliced

1 tablespoon margarine or butter

7 cups reduced-sodium fat-free beef broth

1 can (16 ounces) reduced-sodium whole tomatoes, undrained, coarsely chopped

6 cups thinly sliced red cabbage

4 large beets, peeled, cubed

1 cup each: sliced carrots, cubed turnip, potato

1 tablespoon cider vinegar

Salt and pepper, to taste

8 tablespoons fat-free sour cream

Per Serving:
Calories: 109
% of calories from fat: 17
Fat (gm): 2.2
Saturated fat (gm): 0.4
Cholesterol (mg): 0
Sodium (mg): 91
Protein (gm): 4
Carbohydrate (gm): 20.7

Exchanges:
Milk: 0.0
Vegetable: 3.0
Fruit: 0.0
Bread: 0.5
Meat: 0.0
Fat: 0.0

1. Sauté onions in margarine in Dutch oven until tender, about 5 minutes. Add broth, vegetables, and vinegar; heat to boiling. Reduce heat and simmer, uncovered, 20 to 30 minutes; season to taste with salt and pepper. Top each bowl of soup with a tablespoon of sour cream.

DILLED CARROT SOUP

45 *Carrots team with dill for a fresh, clean flavor. Use canned reduced-sodium vegetable broth, if you like.*

6 first-course servings (about 1½ cups each)

1½ cups chopped onions

2 cloves garlic, minced

6 cups reduced-sodium fat-free chicken broth

1 can (16 ounces) reduced-sodium diced tomatoes, undrained

2 pounds carrots, cut into 2-inch pieces

1 medium Idaho potato, peeled, cubed

2–3 tablespoons lemon juice

1–1½ teaspoons dried dill weed

Salt and white pepper, to taste

6 tablespoons fat-free plain yogurt

Shredded carrot, as garnish

Dill sprigs, as garnish

Per Serving:
Calories: 139
% of calories from fat: 6
Fat (gm): 1
Saturated fat (gm): 0.1
Cholesterol (mg): 0.3
Sodium (mg): 88
Protein (gm): 4.4
Carbohydrate (gm): 30.5

Exchanges:
Milk: 0.0
Vegetable: 6.0
Fruit: 0.0
Bread: 0.0
Meat: 0.0
Fat: 0.0

1. Sauté onions and garlic in lightly greased saucepan until tender, about 5 minutes. Add broth, tomatoes and liquid, carrots, and potato; heat to boiling. Reduce heat and simmer, covered, until vegetables are tender, about 15 minutes.

2. Process soup in food processor or blender until smooth. Add lemon juice and dill weed; season to taste with salt and white pepper. Serve soup warm or chilled. Top each bowl of soup with a tablespoon of yogurt; garnish with shredded carrot and dill sprigs.

CREAM OF CAULIFLOWER SOUP WITH CHEESE

45 *Fat-free half-and-half adds a rich creaminess to the soup.*

6 first-course servings (about 1 cup each)

½ cup chopped onion

2 cloves garlic, minced

2 tablespoons flour

3½ cups reduced-sodium fat-free chicken broth

12 ounces cauliflower, cut into florets

1 large Idaho potato, peeled, cubed

¼–½ cup fat-free half-and-half or fat-free milk

¾ cup (3 ounces) reduced-fat Cheddar cheese

Salt and white pepper, to taste

Ground mace or nutmeg, as garnish

Per Serving:
Calories: 98
% of calories from fat: 22
Fat (gm): 2.4
Saturated fat (gm): 1.1
Cholesterol (mg): 7.6
Sodium (mg): 214
Protein (gm): 5.5
Carbohydrate (gm): 13.6

Exchanges:
Milk: 0.0
Vegetable: 1.0
Fruit: 0.0
Bread: 0.5
Meat: 0.5
Fat: 0.0

1. Sauté onion and garlic in lightly greased saucepan until tender, about 10 minutes. Stir in flour; cook about 1 minute longer. Add broth, cauliflower, and potato and heat to boiling; reduce heat and simmer, covered, until vegetables are tender, 10 to 15 minutes. Remove about half the vegetables from the soup with a slotted spoon and reserve. Puree remaining soup in food processor or blender until smooth.

2. Return soup to saucepan; stir in reserved vegetables, half-and-half, and cheese. Cook over low heat, stirring, until cheese is melted, 3 to 4 minutes. Season to taste with salt and white pepper; sprinkle each bowl of soup with mace.

CREAMED CORN SOUP

45 *For a flavor accent, garnish bowls of soup generously with finely chopped cilantro or parsley.*

4 first-course servings (about 1 cup each)

½ cup chopped onion

1 medium Idaho potato, peeled, cubed

2 cloves garlic, minced

1 can (15½ ounces) whole kernel corn, drained

3 tablespoons flour

½ teaspoon ground coriander

⅛ teaspoon cayenne pepper

2 cans (14½ ounces each) vegetable or chicken broth

1 cup fat-free milk

2 medium tomatoes, seeded, chopped

Salt and pepper, to taste

Per Serving:
Calories: 238
% of calories from fat: 8
Fat (gm): 2.3
Saturated fat (gm): 0.4
Cholesterol (mg): 1
Sodium (mg): 443
Protein (gm): 7.7
Carbohydrate (gm): 45.7

Exchanges:
Milk: 0.0
Vegetable: 3.0
Fruit: 0.0
Bread: 2.0
Meat: 0.0
Fat: 0.5

1. Sauté onion, potato, and garlic in lightly greased saucepan until onion is tender, about 5 minutes. Stir in corn, flour, coriander, and cayenne pepper; cook 1 minute longer. Stir in broth and heat to boiling; reduce heat and simmer, covered, until potato is tender, about 10 minutes.

2. Process soup in food processor or blender until almost smooth; return to saucepan; stir in milk and tomatoes and heat to boiling. Reduce heat and simmer, uncovered, 5 minutes. Season to taste with salt and pepper.

HEARTY CORN AND POTATO CHOWDER

45 *If a thicker soup is desired, mix 2 tablespoons flour with ¼ cup water; stir into boiling soup. Boil, stirring until thickened, about 1 minute.*

4 first-course servings (about 1⅓ cups each)

2 cups whole kernel corn

1 medium onion, chopped

1 tablespoon canola oil

2 cups each: reduced-sodium chicken broth, cubed potatoes

½ cup sliced celery

½ teaspoon dried thyme leaves

1¾ cups fat-free half-and-half or fat-free milk

Salt and pepper, to taste

Per Serving:
Calories: 248
% of calories from fat: 19
Fat (gm): 5.6
Saturated fat (gm): 1.5
Cholesterol (mg): 5.3
Sodium (mg): 447
Protein (gm): 8.2
Carbohydrate (gm): 44.7

Exchanges:
Milk: 0.0
Vegetable: 0.0
Fruit: 0.0
Bread: 3.0
Meat: 0.0
Fat: 1.0

1. Sauté corn and onion in oil in large saucepan until onion is tender, 5 to 8 minutes. Process ½ the vegetable mixture and the broth in food processor or blender until finely chopped; return to saucepan. Add potatoes, celery, and thyme; heat to boiling. Reduce heat and simmer, covered, until vegetables are tender, 10 to 15 minutes. Stir in half-and-half and cook 2 to 3 minutes; season to taste with salt and pepper.

HERBED CUCUMBER SOUP

45 *This soup is very delicate in flavor. Use a serrated grapefruit spoon to seed cucumbers quickly and easily.*

6 first-course servings (about 1⅓ cups each)

½ cup chopped onion

6 medium cucumbers (about 3 pounds), peeled, seeded, chopped

3 tablespoons flour

4 cups reduced-sodium fat-free chicken broth

1 teaspoon dried mint or dill weed

½ cup fat-free half-and-half or fat-free milk

Salt and white pepper, to taste

Paprika, and thin slices cucumber, as garnish

Per Serving:
Calories: 70
% of calories from fat: 8
Fat (gm): 0.6
Saturated fat (gm): 0.1
Cholesterol (mg): 0
Sodium (mg): 33
Protein (gm): 3.1
Carbohydrate (gm): 13.7

Exchanges:
Milk: 0.0
Vegetable: 1.0
Fruit: 0.0
Bread: 0.5
Meat: 0.0
Fat: 0.0

1. Sauté onion in lightly greased skillet until tender, 3 to 5 minutes. Add cucumbers and cook over medium heat 5 minutes; stir in flour and cook about 1 minute longer. Add broth and mint to saucepan; heat to boiling. Reduce heat and simmer, covered, 10 minutes.

2. Process soup in food processor or blender until smooth; stir in half-and-half and season to taste with salt and pepper. Serve warm or chilled; garnish each bowl of soup with paprika and cucumber slices.

CUCUMBER AND SORREL SOUP

45

If cucumbers are mild in flavor, they do not need to be peeled. Spinach or kale can be substituted for the sorrel.

6 first-course servings (about 1¼ cups each)

¼ cup plus 2 tablespoons sliced green onions, divided

1 clove garlic, minced

3 cups (about 1½ pounds) peeled, seeded, chopped cucumbers

1 cup coarsely chopped sorrel

2 cups each: fat-free milk, reduced-sodium fat-free chicken broth

1 tablespoon cornstarch

2 tablespoons water

Salt and white pepper, to taste

1½ cups Herb Croutons (½ recipe) (see p. 533)

Per Serving:
Calories: 70
% of calories from fat: 10
Fat (gm): 0.8
Saturated fat (gm): 0.2
Cholesterol (mg): 1.3
Sodium (mg): 94
Protein (gm): 4.5
Carbohydrate (gm): 11.7

Exchanges:
Milk: 0.0
Vegetable: 2.5
Fruit: 0.0
Bread: 0.0
Meat: 0.0
Fat: 0.0

1. Sauté ¼ cup green onions and garlic in lightly greased saucepan until tender, 3 to 4 minutes. Add cucumbers and sorrel, and cook over medium heat 5 minutes. Add milk and broth; heat to boiling. Reduce heat and simmer, covered, until cucumbers are tender, 5 to 10 minutes.

2. Process soup in food processor or blender until smooth; return to saucepan and heat to boiling. Whisk in combined cornstarch and water, whisking until thickened, about 1 minute. Season to taste with salt and white pepper. Serve chilled; top each bowl of soup with Herb Croutons and remaining green onions.

45-MINUTE PREPARATION TIP: Make Herb Croutons and bake while preparing soup.

EGGPLANT SOUP WITH ROASTED RED PEPPER SAUCE

Grilling gives eggplant a distinctive smoky flavor. For indoor cooking, egg-plant can be oven roasted. Pierce the eggplant in several places with a fork and place in a baking pan. Bake at 350 degrees until soft, 45 to 50 minutes.

4 first-course servings (about 1 cup each)

2 medium eggplants (about 2½ pounds)
¾ cup chopped onion
¼ cup chopped green bell pepper
2 cloves garlic, minced
1 tablespoon olive oil
4–5 cups reduced-sodium fat-free chicken broth
Salt and white pepper, to taste
Roasted Red Pepper Sauce (recipe follows)

Per Serving:
Calories: 250
% of calories from fat: 19
Fat (gm): 6
Saturated fat (gm): 0.7
Cholesterol (mg): 0
Sodium (mg): 25
Protein (gm): 6.8
Carbohydrate (gm): 44.8

Exchanges:
Milk: 0.0
Vegetable: 2.0
Fruit: 0.0
Bread: 2.0
Meat: 0.0
Fat: 1.0

1. Pierce eggplant in several places with fork. Grill over medium hot coals, turning frequently, until eggplant is very soft, about 30 minutes; cool slightly. Cut eggplant in half, scoop out pulp, and chop coarsely.

2. Sauté onion, pepper, and garlic in oil in large saucepan until tender, 5 to 8 minutes. Add broth and eggplant and heat to boiling. Reduce heat and simmer, covered, 10 minutes. Process soup in food processor or blender until smooth. Season to taste with salt and white pepper. Serve chilled; swirl about ¼ cup Roasted Red Pepper Sauce into each bowl of soup.

Roasted Red Pepper Sauce
Makes about ¾ cup

2 large red bell peppers, cut into halves
1 teaspoon sugar

1. Place peppers, skin sides up, on broiler pan. Broil 4 to 6 inches from heat source until skins are blistered and blackened. Place peppers in plastic bag for 5 minutes; remove and peel off skins.

2. Process peppers and sugar in food processor or blender until smooth. Refrigerate until ready to use.

NOTE: 1 jar (12 ounces) roasted red peppers, drained, can be substituted for the peppers in the recipe.

GARLIC SOUP WITH TOASTED BREAD

45 *Often a beaten egg is slowly stirred into this Mexican soup before serving.*

4 first-course servings (about 1 cup each)

4 slices firm bread (French or sourdough)
Vegetable cooking spray
6–8 cloves garlic, finely chopped
½ teaspoon each: ground cumin, dried oregano leaves
1 tablespoon olive oil
2 cans (14½ ounces each) reduced-sodium fat-free chicken broth
Salt and cayenne pepper, to taste
Chopped cilantro, as garnish

Per Serving:
Calories: 162
% of calories from fat: 28
Fat (gm): 5
Saturated fat (gm): 0.7
Cholesterol (mg): 0
Sodium (mg): 202
Protein (gm): 3.2
Carbohydrate (gm): 20.6

Exchanges:
Milk: 0.0
Vegetable: 1.0
Fruit: 0.0
Bread: 1.5
Meat: 0.0
Fat: 0.5

1. Spray both sides of bread slices generously with cooking spray; cook in large skillet, over medium heat, until golden, about 2 minutes on each side.

2. Sauté garlic and herbs in oil in medium saucepan until lightly browned, about 3 minutes. Add broth and heat to boiling; reduce heat and simmer, covered, 5 minutes. Season to taste with salt and cayenne pepper. Place slices of bread in bottoms of shallow bowls; ladle soup over and sprinkle with cilantro.

CREAM OF MUSHROOM SOUP

45 *For a richer soup, use fat-free half-and-half instead of fat-free milk.*

4 first-course servings (about 1¼ cups each)

1 pound mushrooms
2 tablespoons margarine or butter, divided
1 cup chopped onion
2½ cups reduced-sodium chicken broth
2½ cups fat-free milk, divided
2 tablespoons plus 2 teaspoons cornstarch
Salt and pepper, to taste

Per Serving:
Calories: 207
% of calories from fat: 29
Fat (gm): 7
Saturated fat (gm): 1.4
Cholesterol (mg): 2.5
Sodium (mg): 185
Protein (gm): 8.6
Carbohydrate (gm): 25.3

Exchanges:
Milk: 0.5
Vegetable: 2.5
Fruit: 0.0
Bread: 0.5
Meat: 0.0
Fat: 1.5

1. Slice enough mushroom caps to make 2 cups; finely chop stems and remaining mushrooms.

Sauté sliced mushrooms in 1 tablespoon margarine in large sauce-pan until browned, about 5 minutes; remove and reserve.

2. Sauté onion and chopped mushrooms in remaining 1 tablespoon margarine in saucepan until onion is tender, about 5 minutes. Add broth and 2 cups milk and heat to boiling. Mix remaining ½ cup milk and cornstarch and stir into boiling mixture; boil, stirring, until thickened, about 1 minute. Stir in reserved sliced mushrooms. Season to taste with salt and pepper.

SAVORY MUSHROOM AND BARLEY SOUP

45

Use of quick-cooking barley speeds preparation. Other grains, such as wild rice or oat groats, can be substituted for the barley; cook before adding to the soup.

4 first-course servings (about 1½ cups each)

1 cup each: chopped onion, celery, carrots

1 teaspoon dried savory leaves

¾ teaspoon fennel seeds, crushed

1 quart water

1 can (16 ounces) reduced-sodium whole tomatoes, undrained, coarsely chopped

½ cup quick-cooking barley

2 cups sliced cremini or white mushrooms

¼ cup chopped parsley

Salt and pepper, to taste

Per Serving:
Calories: 151
% of calories from fat: 8
Fat (gm): 1.4
Saturated fat (gm): 0.1
Cholesterol (mg): 0
Sodium (mg): 53
Protein (gm): 5.6
Carbohydrate (gm): 32.1

Exchanges:
Milk: 0.0
Vegetable: 2.0
Fruit: 0.0
Bread: 1.5
Meat: 0.0
Fat: 0.0

1. Sauté onion, celery, and carrots in lightly greased saucepan until onion is tender, about 5 minutes. Stir in herbs; cook about 1 minute longer. Add water, tomatoes with liquid, barley, and mushrooms to saucepan; heat to boiling. Cook, covered, until barley is tender, 10 to 15 minutes. Stir in parsley; season to taste with salt and pepper.

TORTELLINI AND MUSHROOM SOUP

Porcini mushrooms, a Tuscan delicacy found fresh in the fall, are available in dried form year round. Porcini impart a wonderful earthy flavor to recipes. Other dried mushrooms can be substituted for a similar flavor.

6 first-course servings (about 1 cup each)

2 ounces dried porcini mushrooms

Hot water

8 ounces fresh white mushrooms, sliced

2 tablespoons finely chopped shallots or green onions

2 cloves garlic, minced

½ teaspoon dried tarragon or thyme leaves

2 cans (14½ ounces each) reduced-sodium
beef broth

¼ cup dry sherry (optional)

1 package (9 ounces) fresh tomato-and-
cheese tortellini

Salt and pepper, to taste

Per Serving:
Calories: 110
% of calories from fat: 16
Fat (gm): 2
Saturated fat (gm): 0.4
Cholesterol (mg): 4.2
Sodium (mg): 184
Protein (gm): 5
Carbohydrate (gm): 17.1

Exchanges:
Milk: 0.0
Vegetable: 1.0
Fruit: 0.0
Bread: 1.0
Meat: 0.0
Fat: 0.5

1. Place dried mushrooms in bowl; pour hot water over to cover. Let stand until mushrooms are soft, about 15 minutes; drain. Slice mushrooms, discarding any tough parts.

2. Sauté dried and white mushrooms, shallots, garlic, and tarragon in lightly greased saucepan until mushrooms are tender, about 5 minutes. Add broth and sherry and heat to boiling; add tortellini, salt, and pepper. Reduce heat and simmer, uncovered, until tortellini are al dente, about 5 minutes; season to taste with salt and pepper.

BLACK MUSHROOM SOUP

Chinese black mushrooms (dried shiitake mushrooms) add a fragrant, woodsy flavor to this soup.

6 first-course servings (about 1¼ cups each)

1½ ounces dried Chinese black mushrooms
1 ounce dried cloud ear mushrooms
2 cups boiling water
¼ cup each: chopped onion, green onions
5 cups reduced-sodium fat-free chicken broth
3 cups sliced cremini mushrooms
Salt and white pepper, to taste

Per Serving:
Calories: 72
% of calories from fat: 16
Fat (gm): 1.4
Saturated fat (gm): 0.1
Cholesterol (mg): 0
Sodium (mg): 10
Protein (gm): 2.9
Carbohydrate (gm): 11.1

Exchanges:
Milk: 0.0
Vegetable: 3.0
Fruit: 0.0
Bread: 0.0
Meat: 0.0
Fat: 0.0

1. Place dried mushrooms in bowl; add boiling water. Let stand until mushrooms are softened, about 15 minutes. Drain, reserving liquid. Slice mushrooms, discarding tough stems from black mushrooms.

2. Sauté onions until tender in lightly greased saucepan, about 5 minutes. Add dried mushrooms, reserved liquid and broth; heat to boiling. Reduce heat and simmer, covered, 20 minutes, adding cremini mushrooms during last 10 minutes. Season to taste with salt and white pepper.

FRENCH ONION SOUP

This classic soup is topped with Bruschetta and fat-free cheese for healthful, delicious dining.

8 first-course servings (about 1¼ cups each)

6 cups (1½ pounds) thinly sliced Spanish onions
2 cloves garlic, minced
1 teaspoon sugar
6 cups reduced-sodium fat-free beef broth
2 bay leaves
Salt and white pepper, to taste
8 Bruschetta (⅓ recipe) (see p. 530)
8 tablespoons (2 ounces) shredded fat-free Swiss
    or mozzarella cheese

Per Serving:
Calories: 126
% of calories from fat: 7
Fat (gm): 1
Saturated fat (gm): 0.1
Cholesterol (mg): 0.0
Sodium (mg): 542
Protein (gm): 4.9
Carbohydrate (gm): 25

Exchanges:
Milk: 0.0
Vegetable: 0.0
Fruit: 0.0
Bread: 1.5
Meat: 0.0
Fat: 0.0

1. Add onions and garlic to lightly greased Dutch oven and cook, covered, over medium-low heat until wilted, 8 to 10 minutes. Stir in sugar and continue cooking, uncovered, until onions are lightly browned, about 10 minutes. Stir in broth and bay leaves; heat to boiling. Reduce heat and simmer, covered, 30 minutes. Discard bay leaves; season to taste with salt and white pepper.

2. Top each Bruschetta with 1 tablespoon cheese; broil 6 inches from heat source until cheese is melted. Top each bowl of soup with a Bruschetta.

VIDALIA ONION SOUP

The mild sweetness of Vidalia onions makes this soup special, but try it with other flavorful onion varieties too.

8 first-course servings (about 1¼ cups each)

6 cups (1½ pounds) thinly sliced Vidalia onions

2 cloves garlic, minced

1 teaspoon sugar

⅓ cup all-purpose flour

6 cups reduced-sodium fat-free chicken or vegetable, broth

1½ teaspoons dried sage leaves

2 bay leaves

Salt, cayenne, and white pepper, to taste

Snipped chives, as garnish

Per Serving:
Calories: 88
% of calories from fat: 3
Fat (gm): 0.3
Saturated fat (gm): 0.1
Cholesterol (mg): 0
Sodium (mg): 13
Protein (gm): 2.2
Carbohydrate (gm): 16.4

Exchanges:
Milk: 0.0
Vegetable: 2.0
Fruit: 0.0
Bread: 0.5
Meat: 0.0
Fat: 0.0

1. Add onions and garlic to lightly greased saucepan and cook, covered, over medium-low heat until wilted, 8 to 10 minutes. Stir in sugar and continue cooking, uncovered, until onions are lightly browned. Stir in flour; cook about 1 minute longer. Add broth and herbs; heat to boiling. Reduce heat and simmer, covered, 30 minutes. Discard bay leaves.

2. Process half the soup in food processor or blender until smooth; return to saucepan and season to taste with salt, cayenne, and white pepper. Serve warm or chilled; sprinkle each bowl of soup with chives.

THREE-ONION SOUP WITH MUSHROOMS

Mushrooms are a flavorful addition to this onion soup. Substitute canned reduced-sodium vegetable broth to speed preparation.

6 first-course servings (about 1½ cups each)

3 cups thinly sliced onions
1½ cups thinly sliced leeks
½ cup chopped shallots or green onions
1 tablespoon margarine or butter
1 teaspoon sugar
2 cups sliced mushrooms
6½ cups reduced-sodium fat-free chicken broth
Salt and pepper, to taste

Per Serving:
Calories: 119
% of calories from fat: 21
Fat (gm): 3
Saturated fat (gm): 0.5
Cholesterol (mg): 0
Sodium (mg): Protein (gm): 2.7
Carbohydrate (gm): 18.5

Exchanges:
Milk: 0.0
Vegetable: 3.0
Fruit: 0.0
Bread: 0.0
Meat: 0.0
Fat: 0.5

1. Cook onions, leeks, and shallots in margarine in large saucepan, covered, over medium-low heat 15 minutes. Stir in sugar; continue cooking, uncovered, until onion mixture is golden, about 15 minutes. Stir in mushrooms; cook over medium heat until tender, about 5 minutes. Add broth and heat to boiling; reduce heat and simmer, uncovered, 15 minutes. Season to taste with salt and pepper.

ONION AND LEEK SOUP WITH MUSHROOMS

Mushrooms add flavor and texture interest to this soup.

6 first-course servings (about 1½ cups each)

3 cups sliced onions
1½ cups sliced leeks
½ cup chopped shallots or green onions
1 tablespoon margarine or butter
1 teaspoon sugar
4 ounces mushrooms, sliced
6½ cups reduced-sodium chicken broth
Salt and pepper, to taste

Per Serving:
Calories: 211
% of calories from fat: 3
Fat (gm): 0.8
Saturated fat (gm): 0.1
Cholesterol (mg): 0
Sodium (mg): 234
Protein (gm): 12.9
Carbohydrate (gm): 37.1

Exchanges:
Milk: 0.0
Vegetable: 2.0
Fruit: 0.0
Bread: 2.0
Meat: 0.0
Fat: 0.0

1. Cook onions, leeks, and shallots in margarine in large saucepan, covered, over medium heat until wilted, 5 to 8 minutes. Stir in sugar and mushrooms; cook, uncovered, over medium-low heat until onion mixture is golden, 10 to 15 minutes. Add broth and heat to boiling; reduce heat and simmer, uncovered, 15 minutes. Season to taste with salt and pepper.

CHILLED PEA SOUP

45

A refreshing soup for hot sultry days; serve with a ripe tomato salad and crusty bread or rolls.

6 entrée servings (about 1 cup each)

½ cup chopped onion
½ teaspoon each: dried marjoram and thyme leaves
2 cups reduced-sodium fat-free chicken broth
2 packages (20 ounces each) frozen peas
2 cups sliced romaine lettuce
Salt and white pepper, to taste
½ cup fat-free sour cream
Paprika, as garnish

Per Serving:
Calories: 257
% of calories from fat: 4
Fat (gm): 1.1
Saturated fat (gm): 0.2
Cholesterol (mg): 0
Sodium (mg): 274
Protein (gm): 17.4
Carbohydrate (gm): 46.6

Exchanges:
Milk: 0.0
Vegetable: 0.0
Fruit: 0.0
Bread: 3.0
Meat: 0.5
Fat: 0.0

1. Sauté onion and herbs in lightly greased large saucepan until onion is tender, about 5 minutes. Stir in broth, peas, and lettuce; heat to boiling. Reduce heat and simmer, covered, until peas are tender, 5 to 8 minutes. Process soup in food processor or blender until smooth; season to taste with salt and pepper. Serve chilled; stir in sour cream before serving and sprinkle with paprika.

SNOW PEA SOUP

45 *Make this soup a day in advance so that flavors can blend.*

6 first-course servings (about 1¼ cups each)

½ cup each: chopped green onions, yellow onion
1 tablespoon margarine or butter
1 pound snow peas, trimmed
4 cups coarsely chopped romaine lettuce
4 cups reduced-sodium fat-free chicken broth
½ teaspoon each: dried tarragon and mint leaves
Salt and white pepper, to taste
6 tablespoons plain fat-free yogurt
Fresh mint or tarragon sprigs

Per Serving:
Calories: 76
% of calories from fat: 28
Fat (gm): 2.5
Saturated fat (gm): 0.5
Cholesterol (mg): 0.3
Sodium (mg): 47
Protein (gm): 4.3
Carbohydrate (gm): 9.8

Exchanges:
Milk: 0.0
Vegetable: 2.0
Fruit: 0.0
Bread: 0.0
Meat: 0.0
Fat: 0.5

1. Sauté onions in margarine in large saucepan until tender, about 5 minutes. Add snow peas and lettuce; sauté 3 to 4 minutes longer. Add broth, tarragon, and mint; heat to boiling. Reduce heat and simmer, covered, 15 minutes or until snow peas are very tender.

2. Process soup in food processor or blender until smooth; strain and discard solids. Season to taste with salt and white pepper. Serve warm or chilled; garnish each bowl of soup with yogurt and fresh mint.

SWEET RED PEPPER SOUP

45 *Use jarred roasted peppers for this soup, or roast 3 medium red bell peppers. (See Roasted Red Pepper Sauce, p. 50, for roasting directions).*

4 first-course servings (about 1 cup each)

1 medium onion, chopped
½ small jalapeño chili, seeded, minced
1 clove garlic, minced
1 jar (15 ounces) roasted red bell peppers, drained
1 cup reduced-sodium tomato juice
1 can (14½ ounces) vegetable or chicken broth
½ teaspoon dried marjoram leaves
Salt and pepper, to taste

Per Serving:
Calories: 77
% of calories from fat: 5
Fat (gm): 0.4
Saturated fat (gm): 0.1
Cholesterol (mg): 0
Sodium (mg): 264
Protein (gm): 2.9
Carbohydrate (gm): 13.4

Exchanges:
Milk: 0.0
Vegetable: 3.0
Fruit: 0.0
Bread: 0.0
Meat: 0.0
Fat: 0.0

¼ cup fat-free sour cream
Sliced green onion, as garnish

1. Sauté onion, jalapeño chili, and garlic in lightly greased saucepan until tender, about 5 minutes. Process onion mixture, bell peppers, and tomato juice in food processor or blender until smooth. Return mixture to saucepan and add broth and marjoram; heat to boiling. Reduce heat and simmer, covered, 15 minutes. Season to taste with salt and pepper. Serve warm or chilled; top each bowl of soup with a dollop of sour cream and sprinkle with green onion.

POTATO CHOWDER

45 *A basic soup that is versatile: substitute any desired vegetables, such as carrots, zucchini, green beans, or corn, for part of the potatoes for a delectable vegetable chowder.*

6 entrée servings (about 1 cup each)

1 cup chopped onion
¼ cup thinly sliced celery
2 tablespoons margarine or butter
3 tablespoons flour
2 cups reduced-sodium chicken broth
3½ cups peeled, cubed Idaho potatoes
¼–½ teaspoon celery seeds
2 cups fat-free milk
Salt and pepper, to taste

Per Serving:
Calories: 212
% of calories from fat: 17
Fat (gm): 4.2
Saturated fat (gm): 0.9
Cholesterol (mg): 1.3
Sodium (mg): 210
Protein (gm): 7.5
Carbohydrate (gm): 37.1

Exchanges:
Milk: 0.0
Vegetable: 1.0
Fruit: 0.0
Bread: 2.0
Meat: 0.0
Fat: 1.0

1. Sauté onion and celery in margarine in large saucepan until tender, 5 to 8 minutes; stir in flour and cook 1 minute longer. Add broth, potatoes, and celery seeds to saucepan; heat to boiling. Reduce heat and simmer, covered, until potatoes are tender, 10 to 15 minutes. Stir in milk and cook until hot, 2 to 3 minutes. Season to taste with salt and pepper.

HOT CHILI VICHYSSOISE

45 *Potato soup will never be boring if served Tex-Mex style. This version, prepared with peppers, packs a punch!*

6 entrée servings (about 1 cup each)

1 each: chopped medium leek (white part only), large poblano and jalapeño chili

1 pound new red potatoes, unpeeled, halved

6 cloves garlic, peeled

Vegetable cooking spray

1½ teaspoons ground cumin

½ teaspoon each: chili powder, dried oregano leaves, pepper

4 cups reduced-sodium fat-free chicken broth, divided

½–¾ cup fat-free half-and-half or fat-free milk

¼ cup chopped cilantro

Salt, to taste

Per Serving:
Calories: 113
% of calories from fat: 2
Fat (gm): 0.3
Saturated fat (gm): 0
Cholesterol (mg): 0
Sodium (mg): 169
Protein (gm): 6.6
Carbohydrate (gm): 20.9

Exchanges:
Milk: 0.0
Vegetable: 1.0
Fruit: 0.0
Bread: 1.0
Meat: 0.0
Fat: 0.0

1. Cut leek and chilies into ¾-inch pieces. Arrange vegetables in single layer greased foil-lined jelly roll pan; spray with cooking spray and sprinkle with herbs and pepper. Roast at 425 degrees until browned and tender, about 40 minutes, removing garlic when tender, after about 30 minutes.

2. Process vegetables and 1 to 2 cups broth in food processor or blender until smooth. Heat vegetable mixture and remaining broth to boiling in large saucepan; reduce heat to medium. Stir in half-and-half and cook until hot, 3 to 4 minutes. Stir in cilantro; season with salt. Serve warm or chilled.

POTATO AND FRESH HERB SOUP

For flavor variation, try another favorite garden herb, such as rosemary, oregano, lemon thyme, or marjoram.

6 side-dish servings (about 1 cup each)

4 cups reduced-sodium vegetable broth
1 cup each: firmly packed basil and parsley
½ cup chopped onion
1 teaspoon sugar
2 cups potatoes, peeled, cubed
1 cup fat-free milk
¼ cup all-purpose flour
1 tablespoon margarine or butter
Salt and white pepper, to taste
Chopped parsley, as garnish

Per Serving:
Calories: 128
% of calories from fat: 17
Fat (gm): 2.5
Saturated fat (gm): 0.5
Cholesterol (mg): 0.8
Sodium (mg): 355
Protein (gm): 4
Carbohydrate (gm): 22.7

Exchanges:
Milk: 0.0
Vegetable: 0.0
Fruit: 0.0
Bread: 1.5
Meat: 0.0
Fat: 0.5

1. Heat broth, basil, parsley, onion, and sugar to boiling in medium saucepan. Simmer, covered, 30 minutes. Strain; return broth to saucepan. Add potatoes and heat to boiling; reduce heat and simmer, covered, until potatoes are tender, about 15 minutes. Mix milk and flour; stir into saucepan and heat to boiling. Boil, stirring, until thickened, about 1 minute; stir in margarine. Season to taste with salt and white pepper; sprinkle each bowl of soup with parsley.

TWO-SEASON SQUASH AND BEAN SOUP

45 *Winter and summer squash are combined with beans in this flavorful soup.*

6 side-dish servings (about 1½ cups each)

1 cup chopped onion

2 cloves garlic, minced

2 teaspoons margarine or butter

3 cups fat-free beef broth

2 cups each: cubed, seeded butternut squash,
   sliced zucchini

1 can (28 ounces) reduced-sodium whole tomatoes,
   undrained, chopped

1 can (15 ounces) Great Northern beans,
   rinsed, drained

3 tablespoons parsley, chopped

1 bay leaf

1 teaspoon low-sodium Worcestershire sauce

1 teaspoon each: dried marjoram and rosemary leaves

Salt and pepper, to taste

Per Serving:
Calories: 119
% of calories from fat: 10
Fat (gm): 1.6
Saturated fat (gm): 0.3
Cholesterol (mg): 0
Sodium (mg): 308
Protein (gm): 8.3
Carbohydrate (gm): 23.2

Exchanges:
Milk: 0.0
Vegetable: 1.0
Fruit: 0.0
Bread: 1.5
Meat: 0.0
Fat: 0.0

1. Sauté onion and garlic in margarine in large saucepan until tender, about 5 minutes. Add remaining ingredients, except salt and pepper. Heat to boiling; reduce heat and simmer, covered, until squash is tender, about 10 minutes. Discard bay leaf; season to taste with salt and pepper.

CINNAMON-SPICED PUMPKIN SOUP

45 *For convenience, 2 cans (16 ounces each) pumpkin can be substituted for the fresh pumpkin. Any yellow winter squash such as butternut, Hubbard, or acorn can also be used.*

4 first-course servings (about 1¼ cups each)

4 cups cubed, seeded, peeled pumpkin

2 cups fat-free half-and-half or fat-free milk

1–2 tablespoons light brown sugar

½ teaspoon ground cinnamon

¼–½ teaspoon ground nutmeg

Snipped chives, as garnish

Per Serving:
Calories: 125
% of calories from fat: 1
Fat (gm): 0.2
Saturated fat (gm): 0.1
Cholesterol (mg): 0
Sodium (mg): 122
Protein (gm): 5.2
Carbohydrate (gm): 23.2

Exchanges:
Milk: 1.0
Vegetable: 0.0
Fruit: 0.0
Bread: 0.5
Meat: 0.0
Fat: 0.0

1. Cook pumpkin in medium saucepan, covered, in 1 inch simmering water until tender, about 15 minutes; drain. Process pumpkin and half-and-half in food processor or blender; return to saucepan. Stir in brown sugar and spices and heat to boiling; reduce heat and simmer, uncovered, 5 minutes. Sprinkle each bowl of soup with chives.

SUMMER SQUASH SOUP

Use any summer squash in this soup.

6 first-course servings (about 1¼ cups each)

4 medium zucchini, chopped

1 cup peeled, cubed Idaho potato

½ cup chopped shallots

¼ cup sliced green onions

2 cloves garlic, minced

4 cups reduced-sodium fat-free chicken broth

1 cup chopped kale or spinach leaves

1–½ teaspoons dried tarragon leaves

¼–½ cup fat-free half-and-half or fat-free milk

Salt and white pepper, to taste

Cayenne pepper, as garnish

1½ cups Sourdough Croutons (½ recipe) (see p. 532)

Per Serving:
Calories: 100
% of calories from fat: 7
Fat (gm): 0.8
Saturated fat (gm): 0.1
Cholesterol (mg): 0
Sodium (mg): 65
Protein (gm): 3.8
Carbohydrate (gm): 20.6

Exchanges:
Milk: 0.0
Vegetable: 1.0
Fruit: 0.0
Bread: 1.0
Meat: 0.0
Fat: 0.0

1. Sauté zucchini, potato, shallots, green onions, and garlic in lightly greased saucepan until lightly browned, about 8 minutes. Add broth, kale, and tarragon. Heat to boiling; reduce heat and simmer, covered, until vegetables are tender, 10 to 15 minutes.

2. Process soup in food processor or blender until smooth; stir in half-and-half and season to taste with salt and white pepper. Serve warm or chilled; sprinkle each of bowl soup with cayenne pepper and top with Sourdough Croutons.

CHAYOTE SQUASH SOUP WITH CILANTRO CREAM

45 *Chayote squash, often called a "vegetable pear," is native to Mexico and readily available here. The squash is light green in color and delicate in flavor.*

6 first-course servings (about 1 cup each)

1 large onion, chopped

2 cloves garlic, minced

3 tablespoons flour

3 large chayote squash, peeled, seeded, sliced

3 cans (14½ ounces each) reduced-sodium fat-free chicken broth, divided

½ cup water

Salt and white pepper, to taste

Cilantro Cream (recipe follows)

Chopped cilantro, as garnish

Per Serving:
Calories: 68
% of calories from fat: 11
Fat (gm): 0.9
Saturated fat (gm): 0.1
Cholesterol (mg): 0.2
Sodium (mg): 27
Protein (gm): 2.9
Carbohydrate (gm): 13.3

Exchanges:
Milk: 0.0
Vegetable: 2.5
Fruit: 0.0
Bread: 0.0
Meat: 0.0
Fat: 0.0

1. Sauté onion and garlic in lightly greased medium skillet until tender, about 5 minutes. Stir in flour; cook over medium heat 2 minutes, stirring constantly. Add squash and 1 can broth to saucepan; heat to boiling; reduce heat and simmer, covered, until squash is tender, 15 to 20 minutes.

2. Process mixture in food processor or blender until smooth; return to saucepan. Add remaining broth and water; season to taste with salt and white pepper. Serve warm or chilled; drizzle each bowl of soup with Cilantro Cream and sprinkle with cilantro.

Cilantro Cream

Makes about ½ cup

⅓ cup fat-free sour cream
1 tablespoon finely chopped cilantro
¼–⅓ cup fat-free milk

1. Mix sour cream and cilantro in small bowl, adding enough milk for desired consistency.

CREAM OF TOMATO SOUP

45 *A soup similar to the favorite-brand canned tomato soup we all remember eating as kids! Canned tomatoes are necessary for the flavor, so don't substitute fresh.*

4 first-course servings (about 1¼ cups each)

2 cans (14½ ounces each) reduced-sodium whole tomatoes, undrained

1–3 teaspoons beef bouillon crystals

2 cups fat-free milk

3 tablespoons cornstarch

⅛ teaspoon baking soda

2 teaspoons sugar

1–2 tablespoons margarine or butter

Salt and pepper, to taste

Per Serving:
Calories: 142
% of calories from fat: 22
Fat (gm): 3.7
Saturated fat (gm): 0.8
Cholesterol (mg): 2
Sodium (mg): 395
Protein (gm): 6.3
Carbohydrate (gm): 22.6

Exchanges:
Milk: 0.5
Vegetable: 2.0
Fruit: 0.0
Bread: 0.5
Meat: 0.0
Fat: 0.5

1. Process tomatoes with liquid in food processor or blender until smooth; heat tomatoes and bouillon crystals to boiling in large saucepan. Mix milk and cornstarch; stir into tomato mixture, stirring until thickened, about 1 minute. Add baking soda, sugar, and margarine, stirring until margarine is melted. Season to taste with salt and pepper.

TWO-TOMATO SOUP

45 *The concentrated flavor of sun-dried tomatoes enhances the taste of garden-ripe tomato soup.*

6 first-course servings (about 1¼ cups each)

1 cup chopped onion

½ cup each: chopped celery, carrot

2 teaspoons minced roasted garlic

4 cups reduced-sodium fat-free chicken broth

4 cups chopped ripe tomatoes or 2 cans (16 ounces each) reduced-sodium whole tomatoes, undrained, coarsely chopped

1 large Idaho potato, peeled, cubed

½ cup sun-dried tomatoes (not in oil)

½ teaspoons dried basil leaves

½ cup fat-free half-and-half or fat-free milk

2–3 teaspoons sugar

Salt and pepper, to taste

Per Serving:
Calories: 117
% of calories from fat: 5
Fat (gm): 0.8
Saturated fat (gm): 0.1
Cholesterol (mg): 0
Sodium (mg): 150
Protein (gm): 3.7
Carbohydrate (gm): 22.6

Exchanges:
Milk: 0.0
Vegetable: 2.0
Fruit: 0.0
Bread: 1.0
Meat: 0.0
Fat: 0.0

1. Sauté onion, celery, carrot, and garlic in lightly greased large saucepan until lightly browned, 5 to 8 minutes. Add broth, tomatoes with liquid, potato, sun-dried tomatoes, and basil; heat to boiling. Reduce heat and simmer, covered, until vegetables are tender, 10 to 15 minutes.

2. Process soup in food processor or blender until smooth; return to saucepan. Stir in half-and-half and heat until hot, 3 to 5 minutes; season to taste with sugar, salt, and pepper.

SUN-DRIED TOMATO AND LINGUINE SOUP

45 *Great soup in less than 30 minutes! One-half cup uncooked orzo can be substituted for the linguine, if preferred.*

4 first-course servings (about 1 cup each)

½ cup thinly sliced celery

2 tablespoons thinly sliced green onions

2 cloves garlic, minced

2 cans (14½ ounces each) reduced-sodium
    chicken broth
2 ounces uncooked linguine, broken into 2- to
    3-inch pieces
2 sun-dried tomatoes (not in oil), softened, chopped
1–2 teaspoons lemon juice
Salt and pepper, to taste

Per Serving:
Calories: 111
% of calories from fat: 10
Fat (gm): 1.3
Saturated fat (gm): 0.1
Cholesterol (mg): 0
Sodium (mg): 155
Protein (gm): 3.3
Carbohydrate (gm): 16.8

Exchanges:
Milk: 0.0
Vegetable: 1.0
Fruit: 0.0
Bread: 1.0
Meat: 0.0
Fat: 0.0

1. Sauté celery, onions, and garlic in lightly
greased medium saucepan until tender, 5 to 7
minutes. Stir in broth and heat to boiling; add
linguine and sun-dried tomatoes. Reduce heat
and simmer, uncovered, until pasta is al dente,
about 10 minutes. Season with lemon juice, salt
and pepper.

RIPE TOMATO AND LEEK SOUP

45 *Use summer's ripest tomatoes for this soup, cooking only briefly to maintain
their sweetness. Peel the tomatoes or not, as you prefer.*

6 first-course servings (about 1¼ cups each)

2 cups sliced leeks
3 cloves garlic, minced
1 tablespoon olive oil
6 large tomatoes (about 2½ pounds)
4 cups reduced-sodium fat-free chicken broth
½–1 teaspoon dried basil leaves
Salt and white pepper, to taste
6 tablespoons fat-free sour cream or plain yogurt
Basil sprigs, as garnish

Per Serving:
Calories: 99
% of calories from fat: 24
Fat (gm): 2.9
Saturated fat (gm): 0.5
Cholesterol (mg): 0
Sodium (mg): 64
Protein (gm): 3.5
Carbohydrate (gm): 17.3

Exchanges:
Milk: 0.0
Vegetable: 3.0
Fruit: 0.0
Bread: 0.0
Meat: 0.0
Fat: 0.5

1. Sauté leeks and garlic in oil in large saucepan until tender, about
8 minutes. Add tomatoes, broth, and basil to saucepan; heat to
boiling. Reduce heat and simmer, covered, 10 minutes. Process
soup in food processor or blender until smooth; season to taste
with salt and white pepper. Serve soup warm or chilled; top each
bowl of soup with a tablespoon of sour cream and garnish with
basil sprigs.

GAZPACHO

45

Easy to make and served cold, Gazpacho is a wonderful soup to keep on hand in summer months.

6 first-course servings (about 1¼ cups each)

5 large tomatoes, halved, seeded
2 cups reduced-sodium tomato juice
2 cloves garlic
2 tablespoons lime juice
1 teaspoon dried oregano leaves
1 cup each: chopped yellow bell pepper,
  celery, cucumber
6 green onions, thinly sliced
2 tablespoons finely chopped cilantro
Salt and pepper, to taste
Avocado Sour Cream (recipe follows)
Hot pepper sauce

Per Serving:
Calories: 76
% of calories from fat: 17
Fat (gm): 1.6
Saturated fat (gm): 0.3
Cholesterol (mg): 0.1
Sodium (mg): 46
Protein (gm): 3.3
Carbohydrate (gm): 15.1

Exchanges:
Milk: 0.0
Vegetable: 2.0
Fruit: 0.0
Bread: 0.0
Meat: 0.0
Fat: 0.5

1. Chop tomatoes, reserving 1 cup. Process remaining tomatoes, tomato juice, garlic, lime juice, and oregano in food processor or blender until smooth. Mix tomato mixture, reserved tomatoes, bell pepper, celery, cucumber, green onions, and cilantro in large bowl; season to taste with salt and pepper. Serve chilled; top each bowl of soup with a dollop of Avocado Sour Cream. Serve with hot pepper sauce.

Avocado Sour Cream

Makes about ⅔ cup

½ medium avocado, chopped
¼ cup fat-free sour cream
2 tablespoons fat-free milk
Salt and white pepper, to taste

1. Process all ingredients in food processor until smooth; season to taste with salt and white pepper.

BEAN GAZPACHO

45

Pureed beans contribute nutritional value, plus a velvety texture, to this delicious gazpacho.

8 entrée servings (about 1⅓ cups each)

2 cans (15 ounces each) pinto beans, rinsed, drained

1 quart reduced-sodium tomato juice

3–4 tablespoons lime juice

2 teaspoons each: reduced-sodium Worcestershire sauce, minced roasted garlic

1 cup each: thick and chunky salsa, peeled, seeded, chopped cucumber, sliced celery

½ cup each: sliced green onions, chopped green bell pepper

½ cup each: chopped avocado, fat-free sour cream

1½ cups (½ recipe) Herb Croutons (see p. 533)

Per Serving:
Calories: 260
% of calories from fat: 13
Fat (gm): 3.8
Saturated fat (gm): 0.2
Cholesterol (mg): 0
Sodium (mg): 642
Protein (gm): 12.9
Carbohydrate (gm): 47.1

Exchanges:
Milk: 0.5
Vegetable: 2.0
Fruit: 0.0
Bread: 2.5
Meat: 0.5
Fat: 0.0

1. Process beans, tomato juice, lime juice, Worcestershire sauce, and garlic in food processor or blender until smooth; pour into large bowl. Mix in remaining ingredients, except avocado, sour cream, and Herb Croutons. Refrigerate until chilled, 3 to 4 hours.

2. Mix avocado into soup; garnish each bowl of soup with a dollop of sour cream and sprinkle with croutons.

45-MINUTE PREPARATION TIP: Make Herb Croutons and bake while preparing the soup.

WHITE GAZPACHO

45

Something different that is sure to please!

4 first-course servings (about 1 cup each)

1 large onion, sliced
4 cloves garlic, minced
2 cups fat-free milk
1 vegetable or chicken bouillon cube
1–1½ cups plain fat-free yogurt
2 teaspoons lemon juice
2 dashes hot pepper sauce
Salt and white pepper, to taste
⅓ cup each: chopped seeded cucumber,
   yellow tomato, avocado
Finely chopped cilantro, as garnish

Per Serving:
Calories: 109
% of calories from fat: 27
Fat (gm): 3.4
Saturated fat (gm): 0.6
Cholesterol (mg): 2
Sodium (mg): 196
Protein (gm): 6.7
Carbohydrate (gm): 14.3

Exchanges:
Milk: 0.5
Vegetable: 2.0
Fruit: 0.0
Bread: 0.0
Meat: 0.0
Fat: 0.5

1. Sauté onion and garlic in lightly greased skillet over medium-low heat until very tender, about 15 minutes. Add milk and bouillon cube; cook over medium-high heat, stirring frequently, until mixture is hot and bouillon cube is dissolved. Process soup, yogurt, lemon juice, and hot pepper sauce in food processor or blender until smooth. Season to taste with salt and white pepper. Serve chilled; stir cucumber, tomato, and avocado into soup before serving and sprinkle with cilantro.

VEGETABLE SOUP WITH ORZO

Escarole lends a unique taste to this hearty soup; kale or spinach can also be used.

4 entrée servings (about 2 cups each)

1 cup each: chopped onion, sliced carrots, celery
3 cloves garlic, minced
2 medium zucchini or summer yellow squash, sliced
1 cup sliced mushrooms
½ teaspoon each: dried thyme and oregano leaves
5 cups reduced-sodium fat-free chicken broth
½ cup (4 ounces) uncooked orzo

½ cup frozen peas

6 medium leaves escarole, sliced or coarsely chopped

Salt and pepper, to taste

2 tablespoons grated Romano cheese

Per Serving:
Calories: 265
% of calories from fat: 10
Fat (gm): 2.9
Saturated fat (gm): 0.9
Cholesterol (mg): 3.6
Sodium (mg): 298
Protein (gm): 9.1
Carbohydrate (gm): 44.3

Exchanges:
Milk: 0.0
Vegetable: 3.0
Fruit: 0.0
Bread: 2.0
Meat: 0.0
Fat: 1.0

1. Sauté onion, carrots, celery, and garlic in lightly greased large sauce–pan until onion is tender, about 5 minutes. Add zucchini, mushrooms, and herbs; cook, covered, 2 to 3 minutes. Add broth and heat to boiling. Stir in orzo, peas, and escarole; reduce heat and simmer, uncovered, until orzo is al dente, about 7 minutes. Season with salt and pepper. Sprinkle each bowl of soup with cheese.

LIGHTLY CREAMED VEGETABLE SOUP

45 *Fat-free milk, whipped with an immersion blender, lends a wonderful rich texture to this fragrant creamed soup. Or, if desired, just stir the milk into the soup near the end of the cooking time.*

6 first-course servings (about 1⅓ cups each)

1 cup each: sliced onion, carrots, yellow
　summer squash

⅔ cup each: chopped green and red bell pepper, celery

1 clove garlic, minced

1½ tablespoons margarine or butter

4 cups reduced-sodium fat-free chicken broth

4 peppercorns

3 whole cloves

1 bay leaf

⅓ cup all-purpose flour

⅔ cup water

Salt and pepper, to taste

½ cup fat-free milk

Ground nutmeg, as garnish

Per Serving:
Calories: 112
% of calories from fat: 27
Fat (gm): 3.6
Saturated fat (gm): 0.7
Cholesterol (mg): 0.3
Sodium (mg): 73
Protein (gm): 3.4
Carbohydrate (gm): 18

Exchanges:
Milk: 0.0
Vegetable: 2.0
Fruit: 0.0
Bread: 0.5
Meat: 0.0
Fat: 0.5

1. Sauté vegetables in margarine in large saucepan until onion is tender, 8 to 10 minutes. Add broth and herbs, tied in a cheesecloth bag; heat to boiling. Reduce heat and simmer, covered, until vegetables are tender, 10 to 15 minutes; discard herb bag. Heat soup to boiling; stir in combined flour and water. Boil, stirring, until thickened, about 1 minute. Season to taste with salt and pepper.

2. Just before serving, whip fat-free milk with an immersion blender, or process in blender at high speed 30 seconds; stir into soup. Sprinkle each bowl of soup with nutmeg.

LIME-SCENTED VEGETABLE SOUP

A soup with a fresh flavor, accented with lime and cilantro.

6 first-course servings (about 1¼ cups each)

2 cups sliced carrots
¾ cup each: chopped red bell pepper, sliced celery
½ cup sliced green onions
6 cloves garlic, minced
1 small jalapeño chili, finely chopped
6 cups reduced-sodium fat-free chicken broth
½–¾ cup lime juice
½ teaspoon ground cumin
1 cup chopped tomato
½ cup each: chopped cucumber, avocado
3–4 tablespoons finely chopped cilantro
1½ cups Herb Croutons (½ recipe) (see p. 533)

Per Serving:
Calories: 106
% of calories from fat: 29
Fat (gm): 3.9
Saturated fat (gm): 0.1
Cholesterol (mg): 0
Sodium (mg): 100
Protein (gm): 3.3
Carbohydrate (gm): 17.6

Exchanges:
Milk: 0.0
Vegetable: 2.0
Fruit: 0.0
Bread: 0.5
Meat: 0.0
Fat: 0.5

1. Sauté carrots, bell pepper, celery, green onions, garlic, and jalapeño chili in lightly greased saucepan 5 minutes. Add broth, lime juice, and cumin to saucepan; heat to boiling. Reduce heat and simmer, covered, until vegetables are tender, 10 to 15 minutes. Add tomato, cucumber, and avocado to each bowl of soup; sprinkle with cilantro and Herb Croutons.

GARDEN HARVEST SOUP

Vary the vegetables according to your garden's or greengrocer's bounty.

6 first-course servings (about 1½ cups each)

2 small onions, sliced
2 cloves garlic, minced
1 tablespoon olive oil
¾ cup each: sliced carrots, red and yellow bell pepper
½ cup whole kernel corn
5 cups reduced-sodium fat-free chicken broth
1 cup each: cut green beans, sliced zucchini,
   yellow summer squash
½ teaspoon each: dried basil and oregano leaves
⅓ cup fat-free half-and-half or fat-free milk (optional)
Salt and pepper, to taste

Per Serving:
Calories: 136
% of calories from fat: 17
Fat (gm): 2.8
Saturated fat (gm): 0.4
Cholesterol (mg): 0
Sodium (mg): 161
Protein (gm): 8.4
Carbohydrate (gm): 21.3

Exchanges:
Milk: 0.0
Vegetable: 4.0
Fruit: 0.0
Bread: 0.0
Meat: 0.0
Fat: 0.5

1. Sauté onions and garlic in oil in large saucepan until tender, about 5 minutes. Add carrots, bell peppers, and corn and sauté 5 minutes. Add broth, remaining vegetables, and herbs; heat to boiling. Reduce heat and simmer, covered, until vegetables are tender, about 15 minutes; stir in half-and-half and simmer 2 minutes. Season to taste with salt and pepper.

CHICKEN-VEGETABLE SOUP WITH ORZO

Escarole lends a unique flavor to this hearty soup; kale or spinach can also be used.

4 entrée servings (about 2 cups each)

12 ounces boneless, skinless chicken breast, cubed (½-inch)

½ cup each: sliced onion, carrots, celery, mushrooms, zucchini

3 cloves garlic, minced

½ teaspoon each: dried thyme and oregano leaves

2 cans (14½ ounces each) reduced-sodium fat-free chicken broth

½ cup (4 ounces) uncooked orzo

½ cup frozen peas

6 medium leaves escarole, sliced or coarsely chopped

Salt and pepper, to taste

2 tablespoons grated Romano cheese

Per Serving:
Calories: 260
% of calories from fat: 15
Fat (gm): 4.1
Saturated fat (gm): 1.3
Cholesterol (mg): 47.1
Sodium (mg): 281
Protein (gm): 24
Carbohydrate (gm): 29.9

Exchanges:
Milk: 0.0
Vegetable: 1.5
Fruit: 0.0
Bread: 1.5
Meat: 2.0
Fat: 0.0

1. Sauté chicken in lightly greased saucepan until no longer pink in the center, about 8 minutes; remove from saucepan. Add onion, carrots, celery, mushrooms, zucchini, garlic, and herbs to saucepan; sauté until onion is tender, about 5 minutes. Return chicken to saucepan; add chicken broth and heat to boiling. Stir in orzo, peas, and escarole; reduce heat and simmer, uncovered, until orzo is al dente, about 7 minutes. Season to taste with salt and pepper. Sprinkle with cheese.

CHICKEN NOODLE SOUP

Comfort food at its best!

4 entrée servings (about 1¼ cups each)

4 ounces each: boneless, skinless chicken breast and thighs, fat trimmed, cubed (¾-inch)

2 cups sliced celery, including some leaves

1 cup each: sliced carrots, chopped onion

2 cans (14½ ounces each) reduced-sodium chicken broth

1 teaspoon dried marjoram leaves

1 bay leaf

1 cup uncooked wide noodles

Salt and pepper, to taste

Per Serving:
Calories: 307
% of calories from fat: 14
Fat (gm): 5
Saturated fat (gm): 0.8
Cholesterol (mg): 32.9
Sodium (mg): 409
Protein (gm): 22.8
Carbohydrate (gm): 44.3

Exchanges:
Milk: 0.0
Vegetable: 1.0
Fruit: 0.0
Bread: 2.5
Meat: 2.0
Fat: 0.0

1. Sauté chicken, celery, carrots, and onion in lightly greased large saucepan until lightly browned, about 7 minutes. Add chicken broth and herbs; heat to boiling. Reduce heat and simmer, covered, until chicken and vegetables are tender, 15 to 20 minutes. Add noodles. Cook, uncovered, until noodles are tender, 7 to 10 minutes. Discard bay leaf; season to taste with salt and pepper.

CHICKEN AND CHILIES SOUP

45

The green chilies add extra zip and give the soup its spicy South-of-the-Border flavor.

6 first-course servings (about 1⅓ cups each)

Per Serving:
Calories: 176
% of calories from fat: 25
Fat (gm): 4.9
Saturated fat (gm): 2.4
Cholesterol (mg): 24.8
Sodium (mg): 341
Protein (gm): 18.2
Carbohydrate (gm): 14

Exchanges:
Milk: 0.0
Vegetable: 0.0
Fruit: 0.0
Bread: 1.0
Meat: 2.0
Fat: 0.0

1 each: finely chopped medium onion, rib celery, garlic clove

1 teaspoon margarine or butter

1 quart fat-free chicken broth

¾ cup cubed skinless cooked chicken breast (½-inch)

1 can (4 ounces) chopped green chilies, drained

1½ cups small cauliflower florets

1 cup cooked kidney beans

2 tablespoons cornstarch

¼ cup cold water

½ cup (2 ounces) each: shredded mild Cheddar cheese and fat-free Cheddar cheese

Chopped chives, as garnish

1. Sauté onion, celery, and garlic, in margarine in large saucepan until onion is tender, about 5 minutes. Add chicken broth, chicken, chilies, cauliflower, and beans; heat to boiling. Reduce heat and simmer, covered, 10 minutes. Heat soup to boiling; stir in combined cornstarch and water. Boil, stirring, until thickened, about 1 minute. Reduce heat to low; add cheeses, stirring until melted. Sprinkle each serving with chives.

COUNTRY LENTIL SOUP

A light soup that is wholesome in flavor and texture. This soup freezes well, so make extra.

6 entrée servings (about 1½ cups each)

1½ cups chopped onions

1 cup each: sliced celery, carrots

2 teaspoons minced garlic

1 tablespoon olive oil

3 cups vegetable broth

2 cups water

1 cup dried lentils

1 can (14½ ounces) reduced-sodium whole
   tomatoes, undrained, crushed

2 tablespoons chopped parsley

1 teaspoon dried marjoram leaves

½ teaspoon each: dried oregano and thyme leaves

Salt and pepper, to taste

4 tablespoons grated fat-free Parmesan cheese

Per Serving:
Calories: 275
% of calories from fat: 14
Fat (gm): 4.4
Saturated fat (gm): 0.6
Cholesterol (mg): 0
Sodium (mg): 109
Protein (gm): 15.8
Carbohydrate (gm): 42.8

Exchanges:
Milk: 0.0
Vegetable: 3.0
Fruit: 0.0
Bread: 2.0
Meat: 0.5
Fat: 0.5

1. Sauté onions, celery, carrots, and garlic in oil in large saucepan 5 to 8 minutes. Add broth, water, lentils, tomatoes, and herbs; heat to boiling. Reduce heat and simmer, covered, until lentils are tender, about 30 minutes. Season to taste with salt and pepper. Sprinkle each bowl of soup with 1 tablespoon cheese.

INDIAN LENTIL SOUP

45 *This soup (Dal Shorba) from India is flavored with curry powder and sweet coriander. Red, green, or brown lentils can be used.*

8 first-course servings (about 1 cup each)

½ cup chopped onion

1 clove garlic, minced

2 teaspoons curry powder

1 teaspoon each: crushed coriander and cumin seeds

½ teaspoon ground turmeric

¼ teaspoon crushed red pepper flakes

1 tablespoon olive oil

5 cups reduced-sodium fat-free chicken broth

4 cups water

2 cups dried red or brown lentils

Salt and pepper, to taste

6 tablespoons fat-free plain yogurt

Per Serving:
Calories: 193
% of calories from fat: 11
Fat (gm): 2.4
Saturated fat (gm): 0.3
Cholesterol (mg): 0.3
Sodium (mg): 121
Protein (gm): 16
Carbohydrate (gm): 27.6

Exchanges:
Milk: 0.0
Vegetable: 0.0
Fruit: 0.0
Bread: 2.0
Meat: 1.0
Fat: 0.0

1. Sauté onion, garlic, curry powder, herbs, and red pepper in oil in large saucepan until onion is tender, about 5 minutes, stirring frequently. Add broth, water, and lentils; heat to boiling. Reduce heat and simmer, covered, until lentils are tender, about 30 minutes. Season to taste with salt and pepper. Top each bowl of soup with a tablespoon of yogurt.

SPLIT PEA SOUP WITH HAM

*A perfect entrée soup for hearty appetites on a crisp autumn or winter day.
Serve with thick slices of Garlic Bread (see p. 531).*

6 entrée servings (about 1⅓ cups each)

1½ cups each: chopped onions, cubed lean
    smoked ham (8 ounces), fat trimmed
1 cup chopped carrots
½ cup sliced celery
1 tablespoon canola oil
6 cups water
1 can (14½ ounces) reduced-sodium fat-free
    chicken broth
1 pound dried split peas
1 teaspoon dried marjoram leaves
Salt and pepper, to taste

Per Serving:
Calories: 264
% of calories from fat: 11
Fat (gm): 3.4
Saturated fat (gm): 0.6
Cholesterol (mg): 16.2
Sodium (mg): 513
Protein (gm): 21.6
Carbohydrate (gm): 39.9

Exchanges:
Milk: 0.0
Vegetable: 1.0
Fruit: 0.0
Bread: 2.0
Meat: 2.0
Fat: 0.0

1. Sauté onions, ham, carrots, and celery in oil in large saucepan
until tender, 8 to 10 minutes. Add water, chicken broth, split peas,
and marjoram; heat to boiling. Reduce heat and simmer, covered,
until peas are tender, 1 to 1¼ hours. Season to taste with salt
and pepper.

POBLANO CHILI SOUP

45

*Poblano chilies give this soup extraordinary flavor. Taste the peppers, as they
can vary in flavor from mild to very hot; if they are too hot for your taste,
substitute some green bell peppers.*

8 first-course servings (about 1 cup each)

2 medium onions, chopped
4 medium poblano chilies, seeded, chopped
½–1 small jalapeño chili, seeded, finely chopped
2 cans (14½ ounces each) reduced-sodium fat-free
    chicken broth
3 cups tomato juice
½ teaspoon ground cumin

Per Serving:
Calories: 88
% of calories from fat: 3
Fat (gm): 0.4
Saturated fat (gm): 0
Cholesterol (mg): 0
Sodium (mg): 498
Protein (gm): 6.4
Carbohydrate (gm): 18.2

Exchanges:
Milk: 0.0
Vegetable: 3.5
Fruit: 0.0
Bread: 0.0
Meat: 0.0
Fat: 0.0

Salt and pepper, to taste

Chopped cilantro, as garnish

1. Sauté onions and chilies in lightly greased skillet until onions are tender, about 5 minutes. Add broth, tomato juice, and cumin and heat to boiling; reduce heat and simmer, covered, until chilies are very tender, about 10 minutes. Process in food processor or blender until smooth; season to taste with salt and pepper. Serve warm or chilled; sprinkle each bowl of soup with cilantro.

TORTILLA SOUP

Cubed chicken can be added to the soup, if desired, to make this a more substantial dish.

6 first-course servings (about 1½ cups each)

2 corn or flour tortillas, cut into strips (2 x ¼-inch)

Vegetable cooking spray

¾ cup each: chopped onion, celery, tomato

½ teaspoon each: dried basil leaves, ground cumin

5 cups reduced-sodium fat-free chicken broth

1 can (15 ounces) pinto beans, rinsed, drained

6 ounces cooked chicken breast, shredded or cubed

2 tablespoons finely chopped cilantro

1–2 teaspoons lime juice

Salt and cayenne pepper, to taste

Per Serving:
Calories: 176
% of calories from fat: 10
Fat (gm): 2
Saturated fat (gm): 0.3
Cholesterol (mg): 24.1
Sodium (mg): 386
Protein (gm): 19.1
Carbohydrate (gm): 22.6

Exchanges:
Milk: 0.0
Vegetable: 1.0
Fruit: 0.0
Bread: 1.0
Meat: 2.0
Fat: 0.0

1. Spray tortillas lightly with cooking spray and toss; cook in lightly greased medium skillet over medium heat until browned and crisp, about 5 minutes; reserve.

2. Sauté onion, celery, tomato, basil, and cumin in lightly greased saucepan until onion is tender, 3 to 5 minutes. Add broth, beans, and chicken and heat to boiling; reduce heat and simmer, uncovered, 5 minutes. Stir in cilantro; season to taste with lime juice, salt and cayenne pepper. Add tortilla strips to soup bowls; ladle soup over.

POZOLE

This Mexican soup is traditionally made with a pig's head or pork hocks; our version contains lean pork tenderloin and chicken breast instead. The soup always contains hominy and is served with a variety of crisp vegetable garnishes.

4 first-course servings (about 1⅓ cups each)

2 ancho chilies, stems, seeds, and veins discarded

1 cup each: boiling water, chopped onion

1 clove garlic, minced

2 cans (14½ ounces each) reduced-sodium fat-free chicken broth

8 ounces each: cubed pork tenderloin and boneless, skinless chicken breast (1-inch)

1 can (15 ounces) each: hominy, reduced-sodium tomatoes, drained, coarsely chopped

½ teaspoon each: dried oregano and thyme leaves

Salt and pepper, to taste

6 lime wedges

¼ cup each: thinly sliced lettuce, cabbage, green onion, radish, shredded carrot

Per Serving:
Calories: 181
% of calories from fat: 16
Fat (gm): 3.2
Saturated fat (gm): 0.9
Cholesterol (mg): 44.8
Sodium (mg): 244
Protein (gm): 21.2
Carbohydrate (gm): 16.7

Exchanges:
Milk: 0.0
Vegetable: 1.0
Fruit: 0.0
Bread: 1.0
Meat: 2.5
Fat: 0.0

1. Cover chilies with boiling water in small bowl; let stand until softened, about 10 minutes. Process chilies and water in food processor or blender until smooth; reserve.

2. Sauté onion and garlic in lightly greased saucepan until tender; add broth and meats and heat to boiling. Reduce heat and simmer, covered, until meats are tender, 10 to 15 minutes; strain, returning broth to saucepan. Shred meats with fork. Add meats, reserved chili mixture, hominy, tomatoes, and herbs to saucepan; cook, covered, over low heat 10 to 15 minutes. Season to taste with salt and pepper. Serve with lime wedges and fresh vegetables for each person to add to soup.

CHILI CON CARNE

A flavorful chili that will satisfy the heartiest of appetites!

8 entrée servings (about 1 cup each)

1 pound very lean ground beef
1½ cups chopped onions
1 cup chopped green bell pepper
2 cloves garlic, minced
1–2 tablespoons chili powder
2 teaspoons each: ground cumin, dried oregano leaves
¼ teaspoon ground cloves
2 cans (14½ ounces each) reduced-sodium whole
   tomatoes, undrained, coarsely chopped
1 can (15 ounces) red kidney beans, rinsed, drained
1 can (6 ounces) reduced-sodium tomato paste
¾ cup beer or reduced-sodium beef broth
1 tablespoon each: packed light brown sugar, unsweetened cocoa
Salt and pepper, to taste
½ cup each: shredded fat-free or reduced-fat Cheddar cheese
   (2 ounces), sliced green onions, fat-free sour cream

Per Serving:
Calories: 220
% of calories from fat: 13
Fat (gm): 3.6
Saturated fat (gm): 1
Cholesterol (mg): 32.5
Sodium (mg): 224
Protein (gm): 21.9
Carbohydrate (gm): 28.7

Exchanges:
Milk: 0.0
Vegetable: 2.0
Fruit: 0.0
Bread: 1.0
Meat: 2.0
Fat: 0.0

1. Sauté ground beef, onions, bell pepper, garlic, herbs, and spices in lightly greased large saucepan until meat is brown and vegetables are tender, 5 to 8 minutes. Add tomatoes and liquid, beans, tomato paste, beer, brown sugar, and cocoa; heat to boiling. Reduce heat and simmer, covered, 1 hour. Uncover and simmer to thicken, if desired. Season to taste with salt and pepper. Sprinkle each serving of chili with cheese, green onions, and sour cream.

VARIATIONS

Chili Mac — Add 1 cup uncooked elbow macaroni or chili mac pasta and ½ cup water to chili after 45 minutes cooking time; heat to boiling. Reduce heat and simmer, covered, until macaroni is tender, about 15 minutes.

Southwest Chili — Make recipe as above, substituting black or pinto beans for the red kidney, and adding 1 minced jalapeño chili. Garnish each serving with a generous sprinkling of chopped cilantro.

ORIENTAL WATERCRESS SOUP

45 *Spinach can be substituted for the watercress in this fragrant Cantonese offering.*

6 first-course servings (about 1 cup each)

6 cups reduced-sodium fat-free chicken broth
3 slices gingerroot (¼-inch)
2 cups loosely packed torn watercress
Salt and white pepper, to taste
2 sliced green onions
2 tablespoons shredded carrot

1. Heat broth and gingerroot to boiling in large saucepan; reduce heat and simmer, covered, 5 minutes. Remove gingerroot with slotted spoon and discard. Add watercress and simmer, uncovered, 10 to 15 minutes. Season to taste with salt and white pepper. Sprinkle each bowl of soup with green onions and carrot.

Per Serving:
Calories: 11
% of calories from fat: 9
Fat (gm): 0.1
Saturated fat (gm): 0
Cholesterol (mg): 0
Sodium (mg): 116
Protein (gm): 0.9
Carbohydrate (gm): 1.8

Exchanges:
Milk: 0.0
Vegetable: 0.0
Fruit: 0.0
Bread: 0.0
Meat: 0.0
Fat: 0.0

WONTON SOUP

Your menu need not be Asian to begin with this soup; it goes well with any simple entrée.

6 first-course servings (about 1 cup each)

24 Five-Spice Potstickers (½ recipe) (see p. 23)
6 cups reduced-sodium fat-free chicken broth
1 cup sliced spinach
Reduced-sodium tamari soy sauce
Pepper, to taste

1. Make Five-Spice Potstickers through Step 2 in recipe.

Per Serving:
Calories: 139
% of calories from fat: 5
Fat (gm): 0.8
Saturated fat (gm): 0.1
Cholesterol (mg): 2.9
Sodium (mg): 426
Protein (gm): 10.7
Carbohydrate (gm): 20.3

Exchanges:
Milk: 0.0
Vegetable: 1.0
Fruit: 0.0
Bread: 1.0
Meat: 1.0
Fat: 0.0

2. Heat chicken broth to boiling in large saucepan; add potstickers and simmer, uncovered, until potstickers rise to the surface, 2 to 3 minutes. Stir in spinach and green onion; simmer 2 to 3 minutes longer. Season to taste with soy sauce and pepper.

HOT SOUR SOUP

The contrast in hot and sour flavors makes this Mandarin soup a unique offering. The hot chili sesame oil and Sour Sauce are intensely flavored, so use sparingly.

6 first-course servings (about 1 cup each)

1 ounce dried Chinese black mushrooms (shiitake)

¾ cup boiling water

1 quart reduced-sodium fat-free chicken broth

1½ cups cubed tempeh or light extra-firm tofu

½ cup bamboo shoots

¼ cup distilled white vinegar

2 tablespoons reduced-sodium tamari soy sauce

1 tablespoon each: finely chopped gingerroot, brown sugar, cornstarch

3 tablespoons water

Salt, cayenne, and black pepper, to taste

1 egg, lightly beaten

1 teaspoon Asian sesame oil

12–18 drops hot chili sesame oil or Szechwan chili sauce

Sour Sauce (recipe follows)

Per Serving:
Calories: 176
% of calories from fat: 28
Fat (gm): 6
Saturated fat (gm): 0.8
Cholesterol (mg): 35
Sodium (mg): 630
Protein (gm): 11
Carbohydrate (gm): 21

Exchanges:
Milk: 0.0
Vegetable: 0.0
Fruit: 0.0
Bread: 1.5
Meat: 1.5
Fat: 0.0

1. Combine mushrooms and boiling water in small bowl; let stand until mushrooms are softened, 15 to 20 minutes. Drain, reserving liquid. Slice mushrooms, discarding tough stems.

2. Heat broth, mushrooms and reserved liquid, tempeh, bamboo shoots, vinegar, soy sauce, gingerroot, and sugar to boiling in large saucepan. Reduce heat and simmer, uncovered, 10 minutes. Heat soup to boiling; stir in combined cornstarch and water; boil until thickened, stirring, about 1 minute. Season to taste with salt, cayenne, and black pepper. Stir egg slowly into soup; stir in Asian sesame oil. Serve with hot chili oil and Sour Sauce.

Sour Sauce
Makes about ⅓ cup

3 tablespoons distilled white vinegar
1 tablespoon reduced-sodium tamari soy sauce
2 tablespoons packed light brown sugar

1. Mix all ingredients.

ORIENTAL SOUP WITH NOODLES AND CHICKEN

The dried chow mein noodles in this soup are not the fried ones we have used with chop suey for many years. Be sure the correct noodles are used.

4 first-course servings (about ¾ cup each)

1 ounce dried cloud ear or shiitake mushrooms
½ cup sliced white mushrooms
½ cup julienned carrots
2 cans (14½ ounces each) reduced-sodium chicken broth
2 tablespoons dry sherry (optional)
1½ teaspoons light soy sauce
¼ teaspoon five-spice powder
8 ounces boneless, skinless chicken breast, cooked, shredded
2 ounces snow peas, trimmed
½ package (5-ounce size) dried chow mein noodles
Salt and pepper, to taste

Per Serving:
Calories: 213
% of calories from fat: 30
Fat (gm): 7.6
Saturated fat (gm): 1.2
Cholesterol (mg): 29.2
Sodium (mg): 259
Protein (gm): 16.4
Carbohydrate (gm): 19.7

Exchanges:
Milk: 0.0
Vegetable: 0.5
Fruit: 0.0
Bread: 1.0
Meat: 1.5
Fat: 1.0

1. Place dried mushrooms in bowl; pour hot water over to cover. Let stand until mushrooms are soft, about 15 minutes; drain. Slice mushrooms, discarding any tough parts.

2. Sauté dried and white mushrooms, and carrots in lightly greased medium skillet 3 to 4 minutes. Add chicken broth, sherry, soy sauce, and five-spice powder. Heat to boiling; reduce heat and simmer, covered, 10 minutes. Stir in chicken, snow peas, and noodles; cook until noodles are just tender, about 10 minutes. Season to taste with salt and pepper.

SESAME NOODLE SOUP WITH VEGETABLES

45 *The fresh Chinese-style noodles are sometimes called soup noodles, chow mein noodles, or spaghetti. Caution: Fresh noodles cook very quickly.*

4 entrée servings (about 2 cups each)

½ cup sliced green onions

4 cloves garlic, minced

1 tablespoon Asian sesame oil

2 cups thinly sliced napa cabbage

1 cup chopped red bell pepper

½ cup julienned carrots

3 cans (14½ ounces each) reduced-sodium chicken broth

12 ounces boneless, skinless chicken breast, cooked, shredded

1 package (12 ounces) fresh Chinese-style noodles

Salt and pepper, to taste

Per Serving:
Calories: 302
% of calories from fat: 19
Fat (gm): 6.5
Saturated fat (gm): 1
Cholesterol (mg): 43.5
Sodium (mg): 144
Protein (gm): 23
Carbohydrate (gm): 37.8

Exchanges:
Milk: 0.0
Vegetable: 1.5
Fruit: 0.0
Bread: 2.0
Meat: 2.0
Fat: 0.0

1. Sauté green onions and garlic in sesame oil in large saucepan until tender, about 5 minutes. Add cabbage, bell pepper, and carrots; sauté until vegetables are tender, about 5 minutes. Add chicken broth and heat to boiling. Stir in chicken and noodles; reduce heat and simmer, uncovered, until noodles are just tender, 2 to 3 minutes. Season to taste with salt and pepper.

LIGHT MINESTRONE

Minestrone does not always contain pasta, nor is it always a heavy, hearty soup. Enjoy this light version of an old favorite, selecting vegetables that are freshest and most plentiful.

8 first-course servings (about 1¼ cups each)

1 cup sliced carrots
½ cup each: chopped onion, celery, fennel bulb
2 cloves garlic, minced
1 tablespoon olive oil
5 cups reduced-sodium fat-free beef broth
1 can (19 ounces) garbanzo beans, rinsed, drained
1 cup each: snap peas, broccoli florets, zucchini, sliced
¾–1 teaspoon each: dried basil and oregano leaves
1 cup halved cherry tomatoes
¼ cup finely chopped parsley
Salt and pepper, to taste
1½ cups Parmesan Croutons (½ recipe) (see p. 532)

Per Serving:
Calories: 146
% of calories from fat: 21
Fat (gm): 3.5
Saturated fat (gm): 0.6
Cholesterol (mg): 0.5
Sodium (mg): 447
Protein (gm): 8.6
Carbohydrate (gm): 21.3

Exchanges:
Milk: 0.0
Vegetable: 1.0
Fruit: 0.0
Bread: 1.0
Meat: 0.0
Fat: 0.5

1. Sauté carrots, onion, celery, fennel, and garlic in oil in Dutch oven until onion is tender, 5 to 8 minutes. Add broth, beans, peas, broccoli, zucchini, and herbs; heat to boiling. Reduce heat and simmer, covered, until vegetables are tender, 10 to 15 minutes, adding tomatoes and parsley during last 5 minutes of cooking time. Season to taste with salt and pepper. Sprinkle each bowl of soup with Parmesan Croutons.

SUMMER MINESTRONE

Thick and savory, this traditional Italian soup is always a favorite.

8 first-course servings (about 1 cup each)

2 cups each: cubed potatoes, sliced carrots
1 small zucchini, cubed
1 cup each: halved green beans, sliced zucchini, carrots,
    cabbage, chopped onion

½ cup sliced celery

3–4 cloves garlic, minced

2 teaspoons Italian seasoning

1 teaspoons dried oregano leaves

4 cups reduced-sodium chicken broth

1 can (15 ounces) each rinsed, drained kidney beans, and reduced-sodium stewed tomatoes

2 cups water

1½ cups uncooked mostaccioli

½ teaspoon pepper

2 tablespoons grated Parmesan or Romano cheese

Per Serving:
Calories: 177
% of calories from fat: 9
Fat (gm): 1.8
Saturated fat (gm): 0.6
Cholesterol (mg): 1.2
Sodium (mg): 256
Protein (gm): 8.1
Carbohydrate (gm): 33.7

Exchanges:
Milk: 0.0
Vegetable: 2.0
Fruit: 0.0
Bread: 1.5
Meat: 0.5
Fat: 0.0

1. Sauté fresh vegetables in lightly greased large saucepan until crisp-tender, 10 to 12 minutes. Stir in Italian seasoning and oregano; cook 1 minute longer. Add broth, beans, tomatoes, and water; heat to boiling. Reduce heat and simmer, covered, 10 minutes. Heat soup to boiling and add pasta. Reduce heat and simmer, uncovered, until pasta is al dente, 10 to 12 minutes. Stir in pepper; sprinkle each bowl of soup with cheese.

SPINACH AND TORTELLINI SOUP

Pasta soups can be made 2 to 3 days in advance, enhancing flavors. If desired, cook pasta separately and add to the soup when reheating so it's fresh and perfectly cooked.

6 entrée servings (about 1 cup each)

2 cups sliced carrots

¼ cup sliced green onions

2 cloves garlic, minced

1 teaspoon dried basil leaves

2 cans (14½ ounces) reduced-sodium chicken broth

1½ cups water

1 package (9 ounces) fresh tomato-cheese tortellini

3 cups torn spinach leaves

2–3 teaspoons lemon juice

⅛–¼ teaspoon ground nutmeg

⅛ teaspoon pepper

Per Serving:
Calories: 290
% of calories from fat: 9
Fat (gm): 2.8
Saturated fat (gm): 1
Cholesterol (mg): 3.8
Sodium (mg): 395
Protein (gm): 12.1
Carbohydrate (gm): 48

Exchanges:
Milk: 0.0
Vegetable: 2.0
Fruit: 0.0
Bread: 2.5
Meat: 1.0
Fat: 0.0

1. Sauté carrots, green onions, garlic, and basil in lightly greased large saucepan until onions are tender, about 5 minutes. Add broth and water and heat to boiling; reduce heat and simmer, covered, 10 minutes. Heat soup to boiling; stir in tortellini and spinach; reduce heat and simmer, uncovered, until tortellini are al dente, about 5 minutes. Season with lemon juice, nutmeg, and pepper.

RAVIOLI SOUP

In a hurry? Purchased chicken tortellini can be substituted for the home-made!

6 entrée servings (about 1½ cups each)

½ cup julienned carrot
¼ cup sliced green onions
1 teaspoon margarine or butter
2½ quarts fat-free chicken broth
3 cups thinly sliced bok choy or Napa cabbage
Chicken Ravioli (recipe follows)
Salt and pepper, to taste

Per Serving:
Calories: 252
% of calories from fat: 9
Fat (gm): 2.4
Saturated fat (gm): 0.5
Cholesterol (mg): 27.3
Sodium (mg): 644
Protein (gm): 24
Carbohydrate (gm): 29.7

Exchanges:
Milk: 0.0
Vegetable: 0.0
Fruit: 0.0
Bread: 2.0
Meat: 2.0
Fat: 0.0

1. Sauté carrot and green onions in margarine in large saucepan until tender, about 5 minutes. Add broth and heat to boiling; reduce heat and simmer, covered, 5 minutes. Stir in bok choy and Chicken Ravioli and heat to boiling; reduce heat and simmer, uncovered, 2 to 3 minutes or until ravioli are tender and rise to top of soup. Season to taste with salt and pepper.

Chicken Ravioli
Makes 18 ravioli

8 ounces ground chicken breast
1 tablespoon minced green onion
1 teaspoon each: minced garlic, gingerroot
⅛ teaspoon each: salt, pepper
36 wonton wrappers

1. Combine all ingredients, except wonton wrappers, in small bowl. Place rounded teaspoon of chicken mixture in center of each of 18 wonton wrappers. Moisten edges of wrappers with water. Top with remaining wrappers; press edges to seal. Refrigerate, covered, until ready to cook.

ITALIAN MEATBALL SOUP

Flavorful meatballs for this soup are made with low-fat ground turkey. Substitute other pastas for the spaghetti, if you like, such as orrechiette (little ears) or conchiglie (shells).

8 entrée servings (about 2 cups each)

1½ pounds ground turkey

2 eggs

¼ cup seasoned dry bread crumbs

4 cloves garlic, minced, divided

3 tablespoons Italian seasoning, divided

4 cans (14½ ounces each) reduced-sodium chicken broth

3 cups water

2 cups each: cut green beans, sliced carrots, chopped onions

8 ounces thin spaghetti, uncooked, broken into 2- to 3-inch pieces

2 medium plum tomatoes, coarsely chopped

Salt and pepper, to taste

Per Serving:
Calories: 270
% of calories from fat: 28
Fat (gm): 8.7
Saturated fat (gm): 2
Cholesterol (mg): 31.7
Sodium (mg): 174
Protein (gm): 19
Carbohydrate (gm): 30.2

Exchanges:
Milk: 0.0
Vegetable: 1.0
Fruit: 0.0
Bread: 1.5
Meat: 2.0
Fat: 0.5

1. Mix ground turkey, eggs, bread crumbs, 2 cloves of garlic, and 2 tablespoons Italian seasoning until well blended; shape into 32 meatballs. Sauté in lightly greased medium skillet until browned on all sides, 5 to 7 minutes.

2. Combine chicken broth, water, green beans, carrots, onions, remaining 2 cloves garlic, and remaining 1 tablespoon Italian seasoning in large saucepan; heat to boiling. Reduce heat and simmer, covered, until vegetables are crisp-tender, about 8 minutes. Heat soup to boiling; add pasta, meatballs, and tomatoes. Reduce heat and simmer, uncovered, until pasta is al dente, about 7 minutes. Season to taste with salt and pepper.

MEDITERRANEAN-STYLE SHRIMP AND VEGETABLE SOUP

A fragrant vegetable soup with a citrus accent.

6 first-course servings (about 1½ cups each)

2 cups sliced mushrooms
½ cup each: chopped onion, green bell pepper
3 cloves garlic, minced
1 can (16 ounces) reduced-sodium whole tomatoes, undrained, coarsely chopped,
1 can (8 ounces) reduced-sodium tomato sauce
1 pound peeled, deveined shrimp
1–2 cups vegetable broth
½ cup dry white wine or orange juice
½–1 cup clam juice
2 strips orange zest (3 x ½ inches)
2 bay leaves
¾ teaspoon each: dried marjoram and savory leaves
¼ teaspoon crushed fennel seeds
Salt and pepper, to taste

Per Serving:
Calories: 121
% of calories from fat: 8
Fat (gm): 1.1
Saturated fat (gm): 0.2
Cholesterol (mg): 115.6
Sodium (mg): 211
Protein (gm): 14.8
Carbohydrate (gm): 10.7

Exchanges:
Milk: 0.0
Vegetable: 2.0
Fruit: 0.0
Bread: 0.0
Meat: 1.0
Fat: 0.0

1. Sauté mushrooms, onion, bell pepper, and garlic in lightly greased large saucepan, covered, until vegetables are tender, 8 to 10 minutes. Add remaining ingredients, except salt and pepper, and heat to boiling; reduce heat and simmer, covered, 10 to 15 minutes. Remove bay leaves; season to taste with salt and pepper.

GREEK LEMON-RICE SOUP

45 *Nicely tart; use fresh lemon juice for the best flavor. If making this soup in advance, do not add egg until reheating for serving.*

4 first-course servings (about 1 cup each)

3½ cups reduced-sodium fat-free chicken broth
¼ cup long-grain rice
2 large cloves garlic, minced
¼–⅓ cup lemon juice

1 egg, lightly beaten

2 tablespoons chopped parsley

Salt and white pepper, to taste

Per Serving:
Calories: 106
% of calories from fat: 20
Fat (gm): 2.4
Saturated fat (gm): 0.5
Cholesterol (mg): 53.3
Sodium (mg): 31
Protein (gm): 3
Carbohydrate (gm): 14.4

Exchanges:
Milk: 0.0
Vegetable: 0.0
Fruit: 0.0
Bread: 1.0
Meat: 0.0
Fat: 0.5

1. Heat broth to boiling in medium saucepan; stir in rice and garlic. Reduce heat and simmer, covered, until rice is tender, about 25 minutes; reduce heat to low; Mix lemon juice and egg; slowly stir mixture into soup. Stir in parsley; season to taste with salt and white pepper.

CREAMY PEANUT BUTTER SOUP

45 *African in origin, this soup will tempt peanut butter lovers! In our low-fat version, pureed beans contribute rich texture without detracting from the peanut flavor.*

6 first-course servings (about 1 cup each)

½ cup each: chopped onion, carrot, celery

1 leek, cleaned, sliced

2 cloves garlic, minced

3 cups reduced-sodium fat-free chicken broth

1 can (15 ounces) Great Northern beans,
   rinsed, drained

½ cup reduced-fat peanut butter

½ cup fat-free half-and-half or fat-free milk

½ teaspoon curry powder

2–3 teaspoons lemon juice

1–2 dashes red pepper sauce

Salt, cayenne, and black pepper, to taste

Sliced green onions, as garnish

Per Serving:
Calories: 182
% of calories from fat: 26
Fat (gm): 5.5
Saturated fat (gm): 0.9
Cholesterol (mg): 0
Sodium (mg): 452
Protein (gm): 11.8
Carbohydrate (gm): 22.8

Exchanges:
Milk: 0.0
Vegetable: 2.0
Fruit: 0.0
Bread: 1.0
Meat: 1.0
Fat: 0.0

1. Sauté onion, carrot, celery, leek, and garlic in lightly greased large saucepan 5 minutes. Add broth and beans and heat to boiling; reduce heat and simmer, covered, until vegetables are tender, 10 to 15 minutes.

2. Process soup and peanut butter in food processor or blender until smooth; return soup to saucepan, stir in half-and-half and curry powder and heat until hot. Season to taste with lemon juice, red pepper sauce, salt, cayenne, and black pepper. Sprinkle each bowl of soup with green onions.

BEEF BARLEY AND VEGETABLE SOUP

This hearty, rib-sticking soup is even better if made a day or so in advance. Leftover soup will thicken, so thin with beef broth or water.

8 entrée servings (about 1¼ cups each)

1 pound lean beef stew meat, fat trimmed, cubed

1 cup each: chopped onion, celery, carrots

1 clove garlic, minced

1 tablespoon flour

4 cups water

1 can (14½ ounces) each: reduced-sodium beef
   broth, undrained diced tomatoes

½ teaspoon each: dried marjoram and thyme leaves

1 bay leaf

1 cup each: cut green beans, cubed parsnips
   or potatoes

½ cup each: frozen peas, quick-cooking barley

Salt and pepper, to taste

Per Serving:
Calories: 187
% of calories from fat: 16
Fat (gm): 3.3
Saturated fat (gm): 1.1
Cholesterol (mg): 35.4
Sodium (mg): 153
Protein (gm): 18.8
Carbohydrate (gm): 21.1

Exchanges:
Milk: 0.0
Vegetable: 2.0
Fruit: 0.0
Bread: 0.5
Meat: 2.0
Fat: 0.0

1. Sauté beef in lightly greased Dutch oven until browned, 8 to 10 minutes. Add onion, celery, carrots, and garlic; cook 5 minutes. Stir in flour; cook 1 minute. Add water, broth, tomatoes and liquid, and herbs; heat to boiling. Reduce heat and simmer, covered, until beef is very tender, 1 to 1½ hours. Add green beans and parsnips, peas, and barley; simmer, covered, until vegetables and barley are tender, about 15 minutes. Discard bay leaf; season to taste with salt and pepper.

THREE

Meats

OLD-FASHIONED POT ROAST

Cabbage, turnips, and sweet potatoes are other vegetable choices that can be used in this recipe—use the favorites you remember!

6 servings

2¾ pounds beef chuck pot roast, fat trimmed

Salt and pepper, to taste

3 medium onions, cut into wedges

6 cloves garlic, minced

1 cup reduced-sodium beef broth

1 bay leaf

1 pound potatoes, unpeeled, cut into 1½-inch pieces

8 ounces each: peeled carrots, rutabaga or parsnip,
  cut into 1½-inch pieces

¼ cup all-purpose flour

½ cup water

Per Serving:
Calories: 377
% of calories from fat: 15
Fat (gm): 6.4
Saturated fat (gm): 2.2
Cholesterol (mg): 95.6
Sodium (mg): 110
Protein (gm): 37
Carbohydrate (gm): 42.6

Exchanges:
Milk: 0.0
Vegetable: 2.0
Fruit: 0.0
Bread: 1.5
Meat: 4.0
Fat: 0.0

1. Cook beef in lightly greased Dutch oven over medium heat until browned, 2 to 3 minutes on each side. Remove from pan; sprinkle lightly with salt and pepper. Add onions and garlic to pan; sauté 2 to 3 minutes. Return meat to pan; add broth and bay leaf, and heat to boiling. Transfer to oven and bake, covered, at 325 degrees until beef is fork-tender, 2¾ to 3 hours, adding remaining vegetables to pan during last 45 minutes of cooking time.

2. Place meat and vegetable on large serving platter; discard bay leaf. Pour meat juices into glass measure; spoon off and discard fat. Add water to juices, if necessary, to make 2 cups; heat to boiling in small saucepan. Stir in combined flour and water, stirring until thickened, about 1 minute; season to taste with salt and pepper. Serve gravy with pot roast and vegetables.

VARIATIONS

Bourbon Pot Roast — Make recipe as above, omitting rutabaga, and substituting ⅔ cup tomato juice and ⅓ cup bourbon for the beef broth. Add 1 teaspoon dry mustard and ½ teaspoon beef bouillon crystals with the tomato juice in Step 1.

Italian Pot Roast — Make recipe as above, omitting potatoes, carrots, rutabagas, and flour. Substitute 1 cup dry red wine for the beef broth. Add 1 can (15 ounces) roasted garlic diced tomatoes, 1 can (6 ounces) reduced-sodium tomato paste, and 1 teaspoon dried basil leaves in Step 1. Add ½ cup each chopped carrot and celery, and 1 cup sliced mushrooms during last 45 minutes of cooking time. Serve with Herbed Polenta (see p. 426).

MUSTARD ROAST BEEF

45

The spicy coating makes this roast beef extra juicy and flavorful.

6 servings

¼ cup apricot preserves

2–4 tablespoons spicy brown mustard

2–3 teaspoons reduced-sodium Worcestershire sauce

1 tablespoon each: light brown sugar, prepared horseradish

1 teaspoon each: crushed caraway seeds, black peppercorns

¼ teaspoon ground allspice

1 boneless beef sirloin tip roast, fat trimmed (about 2 pounds)

Per Serving:
Calories: 264
% of calories from fat: 26
Fat (gm): 7.3
Saturated fat (gm): 2.5
Cholesterol (mg): 71.8
Sodium (mg): 185
Protein (gm): 33.9
Carbohydrate (gm): 12.5

Exchanges:
Milk: 0.0
Vegetable: 0.0
Fruit: 0.5
Bread: 0.0
Meat: 4.0
Fat: 0.0

1. Mix all ingredients, except beef; spread on all surfaces of beef. Place beef on rack in roasting pan; roast at 325 degrees to desired doneness, 160 degrees for medium, 45 to 60 minutes. Let stand 10 minutes before slicing.

VARIATION

Crumb-Crusted Roast Beef — Make recipe as above omitting brown sugar, horseradish, caraway seeds, and allspice. Combine 1 cup fresh bread crumbs, 2 teaspoons minced garlic, 1 teaspoon dried basil leaves, ½ teaspoon dried oregano leaves, and ¼ teaspoon dried marjoram leaves with the apricot preserves, mustard, and Worcestershire sauce; pat onto beef. Roast as above.

VEGETABLE-STUFFED FLANK STEAK

45

Serve with oven-roasted potatoes and a salad for a well-rounded and delicious meal.

4 servings

1 pound beef flank steak
1 cup fat-free Italian salad dressing
Vegetable Stuffing (recipe follows)
1 cup reduced-sodium fat-free beef broth

Per Serving:
Calories: 281
% of calories from fat: 29
Fat (gm): 8.8
Saturated fat (gm): 3.6
Cholesterol (mg): 49.8
Sodium (mg): 744
Protein (gm): 33.6
Carbohydrate (gm): 14.4

Exchanges:
Milk: 0.0
Vegetable: 0.0
Fruit: 0.0
Bread: 1.0
Meat: 4.0
Fat: 0.0

1. Pound flank steak with meat mallet until even in thickness; score steak diagonally in diamond pattern on both sides. Pour dressing over steak in glass baking dish; refrigerate, covered, 1½ to 2 hours, turning occasionally. Drain; reserve marinade. Spread Vegetable Stuffing on steak, leaving 2-inch margin along sides. Roll up lengthwise; secure edge with wooden picks, or tie with kitchen string.

2. Brown beef on all sides in lightly greased large ovenproof skillet; add broth and reserved marinade. Bake, covered, at 325 degrees to medium doneness (160 degrees) about 45 minutes.

Vegetable Stuffing

Makes about 1¼ cups

8 ounces sliced mushrooms
¼ cup each: chopped carrot, thinly sliced celery, green onions
1 clove garlic, minced
¼ cup unseasoned dry bread crumbs
1½ teaspoons dried Italian seasoning
Salt and pepper, to taste

1. Sauté mushrooms, carrot, celery, green onions, and garlic in lightly greased large skillet until tender, about 5 minutes. Add bread crumbs and Italian seasoning and cook until browned, 2 to 3 minutes; season to taste with salt and pepper.

TOURNEDOS BÉARNAISE

45 *Enjoy this healthy, low-fat version of the classic.*

4 servings

4 slices Italian bread (¾-inch)
Vegetable cooking spray
1 clove garlic, halved
4 beef tenderloin steaks (4 ounces each), fat trimmed
Salt and pepper, to taste
Mock Béarnaise Sauce (recipe follows)

Per Serving:
Calories: 335
% of calories from fat: 29
Fat (gm): 10.4
Saturated fat (gm): 3.9
Cholesterol (mg): 76.1
Sodium (mg): 488
Protein (gm): 35.1
Carbohydrate (gm): 22.7

Exchanges:
Milk: 0.0
Vegetable: 0.0
Fruit: 0.0
Bread: 1.5
Meat: 4.0
Fat: 0.0

1. Spray bread slices with cooking spray; broil 6 inches from heat source until browned, 2 to 3 minutes on each side. Rub bread slices with cut sides of garlic.

2. Sauté steaks in lightly greased medium skillet to desired degree of doneness, 3 to 4 minutes on each side for medium; season to taste with salt and pepper. Arrange steaks on bread slices; spoon Mock Béarnaise Sauce over.

Mock Béarnaise Sauce

Makes about 1½ cups

6 ounces fat-free cream cheese
⅓ cup fat-free sour cream
3–4 tablespoons fat-free milk
2 teaspoons each: minced shallot, lemon juice
½–1 teaspoon Dijon mustard
1½ teaspoons dried tarragon leaves
Salt and white pepper, to taste

1. Heat all ingredients, except salt and pepper, in small saucepan over medium-low heat until melted and smooth, stirring constantly; season to taste with salt and pepper. Serve immediately.

FILET MIGNON STROGANOFF

45 *A creamy mushroom sauce makes these steaks very special.*

4 servings

4 beef tenderloin steaks (4 ounces each), fat trimmed
Salt and pepper, to taste
Mushrooms Stroganoff (recipe follows)
3 cups cooked rice, warm

Per Serving:
Calories: 398
% of calories from fat: 22
Fat (gm): 9.5
Saturated fat (gm): 3.5
Cholesterol (mg): 73.7
Sodium (mg): 157
Protein (gm): 32.6
Carbohydrate (gm): 43.5

Exchanges:
Milk: 0.0
Vegetable: 3.0
Fruit: 0.0
Bread: 2.0
Meat: 3.0
Fat: 0.0

1. Sauté steaks in lightly greased medium skillet to desired degree of doneness, 3 to 4 minutes on each side for medium. Season to taste with salt and pepper; spoon Mushrooms Stroganoff over. Serve with rice.

Mushrooms Stroganoff
Makes about 1½ cups

3 cups sliced mushrooms
¾ cup chopped red bell pepper
2 ounces fat-free cream cheese
½ teaspoon each: dried marjoram and thyme leaves
⅓ cup reduced-fat sour cream
Salt and pepper, to taste

1. Sauté mushrooms and bell pepper in lightly greased skillet until tender, 5 to 8 minutes. Add cream cheese and herbs, stirring until cream cheese is melted; stir in sour cream and cook 2 to 3 minutes. Season to taste with salt and pepper.

45-MINUTE PREPARATION TIP: Begin cooking rice and make Mushrooms Stroganoff before cooking the steaks.

STEAK AU POIVRE

45 *Beef eye of round steak is a healthy choice for this entrée as it has less than 30% calories from fat.*

4 servings

4 teaspoons coarsely crushed black peppercorns

4 beef eye of round or tenderloin steaks (4 ounces each), fat trimmed

Salt, to taste

⅓ cup brandy or beef broth

¼ cup fat-free sour cream

Per Serving:
Calories: 212
% of calories from fat: 20
Fat (gm): 4.5
Saturated fat (gm): 1.6
Cholesterol (mg): 64
Sodium (mg): 68
Protein (gm): 27.7
Carbohydrate (gm): 2.1

Exchanges:
Milk: 0.0
Vegetable: 0.0
Fruit: 0.0
Bread: 0.0
Meat: 3.5
Fat: 0.0

1. Press peppercorns onto both sides of steaks; sprinkle lightly with salt. Sauté in lightly greased medium skillet over medium heat to desired degree of doneness, 3 to 4 minutes on each side for medium. Remove steaks and keep warm.

2. Add brandy to skillet; heat to boiling. Boil, scraping bottom of skillet to loosen cooked particles, until reduced to about 2 tablespoons, 2 to 3 minutes. Stir in sour cream and cook over low heat 1 to 2 minutes. Spoon over steaks.

NOTE: A mixture of white, pink, green, and black peppercorns can be used.

CHICKEN-FRIED STEAK

45 *The beef steaks are pounded until thin for faster cooking and tenderness.*

4 servings

4 beef eye of round steaks (4 ounces each), fat trimmed

2 tablespoons flour

1 egg, lightly beaten

¼ cup each: fat-free milk, seasoned dry bread crumbs

Salt and pepper, to taste

Cream Gravy (see p. 123)

1. Pound steaks with flat side of mallet to ¼ inch thickness. Coat steaks lightly with flour; dip in combined egg and milk and coat with bread crumbs. Cook steaks in lightly greased large skillet over medium heat until browned, about 5 minutes on each side. Cook, covered, over low heat until steaks are tender, turning occasionally, 20 to 25 minutes. Season to taste with salt and pepper. Serve with Cream Gravy.

Per Serving:
Calories: 349
% of calories from fat: 29
Fat (gm): 11
Saturated fat (gm): 3
Cholesterol (mg): 66.2
Sodium (mg): 309
Protein (gm): 36.5
Carbohydrate (gm): 23.8

Exchanges:
Milk: 0.5
Vegetable: 0.0
Fruit: 0.0
Bread: 1.5
Meat: 3.5
Fat: 0.0

MOCK CHICKEN LEGS

Looking a little like lumpy chicken legs, these kebabs are also known as City Chicken.

6 servings

1 pound pork tenderloin, fat trimmed, cubed (1-inch)
8 ounces boneless beef sirloin steak, fat trimmed, cubed (1-inch)
¼ cup all-purpose flour
Salt and pepper, to taste
Cream Gravy (see p. 123)
4½ cups cooked rice or noodles, warm

Per Serving:
Calories: 397
% of calories from fat: 20
Fat (gm): 8.7
Saturated fat (gm): 2.5
Cholesterol (mg): 66.6
Sodium (mg): 140
Protein (gm): 30.7
Carbohydrate (gm): 46.3

Exchanges:
Milk: 0.5
Vegetable: 0.0
Fruit: 0.0
Bread: 2.5
Meat: 3.0
Fat: 0.0

1. Arrange meats on small wooden skewers, alternating beef and pork cubes. Coat meat with flour; let stand 15 minutes. Cook in lightly greased medium skillet over medium heat until browned on all sides, about 10 minutes. Add ½ inch water to skillet; heat to boiling. Reduce heat and simmer, covered, until meat is fork-tender, 15 to 20 minutes. Remove from skillet; sprinkle lightly with salt and pepper. Serve with Cream Gravy and rice.

BEEF STEAK WITH RED AND GREEN STIR-FRY

If available, use red Swiss chard for its beautiful red and green color.

4 servings

2 cups sliced red onions

1 cup sliced celery

2 teaspoons each: minced garlic, gingerroot

6 cups sliced Swiss chard or spinach

2 cups each: sliced red bell pepper, reduced-sodium
fat-free beef broth

2 tablespoons cornstarch

4 teaspoons reduced-sodium tamari soy sauce, divided

½–¾ teaspoon hot chili paste

Salt and pepper, to taste

4 beef eye of round steaks (4 ounces each), fat trimmed

Per Serving:
Calories: 210
% of calories from fat: 17
Fat (gm): 4.1
Saturated fat (gm): 1.4
Cholesterol (mg): 54.9
Sodium (mg): 494
Protein (gm): 26.3
Carbohydrate (gm): 17.1

Exchanges:
Milk: 0.0
Vegetable: 2.0
Fruit: 0.0
Bread: 0.0
Meat: 3.0
Fat: 0.0

1. Stir-fry onions, celery, garlic, and gingerroot in lightly greased large skillet 2 to 3 minutes. Add Swiss chard and bell pepper; stir-fry until vegetables are crisp-tender, 2 to 3 minutes. Stir in combined broth, cornstarch, 2 teaspoons soy sauce, and chili paste; heat to boiling, stirring until thickened, about 1 minute. Season to taste with salt and pepper.

2. Brush steaks with remaining 2 teaspoons soy sauce; cook in lightly greased medium skillet over medium heat to desired degree of doneness, 3 to 4 minutes on each side for medium. Spoon vegetable mixture over steaks.

THAI STIR-FRY

45 *Basmati or jasmine rice can be substituted for the Thai rice; cook with light coconut milk, if desired, or sprinkle with flaked coconut when serving.*

4 servings

1 pound beef round steak, fat trimmed, cut into strips

8 green onions, sliced

2 cups each: broccoli florets, thinly sliced carrots

⅓–⅔ cup Thai peanut sauce

½ cup reduced-sodium fat-free beef broth

2 teaspoons cornstarch

1 package (6.4 ounces) Thai coconut ginger rice, cooked, warm

¼ cup each: chopped cilantro, dry-roasted peanuts

Per Serving:
Calories: 289
% of calories from fat: 19
Fat (gm): 6.2
Saturated fat (gm): 1.7
Cholesterol (mg): 55
Sodium (mg): 788
Protein (gm): 28
Carbohydrate (gm): 30.1

Exchanges:
Milk: 0.0
Vegetable: 3.0
Fruit: 0.0
Bread: 1.0
Meat: 3.0
Fat: 0.0

1. Stir-fry beef in lightly greased wok or large skillet until cooked, 5 to 8 minutes; remove from wok. Add onions, broccoli, and carrots to wok; stir-fry until crisp-tender, 4 to 5 minutes. Stir in peanut sauce and beef; stir in combined vegetable broth and cornstarch and heat to boiling. Boil, stirring until thickened, about 1 minute. Serve over rice; sprinkle with cilantro and peanuts.

PEPPER STEAK

Perfect for buffet-style entertaining.

6 servings

3 cups thickly sliced green, red, and yellow bell peppers

2½ cups sliced onions

4 cloves garlic, minced

1 pound beef eye of round or sirloin, fat trimmed, cut into strips (3 x ¼-inch)

3 tablespoons flour

2 cups reduced-sodium beef broth, divided

1 tablespoon tomato paste

½ teaspoon dried Italian seasoning

Per Serving:
Calories: 383
% of calories from fat: 13
Fat (gm): 5.8
Saturated fat (gm): 1.2
Cholesterol (mg): 42.6
Sodium (mg): 127
Protein (gm): 28.7
Carbohydrate (gm): 56.2

Exchanges:
Milk: 0.0
Vegetable: 3.0
Fruit: 0.0
Bread: 2.5
Meat: 2.5
Fat: 0.0

1½ cups halved cherry tomatoes
1–2 tablespoons Worcestershire sauce
Salt and pepper, to taste
4 cups cooked noodles, warm

1. Sauté bell peppers in lightly greased Dutch oven until tender, about 5 minutes; remove from pan and reserve. Add onions and garlic to skillet; sauté until tender, 5 to 8 minutes. Add beef to pan and cook over medium heat until lightly browned, about 5 minutes, stirring frequently. Stir in flour and cook 1 minute.

2. Add broth, tomato paste, and Italian seasoning; heat to boiling. Reduce heat and simmer, covered, until beef is tender, about 45 minutes, adding tomatoes and reserved peppers during last 10 minutes. Season to taste with Worcestershire sauce, salt, and pepper. Serve with noodles.

VARIATION

Sweet-Sour Pepper Steak — Make recipe as above, substituting 1½ cups snow peas for half the bell peppers and reduced-sodium soy sauce for the Worcestershire sauce. Stir in ¼ cup apricot preserves, ½ cup sliced water chestnuts, and 2 to 3 teaspoons cider vinegar at the end of cooking time. Serve over rice.

BEEF AND VEGETABLE LO MEIN

Fresh Chinese egg noodles are in the produce section of the supermarket.

4 servings

4 dried Chinese black (shiitake) mushrooms
1 tablespoon each: minced gingerroot, garlic, Asian sesame oil
12 ounces beef eye of round, fat trimmed, cut into strips (½-inch)
2 cups broccoli florets
1 cup sliced carrots
⅓ cup water
2 tablespoons dry sherry or water
1 tablespoon black bean paste, soy sauce
2 teaspoons cornstarch
1 package (12 ounces) fresh Chinese egg noodles, cooked

1. Cover dried mushrooms with boiling water in bowl. Let stand until mushrooms are softened, about 15 minutes; drain. Slice mushrooms, discarding tough stems.

2. Stir-fry mushrooms, gingerroot, and garlic in oil in wok or large skillet 2 minutes. Add beef and stir-fry until cooked, about 5 minutes; remove from wok. Add broccoli and carrots to wok; stir-fry until crisp-tender, 5 to 8 minutes. Return beef to wok; stir in combined water, sherry, black bean paste, soy sauce, and cornstarch. Heat to boiling, stirring until thickened, about 1 minute; stir in noodles. Cook until hot, 2 to 3 minutes.

Per Serving:
Calories: 300
% of calories from fat: 18
Fat (gm): 6
Saturated fat (gm): 1.4
Cholesterol (mg): 41.2
Sodium (mg): 153
Protein (gm): 22.1
Carbohydrate (gm): 37.9

Exchanges:
Milk: 0.0
Vegetable: 1.0
Fruit: 0.0
Bread: 2.0
Meat: 2.5
Fat: 0.0

BEEF GOULASH

In Hungary, this paprika seasoned stew is called "gulyas" and it's often served with dollops of sour cream.

4 servings

12 ounces boneless beef round steak, fat trimmed, cubed (¾-inch)

1 teaspoon olive oil

3 large onions, cut into thin wedges

1 cup chopped portobello mushrooms

1 can (15 ounces) diced tomatoes, undrained

1 tablespoon paprika

1 teaspoon unsweetened cocoa

2 cups coarsely sliced cabbage

1 tablespoon caraway seeds

Salt and pepper, to taste

8 ounces medium egg noodles, cooked, warm

Per Serving:
Calories: 407
% of calories from fat: 17
Fat (gm): 7.7
Saturated fat (gm): 2
Cholesterol (mg): 90.9
Sodium (mg): 473
Protein (gm): 29.9
Carbohydrate (gm): 55.2

Exchanges:
Milk: 0.0
Vegetable: 2.0
Fruit: 0.0
Bread: 3.0
Meat: 2.0
Fat: 0.5

1. Sauté beef in oil in large saucepan until browned; add onions and mushrooms and sauté 5 minutes. Add tomatoes with liquid, paprika, and cocoa and heat to boiling; reduce heat and simmer, covered, until beef is tender, 45 to 60 minutes, adding cabbage and caraway seeds during last 10 minutes. Season to taste with salt and pepper; serve over noodles.

GOULASH CASSEROLE

45

This sauerkraut dish, creamy with sour cream and seasoned with caraway, is excellent served with Real Mashed Potatoes (see p. 485).

6 servings (about 1⅓ cups each)

1 pound ground beef eye of round
2 medium onions, chopped
1½ cups chopped red and green bell pepper
2 cloves garlic, minced
1 tablespoon flour
2 teaspoons paprika
1 teaspoon crushed caraway seeds
1 can (14 ounces) sauerkraut, rinsed, drained
1 large tomato, coarsely chopped
1 cup fat-free sour cream
Salt and pepper, to taste

Per Serving:
Calories: 174
% of calories from fat: 15
Fat (gm): 2.8
Saturated fat (gm): 0.9
Cholesterol (mg): 36.6
Sodium (mg): 530
Protein (gm): 17.6
Carbohydrate (gm): 18.1

Exchanges:
Milk: 0.0
Vegetable: 3.0
Fruit: 0.0
Bread: 0.0
Meat: 2.0
Fat: 0.0

1. Cook ground beef in lightly greased large skillet until browned, about 8 minutes; add onions, bell peppers, and garlic and cook until tender, 8 to 10 minutes. Stir in flour, paprika, and caraway seeds; cook 1 minute. Spoon into greased 2-quart casserole. Stir in sauerkraut, tomato, and sour cream; season to taste with salt and pepper. Bake, covered, at 350 degrees until hot, about 30 minutes.

ROAST BEEF HASH

45

Any leftover lean beef or pork can be used in this recipe.

4 servings (about 1 cup each)

½ cup each: chopped onion, green bell pepper
2 cloves garlic, minced
2 cups each: shredded cooked lean beef, cooked, cubed potatoes (½-inch)
½ teaspoon each: dried marjoram and thyme leaves
Salt and pepper, to taste

1. Sauté onion, bell pepper, and garlic in large lightly greased skillet until tender, about 5 minutes. Add beef, potatoes, and herbs; cook over medium heat until meat and potatoes are browned, about 10 minutes. Season to taste with salt and pepper.

VARIATION

Corned Beef Hash — Make recipe as above, substituting lean corned beef for the roast beef.

Per Serving:
Calories: 244
% of calories from fat: 22
Fat (gm): 6
Saturated fat (gm): 2.3
Cholesterol (mg): 50.7
Sodium (mg): 44
Protein (gm): 19.9
Carbohydrate (gm): 27.5

Exchanges:
Milk: 0.0
Vegetable: 1.0
Fruit: 0.0
Bread: 1.5
Meat: 2.0
Fat: 0.0

MEXICAN HASH

Leftover meats or poultry can be used in this dish. Serve with fried eggs for a heartier meal.

4 servings

1 pound beef eye of round, fat trimmed, cubed (½-inch)

1 cup each: chopped tomato, onion

2 large poblano chilies, sliced

1 pound Idaho potatoes, unpeeled, cooked, cubed (½-inch)

Chili powder, to taste

Salt and pepper, to taste

Per Serving:
Calories: 242
% of calories from fat: 15
Fat (gm): 4
Saturated fat (gm): 1.3
Cholesterol (mg): 54.7
Sodium (mg): 55
Protein (gm): 23.4
Carbohydrate (gm): 27.90

Exchanges:
Milk: 0.0
Vegetable: 1.5
Fruit: 0.0
Bread: 1.0
Meat: 2.5
Fat: 0.0

1. Cook beef in 2 inches simmering water in large saucepan, covered, until beef is tender, 20 to 25 minutes; drain. Cool slightly and shred. Sauté beef in lightly greased large skillet over until beginning to brown and crisp, about 5 minutes. Add tomato; cook over medium heat 5 minutes. Remove from skillet and reserve.

2. Add onion and poblano chilies to skillet; cook until tender, 5 to 8 minutes. Add potatoes and cook until browned, about 5 minutes. Add reserved meat mixture to skillet; cook until hot, 3 to 4 minutes. Season to taste with chili powder, salt, and pepper.

BEEF STEAKS WITH TOMATILLO AND AVOCADO SAUCE

45 *The Tomatillo and Avocado Sauce is also excellent with grilled or roasted poultry or pork.*

6 servings

1 medium onion, thinly sliced

6 beef eye of round or tenderloin steaks (4 ounces each), fat trimmed

Salt and pepper, to taste

1 cup Tomatillo Sauce (½ recipe) (see p. 188)

¼ cup each: mashed avocado, fat-free sour cream

6 flour or corn tortillas, warm

Per Serving:
Calories: 271
% of calories from fat: 30
Fat (gm): 8.9
Saturated fat (gm): 3.1
Cholesterol (mg): 56.3
Sodium (mg): 101
Protein (gm): 28.2
Carbohydrate (gm): 19.2

Exchanges:
Milk: 0.0
Vegetable: 1.0
Fruit: 0.0
Bread: 1.0
Meat: 3.0
Fat: 0.0

1. Sauté onion in lightly greased large skillet 2 to 3 minutes; reduce heat to medium-low and cook until onion is very soft, 5 to 8 minutes. Remove from skillet. Add steaks to skillet; cook over medium heat to desired degree of doneness, 3 to 4 minutes on each side for medium. Season to taste with salt and pepper.

2. Heat Tomatillo Sauce in small saucepan until hot. Stir in avocado and sour cream; cook 2 minutes. Top steaks with onions and sauce. Serve with tortillas.

BEEF AND ROASTED PEPPER FAJITAS

45

The beef in these fajitas is cooked with the flavorful pasilla chili for great flavor.

4 servings (2 fajitas each)

1 each: large red, green, yellow bell pepper, cubed (¾-inch)

Vegetable cooking spray

½–1 teaspoon ground cumin

¼ teaspoon ground cloves

1 dried pasilla chili, stem, seeds, and veins discarded

1 pound beef eye of round, fat trimmed, cut into strips (1½ x ½-inch)

3 cloves garlic, minced

¼ small jalapeño chili, seeds and veins discarded, minced

¼ cup finely chopped cilantro

Salt, to taste

8 flour or corn tortillas (6-inch), warm

½ cup fat-free sour cream

Per Serving:
Calories: 365
% of calories from fat: 19
Fat (gm): 7.8
Saturated fat (gm): 1.9
Cholesterol (mg): 54.7
Sodium (mg): 355
Protein (gm): 28.9
Carbohydrate (gm):
Exchanges:
Milk: 0.0
Vegetable: 2.0
Fruit: 0.0
Bread: 2.0
Meat: 3.0
Fat: 0.0

1. Arrange bell peppers in single layer on greased aluminum foil-lined jelly roll pan; spray with cooking spray. Bake at 425 degrees until tender and browned, 20 to 25 minutes. Toss with cumin and cloves.

2. Cover pasilla chili with hot water in small bowl; let stand until softened, about 15 minutes. Drain and chop. Cook beef, garlic, jalapeño, and pasilla chilies in lightly greased large skillet over medium heat until beef is desired doneness, about 5 minutes for medium; stir in bell peppers and cilantro. Season to taste with salt. Spoon onto tortillas. Top with sour cream, and roll up; fold one end up to prevent filling from leaking out.

BLACK BEAN AND BEEF BURRITOS

Another favorite that's a Tex-Mex adaptation of Mexican cooking.

4 servings

½ cup each: chopped poblano chili, onion
1 clove garlic, minced
1 bay leaf, crumbled
1 can (15 ounces) black beans, rinsed, drained
1 can (8 ounces) reduced-sodium tomato sauce
Salt and pepper, to taste
Beef Filling (recipe follows)
4 large flour tortillas (10-inch), warm
½ cup each: shredded fat-free Cheddar cheese
   (2 ounces), fat-free sour cream
2 tablespoons finely chopped cilantro

Per Serving:
Calories: 379
% of calories from fat: 14
Fat (gm): 6.5
Saturated fat (gm): 1.4
Cholesterol (mg): 43.6
Sodium (mg): 677
Protein (gm): 35.5
Carbohydrate (gm): 51.8

Exchanges:
Milk: 0.0
Vegetable: 2.0
Fruit: 0.0
Bread: 2.5
Meat: 2.5
Fat: 0.0

1. Sauté poblano chili, onion, garlic, and bay leaf in lightly greased large skillet until onion is tender, about 5 minutes. Add beans and tomato sauce; heat until hot. Season to taste with salt and pepper. Spoon bean mixture and Beef Filling onto tortillas; top with cheese, sour cream, and cilantro. Roll up; fold one end up to prevent filling from leaking out.

Beef Filling

Makes about 2 cups

12 ounces beef eye of round, fat trimmed, cubed (2-inch)
2 medium tomatoes, coarsely chopped
½ teaspoon ground cinnamon
Salt and pepper, to taste

1. Cook beef in 2 inches simmering water in medium saucepan, covered, until tender, 15 to 20 minutes; drain. Cool slightly; shred finely. Sauté beef in lightly greased medium skillet until beginning to brown, 3 to 4 minutes. Add tomatoes and cinnamon; cook until tomatoes are wilted. Season to taste with salt and pepper.

BEEF AND VEGETABLE ENCHILADAS

Vary these healthful enchiladas by substituting shredded chicken or pork tenderloin for the beef.

6 servings (2 each)

1½ cups each: chopped zucchini, tomatoes

¾ cup chopped carrots

¼ cup each: sliced green onions, chopped poblano chili or green bell pepper

4 cloves garlic, minced

1 teaspoon each: minced jalapeño chili, dried oregano leaves, ground cumin

1½ pounds beef eye of round, fat trimmed, cooked, shredded

Salt and pepper, to taste

12 corn or flour tortillas (6-inch)

Enchilada Sauce (see p. 439)

¾ cup (3 ounces) shredded fat-free Cheddar cheese

3 tablespoons finely chopped cilantro

Per Serving:
Calories: 305
% of calories from fat: 16
Fat (gm): 5.5
Saturated fat (gm): 1.5
Cholesterol (mg): 57.2
Sodium (mg): 244
Protein (gm): 30.2
Carbohydrate (gm): 34.8

Exchanges:
Milk: 0.0
Vegetable: 2.0
Fruit: 0.0
Bread: 1.5
Meat: 3.0
Fat: 0.0

1. Sauté vegetables and herbs in lightly greased large skillet until tender, about 10 minutes. Add beef; cook over medium heat until hot, 5 to 8 minutes. Season to taste with salt and pepper.

2. Dip tortillas in Enchilada Sauce to coat lightly and fill each with about ⅓ cup beef mixture; roll up and place, seam sides down, in large baking pan. Spoon remaining Enchilada Sauce over enchiladas; sprinkle with cheese. Bake, uncovered, at 350 degrees until hot 15 to 20 minutes. Sprinkle with cilantro.

BEEF AND ANCHO CHILI STEW

This stew has lots of delicious sauce, so serve with crusty warm rolls or tortillas, or serve over Black Beans and Rice (see p. 388).

8 servings

3 cups boiling water

4–6 ancho chilies, stems, seeds, and veins discarded

4 medium tomatoes, cut into wedges

2 pounds beef eye of round, fat trimmed, cubed (¾-inch)

1 large onion, chopped

2 cloves garlic, minced

1 teaspoon each: minced jalapeño chili, dried oregano leaves, crushed cumin seeds

2 tablespoons flour

Salt and pepper, to taste

Per Serving:
Calories: 159
% of calories from fat: 23
Fat (gm): 4
Saturated fat (gm): 1.3
Cholesterol (mg): 54.7
Sodium (mg): 56
Protein (gm): 22.1
Carbohydrate (gm): 8.3

Exchanges:
Milk: 0.0
Vegetable: 1.0
Fruit: 0.0
Bread: 0.0
Meat: 2.5
Fat: 0.0

1. Pour boiling water over chilies in bowl; let stand until softened, about 10 minutes. Process chilies and water and tomatoes in blender or food processor until smooth.

2. Sauté beef in lightly greased Dutch oven until browned, about 5 minutes. Add onion, garlic, jalapeno chili, and herbs; cook until onion is tender, about 5 minutes. Stir in flour; cook over medium heat 1 minute. Add ancho chili mixture; heat to boiling. Reduce heat and simmer, covered, until beef is tender, 45 to 60 minutes. Season to taste with salt and pepper.

COUNTRY BEEF STEW

Serve this delicious long simmered stew over noodles or rice.

4 servings (about 1 cup each)

2 pounds cubed lean beef for stew, fat trimmed

1 cup each: chopped onion, celery

3 cloves garlic, minced

2½ cups reduced-sodium beef broth

½ cup dry red wine or reduced-sodium beef broth

2 tablespoons tomato paste

½ teaspoon each: dried thyme and rosemary leaves

1 large bay leaf

2 cups each: cubed unpeeled potato, sliced carrots (1-inch)

1 cup cubed parsnip or turnip

½ cup frozen peas

¼ cup all-purpose flour

½ cup cold water

Salt and pepper, to taste

Per Serving:
Calories: 326
% of calories from fat: 16
Fat (gm): 5.8
Saturated fat (gm): 2
Cholesterol (mg): 70.9
Sodium (mg): 171
Protein (gm): 33.5
Carbohydrate (gm): 29.6

Exchanges:
Milk: 0.0
Vegetable: 2.0
Fruit: 0.0
Bread: 1.5
Meat: 3.0
Fat: 0.0

1. Cook beef in lightly greased large saucepan until browned, 5 to 8 minutes. Add onion, celery, and garlic; cook until tender, about 5 minutes. Add broth, wine, tomato paste, and herbs; heat to boiling. Reduce heat and simmer, covered, until beef is tender, 1½ to 2 hours adding remaining vegetables during last 30 minutes of cooking time. Heat stew to boiling; stir in combined flour and water, stirring until thickened, about 1 minute. Discard bay leaf; season to taste with salt and pepper.

CURRIED BEEF STEW WITH CHIVE DUMPLINGS

Part of the beef in this aromatic stew is coarsely chopped, giving the stew an extra-rich texture.

8 servings

1 pounds cubed lean beef for stew

1 tablespoon vegetable oil

1½ cups chopped onions

3 tablespoons flour

1½ teaspoons curry powder

2 cups reduced-sodium beef broth

1 cup chopped tomato

1 bay leaf

1 package (10 ounces) frozen peas

Salt and pepper, to taste

Chive Dumplings (recipe follows)

Per Serving:
Calories: 297
% of calories from fat: 22
Fat (gm): 7.3
Saturated fat (gm): 1.9
Cholesterol (mg): 55.3
Sodium (mg): 416
Protein (gm): 27.1
Carbohydrate (gm): 29.4

Exchanges:
Milk: 0.0
Vegetable: 0.0
Fruit: 0.0
Bread: 2.0
Meat: 3.0
Fat: 0.0

1. Coarsely chop 1 pound beef; sauté cubed and chopped beef in oil in Dutch oven until browned, about 5 minutes; add onions and cook until browned, 5 to 8 minutes. Stir in flour and curry powder and cook 1 minute. Add beef broth, tomato, and bay leaf; heat to boiling. Reduce heat and simmer, covered, until beef is tender, about 1 hour, adding peas during last 10 minutes. Discard bay leaf; season to taste with salt and pepper.

2. Heat stew to boiling; drop dumpling dough onto top of stew. Cook, uncovered, 10 minutes; cook, covered, 10 minutes longer or until dumplings are dry.

Chive Dumplings

Makes 8 dumplings

1⅔ cups reduced-fat all-purpose baking mix

2 tablespoons finely chopped chives

¼–½ teaspoon curry powder

⅔ cup fat-free milk

1. Combine baking mix, chives, and curry powder in bowl; mix in milk, forming a soft dough.

PAPRIKA-SIRLOIN STEW WITH SOUR CREAM

Imagine tender beef, Italian green beans, and red potatoes cloaked in a heavenly paprika-spiked sour cream sauce. And suppose that such a dinner could be ready to eat in about 30 minutes. Daydream no more—here's the real meal!

4 servings

1 cup reduced-sodium fat-free beef broth

2 cups Italian flat green beans

¾ pound red potatoes, cubed

2 bay leaves

1 pound boneless beef sirloin steak, fat trimmed,
   cut into very thin strips (1 x ½-inch)

1 cup pearl onions, peeled

1 can (15 ounces) diced tomatoes, undrained

1 tablespoon paprika

½ cup fat-free sour cream

Salt and pepper, to taste

Per Serving:
Calories: 286
% of calories from fat: 17
Fat (gm): 5.4
Saturated fat (gm): 2
Cholesterol (mg): 59.5
Sodium (mg): 768
Protein (gm): 27.4
Carbohydrate (gm): 32.9

Exchanges:
Milk: 0.0
Vegetable: 0.0
Fruit: 0.0
Bread: 2.0
Meat: 3.0
Fat: 0.0

1. Heat beef broth, beans, potatoes, and bay leaves to boiling in large saucepan; reduce heat and simmer, covered, until vegetables are tender, about 10 minutes.

2. Sauté beef and onions in large skillet until lightly browned, 8 to 10 minutes; stir into vegetable mixture. Stir in tomatoes with liquid and paprika. Simmer, uncovered, 5 minutes, or until slightly thickened. Stir in sour cream; season to taste with salt and pepper.

BEEF BRAISED IN RED WINE

45

A good-quality Chianti works well in this traditional Italian recipe.

6 servings

1½ pounds boneless beef round steak, fat trimmed, cubed (1-inch)

1 tablespoon olive oil

1 cups sliced mushrooms

1 cup each: chopped onion, celery

1 large clove garlic, minced

2 tablespoons flour

1 cup each: reduced-sodium fat-free beef broth, dry red wine or water

1 can (15 ounces) reduced-sodium tomato sauce

12 baby carrots

6 medium potatoes, halved

1 teaspoon dried thyme leaves

2 large bay leaves

½ teaspoon dry mustard

Salt and pepper, to taste

Per Serving:
Calories: 366
% of calories from fat: 18
Fat (gm): 7.4
Saturated fat (gm): 2.2
Cholesterol (mg): 55.9
Sodium (mg): 115
Protein (gm): 31.2
Carbohydrate (gm): 36.9

Exchanges:
Milk: 0.0
Vegetable: 2.0
Fruit: 0.0
Bread: 2.0
Meat: 3.0
Fat: 0.0

1. Sauté beef in oil in Dutch oven until browned, about 5 minutes; remove from pan. Add mushrooms, onion, celery, and garlic to pan; cook 5 minutes. Stir in flour and cook 1 minute. Add beef, broth and remaining ingredients, except salt and pepper, and heat to boiling; transfer to oven and bake, covered, at 350 degrees until beef is tender, about 1 hour. Season to taste with salt and pepper; discard bay leaves.

BEEF BOURGUIGNON

45

Try this French inspired stew for special occasions, when ordinary beef stew is not quite elegant enough!

6 servings

1½ pounds beef eye of round, fat trimmed, cubed (1½-inch)

1 tablespoon olive oil

¼ cup all purpose flour

1 cup each: reduced-sodium beef broth, Burgundy wine or water

1½ cups peeled pearl onions

3 cups sliced carrots

8 ounces small whole mushrooms

1 teaspoon each: dried marjoram and thyme leaves

2 bay leaves

½ teaspoon each: salt and pepper

12 ounces egg noodles, cooked, warm

Per Serving:
Calories: 522
% of calories from fat: 25
Fat (gm): 14.3
Saturated fat (gm): 4.6
Cholesterol (mg): 96.5
Sodium (mg): 309
Protein (gm): 35.3
Carbohydrate (gm): 55

Exchanges:
Milk: 0.0
Vegetable: 1.0
Fruit: 0.0
Bread: 3.0
Meat: 4.0
Fat: 1.0

1. Sauté beef in oil in Dutch oven until browned, about 10 minutes; stir in flour and cook 1 minute. Add broth and wine; heat to boiling. Transfer to oven and bake, covered, at 350 degrees until beef is very tender, 1 to 1½ hours, adding vegetables, herbs, salt, and pepper during last 30 minutes. Discard bay leaves. Serve over noodles.

BEEF STROGANOFF

A favorite for buffet entertaining, this dish enjoys well-deserved popularity.

4 servings

1 pound beef eye of round or sirloin steak, fat trimmed, cut into strips (1½ x ½-inch)

1 tablespoon margarine or butter

3 cups sliced mushrooms

½ cup sliced onion

2 cloves garlic, minced

2 tablespoons flour

1½ cups reduced-sodium beef broth

1 teaspoon Dijon mustard

¼ teaspoon dried thyme leaves

½ cup fat-free sour cream

Salt and pepper, to taste

3 cups cooked noodles, warm

Per Serving:
Calories: 423
% of calories from fat: 21
Fat (gm): 10
Saturated fat (gm): 2.2
Cholesterol (mg): 64
Sodium (mg): 167
Protein (gm): 39
Carbohydrate (gm): 45.1

Exchanges:
Milk: 0.0
Vegetable: 1.0
Fruit: 0.0
Bread: 2.5
Meat: 4.0
Fat: 0.0

1. Sauté beef in margarine in large saucepan until browned, about 5 minutes; remove from pan. Add mushrooms, onion, and garlic to pan; cook until tender, 5 to 8 minutes. Stir in flour and cook 1 minute. Add beef, beef broth, mustard, and thyme. Heat to boiling; reduce heat and simmer, covered, until beef is tender, 45 to 60 minutes. Reduce heat to low; stir in sour cream and cook 2 to 3 minutes. Season to taste with salt and pepper and serve over noodles.

GREEK BEEF AND LENTIL STEW

Lentils and fresh vegetables partner deliciously in this easy stew.

6 servings (about 1½ cups each)

1 cup each: chopped onion, green bell pepper,
    cubed zucchini

2 teaspoons minced garlic

2 cups each: cubed Idaho potatoes, cut green beans

1 cup lentils

1 can (15 ounces) reduced-sodium diced tomatoes,
    undrained

3 cups reduced-sodium fat-free beef broth

1 teaspoon each: dried oregano and mint leaves

½ teaspoon each: ground turmeric, coriander

12 ounces cooked cubed beef eye of round

Salt and pepper, to taste

Per Serving:
Calories: 302
% of calories from fat: 7
Fat (gm): 2.6
Saturated fat (gm): 0.8
Cholesterol (mg): 27.5
Sodium (mg): 122
Protein (gm): 25.5
Carbohydrate (gm): 46.7

Exchanges:
Milk: 0.0
Vegetable: 3.0
Fruit: 0.0
Bread: 2.0
Meat: 1.5
Fat: 0.0

1. Sauté onion, bell pepper, zucchini, and garlic in lightly greased large saucepan until tender, about 5 minutes. Add remaining ingredients, except salt and pepper; heat to boiling. Reduce heat and simmer, covered, until lentils are just tender and stew is thickened, about 30 minutes. Season to taste with salt and pepper.

CHILI STEW

A squeeze of lime adds a fresh flavor to this spicy favorite.

6 servings (about 2 cups each)

1 pound lean ground beef
1 cup coarsely chopped onion
½ cup coarsely chopped red bell pepper
½ jalapeño chili, finely chopped
2 cloves garlic, minced
1 can (15 ounces) each: reduced-sodium chunky
  tomato sauce, rinsed, drained red kidney beans
3 cups reduced-sodium tomato juice
2 cups each: chopped celery, cubed butternut squash
1 cup each: cubed zucchini, sliced mushrooms
1½ teaspoons each: chili powder, ground cumin
Salt and pepper, to taste
6 lime wedges

Per Serving:
Calories: 317
% of calories from fat: 30
Fat (gm): 10.8
Saturated fat (gm): 4
Cholesterol (mg): 46.6
Sodium (mg): 357
Protein (gm): 21.2
Carbohydrate (gm): 36.1

Exchanges:
Milk: 0.0
Vegetable: 1.0
Fruit: 0.0
Bread: 2.0
Meat: 2.0
Fat: 1.0

1. Cook ground beef in lightly greased Dutch oven until browned, about 8 minutes; add onion, bell pepper, jalapeño chili, and garlic. Sauté until tender, 8 to 10 minutes. Add remaining ingredients, except salt, pepper, and lime wedges; heat to boiling. Reduce heat and simmer, covered, until vegetables are tender, about 15 minutes; cook, uncovered until stew is desired consistency, 15 to 20 minutes. Season to taste with salt and pepper; squeeze lime wedge into each bowl of stew.

HUNGARIAN GOULASH

45

All the traditional flavors of Hungarian goulash in an easy casserole.

6 servings

2 pounds boneless beef round steak,
   fat trimmed, cubed

1 medium onion, finely chopped

1 teaspoon minced garlic

2 tablespoons flour

1½ teaspoons paprika

¼ teaspoon dried thyme leaves

1 bay leaf

1 can (14½ ounces) diced tomatoes, undrained

1 container (8 ounces) fat-free sour cream

Salt and pepper, to taste

12 ounces egg noodles, cooked, warm

Per Serving:
Calories: 471
% of calories from fat: 17
Fat (gm): 8.7
Saturated fat (gm): 2.9
Cholesterol (mg): 123.5
Sodium (mg): 367
Protein (gm): 44.6
Carbohydrate (gm): 50.5

Exchanges:
Milk: 0.0
Vegetable: 1.0
Fruit: 0.0
Bread: 3.0
Meat: 4.0
Fat: 0.0

1. Combine beef, onion, and garlic in greased 2½-quart casserole; sprinkle with flour, paprika, and thyme and toss. Stir in bay leaf and tomatoes with liquid. Bake, covered, at 325 degrees, until beef is tender, 1 to 1½ hours, stirring in sour cream during last 10 minutes. Season to taste with salt and pepper. Serve over noodles.

VARIATION

Three-Meat Goulash — Make recipe as above, using ¾ pound each: cubed lean beef, pork, and veal in place of the beef round steak. Add 8 ounces sliced mushrooms, 1 teaspoon caraway seeds, and ½ teaspoon dried dill weed with the tomatoes.

GROUND BEEF AND VEGETABLE STROGANOFF

45 *Fat-free half-and-half and sour cream contribute wonderful rich flavor and creamy texture to this favorite.*

8 servings (about 1 cup each)

1½ pounds lean ground beef

2 medium onions, thinly sliced

12 ounces mixed wild mushrooms (shiitake, oyster, enoki, or cremini), sliced

2 cloves garlic, minced

¼ cup dry red wine or beef broth

12 ounces broccoli florets and sliced stalks

1 cup fat-free half-and-half or fat-free milk

2 tablespoons flour

1½ teaspoons Dijon mustard

1 cup fat-free sour cream

½ teaspoon dried dill weed

Salt and pepper, to taste

16 ounces noodles, cooked, warm

Per Serving:
Calories: 467
% of calories from fat: 22
Fat (gm): 11.3
Saturated fat (gm): 4.1
Cholesterol (mg): 52.9
Sodium (mg): 468
Protein (gm): 27.7
Carbohydrate (gm): 61.5

Exchanges:
Milk: 0.0
Vegetable: 3.0
Fruit: 0.0
Bread: 3.0
Meat: 2.0
Fat: 1.0

1. Cook ground beef in large skillet until browned, about 10 minutes; drain. Add onions, mushrooms, and garlic to skillet and sauté until tender, about 5 minutes. Add wine and broccoli; cook over medium heat, covered, until broccoli is tender, 8 to 10 minutes. Stir in combined half-and-half, flour, and mustard; heat to boiling, stirring until thickened, about 1 minute. Reduce heat to low; stir in sour cream and dill weed and cook 1 to 2 minutes. Season to taste with salt and pepper; serve over noodles.

SICILIAN BEEF AND RICE

45 *Using frozen pepper and onion blend minimizes kitchen prep time in this easy recipe.*

4 servings

1 package (16 ounces) frozen pepper and onion blend

1 teaspoon minced garlic

12 ounces ground beef round

2 cans (15 ounces each) reduced-sodium
   tomato sauce

2–3 teaspoons dried Italian seasoning

Salt and pepper, to taste

3 cups cooked long-grain rice or pasta, warm

3 tablespoons grated Parmesan cheese

Per Serving:
Calories: 422
% of calories from fat: 11
Fat (gm): 5
Saturated fat (gm): 2.2
Cholesterol (mg): 44.9
Sodium (mg): 186
Protein (gm): 29.3
Carbohydrate (gm): 61.7

Exchanges:
Milk: 0.0
Vegetable: 3.0
Fruit: 0.0
Bread: 3.0
Meat: 2.0
Fat: 0.0

1. Cook pepper and onion blend, garlic, and
ground beef in lightly greased large skillet over
medium heat until beef is browned and vegetables are tender, about 6 minutes. Stir in tomato
sauce and Italian seasoning; simmer, uncovered,
until thickened, about 20 minutes. Season to
taste with salt and pepper. Serve with rice;
sprinkle with Parmesan cheese.

45-MINUTE PREPARATION TIP: Begin cooking
rice before preparing the rest of the recipe.

MEATBALLS IN TOMATO CHILI SAUCE

*The meatballs can be made in advance and frozen; thaw before using.
Pasilla chilies are picante—use 2 only if you enjoy a truly hot sauce!*

4 servings

1–2 pasilla chilies

1 can (28 ounces) reduced-sodium diced tomatoes,
   undrained

Jalapeño Meatballs (recipe follows)

Salt and pepper, to taste

Per Serving:
Calories: 240
% of calories from fat: 24
Fat (gm): 6.5
Saturated fat (gm): 2.3
Cholesterol (mg): 60.9
Sodium (mg): 435
Protein (gm): 29.3
Carbohydrate (gm): 15.9

Exchanges:
Milk: 0.0
Vegetable: 3.0
Fruit: 0.0
Bread: 0.0
Meat: 3.0
Fat: 0.0

1. Cook pasilla chilies in large lightly greased
saucepan over medium heat until softened;
discard stems, seeds, and veins. Process chilies
and tomatoes with liquid in blender until
smooth; heat to boiling in large saucepan. Add
Jalapeño Meatballs; reduce heat and simmer,
covered, until meatballs are cooked, about 10
minutes. Season to taste with salt and pepper.

Jalapeno Meatballs
Makes 16

8 ounces each: ground pork tenderloin, lean beef

1 egg

¼ cup each: unseasoned dry bread crumbs, finely chopped onion

½ cup shredded zucchini

2 cloves garlic, minced

1 teaspoon minced jalapeño chili

½ teaspoon each: dried oregano leaves, salt

¼ teaspoon dried thyme leaves, pepper

1. Mix all ingredients; shape into 16 meatballs.

SWEDISH MEATBALLS WITH NOODLES

Serve the meatballs in cream gravy as an appetizer to serve 8-12 people.

4 servings

1 pound very lean ground beef

½ cup each: finely chopped onion, unseasoned
   dry bread crumbs

⅓ cup fat-free milk

1 egg

1 teaspoon dried dill weed

¼ teaspoon ground allspice

Pinch ground cardamom

½ teaspoon salt

⅛ teaspoon pepper

Cream Gravy (recipe follows)

3 cups cooked noodles, warm

Chopped fresh dill weed or parsley, as garnish

Per Serving:
Calories: 497
% of calories from fat: 24
Fat (gm): 13
Saturated fat (gm): 3.6
Cholesterol (mg): 67.3
Sodium (mg): 814
Protein (gm): 37.9
Carbohydrate (gm): 56.6

Exchanges:
Milk: 0.5
Vegetable: 0.0
Fruit: 0.0
Bread: 3.5
Meat: 3.5
Fat: 0.0

1. Combine ground beef, onion, bread crumbs, milk, egg, and seasonings; shape into 24 meatballs. Bake in baking pan at 425 degrees until meatballs are cooked and browned, 15 to 20 minutes. Combine meatballs with Cream Gravy. Spoon over noodles, and sprinkle with dill weed.

Cream Gravy
Makes about 2 cups

2 tablespoons margarine or butter
¼ cup all-purpose flour
2 cups fat-free half-and-half or milk
½ teaspoon beef bouillon crystals
¼ cup fat-free sour cream
Salt and pepper, to taste

1. Melt margarine in medium saucepan; stir in flour and cook 1 minute. Whisk in half-and-half and bouillon crystals; heat to boiling, stirring until thickened, about 1 minute. Stir in sour cream and cook over low heat 1 to 2 minutes; season to taste with salt and pepper.

JUST PLAIN MEAT LOAF

Moist, the way meatloaf should be, with plenty of leftovers for sandwiches, too! Serve with Real Mashed Potatoes (see p. 485).

6 servings

1½ pounds very lean ground beef
1 cup quick-cooking oats
½ cup fat-free milk
1 egg
¼ cup catsup or chili sauce
½ cup each: chopped onion, green bell pepper
1 teaspoon each: minced garlic, dried Italian
   seasoning
¾ teaspoon salt
½ teaspoon pepper

Per Serving:
Calories: 241
% of calories from fat: 21
Fat (gm): 5.5
Saturated fat (gm): 1.8
Cholesterol (mg): 64.3
Sodium (mg): 489
Protein (gm): 31.2
Carbohydrate (gm): 15.3

Exchanges:
Milk: 0.0
Vegetable: 0.0
Fruit: 0.0
Bread: 1.0
Meat: 3.0
Fat: 0.0

1. Mix all ingredients until blended. Pat mixture into ungreased loaf pan, 9 x 5 inches, or shape into a loaf in baking pan. Bake at 350 degrees until juices run clear and meat thermometer registers 170 degrees, about 1 hour. Let stand in pan 10 minutes; invert onto serving plate.

VARIATIONS

Stuffed Green Peppers — Cut 6 medium green bell peppers lengthwise into halves; discard seeds. Cook peppers in simmering water 3 minutes; drain. Make recipe as above, substituting 1 cup cooked rice for the oats. Fill peppers with mixture and place in baking pan. Bake, covered, at 350 degrees until beef mixture is cooked, about 45 minutes.

Italian Meat Loaf — Make recipe as above, adding ¼ cup (1 ounce) grated fat-free Parmesan cheese, ½ cup (2 ounces) shredded reduced-fat mozzarella cheese, and 2 tablespoons chopped pitted ripe olives. After baking, spread meat loaf with 2 tablespoons seasoned tomato sauce and sprinkle with 2 tablespoons each fat-free Parmesan and shredded reduced-fat mozzarella cheeses. Let stand, loosely covered, 10 minutes.

Savory Cheese Meat Loaf — Make recipe as above, substituting ½ pound ground lean pork for ½ pound of the beef, and adding 4 ounces fat-free cream cheese, ½ cup (2 ounces) shredded reduced-fat Cheddar cheese, and 2 tablespoons Worcestershire sauce. Spread top of loaf with ¼ cup of catsup before baking. Sprinkle ¼ cup (1 ounce) shredded reduced-fat Cheddar cheese on top of meat loaf after baking. Let stand, loosely covered, 10 minutes.

Chutney-Peanut Meat Loaf — Make recipe as above, substituting ½ cup chopped chutney for the catsup, and adding ⅓ cup chopped peanuts, 1 teaspoon curry powder, and ½ teaspoon ground ginger.

LEMON MEAT LOAF

Meat loaf takes on a new dimension with lemon flavor and a smooth Egg Lemon Sauce.

6 servings (2 slices each)

1½ pounds very lean ground beef
1 cup fresh bread crumbs
1 egg
⅓ cup each: chopped onion, green bell pepper
1 clove garlic, minced
1 tablespoon each: lemon juice, grated lemon zest

1 teaspoon Dijon mustard

½ teaspoon each: dried savory leaves, pepper

¾ teaspoon salt

Egg Lemon Sauce (recipe follows)

Per Serving:
Calories: 228
% of calories from fat: 29
Fat (gm): 7.2
Saturated fat (gm): 2.2
Cholesterol (mg): 94.4
Sodium (mg): 463
Protein (gm): 29.4
Carbohydrate (gm): 10.2

Exchanges:
Milk: 0.0
Vegetable: 0.0
Fruit: 0.0
Bread: 1.0
Meat: 3.0
Fat: 0.0

1. Mix all ingredients except Egg Lemon Sauce; pat mixture into ungreased loaf pan, 9 x 5 inches, or shape into a loaf in baking pan. Bake at 350 degrees until juices run clear and meat thermometer registers 170 degrees, about 1 hour. Let stand in pan 5 minutes; invert onto serving plate. Serve with Egg Lemon Sauce.

Egg Lemon Sauce

Makes about 1¼ cups

1 tablespoon margarine or butter

2 tablespoons flour

½ cup each: reduced-sodium fat-free chicken broth, fat-free milk

1 egg, lightly beaten

3–4 tablespoons lemon juice

1 teaspoon grated lemon zest

Salt and white pepper, to taste

1. Melt margarine in medium saucepan; whisk in flour and cook 1 minute. Whisk in broth and milk; heat to boiling, whisking until thickened, about 1 minute. Whisk about ½ the broth mixture into the egg; whisk mixture into saucepan. Whisk over medium heat 1 minute. Add lemon juice and zest; season to taste with salt and white pepper.

VARIATION

Sweet-Sour Ham Loaf — Make recipe as above, substituting ½ pound ground smoked ham for ½ pound of the ground beef, and omitting lemon juice, lemon zest, savory, and Egg Lemon Sauce. Add 2 chopped sweet pickles, ⅓ cup each coarsely chopped almonds, mixed dried fruit, apricot preserves, 2 tablespoons catsup, 1 tablespoon cider vinegar, and 2 teaspoons soy sauce.

PORCUPINE PEPPERS

45

An old favorite—the rice pokes out of the meat like porcupine quills!

4 servings

1 pound very lean ground beef

1 egg, lightly beaten

¼ cup uncooked rice

½ teaspoon Worcestershire sauce

¼ teaspoon each: paprika, celery salt

4 large green bell peppers, halved lengthwise, seeded

1 can (14 ounces) diced tomatoes with chilies, undrained

Per Serving:
Calories: 283
% of calories from fat: 30
Fat (gm): 9.3
Saturated fat (gm): 3.5
Cholesterol (mg): 95.1
Sodium (mg): 469
Protein (gm): 29.2
Carbohydrate (gm): 19.9

Exchanges:
Milk: 0.0
Vegetable: 1.0
Fruit: 0.0
Bread: 1.0
Meat: 3.0
Fat: 0.0

1. Mix beef, egg, rice, and seasonings. Spoon meat mixture into peppers and place in lightly greased baking dish; pour tomatoes with liquid over. Bake, covered, at 350 degrees until beef is cooked and peppers are tender, about 1 hour.

SALISBURY STEAKS WITH MUSHROOM GRAVY

45

Rich Mushroom Gravy is a flavorful complement to moist Salisbury steaks.

4 servings

1 pound ground beef eye of round

2–4 tablespoons finely chopped onion

3 tablespoons water

½ teaspoon salt

¼ teaspoon pepper

Mushroom Gravy (recipe follows)

Per Serving:
Calories: 184
% of calories from fat: 24
Fat (gm): 4.6
Saturated fat (gm): 1.7
Cholesterol (mg): 64
Sodium (mg): 341
Protein (gm): 28.7
Carbohydrate (gm): 5.2

Exchanges:
Milk: 0.0
Vegetable: 1.0
Fruit: 0.0
Bread: 0.0
Meat: 3.0
Fat: 0.0

1. Mix all ingredients, except Mushroom Gravy; shape into four 1-inch thick oval patties. Cook patties in lightly greased large skillet to desired degree of doneness, 3 to 4 minutes per side for medium. Serve with Mushroom Gravy.

Mushroom Gravy
Makes about 1¼ cups

1 cup sliced mushrooms
¼ cup finely chopped onion
2 tablespoons flour
1 cup reduced-sodium beef broth
Salt and pepper, to taste

1. Sauté mushrooms and onion in lightly greased medium skillet until tender; stir in flour and cook 1 minute. Stir in beef broth and heat to boiling; boil, stirring until thickened, about 1 minute. Season to taste with salt and pepper.

GYROS BURGERS

45 *Delicious burgers of lamb and beef, with Greek accents.*

4 servings

8 ounces each: lean ground beef, ground lamb
2 tablespoons chopped onion
2 cloves garlic, minced
½ teaspoon each: dried oregano leaves, dill weed
1 teaspoon salt
4 pita breads
Gyros Relish (recipe follows)

1. Combine ground meats, onion, garlic, herbs, and salt; shape into 4 patties. Cook in large skillet over medium heat to desired degree of doneness, about 5 minutes on each side for medium. Serve in pitas with Gyros Relish.

Per Serving:
Calories: 435
% of calories from fat: 29
Fat (gm): 13.9
Saturated fat (gm): 5
Cholesterol (mg): 87.8
Sodium (mg): 1011
Protein (gm): 34.6
Carbohydrate (gm): 41.2

Exchanges:
Milk: 0.0
Vegetable: 0.0
Fruit: 0.0
Bread: 3.0
Meat: 3.0
Fat: 1.0

Gyros Relish

makes about 2 cups

1 each: seeded, chopped small cucumber, medium tomato, sliced green
  onion
⅔ cup plain fat-free yogurt
½ teaspoon each: dried mint and oregano leaves

1. Mix all ingredients.

CORNED BEEF AND RED CABBAGE DINNER

45 *Don't wait until St. Patrick's Day to enjoy this luck-of-the-Irish stew.
It's fast. It's easy. It's delicious.*

4 servings

16 ounces deli corned beef, cubed
8 medium red potatoes, cubed
2 cups sliced carrots
2 cups cubed, peeled turnips
1 can (14 ounces) reduced-sodium fat-free chicken
  broth
1 tablespoon apple cider vinegar
1 teaspoon pickling spice
1 pound red cabbage, coarsely sliced

Per Serving:
Calories: 440
% of calories from fat: 24
Fat (gm): 11.9
Saturated fat (gm): 4.9
Cholesterol (mg): 64.0
Sodium (mg): 1847
Protein (gm): 29.2
Carbohydrate (gm): 56.6

Exchanges:
Milk: 0.0
Vegetable: 2.0
Fruit: 0.0
Bread: 3.0
Meat: 3.0
Fat: 0.0

1. Combine all ingredients, except cabbage, in large saucepan.
Heat to boiling; reduce heat and simmer, covered, 10 minutes.
Add cabbage and simmer until tender, about 10 minutes.

VEAL LADY SHARON

45

Veal chops are enhanced with a sauce flavored with mushrooms, herbs, and black olives.

4 servings

4 lean veal chops (about 4 ounces each), fat trimmed

1–3 teaspoons margarine or butter

2 medium onions, chopped

1 pound mushrooms, sliced

1 tablespoon each: flour, tomato paste

¾ cup reduced-sodium fat-free chicken broth

⅔ cup dry white wine

1 teaspoon herbes de Provence or dried Italian seasoning

1 small bay leaf

¼–½ cup sliced black olives

Salt and pepper, to taste

Per Serving:
Calories: 302
% of calories from fat: 30
Fat (gm): 10.2
Saturated fat (gm): 2.2
Cholesterol (mg): 100.1
Sodium (mg): 439
Protein (gm): 32
Carbohydrate (gm): 14.5

Exchanges:
Milk: 0.0
Vegetable: 3.0
Fruit: 0.0
Bread: 0.0
Meat: 3.0
Fat: 1.0

1. Cook veal chops in margarine in large skillet over high heat until browned on both sides; transfer to shallow baking dish. In same skillet, sauté onions and mushrooms until tender; sprinkle with flour and cook 2 to 3 minutes, stirring well. Stir in remaining ingredients, except salt and pepper, and heat to boiling. Reduce heat and simmer, covered, 5 minutes. Season to taste with salt and pepper. Pour over veal in baking dish. Bake, uncovered, at 325 degrees until veal is tender, about 45 minutes.

VEAL CHILI POBLANO

45 *Ground veal, poblano chili, and purchased seasoning mix make this fast-track chili an almost-instant favorite.*

4 servings

1 pound ground lean veal or turkey

1 each: chopped large onion, small poblano chili, rib celery

1 can (15 ounces) each: reduced-sodium crushed tomatoes, rinsed drained Great Northern beans

½–1 package (1¼ ounce-size) chili seasoning mix

Per Serving:
Calories: 282
% of calories from fat: 18
Fat (gm): 6.1
Saturated fat (gm): 1.6
Cholesterol (mg): 99.5
Sodium (mg): 659
Protein (gm): 34.2
Carbohydrate (gm): 26.4

Exchanges:
Milk: 0.0
Vegetable: 0.0
Fruit: 0.0
Bread: 2.0
Meat: 3.0
Fat: 0.0

1. Cook veal in lightly greased large saucepan until browned and crumbly, about 8 minutes; add onion, poblano chili, and celery, and sauté until tender, about 5 minutes. Stir in tomatoes, beans, and seasoning mix; heat to boiling. Reduce heat and simmer, uncovered, 15 minutes.

VEAL SAUVIGNON WITH SWISS CHARD

45 *Delight your taste buds with this sophisticated stew. It's a gourmet experience with melt-in-your-mouth veal, tender cauliflower florets, dry white wine, and pasta.*

4 servings

1 pound boneless veal cutlets, cut into strips (2 x ½-inch)

2 teaspoons olive oil, divided

1 medium onion, thinly sliced

1 teaspoon minced garlic

1½ cups sauvignon blanc or other dry white wine

1 tablespoon tomato paste

3 cups cauliflower florets

1 teaspoon dried marjoram leaves

2 cups torn Swiss chard leaves

Salt and pepper, to taste

8 ounces ziti or other pasta, cooked, warm

Per Serving:
Calories: 455
% of calories from fat: 16
Fat (gm): 8
Saturated fat (gm): 1.7
Cholesterol (mg): 74.6
Sodium (mg): 148
Protein (gm): 30
Carbohydrate (gm): 51

Exchanges:
Milk: 0.0
Vegetable: 1.0
Fruit: 0.0
Bread: 3.0
Meat: 2.0
Fat: 2.0

1. Sauté veal in 1 teaspoon oil in large saucepan until lightly browned; remove meat, and keep warm. Sauté onion in remaining 1 teaspoon oil in saucepan until tender; stir in garlic and cook 1 minute. Add wine, tomato paste, cauliflower, and marjoram and heat to boiling; reduce heat and simmer, covered, until tender, about 5 minutes. Stir in Swiss chard and veal; cook 1 to 2 minutes. Season to taste with salt and pepper. Serve over ziti.

VEAL AND VEGETABLE PAPRIKASH

45 *Your preference of hot or sweet paprika can be used in this recipe.*

6 servings

1½ pounds veal scallopine, cut into strips (1-inch)

1 tablespoon olive oil

2 cups thinly sliced cabbage

1 cup each: sliced onion, zucchini, carrots, green bell peppers

1½ cups sliced mushrooms

1 medium tomato, chopped

3 tablespoons flour

1 tablespoon paprika

¾ cup reduced-sodium chicken broth

½ cup fat-free sour cream

Salt and pepper, to taste

12 ounces noodles, cooked, warm

Per Serving:
Calories: 419
% of calories from fat: 20
Fat (gm): 9.1
Saturated fat (gm): 3.2
Cholesterol (mg): 138.5
Sodium (mg): 264
Protein (gm): 33.5
Carbohydrate (gm): 49.8

Exchanges:
Milk: 0.0
Vegetable: 2.0
Fruit: 0.0
Bread: 3.0
Meat: 3.0
Fat: 0.0

1. Sauté veal in oil in large skillet until browned, 3 to 5 minutes; add vegetables and sauté until tender, 8 to 10 minutes. Stir in flour and paprika; cook 1 minute. Stir in broth and heat to boiling; boil, stirring until thickened, about 1 minute. Stir in sour cream; season to taste with salt and pepper. Serve over noodles.

ROSEMARY ROAST PORK TENDERLOIN

45

So easy to prepare, you'll make this delicious entrée often.

4 servings

1 pound pork tenderloin, fat trimmed
1 clove garlic, cut into 8 to 10 slivers
Vegetable cooking spray
1 teaspoon crushed dried rosemary leaves
Salt and pepper, to taste

Per Serving:
Calories: 139
% of calories from fat: 28
Fat (gm): 4
Saturated fat (gm): 1.4
Cholesterol (mg): 66
Sodium (mg): 47
Protein (gm): 23.5
Carbohydrate (gm): .44

Exchanges:
Milk: 0.0
Vegetable: 0.0
Fruit: 0.0
Bread: 0.0
Meat: 3.0
Fat: 0.0

1. Cut small slits in pork and insert garlic slivers. Place pork in small roasting pan and spray lightly with cooking spray. Rub surface of pork with rosemary leaves. Sprinkle lightly with salt and pepper. Roast at 425 degrees to desired degree of doneness, 160 degrees (slightly pink), 20 to 30 minutes.

NOTE: Pork can be eaten slightly pink; it is safe to eat after the internal temperature has reached 140 degrees.

APRICOT STUFFED PORK TENDERLOIN

45

This elegant dish is party-perfect; serve with an aromatic rice, such as jasmine or basmati.

4 servings

1 pound pork tenderloin, fat trimmed
1 can (8½ ounces) apricot halves, drained, chopped (½-inch)
1 each: rib celery, small onion, finely chopped
⅛ teaspoon each: ground cinnamon, black pepper
2 cups seasoned croutons
⅔ cup reduced-sodium fat-free chicken broth

Per Serving:
Calories: 257
% of calories from fat: 25
Fat (gm): 7.0
Saturated fat (gm): 2.2
Cholesterol (mg): 74
Sodium (mg): 396
Protein (gm): 27.2
Carbohydrate (gm): .19.9

Exchanges:
Milk: 0.0
Vegetable: 0.0
Fruit: 1.5
Bread: 0.0
Meat: 3.0
Fat: 0.0

1. Slice tenderloin lengthwise, cutting to, but not through, opposite side. Pound meat with flat side of meat mallet to rectangle about 10 x 6 inches.

2. Combine remaining ingredients, except broth in bowl; pour broth over and toss. Spoon mixture evenly over tenderloin; roll up, starting from short side. Tie meat with kitchen string at 1-inch intervals. Bake at 325 degrees until pork is cooked, 45 to 60 minutes.

PORK TENDERLOIN WITH GREMOLATA

Gremolata is a refreshing blend of garlic, lemon peel, and parsley that is often used to flavor stews and soups.

4 servings

1 pound pork tenderloin, fat trimmed, cubed (1-inch)
1 teaspoon olive oil
4 shallots, thinly sliced
1 cup reduced-sodium fat-free beef broth
2 medium potatoes, cubed
1 can (15 ounces) diced tomatoes, undrained
Salt and pepper, to taste
Gremolata (recipe follows)

Per Serving:
Calories: 289
% of calories from fat: 17
Fat (gm): 5.5
Saturated fat (gm): 1.6
Cholesterol (mg): 65.7
Sodium (mg): 523
Protein (gm): 28.6
Carbohydrate (gm): 31.2

Exchanges:
Milk: 0.0
Vegetable: 0.0
Fruit: 0.0
Bread: 2.0
Meat: 3.0
Fat: 0.0

1. Sauté pork in oil in large saucepan until lightly browned; add shallots and sauté 3 to 4 minutes. Stir in broth and heat to boiling; reduce heat and simmer, covered, 10 minutes. Add potatoes and tomatoes with liquid; simmer, covered, until potatoes are tender, about 15 minutes. Season to taste with salt and pepper. Pass Gremolata to stir into stew.

Gremolata
Makes about ½ cup

1 cup packed parsley sprigs
1–2 tablespoons grated lemon zest
4 large cloves garlic, minced

1. Process all ingredients in food processor until finely minced. Refrigerate until ready to use.

PORK MEDALLIONS WITH YOGURT-SAUCED FETTUCCINE

45 *Pork medallions cook quickly for this delicious easy dinner.*

4 servings

12 ounces pork tenderloin, sliced (½-inch)

½ cup apple juice

1 small onion, chopped

4 small shallots, quartered

¼ teaspoon dried sage leaves

2 tablespoons flour

1 container (8 ounces) plain low-fat yogurt

Salt and pepper, to taste

8 ounces spinach fettuccine, cooked, warm

Per Serving:
Calories: 355
% of calories from fat: 14
Fat (gm): 5.4
Saturated fat (gm): 2.1
Cholesterol (mg): 108.2
Sodium (mg): 150
Protein (gm): 30
Carbohydrate (gm): 45.1

Exchanges:
Milk: 0.0
Vegetable: 0.0
Fruit: 0.0
Bread: 3.0
Meat: 2.5
Fat: 0.0

1. Sauté pork medallions in lightly greased skillet until browned and cooked, 3 to 4 minutes on each side; remove from skillet. Add apple juice, onion, shallots, and sage; heat to boiling. Reduce heat and simmer, covered, until onion is tender, about 5 minutes. Stir in combined flour and yogurt, stirring until thickened, about 1 minute; season to taste with salt and pepper. Add pork and cook over low heat 2 minutes; serve over fettuccine.

45-MINUTE PREPARATION TIP: Begin cooking fettuccine before preparing rest of the recipe.

PORK TENDERLOIN WITH GREEN PEANUT SAUCE

Although the Mexican version of Green Peanut Sauce uses a much larger quantity of peanuts, this lower-fat version is very flavorful with a pleasing crunchy texture.

6 servings

1½ pounds pork tenderloin, fat trimmed, sliced (¼-inch)

Salt and pepper, to taste

1 cup Tomatillo Sauce (½ recipe) (see p. 188)

⅓ cup chopped dry-roasted peanuts

4 cups cooked rice, warm

1. Sauté pork in lightly greased large skillet until cooked, 3 to 4 minutes on each side. Sprinkle lightly with salt and pepper. Add Tomatillo Sauce and peanuts to skillet; heat until hot. Serve over rice.

Per Serving:
Calories: 347
% of calories from fat: 23
Fat (gm): 8.9
Saturated fat (gm): 2
Cholesterol (mg): 65.4
Sodium (mg): 115
Protein (gm): 28.9
Carbohydrate (gm): 36.6

Exchanges:
Milk: 0.0
Vegetable: 1.0
Fruit: 0.0
Bread: 2.0
Meat: 3.0
Fat: 0.0

PORK WITH PEPPERS AND ONIONS

45

This dish can also be made with boneless loin of pork instead of tenderloin.

4 servings

1 pound pork tenderloin, fat trimmed cut into strips (1½ x ½-inch)

1 tablespoon olive oil

1 can (15 ounces) reduced-sodium tomato sauce

1 package (16 ounces) frozen pepper and onion blend

2 tablespoons dry sherry (optional)

1 teaspoon each: minced garlic, dried basil and thyme leaves

Salt and pepper, to taste

8 ounces tricolor rotini, cooked, warm

Per Serving:
Calories: 464
% of calories from fat: 17
Fat (gm): 8.4
Saturated fat (gm): 2
Cholesterol (mg): 65.7
Sodium (mg): 99
Protein (gm): 33.9
Carbohydrate (gm): 58.6

Exchanges:
Milk: 0.0
Vegetable: 3.0
Fruit: 0.0
Bread: 3.0
Meat: 3.0
Fat: 0.0

1. Cook pork in olive oil in large skillet until browned, about 5 minutes; add tomato sauce, pepper and onion blend, sherry, garlic, and herbs. Heat to boiling; reduce heat and simmer, covered, until pork is tender, about 10 minutes. Simmer, uncovered, until thickened, 2 to 3 minutes. Season to taste with salt and pepper. Serve over pasta.

45-minute preparation tip: Begin cooking the rotini before preparing rest of the recipe.

PORK AND SQUASH RAGOUT

45 *Stews don't have to be long-cooked to be good—this delicious stew is ready to eat in less than 45 minutes. Serve with Garlic Bread (see p. 531).*

4 servings (about 1¼ cups each)

1 pound pork tenderloin, cubed

1½ cups each: chopped onions, green bell peppers

2 teaspoons minced roasted garlic

1 tablespoon flour

2 cups cubed, peeled, butternut or acorn squash

2 cans (16 ounces) reduced-sodium diced tomatoes, undrained

1 can (15 ounces) red kidney beans, rinsed, drained

¾ teaspoon dried Italian seasoning

Salt and pepper, to taste

Per Serving:
Calories: 344
% of calories from fat: 10
Fat (gm): 3.8
Saturated fat (gm): 1.3
Cholesterol (mg): 73.1
Sodium (mg): 504
Protein (gm): 33.2
Carbohydrate (gm): 46.2

Exchanges:
Milk: 0.0
Vegetable: 0.0
Fruit: 0.0
Bread: 3.0
Meat: 3.0
Fat: 0.0

1. Sauté pork in lightly greased large saucepan until browned, 8 to 10 minutes; remove from skillet. Add onions, bell peppers, and garlic and sauté until tender, about 8 minutes. Stir in flour; cook 1 minute. Return pork to saucepan; add remaining ingredients, except salt and pepper. Heat to boiling; reduce heat and simmer until pork is cooked, 15 to 20 minutes. Season to taste with salt and pepper.

FETTUCCINE WITH PORK, GREENS, AND CARAMELIZED ONIONS

Cooked chicken breast or shrimp can be used as delicious alternatives to the pork in this recipe.

4 servings

4 medium onions, sliced

1 tablespoon olive oil

1 teaspoon sugar

2 cans (14½ ounces each) reduced-sodium fat-free chicken broth

4 cups thinly sliced greens (kale, Swiss chard, curly endive or spinach)

¼ teaspoon each: salt, pepper

8 ounces fettuccine, cooked, warm

12 ounces pork tenderloin, fat trimmed, sliced (¼-inch)

1. Sauté onions in oil in large skillet 5 minutes; reduce heat to low and stir in sugar. Cook over medium-low heat until onions are golden in color and very soft, about 20 minutes. Stir in chicken broth and heat to boiling; reduce heat and simmer, uncovered, until broth is reduced by ⅓, about 10 minutes. Add greens; simmer, covered, until wilted, 5 to 7 minutes. Simmer, uncovered, until broth is almost evaporated, about 5 minutes. Stir in salt and pepper. Toss with pasta.

Per Serving:
Calories: 385
% of calories from fat: 20
Fat (gm): 8.8
Saturated fat (gm): 1.6
Cholesterol (mg): 59.3
Sodium (mg): 354
Protein (gm): 31.2
Carbohydrate (gm): 44.6

Exchanges:
Milk: 0.0
Vegetable: 3.0
Fruit: 0.0
Bread: 3.0
Meat: 3.0
Fat: 0.0

2. Sauté pork slices in lightly greased large skillet until cooked and browned, about 5 minutes. Arrange on pasta.

CHOP SUEY

Chop Suey can also be served over crisp chow mein noodles or Chinese egg noodles.

4 servings

1 pound pork tenderloin, fat trimmed, cubed (1-inch)
1 tablespoon vegetable oil
2 cups thinly sliced Chinese cabbage
1 cup each: sliced mushrooms, chopped onion, chopped red or green bell pepper
2 cloves garlic, minced
½ cup reduced-sodium chicken broth
2 tablespoons cornstarch
½–1 tablespoon bead molasses
2 cups fresh or canned bean sprouts, rinsed
½–1 can (8 ounces) each: rinsed, drained bamboo shoots, water chestnuts
Reduced-sodium soy sauce, to taste
Salt and pepper, to taste
3 cups cooked rice, warm

Per Serving:
Calories: 428
% of calories from fat: 18
Fat (gm): 8.4
Saturated fat (gm): 2
Cholesterol (mg): 65.4
Sodium (mg): 467
Protein (gm): 31.8
Carbohydrate (gm): 56.8

Exchanges:
Milk: 0.0
Vegetable: 3.0
Fruit: 0.0
Bread: 2.5
Meat: 3.0
Fat: 0.0

1. Stir-fry pork in oil in wok or large skillet until browned, 3 to 5 minutes. Add cabbage, mushrooms, onion, bell pepper, and garlic;

stir-fry until vegetables are crisp-tender, 3 to 5 minutes longer. Stir combined broth, cornstarch, and molasses into wok and heat to boiling. Boil, stirring until thickened, about 1 minute. Stir in bean sprouts, bamboo shoots, and water chestnuts; cook until hot, 1 to 2 minutes. Season to taste with soy sauce, salt, and pepper. Serve over rice.

MOO SHU PORK

Mandarin Pancakes are fabulous and can be made in advance. If you are short on time, however, flour tortillas can be substituted.

6 servings (2 each)

1½ ounces dried Chinese mushrooms

2–3 tablespoons reduced-sodium tamari soy sauce

2 teaspoons each: Asian sesame oil, minced gingerroot, sugar

1 pound pork tenderloin, fat trimmed, cut into strips (1½ x ½-inch)

2 eggs, lightly beaten

½ cup julienned bamboo shoots

2 sliced green onions

½ cup water

2 teaspoons cornstarch

Mandarin Pancakes (recipe follows)

½–¾ cup Oriental plum sauce

12 medium green onions

Per Serving:
Calories: 278
% of calories from fat: 20
Fat (gm): 6.2
Saturated fat (gm): 1.7
Cholesterol (mg): 114.5
Sodium (mg): 266
Protein (gm): 21.7
Carbohydrate (gm): 33

Exchanges:
Milk: 0.0
Vegetable: 4.0
Fruit: 0.0
Bread: 1.0
Meat: 2.0
Fat: 0.0

1. Cover mushrooms with boiling water in bowl; let stand until softened, about 15 minutes; drain. Slice mushrooms, discarding tough centers.

2. Pour combined soy sauce, Asian sesame oil, gingerroot, and sugar over pork in bowl. Let stand 30 minutes, stirring occasionally. Scramble eggs in lightly greased wok or large skillet, breaking into small pieces with a fork; remove from wok and reserve.

3. Add pork mixture, mushrooms, bamboo shoots and sliced green onions to wok; cook over medium heat until pork is browned, 3 to 4 minutes. Stir in combined water and cornstarch; heat to boiling. Boil, stirring until thickened, about 1 minute. Stir in reserved egg.

4. Spread 1 Mandarin Pancake with 2 to 3 teaspoons plum sauce; spoon about ⅓ cup pork mixture onto pancake. Top with a green onion and roll up. Repeat with remaining ingredients.

Mandarin Pancakes
Makes 12 pancakes

⅓ cup boiling water
1 cup all-purpose flour
Vegetable cooking spray

1. Stir water into flour in small bowl until crumbly; shape into a ball. Knead on lightly floured surface until smooth and satiny, about 10 minutes. Let stand, covered, 30 minutes. Divide dough into 12 equal pieces; shape into 12 balls.

2. Roll 2 balls into 3-inch circles with lightly floured rolling pin; spray 1 circle lightly with cooking spray and cover with remaining circle. Roll both circles together into a 6-inch circle being careful not to wrinkle dough. Cook dough circle in lightly greased skillet over medium to medium-high heat until it blisters and is the color of parchment paper, turning frequently with chop sticks or tongs. Remove from skillet; separate into 2 pancakes with pointed knife. Repeat process with remaining dough, making only 1 or 2 dough circles at a time.

NOTES: As pancakes are cooked and separated, they can be covered and kept warm in a 200 degree oven. Pancakes can be cooled, stacked with plastic wrap, and frozen in a freezer bag or aluminum foil for up to 2 months.

SWEET AND SPICY PORK STIR-FRY

45 *Serve over rice, or Chinese egg noodles, if desired.*

4 servings

8 ounces pork, fat trimmed, cubed (¾-inch)
3 cups thinly sliced cabbage
1 cup potato, cubed
½ cup each: chopped onion, sliced celery, carrot
1 tablespoon cornstarch
⅓ cup cold water
¼ cup each: reduced-sodium soy sauce, catsup
2 tablespoons brown sugar

Per Serving:
Calories: 243
% of calories from fat: 19
Fat (gm): 5.3
Saturated fat (gm): 1.8
Cholesterol (mg): 26.5
Sodium (mg): 781
Protein (gm): 16.2
Carbohydrate (gm): 33.7

Exchanges:
Milk: 0.0
Vegetable: 0.0
Fruit: 0.0
Bread: 2.0
Meat: 2.0
Fat: 0.0

1. Stir-fry pork in lightly greased wok or large saucepan over medium-high heat until browned, about 5 minutes. Add vegetables; stir-fry until tender, about 10 minutes. Stir in combined remaining ingredients; heat to boiling, stirring until thickened, about 1 minute.

CHORIZO

45 *Serve Chorizo as patties, or cook and crumble to serve in quesadillas, enchiladas, and other dishes.*

4 servings

¼ teaspoon crushed coriander and cumin seeds
1 dried ancho chili
12 ounces pork tenderloin, fat trimmed, finely
   chopped or ground
1 tablespoon each: paprika, minced garlic, cider
   vinegar, water
½ teaspoon each: dried oregano leaves, salt

Per Serving:
Calories: 112
% of calories from fat: 27
Fat (gm): 3.3
Saturated fat (gm): 1.1
Cholesterol (mg): 49.1
Sodium (mg): 308
Protein (gm): 17.9
Carbohydrate (gm): 2.1

Exchanges:
Milk: 0.0
Vegetable: 0.0
Fruit: 0.0
Bread: 0.0
Meat: 2.0
Fat: 0.0

1. Cook herb seeds in lightly greased small skillet, stirring frequently, until toasted. Remove from skillet. Add ancho chili to skillet; cook over medium heat until softened, about 1 minute on each side, turning so chili does not burn. Remove and discard stem, veins, and seeds. Chop chili finely.

2. Combine pork and all ingredients in small bowl, mixing well. Refrigerate, covered, at least 4 hours or overnight for flavors to blend. Shape mixture into 4 patties; cook in small lightly greased skillet over medium heat until cooked, 4 to 5 minutes on each side.

TOMATILLO PORK STEW

Tomatillos add a special flavor to this South-of-the-Border pork stew.

8 servings

1½ cups chopped onions

1 small poblano chili or green bell pepper, chopped

4 cloves garlic, minced

1–2 tablespoons vegetable oil

2 pounds boneless lean pork, fat trimmed, cubed (¾-inch)

2 tablespoons flour

¾ teaspoon each: dried oregano leaves, ground cumin

½ cup reduced-sodium fat-free chicken broth

2 large tomatoes, chopped

12 ounces tomatillos, husked, chopped

1 can (4 ounces) mild or hot chopped green chilies

1–2 teaspoons lime juice

Salt and pepper, to taste

5 cups cooked rice, warm

Chopped cilantro, as garnish

Toasted pine nuts or almonds, as garnish

Per Serving:
Calories: 374
% of calories from fat: 24
Fat (gm): 9.9
Saturated fat (gm): 2.9
Cholesterol (mg): 64.4
Sodium (mg): 118
Protein (gm): 32.1
Carbohydrate (gm): 37.6

Exchanges:
Milk: 0.0
Vegetable: 2.0
Fruit: 0.0
Bread: 2.0
Meat: 3.0
Fat: 0.0

1. Sauté onions, poblano chili, and garlic in oil in large saucepan 2 to 3 minutes; add pork and sauté until browned, about 5 minutes. Stir in flour and herbs and cook 1 minute. Add chicken broth, tomatoes, tomatillos, and green chilies; heat to boiling. Reduce heat and simmer, covered, until pork is tender, 40 to 50 minutes. Season to taste with lime juice, salt, and pepper. Serve over rice; sprinkle with cilantro and pine nuts.

SAVORY STEWED PORK AND CHORIZO

This versatile dish is often served rolled in a tortilla or used as a topping for tostadas

6 servings

12 ounces pork tenderloin, fat trimmed, cubed (1-inch)

Chorizo (see p. 140)

1 small onion, sliced

1 clove garlic, minced

2 large tomatoes, chopped

¼ teaspoon each: dried oregano and thyme leaves

1 bay leaf

2–3 pickled jalapeño chilies, finely chopped

1 tablespoon pickled jalapeño chili juice

Salt and pepper, to taste

4 cups cooked rice, warm

Per Serving:
Calories: 298
% of calories from fat: 15
Fat (gm): 4.7
Saturated fat (gm): 1.5
Cholesterol (mg): 65.7
Sodium (mg): 313
Protein (gm): 27.2
Carbohydrate (gm): 35

Exchanges:
Milk: 0.0
Vegetable: 0.0
Fruit: 0.0
Bread: 2.0
Meat: 3.0
Fat: 0.0

1. Cover pork with 2 inches simmering water in medium saucepan, covered, until tender, 20 to 30 minutes. Cool; drain, reserving ½ cup broth. Finely shred pork.

2. Cook Chorizo in lightly greased large skillet over medium heat until browned; remove from skillet and crumble. Add onion and garlic to skillet; sauté 2 to 3 minutes. Add tomatoes and herbs and cook over medium heat 5 minutes, stirring occasionally. Add pork, Chorizo, reserved broth, jalapeño chilies, and jalapeño juice to skillet. Cook, uncovered, over medium heat, about 10 minutes, stirring occasionally (mixture should be moist). Discard bay leaf; season to taste with salt and pepper. Serve over rice.

PORK LOIN, POTATO, AND CABBAGE STEW

Shredded potatoes thicken the sauce in this robust pork stew.

4 servings

1 pound boneless pork loin, fat trimmed, cut into strips (1½ x ½-inch)

1 pound red potatoes, peeled, coarsely shredded

1 can (14½ ounces) reduced-sodium stewed tomatoes, undrained

1 can (15 ounces) reduced-sodium tomato sauce

3 cups thinly sliced cabbage

1 cup chopped onion

1 tablespoon each: minced garlic, brown sugar

2 teaspoons each: balsamic vinegar, dried
thyme leaves

1 bay leaf

Salt and pepper, to taste

Per Serving:
Calories: 328
% of calories from fat: 18
Fat (gm): 6.8
Saturated fat (gm): 2.2
Cholesterol (mg): 49.3
Sodium (mg): 101
Protein (gm): 23.4
Carbohydrate (gm): 45.4

Exchanges:
Milk: 0.0
Vegetable: 3.0
Fruit: 0.0
Bread: 2.0
Meat: 2.0
Fat: 0.0

1. Combine all ingredients, except salt and
pepper, in large saucepan; heat to boiling.
Reduce heat and simmer, covered, until pork
is tender, about 30 minutes. Discard bay leaf;
season to taste with salt and pepper.

SHREDDED PORK CHILI

45 *This super-fast chili, spiked with chilies and cumin, can also be made with
shredded cooked chicken or beef.*

4 servings

12 ounces cooked pork tenderloin, shredded

1 can (15 ounces) each: reduced-sodium fat-free
beef broth, rinsed drained pinto beans

1 pound plum tomatoes, sliced

2 jalapeño chilies, minced

1 tablespoon chili powder

1 teaspoon each toasted cumin seeds,
Worcestershire sauce

Per Serving:
Calories: 274
% of calories from fat: 19
Fat (gm): 5.8
Saturated fat (gm): 1.7
Cholesterol (mg): 67.1
Sodium (mg): 475
Protein (gm): 32.7
Carbohydrate (gm): 23.4

Exchanges:
Milk: 0.0
Vegetable: 2.0
Fruit: 0.0
Bread: 1.0
Meat: 3.0
Fat: 0.0

1. Heat all ingredients to boiling in large saucepan; reduce heat and
simmer, covered, 15 minutes.

HAM AND POTATO CASSEROLE AU GRATIN

45

This old-fashioned casserole has been modified to meet today's healthy standards.

6 servings

6 large red potatoes, peeled, thinly sliced, divided

12–16 ounces reduced-sodium ham, fat trimmed, cubed (¾-inch)

1 small green bell pepper, finely chopped

3 green onions, sliced

½–1 cup (2–4 ounces) shredded reduced-fat Cheddar cheese

White Sauce (recipe follows)

¼–½ cup unseasoned dry bread crumbs

Per Serving:
Calories: 301
% of calories from fat: 30
Fat (gm): 10.4
Saturated fat (gm): 3.6
Cholesterol (mg): 40.5
Sodium (mg): 796
Protein (gm): 20.9
Carbohydrate (gm): 32.9

Exchanges:
Milk: 0.0
Vegetable: 0.0
Fruit: 0.0
Bread: 2.0
Meat: 2.0
Fat: 1.0

1. Arrange half the potatoes in greased 2-quart casserole, overlapping slightly; sprinkle with ham, bell pepper, and green onions. Top with remaining potatoes and sprinkle with cheese. Pour White Sauce over. Bake, covered, at 375 degrees for 45 minutes. Sprinkle with bread crumbs and bake, uncovered, until potatoes are tender and casserole is golden brown, 15 to 20 minutes.

White Sauce
Makes about 2 cups

2 tablespoons margarine or butter

3 tablespoons flour

¾ teaspoon dry mustard

2 cups fat-free milk

¼ teaspoon paprika

Salt and pepper, to taste

1. Melt margarine in small saucepan; add flour and dry mustard, stirring over medium heat 1 minute. Whisk in milk and paprika and heat to boiling, whisking until thickened, about 1 minute. Season to taste with salt and pepper.

HEARTY ROSEMARY LAMB
WITH SWEET POTATOES

The pairing of rosemary and lamb is classic, distinctive, and delightful.

4 servings

1 pound boneless lamb shoulder, fat trimmed,
  cubed (¾-inch)

1 teaspoon olive oil

1 large onion, cut into thin wedges

2 tablespoons chopped fresh or 1 teaspoon dried
  rosemary leaves

3 cups reduced-sodium fat-free beef broth

2 bay leaves

1¼ pounds sweet potatoes, peeled, cubed (¾-inch)

1½ cups cut green beans

Salt and pepper, to taste

Per Serving:
Calories: 285
% of calories from fat: 23
Fat (gm): 7.4
Saturated fat (gm): 2.5
Cholesterol (mg): 47.2
Sodium (mg): 171
Protein (gm): 20.6
Carbohydrate (gm): 34.7

Exchanges:
Milk: 0.0
Vegetable: 1.0
Fruit: 0.0
Bread: 2.0
Meat: 2.0
Fat: 0.0

1. Sauté lamb in oil in large saucepan until lightly browned, about 8 minutes. Add onion and rosemary; cook 5 minutes. Add broth and bay leaves; heat to boiling. Reduce heat and simmer, covered, until lamb is tender, 1 to 1½ hours; minutes, adding sweet potatoes and green beans during last 15 minutes. Discard bay leaves; season to taste with salt and pepper.

SHEPHERD'S PIE

Usually the recipient of the week's leftovers, this hearty dish may be different each time it is made.

6 servings

1½ pounds boneless leg of lamb, fat trimmed,
    cubed (½-inch)
1 tablespoon margarine or butter
¾ cup each: chopped onion, green bell pepper,
    sliced celery
3 cloves garlic, minced
3 tablespoons flour
2½ cups reduced-sodium beef broth
1½ cups sliced carrots
1 tablespoon tomato paste
½ teaspoon each: dried rosemary and thyme leaves
1 bay leaf
¾ cup frozen peas
Salt and pepper, to taste
2 cups Real Mashed Potatoes (½ recipe) (see p. 485)

Per Serving:
Calories: 274
% of calories from fat: 27
Fat (gm): 8.4
Saturated fat (gm): 2.3
Cholesterol (mg): 48.5
Sodium (mg): 179
Protein (gm): 21.7
Carbohydrate (gm): 28.5

Exchanges:
Milk: 0.0
Vegetable: 2.0
Fruit: 0.0
Bread: 1.0
Meat: 2.5
Fat: 0.5

1. Sauté lamb in margarine or butter in large saucepan until browned, 5 to 8 minutes; remove from pan. Add onion, bell pepper, celery, and garlic; sauté until lightly browned, 5 to 8 minutes. Stir in flour; cook 1 minute. Return lamb to saucepan; add broth, carrots, tomato paste, and herbs. Heat to boiling; reduce heat and simmer, covered, until lamb is tender, about 1 hour. Discard bay leaf and stir in peas; season to taste with salt and pepper.

2. Pour stew into 1½-quart casserole. Spoon Real Mashed Potatoes around edge of casserole. Bake, uncovered, at 400 degrees until potatoes are browned, about 10 minutes.

PASTITSIO

45

Sweet cinnamon and nutmeg season this Greek favorite.

6 servings

1 pound lean ground lamb or beef

1 cup chopped onion

1 can (8 ounces) reduced-sodium tomato paste

⅓ cup water

Salt and pepper, to taste

2 cups elbow macaroni, cooked

⅓ cup grated fat-free Parmesan cheese

¼ teaspoon each: ground cinnamon and nutmeg

2⅓ cups fat-free milk

2 tablespoons margarine or butter

1 egg

½ cup no-cholesterol real egg product or 4 egg whites

Per Serving:
Calories: 361
% of calories from fat: 23
Fat (gm): 9.3
Saturated fat (gm): 2.5
Cholesterol (mg): 104.7
Sodium (mg): 266
Protein (gm): 25.6
Carbohydrate (gm): 42.8

Exchanges:
Milk: 0.0
Vegetable: 0.0
Fruit: 0.0
Bread: 3.0
Meat: 3.0
Fat: 0.0

1. Cook lamb and onion in lightly greased large skillet over medium heat until lamb is browned, about 5 minutes. Stir in tomato paste and water; cook 2 to 3 minutes longer. Season to taste with salt and pepper. Spoon ½ of the macaroni into greased 13 x 9-inch baking pan; spoon meat mixture over macaroni. Sprinkle combined cheese and spices over lamb; spoon remaining macaroni over the top.

2. Heat milk and margarine or butter in medium saucepan, stirring until margarine is melted. Beat eggs and egg product in small bowl until blended; whisk milk into egg mixture. Pour over macaroni. Bake, uncovered, at 350 degrees until casserole is bubbly, 50 to 60 minutes.

45-MINUTE PREPARATION TIP: Begin cooking macaroni before preparing the rest of the recipe.

VEGETABLE MOUSSAKA

Vegetables and barley are added to traditional moussaka to make this delicious casserole.

12 servings

1 large eggplant, unpeeled, sliced

Olive oil cooking spray

1 pound potatoes, unpeeled, sliced

3 cups chopped onions

2 cups sliced carrots

3 cloves garlic, minced

1 teaspoon each: ground cinnamon, dried oregano and thyme leaves

¾ cup reduced-sodium fat-free beef broth

2 cups each: chopped tomatoes, sliced mushrooms, cooked barley

1 pound ground lean lamb or beef, cooked, drained

1 small zucchini, sliced

Salt and pepper, to taste

Custard Topping (recipe follows)

Ground nutmeg, to taste

Per Serving:
Calories: 265
% of calories from fat: 29
Fat (gm): 8.9
Saturated fat (gm): 2.3
Cholesterol (mg): 44.7
Sodium (mg): 152
Protein (gm): 15
Carbohydrate (gm): 32.7

Exchanges:
Milk: 0.0
Vegetable: 3.0
Fruit: 0.0
Bread: 1.0
Meat: 1.0
Fat: 1.0

1. Arrange eggplant in single layer on greased aluminum foil-lined jelly roll pan and spray with cooking spray. Bake at 350 degrees until eggplant is tender but still firm, about 20 minutes. Arrange eggplant on bottom of 13 x 9-inch baking pan.

2. Heat potatoes, onions, carrots, garlic, seasonings, and broth to boiling in large skillet; reduce heat and simmer, uncovered, 5 minutes. Add tomatoes and mushrooms; simmer, uncovered, until tomatoes are soft. Add barley, lamb, and zucchini; cook, uncovered, until mixture is thick, about 5 minutes. Season to taste with salt and pepper. Spoon mixture over eggplant.

3. Pour Custard Topping over casserole and sprinkle with nutmeg. Bake at 350 degrees until lightly browned on the top, about 45 minutes. Cool 5 to 10 minutes before cutting.

Custard Topping

⅓ cup margarine or butter
½ cup all-purpose flour
3 cups fat-free milk
2 eggs, lightly beaten
Salt and white pepper, to taste

1. Melt margarine in medium saucepan; whisk in flour and cook over medium heat 2 minutes. Whisk in milk and heat to boiling, whisking until thickened, about 1 minute. Whisk about 1 cup milk mixture into eggs; whisk egg mixture back into saucepan. Cook over low heat, whisking until thickened, 2 to 3 minutes. Season to taste with salt and white pepper.

VEAL WITH HERBED MUSHROOMS

45

Veal chops are topped with herb-seasoned mushrooms and black olives.

4 servings

4 boneless veal chops (4 ounces each), fat trimmed
1–2 teaspoons margarine or butter
2 medium onions, chopped
1 pound mushrooms, sliced
1 tablespoon each: flour, tomato paste
1 cup reduced-sodium chicken broth
½ cup dry white wine or reduced-sodium chicken broth
1 teaspoon dried Italian seasoning
1 small bay leaf
¼–½ cup sliced black olives
¼ teaspoon each: salt and pepper

Per Serving:
Calories: 302
% of calories from fat: 30
Fat (gm): 10.2
Saturated fat (gm): 2.2
Cholesterol (mg): 100.1
Sodium (mg): 439
Protein (gm): 32
Carbohydrate (gm): 14.5

Exchanges:
Milk: 0.0
Vegetable: 3.0
Fruit: 0.0
Bread: 0.0
Meat: 3.0
Fat: 1.0

1. Cook veal chops in margarine in large skillet over medium heat until browned, 3 to 4 minutes on each side; transfer to baking dish. Add onions and mushrooms to skillet; sauté until tender, about 10 minutes; sprinkle with flour and cook 1 minute. Stir in remaining ingredients and heat to boiling; spoon mixture over veal chops. Bake, covered, at 325 degrees until veal is tender, about 30 minutes.

EASIEST LAMB STEW

45

This stew is baked, but can also be simmered on the range top if you prefer.

6 servings

2 pounds boneless lean lamb, fat trimmed, cubed (1-inch)

¾ cup each: sliced carrot, chopped onion

2 tablespoons flour

2 cups reduced-sodium chicken broth

4 medium potatoes, peeled, cubed (1-inch)

1 teaspoon dried rosemary leaves

1 bay leaf

½ package (10-ounce size) frozen peas

Salt and pepper, to taste

Per Serving:
Calories: 338
% of calories from fat: 18
Fat (gm): 6.7
Saturated fat (gm): 2.5
Cholesterol (mg): 95.8
Sodium (mg): 213
Protein (gm): 34.3
Carbohydrate (gm): 33.9

Exchanges:
Milk: 0.0
Vegetable: 0.0
Fruit: 0.0
Bread: 2.0
Meat: 4.0
Fat: 0.0

1. Cook lamb in lightly greased Dutch oven over medium heat until browned, about 10 minutes. Add carrot and onion; cook 5 minutes; stir in flour and cook 1 minute. Add broth, potatoes, and herbs; heat to boiling. Transfer to oven and bake, covered, at 325 degrees until lamb is tender, 1 to 1½ hours, adding peas during last 15 minutes. Discard bay leaf; season to taste with salt and pepper.

LAMB AND TURNIP STEW WITH CILANTRO

This homestyle lamb dish has been updated with fresh sage and cilantro.

4 servings

1 pound boneless lamb shoulder, fat trimmed, cubed (1-inch)

1 medium onion, chopped

1 tablespoon minced garlic

1 teaspoon olive oil

¼ cup all-purpose flour

2½ cups reduced-sodium tomato juice

½ cup dry red wine or beef broth

1 tablespoon fresh or 1 teaspoon dried sage leaves

2 cups cubed potatoes

Per Serving:
Calories: 269
% of calories from fat: 24
Fat (gm): 7.3
Saturated fat (gm): 2.4
Cholesterol (mg): 47.2
Sodium (mg): 81
Protein (gm): 17.4
Carbohydrate (gm): 30

Exchanges:
Milk: 0.0
Vegetable: 0.0
Fruit: 0.0
Bread: 2.0
Meat: 2.0
Fat: 0.0

1½ cups cubed turnips
Salt and pepper, to taste
½ cup chopped cilantro

1. Sauté lamb, onion, and garlic in oil in large saucepan until browned, about 8 minutes; stir in flour and cook 1 minute. Add tomato juice, wine, and sage and heat to boiling; reduce heat and simmer, covered, until lamb is tender 1 to 1½ hours, adding vegetables during last 20 minutes. Season to taste with salt and pepper; stir in cilantro.

MOROCCAN LAMB STEW

Sweet spices season this stew; raisins, almonds, and hard-cooked eggs provide colorful garnishes.

8 servings

2 pounds boneless lean lamb, fat trimmed, cubed (¾-inch)
1½ cups chopped onions
2 teaspoons each: minced garlic, gingerroot
1½ cups reduced-sodium fat-free chicken broth
1 cup reduced-sodium tomato puree
½ teaspoon each: ground cinnamon, turmeric
Generous pinch ground cloves
1 bay leaf
⅓ cup raisins
Salt and pepper, to taste
2 hard-cooked eggs, cut into wedges
2–4 tablespoons slivered almonds, toasted
Finely chopped cilantro or parsley as garnish
5 cups cooked couscous or rice, warm

Per Serving:
Calories: 308
% of calories from fat: 20
Fat (gm): 6.6
Saturated fat (gm): 2
Cholesterol (mg): 101.5
Sodium (mg): 103
Protein (gm): 23.8
Carbohydrate (gm): 37.4

Exchanges:
Milk: 0.0
Vegetable: 1.0
Fruit: 0.0
Bread: 2.0
Meat: 2.5
Fat: 0.0

1. Sauté lamb in lightly greased Dutch oven until browned, 5 to 8 minutes; remove from pan. Add onions, garlic, and gingerroot and sauté until onions are tender, about 5 minutes. Return lamb to pan; add broth, tomato puree, and spices; heat to boiling. Reduce heat and simmer, covered, until lamb is tender, 45 to 60 minutes. Stir in raisins. Simmer, uncovered, until sauce is thickened, about 10 minutes. Discard bay leaf; season to taste with salt and pepper.

2. Spoon stew onto rimmed serving platter; arrange egg wedges around edge of platter and sprinkle with almonds and cilantro. Serve with couscous.

CURRIED LAMB STEW

Known in India as Rogan Josh, this flavorful stew is best prepared 1 to 2 days in advance for flavors to meld. The variety of condiments add flavor and color contrast

12 servings

3 pounds boneless leg of lamb, fat trimmed, cubed (1-inch)

1¼ cups low-fat plain yogurt

¼ teaspoon crushed red pepper

2 cups chopped onions

1 tablespoon each: minced gingerroot, garlic

1 teaspoon each: crushed coriander seeds, cumin seeds, ground turmeric

½ teaspoon each: lightly crushed cardamom seeds, pepper

1–2 tablespoons margarine or butter

1 cup reduced-sodium fat-free chicken broth

Salt and pepper, to taste

Turmeric Rice (recipe follows)

Condiments: raisins, toasted slivered almonds, chopped onion and cucumber, finely chopped cilantro or parsley

Per Serving:
Calories: 257
% of calories from fat: 21
Fat (gm): 5.9
Saturated fat (gm): 2
Cholesterol (mg): 49.9
Sodium (mg): 82
Protein (gm): 19.8
Carbohydrate (gm): 29.4

Exchanges:
Milk: 0.0
Vegetable: 0.0
Fruit: 0.0
Bread: 2.0
Meat: 2.0
Fat: 0.0

1. Combine lamb, yogurt, and red pepper in bowl; refrigerate several hours or overnight, stirring occasionally.

2. Sauté onions, gingerroot, garlic, and spices in margarine in Dutch oven until onions are tender, 5 to 8 minutes. Stir in lamb mixture and chicken broth; heat to boiling. Reduce heat and simmer, covered, until lamb is tender, about 1 hour. Season to taste with salt and pepper. Serve over Turmeric Rice with assorted condiments (not included in nutritional data).

Turmeric Rice

4½ cups water
¾ teaspoon ground turmeric
¼ teaspoon salt
2 cups uncooked long-grain rice

1. Heat water to boiling in large saucepan; stir in turmeric and salt. Stir in rice; reduce heat and simmer, covered, until rice is tender, 20 to 25 minutes.

FOUR

Poultry

CHICKEN CORN CHOWDER WITH SWEET PEPPERS

45 *Red bell peppers and picante sauce transform an ordinary corn chowder into an extra special dish.*

6 servings

1 pound boneless, skinless chicken breast, cubed

1 teaspoon olive oil

½ cup each: chopped onion, red bell pepper

2 teaspoons minced garlic

2 cups cubed, peeled potatoes

½ cup reduced-sodium fat-free chicken broth

2 cans (15 ounces each) cream-style corn

⅓ cup picante sauce

Salt and pepper, to taste

Chopped black olives, as garnish

Per Serving:
Calories: 291
% of calories from fat: 17
Fat (gm): 3.9
Saturated fat (gm): 0.7
Cholesterol (mg): 46
Sodium (mg): 536
Protein (gm): 22
Carbohydrate (gm): 45.6

Exchanges:
Milk: 0.0
Vegetable: 0.0
Fruit: 0.0
Bread: 2.5
Meat: 2.0
Fat: 0.0

1. Sauté chicken in oil in large saucepan until browned, 8 to 10 minutes; add onion, bell pepper, and garlic and sauté 5 minutes. Stir in potatoes and broth; heat to boiling. Reduce heat and simmer, covered, until potatoes are tender, about 10 minutes. Stir in corn and picante sauce; simmer, uncovered, until slightly thickened, about 5 minutes. Season to taste with salt and pepper. Sprinkle each bowl of chowder with olives.

CALIFORNIA CHILI

45 *This chili sports some California-style touches!*

6 servings

1 pound boneless, skinless chicken breast, cubed (1-inch)

1 teaspoon crushed mixed peppercorns

4 cups sliced plum tomatoes

1 cup each: diced sun-dried tomatoes (not in oil), Zinfandel
  or other dry red wine

2 dried California chilies, chopped

4 teaspoons chili powder

1 avocado, chopped

2 tablespoons sunflower seeds, toasted

Salt, to taste

6 tablespoons chopped basil

1. Sauté chicken and peppercorns in lightly greased large saucepan until browned, 8 to 10 minutes. Add plum and sun-dried tomatoes, wine, chilies, and chili powder; heat to boiling. Reduce heat and simmer, covered, 10 minutes; simmer, uncovered, until thickened to desired consistency, 5 to 10 minutes. Stir in avocado and sunflower seeds; season to taste with salt. Sprinkle each bowl of chili with basil.

Per Serving:
Calories: 258
% of calories from fat: 30
Fat (gm): 9.2
Saturated fat (gm): 1.8
Cholesterol (mg): 46
Sodium (mg): 272
Protein (gm): 21.5
Carbohydrate (gm): 19.7

Exchanges:
Milk: 0.0
Vegetable: 4.0
Fruit: 0.0
Bread: 0.0
Meat: 2.0
Fat: 1.0

GLAZED CORNISH HENS WITH WILD RICE

45

Cornish hens are marmalade-glazed and served with a fruited wild rice mixture for company fare.

4 servings

2 Rock Cornish game hens (1 to 1¼ pounds each)

Vegetable cooking spray

Paprika

½ cup no-sugar-added orange marmalade, warm

¼ cup each: sliced green onions, celery

1 package (6.25 ounces) quick-cooking long-grain white and wild rice, (spice packet discarded)

1 can (14½ ounces) reduced-sodium chicken broth

1 can (11 ounces) unsweetened Mandarin orange segments, drained

2 tablespoons each: raisins, finely chopped mint or parsley, toasted pecan halves

Salt and pepper, to taste

Per Serving:
Calories: 716
% of calories from fat: 7
Fat (gm): 6.2
Saturated fat (gm): 1.2
Cholesterol (mg): 108.5
Sodium (mg): 273
Protein (gm): 41.1
Carbohydrate (gm): 125.8

Exchanges:
Milk: 0.0
Vegetable: 0.0
Fruit: 4.0
Bread: 4.0
Meat: 4.0
Fat: 0.0

1. Cut Cornish hens into halves with poultry shears and place, cut sides down, on rack in roasting pan. Spray with cooking spray and sprinkle with paprika. Roast at 350 degrees until drumstick meat feels soft when pressed and juices run clear, 1 to 1¼ hours; baste with marmalade during last 30 minutes of roasting time.

2. Sauté green onions and celery in lightly greased medium sauce-pan until tender, about 5 minutes. Add remaining ingredients, except salt and pepper, and simmer, covered, until rice is tender, about 5 minutes. Season to taste with salt and pepper. Serve with Cornish hens.

ROAST CHICKEN WITH CORN BREAD DRESSING

We've baked the dressing in a casserole; if baked in the chicken, it would absorb unwanted fat from the chicken juices.

6 servings

1 roasting chicken (about 3 pounds)
Vegetable cooking spray
1 teaspoon dried rosemary leaves
Corn Bread Dressing (recipe follows)

Per Serving:
Calories: 258
% of calories from fat: 22
Fat (gm): 6.1
Saturated fat (gm): 1.6
Cholesterol (mg): 57.9
Sodium (mg): 548
Protein (gm): 24.4
Carbohydrate (gm): 25.3

Exchanges:
Milk: 0.0
Vegetable: 0.5
Fruit: 0.0
Bread: 1.5
Meat: 2.5
Fat: 0.0

1. Spray chicken with cooking spray; sprinkle with rosemary. Roast chicken on rack in roasting pan at 375 degrees until meat thermometer inserted in thickest part of thigh registers 170 degrees (chicken leg will move freely and juices will run clear), about 1½ hours. Let chicken stand 10 minutes before carving. Serve with Corn Bread Dressing

Corn Bread Dressing
Makes about 3 cups

¾ cup each: chopped onion, sliced celery
¼ cup coarsely chopped pecans
½ teaspoon each: dried sage, rosemary, and thyme leaves
Salt and pepper, to taste
3 cups corn bread stuffing mix
1½ cups reduced-sodium chicken broth
1 egg, lightly beaten

1. Sauté onion, celery, pecans, and herbs in lightly greased large skillet until vegetables are tender, about 5 minutes; season to taste with salt and pepper. Combine with stuffing mix in large bowl; add chicken broth and egg and toss. Spoon into greased 2-quart casserole and cover. Bake, covered, at 375 degrees until hot, about 45 minutes.

VARIATION

Pork Chops with Bread Stuffing — Make stuffing as above, substituting white or whole wheat stuffing mix for the corn bread mix. Trim fat from 6 loin pork chops (about 5 ounces each); cook in lightly greased skillet until well browned, about 5 minutes on each side. Arrange pork chops on top of stuffing in casserole; bake, covered, at 350 degrees until pork chops are tender, 30 to 40 minutes.

45-MINUTE PREPARATION TIP: Place Corn Bread Dressing in oven with chicken during last 45 minutes of roasting time.

CRISP OVEN-FRIED CHICKEN

Serve with Real Mashed Potatoes and Cream Gravy, if you like (see pp. 485, 123), substituting chicken bouillon crystals for the beef bouillon in the gravy.

6 servings

6 skinless chicken breast halves (6 ounces each)

Flour

4 egg whites or ½ cup no-cholesterol real egg product, lightly beaten

¼ cup 2% reduced-fat milk

1½ cups finely crushed corn flakes cereal

¾ cup unseasoned dry bread crumbs

½ teaspoon each: dried rosemary and thyme leaves, crushed

Vegetable cooking spray

Salt and pepper, to taste

Per Serving:
Calories: 387
% of calories from fat: 13
Fat (gm): 5.4
Saturated fat (gm): 1.5
Cholesterol (mg): 104.2
Sodium (mg): 557
Protein (gm): 44.8
Carbohydrate (gm): 36

Exchanges:
Milk: 0.0
Vegetable: 0.0
Fruit: 0.0
Bread: 2.5
Meat: 4.0
Fat: 0.0

1. Coat chicken breasts lightly with flour; dip in combined egg whites and milk, then coat generously with combined corn flakes, bread crumbs, and herbs.

2. Place chicken, meat sides up, in greased baking pan; spray generously with cooking spray and sprinkle lightly with salt and pepper. Bake at 350 degrees until chicken is browned and juices run clear, 45 to 60 minutes.

CHICKEN WITH GINGERED HONEY-ORANGE SAUCE

45

The sauce combines gingerroot, honey, and orange for delicious flavor.

8 servings

8 skinless chicken breast halves (6 ounces each)
Vegetable cooking spray
Paprika, salt, and pepper
Gingered Honey-Orange Sauce (recipe follows)

Per Serving:
Calories: 220
% of calories from fat: 9
Fat (gm): 2.1
Saturated fat (gm): 0.5
Cholesterol (mg): 99
Sodium (mg): 89
Protein (gm): 39.6
Carbohydrate (gm): 8.4

Exchanges:
Milk: 0.0
Vegetable: 0.0
Fruit: 0.5
Bread: 0.0
Meat: 5.0
Fat: 0.0

1. Place chicken in greased baking pan; spray lightly with cooking spray and sprinkle with paprika, salt and pepper. Bake, uncovered, at 350 degrees until chicken browned and juices run clear, 30 to 40 minutes, basting occasionally with Gingered Honey-Orange Sauce. Serve with remaining sauce.

Gingered Honey-Orange Sauce
Makes about 1¼ cups

1 cup orange juice
2 tablespoons honey
Grated zest of 1 orange
1–2 tablespoon finely chopped gingerroot
1 tablespoon flour
1 orange, peeled, cut into segments

1. Combine all ingredients, except orange segments, in small saucepan; heat to boiling. Boil, whisking until thickened, about 1 minute; stir in orange segments and cook over low heat 2 to 3 minutes.

CHICKEN BREASTS WITH ROSEMARY

45 *Easy, yet elegant, this healthful entrée is good served with a risotto (see Index) and a simple vegetable or salad.*

4 servings

1 tablespoon olive oil
1½ teaspoons balsamic vinegar
1 teaspoon minced garlic
1 tablespoon finely grated lemon zest
¼ teaspoon each: salt, pepper
4 boneless, skinless chicken breast halves
   (4 ounces each)
½–¾ cup dry white wine or reduced-sodium
   chicken broth
½ cup chopped tomato
1 teaspoon finely chopped fresh or ½ teaspoon
   dried rosemary leaves

Per Serving:
Calories: 188
% of calories from fat: 31
Fat (gm): 6.4
Saturated fat (gm): 1.3
Cholesterol (mg): 69
Sodium (mg): 209
Protein (gm): 25.6
Carbohydrate (gm): 2.6

Exchanges:
Milk: 0.0
Vegetable: 0.5
Fruit: 0.0
Bread: 0.0
Meat: 3.0
Fat: 0.0

1. Brush combined olive oil, vinegar, garlic, lemon zest, salt, and pepper over chicken; let stand 10 minutes. Cook chicken in lightly greased large skillet over medium heat until browned, about 5 minutes on each side. Add wine, tomato, and rosemary to skillet and heat to boiling; reduce heat and simmer, covered, until chicken is cooked, about 15 minutes.

TANDOORI CHICKEN WITH ORANGE CILANTRO RICE

Chicken pieces are marinated in a seasoned yogurt mixture, then grilled or roasted.

4 servings

1 pound chicken pieces
Tandoori Marinade (recipe follows)
2½ cups Orange Cilantro Rice (⅔ recipe) (see p. 412)

1. Spread chicken with Tandoori Marinade; place in shallow glass baking dish and refrigerate 3 to 4 hours, or overnight.

2. Grill chicken over medium hot coals, covered, until browned and cooked, 10 to 15 minutes on each side. Or, roast in greased, aluminum foil-lined baking pan, covered, at 350 degrees until juices run clear, 25 to 35 minutes. Serve with Orange Cilantro Rice.

Per Serving:
Calories: 272
% of calories from fat: 12
Fat (gm): 3.6
Saturated fat (gm): 0.9
Cholesterol (mg): 69.3
Sodium (mg): 80
Protein (gm): 29.3
Carbohydrate (gm): 28.7

Exchanges:
Milk: 0.0
Vegetable: 2.0
Fruit: 0.0
Bread: 1.0
Meat: 3.0
Fat: 0.0

Tandoori Marinade

Makes about ½ cup

⅓ cup plain fat-free yogurt

1 small jalapeño chili, minced

2 teaspoons each: finely chopped cilantro, garlic, gingerroot, lime zest, paprika

1 teaspoon each: ground cumin, coriander

1. Combine all ingredients.

CAJUN CHICKEN

Packaged Cajun seasoning can be purchased, but we particularly like our homemade blend — try it with beef and pork too!

4 servings

4 boneless, skinless chicken breast halves
  (4 ounces each)
Butter-flavored vegetable cooking spray
Cajun Seasoning (recipe follows)

Per Serving:
Calories: 144
% of calories from fat: 20
Fat (gm): 3.1
Saturated fat (gm): 0.9
Cholesterol (mg): 69
Sodium (mg): 206
Protein (gm): 25.7
Carbohydrate (gm): 2

Exchanges:
Milk: 0.0
Vegetable: 0.0
Fruit: 0.0
Bread: 0.0
Meat: 3.0
Fat: 0.0

1. Spray both sides of chicken pieces with cooking spray; sprinkle with Cajun Seasoning. Grill chicken over medium-hot coals, or broil 6 inches from heat source, until chicken is cooked and juices run clear, about 5 to 8 minutes on each side.

Cajun Seasoning
Makes about 2 tablespoons

2 teaspoons paprika

1 teaspoon each: onion powder, garlic powder

½ teaspoon each: dried thyme and oregano leaves, cayenne
and black pepper

¼ teaspoon salt

1. Mix all ingredients; store in airtight container.

CHICKEN CORDON BLEU

45

A favorite gourmet entrée, the ham and cheese-stuffed chicken breasts are delicious in their new low-fat form!

6 servings

6 boneless, skinless chicken breast halves
(4 ounces each)

4 ounces sliced fat-free Swiss cheese

3 ounces lean smoked ham

Flour

1 egg , lightly beaten

⅓ cup unseasoned dry bread crumbs

Vegetable cooking spray

Per Serving:
Calories: 210
% of calories from fat: 18
Fat (gm): 3.9
Saturated fat (gm): 1.1
Cholesterol (mg): 73.2
Sodium (mg): 540
Protein (gm): 34.6
Carbohydrate (gm): 6.3

Exchanges:
Milk: 0.0
Vegetable: 0.0
Fruit: 0.0
Bread: 0.0
Meat: 4.0
Fat: 0.0

1. Pound chicken breasts with flat side of meat mallet until very thin and even in thickness. Layer cheese and ham on chicken, cutting to fit; roll up and secure with toothpicks. Coat chicken rolls lightly with flour; dip in egg and coat with bread crumbs. Spray rolls generously with cooking spray and cook in large oven-proof skillet over medium heat until browned on all sides, 8 to 10 minutes. Transfer to oven and bake at 350 degrees, uncovered, until cooked, about 25 minutes.

CHICKEN AND RICE ROLL-UPS

45 *Colorful rice fills these moist baked chicken rolls.*

4 servings

4 boneless, skinless chicken breast halves
  (4 ounces each)
3 cups cooked rice
1 cup each: whole kernel corn, finely chopped
  green bell peppers
¼ cup diced pimientos
½ cup (2 ounces) shredded Monterey Jack cheese
Paprika, salt and pepper, to taste

Per Serving:
Calories: 391
% of calories from fat: 18
Fat (gm): 7.8
Saturated fat (gm): 3.7
Cholesterol (mg): 81.6
Sodium (mg): 142
Protein (gm): 33.6
Carbohydrate (gm): 45.6

Exchanges:
Milk: 0.0
Vegetable: 0.0
Fruit: 0.0
Bread: 3.0
Meat: 3.0
Fat: 0.0

1. Pound chicken breasts with flat side of meat mallet to about ¼ inch thickness. Combine rice, corn, bell peppers, pimientos, and cheese medium bowl. Spoon about ⅓ cup rice mixture on each breast; roll up and secure with toothpicks. Spoon remaining rice mixture in greased 11 x 7-inch baking dish; place chicken, seam sides down, on rice. Sprinkle lightly with paprika, salt, and pepper. Bake, covered, at 325 degrees 30 minutes; uncover and bake until cooked, 15 to 20 minutes.

CHICKEN DIVAN

45 *Mayonnaise adds the "tang" to this flavorful sauce!*

6 servings

4 cups cooked rice
1 pound broccoli florets, cooked crisp-tender
Tangy Cheese Sauce (recipe follows)
1 pound boneless, skinless chicken breasts, cooked,
  sliced (½-inch)
½ cup grated fat-free Parmesan cheese

Per Serving:
Calories: 483
% of calories from fat: 26
Fat (gm): 13.7
Saturated fat (gm): 4.4
Cholesterol (mg): 87.4
Sodium (mg): 493
Protein (gm): 40.6
Carbohydrate (gm): 48.4

Exchanges:
Milk: 0.0
Vegetable: 1.0
Fruit: 0.0
Bread: 3.0
Meat: 4.0
Fat: 0.0

1. Spoon rice into greased 13 x 9-inch baking pan; arrange broccoli over rice and top with half the Tangy Cheese Sauce. Top with chicken and remaining sauce; sprinkle with Parmesan cheese. Bake, loosely covered, at 375 degrees until hot and bubbly, about 30 minutes.

Tangy Cheese Sauce
Makes about 3½ cups

½ cup reduced-fat mayonnaise
¼ cup all-purpose flour
1½ cups fat-free milk
1 cup (4 ounces) shredded reduced-fat Cheddar cheese
Salt and pepper, to taste

1. Whisk mayonnaise and flour in medium saucepan; whisk in milk. Heat to boiling; whisk until thickened, about 1 minute. Add cheese, whisking until melted. Season to taste with salt and pepper.

DIJON CHICKEN CASSEROLE

45

Dinner in a dish — what could be easier?

6 servings

1 cup uncooked rice
6 boneless, skinless chicken breast halves
   (4 ounces each)
1 each: medium zucchini, large red bell pepper,
   sliced (¼-inch)
½ cup each: dry white wine, reduced-sodium
   chicken broth
¼ cup Dijon mustard
Salt and pepper, to taste
1 cup unseasoned dry bread crumbs
½ cup (2 ounces) grated Parmesan cheese
2 tablespoons dried tarragon leaves

Per Serving:
Calories: 378
% of calories from fat: 12
Fat (gm): 4.6
Saturated fat (gm): 1.8
Cholesterol (mg): 71.6
Sodium (mg): 530
Protein (gm): 34.3
Carbohydrate (gm): 41.5

Exchanges:
Milk: 0.0
Vegetable: 0.0
Fruit: 0.0
Bread: 3.0
Meat: 3.0
Fat: 0.0

1. Spread rice in greased 12 x 8-inch baking dish. Arrange chicken over rice and top with vegetables. Pour combined wine, broth, and mustard over vegetables and chicken. Sprinkle lightly with salt and pepper. Combine remaining ingredients; sprinkle over vegetables. Bake, covered, at 350 degrees 40 minutes; uncover and bake until rice and chicken are tender with liquid is absorbed, about 10 minutes longer.

CHICKEN AND BROCCOLI CASSEROLE

45

A very easy casserole for those no-time-to-cook days.

6 servings

4 tablespoons margarine or butter, melted

2 cups seasoned stuffing mix

1 can (10¾-ounces) reduced-fat cream of chicken soup

2 cups each: cubed or shredded cooked chicken breast, chopped cooked broccoli

¼ cup chopped onion

⅛ teaspoon black pepper

Per Serving:
Calories: 257
% of calories from fat: 31
Fat (gm): 9
Saturated fat (gm): 2
Cholesterol (mg): Sodium (mg): 795
Protein (gm): 18
Carbohydrate (gm): 26

Exchanges:
Milk: 0.0
Vegetable: 2.0
Fruit: 0.0
Bread: 1.0
Meat: 2.0
Fat: 1.0

1. Drizzle margarine over stuffing mix and toss; spoon ½ the mixture into greased 2-quart casserole. Pour combined soup, chicken, broccoli, onion, and pepper over stuffing; sprinkle with remaining stuffing mixture. Bake, uncovered, at 350 degrees until browned and bubbly, 20 to 25 minutes.

CHICKEN VERONIQUE

45

No one will guess this elegant entrée is so easy to prepare!

4 servings

1 cup sliced mushrooms

2 tablespoons each: sliced green onions, vegetable oil

1 pound boneless, skinless chicken breast, cubed

1 tablespoon flour

¼ cup dry white wine or reduced-sodium chicken broth

1 cup each: reduced-sodium fat-free chicken broth, halved seedless green grapes

1 tablespoon drained capers

Salt and pepper, to taste

2 cups cooked rice, warm

Per Serving:
Calories: 341
% of calories from fat: 27
Fat (gm): 10.1
Saturated fat (gm): 1.8
Cholesterol (mg): 69
Sodium (mg): 184
Protein (gm): 29.6
Carbohydrate (gm): 28.8

Exchanges:
Milk: 0.0
Vegetable: 0.0
Fruit: 0.5
Bread: 1.5
Meat: 3.0
Fat: 0.5

1. Sauté mushrooms and green onions in oil in large skillet until tender, about 5 minutes; add chicken and sauté until browned, about 5 minutes. Sprinkle with flour and cook 1 minute. Stir in white wine and broth; heat to boiling. Reduce heat and simmer, covered, until chicken is cooked, 5 to 8 minutes. Stir in grapes and capers; season to taste with salt and pepper. Serve over rice.

45-MINUTE PREPARATION TIP: Begin cooking rice before preparing the rest of the recipe.

CHICKEN WITH ONIONS AND PEPPERS

45 *Serve this Italian-inspired dish over rice or your favorite pasta.*

4 servings

1 pound boneless, skinless chicken breast, cubed
½ teaspoon minced garlic
1 tablespoon olive oil
2 cups frozen stir-fry pepper blend
1 can (15 ounces) chunky Italian-seasoned
   tomato sauce
Salt and pepper, to taste
2 tablespoons grated Parmesan cheese

Per Serving:
Calories: 215
% of calories from fat: 29
Fat (gm): 7
Saturated fat (gm): 1.8
Cholesterol (mg): 71
Sodium (mg): 674
Protein (gm): 28.5
Carbohydrate (gm): 9.7

Exchanges:
Milk: 0.0
Vegetable: 2.0
Fruit: 0.0
Bread: 0.0
Meat: 3.0
Fat: 0.0

1. Sauté chicken and garlic in oil in large skillet until lightly browned, about 8 minutes. Move chicken to side of pan; add stir-fry pepper blend and cook until softened, 3 to 4 minutes. Stir in tomato sauce; heat to boiling. Reduce heat and simmer, covered, until chicken is cooked, about 10 minutes. Season to taste with salt and pepper; sprinkle with Parmesan cheese.

THAI-SPICED CHICKEN AND CARROTS

45 *Peanut sauce, gingerroot, and sesame oil give this easy dish plenty of Asian-style pizzazz!*

4 servings

1 pound boneless, skinless chicken breast, cubed (½-inch)

4 carrots, diagonally sliced

1 tablespoon each: minced gingerroot, garlic, reduced-sodium soy sauce

1 can (14½ ounces) reduced-sodium fat-free chicken broth

¾ cup sliced green onions

1 tablespoon Thai peanut sauce

1 teaspoon sugar

½ - 1 teaspoon Asian sesame oil

3 cups cooked rice, warm

Per Serving:
Calories: 250
% of calories from fat: 11
Fat (gm): 3.1
Saturated fat (gm): 0.7
Cholesterol (mg): 51.7
Sodium (mg): 203
Protein (gm): 28.4
Carbohydrate (gm): 29

Exchanges:
Milk: 0.0
Vegetable: 2.0
Fruit: 0.0
Bread: 1.0
Meat: 2.0
Fat: 0.0

1. Combine chicken, carrots, gingerroot, garlic, soy sauce, and broth in large saucepan. Heat to boiling; reduce heat and simmer, covered, until chicken is cooked and carrots are tender, about 15 minutes. Stir in green onions, peanut sauce, sugar, and sesame oil; simmer 5 minutes. Serve over rice.

NOTE: 1 tablespoon peanut butter and ¼–½ teaspoon crushed red pepper can be substituted for the Thai peanut sauce.

45-MINUTE PREPARATION TIP: Begin cooking rice before preparing the rest of the recipe.

CHICKEN AND VEGETABLE CURRY

45 *A variety of spices and herbs combine to make the fragrant curry that seasons this dish.*

4 servings

12–16 ounces boneless, skinless chicken breast, cubed

½ cup chopped onion

2 cloves garlic

1 tablespoon flour

1 small head cauliflower, cut into florets

1 cup each: cubed peeled potatoes, chopped tomato, thickly sliced carrots

1½ cups reduced-sodium fat-free chicken broth,

¾ teaspoon ground turmeric

¼ teaspoon each: dry mustard, ground cumin, ground coriander

1–2 tablespoons lemon juice

Salt and cayenne pepper, to taste

Per Serving:
Calories: 250
% of calories from fat: 11
Fat (gm): 3.1
Saturated fat (gm): 0.7
Cholesterol (mg): 51.7
Sodium (mg): 203
Protein (gm): 28.4
Carbohydrate (gm): 29

Exchanges:
Milk: 0.0
Vegetable: 2.0
Fruit: 0.0
Bread: 1.0
Meat: 2.0
Fat: 0.0

1. Sauté chicken, onion, and garlic in lightly greased large saucepan until chicken is browned, 5 to 6 minutes; stir in flour and cook 1 minute. Add vegetables, broth, and herbs; heat to boiling. Reduce heat and simmer, covered, until chicken and vegetables are tender, 10 to 15 minutes. Season to taste with lemon juice, salt, and cayenne pepper.

CHICKEN IN WINE SAUCE

45

This can be assembled in advance and refrigerated if you like; just increase cooking time by 10 minutes.

6 servings

6 boneless, skinless chicken breast halves (4 ounces each)

4 ounces small mushrooms

12 pearl onions, peeled, halved

1 teaspoon minced garlic

1 tablespoon flour

6 small new potatoes, halved

4 slices bacon, cooked crisp, crumbled

½ teaspoon each: dried thyme leaves, salt

¼ teaspoon pepper

½ cup each: reduced sodium chicken broth, dry red wine

Per Serving:
Calories: 276
% of calories from fat: 13
Fat (gm): 4.0
Saturated fat (gm): 1.4
Cholesterol (mg): 69.9
Sodium (mg): 334
Protein (gm): 30.6
Carbohydrate (gm): 25.1

Exchanges:
Milk: 0.0
Vegetable: 0.0
Fruit: 0.0
Bread: 1.5
Meat: 3.0
Fat: 0.0

1. Sauté chicken in lightly greased large skillet until browned, about 5 minutes on each side; remove from skillet. Add mushrooms, pearl onions, and garlic; sauté until mushrooms are tender, about 5 minutes. Sprinkle with flour and cook 1 minute. Combine all ingredients in 2½-quart casserole. Bake, covered, at 350 degrees until chicken and vegetables are tender, about 1 hour.

ORANGE CHICKEN AND VEGETABLES

45

Both orange juice and zest are used to accent this flavorful dish.

6 servings

6 boneless, skinless chicken breast halves
   (4 ounces each)
1 cup each: cubed potatoes, sliced carrots, onion
2 cloves garlic, chopped
½ teaspoon each: dried marjoram and thyme leaves
1-inch piece cinnamon stick
1 tablespoon flour
3 medium tomatoes, chopped
1½ cups orange juice
2 teaspoons grated orange zest
Salt and pepper, to taste

Per Serving:
Calories: 318
% of calories from fat: 10
Fat (gm): 3.5
Saturated fat (gm): 0.9
Cholesterol (mg): 69
Sodium (mg): 87
Protein (gm): 29.4
Carbohydrate (gm): 42.4

Exchanges:
Milk: 0.0
Vegetable: 2.0
Fruit: 0.5
Bread: 1.5
Meat: 2.5
Fat: 0.0

1. Sauté chicken in lightly greased large skillet until browned, about 5 minutes on each side; arrange in 12 x 8-inch baking dish with potatoes and carrots. Add onion, garlic, herbs and cinnamon stick to skillet; sauté until onion is tender, about 5 minutes; add flour and cook 1 minute. Add tomatoes, orange juice, and zest; heat to boiling. Reduce heat and simmer, uncovered, 5 minutes; season to taste with salt and pepper. Pour over chicken and vegetables in baking dish. Bake, covered, at 350 degrees until chicken is tender, about 30 minutes.

CHICKEN À LA KING IN TOAST CUPS

Great served over baked potatoes too!

4 servings

1½ cups sliced mushrooms

½ cup chopped green bell pepper

2½ tablespoons margarine or butter

⅓ cup all-purpose flour

1¼ cups each: reduced-sodium chicken broth,
fat-free milk

2 tablespoons dry sherry (optional)

2 cups cubed cooked chicken breast

½ cup frozen peas, thawed

1 jar (2 ounces) chopped pimiento, drained

Salt and pepper, to taste

Toast Cups (recipe follows)

Per Serving:
Calories: 386
% of calories from fat: 24
Fat (gm): 11.7
Saturated fat (gm): 2.3
Cholesterol (mg): 55.7
Sodium (mg): 578
Protein (gm): 32.1
Carbohydrate (gm): 39.1

Exchanges:
Milk: 0.0
Vegetable: 1.0
Fruit: 0.0
Bread: 2.5
Meat: 3.0
Fat: 0.5

1. Sauté mushrooms and bell pepper in margarine in large sauce-pan until tender, 5 to 8 minutes. Stir in flour and cook 1 minute; stir in broth, milk, and sherry and heat to boiling, stirring until thickened, about 1 minute. Stir in chicken, peas, and pimiento; cook until hot, 3 to 4 minutes. Season to taste with salt and pepper; spoon into Toast Cups.

Toast Cups

Makes 8 (2 per serving)

Vegetable cooking spray
8 slices whole wheat or white bread, crusts trimmed

1. Spray 1 side of bread slices with cooking spray. Press bread slices in greased muffin cups with 4 corners sticking up. Bake, uncovered, at 350 degrees until browned, 10 to 15 minutes.

VARIATION

Ham and Eggs à la King — Make recipe as above, substituting smoked ham for the chicken and adding 2 chopped hard-cooked eggs. Serve over biscuits or squares of cornbread.

CHICKEN OSCAR

45

Easy to make company-fare that will win raves!

6 servings

2 cups seasoned stuffing mix
½ cup reduced-sodium fat-free chicken broth
6 boneless, skinless chicken breast halves
  (4 ounces each)
24 asparagus spears, cooked crisp-tender, warm
6 slices (½ ounce each) provolone cheese

1. Combine stuffing mix and broth; spoon stuffing into 6 mounds in greased 13 x 9-inch baking pan. Top with chicken breasts. Bake, covered, at 350 degrees until chicken is cooked about 30 minutes. Uncover and top with asparagus and cheese slices; bake, uncovered, until cheese is melted, about 5 minutes.

Per Serving:
Calories: 238
% of calories from fat: 29
Fat (gm): 7.3
Saturated fat (gm): 2.8
Cholesterol (mg): 75.5
Sodium (mg): 352
Protein (gm): 32.9
Carbohydrate (gm): 8.6

Exchanges:
Milk: 0.0
Vegetable: 0.0
Fruit: 0.0
Bread: 0.5
Meat: 4.0
Fat: 0.0

SPICY CHICKEN AND RICE

45

You'll enjoy flavors of the Southwest in this very easy casserole!

4 servings

1 pound boneless, skinless chicken breast,
  cubed (2-inch)
1 cup chopped onion
1 tablespoon olive oil
3 cups cooked rice
1 can (14½ ounces) diced tomatoes, undrained
1 cup whole kernel corn
3 tablespoons chopped pimiento
1 can (4 ounces) diced green chilies, drained
¼ teaspoon each: chili powder, ground cumin
Salt and pepper, to taste
¾ cup (3 ounces) shredded reduced-fat
  pepper-Jack cheese

Per Serving:
Calories: 459
% of calories from fat: 20
Fat (gm): 10.1
Saturated fat (gm): 3.6
Cholesterol (mg): 81
Sodium (mg): 519
Protein (gm): 37.2
Carbohydrate (gm): 53.5

Exchanges:
Milk: 0.0
Vegetable: 2.0
Fruit: 0.0
Bread: 3.0
Meat: 4.0
Fat: 0.0

1. Sauté chicken and onion in oil in large skillet until browned, 8 to 10 minutes. Combine all ingredients, except salt, pepper, and cheese, in 2-quart casserole; season to taste with salt and pepper. Bake, covered, at 350 degrees until hot, about 30 minutes. Uncover and sprinkle with cheese; bake until melted, about 5 minutes.

SESAME CHICKEN AND ASPARAGUS STIR-FRY

45 *Check the Asian section of your supermarket for the interesting selection of sauces available for noodles and rice.*

6 servings (about ⅔ cup each)

1 pound boneless, skinless chicken breast, cubed

1 can (15 ounces) black beans, rinsed, drained

8 ounces asparagus, sliced (1-inch)

½ jar (14-ounce size) Mandarin sesame sauce for noodles and rice

1 small tomato, coarsely chopped

¼ teaspoon crushed red pepper

1 package (8 ounces) Chinese egg noodles, cooked, warm

Per Serving:
Calories: 285
% of calories from fat: 8
Fat (gm): 2.9
Saturated fat (gm): 0.6
Cholesterol (mg): 46
Sodium (mg): 295
Protein (gm): 24
Carbohydrate (gm): 45.7

Exchanges:
Milk: 0.0
Vegetable: 1.5
Fruit: 0.5
Bread: 1.5
Meat: 2.0
Fat: 0.0

1. Stir-fry chicken in lightly greased wok or large skillet until browned, about 5 minutes. Add remaining ingredients, except noodles; stir-fry until asparagus is tender, 3 to 4 minutes. Serve over noodles.

45-MINUTE PREPARATION TIP: Begin cooking noodles before preparing the rest of the recipe.

CHICKEN STIR-FRY WITH CHINESE NOODLES

45 *Fresh Chinese noodles and Asian flavors make this pasta dish special.*

4 servings

1 pound boneless, skinless chicken breast, cut into strips

2 cups peeled, cubed, sweet potatoes

¾ cup diagonally sliced green onions

1 tablespoon minced garlic

1–2 teaspoons minced gingerroot

3 cups diagonally halved snow peas

½ cup chopped red bell pepper

¾ cup canned, reduced-sodium fat-free chicken broth

1–2 teaspoons reduced-sodium tamari soy sauce

1½ teaspoons cornstarch

1 teaspoon toasted sesame seeds

Salt and pepper, to taste

1 package (12 ounces) Chinese egg noodles, cooked, warm

Per Serving:
Calories: 237
% of calories from fat: 7
Fat (gm): 1.8
Saturated fat (gm): 0.5
Cholesterol (mg): 35
Sodium (mg): 95
Protein (gm): 17.6
Carbohydrate (gm): 36.9

Exchanges:
Milk: 0.0
Vegetable: 1.0
Fruit: 0.0
Bread: 2.0
Meat: 1.5
Fat: 0.0

1. Stir-fry chicken in lightly greased wok or large skillet until browned, about 5 minutes; remove from wok. Add sweet potatoes, green onions, garlic, and gingerroot to wok; stir-fry 2 to 3 minutes. Cook, covered, over low heat until potatoes are almost tender, about 10 minutes, stirring occasionally. Add snow peas and bell pepper; stir-fry over medium heat until peas are crisp-tender, about 5 minutes. Stir in combined broth, soy sauce, and cornstarch, and chicken; heat to boiling. Boil, stirring until thickened, about 1 minute. Stir in sesame seeds; season to taste with salt and pepper. Serve with noodles.

45-MINUTE PREPARATION TIP: Begin cooking noodles before preparing the rest of the recipe.

CHICKEN AND VEGETABLE CREPES

Enjoy Mock Hollandaise Sauce also with Eggs Benedict and Artichokes with Mock Hollandaise (see pp. 297, 462).

4 servings (2 each)

1 pound boneless, skinless chicken breast, cubed

1½ cups thinly sliced cabbage

¾ cup thinly sliced celery

½ cup each: thinly sliced green pepper, mushrooms, green onions

2 tablespoons water

2–3 teaspoons each: sugar, lemon juice

Salt and pepper, to taste

Crepes (see p. 564), warm

Mock Hollandaise Sauce (recipe follows)

Per Serving:
Calories: 348
% of calories from fat: 21
Fat (gm): 8
Saturated fat (gm): 2.3
Cholesterol (mg): 126.2
Sodium (mg): 581
Protein (gm): 40
Carbohydrate (gm): 26.8

Exchanges:
Milk: 0.0
Vegetable: 2.0
Fruit: 0.0
Bread: 1.0
Meat: 4.0
Fat: 0.0

1. Cook chicken in lightly greased large skillet until browned, 5 to 8 minutes; add vegetables and water. Cook, covered, over medium heat until cabbage and mushrooms are wilted, about 5 minutes. Cook, uncovered, until vegetables are tender, about 5 minutes longer. Season to taste with sugar, lemon juice, salt, and pepper. Spoon mixture along centers of crepes; roll up and arrange, seam sides down, on serving plates. Serve with Mock Hollandaise Sauce.

Mock Hollandaise Sauce
Makes about 1½ cups

6 ounces fat-free cream cheese

⅓ cup fat-free sour cream

3–4 tablespoons fat-free milk

1–2 teaspoons lemon juice

½–1 teaspoon Dijon mustard

⅛ teaspoon ground turmeric

1. Heat all ingredients in small saucepan over low heat, stirring until melted and smooth.

CHICKEN RISOTTO

45 *Microwave Risotto requires very little stirring or attention; adding chicken makes it a hearty meal.*

4 servings

Microwave Risotto (see p. 422)

12 ounces boneless, skinless chicken breast, cubed

1 tablespoon olive oil

2 cups frozen stir-fry pepper blend

¼ cup each: reduced-sodium fat-free chicken broth, dry white wine or dry sherry

½ teaspoon each: dried thyme and oregano leaves

Salt and pepper, to taste

Per Serving:
Calories: 391
% of calories from fat: 19
Fat (gm): 7.9
Saturated fat (gm): 2.4
Cholesterol (mg): 57
Sodium (mg): 330
Protein (gm): 30.9
Carbohydrate (gm): 42.8

Exchanges:
Milk: 0.0
Vegetable: 3.0
Fruit: 0.0
Bread: 2.0
Meat: 3.0
Fat: 0.0

1. Make Microwave Risotto, omitting Parmesan cheese.

2. Sauté chicken in oil in large skillet until lightly browned, about 5 minutes; add remaining ingredients, except salt and pepper. Heat to boiling; reduce heat and simmer, covered, until chicken is tender, about 10 minutes. Stir chicken mixture into risotto; season to taste with salt and pepper.

CHICKEN AND CABBAGE STRUDEL

Fennel adds an aromatic flavor to the strudel. If fresh fennel is not available, substitute sliced celery and add ½ teaspoon crushed fennel seeds with the anise and caraway seeds.

6 servings

1 pound boneless, skinless chicken breast, cubed

½ cup each: chopped onion, sliced leek, thinly sliced fennel

3 cloves garlic, minced

3 cups thinly sliced cabbage

1 cup sliced mushrooms, reduced-sodium fat-free chicken broth

½ cup dry white wine or reduced-sodium chicken broth

1 teaspoon anise seeds, crushed

Per Serving:
Calories: 318
% of calories from fat: 12
Fat (gm): 4.3
Saturated fat (gm): 0.9
Cholesterol (mg): 46
Sodium (mg): 432
Protein (gm): 23.6
Carbohydrate (gm): 41.9

Exchanges:
Milk: 0.0
Vegetable: 4.0
Fruit: 0.0
Bread: 1.5
Meat: 2.0
Fat: 0.0

½ teaspoon caraway seeds, crushed

¾ cup cooked brown rice

¼ cup dark raisins

Salt and pepper, to taste

6 sheets frozen fillo pastry, thawed

Anise or caraway seeds, as garnish

Fresh Tomato and Herb Sauce (recipe follows)

1. Cook chicken in lightly greased large skillet until browned, about 5 minutes; add onion, leek, fennel, and garlic and sauté 3 to 5 minutes. Add cabbage, mushrooms, broth, wine, anise and caraway seeds; cook, covered, until cabbage wilts, 5 to 10 minutes. Cook, uncovered, over medium heat until cabbage begins to brown, about 10 minutes. Stir in rice and raisins; season to taste with salt and pepper. Cool.

2. Lay 1 sheet fillo on clean surface; cover remaining fillo with damp towel to keep from drying. Spray fillo with cooking spray; top with 2 more sheets fillo, spraying each with cooking spray. Spoon ½ the cabbage mixture across dough, 2 inches from short edge; roll up and place, seam-side down, on greased cookie sheet. Flatten roll slightly; spray with cooking spray and sprinkle with anise seeds. Repeat with remaining fillo and cabbage mixture.

3. Bake at 375 degrees until strudels are golden, 35 to 45 minutes. Cool 5 to 10 minutes before cutting. Trim ends of strudels, cutting diagonally. Cut strudels diagonally into serving pieces. Serve with Fresh Tomato and Herb Sauce.

Fresh Tomato and Herb Sauce

Makes about 4 cups

5 cups chopped tomatoes

½ cup each, chopped onion, dry red wine or water

2 tablespoons each: tomato paste, minced garlic, finely chopped fresh or 1½ teaspoons dried thyme leaves

1 tablespoon sugar

2 bay leaves

⅛ teaspoon each: crushed red pepper, ground black pepper

½ teaspoon salt

3–4 tablespoons finely chopped fresh or 2 teaspoons dried basil leaves

1. Combine all ingredients, except basil, in large saucepan; heat to boiling. Reduce heat and simmer, covered, 5 minutes. Simmer, uncovered, until sauce is reduced to medium consistency, about 30 minutes, adding basil during last 5 minutes. Discard bay leaves.

SPAGHETTI SQUASH STUFFED WITH CHICKEN AND VEGETABLES

Jerusalem artichokes, or sun chokes, add extra crunch to the sautéed vegetables.

4 servings

2 medium spaghetti squash (about 2 pounds each), halved lengthwise, seeded

12 ounces boneless, skinless chicken breast, cubed

8 ounces cubed peeled Jerusalem artichokes

1½ cups quartered mushrooms

½ cup each: sliced celery, carrot, chopped onion

2 cloves garlic, minced

2 teaspoons flour

2 medium tomatoes, coarsely chopped

½ cup reduced-sodium fat-free chicken broth

1 teaspoon dried marjoram leaves

Salt and pepper, to taste

2 green onions, thinly sliced

Per Serving:
Calories: 243
% of calories from fat: 12
Fat (gm): 3.3
Saturated fat (gm): 0.8
Cholesterol (mg): 51.7
Sodium (mg): 104
Protein (gm): 24.8
Carbohydrate (gm): 30.8

Exchanges:
Milk: 0.0
Vegetable: 6.0
Fruit: 0.0
Bread: 0.0
Meat: 2.0
Fat: 0.0

1. Place squash halves, cut sides down, in large baking pan; add ½ inch water. Bake, covered, at 350 degrees until squash is tender, 30 to 40 minutes. Scrape pulp into large bowl, separating strands with fork; reserve shells.

2. Sauté chicken, Jerusalem artichokes, mushrooms, celery, carrot, onion, and garlic in lightly greased large skillet until chicken is light brown, about 8 minutes. Stir in flour and cook 1 minute. Add tomatoes, broth, and marjoram; heat to boiling. Cook, covered, until vegetables are tender, about 10 minutes. Season to taste with salt and pepper. Toss mixture with squash; spoon into reserved squash shells. Sprinkle with green onions.

SPEEDY CHICKEN AND RAVIOLI

45 *Use any favorite flavor of ravioli with this quick and nutritious bean sauce.*

4 servings

1 pound chicken tenders, halved crosswise

2 teaspoons minced garlic

¾ cup each: chopped onion, rinsed, drained,
canned kidney beans

1 package (9 ounces) fresh sun-dried tomato ravioli,
cooked, warm

1 large tomato, cubed

½ teaspoon dried thyme leaves

Salt and pepper, to taste

Per Serving:
Calories: 262
% of calories from fat: 17
Fat (gm): 5.1
Saturated fat (gm): 2.3
Cholesterol (mg): 63.5
Sodium (mg): 626
Protein (gm): 29.8
Carbohydrate (gm): 25.2

Exchanges:
Milk: 0.0
Vegetable: 0.0
Fruit: 0.0
Bread: 1.5
Meat: 3.0
Fat: 0.0

1. Cook chicken, garlic, and onion in large lightly greased skillet until chicken is browned, 5 to 8 minutes. Stir in beans, ravioli, tomato, and thyme; cook over medium heat until hot, about 5 minutes. Season to taste with salt and pepper.

45-MINUTE PREPARATION TIP: Begin cooking ravioli before preparing the rest of the recipe.

PRAIRIE CHILI WITH CHICKEN

45 *Few dishes have snappier flavor or are simpler to prepare than this chili! And, a perfect way to revitalize leftover chicken!*

4 servings

12 ounces cooked chicken breast, shredded

1 can (14 ounces) reduced-sodium stewed
tomatoes, undrained

1 can (15 ounces) pinto beans, rinsed, drained

¾ cup mild picante sauce

2 ancho chiles, softened, chopped

2 tablespoons dried onion flakes

½ teaspoon crushed red pepper

1 teaspoon paprika

1 cup fresh or canned drained bean sprouts

Salt, to taste

Per Serving:
Calories: 352
% of calories from fat: 29
Fat (gm): 11.5
Saturated fat (gm): 2.9
Cholesterol (mg): 70.5
Sodium (mg): 689
Protein (gm): 34.2
Carbohydrate (gm): 28.8

Exchanges:
Milk: 0.0
Vegetable: 3.0
Fruit: 0.0
Bread: 1.0
Meat: 4.0
Fat: 0.0

1. Heat all ingredients, except salt, to boiling in large saucepan; reduce heat and simmer, covered, 5 minutes. Season to taste with salt.

CHICKEN ATHENOS

45 *Cinnamon and lemon give this tomato-based stew the signature flavors of Greek cooking. Crumbly feta cheese tops the dish off.*

4 servings

1 pound boneless, skinless chicken breast, cubed (¾-inch)

1 teaspoon olive oil

1 can (14 ounces) reduced-sodium stewed tomatoes, undrained

1 tablespoon lemon juice

2 teaspoons minced garlic

1 each: cinnamon stick, bay leaf

¼ cup dry sherry or reduced-sodium chicken broth

Salt and pepper, to taste

8 ounces egg noodles, cooked, warm

¼ cup (1 ounce) crumbled feta cheese

Per Serving:
Calories: 412
% of calories from fat: 17
Fat (gm): 7.9
Saturated fat (gm): 2.5
Cholesterol (mg): 124.2
Sodium (mg): 370
Protein (gm): 34.4
Carbohydrate (gm): 46

Exchanges:
Milk: 0.0
Vegetable: 2.0
Fruit: 0.0
Bread: 2.0
Meat: 4.0
Fat: 0.0

1. Sauté chicken in oil in large saucepan until lightly browned. Add tomatoes with liquid, lemon juice, garlic, cinnamon stick, bay leaf, and sherry. Heat to boiling; reduce heat and simmer, covered, until chicken is cooked, about 15 minutes. Season to taste with salt and pepper; discard bay leaf and cinnamon stick. Toss mixture with noodles; sprinkle with cheese.

SMOKED CHICKEN BREAST AND LINGUINE SALAD

No time to grill? Smoked chicken or turkey breast from the deli can be used in this salad.

4 servings

1 pound boneless, skinless chicken breast
8 ounces linguine, cooked, room temperature
2 cups sliced carrots, cooked crisp-tender
½ can (15-ounce size) quartered artichoke hearts, drained, rinsed
12 cherry tomatoes, halved
¼ cup sliced green onions
Sour Cream Dressing (recipe follows)

Per Serving:
Calories: 404
% of calories from fat: 11
Fat (gm): 5.2
Saturated fat (gm): 0.8
Cholesterol (mg): 58
Sodium (mg): 800
Protein (gm): 34.9
Carbohydrate (gm): 58.5

Exchanges:
Milk: 0.0
Vegetable: 4.0
Fruit: 0.0
Bread: 2.5
Meat: 2.0
Fat: 0.0

1. Smoke chicken in smoker or on grill, using manufacturer's directions. Cool; refrigerate several hours or overnight to allow flavor to mellow. Shred chicken, or cut into pieces; combine with remaining ingredients and toss.

Sour Cream Dressing

Makes about ⅔ cup

⅓ cup each: fat-free sour cream, mayonnaise
1 tablespoon red wine vinegar
1 clove garlic, minced
½ teaspoon each: crushed dried rosemary leaves, salt
¼ teaspoon pepper

1. Mix all ingredients.

CHICKEN PICCATA WITH FETTUCCINE

45 *This low fat version of the classic piccata is sure to please.*

6 servings

6 small boneless, skinless chicken breast halves
   (3 ounces each)

Flour

1 tablespoon margarine or butter

2 tablespoons flour

1 can (14½ ounces) reduced-sodium chicken broth

½ cup dry white wine or chicken broth

2 tablespoons lemon juice

1 tablespoon each: finely chopped parsley, capers

12 ounces fettuccine, cooked, warm

Per Serving:
Calories: 301
% of calories from fat: 18
Fat (gm): 6
Saturated fat (gm): 0.9
Cholesterol (mg): 43.4
Sodium (mg): 175
Protein (gm): 24.3
Carbohydrate (gm): 35

Exchanges:
Milk: 0.0
Vegetable: 0.0
Fruit: 0.0
Bread: 2.5
Meat: 2.0
Fat: 0.0

1. Pound chicken with flat side of meat mallet to ¼ inch thickness; coat lightly with flour. Cook chicken in lightly greased large skillet over medium to medium-high heat until browned and cooked, 3 to 5 minutes. Remove chicken from skillet.

2. Melt margarine in skillet; stir in 2 tablespoons flour and cook over medium heat 1 to 2 minutes. Whisk in chicken broth, wine, and lemon juice; heat to boiling. Reduce heat and simmer, uncovered, until thickened to a medium consistency, about 15 minutes. Add chicken, parsley and capers; simmer until chicken is hot, 2 to 3 minutes. Serve over pasta.

45-MINUTE PREPARATION TIP: Cook fettuccine while sauce is simmering.

CHICKEN AND FETTUCCINE ALFREDO

45

An old favorite, updated the low-fat way.

6 servings

6 small boneless, skinless chicken breast halves
(3 ounces each)

2 cloves garlic, minced

Paprika

Alfredo Sauce (recipe follows)

12 ounces fettuccine, cooked, warm

Per Serving:
Calories: 380
% of calories from fat: 26
Fat (gm): 11
Saturated fat (gm): 2.6
Cholesterol (mg): 48.4
Sodium (mg): 506
Protein (gm): 29.2
Carbohydrate (gm): 41.4

Exchanges:
Milk: 0.5
Vegetable: 0.0
Fruit: 0.0
Bread: 2.5
Meat: 2.0
Fat: 1.0

1. Rub chicken with garlic; sprinkle generously with paprika. Place chicken in baking pan and bake, uncovered, at 350 degrees until juices run clear, about 20 minutes. Spoon Alfredo Sauce over fettuccine and toss; top with chicken breasts.

Alfredo Sauce

Makes about 2 cups

3 tablespoons margarine or butter

¼ cup all-purpose flour

2½ cups fat-free milk

¼ cup (1 ounce) grated Parmesan cheese

⅛ teaspoon ground nutmeg

½ teaspoon salt

¼ teaspoon pepper

1. Melt margarine in medium saucepan; stir in flour and cook over medium heat 1 minute, stirring. Whisk in milk; heat to boiling, whisking until thickened, about 1 minute. Reduce heat to low and stir in remaining ingredients; cook 1 to 2 minutes.

CHICKEN-PASTA SKILLET

45 *Sun-dried tomatoes and black olives lend a rich, earthy flavor to this colorful dish.*

4 servings

½ cup each: chopped onion, green bell pepper

1 tablespoon olive oil

1 pound boneless, skinless chicken breast, cubed (1-inch)

1 large zucchini, cubed

1 can (15½ ounces) Italian-seasoned diced tomatoes, undrained

1 teaspoon dried marjoram leaves

3 tablespoons each: chopped sun-dried tomatoes, pitted black or Greek olives

Salt and pepper, to taste

4 ounces rigatoni, cooked, warm

Per Serving:
Calories: 330
% of calories from fat: 25
Fat (gm): 9.1
Saturated fat (gm): 1.6
Cholesterol (mg): 69
Sodium (mg): 761
Protein (gm): 30.9
Carbohydrate (gm): 30.7

Exchanges:
Milk: 0.0
Vegetable: 1.0
Fruit: 0.0
Bread: 2.0
Meat: 3.0
Fat: 0.0

1. Sauté onion and bell pepper in olive oil in large skillet until tender, about 5 minutes; add chicken and sauté 5 minutes. Stir in zucchini, tomatoes with liquid, marjoram, sun-dried tomatoes, and olives; heat to boiling. Reduce heat and simmer, uncovered, until chicken is cooked and sauce is thickened, about 10 minutes; season to taste with salt and pepper. Serve over pasta.

45-MINUTE PREPARATION TIP: Begin cooking pasta before preparing the rest of the recipe.

FETTUCCINE WITH CHICKEN LIVER SAUCE

45 *Enjoy the interesting counterpoints of flavor and texture in this savory pasta dish.*

6 servings

4 ounces chicken livers

Flour

2 teaspoons olive oil

1 cup each: sliced onion, carrots

3 cloves garlic, minced

2 teaspoons dried sage leaves

1½ cups reduced-sodium fat-free chicken broth

½ cup dry white wine or chicken broth

2 medium apples, peeled, thinly sliced

1 tablespoon tomato paste

¼ teaspoon salt

⅛ teaspoon pepper

12 ounces fettuccine, cooked, warm

Per Serving:
Calories: 311
% of calories from fat: 11
Fat (gm): 3.6
Saturated fat (gm): 0.5
Cholesterol (mg): 65.2
Sodium (mg): 286
Protein (gm): 11.7
Carbohydrate (gm): 54.2

Exchanges:
Milk: 0.0
Vegetable: 0.0
Fruit: 0.0
Bread: 3.5
Meat: 1.0
Fat: 0.0

1. Coat chicken livers lightly with flour; sauté in oil in large skillet until no longer pink in center, about 8 minutes. Remove livers from skillet. Add onion, carrots, garlic, and sage to skillet; sauté until lightly browned, about 5 minutes. Add livers, chicken broth, and wine. Heat to boiling; reduce heat and simmer, uncovered, until vegetables are tender, about 10 minutes. Stir in apples, tomato paste, salt, and pepper; cook until apples are tender, 2 to 3 minutes. Serve over pasta.

45-MINUTE PREPARATION TIP: Begin cooking fettuccine before preparing the rest of the recipe.

CHICKEN AND CHEESE RELLENOS

Our healthy version of chili rellenos eliminates the customary egg coating and frying in oil.

6 servings

6 large poblano chilies

1 each: chopped medium onion, carrot, garlic clove

1 pound boneless, skinless chicken breast, cooked, shredded

½ cup whole kernel corn

½ teaspoon each: ground cumin, dried thyme leaves

½ cup (2 ounces) each: shredded reduced-fat Monterey Jack,
   fat-free Cheddar cheese

Salt and pepper, to taste

1 tablespoon vegetable oil

Chili Tomato Sauce (recipe follows)

1. Cut stems from tops of chilies; remove and discard seeds and veins. Simmer peppers in water to cover until slightly softened, 2 to 3 minutes; drain and cool.

2. Sauté onion, carrot, and garlic in lightly greased large skillet until tender, 3 to 5 minutes. Add chicken, corn, and herbs; cook over medium heat 1 to 2 minutes. Remove from heat and stir in cheeses; season to taste with salt and pepper. Spoon mixture into peppers; sauté in oil in large skillet until tender and browned on all sides, 6 to 8 minutes. Serve with Chili Tomato Sauce.

Per Serving:
Calories: 215
% of calories from fat: 26
Fat (gm): 6.4
Saturated fat (gm): 1.9
Cholesterol (mg): 54.4
Sodium (mg): 213
Protein (gm): 25.2
Carbohydrate (gm): 15.1

Exchanges:
Milk: 0.0
Vegetable: 2.0
Fruit: 0.0
Bread: 0.5
Meat: 3.0
Fat: 0.0

Chili Tomato Sauce

Makes 1 cup

1 cup reduced-sodium tomato sauce
2 tablespoons water
1–1½ tablespoons chili powder
1 clove garlic
Salt and pepper, to taste

1. Heat all ingredients, except salt and pepper, to boiling in small saucepan; reduce heat and simmer, uncovered, 2 to 3 minutes. Season to taste with salt and pepper.

CHICKEN FAJITAS

Fajitas are an American interpretation of a soft taco. If you are grilling fajita ingredients, leave chicken breasts whole and cut peppers in half, then slice before serving.

4 servings (2 each)

1 pound boneless, skinless chicken breast, cut into strips (1½ x ½-inch)
Fajita Marinade (recipe follows)
1 each: sliced medium red bell pepper, onion
1 can (15 ounces) black beans, rinsed, drained
1 teaspoon ground cumin
Salt and pepper, to taste

8 flour or corn tortillas, warm
¼ cup cilantro sprigs
1 cup Red Tomato Salsa (½ recipe) (see p. 591)
½ cup fat-free sour cream

(see p. 591)

Per Serving:
Calories: 424
% of calories from fat: 14
Fat (gm): 7.3
Saturated fat (gm): 1.2
Cholesterol (mg): 51.7
Sodium (mg): 6Protein (gm): 35.9
Carbohydrate (gm): 61.7

Exchanges:
Milk: 0.0
Vegetable: 2.0
Fruit: 0.0
Bread: 3.0
Meat: 2.0
Fat: 0.0

1. Toss chicken with Fajita Marinade in shallow bowl; refrigerate, covered, 1 to 2 hours.

2. Cook chicken in lightly greased large skillet over medium heat until browned, about 5 minutes; move chicken to side of pan. Add bell pepper and onion; cook over medium heat until vegetables are tender and chicken is cooked, about 5 minutes. Stir in black beans and cumin; cook until hot, 2 to 3 minutes. Season to taste with salt and pepper. Spoon mixture into tortillas; top with cilantro, salsa, and sour cream, and roll up.

Fajita Marinade
Makes about ½ cup

¼ cup lime juice
3 cloves garlic, minced
1½ teaspoons dried oregano leaves
½ teaspoon black pepper

1. Mix all ingredients.

CHICKEN FLAUTAS WITH TOMATILLO SAUCE

Flautas are usually deep-fried; these are sautéed to achieve the same crispness.

4 servings (2 each)

1 cup chopped tomato

¼ cup each: chopped onion, poblano chili

½ teaspoon each: ground cumin, dried thyme leaves

1 pound boneless, skinless chicken breast, cooked, shredded

¼ cup chopped cilantro

Salt and pepper, to taste

8 flour or corn tortillas, warm

Vegetable cooking spray

1 cup Tomatillo Sauce (recipe follows)

4 tablespoons crumbled Mexican white or feta cheese

¼ cup fat-free sour cream

Per Serving:
Calories: 388
% of calories from fat: 23
Fat (gm): 9.8
Saturated fat (gm): 1.4
Cholesterol (mg): 75.7
Sodium (mg): 361
Protein (gm): 34
Carbohydrate (gm): 40.6

Exchanges:
Milk: 0.0
Vegetable: 2.0
Fruit: 0.0
Bread: 2.0
Meat: 3.5
Fat: 0.0

1. Sauté tomato, onion, poblano chili, cumin, and thyme in lightly greased large skillet until onion is tender, about 5 minutes. Add chicken and cilantro; cook 2 to 3 minutes. Season to taste with salt and pepper. Spoon about ⅓ cup mixture on each tortilla; roll up and secure with toothpicks. Spray flautas lightly with cooking spray; cook over medium heat in large skillet until browned on all sides, 5 to 8 minutes. Serve with Tomatillo Sauce, cheese, and sour cream.

Tomatillo Sauce
Makes about 2 cups

1½ pounds tomatillos, husked

½ cup chopped onion

1 teaspoon each: chopped garlic, serrano chili

3 tablespoons chopped cilantro

2–3 teaspoons sugar

Salt and white pepper, to taste

1. Cook tomatillos in 2-inches simmering water in large saucepan until tender, 5 to 8 minutes; drain and cool. Process tomatillos, onion, garlic, chili, and cilantro in food processor or blender until almost smooth. Heat sauce to boiling in lightly greased large skillet; reduce heat and simmer until slightly thickened, about 5 minutes. Season to taste with sugar, salt, and pepper.

CHICKEN BURRITOS WITH POBLANO CHILI SAUCE

Brushed with Poblano Chili Sauce for extra flavor, these burritos are a beautiful adobe red color.

4 servings

12–16 ounces boneless, skinless chicken breast

Salt and pepper, to taste

3 arbol or New Mexico chilies, stems, seeds, and veins discarded

1 small onion, finely chopped

3 cloves garlic, minced

2 tablespoons finely chopped cilantro

1 teaspoon each: dried marjoram and oregano leaves

1 can (15 ounces) pinto beans, rinsed, drained

Cayenne pepper, to taste

4 large flour tortillas (10-inch)

Poblano Chili Sauce (recipe follows)

½ cup fat-free sour cream

Medium or hot salsa (not included in nutritional data)

Per Serving:
Calories: 385
% of calories from fat: 14
Fat (gm): 6.1
Saturated fat (gm): 1.1
Cholesterol (mg): 51.7
Sodium (mg): 661
Protein (gm): 33.1
Carbohydrate (gm): 52.6

Exchanges:
Milk: 0.0
Vegetable: 2.0
Fruit: 0.0
Bread: 3.0
Meat: 2.0
Fat: 0.0

1. Simmer chicken in water to cover in medium saucepan until chicken is tender and cooked, 8 to 10 minutes. Drain, reserving ¼ cup cooking liquid. Shred chicken into small pieces; season to taste with salt and pepper. Cover arbol chilies with hot water in small bowl; let stand until softened, 10 to 15 minutes. Drain; chop finely.

2. Sauté onion, garlic, and herbs in lightly greased medium skillet until onion is tender, 3 to 4 minutes. Add beans, ¼ cup reserved cooking liquid, and arbol chilies; mash coarsely. Cook over medium heat until hot; season to taste with salt and cayenne pepper.

3. Spoon bean mixture and chicken along centers of tortillas; top each with ¼ cup Poblano Chili Sauce. Fold sides of tortillas in, overlapping filling; fold ends in, overlapping to make a square "package"; secure with toothpicks. Cook burritos in lightly greased large skillet until browned on all sides, brushing with remaining Poblano Chili Sauce. Serve with sour cream and salsa.

Poblano Chili Sauce

Makes about 2 cups

2 medium tomatoes, chopped
⅓ cup each: chopped onion, poblano chili
1–2 tablespoons each: minced garlic, chili powder
Salt and pepper, to taste

1. Cook all ingredients, except salt and pepper, in greased medium skillet until tender, 8 to 10 minutes; process in food processor or blender until smooth. Season to taste with salt and pepper.

CHICKEN MOLE

Mole, the most popular and traditional of all the Mexican sauces, is usually served with turkey or chicken. Picante with chilies and fragrant with sweet spices, the sauce is also flavored with unsweetened chocolate or cocoa. Even this simplified version of the delicious mole is somewhat time consuming to make, so double the recipe and freeze half!

6 servings

6 skinless chicken breast halves (6 ounces each)
Mole Sauce (recipe follows)
3 tablespoons finely chopped cilantro

1. Cook chicken in lightly greased large skillet over medium heat until browned, 8 to 10 minutes; arrange in large baking pan. Spoon Mole Sauce over chicken; bake, loosely covered, until chicken is tender and no longer pink in the center, about 30 minutes. Sprinkle with cilantro.

Per Serving:
Calories: 192
% of calories from fat: 25
Fat (gm): 5.1
Saturated fat (gm): 1
Cholesterol (mg): 68.6
Sodium (mg): 82
Protein (gm): 27.7
Carbohydrate (gm): 6.8

Exchanges:
Milk: 0.0
Vegetable: 1.0
Fruit: 0.0
Bread: 0.0
Meat: 3.0
Fat: 0.0

Mole Sauce

Makes about 1½ cups

2 each: mulato, ancho, pasilla chilies
1 tablespoon sesame seeds
2 each: whole peppercorns, cloves
¼ teaspoon coriander seeds
1½-inch piece cinnamon stick
1 tablespoon each: raisins, slivered almonds, pumpkin seeds
¼ cup chopped onion
2 cloves garlic, finely chopped
½ small corn tortilla
Vegetable cooking spray
½ small tomato, chopped
¾ cup reduced-sodium fat-free chicken broth
1 tablespoon unsweetened cocoa
Salt, to taste

1. Cook chilies in lightly greased medium skillet over medium heat until softened; remove and discard stems, seeds, and veins. (If chilies are already soft, the cooking step can be omitted.) Pour boiling water over chilies to cover in bowl; let stand until softened, about 15 minutes. Drain, reserving ¾ cup liquid.

2. Cook sesame seeds and spices in lightly greased small skillet over medium heat until toasted, 1 to 2 minutes; remove from skillet. Add raisins, almonds, and pumpkin seeds and cook over medium heat until toasted, 1 to 2 minutes; remove from skillet. Add onion and garlic to skillet and sauté until tender, 2 to 3 minutes; remove from skillet. Spray tortilla lightly with cooking spray; cook in skillet until browned, about 1 minute on each side. Cool; cut into 1-inch pieces.

3. Process all ingredients, except salt, in blender until smooth. Heat mixture to boiling in medium skillet; reduce heat and simmer, uncovered 5 minutes; season to taste with salt.

CHICKEN ENCHILADAS MOLE

For variation, the enchiladas can also be baked with Tomatillo Sauce (see p. 188). Serve with Jicama Salad (see p. 507) for fresh flavor contrast.

4 servings (2 each)

8 corn or flour tortillas (6-inch)

1 cup mild or medium salsa

1 pound boneless, skinless chicken breast, cooked, shredded

½ cup each: shredded fat-free Cheddar cheese (2 ounces), sliced green onions

4–8 tablespoons fat-free sour cream

¼ cup chopped cilantro

Mole Sauce (see p. 191)

Per Serving:
Calories: 333
% of calories from fat: 15
Fat (gm): 5.9
Saturated fat (gm): 1.1
Cholesterol (mg): 69
Sodium (mg): 752
Protein (gm): 39.1
Carbohydrate (gm): 33.1

Exchanges:
Milk: 0.0
Vegetable: 1.0
Fruit: 0.0
Bread: 2.0
Meat: 3.0
Fat: 0.0

1. Dip tortillas in salsa to coat lightly. Spoon chicken along centers of tortillas; top with cheese, green onions, sour cream, and cilantro. Roll up and place, seam sides down, in baking pan; spoon Mole Sauce over. Bake, loosely covered, at 350 degrees until enchiladas are hot, 20 to 30 minutes.

MESQUITE CHICKEN CHILI

45 *A differently delicious Tex-Mex dish that will appeal to the adventurous and not-so-adventurous alike.*

4 servings

12 ounces boneless, skinless chicken breast, cubed

¾ cup each: chopped onion, poblano chili

1 teaspoon olive oil

1 can (28 ounces) reduced-sodium crushed tomatoes

½ pound tomatillos, husked, coarsely chopped

1 can (15 ounces) red beans, rinsed, drained

2 tablespoons chili powder

2 teaspoons minced garlic

1 teaspoon mesquite smoke flavoring

Salt and pepper, to taste

Per Serving:
Calories: 293
% of calories from fat: 15
Fat (gm): 5.3
Saturated fat (gm): 1.1
Cholesterol (mg): 51.7
Sodium (mg): 469
Protein (gm): 28.1
Carbohydrate (gm): 36.3

Exchanges:
Milk: 0.0
Vegetable: 2.0
Fruit: 0.0
Bread: 2.0
Meat: 2.0
Fat: 0.0

1. Sauté chicken, onion, and poblano chili in oil in large saucepan until chicken is browned, about 8 minutes; add remaining ingredients, except salt and pepper. Heat to boiling; reduce heat and simmer, covered, 10 minutes. Season to taste with salt and pepper.

CHICKEN CACCIATORE

This "Hunter's Stew," of Italian origin, was made from any game brought back from the day's hunting and would vary slightly from kitchen to kitchen.

4 servings

8 ounces each: boneless, skinless chicken breast, thighs

2 teaspoons dried oregano leaves

½ teaspoon each: garlic powder, salt, pepper

3 cups quartered mushrooms

1 cup each: chopped onion, green bell pepper

6 cloves garlic, minced

2 cans (14½ ounces each) reduced-sodium tomatoes, undrained, coarsely chopped

½ cup dry red wine

1 bay leaf

4 teaspoons cornstarch

¼ cup water

Salt and pepper, to taste

3 cups cooked noodles, warm

Per Serving:
Calories: 411
% of calories from fat: 15
Fat (gm): 7.2
Saturated fat (gm): 1.7
Cholesterol (mg): 65.5
Sodium (mg): 199
Protein (gm): 30.9
Carbohydrate (gm): 53.7

Exchanges:
Milk: 0.0
Vegetable: 4.0
Fruit: 0.0
Bread: 2.0
Meat: 3.0
Fat: 0.0

1. Cut each chicken breast into two pieces; sprinkle chicken with combined oregano, garlic powder, salt, and pepper; cook in lightly greased large Dutch oven over medium heat until browned, 5 to 8 minutes; remove from skillet. Add mushrooms, onion, bell pepper, and garlic to Dutch oven; sauté 3 to 4 minutes. Return chicken to pan; add tomatoes with liquid, wine, and bay leaf; heat to boiling. Reduce heat and simmer, covered, until chicken is tender, about 30 minutes.

2. Heat to boiling; stir in combined cornstarch and water. Boil, stirring until sauce is thickened, about 1 minute. Discard bay leaf; season to taste with salt and pepper and serve over noodles.

SWEET-AND-SOUR ISLAND STEW

45 *Sweet-and-sour flavors team with chicken, pineapple, and beans for this island-inspired dish—delicious with jasmine rice or couscous.*

6 servings

1½ pounds chicken tenders

1 tablespoon vegetable oil

3 cups frozen stir-fry pepper blend

2 teaspoons each: minced garlic, gingerroot, jalapeno chili

3 cups reduced-sodium fat-free chicken broth

1 can (20 ounces) unsweetened pineapple chunks, drained, juice reserved

1 can (15 ounces) black beans, rinsed, drained

2 tablespoons each: light brown sugar, apple cider vinegar

2–3 teaspoons curry powder

2 tablespoons cornstarch

Per Serving:
Calories: 288
% of calories from fat: 12
Fat (gm): 3.9
Saturated fat (gm): 0.3
Cholesterol (mg): 48.2
Sodium (mg): 537
Protein (gm): 29.7
Carbohydrate (gm): 34.7

Exchanges:
Milk: 0.0
Vegetable: 1.0
Fruit: 0.5
Bread: 1.0
Meat: 3.0
Fat: 0.0

1. Cook chicken in oil in large skillet over medium heat until browned, about 8 minutes; remove from skillet. Add pepper blend, garlic, gingerroot, and jalapeño chili to skillet; sauté 5 minutes. Stir in chicken and remaining ingredients, except reserved pineapple juice and cornstarch; heat to boiling. Stir in combined cornstarch and reserved pineapple juice; boil, stirring until thickened, about 1 minute.

CARIBBEAN-STYLE CHICKEN STEW

45 *This enticing chowder boasts sofrito, a popular Cuban seasoning found in the ethnic section of many supermarkets.*

4 servings

12 ounces boneless, skinless chicken breast, cubed (¾-inch)

1 medium onion, chopped

1 teaspoon olive oil

1 can (15 ounces) each: rinsed drained garbanzo beans, undrained reduced-sodium diced tomatoes

1 can (14½ ounces) reduced-sodium fat-free chicken broth

2 cups packed spinach leaves

2 tablespoons sofrito sauce (optional)

Salt and pepper, to taste

¼ cup slivered almonds, toasted

Per Serving:
Calories: 346
% of calories from fat: 29
Fat (gm): 10.5
Saturated fat (gm): 1.9
Cholesterol (mg): 54.3
Sodium (mg): 639
Protein (gm): 30.5
Carbohydrate (gm): 28.2

Exchanges:
Milk: 0.0
Vegetable: 3.0
Fruit: 0.0
Bread: 1.0
Meat: 3.0
Fat: 1.0

1. Sauté chicken and onion in oil in large saucepan until chicken is lightly browned, about 8 minutes. Add beans, tomatoes with liquid, and broth and heat to boiling; reduce heat and simmer, covered, 10 minutes. Stir in spinach and sofrito; simmer until spinach is wilted, 5 minutes. Season to taste with salt and pepper. Sprinkle each bowl of stew with almonds.

CHICKEN AND PASTA STEW WITH MUSHROOMS

45

This orange-scented tomato stew actually improves when made ahead of time, giving flavors an opportunity to meld.

6 servings

6 small boneless, skinless chicken breast halves
(3 ounces each)

Flour

1 tablespoon olive oil

2 cups sliced mushrooms

1 small onion, chopped

3 cloves garlic, minced

1 can (14½ ounces) reduced-sodium chicken broth

½ cup dry white wine or reduced-sodium chicken broth

3 tablespoons each: tomato paste, grated orange zest

1 teaspoon each: dried tarragon and thyme leaves

¼ teaspoon each: salt, pepper

12 ounces pappardelle or other flat pasta, cooked, warm

Per Serving:
Calories: 343
% of calories from fat: 16
Fat (gm): 6.1
Saturated fat (gm): 1.1
Cholesterol (mg): 43.5
Sodium (mg): 133
Protein (gm): 25.4
Carbohydrate (gm): 42.7

Exchanges:
Milk: 0.0
Vegetable: 1.0
Fruit: 0.0
Bread: 2.5
Meat: 2.5
Fat: 0.0

1. Coat chicken breasts lightly with flour. Sauté in oil in Dutch oven until browned, about 4 minutes each side; remove from skillet. Add mushrooms, onion, and garlic to pan; sauté until tender, 3 to 4 minutes. Add remaining ingredients, except pasta; heat to boiling. Add chicken and bake, covered, at 350 degrees until chicken is tender, 30 to 40 minutes. Serve over pasta.

CHICKEN AND PORK STEW WITH FRUIT

Enjoy flavor accents of tropical fruit, sweet cinnamon, and piquant ancho chili in this stew; serve over rice or couscous.

6 servings

2 tablespoons slivered almonds

1 tablespoon sesame seeds

1 -inch piece cinnamon stick

3 ancho chilies, stems, seeds, and veins discarded

2 medium tomatoes, coarsely chopped

1 can (14½ ounces) reduced-sodium
fat-free chicken broth, divided

12 ounces each: pork tenderloin and boneless
skinless chicken breast, cubed (1½-inch)

1 cup each: fresh or canned pineapple chunks,
sliced ripe plantain, cubed peeled jicama

Salt and pepper, to taste

Per Serving:
Calories: 239
% of calories from fat: 22
Fat (gm): 5.9
Saturated fat (gm): 1.4
Cholesterol (mg): 67.2
Sodium (mg): 81
Protein (gm): 28.1
Carbohydrate (gm): 19.6

Exchanges:
Milk: 0.0
Vegetable: 1.0
Fruit: 1.0
Bread: 0.0
Meat: 3.0
Fat: 0.0

1. Cook almonds, sesame seeds, and cinnamon in lightly greased small skillet over medium heat until browned, 3 to 4 minutes; remove from skillet. Add chilies and tomatoes to skillet and cook over medium heat until tomatoes are soft, 2 to 3 minutes. Process almond and tomato mixtures and 1 cup broth in blender or food processor until smooth. Transfer to lightly greased large saucepan and cook over medium heat until slightly thickened, 4 to 5 minutes.

2. Sauté pork and chicken in lightly greased large skillet until browned, about 5 minutes. Add meat mixture and remaining broth to saucepan with chilies; heat to boiling. Reduce heat and simmer, covered, until meats are tender, about 30 minutes, adding fruit and jicama during last 10 minutes. Season to taste with salt and pepper.

CHICKEN FRICASSEE

Cloves and bay leaf add a flavor update to this dish; traditional herbs, rosemary and thyme can be substituted.

6 servings

6 skinless chicken breast halves (6 ounces each)

1 cup each: onion wedges, sliced carrots, celery

2 cloves garlic, minced

3 tablespoons flour

2 cans (14½ ounces each) reduced-sodium fat-free chicken broth

16 whole cloves, tied in cheesecloth

2 bay leaves

1 teaspoon lemon juice

½ teaspoon each: sugar, salt

¼ teaspoon pepper

12 ounces fettuccine, cooked, warm

Per Serving:
Calories: 361
% of calories from fat: 13
Fat (gm): 5.1
Saturated fat (gm): 0.9
Cholesterol (mg): 78.6
Sodium (mg): 401
Protein (gm): 35.9
Carbohydrate (gm): 41.5

Exchanges:
Milk: 0.0
Vegetable: 2.0
Fruit: 0.0
Bread: 2.0
Meat: 3.0
Fat: 0.0

1. Cook chicken in lightly greased large skillet over medium heat until browned, about 8 minutes. Remove from skillet. Add vegetables to skillet; sauté 5 minutes. Stir in flour and cook 1 minute. Return chicken to skillet. Add remaining ingredients, except pasta; heat to boiling. Reduce heat and simmer, covered, until chicken is tender, about 20 minutes; simmer, uncovered, until sauce is thickened to medium consistency, about 10 minutes. Discard cloves and bay leaves. Serve with fettuccine.

CHICKEN PAPRIKASH

Lean veal can be used in this recipe instead of chicken.

4 servings

1 pound boneless, skinless chicken breast,
    cubed (¾-inch)
1 tablespoon margarine or butter
1 cup chopped onion
4 cloves garlic, minced
2 tablespoons flour
½ cup reduced-sodium chicken broth
¼ cup dry white wine or chicken broth
1 cup chopped tomato
1 teaspoon paprika
½ cup fat-free sour cream
Salt and white pepper, to taste
3 cups cooked noodles, warm

Per Serving:
Calories: 416
% of calories from fat: 18
Fat (gm): 8.4
Saturated fat (gm): 1.4
Cholesterol (mg): 69
Sodium (mg): 139
Protein (gm): 35.9
Carbohydrate (gm): 47.9

Exchanges:
Milk: 0.0
Vegetable: 1.0
Fruit: 0.0
Bread: 3.0
Meat: 3.0
Fat: 0.0

1. Sauté chicken in margarine in large saucepan until browned, 8 to 10 minutes; add onion and garlic and sauté 5 minutes. Stir in flour and cook 1 minute. Add chicken broth, wine, tomato, and paprika and heat to boiling; reduce heat and simmer, covered, until chicken is tender, 15 to 20 minutes. Stir in sour cream and cook, uncovered, 2 to 3 minutes. Season to taste with salt and white pepper; serve over noodles.

COUNTRY CHICKEN STEW

45 *Serve this hearty stew with warm Multi-Grain Batter Bread or Peasant Bread (see pg. 554, 549).*

6 servings

1½ pounds boneless, skinless chicken breast, cubed (1-inch)
Flour
1½ tablespoons olive oil
1 cup each: chopped onion, red bell peppers
½ cup chopped carrots

2 large cloves garlic, minced

1 can (14½ ounces) reduced-sodium Italian-style chopped tomatoes, undrained

1¾ cups reduced-sodium fat-free chicken broth

¼ cup tomato paste

¾ teaspoon each: dried thyme and marjoram leaves

Salt and pepper, to taste

Per Serving:
Calories: 291
% of calories from fat: 24
Fat (gm): 7.9
Saturated fat (gm): 1.5
Cholesterol (mg): 73.6
Sodium (mg): 393
Protein (gm): 32.1
Carbohydrate (gm): 23.8

Exchanges:
Milk: 0.0
Vegetable: 3.0
Fruit: 0.0
Bread: 0.5
Meat: 3.5
Fat: 0.0

1. Coat chicken with flour; sauté in oil in Dutch oven until browned, about 8 minutes. Stir in onion, bell peppers, carrots, and garlic; sauté until vegetables are tender, about 8 minutes. Add remaining ingredients, except salt, and pepper; heat to boiling. Reduce heat and simmer, covered, until chicken is tender, about 20 minutes. Season to taste with salt and pepper.

CHICKEN STEW WITH PARSLEY DUMPLINGS

For variation, omit the dumplings and serve this savory stew over noodles or Real Mashed Potatoes (see p. 485).

6 servings

1 cup chopped onion

3 carrots, thickly sliced (¾-inch)

½ cup sliced celery

3 cups reduced-sodium chicken broth, divided

1½ cups cubed boneless, skinless chicken breast

¾ teaspoon dried sage leaves

½ cup frozen peas

¼ cup all-purpose flour

Salt and pepper, to taste

Parsley Dumplings (recipe follows)

Per Serving:
Calories: 233
% of calories from fat: 20
Fat (gm): 5.1
Saturated fat (gm): 1.4
Cholesterol (mg): 35.5
Sodium (mg): 383
Protein (gm): 19.2
Carbohydrate (gm): 26.7

Exchanges:
Milk: 0.0
Vegetable: 2.0
Fruit: 0.0
Bread: 1.0
Meat: 1.5
Fat: 0.5

1. Sauté onion, carrots, and celery in lightly greased large saucepan 5 minutes. Add 2½ cups chicken broth, chicken, and sage; heat to boiling. Reduce heat and simmer, covered, until chicken is cooked and vegetables are tender, 10 to 15 minutes; stir in peas. Heat to boiling; stir combined flour and remaining ½ cup chicken broth into stew. Boil, stirring until thickened, 1 to 2 minutes. Season to taste with salt and pepper.

2. Spoon dumpling dough into 6 mounds on top of boiling stew; reduce heat and simmer, covered, 10 minutes. Simmer, uncovered, 10 minutes.

Parsley Dumplings
Makes 6

¾ cup all-purpose flour
1 teaspoon baking powder
¼ teaspoon salt
1½ tablespoons vegetable shortening
⅓ cup 2% reduced-fat milk
2 tablespoons finely chopped parsley

1. Combine flour, baking powder, and salt in small bowl. Cut in shortening with pastry blender until mixture resembles coarse crumbs. Stir in milk to make a soft dough; stir in parsley.

QUICK CHICKEN AND VEGETABLE STEW

45 *Pureed beans provide a perfect thickening for the stew, and canned vegetables speed preparation.*

8 servings

1 pound chicken tenders, halved crosswise
¾ cup each: sliced carrots, chopped onion
2 teaspoons minced garlic
1 can (15 ounces) navy beans, rinsed, drained
2 cups reduced-sodium fat-free chicken broth, divided
2 cans (16 ounces) Italian-style zucchini with
   mushrooms in tomato sauce
1 can (15 ounces) black beans, rinsed, drained
1 cup frozen peas
1½ teaspoons dried Italian seasoning
Salt and pepper, to taste
8 ounces noodles, cooked, warm

Per Serving:
Calories: 326
% of calories from fat: 9
Fat (gm): 3.4
Saturated fat (gm): 0.8
Cholesterol (mg): 59
Sodium (mg): 607
Protein (gm): 26
Carbohydrate (gm): 47.5

Exchanges:
Milk: 0.0
Vegetable: 1.0
Fruit: 0.0
Bread: 3.0
Meat: 1.5
Fat: 0.0

1. Sauté chicken, carrots, onion, and garlic in large lightly greased saucepan until chicken is browned, about 8 minutes. Puree navy beans with 1 cup broth in food processor or blender; return to saucepan. Add remaining 1 cup broth, zucchini, black beans, peas, and Italian seasoning; heat to boiling. Reduce heat and simmer, uncovered, until vegetables are tender, about 10 minutes. Season to taste with salt and pepper. Serve over noodles.

GARDEN STEW WITH CHICKEN AND COUSCOUS

45 *Take advantage of your garden's bounty with this quick and easy stew.*

8 servings

8 boneless, skinless chicken breast halves
   (4 ounces each)
2 medium onions, chopped
4 ounces each: sliced shiitake, cremini mushrooms
1 small jalapeño chili, finely chopped
1 tablespoon flour
2 cups each: reduced-sodium fat-free chicken broth,
   chopped tomatoes
1½ cups each: cubed turnips or parsnips, sliced
   zucchini, baby carrots
1 bay leaf
½ cup loosely packed cilantro leaves
Salt and pepper, to taste
4 cups cooked couscous, warm

Per Serving:
Calories: 472
% of calories from fat: 5
Fat (gm): 2.8
Saturated fat (gm): 0.6
Cholesterol (mg): 88
Sodium (mg): 294
Protein (gm): 45.4
Carbohydrate (gm): 65.0

Exchanges:
Milk: 0.0
Vegetable: 0.0
Fruit: 0.0
Bread: 4.0
Meat: 4.0
Fat: 0.0

1. Sauté chicken over medium heat in lightly greased large skillet until browned, about 5 minutes on each side; remove from skillet. Add onions, mushrooms, and jalapeño chili to skillet; sauté until browned, about 5 minutes. Stir in flour; cook 1 minute. Return chicken to skillet; add broth, tomatoes, turnips, zucchini, carrots, and bay leaf. Heat to boiling; reduce heat and simmer, covered, until vegetables are tender and chicken cooked, about 15 minutes. Stir in cilantro; discard bay leaf and season to taste with salt and pepper. Serve with couscous.

45-MINUTE PREPARATION TIP: Cook couscous while the stew is simmering.

CHICKEN WITH RAVIOLI AND ASPARAGUS

45 *A reduction of broth, white wine, and orange juice creates an elegant and fragrant sauce for chicken and flavorful pasta.*

4 servings

1 boneless, skinless chicken breast halves
  (4 ounces each)
Salt and pepper, to taste
2 cups reduced-sodium fat-free chicken broth
1 cup orange juice
½ cup dry white wine
¼ teaspoon crushed red pepper
1 pound asparagus, sliced (1-inch)
2 tablespoons margarine or butter
1 package (9 ounces) fresh mushroom ravioli,
  cooked, warm

Per Serving:
Calories: 340
% of calories from fat: 34
Fat (gm): 12.5
Saturated fat (gm): 2
Cholesterol (mg): 76.9
Sodium (mg): 454
Protein (gm): 33
Carbohydrate (gm): 11.7

Exchanges:
Milk: 0.0
Vegetable: 1.0
Fruit: 0.0
Bread: 2.0
Meat: 3.0
Fat: 0.5

1. Cook chicken over medium heat in lightly greased large skillet until cooked, about 10 minutes on each side. Sprinkle lightly with salt and pepper; remove from skillet. Add broth, orange juice, white wine, and crushed red pepper and heat to boiling; boil, uncovered, until liquid is reduced to ½ cup, about 10 minutes. Add asparagus; simmer, covered, until crisp-tender, 3 to 4 minutes. Add chicken, margarine, and ravioli; cook until hot, 2 to 3 minutes. Season to taste with salt and pepper.

CHICKEN STEW WITH RED WINE

45 *Serve this stew with warm crusty bread to soak up the delicious broth.*

4 servings

4 boneless, skinless chicken breast halves
2 teaspoons olive oil
1 medium onion, chopped
2 large cloves garlic, minced
1 tablespoon flour
¾ cup each: reduced-sodium fat-free chicken broth, dry red wine

1 bay leaf

1½–1 teaspoons dried Italian seasoning

Salt and pepper, to taste

Per Serving:
Calories: 207
% of calories from fat: 24
Fat (gm): 5.3
Saturated fat (gm): 1.2
Cholesterol (mg): 69
Sodium (mg): 152
Protein (gm): 26.8
Carbohydrate (gm): 4.7

1. Sauté chicken in oil in large skillet until browned on both sides, about 8 minutes. Stir in onion and garlic and sauté until tender, about 5 minutes; sprinkle with flour and cook 1 minute. Add remaining ingredients, except salt and pepper; heat to boiling. Reduce heat and simmer, uncovered, until chicken is tender, about 15 minutes; simmer, uncovered, until thickened to desired consistency, 5 to 10 minutes. Discard bay leaf; season to taste with salt and pepper.

Exchanges:
Milk: 0.0
Vegetable: 1.0
Fruit: 0.0
Bread: 0.0
Meat: 3.0
Fat: 0.0

TURKEY CUTLETS WITH SAGE

45 *Sage adds a robust flavor and aroma to this dish.*

4 servings

1 pound turkey breast cutlets

2 tablespoons red wine vinegar

2 teaspoons each: minced garlic, dried sage leaves

¼ teaspoon each: salt, pepper

Flour

2 teaspoons olive oil

½ cup reduced-sodium fat-free chicken broth

1 tablespoon lemon juice

Per Serving:
Calories: 158
% of calories from fat: 26
Fat (gm): 4.5
Saturated fat (gm): 1
Cholesterol (mg): 44.7
Sodium (mg): 63
Protein (gm): 21.1
Carbohydrate (gm): 7

Exchanges:
Milk: 0.0
Vegetable: 0.0
Fruit: 0.0
Bread: 0.5
Meat: 3.0
Fat: 0.0

1. Pound turkey cutlets with flat side of meat mallet to ¼ inch thickness; brush with combined vinegar, garlic, sage, salt, and pepper. Let stand 5 minutes. Coat both sides of cutlets lightly with flour; sauté in oil in large skillet until browned and cooked, 2 to 3 minutes on each side. Remove cutlets to platter and keep warm. Heat broth and lemon juice to boiling in skillet; boil until slightly thickened. Spoon over cutlets.

TURKEY SAUSAGE-STUFFED ACORN SQUASH

45

A perfect autumn offering.

4 servings

2 acorn squash (about 1 pound each), halved, seeded
1 small onion, chopped
1 clove garlic, minced
8 ounces Italian-style turkey sausage, casing removed
½ cup each: chopped tomato, cooked rice
½ teaspoon each: dried sage and thyme leaves
Salt and pepper, to taste

Per Serving:
Calories: 263
% of calories from fat: 21
Fat (gm): 6.6
Saturated fat (gm): 1.8
Cholesterol (mg): 30.4
Sodium (mg): 472
Protein (gm): 13.7
Carbohydrate (gm): 43.4

Exchanges:
Milk: 0.0
Vegetable: 0.0
Fruit: 0.0
Bread: 3.0
Meat: 1.0
Fat: 0.0

1. Place squash, cut sides down, in baking pan; add ½ inch water. Bake, covered, at 400 degrees until flesh is fork-tender, about 30 minutes. Drain.

2. Sauté onion, garlic, and sausage in lightly greased large skillet until browned, about 5 minutes. Add tomato, rice, sage, and thyme. Cook over medium heat until mixture is hot, about 5 minutes; season to taste with salt and pepper. Serve mixture in squash halves.

45-MINUTE PREPARATION TIP: Prepare filling while squash is baking.

TURKEY DIVAN

45

For real convenience, assemble this casserole in advance and refrigerate up to 24 hours; sprinkle with bread crumbs and bake until bubbly, about 40 minutes.

4 servings

½ cup chopped onion
1 tablespoon margarine or butter
¼ cup all-purpose flour
¾ cup each: reduced-sodium chicken broth, fat-free half-and-half or milk
¼ cup dry white wine (optional)
½ teaspoon each: dried savory and marjoram leaves
2–3 pinches ground nutmeg

1 cup (4 ounces) shredded fat-free Swiss cheese
Salt, cayenne, and white pepper, to taste
1½ cups cubed cooked turkey or chicken breast
2 cups broccoli florets, cooked crisp-tender
3–4 tablespoons unseasoned dry bread crumbs

Per Serving:
Calories: 300
% of calories from fat: 13
Fat (gm): 4.2
Saturated fat (gm): 0.9
Cholesterol (mg): 70.9
Sodium (mg): 566
Protein (gm): 37.4
Carbohydrate (gm): 22.9

1. Sauté onion in margarine in medium saucepan until tender, 2 to 3 minutes. Mix flour and chicken broth until smooth; whisk into saucepan with half-and-half and wine. Heat to boiling, whisking until thickened, 1 minute. Add seasonings and cheese, whisking until cheese is melted. Season to taste with salt, cayenne, and white pepper.

Exchanges:
Milk: 0.5
Vegetable: 1.0
Fruit: 0.0
Bread: 1.0
Meat: 3.0
Fat: 0.0

2. Arrange turkey and broccoli in 10 x 7-inch baking dish; pour sauce over and sprinkle with bread crumbs. Bake at 350 degrees until bubbly, about 25 minutes.

TURKEY POT PIE

Leftovers from Thanksgiving dinner are welcome ingredients in this delectable pot pie.

6 servings

1 cup chopped onion
½ cup chopped green bell pepper
2½ cups reduced-sodium chicken broth
1 cup each: cubed potato, parsnip, sliced carrots, broccoli florets
½ cup each: small mushrooms, whole-kernel corn, peas
1 pound cooked turkey breast, cubed
½ teaspoon each: dried rosemary and thyme leaves
⅓ cup all-purpose flour
⅔ cup fat-free half-and-half or fat-free milk
Salt and pepper, to taste
Pot Pie Pastry (recipe follows)
Fat-free milk
1 tablespoon grated Parmesan cheese

Per Serving:
Calories: 380
% of calories from fat: 17
Fat (gm): 7.1
Saturated fat (gm): 2.1
Cholesterol (mg): 65.5
Sodium (mg): 284
Protein (gm): 32.8
Carbohydrate (gm): 45.1

Exchanges:
Milk: 0.0
Vegetable: 0.0
Fruit: 0.0
Bread: 3.0
Meat: 3.0
Fat: 0.0

1. Sauté onion and bell pepper in lightly greased large saucepan until lightly browned, about 5 minutes. Add chicken broth, remaining vegetables, turkey, and herbs. Heat to boiling; reduce heat and simmer, covered, until vegetables are tender, about 10 minutes. Heat mixture to boiling. Stir in combined flour and fat-free half-and-half; boil, stirring until thickened, 1 to 2 minutes. Season to taste with salt and pepper. Pour into 2-quart casserole or soufflé dish.

2. Roll pastry on floured surface to fit top of casserole; place on casserole, trim, and flute. Cut steam vents in top of pastry. Bake at 425 degrees 20 minutes; brush with milk and sprinkle with cheese. Bake until golden, 5 to 10 minutes. Cool 10 minutes before serving.

Pot Pie Pastry

1 cup all-purpose flour
2 tablespoons grated Parmesan cheese
2½–3 tablespoons vegetable shortening
3–4 tablespoons ice water

1. Combine flour and Parmesan cheese in medium bowl. Cut in shortening with pastry blender until mixture resembles coarse crumbs. Add water, one tablespoon at a time, mixing with fork just until dough holds together. Refrigerate until ready to use.

RIGATONI WITH TURKEY SAUSAGE AND FENNEL PESTO

Fennel Pesto and fresh fennel add a unique twist to a traditional favorite.

6 servings

1 pound Italian-style turkey sausage
1½ cups thinly sliced fennel bulb or celery
1 cup chopped onion
2 cloves garlic, minced
1 can (8 ounces) low-sodium whole tomatoes, drained, chopped
Fennel Pesto (recipe follows)
12 ounces rigatoni or other tube pasta, cooked, warm

1. Cook sausage in lightly greased large skillet over medium heat until browned, about 5 minutes. Remove sausage and slice; return to skillet. Add fennel, onion, and garlic; sauté until onion is tender, about 8 minutes. Stir in tomatoes and Fennel Pesto. Heat to boiling; reduce heat and simmer, covered, about 15 minutes. Spoon over pasta and toss.

Per Serving:
Calories: 406
% of calories from fat: 29
Fat (gm): 13
Saturated fat (gm): 2.9
Cholesterol (mg): 48.2
Sodium (mg): 711
Protein (gm): 24.6
Carbohydrate (gm): 48.3

Exchanges:
Milk: 0.0
Vegetable: 1.0
Fruit: 0.0
Bread: 2.5
Meat: 2.0
Fat: 2.0

Fennel Pesto

Makes about 1⅓ cups

1 tablespoon fennel seeds
3 tablespoons hot water
1 cup chopped fennel bulb
½ cup loosely packed parsley
2 cloves garlic
14 walnut halves
1 tablespoon olive oil
¼ cup (1 ounce) grated Parmesan cheese

1. Pour hot water over fennel seeds in bowl to cover. Let stand 10 minutes. Process fennel seeds and remaining ingredients in food processor or blender until very finely chopped.

ROASTED VEGETABLES, TURKEY SAUSAGE, AND MUSHROOM TORTELLINI

45

Substitute ravioli or a shaped pasta for the tortellini if you wish.

4 servings

1 cup each: cubed plum tomatoes, halved mushrooms, sliced zucchini, yellow summer squash, broccoli florets
12 ounces low-fat smoked turkey sausage, sliced (½-inch)
Vegetable cooking spray
1½ teaspoons dried Italian seasoning
Salt and pepper, to taste
1 package (9 ounces) fresh mushroom or herb tortellini, cooked, warm
1–2 tablespoons olive oil

1. Arrange vegetables and sausage in single layer on greased foil-lined jelly roll pan; spray generously with cooking spray. Sprinkle with Italian seasoning, salt, and pepper. Roast at 425 degrees until vegetables are browned, about 40 minutes, removing broccoli and sausage after about 20 minutes. Combine vegetables, sausage, and tortellini; drizzle with olive oil and toss.

Per Serving:
Calories: 386
% of calories from fat: 30
Fat (gm): 13.5
Saturated fat (gm): 4.1
Cholesterol (mg): 89.1
Sodium (mg): 959
Protein (gm): 28.7
Carbohydrate (gm): 42.2

Exchanges:
Milk: 0.0
Vegetable: 3.0
Fruit: 0.0
Bread: 2.0
Meat: 2.0
Fat: 1.0

HOME-STYLE TURKEY STEW

45 *A great family meal that's very fast to prepare!*

4 servings

12 ounces boneless, skinless turkey breast, cubed (¾-inch)

2 medium onions, cut into thin wedges

4 ounces mushrooms, halved

2 teaspoons olive oil

2 each: sliced carrots, cubed potatoes

1 can (14½ ounces) reduced-sodium fat-free chicken broth

1 teaspoon each: dried thyme leaves, celery seeds

1 cup frozen peas

Salt and pepper, to taste

Per Serving:
Calories: 158
% of calories from fat: 26
Fat (gm): 4.5
Saturated fat (gm): 1
Cholesterol (mg): 44.7
Sodium (mg): 63
Protein (gm): 21.1
Carbohydrate (gm): 7

Exchanges:
Milk: 0.0
Vegetable: 0.0
Fruit: 0.0
Bread: 0.5
Meat: 3.0
Fat: 0.0

1. Sauté turkey, onions, and mushrooms in oil in large saucepan until lightly browned, about 8 minutes. Add remaining ingredients, except peas, salt, and pepper; heat to boiling. Reduce heat and simmer, covered, until turkey and vegetables are tender, about 20 minutes, adding peas during last 5 minutes. Season to taste with salt and pepper.

TURKEY SANCOCHE

45 *Sancoche is a hearty stew of meats, fish, vegetables, and seasonings that hails from Latin America.*

4 servings

1 pound boneless, skinless turkey breast, cubed
(¾-inch)

1 cup each: cubed peeled sweet and white potato,
chopped onion

1 small butternut squash, peeled, cubed (¾-inch)

1 can (15 ounces) black beans, rinsed, drained

1 can (14½ ounces) reduced-sodium fat-free
chicken broth

1 jalapeño chili, minced

1 teaspoon each: annatto seeds, toasted cumin seeds

Salt and pepper, to taste

¼ cup coarsely chopped cashews

Per Serving:
Calories: 324
% of calories from fat: 18
Fat (gm): 7.2
Saturated fat (gm): 1.5
Cholesterol (mg): 44.7
Sodium (mg): 652
Protein (gm): 29.6
Carbohydrate (gm): 43.7

Exchanges:
Milk: 0.0
Vegetable: 0.0
Fruit: 0.0
Bread: 2.5
Meat: 2.0
Fat: 0.0

1. Combine all ingredients, except salt, pepper, and cashews, in large saucepan. Heat to boiling; reduce heat and simmer, covered, until turkey and vegetables are tender, about 20 minutes. Season to taste with salt and pepper. Sprinkle each bowl of stew with cashews.

TURKEY-WILD RICE STEW

In this recipe, we've combined two Native American foods, wild rice and turkey, to create a super supper.

4 servings

1 pound boneless, skinless turkey breast, cubed

½ cup each: chopped onion, sliced carrot

1 teaspoon olive oil

3 cups reduced-sodium fat-free chicken broth

½ cup wild rice

2 cups small broccoli florets

1 tablespoon chopped fresh or 1 teaspoon dried sage
leaves

Salt and pepper, to taste

Per Serving:
Calories: 250
% of calories from fat: 13
Fat (gm): 3.8
Saturated fat (gm): 0.9
Cholesterol (mg): 44.7
Sodium (mg): 196
Protein (gm): 29
Carbohydrate (gm): 24.6

Exchanges:
Milk: 0.0
Vegetable: 1.0
Fruit: 0.0
Bread: 1.0
Meat: 3.0
Fat: 0.0

1. Sauté turkey, onion, and carrot in oil in large saucepan until lightly browned, about 5 minutes. Add broth and wild rice; heat to boiling. Reduce heat and simmer, covered, until rice is tender, about 50 minutes; add broccoli and sage during last 10 minutes. Season to taste with salt and pepper.

EASY BAKED JAMBALAYA

45

This streamlined version of the Louisiana favorite boasts all that Cajun flavor.

8 servings

2 cups long-grain rice
1 pound smoked turkey sausage, sliced
1 pound boneless skinless chicken breast, cubed
1 pound mushrooms, halved
1 cup each: chopped green bell peppers, onion, celery
1 package (10 ounces) frozen sliced okra
1 jar (4 ounces) diced pimientos
2 cans (14½ ounces each) reduced-sodium diced
   tomatoes, undrained
1 teaspoon paprika
½ teaspoon each: salt, cayenne pepper
½ cup chicken broth or water

Per Serving:
Calories: 382
% of calories from fat: 15
Fat (gm): 6.3
Saturated fat (gm): 2.5
Cholesterol (mg): 62.9
Sodium (mg): 632
Protein (gm): 28.6
Carbohydrate (gm): 52.6

Exchanges:
Milk: 0.0
Vegetable: 1.0
Fruit: 0.0
Bread: 3.0
Meat: 3.0
Fat: 0.0

1. Mix all ingredients in greased 2½-quart casserole. Bake, covered, at 325 degrees until rice is tender with liquid absorbed, 1 to 1½ hours.

ITALIAN-STYLE TURKEY SAUSAGE AND FENNEL STEW

45 *Use your preference—sweet or hot Italian sausage—in this harvest garden stew.*

4 servings

12 ounces Italian turkey sausage

1 medium onion, cut into thin wedges

1 can (15 ounces) reduced-sodium diced tomatoes, undrained

1 cup reduced-sodium fat-free chicken broth

1 pound butternut squash, peeled, cubed (¾-inch)

12 Brussels sprouts, halved

2 parsnips, sliced

1 small fennel bulb, sliced

¼ teaspoon crushed red pepper

1 teaspoon dried Italian seasoning

Salt and pepper, to taste

Per Serving:
Calories: 310
% of calories from fat: 26
Fat (gm): 9.7
Saturated fat (gm): 2.6
Cholesterol (mg): 45.6
Sodium (mg): 780
Protein (gm): 21.8
Carbohydrate (gm): 39.4

Exchanges:
Milk: 0.0
Vegetable: 2.0
Fruit: 0.0
Bread: 2.0
Meat: 2.0
Fat: 0.0

1. Cook sausage and onion in lightly greased large saucepan until sausage is browned, about 10 minutes; remove sausage and slice. Return sausage to saucepan with remaining ingredients, except salt and pepper; heat to boiling. Reduce heat and simmer, covered, until vegetables are tender, about 20 minutes. Season to taste with salt and pepper.

FIVE

Fish
and
Seafood

CANNED CLAM CHOWDER

45 *This tasty clam chowder, conveniently made with canned clams, is ready to eat by the time you get the table set!*

6 servings

1 cup each: chopped onion, celery

¼ cup all-purpose flour

2 cups clam juice

2 cans (6½ ounces each) diced clams, undrained

1 can (6½ ounces) whole clams, undrained

1¾ cups peeled, cubed russet potatoes

2 slices turkey bacon, fried crisp, crumbled

1 teaspoon dried thyme leaves

1 bay leaf

1½–2 cups fat-free half-and-half or fat-free milk

Salt and pepper, to taste

Per Serving:
Calories: 195
% of calories from fat: 11
Fat (gm): 2.3
Saturated fat (gm): 0.6
Cholesterol (mg): 59.2
Sodium (mg): 261
Protein (gm): 13.4
Carbohydrate (gm): 30.3

Exchanges:
Milk: 0.0
Vegetable: 0.0
Fruit: 0.0
Bread: 1.5
Meat: 1.0
Fat: 0.0

1. Sauté onion and celery in lightly greased large saucepan until tender, 5 to 8 minutes. Stir in flour; cook 1 minute. Stir in remaining ingredients, except fat-free half-and-half, salt, and pepper; heat to boiling. Reduce heat and simmer, covered, until potatoes are tender, about 15 minutes. Stir in half-and-half; cook over medium heat until hot, about 5 minutes. Discard bay leaf; season to taste with salt and pepper.

EASY MANHATTAN CLAM CHOWDER

45 *Enjoy this quick version of the popular clam chowder.*

4 servings

4 slices bacon, diced

1 cup each: chopped onion, cubed peeled potatoes

¾ cup sliced carrots

2 tablespoons flour

1 cup clam juice

1 can (15 ounces) reduced-sodium diced tomatoes, undrained

½ teaspoon dried thyme leaves

2 cans (6 ounces each) minced clams, undrained

Salt and pepper, to taste

Per Serving:
Calories: 187
% of calories from fat: 11
Fat (gm): 2.4
Saturated fat (gm): 0.4
Cholesterol (mg): 33.4
Sodium (mg): 305
Protein (gm): 14.9
Carbohydrate (gm): 27.5

Exchanges:
Milk: 0.0
Vegetable: 2.0
Fruit: 0.0
Bread: 1.0
Meat: 1.0
Fat: 0.0

1. Cook bacon and onion in lightly greased large saucepan over medium heat until bacon is crisp and onion tender, about 5 minutes. Add potatoes and carrots and cook 5 minutes; add flour and cook 1 minute. Add remaining ingredients, except salt and pepper, and heat to boiling; reduce heat and simmer, covered, until vegetables are tender, about 15 minutes. Season to taste with salt and pepper.

CREAMY CLAM AND BROCCOLI CHOWDER

45 *Pureed white beans give this soup a velvety smooth texture—a nutritional boost too! Use rinsed, drained canned beans, if you prefer.*

4 servings

2 cups cooked navy or other white beans, divided

1 can (14 ounces) reduced-sodium fat-free chicken broth, divided

4 teaspoons minced garlic

1 teaspoon olive oil

1 cup each: broccoli florets, chopped plum tomatoes

2 cans (6½ ounces) minced clams, undrained

2 tablespoons each: dry white wine (optional), chopped fresh or 1 tablespoon dried dill weed

Salt and pepper, to taste

Per Serving:
Calories: 336
% of calories from fat: 11
Fat (gm): 4.1
Saturated fat (gm): 0.6
Cholesterol (mg): 62.2
Sodium (mg): 199
Protein (gm): 36.4
Carbohydrate (gm): 37.6

Exchanges:
Milk: 0.0
Vegetable: 1.0
Fruit: 0.0
Bread: 2.0
Meat: 3.0
Fat: 0.0

1. Process 1 cup beans and ½ cup broth in food processor or blender until smooth. Sauté garlic in oil in large saucepan 1 minute; stir in pureed beans and remaining ingredients, except salt and pepper. Heat to boiling; reduce heat and simmer, covered until broccoli is tender, about 10 minutes. Season to taste with salt and pepper.

SPICY CRAB AND SCALLOP CHOWDER

45 *The flavor kick in this seafood chowder comes from pickling spice!*

4 servings

1 medium onion, chopped

1 rib celery, chopped

1 tablespoon margarine or butter

1½ cups clam juice

1 can (14 ounces) reduced-sodium stewed
tomatoes, undrained

2 teaspoons pickling spice, tied in cheesecloth

1 can (4 ounces) lump crabmeat, drained

8 ounces bay scallops

¼–½ cup 2% reduced-fat milk

Salt and pepper, to taste

Per Serving:
Calories: 144
% of calories from fat: 26
Fat (gm): 4.3
Saturated fat (gm): 0.8
Cholesterol (mg): 50.4
Sodium (mg): 485
Protein (gm): 18.2
Carbohydrate (gm): 8.9

Exchanges:
Milk: 0.0
Vegetable: 1.0
Fruit: 0.0
Bread: 0.0
Meat: 2.0
Fat: 0.0

1. Sauté onion and celery in margarine in large saucepan until softened. Add clam juice, tomatoes with liquid, and pickling spice tied in a cheesecloth bag. Heat to boiling; stir in crabmeat, scallops, and milk. Simmer, covered, until scallops are cooked and opaque, about 5 minutes. Discard pickling spice. Season to taste with salt and pepper.

CRAB CHOWDER WITH SNOW PEAS

45 *This aromatic chowder gets its flavor essence from jasmine rice, gingerroot, and sorrel.*

4 servings

2 cups clam juice

2½ cups water

½ cup jasmine or basmati rice

2 green onions, sliced

1 tablespoon minced gingerroot

2 cans (4 ounces each) lump crabmeat

2 cups each: snow peas, halved crosswise,
torn sorrel or kale leaves

1 tablespoon dry sherry (optional)

Per Serving:
Calories: 209
% of calories from fat: 8
Fat (gm): 1.9
Saturated fat (gm): 0.5
Cholesterol (mg): 52.7
Sodium (mg): 491
Protein (gm): 17.6
Carbohydrate (gm): 28.8

Exchanges:
Milk: 0.0
Vegetable: 1.0
Fruit: 0.0
Bread: 1.0
Meat: 2.0
Fat: 0.0

½ cup 2% reduced-fat milk

Salt and pepper, to taste

1. Heat clam juice and water to boiling in large saucepan. Stir in rice, green onions, and gingerroot; reduce heat and simmer, covered, until rice is tender, about 25 minutes. Stir in remaining ingredients, except salt and pepper; simmer until snow peas are crisp-tender, 3 to 4 minutes. Season to taste with salt and pepper.

LOBSTER AND SHRIMP CHOWDER

45 *For easiest preparation, purchase cooked lobster and shrimp in the seafood department of your supermarket.*

4 servings

2 large Yukon gold potatoes, peeled, cubed

1 medium onion, chopped

1 can (15 ounces) reduced-sodium diced
   tomatoes, undrained

1½ cups clam juice

8 ounces cooked lobster, cut into small chunks

4 ounces cooked peeled, deveined small shrimp

1 teaspoon dried tarragon leaves

1 cup 1% low-fat milk

¼ cup chopped parsley

Salt and pepper, to taste

Per Serving:
Calories: 210
% of calories from fat: 9
Fat (gm): 2.1
Saturated fat (gm): 0.9
Cholesterol (mg): 100.7
Sodium (mg): 519
Protein (gm): 22.4
Carbohydrate (gm): 25.7

Exchanges:
Milk: 0.0
Vegetable: 1.0
Fruit: 0.0
Bread: 1.0
Meat: 2.0
Fat: 0.0

1. Combine potatoes, onion, tomatoes with liquid, and clam juice in large saucepan. Heat to boiling; reduce heat and simmer, covered, until potatoes are tender, about 10 minutes. Add remaining ingredients, except salt and pepper, and simmer, uncovered, until hot, about 5 minutes. Season to taste with salt and pepper.

CURRIED SCALLOP AND POTATO CHOWDER

45 *This chowder has a lively curry flavor and a bright yellow color!*

4 servings

1 bottle (11 ounces) clam juice
½ cup dry white wine or water
1 pound potatoes, peeled, cubed
1 teaspoon curry powder
½ teaspoon minced garlic
1 pound sea scallops
1 cup frozen peas
¼–½ cup 1% low-fat milk
Salt and pepper, to taste

Per Serving:
Calories: 251
% of calories from fat: 7
Fat (gm): 1.8
Saturated fat (gm): 0.2
Cholesterol (mg): 49.3
Sodium (mg): 482
Protein (gm): 25.6
Carbohydrate (gm): 29.4

Exchanges:
Milk: 0.0
Vegetable: 0.0
Fruit: 0.0
Bread: 2.0
Meat: 3.0
Fat: 0.0

1. Heat clam juice, wine, potatoes, curry powder, and garlic to boiling in large saucepan; reduce heat and simmer, covered, until potatoes are tender, about 10 minutes. Process about half the mixture in food processor or blender until smooth; return to pan. Stir in scallops, peas and milk; cook over medium heat until scallops are cooked, about 5 minutes. Season to taste with salt and pepper.

SEAFOOD SAMPLER

45 *This sensibly seasoned chowder is great with Herb Croutons (see p. 533).*

4 servings

½ cup each: chopped yellow bell pepper,
  chopped onion
1 teaspoon olive oil
1 can (15 ounces) reduced-sodium diced tomatoes
  undrained
2 medium potatoes, cubed
½ cup dry white wine or water
½ teaspoon celery seeds
1 teaspoon herbes de Provence or dried
  Italian seasoning
8 ounces haddock or halibut, cubed (1-inch)

Per Serving:
Calories: 231
% of calories from fat: 10
Fat (gm): 2.5
Saturated fat (gm): 0.4
Cholesterol (mg): 88
Sodium (mg): 172
Protein (gm): 23.7
Carbohydrate (gm): 24.7

Exchanges:
Milk: 0.0
Vegetable: 1.0
Fruit: 0.0
Bread: 1.0
Meat: 3.0
Fat: 0.0

4 ounces each: bay scallops, peeled deveined shrimp
½ teaspoon hot pepper sauce
Salt, to taste

1. Sauté pepper and onion in oil in large saucepan until lightly browned, about 5 minutes. Add tomatoes with liquid, potatoes, wine, and herbs; heat to boiling. Reduce heat and simmer, covered, until potatoes are tender, about 10 minutes. Add seafood; simmer until haddock is tender and flakes with a fork, about 5 minutes. Stir in hot pepper sauce; season to taste with salt.

HALIBUT AND POTATO CHOWDER

45 *This chunky chowder has a thick, flavorful base of pureed vegetables.*

4 servings

1 each: chopped large onion, rib celery
1½ cups clam juice
4 cups cubed, peeled potatoes
1 pound halibut, cubed (¾-inch)
1 carrot, shredded
1 cup 1% low-fat milk
1 teaspoon dried savory leaves
½–1 teaspoons hot pepper sauce
Salt, to taste
2 slices bacon, cooked crisp, crumbled

Per Serving:
Calories: 394
% of calories from fat: 12
Fat (gm): 5.4
Saturated fat (gm): 1.4
Cholesterol (mg): 45.7
Sodium (mg): 430
Protein (gm): 31.4
Carbohydrate (gm): 55.4

Exchanges:
Milk: 0.0
Vegetable: 1.0
Fruit: 0.0
Bread: 3.0
Meat: 3.0
Fat: 0.0

1. Sauté onion and celery in lightly greased large saucepan until light browned, about 5 minutes. Stir in clam juice and potatoes and heat to boiling; reduce heat and simmer, covered, until potatoes are tender, about 10 minutes. Process about half the mixture in food processor or blender until smooth; return to saucepan. Heat to boiling; add remaining ingredients, except salt and bacon. Reduce heat and simmer, covered, until halibut is tender and flakes with a fork, about 5 minutes. Season to taste with salt; sprinkle each bowl of soup with bacon.

MONKFISH-CHEDDAR CHOWDER

45 *Use any favorite firm-textured fish in this creamy, cheesy chowder.*

4 servings

½ cup each: chopped onion, sliced carrots

2 teaspoons margarine or butter

1 pound potatoes, peeled, cubed

1 can (14 ounces) reduced-sodium fat-free
   chicken broth

1 pound monkfish, cubed (¾-inch)

½ cup each: fat-free milk, shredded reduced-fat
   Cheddar cheese (2 ounces)

½–1 teaspoon hot pepper sauce

Salt, to taste

Chopped chives, as garnish

Per Serving:
Calories: 274
% of calories from fat: 19
Fat (gm): 5.9
Saturated fat (gm): 1.8
Cholesterol (mg): 35.4
Sodium (mg): 344
Protein (gm): 24.9
Carbohydrate (gm): 29.5

Exchanges:
Milk: 0.0
Vegetable: 0.0
Fruit: 0.0
Bread: 1.5
Meat: 3.0
Fat: 0.0

1. Sauté onion and carrots in margarine in large saucepan until tender, 3 to 4 minutes; add potatoes and broth. Heat to boiling; reduce heat and simmer, covered, until potatoes are tender, about 10 minutes. Process about ½ the mixture in food processor or blender until smooth; return to saucepan and heat to boiling. Add fish and milk; reduce heat and simmer, covered, until fish is tender and flakes with a fork, about 5 minutes. Stir in cheese and hot pepper sauce; stir over low heat until cheese is melted. Season to taste with salt; sprinkle each bowl of soup with chives.

SALMON AND ROASTED PEPPER CHOWDER

45 *Salmon is paired with corn and seasoned with jalapeño chilies, cumin, and oregano for a fast and fabulous feast.*

4 servings

2 cups each: whole kernel corn, reduced-sodium vegetable broth

2 medium potatoes, peeled, cubed

1 cup chopped roasted red pepper

½–1 jalapeño chili, minced

2 teaspoons minced garlic

1 teaspoon each: cumin seeds, dried oregano leaves

12 ounces salmon steaks, cubed (1-inch)

Salt and pepper, to taste

Per Serving:
Calories: 259
% of calories from fat: 12
Fat (gm): 3.4
Saturated fat (gm): 0.5
Cholesterol (mg): 42.8
Sodium (mg): 197
Protein (gm): 20.5
Carbohydrate (gm): 36.4

1. Combine all ingredients, except salmon, salt, and pepper in large saucepan. Heat to boiling; reduce heat and simmer, covered, until potatoes are tender, about 10 minutes. Add salmon; simmer until salmon is tender and flakes with a fork, about 5 minutes. Season to taste with salt and pepper.

Exchanges:
Milk: 0.0
Vegetable: 0.0
Fruit: 0.0
Bread: 2.0
Meat: 2.0
Fat: 0.0

CIOPPINO

Our version of this classic Italian soup is made with shellfish. Clams in their shells are traditionally used, but canned whole clams may be substituted, if you prefer.

6 servings

1 cup each: thinly sliced onion, green onions, green bell pepper

1 tablespoon each: minced garlic, olive oil

1 can (14½ ounces) reduced-sodium diced tomatoes, undrained

1 cup each: clam juice, water

½ cup dry white wine or clam juice

1 teaspoon each: dried tarragon and thyme leaves

¼ teaspoon dried rosemary leaves, crushed

1 bay leaf

1 pound crabmeat or firm white fish, cubed

8–12 ounces shrimp, peeled, deveined

18 clams in shells, scrubbed

Salt and pepper, to taste

Per Serving:
Calories: 210
% of calories from fat: 19
Fat (gm): 4.3
Saturated fat (gm): 0.6
Cholesterol (mg): 130.6
Sodium (mg): 276
Protein (gm): 24.1
Carbohydrate (gm): 10.2

Exchanges:
Milk: 0.0
Vegetable: 2.0
Fruit: 0.0
Bread: 0.0
Meat: 3.0
Fat: 0.0

1. Sauté onion, green onions, bell pepper, and garlic in oil in large saucepan, over low heat, until tender, 5 to 8 minutes. Add tomatoes with liquid, clam juice, water, wine, and herbs. Heat to boiling; reduce heat and simmer, covered, 20 minutes. Add crabmeat, shrimp, and clams; heat to boiling. Reduce heat and simmer until shrimp are cooked, and clams have opened, about 8 minutes. Discard bay leaf and any clams that have not opened. Season to taste with salt and pepper.

EASY ITALIAN FISH SOUP

45 *A surprisingly simple combination of ingredients yields savory results in this healthful, hurry-up meal.*

4 servings

1 each: chopped large onion, rib celery

½ teaspoon minced garlic

1 tablespoon olive oil

1 can (14½ ounces) reduced-sodium diced tomatoes, undrained

1 bottle (8 ounces) clam juice

¼ cup dry white wine or clam juice

¼ teaspoon dried marjoram leaves

1 pound halibut or other lean, firm fish, cubed (1-inch)

¼ cup chopped parsley

Salt and pepper, to taste

Per Serving:
Calories: 206
% of calories from fat: 27
Fat (gm): 6.3
Saturated fat (gm): 0.9
Cholesterol (mg): 36.1
Sodium (mg): 242
Protein (gm): 25.4
Carbohydrate (gm): 9.7

Exchanges:
Milk: 0.0
Vegetable: 2.0
Fruit: 0.0
Bread: 0.0
Meat: 3.0
Fat: 0.0

1. Sauté onion, celery, and garlic in oil in large saucepan over medium heat until lightly browned, about 5 minutes. Stir in tomatoes with liquid, clam juice, wine, and marjoram; heat to boiling. Reduce heat and simmer, covered, 20 minutes; add halibut and simmer until fish is tender and flakes with a fork, about 5 minutes. Stir in parsley; season to taste with salt and pepper.

CRAB CAKES WITH POBLANO CHILI SAUCE

45 *Peeled, cooked shrimp or imitation crabmeat can easily be substituted for all or part of the crab.*

4 servings

12 ounces Alaskan king, lump or claw crabmeat, finely chopped

½ each: finely chopped small onion, medium tomato

½ small jalapeño chili, minced

1 egg white

2–4 tablespoons unseasoned dry bread crumbs

½ teaspoon each: dried oregano leaves, salt

Flour or unseasoned dry bread crumbs

1 cup Poblano Chili Sauce (½ recipe) (see p. 190)

Per Serving:
Calories: 133
% of calories from fat: 10
Fat (gm): 1.4
Saturated fat (gm): 0.2
Cholesterol (mg): 35.7
Sodium (mg): 793
Protein (gm): 18.6
Carbohydrate (gm): 12.1

Exchanges:
Milk: 0.0
Vegetable: 2.0
Fruit: 0.0
Bread: 0.0
Meat: 2.0
Fat: 0.0

1. Combine crabmeat, onion, tomato, jalapeño chili, and egg white in small bowl; mix in bread crumbs, oregano, and salt. Shape into 4 patties about ½ inch thick; coat lightly with flour. Cook patties in lightly greased large skillet over medium heat until cooked through and lightly browned, 3 to 4 minutes on each side. Serve with Poblano Chili Sauce.

PASTA AND CRABMEAT SALAD WITH FRUIT VINAIGRETTE

45 *Any firm-textured fish, such as halibut or haddock, can be substituted for the crabmeat; surimi (imitation crabmeat) can also be used.*

4 servings

6 ounces lump crabmeat

½ cup each: chopped seeded cucumber, medium tomato

1 cup cooked peas

8 ounces farfalle (bow tie) pasta, cooked, room temperature

Fruit Vinaigrette (recipe follows)

Per Serving:
Calories: 330
% of calories from fat: 16
Fat (gm): 6.1
Saturated fat (gm): 0.9
Cholesterol (mg): 42.5
Sodium (mg): 267
Protein (gm): 19.4
Carbohydrate (gm): 50.1

Exchanges:
Milk: 0.0
Vegetable: 1.0
Fruit: 0.0
Bread: 3.0
Meat: 1.0
Fat: 0.5

1. Combine all ingredients and toss.

Fruit Vinaigrette
Makes about ⅔ cup

¼ cup orange juice

3 tablespoons raspberry red wine vinegar

2 tablespoons each: lime juice, finely chopped cilantro, parsley

1 tablespoon olive oil

1 teaspoon grated lime zest, minced garlic

¼ teaspoon each: ground nutmeg, salt

⅛ teaspoon each: cayenne and black pepper

1. Mix all ingredients.

45-MINUTE PREPARATION TIP: Begin cooking farfalle before preparing the rest of the recipe.

SCALLOPS WITH APPLES AND PEA PODS

45 *This colorful dish with an apple accent is delicious served over steamed rice, rice noodles, or Chinese egg noodles.*

4 servings

3 small apples, unpeeled, thinly sliced

1 each: chopped medium onion, red bell pepper

3 ounces snow peas, trimmed

2 tablespoons vegetable oil, divided

12 ounces scallops

¼ cup apple cider

2 teaspoons cornstarch

1 tablespoon reduced-sodium soy sauce

Salt and pepper, to taste

Per Serving:
Calories: 238
% of calories from fat: 30
Fat (gm): 8.3
Saturated fat (gm): 1
Cholesterol (mg): 36.2
Sodium (mg): 315
Protein (gm): 17.5
Carbohydrate (gm): 26

Exchanges:
Milk: 0.0
Vegetable: 0.0
Fruit: 1.5
Bread: 0.0
Meat: 2.0
Fat: 1.0

1. Stir-fry apples, onion, bell pepper, and snow peas in 1 tablespoon oil in wok or large skillet over medium-high heat until crisp-tender, about 3 minutes. Remove from wok. Add scallops and stir-fry in remaining 1 tablespoon oil until cooked and opaque, about 4 minutes. Stir in combined cider, cornstarch, and soy sauce, and cook until mixture boils and thickens, about 1 minute. Stir in apple mixture; stir-fry 2 minutes. Season to taste with salt and pepper.

SHRIMP WITH ARTICHOKES AND PEPPERS

45 *This skillet supper is quick, easy, and brimming with flavor.*

6 servings

2 cups frozen stir-fry pepper blend

1 teaspoon minced garlic

1 tablespoon olive oil

1 can (15 ounces) reduced-sodium chunky
   tomato sauce

1 can (14 ounces) artichoke hearts, drained, quartered

3 tablespoons dry sherry (optional)

2 teaspoons dried Italian seasoning

12 ounces medium shrimp, peeled, deveined

Salt and pepper, to taste

8 ounces penne, cooked, warm

Per Serving:
Calories: 277
% of calories from fat: 11
Fat (gm): 3.4
Saturated fat (gm): 0.5
Cholesterol (mg): 87
Sodium (mg): 292
Protein (gm): 17.4
Carbohydrate (gm): 40.5

Exchanges:
Milk: 0.0
Vegetable: 2.0
Fruit: 0.0
Bread: 2.0
Meat: 1.5
Fat: 0.0

1. Sauté pepper blend and garlic in oil in large skillet until tender, about 5 minutes; add tomato sauce, artichoke hearts, and sherry. Heat to boiling; reduce heat and simmer, covered, 5 minutes. Add Italian seasoning and shrimp; simmer until shrimp are cooked, about 5 minutes. Season to taste with salt and pepper; serve over penne.

SHRIMP DE JONGHE

For an elegant presentation, assemble and bake the shrimp in individual shell dishes.

4 servings

2 tablespoons finely chopped shallots or onion

4 cloves garlic, minced

3 tablespoons margarine or butter

2 tablespoons dry sherry (optional)

1 tablespoon lemon juice

¼ teaspoon each: dried marjoram and tarragon leaves

Pinch each: ground nutmeg, cayenne pepper

1 cup fresh white bread crumbs

¼ cup finely chopped parsley

Salt and pepper, to taste

1 pound peeled, deveined shrimp

3 cups cooked rice, warm

Per Serving:
Calories: 370
% of calories from fat: 27
Fat (gm): 10.8
Saturated fat (gm): 2.1
Cholesterol (mg): 129.1
Sodium (mg): 287
Protein (gm): 22
Carbohydrate (gm): 42.8

Exchanges:
Milk: 0.0
Vegetable: 1.0
Fruit: 0.0
Bread: 2.5
Meat: 2.0
Fat: 1.0

1. Sauté shallots and garlic in margarine in medium skillet until tender, 2 to 3 minutes. Stir in sherry, lemon juice, and seasonings; remove from heat. Add bread crumbs and parsley and toss; season to taste with salt and pepper. Sprinkle crumb mixture over shrimp in shell dishes or 11 x 7-inch baking dish. Bake at 450 degrees until shrimp are cooked, about 10 minutes. Serve with rice.

45-MINUTE PREPARATION TIP: Begin cooking rice before preparing the rest of the recipe.

SHRIMP DIANE

Serve this flavorful shrimp dish over basmati rice, couscous, or angel hair pasta.

4 servings

½ cup sliced mushrooms

2 tablespoons minced shallots

1 tablespoon margarine or butter

1 can (15½ ounces) quartered artichoke hearts, drained

¼ cup each: dry white wine or reduced-sodium
chicken broth, chopped chives, pimiento
12–16 ounces peeled, deveined shrimp
Salt and pepper, to taste
Chopped parsley, as garnish

Per Serving:
Calories: 149
% of calories from fat: 23
Fat (gm): 3.6
Saturated fat (gm): 0.8
Cholesterol (mg): 130
Sodium (mg): 460
Protein (gm): 17.2
Carbohydrate (gm): 8.2

1. Sauté mushrooms and shallots in margarine
in large skillet until tender, about 5 minutes; add
artichoke hearts, wine, chives, and pimiento and
cook, covered, over medium heat 2 minutes. Add
shrimp and cook until shrimp are cooked, 3 to 5
minutes. Season to taste with salt and pepper.
Sprinkle with parsley.

Exchanges:
Milk: 0.0
Vegetable: 1.0
Fruit: 0.0
Bread: 0.0
Meat: 2.0
Fat: 0.0

SHRIMP WITH GARLIC

The garlic is cooked very slowly, until golden and tender, giving the dish it's special flavor.

4 servings

1 large head garlic
2 tablespoons olive or vegetable oil
1 pound peeled, deveined shrimp
½ lime
2 tablespoons finely chopped cilantro
Salt and pepper, to taste
Yellow Salsa Rice (see p. 412)
4 corn or flour tortillas (6-inch)

Per Serving:
Calories: 388
% of calories from fat: 20
Fat (gm): 8.5
Saturated fat (gm): 1.3
Cholesterol (mg): 131.6
Sodium (mg): 340
Protein (gm): 21.7
Carbohydrate (gm): 55.1

Exchanges:
Milk: 0.0
Vegetable: 0.0
Fruit: 0.0
Bread: 3.5
Meat: 2.5
Fat: 0.0

1. Peel garlic cloves and cut into halves; cook in oil in medium
skillet over low heat until garlic is soft and golden, 15 to 20 minutes;
remove from skillet. Add shrimp to skillet; cook over medium heat
until shrimp are cooked, about 5 minutes. Return garlic to skillet;
cook over low heat 1 to 2 minutes. Squeeze lime juice over and
sprinkle with cilantro; season to taste with salt and pepper. Serve
with Yellow Salsa Rice and tortillas.

SPRING VEGETABLE AND SHRIMP STIR-FRY

45 *The best of spring's bounty, seasoned with fresh ginger, sesame oil, and tamari soy sauce.*

4 servings

1 pound asparagus, sliced (1½-inch)

1 cup each: sliced small red potatoes, mushrooms

½ cup each: chopped onion, red bell pepper

2–4 teaspoons minced garlic, gingerroot

½ cup reduced-sodium fat-free chicken broth

12–16 ounces peeled deveined shrimp

4 teaspoons cornstarch

¼ cup cold water

1–2 tablespoons reduced-sodium tamari soy sauce

1–2 teaspoons Asian sesame oil

Salt and pepper, to taste

3 cups cooked brown and wild rice

Per Serving:
Calories: 310
% of calories from fat: 10
Fat (gm): 3.5
Saturated fat (gm): 0.5
Cholesterol (mg): 130
Sodium (mg): 537
Protein (gm): 23
Carbohydrate (gm): 48.9

Exchanges:
Milk: 0.0
Vegetable: 3.0
Fruit: 0.0
Bread: 2.0
Meat: 2.0
Fat: 0.0

1. Stir-fry vegetables, garlic, and gingerroot in lightly greased wok or large skillet until almost tender, about 10 minutes. Add broth and shrimp and heat to boiling; reduce heat and simmer, covered, until vegetables are crisp-tender and shrimp are cooked, 3 to 5 minutes. Heat to boiling; stir in combined cornstarch and water, stirring until thickened, about 1 minute. Stir in soy sauce and sesame oil; season to taste with salt and pepper. Serve with rice.

SHRIMP AND CHEESE ROTOLO WITH MANY-CLOVES GARLIC SAUCE

45 *Some people prefer cutting the lasagne noodles into halves before filling, as they are easier to handle when eating. If cut, spread each noodle half with ½ to 2 tablespoons of the cheese mixture.*

6 servings

1 pound peeled, deveined cooked shrimp, chopped

1¼ cups reduced-fat ricotta cheese

3–4 cloves garlic, minced

¾ teaspoon dried marjoram leaves

½ teaspoon each: dried thyme leaves, salt

¼ teaspoon pepper

12 lasagne noodles (10 ounces), cooked, room temperature

Many-Cloves Garlic Sauce (see p. 17)

Per Serving:
Calories: 323
% of calories from fat: 16
Fat (gm): 5.9
Saturated fat (gm): 1.7
Cholesterol (mg): 128.1
Sodium (mg): 403
Protein (gm): 25
Carbohydrate (gm): 40

Exchanges:
Milk: 0.0
Vegetable: 0.0
Fruit: 0.0
Bread: 2.0
Meat: 3.0
Fat: 0.0

1. Mix shrimp, cheese, garlic, herbs, salt, and pepper. Spread 3 to 4 tablespoons of mixture evenly on each noodle; roll up and place, seam sides down in baking dish. Spoon Many Cloves Garlic Sauce over rotolo; bake, loosely covered, at 350 degrees until hot, 20 to 30 minutes.

SPICY SHRIMP AND RICE STEW

This full-bodied shrimp and rice stew is seasoned with a creative combination of spices.

6 servings

1 large onion, chopped

2 large garlic cloves, minced

2 teaspoons olive oil

3 cups reduced-sodium fat-free chicken broth

⅓ cup each: chopped celery, carrot, green bell pepper

1 can (14½ ounces) reduced-sodium diced tomatoes, undrained

1 large bay leaf

1½ teaspoons dried thyme leaves

¾ teaspoon paprika

1 cup uncooked long-grain rice

1 pound medium shrimp, peeled, deveined

Salt and cayenne pepper, to taste

Per Serving:
Calories: 217
% of calories from fat: 9
Fat (gm): 2.1
Saturated fat (gm): 0.4
Cholesterol (mg): 87.5
Sodium (mg): 217
Protein (gm): 14.2
Carbohydrate (gm): 34.6

Exchanges:
Milk: 0.0
Vegetable: 1.0
Fruit: 0.0
Bread: 2.0
Meat: 1.0
Fat: 0.0

1. Sauté onion and garlic in oil in large saucepan until onion is tender, about 5 minutes. Add remaining ingredients, except rice, shrimp, salt, and cayenne pepper and heat to boiling; reduce heat and simmer, covered, 10 minutes. Heat to boiling and add rice; reduce heat and simmer, covered, until rice is tender, about 20 minutes. Add shrimp; simmer, covered, until shrimp are cooked, about 5 minutes. Discard bay leaf; season to taste with salt and cayenne pepper.

SHRIMP AND SAUSAGE GUMBO

45 *Okra plays a dual role in this speedy version of the bayou favorite—it thickens the gumbo while giving it a characteristic Creole flavor.*

4 servings

4 ounces smoked turkey sausage, halved, thinly sliced

1 red bell pepper, chopped

1 clove garlic, minced

1 teaspoon margarine or butter

2 cans (14 ounces each) reduced-sodium stewed tomatoes, undrained

8 ounces each: fresh or frozen sliced okra, peeled deveined shrimp

½ teaspoon crushed red pepper

Salt, to taste

3 cups cooked rice, warm

Per Serving:
Calories: 316
% of calories from fat: 14
Fat (gm): 5
Saturated fat (gm): 1.2
Cholesterol (mg): 104.4
Sodium (mg): 395
Protein (gm): 19.9
Carbohydrate (gm): 48.9

Exchanges:
Milk: 0.0
Vegetable: 3.0
Fruit: 0.0
Bread: 2.0
Meat: 2.0
Fat: 0.0

1. Sauté sausage, bell pepper, and garlic in margarine in large saucepan until browned, about 5 minute. Stir in tomatoes with liquid, okra, shrimp, and crushed red pepper; heat to boiling. Reduce heat and simmer, covered, until shrimp are cooked and pink, about 5 minutes. Season to taste with salt. Serve over rice in bowls.

SHRIMP TOSTADAS

Serve these great tostadas with Zucchini from Puebla, Yellow Salsa Rice or Refried Beans (see pp. 499, 412, 393).

4 servings

12–16 ounces peeled, deveined medium shrimp

1 small onion, chopped

½ serrano chili, finely chopped

1 cup Chili Tomato Sauce (see p. 186), warm

4 corn tortillas (6-inch)

2 cups chopped romaine lettuce

1 medium tomato, chopped

¼ cup crumbled Mexican white or fat-free feta cheese

Guacamole (see p. 7)

Per Serving:
Calories: 283
% of calories from fat: 29
Fat (gm): 9.3
Saturated fat (gm): 1.4
Cholesterol (mg): 129
Sodium (mg): 299
Protein (gm): 23.0
Carbohydrate (gm): 28.9

1. Reserve 4 shrimp for garnish; coarsely chop remaining shrimp. Cook whole and chopped shrimp, onion, and serrano chili in lightly greased medium saucepan until shrimp are cooked, 3 to 5 minutes. Stir Chili Tomato Sauce into shrimp mixture.

Exchanges:
Milk: 0.0
Vegetable: 0.0
Fruit: 0.0
Bread: 2.0
Meat: 2.0
Fat: 0.5

2. Cook tortillas in lightly greased medium skillet until crisp and browned, about 1 minute on each side. Top tortillas with lettuce and tomato; spoon shrimp mixture over. Sprinkle with crumbled cheese; top each tostada with Guacamole and a whole shrimp.

SHRIMP AND CRAB ENCHILADAS WITH PASILLA CHILI SAUCE

The rich Pasilla Chili Sauce is creamy in texture, slightly smoky in flavor; it is also excellent served with grilled chicken breast or lean pork.

4 servings

8 ounces peeled, deveined cooked shrimp, coarsely chopped

4 ounces chopped Alaskan King or lump crabmeat or peeled, deveined shrimp

Pasilla Chili Sauce (recipe follows)

8 flour tortillas (6-inch)

½ cup (2 ounces) shredded fat-free Cheddar cheese

¼ cup finely chopped cilantro

Per Serving:
Calories: 318
% of calories from fat: 13
Fat (gm): 4.5
Saturated fat (gm): 0.7
Cholesterol (mg): 101.9
Sodium (mg): 722
Protein (gm): 28.3
Carbohydrate (gm): 41.2

Exchanges:
Milk: 0.0
Vegetable: 0.5
Fruit: 0.0
Bread: 2.0
Meat: 3.0
Fat: 0.0

1. Combine shrimp, crabmeat, and ¾ cup Pasilla Chili Sauce; divide mixture on tortillas and roll up. Place tortillas, seam sides down, in greased 11 x 7 inch baking dish. Spoon remaining Pasilla Chili Sauce over enchiladas; sprinkle with cheese. Bake, uncovered, at 350 degrees until hot, about 20 minutes. Sprinkle with cilantro.

Pasilla Chili Sauce
Makes about 2 cups

3 pasilla chilies
2 medium tomatoes, coarsely chopped
1 small onion, coarsely chopped
½ teaspoon sugar
1 cup fat-free sour cream
Salt and pepper, to taste

1. Cook chilies in small lightly greased small skillet over medium heat until soft; remove and discard stems, seeds, and veins. Process chilies, tomatoes, onion, and sugar in blender until smooth. Cook mixture in lightly greased medium skillet over medium heat until thickened, about 5 minutes. Reduce heat to low; stir in sour cream and cook until hot, about 2 minutes. Season to taste with salt and pepper.

SEAFOOD NEWBURG

45 *Any shellfish or lean white fish can be used in this classic Newburg.*

4 servings

8 ounces each: peeled deveined shrimp, bay scallops
½ cup water
¼ cup finely chopped shallots or onion
2 tablespoons margarine or butter
¼ cup all-purpose flour
1½ cups fat-free half-and-half or fat-free milk
1 egg yolk
1–2 tablespoons dry sherry (optional)
Pinch each: ground nutmeg, cayenne pepper
Salt, to taste
4 slices toast, cut diagonally into halves
Chopped parsley, as garnish

Per Serving:
Calories: 326
% of calories from fat: 26
Fat (gm): 9.1
Saturated fat (gm): 1.8
Cholesterol (mg): 164.8
Sodium (mg): 495
Protein (gm): 26.7
Carbohydrate (gm): 29.9

Exchanges:
Milk: 0.8
Vegetable: 0.0
Fruit: 0.0
Bread: 2.0
Meat: 3.0
Fat: 0.5

1. Simmer shrimp and scallops in water in medium saucepan, covered, until cooked, 3 to 5 minutes. Drain, reserving liquid.

2. Sauté shallots in margarine in medium saucepan until tender, 2 to 3 minutes; mix in flour and cook 1 minute. Whisk in half-and-half and reserved cooking liquid; heat to boiling, whisking until thickened, about 1 minute. Whisk about half the mixture into egg yolk in small bowl; whisk egg mixture into saucepan. Whisk over low heat 30 seconds. Stir in shrimp, scallops, sherry, nutmeg, and cayenne pepper; cook 2 to 3 minutes. Season to taste with salt. Serve on toast; sprinkle with parsley.

CIOPPINO PASTA

The seafood is added to the sauce toward the end of the cooking time to avoid overcooking. Serve in bowls to accommodate the generous serving of sauce.

8 servings

1 cup each: chopped green bell pepper, onion, mushrooms
4 cloves garlic, minced
1 tablespoon olive oil
3 cups chopped tomatoes
½ cup dry white wine or clam juice
1 tablespoon tomato paste
2 tablespoons chopped parsley
2 teaspoons each: dried oregano and basil leaves
1 teaspoon ground turmeric
8 ounces each: sea scallops, cubed crabmeat (½-inch)
4 ounces halibut or haddock, cubed (1-inch)
12 mussels in the shell, scrubbed
½ teaspoon each: salt, pepper
12 ounces fettuccine, cooked, warm

Per Serving:
Calories: 387
% of calories from fat: 24
Fat (gm): 10.2
Saturated fat (gm): 2.1
Cholesterol (mg): 80.9
Sodium (mg): 514
Protein (gm): 24.5
Carbohydrate (gm): 47

Exchanges:
Milk: 0.0
Vegetable: 2.0
Fruit: 0.0
Bread: 2.0
Meat: 2.0
Fat: 0.75

1. Sauté bell pepper, onion, mushrooms, and garlic in oil in large saucepan until onion is tender, about 5 minutes. Stir in tomatoes, wine, tomato paste, and herbs; heat to boiling. Reduce heat and simmer, covered, 5 minutes; simmer, uncovered, until mixture is thickened to desired consistency, about 20 minutes, adding seafood during last 10 minutes of cooking time. Discard any mussels that have not opened. Stir in salt and pepper. Toss with fettuccine.

FLOUNDER EN PAPILLOTE

Traditionally made with a lean white fish, this recipe is also very delicious with salmon or tuna.

6 servings

6 flounder, sole or other lean white fish fillets
   (4 ounces each)
Salt and pepper, to taste
1 cup each: sliced mushrooms, julienned carrots
¼ cup finely chopped shallots or onion
2 cloves garlic, minced
½ teaspoon dried tarragon leaves
2 teaspoons margarine or butter
½ cup dry white wine or water
¼ cup finely chopped parsley
6 lemon wedges

Per Serving:
Calories: 149
% of calories from fat: 17
Fat (gm): 2.8
Saturated fat (gm): 0.6
Cholesterol (mg): 59.8
Sodium (mg): 118
Protein (gm): 22.3
Carbohydrate (gm): 5.7

Exchanges:
Milk: 0.0
Vegetable: 1.0
Fruit: 0.0
Bread: 0.0
Meat: 2.5
Fat: 0.0

1. Cut six 12-inch squares of parchment paper; fold in half, and cut each into a large heart shape. Open hearts and place 1 fish fillet on each; sprinkle lightly with salt and pepper.

2. Sauté mushrooms, carrots, shallots, garlic, and tarragon in margarine in large skillet until carrots are crisp-tender, about 5 minutes. Stir in wine and parsley; season to taste with salt and pepper. Spoon mixture over fish. Fold packets in half, bringing edges together; crimp edges tightly to seal. Bake on jelly roll pan at 425 degrees until packets puff, 10 to 12 minutes. Serve with lemon wedges.

NOTE: Aluminum foil can be used in place of parchment paper; bake fish 15 minutes.

FLORENTINE FISH DINNER

45 *Pasta, spinach, and fish fillets combine to make this quick, flavorful dinner.*

4 servings

1 can (14 ounces) reduced-sodium diced tomatoes, undrained

2 cups frozen chopped spinach, thawed

1 tablespoon olive oil

½ teaspoon minced garlic

Salt and pepper, to taste

3 tablespoons grated Parmesan cheese

8 ounces linguine, cooked, warm

1 pound skinless flounder fillets

Per Serving:
Calories: 353
% of calories from fat: 18
Fat (gm): 7.5
Saturated fat (gm): 1.6
Cholesterol (mg): 63.1
Sodium (mg): 355
Protein (gm): 32.6
Carbohydrate (gm): 41.7

Exchanges:
Milk: 0.0
Vegetable: 2.0
Fruit: 0.0
Bread: 2.0
Meat: 3.0
Fat: 0.0

1. Combine tomatoes with liquid, spinach, olive oil, and garlic in medium saucepan; heat to boiling. Reduce heat and simmer until thickened to desired consistency, about 10 minutes; season to taste with salt and pepper. Toss sauce and Parmesan cheese with linguine and keep warm.

2. Cook flounder in lightly greased large skillet over medium heat until flounder is tender and flakes with a fork, 3 to 4 minutes on each side. Sprinkle lightly with salt and pepper. Serve with linguine; sprinkle with Parmesan cheese.

45-MINUTE PREPARATION TIP: Begin cooking pasta before preparing the rest of the recipe.

CARIBBEAN-STYLE FLOUNDER

45 *Annatto seeds can be found in the ethnic section of the supermarket; they give the oil a bright yellow color and subtle flavor.*

4 servings

1 tablespoon annatto seeds (optional)

2 teaspoons peanut oil

1 each: sliced medium onion, cubed sweet potato

2 cups reduced-sodium fat-free chicken broth

1 can (14 ounces) reduced-sodium diced tomatoes, undrained

1 teaspoon dried thyme leaves

1 cup frozen peas

1 pound flounder fillets, cubed (¾-inch)

3–4 teaspoons lemon juice

Salt and pepper, to taste

Per Serving:
Calories: 240
% of calories from fat: 16
Fat (gm): 4.2
Saturated fat (gm): 0.8
Cholesterol (mg): 60.1
Sodium (mg): 227
Protein (gm): 28.5
Carbohydrate (gm): 21.4

Exchanges:
Milk: 0.0
Vegetable: 0.0
Fruit: 0.0
Bread: 1.0
Meat: 3.0
Fat: 0.0

1. Cook annatto seeds in oil in large saucepan over medium-high heat 3 minutes; remove and discard annatto seeds. Add onion to saucepan; sauté 2 minutes; add sweet potato, broth, tomatoes with liquid, and thyme. Heat to boiling; reduce heat and simmer, covered, until potato is tender, about 10 minutes. Using potato masher, coarsely mash mixture in pan. Add peas and flounder; simmer until fish is tender and flakes with a fork, about 5 minutes. Season to taste with lemon juice, salt and pepper.

FISH STEW MARSALA

45 *Marsala wine adds a distinctive, appealing note to this simple Italian fish stew. Substitute any lean white fish you prefer.*

4 servings

1 cup each: chopped onion, red and green bell peppers

½ cup chopped celery

1 teaspoon minced garlic

1½ tablespoons olive oil

2½ cups reduced-sodium fat-free chicken broth

⅓ cup dry Marsala wine or fat-free chicken broth

1 teaspoon dried thyme leaves

¼ cup reduced-sodium tomato paste

2 tablespoons lemon juice

1 pound haddock steaks, cut into large chunks

2 cups medium pasta shells, cooked, warm

Salt and pepper, to taste

Per Serving:
Calories: 409
% of calories from fat: 15
Fat (gm): 7
Saturated fat (gm): 1
Cholesterol (mg): 65.2
Sodium (mg): 206
Protein (gm): 33
Carbohydrate (gm): 49

Exchanges:
Milk: 0.0
Vegetable: 1.0
Fruit: 0.0
Bread: 3.0
Meat: 3.0
Fat: 0.0

1. Sauté onion, bell peppers, celery, and garlic in oil in large skillet until tender and lightly browned, about 5 minutes. Add broth, Marsala, and thyme; heat to boiling. Reduce heat and simmer, uncovered, 10 minutes. Stir in tomato paste, lemon juice, and haddock; simmer until fish flakes with a fork, about 5 minutes. Stir in pasta; season to taste with salt and pepper.

45-MINUTE PREPARATION TIP: Begin cooking pasta before preparing the rest of the recipe.

BRAISED FISH WITH SUN-DRIED TOMATO SAUCE

45 *The combination of tomato sauce and sun-dried tomatoes gives this dish rich tomato flavor. Red snapper or other firm fish can be substituted for the halibut.*

4 servings

1 large onion, chopped

1 teaspoon minced garlic

1 tablespoon olive oil

1 cup clam juice or reduced-fat chicken broth

3 tablespoons chopped sun-dried tomatoes

¾ teaspoon each: dried marjoram and oregano leaves

1 can (8 ounces) reduced-sodium tomato sauce

4 halibut steaks (about 4 ounces each)

Salt and pepper, to taste

Per Serving:
Calories: 204
% of calories from fat: 30
Fat (gm): 6.8
Saturated fat (gm): 0.9
Cholesterol (mg): 36.1
Sodium (mg): 232
Protein (gm): 25.4
Carbohydrate (gm): 9.6

Exchanges:
Milk: 0.0
Vegetable: 2.0
Fruit: 0.0
Bread: 0.0
Meat: 3.0
Fat: 0.0

1. Sauté onion and garlic in oil in large skillet until browned, about 5 minutes. Stir in clam juice, sun-dried tomatoes, and herbs. Heat to boiling; boil, uncovered, stirring frequently until liquid is almost evaporated, about 5 minutes. Add tomato sauce and fish; simmer until fish is tender and flakes with a fork, about 5 minutes. Season to taste with salt and pepper.

HALIBUT WITH SOUR CREAM AND POBLANO SAUCE

45 *The picante Sour Cream and Poblano Sauce is also excellent served with shredded chicken breast or lean pork in soft tacos, or over favorite enchiladas.*

4 servings

4 halibut steaks (about 4 ounces each)
3 tablespoons lime juice
1 clove garlic, minced
Salt and pepper, to taste
Sour Cream and Poblano Sauce (recipe follows)
4 lime wedges

Per Serving:
Calories: 184
% of calories from fat: 13
Fat (gm): 2.7
Saturated fat (gm): 0.4
Cholesterol (mg): 36.4
Sodium (mg): 101
Protein (gm): 28.2
Carbohydrate (gm): 11.9

Exchanges:
Milk: 0.0
Vegetable: 1.0
Fruit: 0.0
Bread: 0.0
Meat: 3.0
Fat: 0.0

1. Brush halibut with combined lime juice and garlic; let stand 15 minutes. Cook halibut in lightly greased large skillet over medium heat until halibut is tender and flakes with a fork, 4 to 5 minutes on each side. Sprinkle lightly with salt and pepper. Serve with Sour Cream and Poblano Sauce and lime wedges.

Sour Cream and Poblano Sauce
Makes about 1 cup

1 each: thinly sliced large poblano chili, finely chopped small onion
2 cloves garlic, minced
1 cup fat-free sour cream
¼ teaspoon ground cumin
Salt and pepper, to taste

1. Sauté poblano chili, onion, and garlic in lightly greased small saucepan until very tender, about 5 minutes. Stir in sour cream and cumin; cook over low heat 2 to 3 minutes. Season to taste with salt and pepper.

ASPARAGUS-ROUGHY AU GRATIN

Orange roughy is a light-flavored fish with a nice, firm texture—delicious baked with asparagus.

6 servings

4 cups cooked rice

1 pound fresh asparagus, sliced (1-inch)

6 orange roughy fillets (4 ounces each)

1 medium onion, finely chopped

3 tablespoons margarine or butter

⅓ cup all-purpose flour

1 cup each: fat-free milk, shredded reduced-fat
    Cheddar cheese (4 ounces)

¼ teaspoon each: salt, pepper

1 cup unseasoned dry bread crumbs

Per Serving:
Calories: 468
% of calories from fat: 22
Fat (gm): 11.2
Saturated fat (gm): 2.8
Cholesterol (mg): 44
Sodium (mg): 712
Protein (gm): 37.2
Carbohydrate (gm): 51.3

Exchanges:
Milk: 0.0
Vegetable: 1.0
Fruit: 0.0
Bread: 3.0
Meat: 4.0
Fat: 0.0

1. Spoon rice into 13 x 9-inch baking dish; arrange asparagus over rice and top with fish fillets, overlapping if necessary.

2. Sauté onion in margarine in medium saucepan until tender, about 5 minutes. Stir in flour and cook 1 minute. Whisk in milk and heat to boiling, whisking until thickened, about 1 minute. Whisk in cheese, salt, and pepper. Spoon sauce over fish; sprinkle with bread crumbs. Bake, covered, at 350 degrees until sauce is bubbly, about 20 minutes. Bake, uncovered, until browned, about 10 minutes.

RED SNAPPER BAKED WITH CILANTRO

45

Tuna, salmon, cod, or any firm white fish can be used in this recipe.

6 servings

⅓ cup lime juice

1½ tablespoons pickled jalapeño chili juice

1 teaspoon ground cumin

1½ pounds red snapper fillets or steaks

1 medium onion, thinly sliced

2 pickled jalapeño chilies, minced

2 cloves garlic, minced

1 cup coarsely chopped cilantro

Salt and pepper, to taste

Thinly sliced green onions, as garnish

6 lime wedges

Per Serving:
Calories: 135
% of calories from fat: 12
Fat (gm): 1.7
Saturated fat (gm): 0.3
Cholesterol (mg): 41.6
Sodium (mg): 169
Protein (gm): 24
Carbohydrate (gm): 5

Exchanges:
Milk: 0.0
Vegetable: 0.0
Fruit: 0.0
Bread: 0.0
Meat: 3.0
Fat: 0.0

1. Pour combined lime juice, jalapeño juice, and cumin over fish in glass baking dish; top with onion, jalapeño chilies, garlic, and cilantro. Refrigerate, covered, 2 hours, turning fish once.

2. Bake uncovered, at 400 degrees until red snapper is tender and flakes with a fork, about 10 minutes. Sprinkle fish lightly with salt and pepper; sprinkle with green onions and serve with lime wedges.

RED SNAPPER VERACRUZ

45

In this famous dish from Veracruz, Mexico, red snapper is baked in a full-flavored tomato sauce with olives and capers. The fish can also be grilled, then topped with the sauce.

6 servings

1 whole red snapper, dressed (about 2 pounds)

2 tablespoons lime juice

2 cloves garlic, minced

Veracruz Sauce (recipe follows)

6 lime wedges

1. Pierce surfaces of fish with long-tined fork; rub with lime juice and garlic. Refrigerate, covered, in large glass baking dish 2 hours.

2. Spoon Veracruz Sauce over fish. Bake, uncovered, at 400 degrees until fish is tender and flakes with a fork, 25 to 35 minutes. Serve with lime wedges.

Per Serving:
Calories: 198
% of calories from fat: 15
Fat (gm): 3.3
Saturated fat (gm): 0.6
Cholesterol (mg): 55.5
Sodium (mg): 311
Protein (gm): 32.6
Carbohydrate (gm): 9.2

Exchanges:
Milk: 0.0
Vegetable: 2.0
Fruit: 0.0
Bread: 0.0
Meat: 3.0
Fat: 0.0

Veracruz Sauce

Makes about 2 cups

1 cup chopped onion
3 cloves garlic, minced
1 pickled jalapeño chili, minced
2-inch piece cinnamon stick
1 bay leaf
½ teaspoon each: dried oregano and thyme leaves, ground cumin
3 cups chopped tomatoes
¼ cup sliced pitted green olives
1–2 tablespoons capers
Salt and pepper, to taste

1. Sauté onion, garlic, jalapeño chili, cinnamon, and herbs in large lightly greased skillet until onion is tender, 5 to 8 minutes. Add tomatoes, olives, and capers; simmer, uncovered, until sauce is a medium consistency, about 10 minutes. Discard bay leaf; season to taste with salt and pepper.

GRILLED RED SNAPPER WITH TROPICAL SALSA

Trendy salsas are making the scene—you'll enjoy our fruit and black bean version.

6 servings

1 whole red snapper, dressed (about 2 pounds)

3 tablespoons lime juice

2 cloves garlic, minced

Tropical Salsa (recipe follows)

Lime wedges, as garnish

Cilantro or parsley sprigs, as garnish

Per Serving:
Calories: 189
% of calories from fat: 11
Fat (gm): 2.2
Saturated fat (gm): 0.5
Cholesterol (mg): 55.5
Sodium (mg): 75
Protein (gm): 32.1
Carbohydrate (gm): 9

Exchanges:
Milk: 0.0
Vegetable: 0.0
Fruit: 0.0
Bread: 0.0
Meat: 3.0
Fat: 0.0

1. Pierce surfaces of fish with long-tined fork; rub with lime juice and garlic. Refrigerate, covered, in large glass baking dish 2 hours.

2. Grill fish over medium-hot coals, or bake, uncovered, at 400 degrees, until fish is tender and flakes with a fork, 20 to 25 minutes. Serve with Tropical Salsa; garnish with lime wedges and cilantro.

Tropical Salsa

Makes about 1½ cups

½ cup each: chopped papaya or mango, pineapple, tomato

¼ cup each: chopped, seeded cucumber, rinsed, drained canned black beans, orange juice

½ teaspoon minced jalapeño chili

2 tablespoons finely chopped cilantro

1 tablespoon lime juice

2 teaspoons sugar

1. Combine all ingredients.

POACHED SALMON WITH MOCK HOLLANDAISE SAUCE

45 *Poached salmon can be served warm or cold depending upon the occasion and the season of the year.*

6 servings

¾ cup dry white wine or clam juice

½ cup water

2 thin slices onion

4 dill or parsley sprigs

¼ teaspoon each: dried thyme and tarragon leaves

1 bay leaf

4 peppercorns

½ teaspoon salt

4 small salmon steaks (4 ounces each)

Mock Hollandaise Sauce (see p. 175)

Chopped parsley, as garnish

4 lemon wedges

Per Serving:
Calories: 195
% of calories from fat: 30
Fat (gm): 6.2
Saturated fat (gm): 0.9
Cholesterol (mg): 53.3
Sodium (mg): 351
Protein (gm): 26.9
Carbohydrate (gm): 4.2

Exchanges:
Milk: 0.5
Vegetable: 0.0
Fruit: 0.0
Bread: 0.0
Meat: 3.0
Fat: 0.0

1. Heat wine, water, onion, herbs, peppercorns, and salt to boiling in medium skillet. Reduce heat and simmer, covered, 5 minutes. Add salmon to skillet; simmer, covered, until salmon is cooked and flakes with a fork, 6 to 10 minutes. Serve Mock Hollandaise Sauce over salmon; sprinkle with parsley. Serve with lemon wedges.

SALMON WITH CILANTRO PESTO FETTUCCINE

45 *Tuna or halibut can substitute nicely for the salmon.*

6 servings

6 salmon steaks (4 ounces each)

2–3 teaspoons Dijon mustard

12 ounces spinach fettuccine, cooked, warm

Cilantro Pesto (recipe follows)

1. Brush salmon with mustard; broil 6 inches from heat source until salmon is tender and flakes with fork, 10 to 12 minutes, turning once. Toss fettuccine with Cilantro Pesto; serve with salmon.

Per Serving:
Calories: 372
% of calories from fat: 30
Fat (gm): 12.3
Saturated fat (gm): 2.6
Cholesterol (mg): 126.7
Sodium (mg): 319
Protein (gm): 32.7
Carbohydrate (gm): 31.1

Cilantro Pesto

Makes about ¾ cup

1½ cups packed cilantro leaves

½ cup packed parsley

1 clove garlic, minced

¼ cup grated Parmesan cheese

3 tablespoons pine nuts or walnuts

1 tablespoon each: olive oil, lemon juice

¼ teaspoon each: salt, pepper

Exchanges:
Milk: 0.0
Vegetable: 0.0
Fruit: 0.0
Bread: 2.0
Meat: 3.0
Fat: 1.0

1. Process all ingredients in food processor or blender until mixture is very finely chopped.

SALMON RISOTTO

45 *The salmon and sauce are prepared while the risotto is cooking in the microwave oven—a real time-saver!*

6 servings

Microwave Risotto (see pg. 422)

12–16 ounces salmon steaks

¾ cup sliced green onions

¼ cup dry sherry or reduced-fat chicken broth

1 cup reduced-fat sour cream

½ cup 1% low-fat milk

1 tablespoon chopped fresh or 2 teaspoons dried dill weed

Salt and pepper, to taste

Per Serving:
Calories: 291
% of calories from fat: 23
Fat (gm): 7.1
Saturated fat (gm): 3.4
Cholesterol (mg): 42.7
Sodium (mg): 175
Protein (gm): 20
Carbohydrate (gm): 31.2

Exchanges:
Milk: 0.0
Vegetable: 0.0
Fruit: 0.0
Bread: 2.0
Meat: 2.0
Fat: 0.5

1. Make Microwave Risotto.

2. While risotto is cooking, cook salmon in lightly greased large skillet over medium heat until salmon is tender and flakes with

fork, about 10 minutes. Remove and discard skin; cut salmon into large pieces. Add green onions and sherry to skillet; cook over medium heat until green onions are tender, 2 to 3 minutes. Stir in sour cream, milk, and dill weed; add salmon and stir into risotto. Season to taste with salt and pepper.

SALMON CASSEROLE

45

This light and flavorful casserole is great for brunch, lunch, or dinner.

8 servings

2 cans (14¾ ounces each) salmon, drained, flaked

1 pound mushrooms, coarsely chopped

¼ teaspoon each: ground nutmeg, pepper

¼ cup finely chopped onion

1–2 tablespoons margarine or butter

2 tablespoons flour

1½ cups fat-free milk

½ cup unseasoned dry bread crumbs

Per Serving:
Calories: 219
% of calories from fat: 29
Fat (gm): 7.1
Saturated fat (gm): 1.4
Cholesterol (mg): 86.6
Sodium (mg): 505
Protein (gm): 28.6
Carbohydrate (gm): 10.9

Exchanges:
Milk: 0.0
Vegetable: 2.0
Fruit: 0.0
Bread: 0.0
Meat: 3.0
Fat: 0.0

1. Combine salmon, mushrooms, nutmeg, and pepper in 12 x 8-inch baking dish.

2. Sauté onion in margarine in medium saucepan 1 minute; stir in flour and cook 1 minute. Whisk in milk; heat to boiling, whisking until thickened, about 1 minute. Pour over salmon and sprinkle with bread crumbs. Bake, uncovered, at 375 degrees until lightly browned, about 35 minutes.

SALMON SOUFFLÉ

45

This casserole requires some care in preparation, but the results are well worth it.

6 servings

⅔ cup each: chopped green and red bell pepper

1 tablespoon margarine or butter

¼ cup all-purpose flour

1½ cups fat-free milk

¾ teaspoon dried dill weed

¼ teaspoon salt

⅛ teaspoon white pepper

2–3 egg yolks, lightly beaten

1 can (6½ ounces) salmon, drained, flaked

1 cup whole kernel corn

5 egg whites

Pinch cream of tartar

Per Serving:
Calories: 183
% of calories from fat: 30
Fat (gm): 6.2
Saturated fat (gm): 1.5
Cholesterol (mg): 85.6
Sodium (mg): 367
Protein (gm): 14.3
Carbohydrate (gm): 18.2

Exchanges:
Milk: 0.0
Vegetable: 0.0
Fruit: 0.0
Bread: 1.0
Meat: 2.0
Fat: 0.0

1. Sauté bell peppers in margarine in large saucepan until tender, about 5 minutes. Stir in flour and cook 1 minute. Whisk in milk, dill weed, salt, and pepper; heat to boiling. Whisk about half the mixture into egg yolks; whisk mixture into saucepan. Mix in salmon and corn.

3. Beat egg whites and cream of tartar in large bowl to stiff but not dry peaks; fold into salmon mixture. Pour into lightly greased 2-quart soufflé dish. Bake, uncovered, at 350 degrees until golden brown and knife inserted near center comes out clean, about 45 minutes. Serve immediately.

SOLE, MEDITERRANEAN STYLE

45 *This fast and flavorful fish dinner features sole, but any mild-flavored white fish, such as flounder, halibut, or turbot, can be substituted.*

4 servings

½ cup sun-dried tomatoes (not in oil), softened

1 package (16 ounces) frozen stir-fry pepper blend

½ cup reduced-sodium fat-free chicken broth

2 teaspoons olive oil

1 teaspoon each: minced garlic, dried basil leaves

Salt and pepper, to taste

8 ounces penne or mostaccioli, cooked, warm

¼ cup (1 ounce) grated Parmesan cheese

12–16 ounces skinless sole fillets

Chopped parsley, as garnish

Per Serving:
Calories: 387
% of calories from fat: 14
Fat (gm): 6
Saturated fat (gm): 1.7
Cholesterol (mg): 49
Sodium (mg): 347
Protein (gm): 28.3
Carbohydrate (gm): 53.3

Exchanges:
Milk: 0.0
Vegetable: 2.0
Fruit: 0.0
Bread: 3.0
Meat: 2.0
Fat: 0.0

1. Combine tomatoes, stir-fry blend, broth, olive oil, garlic, and basil in large skillet; heat to boiling. Reduce heat and simmer, uncovered, until vegetables are very tender, about 5 minutes; season to taste with salt and pepper. Toss with penne and Parmesan in large bowl; keep warm.

2. Cook sole in large lightly greased skillet over medium heat until browned on the bottom, 3 to 4 minutes; turn and cook until fish is tender and flakes with fork, 3 to 4 minutes. Sprinkle lightly with salt and pepper. Serve over pasta mixture; sprinkle with parsley.

45-MINUTE PREPARATION TIP: Begin cooking pasta before preparing the rest of the recipe.

TUNA STEAKS WITH GARLIC PASTA

45 *Slow cooking gives the garlic a sweet, mellow flavor.*

4 servings

⅓ cup thinly sliced garlic

2–3 teaspoons olive oil

1 cup frozen peas

1 tablespoon minced fresh or 1 teaspoon dried
   rosemary leaves

Salt and pepper, to taste

4 tuna steaks (4 ounces each)

2 cups (8 ounces) orecchiette (little ears) pasta,
   cooked, warm

¼–⅓ cup freshly grated Parmesan cheese

Per Serving:
Calories: 430
% of calories from fat: 13
Fat (gm): 6
Saturated fat (gm): 1.7
Cholesterol (mg): 53.4
Sodium (mg): 173
Protein (gm): 37.9
Carbohydrate (gm): 54.1

Exchanges:
Milk: 0.0
Vegetable: 2.0
Fruit: 0.0
Bread: 3.0
Meat: 3.0
Fat: 0.0

1. Cook garlic in oil in small skillet over medium heat 2 minutes;
reduce heat to medium-low and cook, uncovered, until garlic is
golden, about 10 minutes. Stir in peas and rosemary and cook until
hot, 1 to 2 minutes; season to taste with salt and pepper.

2. While garlic is cooking, broil tuna 6 inches from heat source
until fish is tender and flakes with a fork, 4 to 5 minutes on each
side; season to taste with salt and pepper. Toss garlic mixture with
orecchiette and Parmesan cheese; top with tuna.

GRILLED FISH WITH CHILI PASTE

*Dried ancho and pasilla chilies and vinegar combine to create a piquant
seasoning for the fish.*

4 servings

1 pound fish fillets (red snapper, tuna, or any firm fish)

Chili Paste (recipe follows)

4 lime wedges

1. Spread top of fillets with Chili Paste. Grill over medium-hot coals
or broil 6 inches from heat source until fish is tender and flakes

with a fork, 10 to 15 minutes, depending upon thickness of fish. Serve with lime wedges.

Chili Paste

Makes about ¼ cup

1 each: ancho and pasilla chili
2 cloves garlic
½ teaspoon salt
1 tablespoon white wine vinegar
Water

Per Serving:
Calories: 133
% of calories from fat: 11
Fat (gm): 1.5
Saturated fat (gm): 0.3
Cholesterol (mg): 41.6
Sodium (mg): 377
Protein (gm): 23.4
Carbohydrate (gm): 4.6

Exchanges:
Milk: 0.0
Vegetable: 0.5
Fruit: 0.0
Bread: 0.0
Meat: 2.5
Fat: 0.0

1. Cook chilies in lightly greased medium skillet over medium heat until softened, l to 2 minutes. Remove and discard stems, seeds, and veins. Process chilies, garlic, salt, and vinegar in food processor or blender, adding small amount of water, if necessary, to make smooth paste.

TUNA STEAKS WITH SWEET-SOUR TOMATO-BASIL RELISH

45 *Spicy tomato relish nicely complements grilled tuna in this easy but elegant recipe.*

4 servings

2 teaspoons olive oil
1 teaspoon each: minced garlic, lemon juice
½ teaspoon each: dried basil and thyme leaves
4 tuna steaks (4 ounces each)
Salt and pepper, to taste
Sweet-Sour Tomato-Basil Relish (recipe follows)

Per Serving:
Calories: 182
% of calories from fat: 23
Fat (gm): 4.6
Saturated fat (gm): 0.7
Cholesterol (mg): 49.4
Sodium (mg): 108
Protein (gm): 26.2
Carbohydrate (gm): 8.4

Exchanges:
Milk: 0.0
Vegetable: 1.0
Fruit: 0.0
Bread: 0.0
Meat: 3.0
Fat: 0.0

1. Combine olive oil, garlic, lemon juice, and herbs in small bowl; brush on tuna. Let stand 15 minutes. Broil tuna 6 inches from heat source until fish is tender and flakes with a fork, 6 to 8 minutes on each side, for well-done. Sprinkle lightly with salt and pepper; serve with Sweet-Sour Tomato-Basil Relish.

Sweet-Sour Tomato-Basil Relish

Makes about 1 cup

1 large tomato, seeded, cubed

2 tablespoons tomato paste

½ tablespoon water

1½ tablespoons each: red wine vinegar, sugar

1 teaspoon olive oil

¼ teaspoon each: dried basil and thyme leaves

1. Sauté tomato in lightly greased small skillet until softened, 3 to 4 minutes; combine with remaining ingredients.

45-MINUTE PREPARATION TIP: Make Sweet-Sour Tomato-Basil Relish before preparing the rest of the recipe.

NIÇOISE PLATTER

This tuna and vegetable medley is drizzled with vinaigrette and served with garlic-spiked aioli.

6 servings

12 small red potatoes, cooked, quartered

12 ounces green beans, cooked

2 large beets, cooked, cubed

4 Braised Whole Artichokes (see p. 462)

3 hard-cooked eggs, halved

2 medium tomatoes, cut into wedges

2 cans (6⅛ ounces each) white tuna in water, drained, flaked

3 cups mixed salad greens

2 tablespoons sliced ripe olives

1 tablespoon capers

½ cup fat-free Italian dressing

Salt and pepper, to taste

Aioli (recipe follows)

Per Serving:
Calories: 451
% of calories from fat: 19
Fat (gm): 10.0
Saturated fat (gm): 2.3
Cholesterol (mg): 204.5
Sodium (mg): 1389
Protein (gm): 35.6
Carbohydrate (gm): 59.6

Exchanges:
Milk: 0.0
Vegetable: 0.0
Fruit: 0.0
Bread: 4.0
Meat: 3.0
Fat: 0.0

1. Arrange cooked vegetables, Braised Whole Artichokes, eggs, tomatoes, and tuna on greens-lined plates; sprinkle with olives and capers. Drizzle with Italian dressing; sprinkle lightly with salt and pepper. Serve with Aioli.

Aioli

Makes about ¾ cup

¾ cup fat-free mayonnaise
1 teaspoon each: tarragon vinegar, lemon juice, Dijon mustard
3 cloves garlic, minced
Salt and white pepper, to taste

1. Mix all ingredients, except salt and pepper; season to taste with salt and pepper.

TUNA PASTA SALAD

45 *A tuna salad with a difference! Purchased low-fat dressing may be substituted for the homemade Italian Dressing.*

6 servings

12 ounces penne or mostaccioli, cooked, room
  temperature
1 can (15 ounces) quartered artichoke hearts, drained
4 plum tomatoes, coarsely chopped
1½ cups cubed zucchini
¼ cup each: sliced green onion tops, black olives
Italian Dressing (recipe follows)
2 cans (6⅛ ounces each) white tuna in water,
  drained, flaked
Salt and pepper, to taste

Per Serving:
Calories: 435
% of calories from fat: 29
Fat (gm): 14.1
Saturated fat (gm): 2.1
Cholesterol (mg): 24.3
Sodium (mg): 590
Protein (gm): 23.9
Carbohydrate (gm): 52.7

Exchanges:
Milk: 0.0
Vegetable: 3.0
Fruit: 0.0
Bread: 2.0
Meat: 2.0
Fat: 2.0

1. Combine all ingredients, except salt and pepper, in large bowl, tossing lightly; season to taste with salt and pepper.

Italian Dressing

Makes about ½ cup

¼ cup olive oil

1 tablespoon each: lemon juice, red wine vinegar, water

½ teaspoon each: minced garlic, dry mustard, sugar, dried oregano and thyme leaves

1. Combine all ingredients.

45-MINUTE PREPARATION TIP: Begin cooking penne before preparing the rest of the recipe.

TUNA, FENNEL, AND PASTA SALAD WITH ORANGE VINAIGRETTE

Haddock, halibut, or salmon are tasty alternatives to the tuna in this orange and fennel scented dish.

6 servings

1 pound tuna steaks, grilled or broiled, warm

1½ cups (6 ounces) pasta shells, cooked, room temperature

3 cups torn leaf lettuce, Belgium endive

2 medium oranges, peeled, cut into segments

½ cup very thinly sliced fennel bulb or celery

1 small red bell pepper, sliced

Orange Vinaigrette (recipe follows)

Per Serving:
Calories: 296
% of calories from fat: 26
Fat (gm): 8.6
Saturated fat (gm): 1.2
Cholesterol (mg): 33.9
Sodium (mg): 140
Protein (gm): 23.4
Carbohydrate (gm): 31.6

Exchanges:
Milk: 0.0
Vegetable: 1.0
Fruit: 0.5
Bread: 1.5
Meat: 2.0
Fat: 0.5

1. Remove skin and any bones from tuna; break tuna into large chunks. Combine tuna and remaining ingredients and toss.

Orange Vinaigrette
Makes about ⅔ cup

¼ cup orange juice

3 tablespoons each: olive oil, balsamic or red wine vinegar

2 tablespoons finely chopped shallots or green onion

2 cloves garlic, minced

1 teaspoon dried rosemary leaves

½ teaspoon fennel seeds, crushed

¼ teaspoon salt

⅛ teaspoon white pepper

1. Mix all ingredients.

TUNA PATTIES WITH CREAMED PEA SAUCE

45

These generous patties can also be served in buns, or the mixture can be baked in a small loaf pan.

4 servings

2 cans (6⅛ ounces each) light tuna packed in water, drained

¾ cup unseasoned dry bread crumbs, divided

¼ cup each: finely chopped onion, celery

2 tablespoons chopped green bell pepper

3 tablespoons fat-free mayonnaise

2 teaspoons Worcestershire sauce

Salt and cayenne pepper, to taste

1 egg

Creamed Pea Sauce (recipe follows)

Per Serving:
Calories: 325
% of calories from fat: 25
Fat (gm): 8.9
Saturated fat (gm): 2
Cholesterol (mg): 79.2
Sodium (mg): 726
Protein (gm): 30
Carbohydrate (gm): 28.6

Exchanges:
Milk: 0.5
Vegetable: 1.0
Fruit: 0.0
Bread: 1.0
Meat: 3.5
Fat: 0.0

1. Combine tuna, ½ cup bread crumbs, onion, celery, bell pepper, mayonnaise, and Worcestershire sauce in medium bowl; season to taste with salt and cayenne pepper. Mix in egg; shape into 4 patties, about ½ inch thick and coat with remaining ¼ cup bread crumbs. Cook patties in lightly greased medium skillet over medium heat until browned, about 5 minutes on each side. Serve with Creamed Pea Sauce.

Creamed Pea Sauce

Makes about 1 cup

2 tablespoons each: margarine or butter, flour
1 cup each: fat-free half-and-half or fat-free milk, frozen, thawed peas
Salt and pepper, to taste

1. Melt margarine in small saucepan; stir in flour and cook 1 minute. Whisk in half-and-half; heat to boiling. Boil, whisking until thickened, about 1 minute. Stir in peas; cook over low heat 2 to 3 minutes. Season to taste with salt and pepper.

45-MINUTE PREPARATION TIP: Make Creamed Pea Sauce and keep warm while preparing Tuna Patties.

TUNA CASSEROLE

45

Just like Mom used to make, but a healthier version!

8 servings

12 ounces thin egg noodles, cooked
2 cans (12 ounces each) solid white tuna in water, drained, flaked
1 jar (2½ ounces) diced pimientos, drained
8 ounces mushrooms, sliced
1 can (10½ ounces) each: reduced-fat cream of mushroom soup, reduced-fat cream of celery soup
1 cup water
½ cup dry bread crumbs

Per Serving:
Calories: 364
% of calories from fat: 15
Fat (gm): 5.6
Saturated fat (gm): 1.3
Cholesterol (mg): 77.7
Sodium (mg): 684
Protein (gm): 28.5
Carbohydrate (gm): 44.2

Exchanges:
Milk: 0.0
Vegetable: 0.0
Fruit: 0.0
Bread: 3.0
Meat: 2.0
Fat: 0.0

1. Place half the noodles in 2½-quart casserole. Layer half the tuna, pimientos, and mushrooms on noodles. Repeat layers. Pour combined soups and water over casserole; top with bread crumbs. Bake, covered, at 375 degrees for 20 minutes; bake uncovered until browned and bubbly, about 15 minutes.

FISH BAKED WITH STUFFING

45

Fish fillets are cooked on a bed of seasoned bread stuffing—add a salad and vegetable, and dinner is served!

4 servings

1 cup each: chopped onion, sliced mushrooms
½ teaspoon minced garlic
1½ cups crumb-type seasoned stuffing mix
3 tablespoons grated Parmesan cheese
1 pound lean white fish fillets
¼ teaspoon dried basil leaves
Salt and pepper, to taste
¼ cup dry white wine or chicken broth

Per Serving:
Calories: 241
% of calories from fat: 13
Fat (gm): 3.5
Saturated fat (gm): 1.1
Cholesterol (mg): 63.1
Sodium (mg): 584
Protein (gm): 27.5
Carbohydrate (gm): 22.4

Exchanges:
Milk: 0.0
Vegetable: 0.0
Fruit: 0.0
Bread: 1.5
Meat: 3.0
Fat: 0.0

1. Sauté onion, mushrooms, and garlic in lightly greased large skillet until onion is tender, 5 to 8 minutes. Stir in stuffing mix and Parmesan cheese; spoon into baking dish. Arrange fish on stuffing, overlapping if necessary; sprinkle with basil, salt, and pepper. Pour wine over fish. Bake, covered, at 375 degrees until fish is tender and flakes with a fork, about 20 minutes.

WHITEFISH AND LINGUINE WITH LEMON-CAPER SAUCE

Any white-fleshed fish, such as cod, halibut, haddock, or orange roughy, can be used.

6 servings

6 whitefish fillets (about 3 ounces each)

1 tablespoon Dijon mustard

2 cloves garlic, minced

1 teaspoon dried tarragon leaves

2–3 tablespoons margarine or butter

3 tablespoons flour

1 can (14½ ounces) reduced-sodium fat-free chicken broth

2–3 teaspoons lemon juice

3 tablespoons capers

¼ teaspoon salt

⅛ teaspoon white pepper

12 ounces linguine, cooked, warm

Per Serving:
Calories: 326
% of calories from fat: 28
Fat (gm): 10
Saturated fat (gm): 1.5
Cholesterol (mg): 49.3
Sodium (mg): 505
Protein (gm): 23.7
Carbohydrate (gm): 35.4

Exchanges:
Milk: 0.0
Vegetable: 0.0
Fruit: 0.0
Bread: 2.5
Meat: 2.0
Fat: 1.0

1. Brush fish fillets with combined mustard, garlic, and tarragon. Bake at 350 degrees until fish is tender and flakes with fork, 10 to 12 minutes.

2. Melt margarine in small saucepan; stir in flour and cook over medium heat 1 minute. Stir in chicken broth and lemon juice; heat to boiling, stirring until thickened, about 1 minute. Stir in capers, salt, and pepper. Serve fish on linguine; spoon sauce over.

SIX

Vegetarian Entrées

BEAN AND BARLEY SOUP

45

V

A soup that can be easily increased to serve a crowd; make it a day ahead of time for best flavor.

6 servings

¾ cup each: chopped onion, red bell pepper

2 teaspoons minced garlic

2 tablespoons olive oil

1 tablespoon flour

1½ teaspoons dried Italian seasoning

7 cups low-sodium vegetable broth

2 cans (15 ounces) cannellini or Great Northern beans, rinsed, drained

2 tablespoons reduced-sodium tomato paste

½ cup quick-cooking barley

1 cup each: cubed unpeeled Idaho potato, sliced carrots, packed baby spinach leaves

Salt and pepper, to taste

Per Serving:
Calories: 297
% of calories from fat: 17
Fat (gm): 5.6
Saturated fat (gm): 0.7
Cholesterol (mg): 0
Sodium (mg): 325
Protein (gm): 10
Carbohydrate (gm): 52.1

Exchanges:
Milk: 0.0
Vegetable: 1.0
Fruit: 0.0
Bread: 3.0
Meat: 0.0
Fat: 1.0

1. Sauté onion, bell pepper, and garlic in oil in Dutch oven 5 minutes. Add flour and Italian seasoning; cook 1 to 2 minutes longer. Add remaining ingredients, except spinach, salt, and pepper; heat to boiling. Reduce heat and simmer, uncovered, 20 to 25 minutes, adding spinach during last 5 minutes of cooking time. Season to taste with salt and pepper.

SHIITAKE-PORTOBELLO CHOWDER

45

L

Celebrate the rich mushroom, cheese and wine flavors in this chowder.

4 servings

4 shallots, thinly sliced

2 teaspoons margarine or butter, divided

2 large potatoes, cubed (¼-inch)

3 cups reduced-sodium vegetable broth

2 cups each: sliced shiitake mushroom caps, cubed portobello mushrooms

¼ cup (1 ounce) shredded Gruyère or Swiss cheese

2 tablespoons Marsala wine (optional)

Salt and white pepper, to taste

Per Serving:
Calories: 162
% of calories from fat: 26
Fat (gm): 5
Saturated fat (gm): 1.8
Cholesterol (mg): 7.8
Sodium (mg): 114
Protein (gm): 5.6
Carbohydrate (gm): 24.7

Exchanges:
Milk: 0.0
Vegetable: 2.0
Fruit: 0.0
Bread: 1.0
Meat: 0.0
Fat: 1.0

1. Sauté shallots in 1 teaspoon margarine in large saucepan 2 to 3 minutes; add potatoes and broth and heat to boiling. Reduce heat and simmer, covered, until potatoes are tender, about 15 minutes. Process mixture in blender or food processor until smooth; return to saucepan.

2. Sauté mushrooms in remaining 1 teaspoon margarine in large skillet until lightly browned, about 8 minutes; stir into potato mixture. Cook, uncovered, over medium heat until hot, about 5 minutes. Remove from heat; add cheese and wine, stirring until cheese is melted. Season to taste with salt and white pepper.

VIETNAMESE CURRIED COCONUT SOUP

45

V

Rice stick noodles, made with rice flour, can be round or flat. They must be softened in water before cooking. Cooked angel hair pasta can be substituted.

6 servings

Per Serving:
Calories: 218
% of calories from fat: 28
Fat (gm): 7.2
Saturated fat (gm): 0.1
Cholesterol (mg): 0
Sodium (mg): 627
Protein (gm): 4.1
Carbohydrate (gm): 37.1

Exchanges:
Milk: 0.0
Vegetable: 1.0
Fruit: 0.0
Bread: 2.0
Meat: 0.0
Fat: 1.0

1 cup each: chopped onion, red bell peppers

2 tablespoons minced gingerroot

1 tablespoon minced garlic

3–4 tablespoons curry powder

3 cups each: vegetable broth, coconut milk

1 cup each: broccoli florets, cubed, peeled, seeded butternut squash

1 tablespoon each: grated lime zest, Oriental chili paste

½ package (8-ounce size) rice stick noodles

¼ cup each: all-purpose flour, cold water, lime juice

Salt, to taste

Chopped cilantro, as garnish

1. Sauté onion, bell peppers, gingerroot, and garlic in lightly greased large skillet until tender, about 5 minutes. Stir in curry powder; cook 1 minute. Add broth, coconut milk, vegetables, lime zest, and chili paste; heat to boiling. Reduce heat and simmer, covered, until vegetables are tender, about 15 minutes.

2. While stew is cooking, pour cold water over noodles in large bowl; let stand until noodles are separate and soft, about 5 minutes. Stir noodles into 4 quarts boiling water in large saucepan; reduce heat and simmer, uncovered, until tender, about 5 minutes. Drain.

3. Heat stew to boiling; stir in combined flour, cold water, and lime juice. Boil, stirring until thickened, about 1 minute. Season to taste with salt. Serve over noodles in shallow bowls; sprinkle generously with cilantro.

MONTEREY CHILI ACINI DE PEPE

45

L

Bulgur or cracked wheat can be substituted for the acini de pepe, in this flavorful chili.

4 servings

½ cup each: chopped onion, green bell pepper

1 teaspoon olive oil

1 can (15 ounces) pinto beans, rinsed drained

1 can (14 ounces) reduced-sodium diced
   tomatoes, undrained

1 tablespoon chili powder

1 teaspoon each: dried oregano leaves,
   unsweetened cocoa

½ cup acini de pepe, cooked

¼ cup chopped cilantro

Salt and pepper, to taste

¾ cup (3 ounces) shredded Monterey Jack cheese

Per Serving:
Calories: 275
% of calories from fat: 29
Fat (gm): 9.2
Saturated fat (gm): 4.5
Cholesterol (mg): 18.9
Sodium (mg): 461
Protein (gm): 14
Carbohydrate (gm): 36

Exchanges:
Milk: 0.0
Vegetable: 1.0
Fruit: 0.0
Bread: 2.0
Meat: 1.0
Fat: 1.0

1. Sauté onion and bell pepper in oil in large saucepan until tender, 3 to 4 minutes. Add beans, tomatoes with liquid, chili powder, oregano, and cocoa. Heat to boiling; reduce heat and simmer, covered, 10 minutes. Stir in acini de pepe and cilantro; season to taste with salt and pepper. Sprinkle each bowl of chili with cheese.

SWEET POTATO CHIPOTLE CHILI

45

V

Chipotle chilies are dried, smoked jalapeño chilies. When canned, they are in adobo sauce, which is made with ground chilies and spices. The chilies add a distinctive smoky flavor to this robust dish; taste before adding more, as they can be fiercely hot!

4 servings (about 1½ cups each)

1 cup each: chopped onion, green bell pepper

2 teaspoons minced gingerroot

1 teaspoon each: minced garlic, crushed cumin seeds

1 tablespoons peanut or canola oil

3 cups cubed, peeled sweet potatoes

2 cans (15 ounces each) black beans, rinsed, drained

1 can (14½ ounces) chili-style chunky tomatoes, undrained

½–1 chipotle chili in adobo sauce, chopped

1 cup water or vegetable broth

Salt, to taste

Per Serving:
Calories: 213
% of calories from fat: 14
Fat (gm): 3.9
Saturated fat (gm): 0.6
Cholesterol (mg): 0
Sodium (mg): 452
Protein (gm): 8.6
Carbohydrate (gm): 44.8

Exchanges:
Milk: 0.0
Vegetable: 0.0
Fruit: 0.0
Bread: 3.0
Meat: 0.0
Fat: 0.5

1. Sauté onion, bell pepper, gingerroot, garlic, and cumin seeds in oil in large saucepan until tender, about 5 minutes. Add remaining ingredients, except salt, and heat to boiling. Reduce heat and simmer, covered, until sweet potatoes are tender, about 15 minutes. Season to taste with salt.

SCOTCH BONNET CHILI

45

L

A true "hot-heads" delight, this chili gets its firepower from the redoubtable habanero chili, often called the Scotch bonnet. Substitute jalapeño chili for a milder flavor.

4 servings

1 each: large onion, medium green bell pepper, chopped

½–1 habanero chili, chopped

4 ounces vegetarian sausage, halved lengthwise, sliced

1 teaspoon olive oil

1 can (14½ ounces) reduced-sodium diced tomatoes, undrained

2 cups refried beans

1 tablespoon chili powder

1 teaspoon ground cumin

Salt, to taste

1 cup fat-free sour cream

Per Serving:
Calories: 293
% of calories from fat: 18
Fat (gm): 5.9
Saturated fat (gm): 1
Cholesterol (mg): 25.6
Sodium (mg): 767
Protein (gm): 17.1
Carbohydrate (gm): 43.8

Exchanges:
Milk: 0.0
Vegetable: 0.0
Fruit: 0.0
Bread: 3.0
Meat: 1.0
Fat: 0.5

1. Sauté onion, bell pepper, habanero chili, and vegetarian sausage in oil in large saucepan until onions are tender. Stir in remaining ingredients, except salt and sour cream; heat to boiling. Reduce heat and simmer, uncovered, until slightly thickened, about 15 minutes, season to taste with salt. Top each bowl of chili with sour cream.

WINTER STEW STROGANOFF

LO

The perfect stew for cold winter evenings.

Makes 6 servings

1½ cups each: thinly sliced onions, halved mushrooms

3 tablespons margarine or butter

1 pound each: Idaho and sweet potatoes, peeled, cooked, cubed

1 cup frozen peas

1½ cups reduced-sodium vegetable broth

1 tablespoon each: dry mustard, sugar

1 cup fat-free sour cream

¼ cup chopped parsley

Salt and pepper, to taste

12 ounces wide noodles, cooked, warm

Per Serving:
Calories: 512
% of calories from fat: 16
Fat (gm): 9.1
Saturated fat (gm): 1.9
Cholesterol (mg): 54.3
Sodium (mg): 288
Protein (gm): 17.0
Carbohydrate (gm): 91.7

Exchanges:
Milk: 0.0
Vegetable: 0.0
Fruit: 0.0
Bread: 6.0
Meat: 0.0
Fat: 2.0

1. Sauté onions and mushrooms in margarine in large saucepan until onions are tender, 8 to 10 minutes. Stir in potatoes, peas, and vegetable broth; heat to boiling. Reduce heat and simmer, covered, until vegetables are tender, about 10 minutes. Stir in combined dry mustard, sugar, and sour cream; simmer until hot, 3 to 4 minutes. Stir in parsley; season to taste with salt and pepper. Serve over noodles.

CABBAGE RAGOUT WITH REAL MASHED POTATOES

L

Fresh fennel, gingerroot, and apple lend aromatic highlights to this cabbage stew. If fresh fennel is not available, substitute celery and increase the amount of fennel seeds to 1½ teaspoons.

6 servings (about 1⅓ cups each)

1 medium eggplant (about 1¼ pounds), unpeeled, sliced (1-inch)

1 cup chopped onion

½ cup thinly sliced fennel bulb

1 tablespoon each: minced garlic, gingerroot

1 teaspoon fennel seeds, crushed

8 cups thinly sliced cabbage

2 cups reduced-sodium vegetable broth

2 medium apples, cored, cubed

1 cup fat-free sour cream

Salt and pepper, to taste

Real Mashed Potatoes (see p. 485) or 4 cups cooked whole wheat noodles

Per Serving:
Calories: 249
% of calories from fat: 10
Fat (gm): 3
Saturated fat (gm): 0.5
Cholesterol (mg): 8.8
Sodium (mg): 255
Protein (gm): 8.5
Carbohydrate (gm): 50

Exchanges:
Milk: 0.0
Vegetable: 0.0
Fruit: 0.0
Bread: 3.0
Meat: 0.0
Fat: 0.5

1. Cook 5 or 6 eggplant slices over medium heat in lightly greased large skillet until browned on the bottom, 3 to 5 minutes. Spray tops of slices with cooking spray and turn; cook until browned, 3 to 5 minutes. Repeat with remaining eggplant. Cut eggplant into 1-inch cubes and reserve.

2. Sauté onion, fennel, garlic, gingerroot, and fennel seeds in lightly greased large saucepan until onion is tender, 3 to 5 minutes. Add cabbage and broth and heat to boiling; reduce heat and simmer, covered, until cabbage is wilted and crisp-tender, about 5 minutes. Stir in apples and cook, covered, until apples are tender, about 5 minutes. Stir in reserved eggplant and sour cream; cook over medium heat until hot through, 3 to 4 minutes. Season to taste with salt and pepper. Serve stew over potatoes or noodles.

VEGETABLES MARENGO

45 *Flavors of the Mediterranean accent this colorful dish.*

V

6 servings (about 1 cup each)

1½ packages (8-ounce size) tempeh or firm tofu, cubed (¾-inch)

2 cups cubed zucchini

1 cup each: onion wedges, halved small mushrooms

2 cloves minced garlic

1 tablespoon flour

1 can (16 ounces) reduced-sodium diced tomatoes, undrained

¾ cup vegetable broth

1 strip orange zest (3 x 1-inch)

½ teaspoon each: dried thyme and oregano leaves

1 bay leaf

Salt and pepper, to taste

2 cups cooked brown rice, warm

Per Serving:
Net carbohydrate (gm): 27
Calories: 228
% of calories from fat: 26
Fat (gm): 7
Saturated fat (gm): 1.4
Cholesterol (mg): 0.0
Sodium (mg): 101
Protein (gm): 14
Carbohydrate (gm): 31

Exchanges:
Milk: 0.0
Vegetable: 0.0
Fruit: 0.0
Bread: 2.0
Meat: 1.0
Fat: 0.5

1. Sauté tempeh, vegetables, and garlic in lightly greased large skillet until tempeh is beginning to brown, 5 to 8 minutes; stir in flour and cook 1 minute longer. Add remaining ingredients, except salt, pepper, and rice; heat to boiling; reduce heat and simmer, covered, until vegetables are tender, about 5 minutes. Discard bay leaf; season to taste with salt and pepper. Serve over rice.

MEATLESS SLOPPY JOES

45

V

A great sandwich for kids of all ages! Serve with lots of pickles and fresh vegetable relishes.

4 servings

¾ cup sliced mushrooms

½ cup each: chopped onion, green or red bell pepper

1 teaspoon minced garlic

½ cup each: reduced-sodium catsup, textured vegetable protein

⅔ cup water

2 tablespoons light brown sugar

1 tablespoon prepared mustard

1 teaspoon each: celery seeds, chili powder

Salt and pepper, to taste

4 whole wheat hamburger buns, toasted

8 sweet or dill pickle spears

Per Serving:
Calories: 264
% of calories from fat: 11
Fat (gm): 3.5
Saturated fat (gm): 0.7
Cholesterol (mg): 0
Sodium (mg): 428
Protein (gm): 15.1
Carbohydrate (gm): 48.9

Exchanges:
Milk: 0.0
Vegetable: 1.0
Fruit: 0.0
Bread: 2.0
Meat: 2.0
Fat: 0.0

1. Sauté mushrooms, onion, bell pepper, and garlic in lightly greased medium saucepan until tender, 5 to 8 minutes. Stir in remaining ingredients, except salt, pepper, buns, and pickles; heat to boiling. Reduce heat and simmer, covered, 10 minutes. Season to taste with salt and pepper. Serve in buns with pickles.

HASH BROWN LOAF WITH EGGS

45

LO

This is a perfect entrée for brunch or a light supper.

4 servings

¾ cup each: textured vegetable protein, vegetable broth

1 cup shredded carrots

⅓ cup each: finely chopped onion, red bell pepper

2 cloves garlic, minced

¾ cup shredded Idaho potato

1½ teaspoons each: dried chives, thyme leaves

Salt and pepper, to taste

1 cup each: no-cholesterol real egg product, shredded fat-free Cheddar cheese (4 ounces), divided

4 fried or poached eggs

1. Combine vegetable protein and broth in medium bowl; let stand until broth is absorbed, 5 to 10 minutes. Sauté carrots, onion, bell pepper, and garlic in lightly greased skillet until tender, about 5 minutes. Stir in potato and herbs; season to taste with salt and pepper. Mix in egg product and ¾ cup cheese.

2. Pack mixture into greased 7 x 4-inch loaf pan. Bake, loosely covered, at 350 degrees until loaf is set, 45–60 minutes; uncover and sprinkle with remaining ¼ cup cheese. Bake until cheese melted, about 5 minutes. Let stand 10 minutes; loosen sides of loaf with sharp knife and unmold onto serving plate. Serve with eggs.

Per Serving:
Calories: 310
% of calories from fat: 21
Fat (gm): 7.4
Saturated fat (gm): 2
Cholesterol (mg): 211
Sodium (mg): 493
Protein (gm): 36.2
Carbohydrate (gm): 26

Exchanges:
Milk: 0.0
Vegetable: 2.0
Fruit: 0.0
Bread: 1.0
Meat: 3.0
Fat: 0.0

ROASTED EGGPLANT AND VEGETARIAN SAUSAGE WITH ZITI

45

V

Enjoy with any pasta or soft polenta, or in a warm pita.

6 servings

1 medium eggplant, unpeeled, sliced (½-inch)
3 medium onions, cut into wedges (½-inch)
Vegetable cooking spray
½ teaspoon each: dried thyme, marjoram and savory leaves
Salt and pepper, to taste
12 ounces Italian-style vegetarian sausage, cooked, crumbled
1 can (14½ ounces) reduced-sodium diced tomatoes, undrained
1 tablespoon roasted garlic
8 ounces ziti, cooked, warm

Per Serving:
Calories: 298
% of calories from fat: 21
Fat (gm): 7.1
Saturated fat (gm): 1.9
Cholesterol (mg): 30.4
Sodium (mg): 473
Protein (gm): 17.1
Carbohydrate (gm): 44.1

Exchanges:
Milk: 0.0
Vegetable: 2.0
Fruit: 0.0
Bread: 2.0
Meat: 2.0
Fat: 0.0

1. Cut eggplant slices into fourths; arrange eggplant and onions in single layer on foil-lined greased jelly roll pan. Spray vegetables with cooking spray; sprinkle with herbs, salt, and pepper. Roast at 425 degrees 25 minutes. Spoon combined vegetarian sausage, tomatoes with liquid, and roasted garlic over vegetables; roast until eggplant and onions are tender, about 15 minutes. Serve over ziti.

ROASTED VEGETABLES AND BEANS WITH PORTOBELLO MUSHROOMS

45

◊

L

Complement this full-flavored entrée with warm garlic bread.

6 servings

1 package (1 pound, 10 ounces) frozen Parmesan-herb oven-roasted vegetables

1 can (15 ounces) each: pinto and dark kidney beans, rinsed, drained

1 red or green bell pepper, thickly sliced

1 small onion, cut into thin wedges

2 tablespoons olive or vegetable oil, divided

4 large portobello mushrooms, stems removed

Per Serving:
Calories: 299
% of calories from fat: 18
Fat (gm): 5.5
Saturated fat (gm): 0.8
Cholesterol (mg): 3.3
Sodium (mg): 764
Protein (gm): 9.8
Carbohydrate (gm): 47.2

Exchanges:
Milk: 0.0
Vegetable: 2.0
Fruit: 0.0
Bread: 3.0
Meat: 0.0

1. Toss vegetables, except mushrooms, with 1 tablespoon oil and arrange in single layer on greased aluminum foil-lined large jelly roll pan; sprinkle with Parmesan-herb seasoning packet. Arrange mushrooms on end of pan and brush with remaining 1 tablespoon oil. Bake at 450 degrees until browned, about 30 minutes. Arrange mushrooms on plates; spoon vegetables over.

SPINACH CHEESE CREPES

LO

For variation, add ½ cup sautéed chopped portobello mushrooms to the cottage cheese mixture.

4 servings (2 crepes each)

¼ cup chopped onion

1 package (10 ounces) frozen chopped spinach, thawed, well drained

1 cup fat-free cottage cheese

½ teaspoon dried thyme leaves

2–3 pinches ground nutmeg

Salt and pepper, to taste

8 slices (4 ounces) fat-free mozzarella or Swiss cheese

8 Crepes (see p. 564), warm

1½ cups (½ recipe) Fresh Tomato and Herb Sauce (see p. 177)

Per Serving:
Net carbohydrate (gm): 20
Calories: 342
% of calories from fat: 28
Fat (gm): 11
Saturated fat (gm): 2.6
Cholesterol (mg): 123
Sodium (mg): 905
Protein (gm): 36
Carbohydrate (gm): 27

Exchanges:
Milk: 0.0
Vegetable: 0.0
Fruit: 0.0;
Bread: 1.5
Meat: 4.0
Fat: 0.0

1. Sauté onion in lightly greased medium skillet until tender, 3 to 4 minutes. Add spinach and cook until very dry, about 5 minutes. Mix with cottage cheese, thyme, and nutmeg; season to taste with salt and pepper.

2. Place cheese slices on crepes; top with spinach-cheese mixture. Roll up crepes and place, seam sides down, in greased baking dish. Bake, loosely covered, at 325 degrees until hot, about 10 minutes. Serve with Fresh Tomato and Herb Sauce.

VEGETABLE STRUDEL WITH CHEESE

L   *A special dish for festive occasions that's easy enough for family dinners, too.*

4 servings

2 packages (1.25 ounces each) cheese sauce mix

1 cup each: sliced shiitake or cremini mushrooms, red bell peppers

¼ cup chopped shallots

1 teaspoon minced garlic

1 tablespoon margarine or butter

1½ cups each: small broccoli florets, cubed butternut or acorn squash, cooked crisp-tender

¾ cup (3 ounces) shredded reduced-fat brick or Swiss cheese

Salt and pepper, to taste

5 sheets frozen fillo pastry, thawed

Vegetable cooking spray

Per Serving:
Calories: 245
% of calories from fat: 25
Fat (gm): 7.7
Saturated fat (gm): 3.3
Cholesterol (mg): 11.1
Sodium (mg): 724
Protein (gm): 12.1
Carbohydrate (gm): 38.6

Exchanges:
Milk: 0.0
Vegetable: 1.0
Fruit: 0.0
Bread: 2.0
Meat: 1.0
Fat: 0.5

1. Make cheese sauce according to package directions. Sauté mushrooms, bell peppers, shallots, and garlic in margarine in large skillet 5 minutes. Stir in broccoli, squash, and half the cheese sauce; remove from heat. Stir in shredded cheese; season to taste with salt and pepper.

2. Lay 1 sheet fillo on clean kitchen towel; spray lightly with cooking spray. Cover with second sheet fillo and spray with cooking spray; repeat with remaining fillo. Spoon vegetable mixture along long side of fillo, 3 to 4 inches from the edge. Fold edge of fillo over filling and roll up, using towel to help lift and roll; place seam side down on greased cookie sheet. Spray top of fillo lightly with cooking spray.

3. Bake at 400 degrees until golden, about 20 minutes. Let stand 5 minutes before cutting. Trim ends; cut strudel into 4 pieces and arrange on plates. Serve with remaining cheese sauce.

STUFFED CABBAGE WITH CHILI TOMATO SAUCE

V *This dish can be served in smaller portions as a side dish.*

6 servings

1 large head green cabbage

1 cup chopped onion

1 teaspoon each: minced jalapeño chili, garlic

1 tablespoon canola oil

1 can (15 ounces) black beans, rinsed, drained

2 medium tomatoes, chopped

½ teaspoon each: dried oregano and thyme leaves

½ cup each: raisins, cooked rice

1 tablespoon finely chopped cilantro

Salt and pepper, to taste

Chili Tomato Sauce (see p. 186)

Per Serving:
Calories: 228
% of calories from fat: 14
Fat (gm): 4
Saturated fat (gm): 0.4
Cholesterol (mg): 0
Sodium (mg): 313
Protein (gm): 11.9
Carbohydrate (gm): 45.5

Exchanges:
Milk: 0.0
Vegetable: 4.0
Fruit: 0.5
Bread: 1.0
Meat: 0.0
Fat: 0.5

1. Trim cabbage, discarding any wilted outside leaves. Place cabbage in large saucepan with water to cover; heat to boiling. Reduce heat and simmer, covered, 10 minutes. Drain cabbage; cool until warm enough to handle.

2. Sauté onion, jalapeño chili, and garlic in oil in large skillet until tender, about 5 minutes. Add beans, tomatoes, and herbs to skillet; lightly mash beans. Cook, covered, over medium heat, 10 minutes. Stir in raisins, rice, and cilantro; season to taste with salt and pepper.

3. Place cabbage on large square of double-thickness cheesecloth. Spread outer cabbage leaves as flat as possible without breaking them off. Cut out inner leaves of cabbage, chop finely, and add to rice mixture; remove and discard core of cabbage. Pack rice mixture in center of cabbage; fold outer leaves up over mixture, reshaping cabbage. Gather cheesecloth around cabbage and tie with string.

Place cabbage in large saucepan and add water to cover; heat to boiling. Reduce heat and simmer, covered, 1 hour. Lift cabbage from saucepan and remove cheesecloth. Place cabbage on plate and cut into wedges; serve with Chili Tomato Sauce.

Chili Tomato Sauce
Makes about 2 cups

1 can (16 ounces) reduced-sodium tomato sauce
¼ cup water
2–2½ tablespoons chili powder
2 cloves garlic, minced
Salt and pepper, to taste

1. Heat all ingredients, except salt and pepper, to boiling in small saucepan. Reduce heat and simmer, uncovered, 2 to 3 minutes. Season to taste with salt and pepper.

ROASTED STUFFED PORTOBELLO MUSHROOMS WITH SPINACH-CILANTRO PESTO

L   *Serve one mushroom as a hearty appetizer or first course.*

4 servings

8 large portobello mushrooms
1 cup each: finely chopped zucchini, shredded carrots
3 green onions, thinly sliced
¼ cup unseasoned dry bread crumbs
Spinach-Cilantro Pesto (recipe follows)
Salt and pepper, to taste
½ cup (2 ounces) shredded reduced-fat
    mozzarella cheese

Per Serving:
Calories: 185
% of calories from fat: 20
Fat (gm): 3.9
Saturated fat (gm): 1.8
Cholesterol (mg): 7.6
Sodium (mg): 206
Protein (gm): 16
Carbohydrate (gm): 19.1

Exchanges:
Milk: 0.0
Vegetable: 4.0
Fruit: 0.0
Bread: 0.5
Meat: 1.0
Fat: 0.0

1. Remove mushroom stems and chop. Sauté mushroom stems, zucchini, carrots, and green onions in lightly greased skillet until crisp-tender, about 8 minutes. Stir in bread crumbs and pesto; season to taste with salt and pepper. Spoon vegetable mixture onto mushrooms. Bake on greased jelly roll pan at 425 degrees until tender, about 20 minutes, sprinkling with cheese the last 5 minutes of roasting time.

Spinach-Cilantro Pesto
Makes about ½ cup

1 cup loosely packed spinach
¼ cup packed cilantro leaves
3 cloves garlic
¼ teaspoon ground cumin
1 tablespoon grated fat-free Parmesan cheese
1–2 teaspoons each: olive oil, lime juice
1–2 tablespoons water
Salt and pepper, to taste

1. Process all ingredients, except water, salt, and pepper, in food processor or blender until almost smooth; add water if necessary for consistency. Season to taste with salt and pepper. Serve at room temperature.

STIR-FRIED RICE NOODLES WITH VEGETABLES

45

V

Rice noodles are also called cellophane noodles, or "bihon." The dried noodles are soaked in cold water to soften, then drained before using.

4 servings (about 1½ cups each)

1 package (8 ounces) rice noodles
1 cup each: cut green beans, cubed yellow summer squash
½ cup each: thinly sliced celery, red bell pepper
4 green onions, thinly sliced
1 tablespoon finely chopped gingerroot
1 tablespoon canola oil
2 cups shredded napa cabbage
1 cup reduced-sodium vegetable broth
2 tablespoons dry sherry (optional)
2–3 teaspoons light soy sauce
½–1 teaspoon Szechuan chili sauce

Per Serving:
Calories: 161
% of calories from fat: 20
Fat (gm): 3.8
Saturated fat (gm): 0.5
Cholesterol (mg): 0
Sodium (mg): 137
Protein (gm): 4.2
Carbohydrate (gm): 29.4

Exchanges:
Milk: 0.0
Vegetable: 1.0
Fruit: 0.0
Bread: 1.5
Meat: 0.0
Fat: 0.5

1. Place noodles in large bowl; pour cold water over to cover. Let stand until noodles separate and are soft, about 15 minutes; drain.

2. Stir-fry green beans, squash, celery, bell pepper, green onions, and gingerroot in oil in large wok or skillet until tender, 8 to

10 minutes. Add cabbage and stir-fry 1 minute. Stir in noodles and remaining ingredients. Heat to boiling; reduce heat and simmer, uncovered, until noodles have absorbed all liquid, about 5 minutes.

BUCATINI WITH BRUSSELS SPROUTS AND WALNUTS

45 *Bucatini is a spaghetti-type pasta with a hole in the center.*

L

4 servings

12 ounces Brussels sprouts, cooked crisp-tender, halved

2 teaspoons minced garlic

8 ounces bucatini or spaghetti, cooked, warm

2 cups seeded, chopped Italian plum tomatoes

⅔ cup minced parsley

¼ cup each: toasted unseasoned dry bread crumbs, chopped walnuts

2–4 tablespoons grated fat-free Parmesan cheese

Salt and pepper, to taste

Per Serving:
Calories: 367
% of calories from fat: 16
Fat (gm): 6.7
Saturated fat (gm): 0.7
Cholesterol (mg): 0
Sodium (mg): 118
Protein (gm): 14.9
Carbohydrate (gm): 65.4

Exchanges:
Milk: 0.0
Vegetable: 3.0
Fruit: 0.0
Bread: 3.0
Meat: 0.5
Fat: 1.0

1. Sauté Brussels sprouts and garlic in lightly greased skillet until hot, 3 to 4 minutes. Toss with remaining ingredients, except salt and pepper. Season to taste with salt and pepper.

45-MINUTE PREPARATION TIP: Begin cooking the bucatini before preparing the rest of the recipe.

ANGEL HAIR PASTA WITH VEGETABLES AND GOAT CHEESE

45 *Goat cheese adds a creamy texture and piquant accent to this flavorful pasta dish.*

L

6 servings

8 ounces each: snow peas, sliced mushrooms

1 cup each: sliced carrots, tomatoes

1 teaspoon each: dried basil and tarragon leaves

½ cup each: reduced-sodium vegetable broth, fat-free milk

2 teaspoons tomato paste

Salt and pepper, to taste

3 ounces goat cheese or reduced-fat cream cheese

12 ounces capellini (angel hair) or thin spaghetti, cooked, warm

Per Serving:
Calories: 293
% of calories from fat: 13
Fat (gm): 4.3
Saturated fat (gm): 2.5
Cholesterol (mg): 12.9
Sodium (mg): 190
Protein (gm): 13.2
Carbohydrate (gm): 50.7

Exchanges:
Milk: 0.0
Vegetable: 2.5
Fruit: 0.0
Bread: 2.5
Meat: 0.0
Fat: 0.5

1. Sauté vegetables and herbs in lightly greased large skillet until snow peas are crisp-tender, 6 to 8 minutes. Stir in vegetable broth, milk, and tomato paste; heat to boiling. Reduce heat and simmer, uncovered, until thickened to desired sauce consistency, about 10 minutes; stirring occasionally; season to taste with salt and pepper. Stir goat cheese into warm pasta until melted; add vegetable mixture and toss.

45-MINUTE PREPARATION TIP: Begin cooking pasta while sauce is simmering.

PASTA WITH OYSTER MUSHROOMS

45

L

Although this recipe specifies oyster mushrooms, feel free to substitute any other type.

6 servings

16 ounces oyster mushrooms, separated into pieces

1–2 tablespoons minced garlic

4 tablespoons margarine or butter

2 tablespoons flour

2 cups fat-free milk

½ cup reduced-sodium vegetable broth

2 teaspoons lemon juice

1 cup chopped, seeded tomato

½ teaspoon each: salt, pepper

12 ounces fettuccine, cooked, warm

2 tablespoons grated Parmesan cheese

Per Serving:
Calories: 328
% of calories from fat: 30
Fat (gm): 11.0
Saturated fat (gm): 2
Cholesterol (mg): 3.0
Sodium (mg): 454
Protein (gm): 15.0
Carbohydrate (gm): 44.4

Exchanges:
Milk: 0.0
Vegetable: 3.0
Fruit: 0.0
Bread: 2.0
Meat: 0.0
Fat: 2.0

1. Sauté mushrooms and garlic in margarine in large skillet until soft, about 5 minutes. Stir in flour; cook 1 minute. Add milk, broth, and lemon juice; heat to boiling. Reduce heat and simmer, uncovered, until liquid is reduced to about 1¼ cups, about 10 minutes. Stir in tomato, salt, and pepper. Spoon sauce over pasta; sprinkle with Parmesan cheese.

45-MINUTE PREPARATION TIP: Begin cooking pasta while sauce is simmering.

FETTUCCINE WITH EGGPLANT PERSILLADE

45

L

"Persillade" is a French term meaning "with lots of parsley," which this fragrant dish has.

4 servings

1 each: chopped medium onion, green and red bell pepper

1 small eggplant, unpeeled, cubed

2 teaspoons minced roasted garlic

½ cup canned reduced-sodium vegetable broth

Salt and pepper, to taste

½ cup finely chopped parsley

8 ounces whole wheat fettuccine, cooked, warm

2–4 tablespoons grated fat-free Parmesan cheese

Per Serving:
Calories: 246
% of calories from fat: 9
Fat (gm): 2.5
Saturated fat (gm): 0.1
Cholesterol (mg): 0
Sodium (mg): 136
Protein (gm): 11.0
Carbohydrate (gm): 48.7

Exchanges:
Milk: 0.0
Vegetable: 3.0
Fruit: 0.0
Bread: 2.0
Meat: 0.5
Fat: 0.0

1. Sauté onion, bell peppers, eggplant, and garlic in lightly greased large skillet 5 minutes, stirring occasionally. Add broth and heat to boiling; reduce heat and simmer, covered, until eggplant is tender and broth absorbed, about 5 minutes. Season to taste with salt and pepper. Toss vegetable mixture with parsley, pasta, and cheese.

45-MINUTE PREPARATION TIP: Begin cooking the fettuccine before preparing the rest of the recipe.

FETTUCCINE WITH GREENS AND CARAMELIZED ONIONS

45 | *This pasta dish is healthy and delicious!*

V | **4 servings**

4 medium onions, sliced

1 tablespoon olive oil

1 teaspoon sugar

1 can (14½ ounces) reduced-sodium vegetable broth

4 cups thinly sliced kale, mustard greens, Swiss chard or spinach

Salt and pepper, to taste

8 ounces fettuccine, cooked, warm

Per Serving:
Calories: 281
% of calories from fat: 18
Fat (gm): 5.8
Saturated fat (gm): 0.5
Cholesterol (mg): 0
Sodium (mg): 151
Protein (gm): 10.3
Carbohydrate (gm): 49.9

Exchanges:
Milk: 0.0
Vegetable: 2.0
Fruit: 0.0
Bread: 2.5
Meat: 0.0
Fat: 1.0

1. Cook onions in oil over medium heat in large skillet 5 minutes; reduce heat to low and stir in sugar. Cook until onions are golden in color and very soft, about 20 minutes. Stir in broth; heat to boiling. Reduce heat and simmer, uncovered, until broth is reduced by ⅓, about 10 minutes. Add kale and simmer, covered, until wilted, 5 to 7 minutes. Simmer, uncovered, until broth is almost evaporated, about 5 minutes. Season to taste with salt and pepper. Toss with pasta.

45-MINUTE PREPARATION TIP: Begin cooking the fettuccine before preparing the rest of the recipe.

MIXED VEGETABLE FETTUCCINE

45 *Roasting is an effortless way to cook many vegetables at the same time!*

L   **6 servings**

2 sweet potatoes, peeled, thickly sliced

1 each: thickly sliced yellow summer squash, green bell pepper, medium tomato

4 green onions, very thinly sliced

Vegetable cooking spray

¼ cup cider vinegar

2 tablespoons olive oil

1 teaspoon lemon juice

1 tablespoon each: chopped fresh or 1 teaspoon dried oregano leaves and tarragon leaves

8 ounces fettuccine, cooked, warm

1 tablespoon grated Parmesan cheese

Per Serving:
Calories: 267
% of calories from fat: 26
Fat (gm): 8.5
Saturated fat (gm): 1.1
Cholesterol (mg): 1.1
Sodium (mg): 119
Protein (gm): 9.1
Carbohydrate (gm): 46.4

Exchanges:
Milk: 0.0
Vegetable: 1.5
Fruit: 0.0
Bread: 2.5
Meat: 0.0
Fat: 1.5

1. Arrange vegetables in single layer on greased foil-lined jelly roll pan; spray with cooking spray. Roast at 425 degrees until vegetables are browned and tender, about 30 minutes. Toss with combined vinegar, olive oil, lemon juice, and herbs; toss with pasta. Sprinkle with Parmesan cheese.

MAFALDE WITH GARBANZO BEANS, TOMATOES, AND CROUTONS

45 *Serve with Italian-style vegetarian sausage, if you like.*

L   **8 servings**

½ cup each: chopped onion, poblano chili or green bell pepper

1 teaspoon minced garlic

1 can (15½ ounces) garbanzo beans, rinsed, drained

2 cups seeded, chopped Italian plum tomatoes

¼ cup each: chopped basil leaves, fat-free Italian salad dressing

8 ounces mafalde or other flat pasta, cooked, warm

1½ cups (½ recipe) Herb or Parmesan Croutons (see pp. 532, 533)

Grated Parmesan cheese, as garnish

1. Sauté onion, poblano chili, and garlic in lightly greased medium skillet until tender, 5 to 8 minutes. Add beans, tomatoes, and basil; cook, covered, over medium heat until hot, 3 to 4 minutes. Toss with pasta and croutons; sprinkle with Parmesan cheese.

45-MINUTE PREPARATION TIP: Begin cooking the mafalde before preparing the rest of the recipe.

Per Serving:
Calories: 393
% of calories from fat: 18
Fat (gm): 7.7
Saturated fat (gm): 1.0
Cholesterol (mg): 0.0
Sodium (mg): 531
Protein (gm): 12.3
Carbohydrate (gm): 69

Exchanges:
Milk: 0.0
Vegetable: 0.0
Fruit: 0.0
Bread: 4.0
Meat: 1.0
Fat: 1.0

MARINATED TORTELLINI AND VEGETABLE KABOBS

45
❄

Broccoli, cauliflower, carrots, or winter squash are also delicious in this recipe; cook until crisp-tender before skewering.

LO

4 servings

1 large red bell pepper, cubed (1-inch)
1 each: thickly sliced small yellow summer squash, zucchini, cucumber
24 each: cherry tomatoes, medium mushroom caps
16 pitted Greek or ripe olives
4 ounces each: cubed fat-free mozzarella cheese, fat-free Cheddar cheese
½ package (9 ounce-size) mushroom, herb or cheese tortellini, cooked
1¼ cups fat-free Italian salad dressing
3 cloves garlic, minced
2 tablespoons grated fat-free Parmesan cheese
4 cups torn salad greens

Per Serving:
Calories: 362
% of calories from fat: 16
Fat (gm): 6.2
Saturated fat (gm): 1.6
Cholesterol (mg): 13.3
Sodium (mg): 606
Protein (gm): 30.6
Carbohydrate (gm): 44.3

Exchanges:
Milk: 0.0
Vegetable: 5.0
Fruit: 0.0
Bread: 1.5
Meat: 2.5
Fat: 0.0

1. Arrange vegetables, olives, cubed cheese, and tortellini on wooden skewers and place in large baking dish; pour combined salad dressing, garlic, and Parmesan cheese over. Refrigerate, covered, 4 to 6 hours, turning kabobs occasionally. Drain kabobs; reserving ¾ cup marinade. Arrange kabobs on lettuce on plates; drizzle reserved marinade.

POTATO GNOCCHI WITH SAGE CREAM

45   *Fat-free half-and-half is the secret to the rich creaminess of the sauce.*

L   **6 servings**

2 cups fat-free half-and-half or fat-free milk

16–20 thinly sliced medium sage leaves or 1
   teaspoon dried sage leaves

2 tablespoons all-purpose flour

½ teaspoon ground nutmeg

¾ cup water, divided

1 cup chopped onion

2 teaspoons margarine or butter

4 cups small broccoli florets

1 package (16 ounces) potato gnocchi, cooked, warm

Salt and pepper, to taste

Shredded Parmesan cheese, as garnish

Per Serving:
Calories: 263
% of calories from fat: 2
Fat (gm): 0.6
Saturated fat (gm): 0.2
Cholesterol (mg): 0.9
Sodium (mg): 150
Protein (gm): 13.4
Carbohydrate (gm): 52.4

Exchanges:
Milk: 0.0
Vegetable: 2.0
Fruit: 0.0
Bread: 2.5
Meat: 0.0
Fat: 0.0

1. Heat half-and-half and sage (if using dried sage, tie leaves in small cheesecloth bag) to boiling in medium saucepan; reduce heat and simmer, covered, 10 minutes. Strain, discarding sage. Return half-and-half to saucepan and heat to boiling; whisk in combined flour, nutmeg, and ¼ cup water. Boil, whisking, until thickened, about 1 minute; keep warm.

2. Sauté onion in margarine in large skillet 2 to 3 minutes; add broccoli and remaining ½ cup water and heat to boiling. Reduce heat and simmer, covered, until broccoli is crisp-tender, about 5 minutes; drain. Add sauce and gnocchi and cook 2 to 3 minutes; season to taste with salt and pepper. Sprinkle with cheese.

45-MINUTE PREPARATION TIP: Begin cooking the gnocchi before preparing the rest of the recipe.

TUSCAN BEAN BAKE

V | *Easy to make, these beans are lemon-scented and seasoned with sun-dried tomatoes, garlic, and herbs.*

4 servings (about 1 cup each)

1 cup dried cannellini or Great Northern beans

1 cup reduced-sodium vegetable broth

½ cup each: chopped onion, red bell pepper

2 teaspoons minced garlic

1 teaspoon each: dried sage and rosemary leaves

2–3 teaspoons grated lemon zest

6 sun-dried tomatoes (not in oil), softened, sliced

Salt and pepper, to taste

1 cup fresh whole wheat bread crumbs

¼ cup minced parsley

Per Serving:
Calories: 250
% of calories from fat: 6
Fat (gm): 1.7
Saturated fat (gm): 0.3
Cholesterol (mg): 0
Sodium (mg): 220
Protein (gm): 14.3
Carbohydrate (gm): 45.4

Exchanges:
Milk: 0.0
Vegetable: 1.5
Fruit: 0.0
Bread: 2.5
Meat: 0.5
Fat: 0.0

1. Cover beans with 2 inches water in large saucepan; heat to boiling and boil, uncovered, 2 minutes. Remove from heat and let stand, covered, 1 hour; drain.

2. Combine beans and remaining ingredients, except bread crumbs and parsley, in 1½-quart casserole. Bake, covered, at 350 degrees, until beans are tender, about 1 hour; season to taste with salt and pepper. Sprinkle combined bread crumbs and parsley over top, pressing lightly onto beans to moisten. Bake, uncovered, until thickened, about 20 minutes.

VEGETABLE SALAD WITH MILLET

45

V

Serve this salad in bowls, in beefsteak tomato halves, or use it as a filling for warm pita pockets.

6 servings

1¼ cups millet

3⅓ cups water

½ cup each: sliced celery, red bell pepper

¼ cup each: sliced green onions, carrot, parsley, and basil leaves

½ small head iceberg lettuce, sliced

1 medium tomato, coarsely chopped

Oregano Vinaigrette (recipe follows)

Salt and pepper, to taste

4 pita breads

Per Serving:
Calories: 350
% of calories from fat: 24
Fat (gm): 9.2
Saturated fat (gm): 1.3
Cholesterol (mg): 0.0
Sodium (mg): 237
Protein (gm): 9.3
Carbohydrate (gm): 57.0

Exchanges:
Milk: 0.0
Vegetable: 0.0
Fruit: 0.0
Bread: 4.0
Meat: 0.0
Fat: 1.5

1. Cook millet in large saucepan over medium heat until toasted, 2 to 3 minutes, stirring frequently. Add water and heat to boiling; reduce heat and simmer, covered, until millet is tender and liquid absorbed, about 15 minutes. Remove from heat and let stand, covered, 10 minutes; cool.

2. Process celery, bell pepper, green onions, carrot, parsley, and basil in food processor until finely chopped; transfer to large bowl. Process lettuce until finely chopped; add to vegetables. Add tomato, millet, and Oregano Vinaigrette; toss. Season to taste with salt and pepper. Serve with pitas.

Oregano Vinaigrette
Makes about ⅓ cup

3 tablespoons each: olive oil, white wine vinegar

1 teaspoon dried oregano leaves

1. Mix all ingredients.

WHEAT AND BARLEY BOWL

Grains and greens are cooked together, then combined with tomatoes and toasted nuts.

4 servings (about 1 cup each)

¾ cup quick-cooking barley

2 cups reduced-sodium vegetable broth

¼ cup bulgur

½ teaspoon dried thyme leaves

3 cups thinly sliced turnip greens, kale or spinach

½ cup thinly sliced green onions

1 large tomato, coarsely chopped

¼ cup coarsely chopped walnuts, toasted

1–2 tablespoons lemon juice

Salt and pepper, to taste

Per Serving:
Calories: 257
% of calories from fat: 20
Fat (gm): 6
Saturated fat (gm): 0.6
Cholesterol (mg): 0
Sodium (mg): 66
Protein (gm): 8.6
Carbohydrate (gm): 41.7

Exchanges:
Milk: 0.0
Vegetable: 1.0
Fruit: 0.0
Bread: 2.5
Meat: 0.0
Fat: 1.0

1. Add barley to lightly greased large saucepan and cook over medium heat, stirring occasionally, until golden, about 5 minutes. Add broth, bulgur, and thyme and heat to boiling: reduce heat and simmer, covered, until barley is tender, about 10 minutes. Stir in greens and green onions; cook, covered, until all liquid is gone, about 10 minutes. Stir in tomato, walnuts, and lemon juice; cook 5 minutes longer. Season to taste with salt and pepper.

EGGPLANT POLENTA STACK

Packaged polenta comes in several flavors; choose your favorite for this dish.

4 servings

8 slices eggplant (¾-inch)

1 egg, lightly beaten

½ cup seasoned dry bread crumbs

¼ cup (1 ounce) grated Parmesan cheese

8 slices (½-inch) tomato

Salt and pepper, to taste

1 package (16 ounces) prepared Italian-herb polenta, cut into 8 slices

2–4 ounces reduced-fat feta, crumbled

1. Dip eggplant slices in egg and coat with combined bread crumbs and Parmesan cheese. Cook in lightly greased large skillet until browned, 6 to 8 minutes on each side. Arrange eggplant in baking pan; top with tomato slices and sprinkle lightly with salt and pepper. Top tomato slices with polenta and sprinkle with feta cheese. Bake at 500 degrees, loosely covered, until polenta is warm and cheese softened, about 5 minutes.

Per Serving:
Calories: 222
% of calories from fat: 18
Fat (gm): 4.5
Saturated fat (gm): 2.4
Cholesterol (mg): 9
Sodium (mg): 624
Protein (gm): 10.9
Carbohydrate (gm): 35.1

Exchanges:
Milk: 0.0
Vegetable: 0.0
Fruit: 0.0
Bread: 2.0
Meat: 1.0
Fat: 0.0

FALAFEL PATTIES

45

L

The falafel mixture can also be shaped into 1-inch balls and cooked as below; serve with Yogurt Cucumber Sauce as appetizers, or in pitas for sandwiches.

4 servings (2 each)

1 package (6 ounces) falafel mix
½ cup shredded carrots
¼ cup sunflower kernels
1 tablespoons thinly sliced green onions
Yogurt Cucumber Sauce (recipe follows)

Per Serving:
Calories: 255
% of calories from fat: 30
Fat (gm): 7.7
Saturated fat (gm): 0.5
Cholesterol (mg): 1
Sodium (mg): 586
Protein (gm): 11.7
Carbohydrate (gm): 28.6

Exchanges:
Milk: 0.0
Vegetable: 0.0
Fruit: 0.0
Bread: 2.0
Meat: 1.0
Fat: 1.0

1. Prepare falafel mix with water according to package directions; mix in carrots, sunflower kernels, and green onions. Shape mixture into 8 patties about ½ inch thick; sauté in lightly greased skillet until browned, 4 to 5 minutes on each side. Serve with Yogurt Cucumber Sauce.

Yogurt Cucumber Sauce
Makes about 1⅔ cups

1 cup each: plain fat-free yogurt, finely chopped cucumber
½ teaspoon each: dried dill weed, mint leaves
Salt and white pepper, to taste

1. Mix yogurt, cucumber, and herbs. Season to taste with salt and white pepper.

45-MINUTE PREPARATION TIP: Make Yogurt Cucumber Sauce while patties are cooking.

FALAFEL DINNER LOAF

45

LO

Dried fruit provides a marvelous sweet accent in this easy-to-make loaf. It's also terrific served cold for summer dining.

4 servings

1 package (6 ounces) falafel mix
½ cup each: shredded zucchini, chopped mixed
 dried fruit
3 tablespoons each: coarsely chopped toasted pecans,
 thinly sliced green onion
2 eggs
¾ cup plain fat-free yogurt

Per Serving:
Calories: 311
% of calories from fat: 29
Fat (gm): 9.5
Saturated fat (gm): 1.1
Cholesterol (mg): 106.8
Sodium (mg): 603
Protein (gm): 12.9
Carbohydrate (gm): 38.3

Exchanges:
Milk: 0.0
Vegetable: 0.0
Fruit: 0.5
Bread: 2.0
Meat: 0.0
Fat: 2.0

1. Prepare falafel mix with water according to package directions; mix in remaining ingredients, except yogurt. Pack mixture into greased 7 x 4-inch loaf pan. Bake, uncovered, at 350 degrees until set, about 30 minutes. Invert loaf onto serving plate; serve with yogurt.

GINGER COCONUT RICE AND SWEET POTATOES

45

Jasmine rice, scented with lemon grass and coconut, enhances this Asian-inspired entrée offering.

V

4 servings

½ cup finely chopped onion

1½–2 tablespoons each: minced gingerroot, lemon grass

1 teaspoon minced garlic

1¼ cups each: water, reduced-fat coconut milk

1 cup jasmine or long-grain rice

1 sweet potato, peeled, quartered, sliced (¼-inch)

2 cups frozen stir-fry vegetable blend with asparagus

¼ cup finely chopped cilantro

1–2 tablespoons lime juice

Salt and pepper, to taste

Per Serving:
Calories: 270
% of calories from fat: 13
Fat (gm): 3.9
Saturated fat (gm): 0
Cholesterol (mg): 0
Sodium (mg): 12
Protein (gm): 4.8
Carbohydrate (gm): 52.8

Exchanges:
Milk: 0.0
Vegetable: 1.0
Fruit: 0.0
Bread: 3.0
Meat: 0.0
Fat: 0.5

1. Sauté onion, gingerroot, lemon grass, and garlic in lightly greased medium skillet until onion is tender, about 5 minutes. Stir in water, coconut milk, rice, and sweet potato; heat to boiling. Reduce heat and simmer, covered, until sweet potato is almost tender, about 10 minutes. Mix in stir-fry blend; simmer, covered, until vegetables are tender and liquid absorbed, 8 to 10 minutes. Stir in cilantro; season to taste with lime juice, salt, and pepper.

ASIAN FRIED RICE

45

The combination of wild and white rice adds a new dimension to an Asian favorite. Lightly scrambled egg is a traditional addition to many fried rice recipes; it can be omitted, if desired.

O

4 servings

2 cups broccoli florets and sliced stalks

1 cup halved snow peas

¾ cup each: bean sprouts, sliced carrots, shiitake mushrooms, chopped celery, green bell pepper

1 teaspoon each: minced garlic, gingerroot

½ cup reduced-sodium vegetable broth

2 tablespoons reduced-sodium soy sauce

1½ cups each: cooked white and wild rice

1 egg, lightly scrambled, crumbled

Salt and pepper, to taste

Per Serving:
Calories: 236
% of calories from fat: 8
Fat (gm): 2.1
Saturated fat (gm): 0.5
Cholesterol (mg): 53.3
Sodium (mg): 340
Protein (gm): 10.2
Carbohydrate (gm): 46.9

1. Stir-fry vegetables, garlic, and gingerroot in lightly greased large wok or skillet until crisp-tender, 5 to 8 minutes. Add broth and soy sauce; stir in rice and scrambled egg and stir-fry 2 to 3 minutes longer. Season to taste with salt and pepper.

Exchanges:
Milk: 0.0
Vegetable: 2.0
Fruit: 0.0
Bread: 2.5
Meat: 0.0
Fat: 0.0

CURRIED COUSCOUS WITH SMOKED TOFU

45

L

A delicious combination of flavors and textures. Serve with a green salad and crusty bread.

6 servings

½ cup each: finely chopped onion, red or green bell pepper

1½ teaspoons minced garlic

1 tablespoon olive oil

1½ teaspoons curry powder

1¼ cups vegetable broth

1 package (10 ounces) couscous (spice packet discarded)

2 packages (6 ounces each) smoked tofu, cubed

1 can (11 ounces) Mandarin orange segments, drained

Salt and pepper, to taste

6 tablespoons (1½ ounces) crumbled reduced-fat feta cheese

Per Serving:
Calories: 328
% of calories from fat: 23
Fat (gm): 8.8
Saturated fat (gm): 1.7
Cholesterol (mg): 2.5
Sodium (mg): 318
Protein (gm): 17.3
Carbohydrate (gm): 46.8

Exchanges:
Milk: 0.0
Vegetable: 0.0
Fruit: 0.0
Bread: 3.0
Meat: 1.0
Fat: 1.0

1. Sauté onion, bell pepper, and garlic in oil in large saucepan until tender, about 5 minutes. Stir in curry powder; add broth and heat to boiling. Stir in couscous and tofu; remove from heat and let stand, covered, 5 minutes. Stir in orange segments; season to taste with salt and pepper and sprinkle with cheese.

GREEN ON GREEN STIR-FRY WITH TOFU

45 *The variety of green vegetables creates a beautiful presentation.*

V **6 servings**

3 cups sliced leeks (white parts only)

1 cup sliced celery

1 teaspoon each: minced garlic, gingerroot

½ teaspoon crushed red pepper

3 cups each: snow peas, sliced bok choy

1 cup chopped green bell pepper

2 cups reduced-sodium vegetable broth

2 tablespoons cornstarch

2 teaspoons reduced-sodium soy sauce

Salt and pepper, to taste

1 package (10 ounces) light firm tofu, cubed

4 cups cooked rice, warm

Per Serving:
Calories: 236
% of calories from fat: 4.8
Fat (gm): 1.3
Saturated fat (gm): 0.2
Cholesterol (mg): 0.0
Sodium (mg): 319
Protein (gm): 9.3
Carbohydrate (gm): 47

Exchanges:
Milk: 0.0
Vegetable: 2.0
Fruit: 0.0
Bread: 2.0
Meat: 1.0
Fat: 0.0

1. Stir-fry leeks, celery, garlic, gingerroot, and crushed red pepper in lightly greased large wok or skillet 2 to 3 minutes. Add snow peas, bok choy, and bell pepper and stir-fry until crisp-tender, 3 to 5 minutes.

2. Stir combined broth, cornstarch, and soy sauce into wok and heat to boiling. Boil, stirring until thickened, about 1 minute. Season to taste with salt and pepper. Stir in tofu; cook 1 to 2 minutes longer. Serve over rice.

45-MINUTE PREPARATION TIP: Begin cooking the rice before preparing the rest of the recipe.

BLACK BEAN AND SMOKED TOFU SALAD

 The smoky flavor of the tofu is a pleasant contrast to the picante chili, fresh cilantro, and Mustard-Honey Dressing.

4 servings

2 cans (15 ounces each) black beans, rinsed, drained

2 packages (6 ounces each) smoked tofu, cubed

1 cup each: chopped tomato, red bell pepper

½ cup sliced red onion
¼ cup each: finely chopped cilantro, parsley
2 teaspoons each: finely chopped jalapeno chili,
   roasted garlic
Mustard-Honey Dressing (recipe follows)

Per Serving:
Calories: 309
% of calories from fat: 30
Fat (gm): 12
Saturated fat (gm): 2
Cholesterol (mg): 0.0
Sodium (mg): 1024
Protein (gm): 19
Carbohydrate (gm): 42

1. Combine all ingredients in salad bowl and toss.

Exchanges:
Milk: 0.0
Vegetable: 0.0
Fruit: 0.0
Bread: 2.5
Meat: 2.5
Fat: 0.0

Mustard-Honey Dressing

Makes about ½ cup

3–4 tablespoons each: olive oil, cider vinegar
1 tablespoon Dijon mustard
1–2 tablespoons honey
½ teaspoon dried oregano leaves
1–2 dashes red pepper sauce

1. Mix all ingredients.

SWEET POTATO AND TEMPEH PATTIES

45 *Cornbread stuffing crumbs add great flavor and texture to the patties.*

L **4 servings**

Per Serving:
Calories: 336
% of calories from fat: 23
Fat (gm): 8.8
Saturated fat (gm): 3
Cholesterol (mg): 10
Sodium (mg): 224
Protein (gm): 17.2
Carbohydrate (gm): 48.9

1 package (8 ounces) tempeh, crumbled
½ cup each: chopped onion, red bell pepper
2 teaspoons each: minced jalapeno chili, garlic
1–2 teaspoons vegetable oil
1 can (15 ounces) sweet potatoes, drained, mashed
1 cup corn bread stuffing crumbs, finely crushed,
   divided
2 tablespoons sugar-free apricot preserves
Salt and pepper, to taste
½ cup each: applesauce, reduced-fat sour cream

Exchanges:
Milk: 0.0
Vegetable: 1.0
Fruit: 0.0
Bread: 3.0
Meat: 1.0
Fat: 1.0

1. Sauté tempeh, onion, bell pepper, jalapeño chili, and garlic in oil in large skillet until vegetables are tender, about 5 minutes; stir in sweet potatoes, ⅔ cup corn bread crumbs, and apricot preserves.

Season to taste with salt and pepper. Shape mixture into 4 patties; coat with reserved ⅓ cup crumbs. Cook patties in lightly greased large skillet over medium heat until browned, about 5 minutes on each side. Serve warm with applesauce and sour cream.

GARDEN VEGETABLES AND TEMPEH SAUTÉ

45

Excellent served over rice, fresh Chinese-style noodles, or pasta.

V

4 servings

Tamari Marinade (see p. 290)

2 tablespoons red wine vinegar

1 teaspoon dried Italian seasoning

1 package (8 ounces) tempeh

½ cup each: sliced onion, red bell pepper

1 teaspoon minced garlic

1 cup reduced-sodium tomato juice, sliced zucchini

2 cups sliced mushrooms, tomato wedges

1 teaspoon each: dried basil and oregano leaves

¼ teaspoon cayenne pepper

Salt and pepper, to taste

Per Serving:
Net carbohydrate (gm): 16
Calories: 180
% of calories from fat: 30
Fat (gm): 6.8
Saturated fat (gm): 1.4
Cholesterol (mg): 0.0
Sodium (mg): 323
Protein (gm): 15
Carbohydrate (gm): 20

Exchanges:
Milk: 0.0
Vegetable: 1.0
Fruit: 0.0
Bread: 1.0
Meat: 1.5
Fat: 0.0

1. Make marinade, substituting red wine vinegar for the cider vinegar and Italian seasoning for the chili powder. Pour over tempeh in shallow glass bowl. Refrigerate, covered, 4 hours or overnight. Drain; reserve marinade. Cut tempeh into ½-inch cubes.

2. Sauté tempeh, onion, bell pepper, and garlic in lightly greased large skillet until vegetables are crisp-tender, about 5 minutes. Stir in reserved marinade and remaining ingredients, except salt and pepper; heat to boiling. Reduce heat and simmer, covered, until vegetables are tender, 5 to 8 minutes; season to taste with salt and pepper.

TEMPEH STEAK WITH RED AND GREEN STIR-FRY

45 *If available, use red Swiss chard for its intense red and green color.*

V **6 servings**

2 cups each: sliced red onions, red bell peppers

1 cup sliced celery

2 teaspoons minced garlic

1 teaspoon minced gingerroot

6 cups thinly sliced red or green Swiss chard
or spinach

2 cups reduced-sodium vegetable broth

2 tablespoons cornstarch

½–¾ teaspoon hot chili paste

Salt and pepper, to taste

16 ounces tempeh, cut into 6 pieces

4 teaspoons reduced-sodium tamari soy sauce

Per Serving:
Calories: 302
% of calories from fat: 26
Fat (gm): 9.4
Saturated fat (gm): 1.5
Cholesterol (mg): 0
Sodium (mg): 272
Protein (gm): 27.3
Carbohydrate (gm): 32

Exchanges:
Milk: 0.0
Vegetable: 3.0
Fruit: 0.0
Bread: 1.0
Meat: 2.0
Fat: 1.0

1. Stir-fry onions, bell peppers, celery, garlic, and gingerroot in lightly greased large wok or skillet until crisp-tender 5 to 8 minutes. Add Swiss chard and stir-fry until wilted, 1 to 2 minutes. Stir in combined broth, cornstarch, and chili paste; heat to boiling. Boil, stirring, until thickened, about 1 minute. Season to taste with salt and pepper.

2. Brush tempeh with soy sauce; cook in lightly greased wok over medium heat until browned, 2 to 3 minutes on each side. Serve vegetables over tempeh.

BARBECUED TEMPEH AND PEPPERS

V *Serve in toasted multigrain buns for fabulous sandwiches, too!*

4 servings

1 package (8 ounces) tempeh, cubed
Tamari Marinade (recipe follows)
1 cup each: sliced onion, green bell pepper
1 teaspoon minced garlic
1 cup water
¼ cup reduced-sodium tomato paste
1–2 tablespoons each: unsulphured molasses, brown sugar
2 teaspoons each: prepared mustard, cider vinegar
1 teaspoon chili powder
Salt and pepper, to taste
3 cups cooked brown basmati rice, warm

Per Serving:
Calories: 371
% of calories from fat: 15
Fat (gm): 6.4
Saturated fat (gm): 0.8
Cholesterol (mg): 0
Sodium (mg): 394
Protein (gm): 20.1
Carbohydrate (gm): 64.1

Exchanges:
Milk: 0.5
Vegetable: 3.0
Fruit: 0.0
Bread: 3.0
Meat: 1.0
Fat: 0.5

1. Place tempeh in shallow glass bowl; pour Tamari Marinade over and toss. Refrigerate, covered, several hours or overnight, tossing occasionally. Drain; reserve marinade.

2. Sauté onion, bell peppers, and garlic in lightly greased skillet until tender, 5 to 8 minutes. Add reserved marinade and remaining ingredients, except salt, pepper and rice, to skillet; heat to boiling. Reduce heat and simmer, uncovered, until mixture is thickened, mashing cubes of tempeh slightly with a fork. Season to taste with salt and pepper; serve over rice.

Tamari Marinade
Makes about ¼ cup

2 tablespoons each: reduced-sodium tamari soy sauce, cider vinegar
1½ teaspoons minced garlic
½–1 teaspoon chili powder

1. Mix all ingredients.

TEMPEH FAJITAS

45

❅

L

Fajitas are an American interpretation of soft tacos.

4 servings

8–12 ounces tempeh, cut into strips (2 x ½-inch)
Fajita Marinade (recipe follows)
1 each sliced medium red bell pepper, onion
1 can (15 ounces) black beans, rinsed, drained
2 tablespoons finely chopped cilantro
1 teaspoon each: ground cumin, dried marjoram
  leaves
Salt and pepper, to taste
8 flour or corn tortillas (6-inch), warm
1 cup hot or mild salsa
½ cup fat-free sour cream

Per Serving:
Calories: 441
% of calories from fat: 18
Fat (gm): 9.7
Saturated fat (gm): 1.4
Cholesterol (mg): 0
Sodium (mg): 601
Protein (gm): 29.1
Carbohydrate (gm): 70.8

Exchanges:
Milk: 0.0
Vegetable: 2.0
Fruit: 0.0
Bread: 4.0
Meat: 2.0
Fat: 0.0

1. Combine tempeh and Fajita Marinade in glass baking dish; refrigerate, covered, 1 to 2 hours; drain. Cook tempeh in lightly greased large skillet over medium heat until browned, 5 to 8 minutes; move tempeh to side of pan. Add bell pepper and onion; cook until tender, about 5 minutes. Add beans, cilantro, cumin, and marjoram; cook until hot, 2 to 3 minutes. Season to taste with salt and pepper; serve in tortillas with salsa and sour cream.

Fajita Marinade
Makes about ⅓ cup

⅓ cup lime juice
4 cloves garlic, minced
1½ teaspoons dried oregano leaves
½ teaspoon ground allspice
¼ teaspoon black pepper

1. Mix all ingredients.

MEXICAN-STYLE VEGETABLES AND RICE

45

Rice combines with vegetables and south-of-the-border flavors. Toast the millet in a skillet over medium heat, about 5 minutes, to maximize flavor.

L

6 servings

⅔ cup each: chopped red bell pepper, onion

3 cloves garlic, minced

1 jalapeño chili, finely chopped

2 cups each: cubed peeled chayote squash, halved small cremini mushrooms

1 cup whole kernel corn

½ teaspoon each: dried oregano leaves, ground cumin, chili powder

Salt and pepper, to taste

4 cups cooked white or brown rice

1 cup fat-free sour cream

¾ cup (3 ounces) shredded reduced-fat Monterey Jack cheese

2 green onions, sliced

Per Serving:
Calories: 293
% of calories from fat: 12
Fat (gm): 4.1
Saturated fat (gm): 1.7
Cholesterol (mg): 10.1
Sodium (mg): 156
Protein (gm): 14
Carbohydrate (gm): 52.6

Exchanges:
Milk: 0.0
Vegetable: 2.0
Fruit: 0.0
Bread: 3.0
Meat: 0.5
Fat: 0.0

1. Sauté bell pepper, onion, garlic, and jalapeño chili in lightly greased large skillet 5 minutes; add squash, mushrooms, corn, and herbs. Cook, covered, over medium heat until squash and mushrooms are tender, about 8 minutes, stirring occasionally. Season to taste with salt and pepper.

2. Spoon half of the rice into greased 2-quart casserole. Top with vegetable mixture and sour cream; spoon remaining rice on top. Bake, loosely covered, at 300 degrees until hot, 30 to 40 minutes. Sprinkle with cheese, and bake, uncovered, until cheese is melted, 5 to 10 minutes; sprinkle with green onions.

45-MINUTE PREPARATION TIP: Begin cooking rice before preparing the rest of the recipe.

ROASTED VEGETABLE FAJITAS

The vegetables can also be grilled over mesquite chips for a smoky accent; cut vegetables in large enough pieces so they don't fall through the grill rack!

4 servings

2 each: thickly sliced medium red bell peppers, poblano chilies or green bell peppers, carrots, zucchini, chayote squash

2 each: medium tomatoes and onions, cut into wedges

8 ounces large mushrooms, halved

Vegetable cooking spray

2 teaspoons each: ground cumin, dried oregano leaves

Fajita Dressing (recipe follows)

Salt and pepper, to taste

8 flour or corn tortillas (6-inch), warm

Per Serving:
Calories: 300
% of calories from fat: 30
Fat (gm): 11.5
Saturated fat (gm): 1.6
Cholesterol (mg): 0
Sodium (mg): 264
Protein (gm): 8.8
Carbohydrate (gm): 51.7

Exchanges:
Milk: 0.0
Vegetable: 4.0
Fruit: 0.0
Bread: 2.0
Meat: 0.0
Fat: 2.0

1. Arrange vegetables in single layer in greased aluminum foil-lined pan; spray generously with cooking spray and sprinkle with herbs. Bake vegetables at 425 degrees until tender and browned, 40 to 45 minutes. Toss with Fajita Dressing and toss; season to taste with salt and pepper. Spoon vegetable mixture onto tortillas and roll up.

Fajita Dressing
Makes about ¼ cup

2 tablespoons olive oil

1 tablespoon lime juice

2–3 teaspoons cider vinegar

2–3 cloves garlic, minced

1. Mix all ingredients.

SEVEN

Eggs
and
Cheese

CHEESE FONDUE

45 *Flavored with wine and a hint of garlic, this creamy fondue is made with fat-free cheese!*

8 servings (¼ cup each)

1½ cups dry white wine or fat-free milk
2–3 large cloves garlic, peeled
2 packages (3 ounces each) fat-free cream cheese
2 cups (8 ounces) shredded fat-free Swiss cheese
1 tablespoon flour
Salt and cayenne pepper, to taste
French bread, cubed, for dipping

Per Serving:
Calories: 100
% of calories from fat: 0
Fat (gm): 0
Saturated fat (gm): 0
Cholesterol (mg): 0
Sodium (mg): 547
Protein (gm): 10.8
Carbohydrate (gm): 5

Exchanges:
Milk: 0.0
Vegetable: 0.0
Fruit: 0.0
Bread: 0.0
Meat: 1.5
Fat: 0.0

1. Heat wine and garlic to boiling in medium saucepan; reduce heat and simmer rapidly, uncovered, until reduced to ¾ cup, about 15 minutes; discard garlic. Add cream cheese and stir over low heat until melted. Toss shredded Swiss cheese with flour; add to saucepan and stir until melted. Season to taste with salt and cayenne pepper. Serve in fondue pot or bowl with bread cubes for dipping.

NOTE: If fondue becomes too thick, it can be thinned with wine or milk.

WELSH RAREBIT

45 *Rarebit is also delicious served over sliced ham or chicken breast and asparagus spears on toast.*

6 servings (about ½ cup sauce each)

¼ cup finely chopped onion
2 tablespoons margarine or butter
¼ cup all-purpose flour
2 cups fat-free milk
½ cup white wine or fat-free milk
2 ounces light pasteurized processed cheese, cubed
½ cup (2 ounces) reduced-fat sharp Cheddar cheese, cubed
¼–½ teaspoon dry mustard

White and cayenne pepper, to taste
6 slices sourdough or multigrain bread
Butter-flavored vegetable cooking spray
6 thick slices tomato
Paprika, as garnish

Per Serving:
Calories: 219
% of calories from fat: 31
Fat (gm): 7.6
Saturated fat (gm): 3.4
Cholesterol (mg): 11.5
Sodium (mg): 502
Protein (gm): 9.9
Carbohydrate (gm): 24.1

Exchanges:
Milk: 0.0
Vegetable: 0.0
Fruit: 0.0
Bread: 1.5
Meat: 1.0
Fat: 1.0

1. Sauté onion in margarine in medium saucepan until tender, 2 to 3 minutes. Stir in flour and cook 1 minute. Whisk in milk and wine; heat to boiling. Boil, whisking until thickened, about 1 minute. Stir in cheeses and dry mustard; whisk over low heat until cheeses are melted. Season to taste with white and cayenne pepper.

2. Spray both sides of bread with cooking spray; cook over medium heat in large skillet until browned, 2 to 3 minutes on each side. Sauté tomato slices in lightly greased medium skillet until hot, 2 to 3 minutes. Top bread with tomato slices and spoon cheese sauce over. Sprinkle with paprika.

VARIATION

Cheese and Vegetable Rarebit — Make recipe as above, stirring ½ cup each sautéed chopped portobello mushrooms, yellow summer squash, and broccoli florets into the cheese sauce in step 1; delete tomato in step 2.

EGGS BENEDICT

45 *Six slices of English Muffin Bread (see p. 543) can be substituted for the English muffins.*

6 servings

6 ounces sliced lean Canadian bacon
3 English muffins, halved, toasted
Spinach leaves
6 each: tomato slices, poached eggs
Mock Hollandaise Sauce (see p. 175)
Paprika and chopped parsley, as garnish

1. Heat Canadian bacon in lightly greased small skillet until hot and lightly browned. Arrange Canadian bacon on muffin halves; top with spinach leaves, tomato slices, and poached eggs. Spoon Mock Hollandaise Sauce over eggs; sprinkle with paprika and parsley.

45-MINUTE PREPARATION TIP: Make Mock Hollandaise Sauce before preparing the rest of the recipe.

Per Serving:
Calories: 204
% of calories from fat: 27
Fat (gm): 5.6
Saturated fat (gm): 1.7
Cholesterol (mg): 228.3
Sodium (mg): 786
Protein (gm): 19
Carbohydrate (gm): 17

Exchanges:
Milk: 0.0
Vegetable: 0.0
Fruit: 0.0
Bread: 1.0
Meat: 2.5
Fat: 0.0

EGGS IN A CUMULUS CLOUD

45 *Delicious flavors in a unique presentation.*

4 servings

2 pumpernickel bagels, split, toasted
8 tablespoons fat-free cream cheese
4 eggs, separated
Salt and pepper, to taste
Paprika, as garnish

1. Spread bagel halves with cream cheese. Beat egg whites to stiff, but not dry peaks in large bowl; spoon over bagel halves. Make a depression in center of egg whites with a spoon and place 1 yolk in each. Broil 6 inches from heat source until egg white is lightly browned and yolks are set on top, 2 to 3 minutes. Sprinkle lightly with salt, pepper, and paprika.

Per Serving:
Calories: 188
% of calories from fat: 26
Fat (gm): 6.4
Saturated fat (gm): 1.8
Cholesterol (mg): 214.4
Sodium (mg): 332
Protein (gm): 15.1
Carbohydrate (gm): 26.4

Exchanges:
Milk: 0.0
Vegetable: 0.0
Fruit: 0.0
Bread: 1.5
Meat: 1.0
Fat: 0.5

DRUNKEN EGGS

45 *A novel brunch offering with a flavor kick!*

4 servings

1½ cups reduced-sodium vegetable juice cocktail

6–8 drops hot pepper sauce

2 teaspoons Worcestershire sauce

4 eggs

⅓ cup light beer

4 slices whole wheat bread, toasted

Chopped parsley, as garnish

Per Serving:
Calories: 169
% of calories from fat: 32
Fat (gm): 6.1
Saturated fat (gm): 1.8
Cholesterol (mg): 212
Sodium (mg): 323
Protein (gm): 9.6
Carbohydrate (gm): 17.5

Exchanges:
Milk: 0.0
Vegetable: 1.0
Fruit: 0.0
Bread: 1.0
Meat: 1.0
Fat: 0.5

1. Heat vegetable juice, hot pepper sauce, and Worcestershire sauce to simmering in small skillet. Break eggs into a saucer, and slide into juice mixture. Simmer gently, spooning juice over eggs. When eggs are almost done, pour beer over and heat just until warm, 1 to 2 minutes. Remove eggs with slotted spoon; drain. Serve on toast; garnish with parsley.

OMELET PUFF WITH VEGETABLE MÉLANGE

45 *Beaten egg whites make this oven-baked omelet soar to new heights.*

2 servings

2 eggs

¼ teaspoon each: dried tarragon leaves, salt, pepper

5 egg whites

¼ cup water

Vegetable Mélange (recipe follows)

Per Serving:
Calories: 130
% of calories from fat: 4
Fat (gm): 0.5
Saturated fat (gm): 0.1
Cholesterol (mg): 0
Sodium (mg): 553
Protein (gm): 16.2
Carbohydrate (gm): 16.3

Exchanges:
Milk: 0.0
Vegetable: 0.0
Fruit: 0.0
Bread: 2.0
Meat: 2.0
Fat: 0.0

1. Beat eggs, tarragon, salt, and pepper at high speed in small bowl until thick and lemon colored, about 5 minutes. Beat egg whites and water in large bowl with clean beaters until stiff, but not dry, peaks form; fold into beaten eggs.

2. Spread egg mixture evenly in lightly greased ovenproof 10-inch skillet; cook over medium heat until bottom of omelet is lightly browned, about 5 minutes. Bake at 325 degrees, uncovered, until puffed and lightly browned, about 15 minutes. Loosen edge of omelet with spatula; slide onto serving plate, carefully folding omelet in half. Spoon Vegetable Mélange over omelet.

Vegetable Mélange
Makes about 3 cups

1 cup each: small whole okra, tomato wedges, sliced zucchini, onion
½ cup sliced green bell pepper
1 teaspoon dried Italian seasoning
Salt and pepper, to taste

1. Sauté vegetables and Italian seasoning in lightly greased large skillet until tender, 5 to 7 minutes. Season to taste with salt and pepper.

45-MINUTE PREPARATION TIP: Slice vegetables for Vegetable Mélange before preparing the rest of the recipe.

VEGETABLE PUFF

Perfect for brunch or lunch, sautéed vegetables are baked with eggs in a casserole.

6 servings

2 cups each: sliced mushrooms, coarsely chopped
　broccoli florets
1 cup shredded carrots
½ cup each: chopped red bell pepper, green onions
¼ cup whole kernel corn
2 cloves garlic, minced
2 teaspoons lemon juice
¾ teaspoon dried thyme leaves
Salt and pepper, to taste
1 cup fat-free half-and-half or fat-free milk
2 tablespoons flour
4 eggs, lightly beaten
4 large egg whites, beaten to stiff peaks

Per Serving:
Calories: 139
% of calories from fat: 27
Fat (gm): 4.3
Saturated fat (gm): 1.4
Cholesterol (mg): 143
Sodium (mg): 169
Protein (gm): 10
Carbohydrate (gm): 16

Exchanges:
Milk: 0.0
Vegetable: 3.0
Fruit: 0.0
Bread: 0.0
Meat: 1.0
Fat: 5.0

1. Sauté vegetables and garlic in lightly greased large skillet until tender, about 8 minutes. Stir in lemon juice, and thyme; season to taste with salt and pepper. Remove from heat.

2. Whisk half-and-half and flour in small saucepan; heat to boiling. Boil, whisking until thickened, about 1 minute. Whisk mixture into beaten eggs; stir into vegetable mixture. Fold beaten egg whites into vegetable mixture and spoon into greased 1½-quart casserole. Place casserole in a large roasting pan on center oven rack; add 2 inches hot water to pan. Bake, uncovered, at 375 degrees until puffed and browned, about 35 minutes. Serve immediately.

EASY CHEESE PUFF

45

A delicious casserole that tastes like cheese blintzes, but requires much less time and effort to prepare.

8 servings

4 eggs

1¼ cups fat-free milk

2 tablespoons each: fat-free sour cream, melted margarine or butter

1 teaspoon vanilla

1⅓ cups all-purpose flour

1 tablespoon each: sugar, baking powder

Sweet Cheese Filling (recipe follows)

Powdered sugar, as garnish

2 cups sliced strawberries

Per Serving:
Calories: 299
% of calories from fat: 31
Fat (gm): 10.8
Saturated fat (gm): 4.8
Cholesterol (mg): 141.4
Sodium (mg): 556
Protein (gm): 20.9
Carbohydrate (gm): 32

Exchanges:
Milk: 0.0
Vegetable: 0.0
Fruit: 0.0
Bread: 2.0
Meat: 2.0
Fat: 1.0

1. Combine all ingredients, except Sweet Cheese Filling, powdered sugar, and strawberries in large bowl; beat with mixer until very smooth. Pour 1½ cups batter into lightly greased 13 x 9-inch baking dish. Bake at 350 degrees until set, about 10 minutes.

2. Spread Sweet Cheese Filling over baked layer. Whisk remaining batter to combine; pour over cheese, covering completely. Bake at 350 degrees until top is puffed and browned, about 45 minutes; sprinkle with powdered sugar. Cut into squares and top with strawberries.

Sweet Cheese Filling
Makes about 3½ cups

2 containers (15 ounces each) reduced-fat ricotta cheese

2 eggs

2 tablespoons each: sugar, lemon juice

1. Mix all ingredients.

BEER-CHEESE PUFF

45 *Just a touch of beer flavors the cheese topping on this open-face sandwich.*

2 servings

¾ cup fat-free cottage cheese

½ cup (2 ounces) shredded reduced-fat
  Cheddar cheese

1 tablespoon grated Parmesan cheese

¼ cup minced green onion

2 tablespoons beer, apple juice, or cider

2–3 dashes each: Worcestershire sauce, hot
  pepper sauce

2 large slices pumpernickel bread, toasted

Per Serving:
Calories: 226
% of calories from fat: 24
Fat (gm): 6.3
Saturated fat (gm): 3.7
Cholesterol (mg): 12.1
Sodium (mg): 782
Protein (gm): 22.6
Carbohydrate (gm): 19.9

Exchanges:
Milk: 0.0
Vegetable: 0.0
Fruit: 0.0
Bread: 1.0
Meat: 3.0
Fat: 0.0

1. Combine all ingredients, except bread, in bowl; spread half the cheese mixture on each bread slice. Broil 6 inches from heat source until bubbly, 3 to 4 minutes.

CHEDDAR CHEESE SOUFFLÉ

45 *This spectacular soufflé soars above the soufflé dish!*

4 servings

1–2 tablespoons grated fat-free Parmesan cheese

1 cup fat-free milk

3 tablespoons flour

½ teaspoon each: dry mustard, dried marjoram leaves

¼ teaspoon cayenne pepper

2 pinches ground nutmeg

3 egg yolks

¼ cup (1 ounce) shredded fat-free Cheddar cheese

Salt and white pepper, to taste

3 egg whites

¼ teaspoon cream of tartar

Per Serving:
Calories: 162
% of calories from fat: 23
Fat (gm): 4.1
Saturated fat (gm): 1.3
Cholesterol (mg): 160.8
Sodium (mg): 340
Protein (gm): 19.3
Carbohydrate (gm): 11.2

Exchanges:
Milk: 0.0
Vegetable: 0.0
Fruit: 0.0
Bread: 0.5
Meat: 2.5
Fat: 0.0

1. Coat greased 1-quart soufflé dish with Parmesan cheese. Attach a foil collar, extending foil 3 inches above top of dish; lightly grease inside of collar.

2. Whisk milk, flour, and seasonings until blended in small saucepan. Heat to boiling; whisk until thickened, about 1 minute. Whisk about ½ cup mixture into egg yolks; whisk mixture into saucepan. Add cheese and whisk over low heat until melted; season to taste with salt and white pepper.

3. Beat egg whites and cream of tartar in medium bowl to stiff, but not dry, peaks. Stir about ⅓ the egg whites into cheese mixture; fold cheese mixture into remaining whites. Spoon into prepared soufflé dish. Bake at 350° until soufflé is puffed, browned, and just set in the center, 35 to 40 minutes. Serve immediately.

SPINACH SOUFFLÉ

45

Any cooked vegetable can be substituted for the spinach in this recipe

4 servings

1 small onion, minced

1 teaspoon margarine or butter

3 tablespoons flour

½ teaspoon ground nutmeg

½ cup each: fat-free milk, reduced-sodium fat-free chicken or vegetable broth

2 egg yolks, lightly beaten

1 package (10 ounces) frozen chopped spinach, thawed, well drained

⅛ teaspoon white pepper

4 egg whites

Pinch cream of tartar

Per Serving:
Calories: 118
% of calories from fat: 28
Fat (gm): 3.9
Saturated fat (gm): 1.1
Cholesterol (mg): 107.1
Sodium (mg): 167
Protein (gm): 9.7
Carbohydrate (gm): 12.1

Exchanges:
Milk: 0.0
Vegetable: 1.0
Fruit: 0.0
Bread: 0.5
Meat: 1.0
Fat: 0.0

1. Sauté onion in margarine in medium saucepan until tender, 3 to 4 minutes; stir in flour and nutmeg and cook 1 minute. Whisk in milk and broth and heat to boiling, whisking until thickened, about 1 minute. Whisk about half the sauce into egg yolks; whisk yolk mixture into saucepan. Mix in spinach and white pepper.

2. Beat egg whites and cream of tartar in large bowl to stiff, but not dry, peaks; fold into spinach mixture and spoon into greased 1-quart soufflé dish. Bake, uncovered, at 350 degrees until puffed and browned, about 40 minutes. Serve immediately.

PANCAKE PUFF WITH EGGS PIPERADE

A puffed Dutch Pancake makes a tasty serving bowl for chili-inspired scrambled eggs.

4 servings

2 cups frozen stir-fry pepper blend
½–1 jalapeño chili, minced
1 teaspoon minced garlic
1 small tomato, chopped
6 eggs
4 egg whites or 1 cup no-cholesterol real egg product
2 tablespoons fat-free milk
Salt and pepper, to taste
Dutch Pancake (recipe follows)
Minced chives or parsley, as garnish

Per Serving:
Calories: 315
% of calories from fat: 30
Fat (gm): 10.3
Saturated fat (gm): 3.2
Cholesterol (mg): 424
Sodium (mg): 430
Protein (gm): 24.1
Carbohydrate (gm): 29.3

Exchanges:
Milk: 0.0
Vegetable: 0.0
Fruit: 0.0
Bread: 2.0
Meat: 3.0
Fat: 0.0

1. Sauté stir-fry blend, jalapeño chili, and garlic in lightly greased large skillet until tender, 5 to 8 minutes; stir in tomato. Whisk eggs, egg whites, and milk until well blended; add to skillet and cook over medium heat until set, about 5 minutes, stirring frequently. Sprinkle lightly with salt and pepper. Spoon into hot Dutch Pancake; sprinkle with chives.

Dutch Pancake
Makes 1 pancake

2 eggs
4 egg whites or ½ cup no-cholesterol real egg product
¾ cup each: fat-free milk, all-purpose flour
1 tablespoon sugar
¼ teaspoon salt
Vegetable cooking spray

1. Whisk all ingredients, except cooking spray, in large bowl until almost smooth (batter will be slightly lumpy). Spray large oven-proof skillet with cooking spray and heat over medium heat until hot; pour in batter. Bake, uncovered, at 425 degrees until pancake is puffed and browned, 20 to 25 minutes (do not open door during first 15 minutes).

45-MINUTE PREPARATION TIP: Begin cooking vegetable-egg mixture when Dutch Pancake goes into the oven.

PASTA FRITTATA

45 *A pasta frittata is a delicious way to use leftover pasta and vegetables.*

4 servings

2 cups cooked thin spaghetti
2 eggs, lightly beaten
2 tablespoons grated Parmesan cheese
½ teaspoon salt
¼ teaspoon pepper
1 cup cauliflower florets
¾ cup each: sliced carrots, red bell peppers
½ cup each: sliced zucchini, chopped tomato
¼ cup sliced green onions
1½ teaspoons dried Italian seasoning
1 tablespoon each: minced garlic, olive oil
Salt and pepper, to taste

Per Serving:
Calories: 228
% of calories from fat: 26
Fat (gm): 7
Saturated fat (gm): 1.4
Cholesterol (mg): 106
Sodium (mg): 83
Protein (gm): 10
Carbohydrate (gm): 34

Exchanges:
Milk: 0.0
Vegetable: 1.0
Fruit: 0.0
Bread: 2.0
Meat: 0.0
Fat: 1.0

1. Mix spaghetti, eggs, cheese, salt, and pepper; spread evenly in lightly greased medium skillet. Cook, uncovered, over medium heat until browned on bottom, about 5 minutes. Slide frittata onto plate; invert into skillet and cook until browned on other side, about 5 minutes; keep warm on low heat.

2. Sauté vegetables and herbs in oil in large skillet until tender, 8 to 10 minutes; season to taste with salt and pepper. Serve vegetables over fritatta.

45-MINUTE PREPARATION TIP: Prepare recipe ingredients while spaghetti is cooking.

VEGETABLE FRITTATA WITH PARMESAN TOAST

45 *This Italian-style omelet is quick and easy to prepare, and delicious to eat!*

4 servings

2 cups sliced mushrooms

½ cup each: sliced poblano chili, onion

2 cloves garlic, minced

6 eggs, lightly beaten

¼ cup fat-free milk

½ cup each: cooked brown rice, shredded fat-free Cheddar cheese

¼ teaspoon salt

⅛ teaspoon pepper

4 slices Italian or French bread

4 teaspoons grated Parmesan cheese

Per Serving:
Calories: 285
% of calories from fat: 30
Fat (gm): 9.5
Saturated fat (gm): 3
Cholesterol (mg): 319
Sodium (mg): 732
Protein (gm): 19
Carbohydrate (gm): 30

Exchanges:
Milk: 0.0
Vegetable: 0.0
Fruit: 0.0
Bread: 2.0
Meat: 2.0
Fat: 1.0

1. Sauté vegetables and garlic in lightly greased medium ovenproof skillet until tender, about 8 minutes. Pour combined eggs, milk, rice, cheese, salt, and pepper over vegetables; cook, without stirring, over medium-low heat until eggs are set and lightly browned on bottom, about 10 minutes.

2. Sprinkle bread with Parmesan cheese. Broil bread and frittata 6 inches from heat source until bread is browned and frittata is cooked on top, 2 to 4 minutes. Serve frittata with Parmesan bread.

QUICHE LORRAINE

Enjoy the rich texture and flavor of this classic quiche, modified to low-fat goodness.

6 servings

Basic Pie Crust (see p. 626)

¼ cup finely chopped onion

¾ cup each: fat-free milk

½ can (12-ounce size) evaporated fat-free milk

2 eggs, lightly beaten

¼ cup fat-free sour cream

2 slices bacon, cooked crisp, crumbled

¼ teaspoon salt

⅛ teaspoon each: cayenne pepper, ground nutmeg

1 cup (4 ounces) shredded fat-free Swiss cheese

1 tablespoon flour

Per Serving:
Calories: 276
% of calories from fat: 26
Fat (gm): 7.9
Saturated fat (gm): 2.1
Cholesterol (mg): 38.7
Sodium (mg): 562
Protein (gm): 14.4
Carbohydrate (gm): 34.7

Exchanges:
Milk: 0.0
Vegetable: 0.0
Fruit: 0.0
Bread: 2.0
Meat: 2.0
Fat: 0.5

1. Make Basic Pie Crust in 8-inch pie pan and bake.

2. Sauté onion in lightly greased small skillet until tender, 3 to 5 minutes. Mix onion and remaining ingredients, except cheese and flour, in medium bowl until smooth. Toss cheese with flour; stir into milk mixture and pour into pie crust. Bake at 350 degrees until quiche is set and a sharp knife inserted near center comes out clean, about 40 minutes. Cover edge of pie crust with aluminum foil if becoming too brown. Cool on wire rack 5 minutes.

VARIATION

Spinach Quiche — Make recipe as above, adding ½ package (10-ounce size) frozen, thawed, well drained spinach to sautéed onion; cook over medium heat until mixture is quite dry, 3 to 4 minutes.

EGG AND BROCCOLI CASSEROLE

45

This delicious casserole can be assembled up to 1 day ahead and refrigerated; add 10 minutes to the baking time.

4 servings

2 packages (10 ounces each) frozen chopped broccoli, cooked, well drained
4 hard-cooked eggs, thinly sliced
1 cup fat-free sour cream
½ cup fat-free mayonnaise
2 tablespoons tarragon vinegar or white wine vinegar
1½ teaspoons dried tarragon leaves
Paprika, as garnish

Per Serving:
Calories: 205
% of calories from fat: 23
Fat (gm): 5.2
Saturated fat (gm): 1.6
Cholesterol (mg): 212
Sodium (mg): 357
Protein (gm): 14.7
Carbohydrate (gm): 24.3

Exchanges:
Milk: 0.0
Vegetable: 2.0
Fruit: 0.0
Bread: 1.0
Meat: 1.0
Fat: 0.5

1. Arrange broccoli in lightly greased 13 x 9-inch baking dish; top with egg slices. Heat combined sour cream, mayonnaise, vinegar, and tarragon in small saucepan over low heat, stirring until warm, about 4 minutes. Pour over broccoli and eggs; sprinkle with paprika. Bake, uncovered, at 325 degrees 15 to 20 minutes.

FRENCH TOAST CASSEROLE

45

Your favorite fruit, such as bananas, blueberries, strawberries, or golden raisins, can be used instead of raspberries.

6 servings

2 cups fat-free milk
3 eggs, lightly beaten
12 slices whole-grain or sourdough bread, halved, divided
3 tablespoons melted margarine or butter, divided
9 tablespoons powdered sugar, divided
2 cups fresh or frozen, thawed, drained, raspberries, divided
1 tablespoon ground cinnamon
Lite Pancake Syrup, warm (optional)

Per Serving:
Calories: 328
% of calories from fat: 29
Fat (gm): 11.3
Saturated fat (gm): 2
Cholesterol (mg): 107.4
Sodium (mg): 316
Protein (gm): 14.4
Carbohydrate (gm): 47.4

Exchanges:
Milk: 0.0
Vegetable: 0.0
Fruit: 0.0
Bread: 3.0
Meat: 1.0
Fat: 1.0

1. Beat milk and eggs in 11 x 7-inch baking dish. Dip bread halves into egg mixture, coating both sides well. Arrange 8 bread halves in lightly greased 9-inch square baking dish. Drizzle with 1 table-spoon margarine; sprinkle with 3 tablespoons sugar and 1 cup raspberries. Repeat layers 1 more time, arranging bread halves in opposite direction from bottom layer. Top with remaining 8 bread halves, margarine, and sugar. Sprinkle with cinnamon.

2. Bake, covered, 25 minutes at 400 degrees; uncover and bake until browned, about 10 minutes longer. Serve with syrup, if desired.

COUNTRY-STYLE POTATO KUGEL

45

This hash brown kugel owes its light texture to beaten egg whites. It would be excellent served with a tomato sauce (see Index).

6 servings

2 packages (5½ ounces each) hash brown potato mix with onions

3 cups boiling water

6 egg yolks, lightly beaten

1½ cups cold water

1 teaspoon each: baking powder, dried basil and oregano leaves, salt

2 tablespoons snipped chives

½ teaspoon pepper

6 egg whites, beaten to stiff peaks

Per Serving:
Calories: 123
% of calories from fat: 28
Fat (gm): 3.9
Saturated fat (gm): 1.2
Cholesterol (mg): 159.8
Sodium (mg): 559
Protein (gm): 6.3
Carbohydrate (gm): 15.8

Exchanges:
Milk: 0.0
Vegetable: 0.0
Fruit: 0.0
Bread: 1.0
Meat: 1.0
Fat: 0.0

1. Place potato mix in large bowl; pour boiling water over. Let stand 20 to 25 minutes, stirring occasionally. Mix combined remaining ingredients, except egg whites, into potatoes. Fold potato mixture into egg whites. Spoon mixture into lightly greased 11 x 7-inch baking dish; bake at 300 degrees until browned and set, about 1 hour.

HASH AND EGGS

45 *You'll enjoy the variety of vegetables in this hearty hash.*

4 servings

1 cup chopped onion
4 medium Idaho potatoes, unpeeled, cooked, cubed
Vegetable cooking spray
1 cup each: frozen peas, whole kernel corn
½ teaspoon dried thyme leaves
Salt and pepper, to taste
4 eggs

Per Serving:
Calories: 180
% of calories from fat: 29
Fat (gm): 5.6
Saturated fat (gm): 1.6
Cholesterol (mg): 212.1
Sodium (mg): 461
Protein (gm): 13.7
Carbohydrate (gm): 17.1

Exchanges:
Milk: 0.0
Vegetable: 0.0
Fruit: 0.0
Bread: 1.5
Meat: 1.0
Fat: 0.5

1. Sauté onion and potatoes in lightly greased large skillet 2 to 3 minutes; spray with cooking spray and cook until potatoes are browned, about 5 minutes. Add peas, corn, and thyme; cook until hot, 2 to 3 minutes. Season to taste with salt and pepper. Move hash to side of skillet; add eggs and cook, covered, over medium-low heat until set, 3 to 4 minutes. Season to taste with salt and pepper.

VARIATION

Herbed Bean and Sweet Potato Hash — Make recipe as above, substituting sweet potatoes for the Idaho potatoes, 1 can (15 ounces) drained dark kidney beans for the peas and corn, and adding ¾ teaspoon crushed dried rosemary leaves.

SWEET POTATO HASH WITH POACHED EGGS

45 *A colorful hash dish that's perfect for a breakfast, brunch, or light supper.*

4 servings (scant 1 cup each)

2 cups each: cubed, peeled cooked sweet potatoes, Idaho potatoes
½ cup each: chopped onion, red bell pepper
1 teaspoon dried rosemary leaves
½ teaspoon dried thyme leaves
Vegetable cooking spray

Salt and pepper, to taste

4 poached or fried eggs

Per Serving:
Calories: 393
% of calories from fat: 13
Fat (gm): 5.8
Saturated fat (gm): 1.7
Cholesterol (mg): 212
Sodium (mg): 171
Protein (gm): 12.3
Carbohydrate (gm): 74.4

Exchanges:
Milk: 0.0
Vegetable: 0.5
Fruit: 0.0
Bread: 4.5
Meat: 1.0
Fat: 0.0

1. Sauté vegetables and herbs in lightly greased large skillet 5 minutes; spray with cooking spray and cook until potatoes are browned, about 5 minutes. Season to taste with salt and pepper. Top each serving of hash with an egg.

SAUSAGE AND EGG PIZZA

45

Tempting for brunch, lunch, or healthy snacking.

6 servings

Per Serving:
Calories: 294
% of calories from fat: 25
Fat (gm): 8.1
Saturated fat (gm): 2.4
Cholesterol (mg): 257.6
Sodium (mg): 449
Protein (gm): 20.2
Carbohydrate (gm): 35.8

Exchanges:
Milk: 0.0
Vegetable: 1.0
Fruit: 0.0
Bread: 2.0
Meat: 2.0
Fat: 0.5

2 large poblano chilies, sliced

1 cup chopped onion

1 clove garlic, minced

8 eggs, lightly beaten

¼ cup fat-free milk

4 ounces Italian-style turkey sausage,
    cooked, crumbled

Salt and pepper, to taste

Potato Pizza Crust (recipe follows)

½–1 cup (2–4 ounces) shredded fat-free
    mozzarella cheese

1. Cook chilies, onion, and garlic in lightly greased large skillet over medium to medium-low heat until chilies are very soft, 20 to 30 minutes. Remove from skillet. Add combined eggs and milk to skillet; cook until eggs are just set, stirring occasionally. Stir in sausage and chili mixture; season to taste with salt and pepper. Spoon mixture onto Potato Pizza Crust and sprinkle with cheese; bake at 400 degrees until cheese is melted, about 5 minutes.

Potato Pizza Crust
Makes 1 crust

1 package (1¼ pounds) refrigerated shredded potatoes for hash browns
⅓ cup finely chopped onion
1 egg
¼ teaspoon each: salt, pepper
Vegetable cooking spray

1. Mix all ingredients, except vegetable cooking spray; press mixture evenly on bottom and 1 inch up side of lightly greased ovenproof skillet. Spray potatoes with cooking spray. Bake at 400 degrees until browned, about 20 minutes.

45-MINUTE PREPARATION TIP: Make Potato Pizza Crust while preparing the rest of the recipe.

HOT CHEESE BAVARIAN

45 *A little German mustard would set this Bavarian sandwich off to perfection!*

2 servings

2 slices rye bread
2 teaspoons margarine or butter
¼ cup each: drained sauerkraut, thinly sliced cabbage
2 slices tomato
4 ounces sliced reduced-fat mozzarella cheese

1. Spread bread with margarine; top unbuttered sides with combined sauerkraut and cabbage. Top with tomato slices and cheese; cook, covered, over medium-low heat in medium skillet until bread is browned on the bottom and cheese is melted, 4 to 5 minutes.

Per Serving:
Calories: 218
% of calories from fat: 21
Fat (gm): 5
Saturated fat (gm): 1
Cholesterol (mg): 0
Sodium (mg): 765
Protein (gm): 21.2
Carbohydrate (gm): 21.9

Exchanges:
Milk: 0.0
Vegetable: 1.0
Fruit: 0.0
Bread: 1.0
Meat: 2.0
Fat: 0.0

FRENCH TOASTED CHERRY-CHEESE SANDWICHES

45 *Crisp on the outside, melty on the inside, with a tart flavor accent of cherry!*

2 servings

2 eggs
½ cup fat-free milk
¼ cup dry white wine or fat-free milk
4 ounces sliced reduced-fat Swiss cheese
4 slices whole wheat bread
¼ cup chopped dried cherries

Per Serving:
Calories: 406
% of calories from fat: 23
Fat (gm): 10.4
Saturated fat (gm): 4
Cholesterol (mg): 232.6
Sodium (mg): 512
Protein (gm): 30.6
Carbohydrate (gm): 44.5

Exchanges:
Milk: 0.0
Vegetable: 0.0
Fruit: 1.0
Bread: 2.0
Meat: 3.0
Fat: 0.5

1. Beat eggs, milk, and wine in pie plate. Arrange cheese on 2 slices bread and sprinkle with dried cherries; top with remaining bread. Dip both sides of sandwiches in egg mixture; cook over medium-low heat in lightly greased skillet until browned, about 5 minutes on each side.

VARIATION

French Toasted Swiss-Mushroom — Make recipe as above, spreading 2 bread slices with Dijon mustard and substituting reduced-fat Cheddar cheese for the Swiss cheese and ⅓ cup chopped mushrooms for the cherries.

CRUNCHY FRENCH TOAST SANDWICH

45

Crushed corn flakes add a crunchy texture to this nouveaux French toast breakfast sandwich.

2 servings

1 egg
¾ cup fat-free milk
1 teaspoon vanilla
1 cup corn flakes, crushed
1 teaspoon ground cinnamon
2 teaspoons granulated sugar
¼ cup fresh or frozen blueberries
⅔ cup fat-free cottage cheese
2 teaspoons grated lemon zest
4 slices day-old sourdough bread

Per Serving:
Calories: 303
% of calories from fat: 11
Fat (gm): 3.8
Saturated fat (gm): 1.1
Cholesterol (mg): 110.9
Sodium (mg): 702
Protein (gm): 20.1
Carbohydrate (gm): 50

Exchanges:
Milk: 0.0
Vegetable: 0.0
Fruit: 0.0
Bread: 3.0
Meat: 2.0
Fat: 0.0

1. Beat egg, milk, and vanilla in pie plate. Combine corn flakes, cinnamon, and granulated sugar on sheet of waxed paper. Combine blueberries, cottage cheese, and lemon zest; spread on 2 slices of bread and top with remaining bread. Dip both sides of sandwiches into egg mixture, then lightly into crumb mixture, coating both sides. Bake sandwiches on lightly greased cookie sheet at 450 degrees until browned, about 10 minutes on each side.

WALNUT-RAISIN FRENCH TOAST WITH RUM SYRUP

45

Warm Rum Syrup is the finishing touch for this sweet brunch treat.

6 servings

3 eggs
¾ cup fat-free milk
½ teaspoon vanilla extract
¼ teaspoon cinnamon
12 slices raisin-walnut bread
Warm Rum Syrup (recipe follows)

1. Beat egg, milk, vanilla, and cinnamon in pie plate; coat both sides of bread slices with egg mixture. Cook bread slices over medium heat in lightly greased large skillet until golden, about 5 minutes on each side. Serve with Warm Rum Syrup.

Warm Rum Syrup

Makes about 1½ cups

¼ cup sugar

1 tablespoon cornstarch

1¼ cups fat-free milk

2 tablespoons light rum or ½ teaspoon rum extract

2 tablespoons margarine or butter

⅛ teaspoon ground nutmeg

1. Mix sugar and cornstarch in small saucepan; whisk in milk and rum and heat to boiling. Boil, whisking until thickened, about 1 minute. Remove from heat; stir in margarine and nutmeg.

Per Serving:
Calories: 364
% of calories from fat: 24
Fat (gm): 9.6
Saturated fat (gm): 2.5
Cholesterol (mg): 107.7
Sodium (mg): 389
Protein (gm): 11.2
Carbohydrate (gm): 56.2

Exchanges:
Milk: 0.0
Vegetable: 0.0
Fruit: 0.0
Bread: 4.0
Meat: 0.0
Fat: 2.0

GOAT CHEESE QUESADILLAS

45

Perfect as a light lunch, teamed with a soup or salad. Or cut into wedges and serve as an appetizer served with Tropical Salsa (see p. 242).

4 servings

1 package (3 ounces) fat-free cream cheese

3 ounces reduced-fat goat cheese

¼ cup sun-dried tomatoes (not in oil), softened, chopped

4 flour tortillas (6-inch)

2 tablespoons chopped mint leaves

1. Combine cheeses and sun-dried tomatoes in small bowl; spread mixture over half of each tortilla and sprinkle with mint. Fold tortillas in half; cook in large skillet over medium heat until browned, 2 to 3 minutes on each side.

Per Serving:
Calories: 287
% of calories from fat: 35
Fat (gm): 11.2
Saturated fat (gm): 6.8
Cholesterol (mg): 23.0
Sodium (mg): 554
Protein (gm): 18.0
Carbohydrate (gm): 30.1

Exchanges:
Milk: 0.0
Vegetable: 0.0
Fruit: 0.0
Bread: 2.0
Meat: 2.0
Fat: 0.5

HUEVOS RANCHEROS

Everyone loves Mexican "country-style eggs" for a hearty breakfast! To speed preparation, canned refried beans can be used.

6 servings

6 corn tortillas
Vegetable cooking spray
6 eggs, fried
Serrano Tomato Sauce (recipe follows)
Refried Beans (see p. 393)

Per Serving:
Calories: 252
% of calories from fat: 22
Fat (gm): 6.2
Saturated fat (gm): 1.7
Cholesterol (mg): 213
Sodium (mg): 109
Protein (gm): 14.3
Carbohydrate (gm): 35.6

Exchanges:
Milk: 0.0
Vegetable: 1.0
Fruit: 0.0
Bread: 2.0
Meat: 1.5
Fat: 0.0

1. Spray tortillas lightly on both sides with cooking spray; cook in large skillet over medium heat until browned, about 1 minute on each side. Top tortillas with eggs; spoon Serrano Tomato Sauce over eggs. Serve with Refried Beans.

Serrano Tomato Sauce

6 servings (about ⅓ cup each)

1 each: finely chopped small onion, clove garlic, serrano chili
2 large tomatoes, pureed
Salt, to taste

1. Sauté onion, garlic, and serrano chili in lightly greased medium skillet until tender, 3 to 4 minutes. Add tomatoes and heat to boiling; cook over medium to medium-high heat until mixture thickens to a medium sauce consistency, 5 to 8 minutes. Season to taste with salt.

MEXICAN SCRAMBLED EGGS WITH CHORIZO

In this recipe, the homemade Chorizo is crumbled, rather than being made into patties. Of course, purchased chorizo can also be used.

6 servings

1 large tomato, chopped
½ cup sliced green onions
2–3 teaspoons finely chopped serrano or jalapeño chilies

2 small cloves garlic, minced

Chorizo (see p. 140), crumbled

9 eggs, lightly beaten

¼ cup fat-free milk

Salt and pepper, to taste

Tomatillo Sauce, warm (see p. 188)

6 corn or flour tortillas (6-inch), warm

Per Serving:
Calories: 347
% of calories from fat: 31
Fat (gm): 12
Saturated fat (gm): 3
Cholesterol (mg): 388
Sodium (mg): 724
Protein (gm): 28
Carbohydrate (gm): 34

Exchanges:
Milk: 0.0
Vegetable: 0.0
Fruit: 0.0
Bread: 2.0
Meat: 3.0
Fat: 0.5

1. Sauté tomato, green onions, chilies, and garlic in lightly greased large skillet until tender, about 5 minutes. Add Chorizo and cook 3 to 4 minutes. Add combined eggs and milk and cook over medium heat until eggs are set, stirring occasionally; season to taste with salt and pepper. Serve with Tomatillo Sauce and tortillas.

Tomatillo Sauce

Makes 8 servings (about ¼ cup each)

1½ pounds tomatillos, husked

½ medium onion, chopped

1 clove garlic, minced

½ small serrano chili, minced

3 tablespoons chopped cilantro

2–3 teaspoons sugar

Salt and white pepper, to taste

1. Simmer tomatillos, covered, in 1- inch water in large saucepan until tender, 5 to 8 minutes. Cool; drain. Process with onion, garlic, serrano chili, and cilantro in food processor or blender until almost smooth. Cook sauce in lightly greased large skillet over medium heat until slightly thickened, about 5 minutes. Season to taste with sugar, salt, and pepper.

MEXICAN SCRAMBLED EGGS WITH SHRIMP

45 *Crabmeat can be substituted for the shrimp in this recipe if you prefer.*

4 servings

1 medium tomato, chopped

¼ cup sliced green onions

1–2 teaspoons finely chopped serrano or jalapeño chili

1 small clove garlic, minced

8 ounces peeled deveined shrimp

6 eggs, lightly beaten

2 tablespoons fat-free milk

Salt and pepper, to taste

1 cup Tomatillo Sauce, warm (see p. 188)

Per Serving:
Calories: 217
% of calories from fat: 39
Fat (gm): 9.4
Saturated fat (gm): 2.7
Cholesterol (mg): 404
Sodium (mg): 196
Protein (gm): 22.6
Carbohydrate (gm): 10.2

Exchanges:
Milk: 0.0
Vegetable: 2.0
Fruit: 0.0
Bread: 0.0
Meat: 3.0
Fat: 0.0

1. Sauté tomato, green onions, serrano chili, and garlic in lightly greased skillet until tender, about 5 minutes. Add shrimp and cook over medium heat until shrimp are pink and cooked, 3 to 4 minutes. Add combined eggs and milk; cook over medium to medium-low heat until eggs are cooked, stirring occasionally. Season to taste with salt and pepper. Serve with Tomatillo Sauce.

EGGS SCRAMBLED WITH CRISP TORTILLA STRIPS

This is a good recipe to use with stale tortillas. Complement this hearty egg dish with Chorizo (see p. 140).

6 servings

6 corn tortillas (6-inch), cut into strips (2 x ½-inch)

Vegetable cooking spray

9 eggs, lightly beaten

3 tablespoons fat-free milk

Salt and pepper, to taste

3 tablespoons each: crumbled Mexican white cheese or farmer's cheese, chopped cilantro

Poblano Chili Sauce, warm (see p. 190)

Black Beans and Rice, warm (see p. 388)

Per Serving:
Calories: 367
% of calories from fat: 18
Fat (gm): 7.7
Saturated fat (gm): 2.2
Cholesterol (mg): 215.7
Sodium (mg): 480
Protein (gm): 22.9
Carbohydrate (gm): 55.9

Exchanges:
Milk: 0.0
Vegetable: 1.0
Fruit: 0.0
Bread: 3.0
Meat: 2.5
Fat: 0.0

1. Spray tortilla strips lightly with cooking spray and toss; cook in large skillet over medium to medium-high heat until browned and crisp, 3 to 4 minutes. Pour combined eggs and milk over tortilla strips; cook over medium to medium-low heat until eggs are cooked, stirring occasionally. Season to taste with salt and pepper; sprinkle with cheese and cilantro. Serve with Poblano Chili Sauce and Black Beans and Rice.

EGGS SCRAMBLED WITH CACTUS

45 *Cactus paddles, or "nopales," are available canned as well as fresh; the canned cactus does not have to be cooked. Poblano chilies or sweet bell peppers can be substituted, if preferred.*

4 servings

1 quart water

8 ounces cactus paddles, sliced

1 teaspoon salt

¼ teaspoon baking soda

¾ cup each: chopped onion, tomato

1 teaspoon finely chopped jalapeño chili

6 eggs, lightly beaten

2 tablespoons fat-free milk

Salt and pepper, to taste

4 corn or flour tortillas (6-inch), warm

Per Serving:
Calories: 182
% of calories from fat: 29
Fat (gm): 6
Saturated fat (gm): 2
Cholesterol (mg): 212
Sodium (mg): 292
Protein (gm): 13
Carbohydrate (gm): 20

Exchanges:
Milk: 0.0
Vegetable: 0.0
Fruit: 0.0
Bread: 1.0
Meat: 2.0
Fat: 0.0

1. Heat water to boiling in medium saucepan; add cactus, salt, and baking soda. Reduce heat and simmer, uncovered, until cactus is crisp-tender, about 20 minutes. Rinse and drain. Sauté cactus, onion, tomato, and jalapeño chili in lightly greased large skillet until onion is tender, 3 to 4 minutes. Add combined eggs and milk; cook over medium heat until set, stirring occasionally. Season to taste with salt and pepper. Serve with tortillas.

CHIPOTLE POTATO AND EGG BAKE

For convenience, this recipe uses frozen vegetable products. For a serving variation, potato mixture can be spooned onto serving plates and topped with poached or fried eggs.

4 servings

2 cups frozen stir-fry pepper blend

1–2 teaspoons minced garlic

½–1 small canned chipotle chili in adobo sauce, chopped

1⅓ cups fat-free milk

2⅔ cups frozen mashed potatoes

Salt, to taste

4 eggs

½–¾ cup (2–3 ounces) shredded reduced-fat Cheddar cheese

Per Serving:
Calories: 242
% of calories from fat: 27
Fat (gm): 7.2
Saturated fat (gm): 2.2
Cholesterol (mg): 213.6
Sodium (mg): 452
Protein (gm): 16.5
Carbohydrate (gm): 27.1

Exchanges:
Milk: 0.0
Vegetable: 2.0
Fruit: 0.0
Bread: 1.0
Meat: 2.0
Fat: 0.5

1. Sauté pepper blend and garlic in lightly greased skillet until peppers begin to brown, about 5 minutes. Add chipotle chili and milk; heat until milk is steaming. Stir in potatoes; cook over medium heat, stirring frequently, until potatoes are thickened, 4 to 5 minutes. Season to taste with salt.

2. Spread potato mixture in greased 8-inch square or round baking pan, or 4 individual gratin dishes. Make 4 indentations in potatoes with back of spoon; break eggs into indentations. Sprinkle cheese over potatoes and eggs. Bake at 350 degrees until eggs are desired doneness, 13 to 15 minutes.

BEAN AND CHEESE CHILI RELLENOS

Chili rellenos are normally coated with a beaten egg white mixture and fried in deep oil; our healthy version omits this fat-laden step.

6 servings

6 medium poblano chilies or green bell peppers

2–3 quarts water

1 tablespoon each: minced garlic, jalapeno chili

1 teaspoon dried oregano leaves

2 packages (8 ounces each) fat-free cream cheese, room temperature

½ cup (2 ounces) Mexican white cheese or farmer's cheese, crumbled

1½ cups cooked pinto beans or 1 can (15 ounces) pinto beans, rinsed, drained

1 tablespoon vegetable oil

Per Serving:
Calories: 204
% of calories from fat: 25
Fat (gm): 5.5
Saturated fat (gm): 0.4
Cholesterol (mg): 22.3
Sodium (mg): 520
Protein (gm): 17.2
Carbohydrate (gm): 19.4

Exchanges:
Milk: 0.0
Vegetable: 1.0
Fruit: 0.0
Bread: 1.0
Meat: 1.5
Fat: 0.5

1. Cut stems from tops of poblano chilies; remove and discard seeds and veins. Cook chilies in simmering water to cover, until chilies are slightly softened, 2 to 3 minutes. Drain.

2. Sauté jalapeño chili, garlic, and oregano in lightly greased skillet until chili is tender, 2 to 3 minutes. Mix chili mixture, cheeses, and beans; stuff poblano chilies with mixture. Sauté chilies in oil in large skillet over medium to medium-high heat until tender and browned on all sides, 6 to 8 minutes.

BREAKFAST BURRITOS

A delicious alternative to standard breakfast fare!

6 servings

3 cups cubed, cooked, unpeeled Idaho potatoes

1 cup each: chopped red or green bell peppers, green onions

1½ cups cubed zucchini

¼ cup whole kernel corn

4 cloves garlic, minced

8 eggs, lightly beaten

¼ cup finely chopped cilantro

¾ teaspoon dried oregano leaves

1 cup (4 ounces) shredded reduced-fat mozzarella or Cheddar cheese

Salt and pepper, to taste

6 flour tortillas (10-inch)

1–1½ cups mild or hot salsa

Per Serving:
Calories: 478
% of calories from fat: 28
Fat (gm): 14.5
Saturated fat (gm): 5
Cholesterol (mg): 292
Sodium (mg): 785
Protein (gm): 20
Carbohydrate (gm): 65

Exchanges:
Milk: 0.0
Vegetable: 1.0
Fruit: 0.0
Bread: 4.0
Meat: 2.0
Fat: 1.0

1. Sauté vegetables and garlic in lightly greased large skillet until potatoes are browned, about 10 minutes. Add combined eggs, cilantro, and oregano to skillet; cook over medium heat until set, stirring occasionally. Remove from heat and stir in cheese; season to taste with salt and pepper. Spoon mixture onto tortillas; fold 2 sides of each tortilla in about 2 inches, then fold in other sides to enclose filling. Serve with salsa.

TOMATO, SPINACH, AND CHEESE BURRITOS

45

A Neapolitan burrito!

4 servings

1 cup each: fat-free and reduced-fat ricotta cheese

1 teaspoon grated Parmesan cheese

¾ teaspoon chili powder

½ teaspoon each: crushed red pepper, ground cumin

4 flour tortillas (10-inch)

4 ounces spinach leaves, thinly sliced

1 large tomato, chopped

Olive oil cooking spray

½ cup each: prepared salsa, fat-free sour cream

Per Serving:
Calories: 285
% of calories from fat: 16
Fat (gm): 5.3
Saturated fat (gm): 1.9
Cholesterol (mg): 16.9
Sodium (mg): 712
Protein (gm): 26.6
Carbohydrate (gm): 34.7

Exchanges:
Milk: 0.0
Vegetable: 2.0
Fruit: 0.0
Bread: 1.0
Meat: 3.0
Fat: 0.0

1. Combine cheeses and seasonings in medium bowl. Spread ½ cup cheese mixture in center of each tortilla; sprinkle with spinach and tomato. Fold 2 sides of each tortilla in about 2 inches, then fold in other sides to enclose filling. Arrange burritos, seam sides down, in greased baking pan; spray lightly with cooking spray. Bake at 400 degrees until browned, about 25 minutes. Serve with salsa and sour cream.

NEW MEXICO EGG TOSTADAS

45

These easy tostadas are baked and served with a simple chili sauce.

4 servings

4 whole wheat tortillas (6-inch)
2 cups fat-free refried beans
2 green onions, thinly sliced
4 eggs
Red Sauce (recipe follows)
4 tablespoons fat-free sour cream
Chopped cilantro, as garnish

Per Serving:
Calories: 251
% of calories from fat: 18
Fat (gm): 5.1
Saturated fat (gm): 1.6
Cholesterol (mg): 212
Sodium (mg): 715
Protein (gm): 15.2
Carbohydrate (gm): 35.1

Exchanges:
Milk: 0.0
Vegetable: 0.0
Fruit: 0.0
Bread: 2.5
Meat: 1.0
Fat: 0.5

1. Quickly immerse tortillas in cold water and drain; bake on greased cookie sheet at 450 degrees until lightly browned, 2 to 3 minutes. Spoon refried beans around outer edge of each tortilla; sprinkle with green onions. Break an egg into center of each tortilla. Bake at 350 degrees until eggs are set, 15 to 20 minutes. Serve with Red Sauce and sour cream; garnish with cilantro.

Red Sauce

Makes about ¾ cup

¼ cup chopped onion
½ cup reduced-sodium fat-free beef broth
¼ cup crushed New Mexico chilies, seeds and stems discarded

1. Heat all ingredients to boiling in small saucepan; reduce heat and simmer, covered, until onion and chilies are soft, about 5 minutes. Process in blender or food processor until smooth.

BLACK BEAN CHEESECAKE WITH SALSA

45

This unusual entrée can also be served in smaller pieces as an appetizer or first course. It can be served at room temperature, or heated as the recipe directs. Make it a day in advance, as overnight chilling is essential.

8 servings

4 flour tortillas (6-inch)

3 packages (8 ounces each) fat-free cream cheese, room temperature

6 eggs

1 can (15 ounces) black beans, rinsed, drained

2 tablespoons finely chopped onion

1 tablespoon each: minced garlic, jalapeño chili

2 teaspoons dried cumin

½ teaspoon each: dried oregano leaves, chili powder, salt, cayenne pepper

1 cup hot or mild salsa

Per Serving:
Calories: 249
% of calories from fat: 25
Fat (gm): 7
Saturated fat (gm): 2
Cholesterol (mg): 165
Sodium (mg): 797
Protein (gm): 21.5
Carbohydrate (gm): 25

Exchanges:
Milk: 0.0
Vegetable: 0.0
Fruit: 0.0
Bread: 1.5
Meat: 2.5
Fat: 0.0

1. Line greased 9-inch springform pan with overlapping tortillas.

2. Beat cream cheese in large bowl until smooth; beat in eggs. Mix in remaining ingredients, except salsa; pour into prepared springform pan. Bake, uncovered, at 300 degrees until center is set and sharp knife inserted halfway between center and edge of cheesecake comes out almost clean, 1¾ to 2 hours. Cool on wire rack; refrigerate 8 hours or overnight.

3. Cook wedges of cheesecake in lightly greased large skillet over medium-low heat until browned on both sides. Serve with salsa.

EIGHT

Pasta

HOMEMADE PASTA

Fresh pasta dough is not difficult to make. A pasta machine is a very simple way of kneading, rolling, and cutting the dough, and it produces a high-quality pasta. Rolling and cutting the dough by hand is somewhat more difficult; it requires practice to make thin, delicate pasta. Be sure to follow cooking directions in Step 4 carefully. Fresh pasta cooks very quickly—much more quickly than purchased fresh or dried pasta.

4 entrée servings

1½ cups all-purpose flour

2 large eggs

Additional flour for rolling

Per Serving:
Calories: 208
% of calories from fat: 13
Fat (gm): 3
Saturated fat (gm): 0.8
Cholesterol (mg): 106.5
Sodium (mg): 32
Protein (gm): 8
Carbohydrate (gm): 36.1

Exchanges:
Milk: 0.0
Vegetable: 0.0
Fruit: 0.0
Bread: 2.5
Meat: 0.0
Fat: 0.5

1. Mound flour on cutting board, making a well in center. Drop eggs into center of well. Mix eggs with a fork. While mixing eggs, gradually start to incorporate flour into the eggs. As flour is incorporated, it will be necessary to move the mound of flour toward the center, using your hands. Continue mixing until all or almost all flour has been incorporated, forming a soft, but not sticky, ball of dough.

2. To knead dough with a pasta machine, set machine rollers on widest setting. Cut dough into 2 equal pieces. Lightly flour outside of 1 piece, and pass it through machine. Fold piece of dough into thirds; pass it through machine again, inserting open edges (not the fold) of dough first. Repeat folding and rolling 8 to 12 times or until dough feels smooth and satiny; lightly flour dough only if it begins to feel sticky.

Move machine rollers to next narrower setting. Pass dough, without folding, through rollers, beginning to roll out and stretch dough. Move machine rollers to next narrower setting; pass dough through rollers. Continue process until pasta is as thin as desired. (Often the narrowest setting on machine makes pasta too thin; 1 or 2 settings from the end is usually best.) Lightly flour dough if it begins to feel even slightly sticky at any time. Repeat above procedures with second piece of dough.

To cut pasta with the machine, set cutting rollers for width of pasta desired; pass dough through cutters. Arrange cut pasta in single layer on lightly floured surface.

3. To knead dough by hand, knead on lightly floured surface until smooth and satiny, about 10 minutes. Cover dough lightly with damp towel and let rest 10 minutes.

Place dough on lightly floured surface. Starting in center of dough, roll with rolling pin from center to edge. Continue rolling, always from center to edge, keeping dough as round as possible, until dough is about $\frac{1}{16}$ inch thick. Lightly flour dough if it begins to feel even slightly sticky at any time.

To cut pasta by hand, flour top of dough lightly and roll up. Cut into desired widths with sharp knife. Immediately unroll cut pasta and arrange in single layer on lightly floured surface.

4. To cook fresh or dried pasta, heat 4 to 5 quarts lightly salted water to boiling. Add pasta and begin testing for doneness as soon as water returns to boil. Cooking time will vary from 0 to 2 minutes once water has returned to boil.

NOTES: Pasta can be cooked fresh, or it can be dried and frozen or stored in an airtight container to be cooked later. To dry pasta, let stand on floured surface (or hang over rack) until completely dried. (Be sure pasta is completely dried or it will turn moldy in storage.) Store at room temperature in airtight container, or freeze.

Fresh homemade pasta can be used with any recipe, but it will result in a higher cholesterol count than stated with the recipe.

PASTA BOLOGNESE

45 *Bolognese is no doubt the favorite of pasta sauces—enjoy this savory healthful version!*

6 servings

1 pound ground beef eye of round

¼ cup each: chopped onion, carrot, celery

3 cloves garlic, minced

1½ teaspoons dried Italian seasoning

⅛ teaspoon ground nutmeg

1 can (8 ounces) each: reduced-sodium tomato sauce, reduced-sodium whole tomatoes, undrained, chopped

¼ cup dry red wine or tomato juice

½ teaspoon salt

¼ teaspoon pepper

12 ounces spaghetti, cooked, warm

Per Serving:
Calories: 361
% of calories from fat: 16
Fat (gm): 6.2
Saturated fat (gm): 2.2
Cholesterol (mg): 28.2
Sodium (mg): 287
Protein (gm): 24.6
Carbohydrate (gm): 50.2

Exchanges:
Milk: 0.0
Vegetable: 1.0
Fruit: 0.0
Bread: 3.0
Meat: 2.0
Fat: 0.0

1. Cook ground beef in lightly greased medium saucepan over medium heat until browned, 5 to 8 minutes; drain well and crumble. Add onion, carrot, celery, garlic, Italian seasoning, and nutmeg to saucepan; sauté until lightly browned, about 5 minutes. Add tomato sauce, tomatoes with liquid, and wine; heat to boiling. Reduce heat and simmer, uncovered, until thick sauce consistency, about 15 minutes; stir in salt and pepper. Serve over spaghetti.

45-MINUTE PREPARATION TIP: Cook pasta while sauce is simmering.

PASTA WITH TOMATO AND MEATBALL SAUCE

Herb-Seasoned Meatballs can be made up to two days in advance, making the sauce very easy to complete.

8 servings

1 cup chopped onion

1 tablespoon each: minced garlic, olive oil

1 can (16 ounces) reduced-sodium whole tomatoes, undrained, chopped

1 can (8 ounces) reduced-sodium tomato sauce
2 teaspoons dried Italian seasoning
⅛ teaspoon crushed red pepper
Herb-Seasoned Meatballs (recipe follows)
Salt and pepper, to taste
12 ounces spaghetti, cooked, warm

Per Serving:
Calories: 355
% of calories from fat: 21
Fat (gm): 8.4
Saturated fat (gm): 1.9
Cholesterol (mg): 42.3
Sodium (mg): 405
Protein (gm): 20.2
Carbohydrate (gm): 48.8

Exchanges:
Milk: 0.0
Vegetable: 3.0
Fruit: 0.0
Bread: 2.0
Meat: 1.5
Fat: 1.0

1. Sauté onion and garlic in oil in large saucepan 2 to 3 minutes. Stir in tomatoes and liquid, tomato sauce, Italian seasoning, and crushed red pepper; heat to boiling. Reduce heat and simmer, uncovered, 10 minutes. Add Herb-Seasoned Meatballs; simmer, uncovered, until medium sauce consistency, 10 to 15 minutes. Season to taste with salt and pepper. Serve over spaghetti.

Herb-Seasoned Meatballs

Makes 6 servings (3 meatballs each)

1 pound ground turkey or lean beef
⅓ cup unseasoned dry bread crumbs
1 egg white
3 cloves garlic, minced
1 teaspoon dried Italian seasoning
½ teaspoon salt
¼ teaspoon pepper

1. Mix all ingredients; shape into 18 meatballs. Cook meatballs over medium heat in lightly greased skillet until cooked and browned on all sides, 8 to 10 minutes. Drain well.

PASTA PUTTANESCA

45 *Ham, olives, and red pepper flakes add distinctive flavor to this popular sauce.*

8 servings

3 large onions, chopped

2 teaspoons minced garlic

2½ tablespoons olive oil

1 cup diced lean ham or Canadian bacon

2 cans (28 ounces each) reduced-sodium tomatoes, undrained, chopped

¼ cup sliced green olives

2 teaspoons dried basil leaves

⅛–¼ teaspoon crushed red pepper

Salt and pepper, to taste

16 ounces spaghetti, cooked, warm

Per Serving:
Calories: 330
% of calories from fat: 18
Fat (gm): 6.5
Saturated fat (gm): 1
Cholesterol (mg): 8.4
Sodium (mg): 278
Protein (gm): 12.8
Carbohydrate (gm): 56

Exchanges:
Milk: 0.0
Vegetable: 2.0
Fruit: 0.0
Bread: 3.0
Meat: 1.0
Fat: 0.5

1. Sauté onions and garlic in olive oil in large saucepan until tender and lightly browned, about 10 minutes. Add remaining ingredients, except salt, pepper, and spaghetti and heat to boiling. Reduce heat and simmer, uncovered, until thickened to medium sauce consistency, about 15 minutes; season to taste with salt and pepper. Serve over spaghetti.

45-MINUTE PREPARATION TIP: Cook pasta while sauce is simmering.

PASTA PEPERONATA

45 *The Peperonata mixture is a great addition to Italian sausage or bratwurst sandwiches.*

4 entrée servings

1½ cups each: sliced red, green, yellow bell peppers

1 cup each: sliced yellow and red onion

8 cloves garlic, minced

2 tablespoons each: olive oil, water

½ teaspoon dried thyme leaves

1 teaspoon sugar

Salt and pepper, to taste

8 ounces spaghetti, cooked, warm

¼ cup (1 ounce) grated Parmesan cheese

Per Serving:
Calories: 426
% of calories from fat: 25
Fat (gm): 11.8
Saturated fat (gm): 1.6
Cholesterol (mg): 0
Sodium (mg): 8
Protein (gm): 11.1
Carbohydrate (gm): 70.3

Exchanges:
Milk: 0.0
Vegetable: 3.0
Fruit: 0.0
Bread: 3.5
Meat: 0.0
Fat: 2.5

1. Sauté peppers, onions, and garlic in oil in large skillet 2 to 3 minutes. Add water; cook, covered, over medium to medium-high heat until vegetables are softened, about 5 minutes. Stir in thyme and sugar; cook, uncovered, over medium-low heat until mixture is very soft and browned, about 20 minutes. Season to taste with salt and pepper. Toss with spaghetti; sprinkle with cheese.

VARIATION

Roasted Peperonta with Italian Sausage — Make recipe above, omitting thyme, pasta, and Parmesan cheese. Arrange vegetables in single layer on greased foil-lined jelly roll pan; spray with olive oil cooking spray and sprinkle with 1½ teaspoons dried Italian seasoning. Roast at 425 degrees until browned and very soft, about 45 minutes; combine in bowl. While vegetables are roasting, cook 1½ pounds Italian-style turkey sausage in greased large skillet until cooked and browned, about 10 minutes; cut into serving pieces and serve with peperonata.

45-MINUTE PREPARATION TIP: Begin cooking the spaghetti before preparing the rest of the recipe.

FETTUCCINE WITH ROASTED GARLIC, ONIONS, AND PEPPERS

45

Deceptively simple to make, and incredibly delicious to eat!

8 side-dish servings

2 bulbs garlic
Olive oil cooking spray
3 medium onions, cut into wedges
2 large red bell peppers, thickly sliced
2 tablespoons each: olive oil, lemon juice
½ teaspoon salt
¼ teaspoon pepper
8 ounces fettuccine, cooked, warm

Per Serving:
Calories: 151
% of calories from fat: 26
Fat (gm): 4.5
Saturated fat (gm): 0.5
Cholesterol (mg): 0
Sodium (mg): 184
Protein (gm): 5
Carbohydrate (gm): 24.4

Exchanges:
Milk: 0.0
Vegetable: 1.5
Fruit: 0.0
Bread: 1.0
Meat: 0.0
Fat: 1.0

1. Cut a scant ½ inch off tops of garlic bulbs, exposing ends of cloves; spray with cooking spray. Wrap garlic bulbs loosely in aluminum foil. Arrange garlic, onions, and bell peppers in single layer on greased foil-lined jelly roll pan. Roast at 425 degrees until garlic is very soft and vegetables are tender, 30 to 40 minutes. Cool garlic slightly; squeeze pulp into small bowl. Stir in oil, lemon juice, salt, and pepper. Toss with pasta and onion mixture.

45-MINUTE PREPARATION TIP: Begin cooking the fettuccine before preparing the rest of the recipe.

FETTUCCINE WITH FENNEL, SPROUTS, AND HAM

45

If fennel is not available, substitute ½ cup thinly sliced celery, and add ½ teaspoon crushed fennel seeds to the sautéed vegetables.

4 entrée servings

4 ounces sliced reduced-sodium ham, cut into thin strips
1 cup each: thinly sliced fennel bulb, onion
8 ounces small Brussels sprouts, halved
¼ cup water
1 tablespoon lemon juice
Salt and pepper, to taste
8 ounces spinach fettuccine, cooked, warm

½ cup (2 ounces) shredded Parmesan cheese

¼ cup toasted pine nuts or slivered almonds

Per Serving:
Calories: 307
% of calories from fat: 24
Fat (gm): 8.4
Saturated fat (gm): 2.7
Cholesterol (mg): 85.6
Sodium (mg): 474
Protein (gm): 18.7
Carbohydrate (gm): 41.2

Exchanges:
Milk: 0.0
Vegetable: 2.0
Fruit: 0.0
Bread: 2.0
Meat: 1.0
Fat: 1.0

1. Sauté ham, fennel, and onion in lightly greased large skillet until onion is tender and browned, about 5 minutes. Add Brussels sprouts and water and heat to boiling; reduce heat and simmer, covered, until sprouts are crisp-tender, 5 to 8 minutes. Stir in lemon juice; season to taste with salt and pepper. Serve over pasta; sprinkle with Parmesan cheese and pine nuts.

45-MINUTE PREPARATION TIP: Begin cooking the fettuccine before preparing the rest of the recipe.

CREAMY FETTUCCINE PRIMAVERA

45 *The sauce for this dish should be somewhat thin, as it thickens once removed from the heat. If reheating, the sauce will require additional milk.*

4 entrée servings

2 cups each: sliced mushrooms, broccoli florets

½ cup each: chopped red bell pepper, water

8 ounces fat-free cream cheese

1 cup fat-free milk, divided

¼ cup sliced green onions

½ teaspoon dried Italian seasoning

2 tablespoons grated fat-free Parmesan cheese

Salt and white pepper, to taste

8 ounces fettuccine, cooked, warm

Per Serving:
Calories: 273
% of calories from fat: 8
Fat (gm): 2.5
Saturated fat (gm): 0.1
Cholesterol (mg): 0.7
Sodium (mg): 491
Protein (gm): 20.4
Carbohydrate (gm): 43.2

Exchanges:
Milk: 0.5
Vegetable: 2.0
Fruit: 0.0
Bread: 2.0
Meat: 0.5
Fat: 0.0

1. Sauté mushrooms, broccoli, and bell pepper in lightly greased large skillet 3 to 4 minutes. Add water and heat to boiling; reduce heat and simmer, covered, until broccoli is tender, about 8 minutes; drain.

2. Heat cream cheese, ⅔ cup milk, green onions, and Italian seasoning in small saucepan over low heat until cream cheese is melted, stirring frequently. Stir in Parmesan cheese and enough remaining ⅓ cup milk to make a thin consistency. Season to taste with salt and pepper. Toss with fettuccine and vegetables.

45-MINUTE PREPARATION TIP: Begin cooking the fettuccine before preparing the rest of the recipe.

FETTUCCINE PAPRIKASH

45 *Use your preference of hot or sweet paprika in this recipe.*

6 servings

1 cup each: sliced red and green bell pepper, onion

1 tablespoon margarine or butter

2 tablespoons flour

1 tablespoon sweet Hungarian paprika

½ teaspoon salt

¼ teaspoon pepper

1 can (8 ounces) reduced-sodium tomato sauce

½ cup each: reduced-sodium fat-free chicken broth, dry white wine or chicken broth, reduced-fat sour cream

12 ounces fettuccine, cooked, warm

Per Serving:
Calories: 264
% of calories from fat: 20
Fat (gm): 5.8
Saturated fat (gm): 1.7
Cholesterol (mg): 16.7
Sodium (mg): 267
Protein (gm): 9.5
Carbohydrate (gm): 41

Exchanges:
Milk: 0.0
Vegetable: 2.0
Fruit: 0.0
Bread: 2.0
Meat: 0.0
Fat: 1.5

1. Sauté bell peppers and onion in margarine in large skillet until peppers are very soft, 10 to 15 minutes. Stir in flour, paprika, salt, and pepper; cook 1 minute. Stir in tomato sauce, broth, and wine; heat to boiling. Reduce heat and simmer, uncovered, until sauce is thickened, 5 to 7 minutes; stir in sour cream. Serve over fettuccine.

45-MINUTE PREPARATION TIP: Cook pasta while sauce is simmering.

FETTUCCINE WITH CHILI-MUSHROOM STROGANOFF SAUCE

45 *Shiitake mushrooms and dried ancho chilies are unique flavor additions to this pasta sauce. The chilies can be quite hot, so adjust amount according to your taste.*

8 servings

3 cups boiling water, divided

1–2 dried ancho chilies

1 package (1¾ ounces) dried shiitake mushrooms

2 cups vegetable broth, divided

1 cup chopped onion

8 ounces white mushrooms, halved or quartered

2 tablespoons margarine or butter

¼ cup all-purpose flour

½ teaspoon dried thyme leaves

1 cup reduced-fat sour cream

1 teaspoon Dijon mustard

Salt and pepper, to taste

16 ounces fettuccine, cooked, warm

Per Serving:
Calories: 333
% of calories from fat: 18
Fat (gm): 6.7
Saturated fat (gm): 2.1
Cholesterol (mg): 10
Sodium (mg): 306
Protein (gm): 11.3
Carbohydrate (gm): 56.5

Exchanges:
Milk: 0.0
Vegetable: 2.0
Fruit: 0.0
Bread: 3.0
Meat: 0.0
Fat: 1.5

1. Pour boiling water over ancho chilies and shiitake mushrooms in bowl. Let stand until softened, about 10 minutes. Drain chilies and mushrooms, reserving liquid. Slice mushrooms, discarding tough centers. Process chilies and 1 cup vegetable broth in blender or food processor until smooth.

2. Sauté onion, white and shiitake mushrooms in margarine in large skillet until wilted, about 5 minutes. Stir in flour; cook 1 minute. Stir in reserved liquid, chili mixture, remaining 1 cup broth, and thyme. Heat to boiling; reduce heat and simmer, covered, until shiitake mushrooms are tender, 10 to 15 minutes. Simmer, uncovered, to desired sauce consistency, about 5 minutes. Stir in sour cream and mustard; cook over low heat until hot, 2 to 3 minutes. Season to taste with salt and pepper. Serve with pasta.

45-MINUTE PREPARATION TIP: Begin cooking pasta while sauce is simmering.

FETTUCCINE WITH GORGONZOLA SAUCE

45 *Gorgonzola lends rich flavor to this creamy sauce.*

6 servings

2 cups fat-free milk
¼ cup each: dry white wine or milk, all-purpose flour
3 ounces Gorgonzola cheese, crumbled
2 tablespoons margarine or butter
¼ teaspoon pepper
12 ounces fettuccine, cooked, warm

Per Serving:
Calories: 298
% of calories from fat: 23
Fat (gm): 10
Saturated fat (gm): 3.5
Cholesterol (mg): 22.1
Sodium (mg): 295
Protein (gm): 12.4
Carbohydrate (gm): 38.4

Exchanges:
Milk: 0.0
Vegetable: 2.0
Fruit: 0.0
Bread: 2.0
Meat: 0.0
Fat: 2.0

1. Whisk milk, wine, and flour in medium saucepan until smooth; heat to boiling, whisking until thickened, 1 to 2 minutes. Reduce heat to low and whisk in cheese, margarine, and pepper; cook until cheese is melted, 1 to 2 minutes. Serve over fettuccine.

45-MINUTE PREPARATION TIP: Begin cooking pasta before preparing the rest of the recipe.

STIR-FRIED RICE NOODLES WITH SHRIMP

45 *Sea or bay scallops can be substituted for the shrimp.*

4 entrée servings (about 1½ cups each)

1 package (8 ounces) rice noodles
4 green onions, thinly sliced
1 tablespoon finely chopped gingerroot
8 ounces peeled, deveined shrimp
1 tablespoon vegetable oil
2 cups shredded napa cabbage
1 cup reduced-sodium chicken broth
2 tablespoons dry sherry (optional)
2–3 teaspoons light soy sauce
½–1 teaspoon Szechuan chili sauce

Per Serving:
Calories: 292
% of calories from fat: 13
Fat (gm): 4.2
Saturated fat (gm): 0.6
Cholesterol (mg): 87.1
Sodium (mg): 223
Protein (gm): 17.1
Carbohydrate (gm): 46.6

Exchanges:
Milk: 0.0
Vegetable: 1.0
Fruit: 0.0
Bread: 3.0
Meat: 1.0
Fat: 0.0

1. Place noodles in large bowl; pour cold water over to cover. Let stand until noodles separate and are soft, about 15 minutes; drain.

2. Stir-fry green onions, gingerroot, and shrimp in oil in wok or large skillet until shrimp are cooked, about 5 minutes; remove from wok. Add cabbage to wok and stir-fry 1 minute; stir in remaining ingredients. Heat to boiling; reduce heat and simmer, uncovered, until noodles have absorbed all liquid, about 5 minutes. Return shrimp mixture to wok; stir-fry until hot, 2 to 3 minutes.

45-MINUTE PREPARATION TIP: Cut vegetables while noodles are soaking.

LINGUINE WITH MIXED HERB PESTO

45 *A ½-ounce package of fresh herbs yields about ¼ cup packed herb leaves. Serve pesto sauce at room temperature, mixing with hot pasta.*

4 servings

½ cup each: packed basil leaves and parsley leaves

¼ cup packed oregano leaves

3–4 tablespoons grated fat-free Parmesan cheese

1 ounce walnuts (about 14 medium)

1 tablespoon olive oil, minced garlic

2 teaspoons lemon juice

2–4 tablespoons reduced-sodium fat-free chicken broth or water

½ teaspoon salt

¼ teaspoon pepper

8 ounces linguine, cooked, warm

Per Serving:
Calories: 253
% of calories from fat: 30
Fat (gm): 8.8
Saturated fat (gm): 0.7
Cholesterol (mg): 0
Sodium (mg): 447
Protein (gm): 9.7
Carbohydrate (gm): 36

Exchanges:
Milk: 0.0
Vegetable: 1.0
Fruit: 0.0
Bread: 2.0
Meat: 0.0
Fat: 1.5

1. Process all ingredients, except linguine, in food processor until mixture is a smooth, spoonable paste; toss with linguine.

45-MINUTE PREPARATION TIP: Make pesto while linguine is cooking.

ROASTED SUMMER VEGETABLES WITH PASTA

45

For attractive serving, the pasta can be shaped into small nests to contain the medley of roasted vegetables.

8 servings

1 medium eggplant, peeled, cubed (1-inch)

1 cup each: sliced zucchini, red or green bell pepper, red onion wedges

Olive oil cooking spray

2 teaspoons crushed caraway seeds

3 tablespoons olive oil

2 tablespoons balsamic or red wine vinegar

1 teaspoon lemon juice

3 cloves garlic, minced

¼ teaspoon each: salt, pepper

16 ounces linguine, cooked, warm

Per Serving:
Calories: 275
% of calories from fat: 21
Fat (gm): 6
Saturated fat (gm): 0.7
Cholesterol (mg): 0.0
Sodium (mg): 258
Protein (gm): 17
Carbohydrate (gm): 38

Exchanges:
Milk: 0.0
Vegetable: 1.0
Fruit: 0.0
Bread: 2.0
Meat: 2.0
Fat: 0.0

1. Arrange vegetables in single layer on greased foil-lined jelly roll pan; spray with cooking spray and sprinkle with caraway seeds. Roast at 425 degrees until vegetables are browned and tender, 30 to 40 minutes. Combine remaining ingredients, except pasta; drizzle over vegetables and toss. Serve with pasta.

45-MINUTE PREPARATION TIP: Cook pasta while vegetables are roasting.

LINGUINE WITH WHITE CLAM SAUCE

45

One of Italy's most treasured dishes!

4 servings

1 tablespoon each: minced garlic, olive oil

2 cups bottled clam juice

1 tablespoons cornstarch

½ cup dry white wine or clam juice

1 pound shucked clams or 2 cans (7½ ounces each) baby clams, undrained

1 tablespoon lemon juice

1 teaspoon dried basil leaves

⅛ teaspoon ground white pepper

8 ounces linguine, cooked, warm

Per Serving:
Calories: 319
% of calories from fat: 18
Fat (gm): 6.5
Saturated fat (gm): 0.6
Cholesterol (mg): 38.6
Sodium (mg): 305
Protein (gm): 23.5
Carbohydrate (gm): 39.1

Exchanges:
Milk: 0.0
Vegetable: 0.5
Fruit: 0.0
Bread: 2.5
Meat: 2.0
Fat: 0.5

1. Sauté garlic in oil in medium saucepan, 1 to 2 minutes. Stir in clam juice and heat to boiling; whisk in combined cornstarch and wine. Boil, whisking until thickened, about 1 minute. Add remaining ingredients, except linguine; simmer, covered, until clams are cooked, 5 to 7 minutes. Serve over linguine.

45-MINUTE PREPARATION TIP: Begin cooking pasta before preparing the rest of the recipe.

LINGUINE WITH RED CLAM SAUCE

45 *This light tomato sauce is rich with succulent clams.*

4 servings

1 tablespoon each: minced garlic, olive oil

1 can (28 ounces) Italian tomatoes, undrained, coarsely chopped

¼ cup dry red wine, clam juice, or water

2 teaspoons dried oregano leaves

1 tablespoon lemon juice

⅛–¼ teaspoon cayenne pepper

¼ teaspoon black pepper

1 pound shucked baby clams or 2 cans (7½ ounces each) baby clams, undrained

8 ounces linguine, cooked, warm

Per Serving:
Calories: 332
% of calories from fat: 16
Fat (gm): 5.8
Saturated fat (gm): 0.6
Cholesterol (mg): 38.1
Sodium (mg): 590
Protein (gm): 22.3
Carbohydrate (gm): 43.8

Exchanges:
Milk: 0.0
Vegetable: 2.0
Fruit: 0.0
Bread: 2.0
Meat: 2.0
Fat: 0.5

1. Sauté garlic in oil in medium saucepan until tender, about 2 minutes. Stir in remaining ingredients, except clams and linguine; heat to boiling. Reduce heat and simmer, uncovered, until mixture is medium sauce consistency, about 10 minutes. Stir in clams; simmer, covered, until clams are cooked, 5 to 7 minutes. Discard any unopened clams. Serve over linguine.

45-MINUTE PREPARATION TIP: Cook pasta while sauce is simmering.

JERK CHICKEN AND SHRIMP WITH LINGUINE

Enjoy the highly seasoned flavors of the Caribbean in this pasta dish!

4 servings

Jerk Sauce (recipe follows)
8 ounces chicken tenders
4 ounces peeled, deveined shrimp
1 can (14½ ounces) reduced-sodium chicken broth
2 teaspoons lime juice
1 pound broccoli florets, cooked crisp-tender
8 ounces linguine, cooked, warm

Per Serving:
Calories: 332
% of calories from fat: 13
Fat (gm): 4.9
Saturated fat (gm): 0.6
Cholesterol (mg): 73
Sodium (mg): 232
Protein (gm): 28
Carbohydrate (gm): 47

Exchanges:
Milk: 0.0
Vegetable: 2.0
Fruit: 0.0
Bread: 2.5
Meat: 2.0
Fat: 0.0

1. Combine Jerk Sauce with chicken and shrimp in glass bowl and toss. Refrigerate, covered, 30 minutes.

2. Cook undrained chicken and shrimp in lightly greased large skillet over medium-high heat until chicken and shrimp are browned, about 5 minutes. Stir in chicken broth and lime juice; heat to boiling. Reduce heat and simmer, uncovered, until liquid is thin sauce consistency, about 5 minutes; add broccoli and cook 2 to 3 minutes. Serve over linguine.

Jerk Sauce

Makes about ⅓ cup

3 tablespoons water
2 tablespoons each: chopped cilantro, gingerroot, light brown sugar
1 tablespoon ground allspice
2 teaspoons each: chopped garlic, black peppercorns
¼ teaspoon each: ground coriander, mace, crushed red pepper

1. Process all ingredients in food processor until coarse paste is formed.

45-MINUTE PREPARATION TIP: Begin cooking linguine before preparing Step 2 of recipe.

PASTA WITH GREENS, RAISINS, AND PINE NUTS

45 *Radicchio, escarole, curly endive, kale, or mustard greens can be substituted for the brightly colored Oriental kale in this sweet-and-bitter Italian favorite.*

4 entrée servings

4 medium onions, sliced

1 tablespoon each: minced garlic, olive oil

1 teaspoon sugar

12 ounces Oriental kale leaves, torn

⅓ cup dark raisins

½ cup reduced-sodium vegetable broth

Salt and pepper, to taste

8 ounces whole wheat spaghetti or linguine, cooked, warm

2 tablespoons pine nuts or slivered almonds

Per Serving:
Calories: 391
% of calories from fat: 17
Fat (gm): 8
Saturated fat (gm): 0.9
Cholesterol (mg): 0.0
Sodium (mg): 127
Protein (gm): 13
Carbohydrate (gm): 75

Exchanges:
Milk: 0.0
Vegetable: 0.0
Fruit: 0.0
Bread: 4.0
Meat: 0.0
Fat: 1.0

1. Sauté onions and garlic in oil in large skillet until tender, 3 to 5 minutes. Stir in sugar; cook over low heat until onions are golden, 10 to 15 minutes, stirring occasionally. Stir in kale, raisins, and broth; cook, covered, over low heat until kale is wilted, about 10 minutes. Season to taste with salt and pepper. Toss with spaghetti and sprinkle with pine nuts.

45-MINUTE PREPARATION TIP: Begin cooking the spaghetti before preparing the rest of the recipe.

PASTA WITH GOAT CHEESE AND ONION CONFIT

45 *Try this dish with flavored specialty pastas such as dried mushroom, herb, or black pepper.*

4 entrée servings

4 cups thinly sliced onions

1 teaspoon each: minced garlic, sugar

½ teaspoon each: dried sage and rosemary leaves

½ cup dry white wine or fat-free milk

2 ounces each: fat-free cream cheese, goat cheese

Salt and pepper, to taste

8 ounces whole wheat thin spaghetti, cooked, warm

2–3 tablespoons coarsely chopped walnuts

Per Serving:
Calories: 395
% of calories from fat: 15
Fat (gm): 6.7
Saturated fat (gm): 2.4
Cholesterol (mg): 6.5
Sodium (mg): 144
Protein (gm): 16
Carbohydrate (gm): 66.9

Exchanges:
Milk: 0.0
Vegetable: 2.0
Fruit: 0.0
Bread: 4.0
Meat: 0.5
Fat: 0.5

1. Sauté onions in lightly greased large skillet 3 to 4 minutes; stir in garlic, sugar, and herbs and cook, uncovered, over medium-low heat until onions are golden, 15 to 20 minutes. Stir in wine; simmer 2 to 3 minutes. Add cream cheese and goat cheese, stirring until melted; season to taste with salt and white pepper. Toss with pasta; sprinkle with walnuts.

45-MINUTE PREPARATION TIP: Cook spaghetti while onions are cooking.

MOLDED CAPELLINI CARBONARA

45

Thin spaghetti or linguine can be substituted for the angel hair pasta. The center of the mold can be filled with a mixture of vegetables.

4 entrée servings

¼ cup minced shallots

1 teaspoon minced garlic

1 cup seeded chopped Italian plum tomatoes

½ teaspoon dried oregano leaves

¼ teaspoon crushed red pepper

2 slices bacon, fried crisp, crumbled

Salt and pepper, to taste

8 ounces capellini (angel hair pasta), cooked

3 eggs, lightly beaten

1. Sauté shallots and garlic in lightly greased skillet until tender, 3 to 4 minutes. Add tomatoes, oregano, and crushed red pepper. Cook, covered, over medium heat until tomatoes soften, about 5 minutes; stir in bacon and season to taste with salt and pepper. Combine with pasta and eggs and spoon into greased 6-cup ring mold. Bake, uncovered, at 350 degrees until set, about 20 minutes. Invert onto serving plate.

Per Serving:
Calories: 249
% of calories from fat: 24
Fat (gm): 6.9
Saturated fat (gm): 2.2
Cholesterol (mg): 224.1
Sodium (mg): 99
Protein (gm): 12.8
Carbohydrate (gm): 34.1

Exchanges:
Milk: 0.0
Vegetable: 1.0
Fruit: 0.0
Bread: 2.0
Meat: 1.0
Fat: 0.5

45-MINUTE PREPARATION TIP: Begin cooking the capellini before preparing the rest of the recipe.

WARM PAPPARDELLE WITH CAJUN SHRIMP

45 *Any of the wide, flat pastas, such as mafalde or trenette, are also appropriate for this highly spiced dish.*

4 entrée servings

⅓ cup each: sliced red bell pepper, onion

12 ounces peeled, deveined shrimp

2 teaspoons each: dried oregano, basil, and thyme leaves

½ teaspoon each: garlic powder, paprika

¼ teaspoon each: cayenne and black pepper, salt

1 cup reduced-sodium chicken broth

¼ cup dry white wine or water

1 tablespoon tomato paste

8 ounces pappardelle, cooked, warm

Per Serving:
Calories: 292
% of calories from fat: 7
Fat (gm): 2.2
Saturated fat (gm): 0.5
Cholesterol (mg): 130.6
Sodium (mg): 329
Protein (gm): 22.7
Carbohydrate (gm): 41.4

Exchanges:
Milk: 0.0
Vegetable: 0.5
Fruit: 0.0
Bread: 3.0
Meat: 1.0
Fat: 0.0

1. Sauté bell pepper and onion in lightly greased large skillet until tender, 3 to 4 minutes. Stir in shrimp and seasonings; cook over medium heat until shrimp just begin to turn pink, about 2 minutes. Stir in broth, wine, and tomato paste; heat to boiling. Reduce heat and simmer, uncovered 5 minutes. Serve over pasta.

45-MINUTE PREPARATION TIP: Begin cooking pappardelle before preparing the rest of the recipe.

PASTA WITH CABBAGE AND POTATOES

45 *Add sautéed cubed ham or sliced smoked turkey sausage to this dish for a heartier entrée.*

8 servings

6 cups thinly sliced cabbage

4 cloves garlic, minced

⅓ cup reduced-sodium chicken broth

4 medium Idaho potatoes, peeled, cubed

1 teaspoon each: dried rosemary and sage leaves

½ teaspoon salt

¼ teaspoon pepper

16 ounces pappardelle or other flat pasta, cooked, warm

¼ cup (1 ounce) grated Parmesan cheese

Per Serving:
Calories: 297
% of calories from fat: 6
Fat (gm): 1.8
Saturated fat (gm): 0.7
Cholesterol (mg): 3.2
Sodium (mg): 215
Protein (gm): 10.5
Carbohydrate (gm): 59.6

Exchanges:
Milk: 0.0
Vegetable: 0.0
Fruit: 0.0
Bread: 4.0
Meat: 0.0
Fat: 0.5

1. Combine cabbage, garlic, and broth in large skillet; heat to boiling; reduce heat and simmer, covered, until cabbage is wilted, about 5 minutes. Add potatoes, herbs, salt, and pepper; cook, covered, over medium heat until potatoes are tender and broth is almost evaporated, about 10 minutes. Toss with pasta; sprinkle with Parmesan cheese.

45-MINUTE PREPARATION TIP: Begin cooking pasta before preparing the rest of the recipe.

PASTA WITH THREE-ONION SAUCE

45 *The vegetables for this sauce are cooked very slowly until the onions are caramelized.*

6 servings

1½ cups each: sliced leeks (white parts only), chopped red onions
6 shallots, sliced
3 tablespoons olive oil
¼ cup all-purpose flour
1 can (14½ ounces) reduced-sodium fat-free chicken broth
¼ teaspoon each: dried thyme leaves, pepper
½ teaspoon salt
12 ounces mafalde or other flat pasta, cooked, warm

Per Serving:
Calories: 327
% of calories from fat: 21
Fat (gm): 7.8
Saturated fat (gm): 1.1
Cholesterol (mg): 0
Sodium (mg): 360
Protein (gm): 9.7
Carbohydrate (gm): 54.4

Exchanges:
Milk: 0.0
Vegetable: 2.0
Fruit: 0.0
Bread: 3.0
Meat: 0.0
Fat: 1.5

1. Sauté leeks, onions, and shallots in oil in medium saucepan 2 to 3 minutes. Reduce heat to medium-low and cook slowly until mixture is golden, about 15 minutes. Stir in flour; cook over medium heat 1 to 2 minutes. Add broth, thyme, salt, and pepper; heat to boiling, stirring until thickened, about 1 minute. Serve over mafalde.

45-MINUTE PREPARATION TIP: Cook mafalde while leek mixture is cooking.

"LITTLE EARS" WITH SHRIMP AND VEGETABLES

45 *For variety, substitute cooked cubed chicken breast, lean beef, or lean pork for the shrimp in this salad.*

4 entrée servings

12 ounces peeled, deveined cooked shrimp
3 cups broccoli florets, cooked crisp-tender, cooled
1 medium yellow or green bell pepper sliced
12 cherry tomatoes, halved
2 cups (8 ounces) orecchiette (little ears) or small pasta shells, cooked, room temperature
Mustard Seed Vinaigrette (recipe follows)

1. Combine all ingredients in salad bowl and toss.

Mustard Seed Vinaigrette

Makes about ⅓ cup

2 tablespoons each: olive oil, white wine vinegar, lemon juice

2 each: cloves garlic, medium shallots, finely chopped

2 tablespoons chopped cilantro

¼ teaspoon each: salt, pepper

1. Mix all ingredients.

45-MINUTE PREPARATION TIP: Begin cooking pasta and broccoli before preparing the rest of the recipe; rinse in cold water to cool.

Per Serving:
Calories: 367
% of calories from fat: 23
Fat (gm): 9.6
Saturated fat (gm): 1.4
Cholesterol (mg): 130.6
Sodium (mg): 451
Protein (gm): 24.7
Carbohydrate (gm): 47.3

Exchanges:
Milk: 0.0
Vegetable: 2.0
Fruit: 0.0
Bread: 2.5
Meat: 2.0
Fat: 0.5

BOW TIE BLACK BEAN PASTA

Any shaped pasta can be used in this recipe.

4 servings

4 ounces dried black beans

½ cup each: chopped onion, red bell pepper

½ tablespoon minced garlic

1½ teaspoons canola oil

¼ cup dry sherry or vegetable broth

2 cups vegetable broth

2 teaspoons dried Italian seasoning

8 ounces tiny bow tie pasta, cooked

Salt and pepper, to taste

Per Serving:
Calories: 269
% of calories from fat: 11
Fat (gm): 2.9
Saturated fat (gm): 0.3
Cholesterol (mg): 0
Sodium (mg): 471
Protein (gm): 10.7
Carbohydrate (gm): 44.5

Exchanges:
Milk: 0.0
Vegetable: 0.0
Fruit: 0.0
Bread: 3.0
Meat: 1.0
Fat: 0.0

1. Cover beans with 2 inches water in large saucepan; heat to boiling and boil, uncovered, 2 minutes. Remove from heat and let stand, covered, 1 hour; drain.

2. Sauté onion, bell pepper, and garlic in oil in large skillet until onion is tender. Add sherry and simmer until liquid is absorbed. Add broth, black beans, and Italian seasoning; heat to boiling. Simmer until beans are tender, about 1 hour. Stir in pasta; simmer until hot, 3 to 4 minutes. Season to taste with salt and pepper.

FUSILLI WITH TOMATOES AND CORN

45 *A perfect salad, especially when homegrown tomatoes, corn, and basil are available!*

8 side-dish servings

2 cups chopped plum tomatoes
1 cup cooked whole-kernel corn
½ cup sliced green onions
6 ounces fusilli (spirals), cooked, room temperature
Fresh Basil Dressing (recipe follows)

1. Combine all ingredients and toss.

Per Serving:
Calories: 135
% of calories from fat: 26
Fat (gm): 4
Saturated fat (gm): 0.6
Cholesterol (mg): 0
Sodium (mg): 141
Protein (gm): 4.1
Carbohydrate (gm): 21.8

Exchanges:
Milk: 0.0
Vegetable: 1.0
Fruit: 0.0
Bread: 1.0
Meat: 0.0
Fat: 1.0

Fresh Basil Dressing

Makes about ⅓ cup

⅓ cup red wine vinegar
2 tablespoons olive or canola oil
3 tablespoons chopped fresh or 1½ teaspoons
   dried basil leaves
2 cloves garlic, minced
½ teaspoon salt
¼ teaspoon pepper

1. Mix all ingredients.

45-MINUTE PREPARATION TIP: Begin cooking the fusilli before preparing the rest of the recipe.

FUSILLI WITH ARTICHOKE SAUCE

45 *Minced jalapeño chilis add a hint of piquancy to this sauce.*

4 servings

1 cup sliced onion

2 cloves garlic, minced

½–1 teaspoon minced jalapeño chili

1 tablespoon olive oil

2 tablespoons flour

1 can (14 ounces) artichoke hearts, drained, sliced

1 cup reduced-sodium fat-free chicken broth

¼ cup (1 ounce) grated Parmesan cheese

¼ teaspoon each: salt, pepper

8 ounces fusilli (spirals), cooked, warm

Per Serving:
Calories: 339
% of calories from fat: 16
Fat (gm): 6
Saturated fat (gm): 1.6
Cholesterol (mg): 3.9
Sodium (mg): 533
Protein (gm): 14.2
Carbohydrate (gm): 55.6

Exchanges:
Milk: 0.0
Vegetable: 2.0
Fruit: 0.0
Bread: 3.0
Meat: 0.0
Fat: 1.5

1. Sauté onion, garlic, and jalapeño chili in oil in medium saucepan until tender, about 5 minutes; stir in flour and cook 1 minute. Add artichoke hearts and broth; heat to boiling, stirring until thickened, about 1 minute. Stir in Parmesan cheese, salt, and pepper; cook 1 to 2 minutes. Serve over fusilli.

45-minute preparation tip: Begin cooking fusilli before preparing the rest of the recipe.

CREAMY TOMATO-PEPPER SAUCE WITH PENNE

45 *This sauce is so creamy you'd swear it's high in fat, but it is really quite low.*

6 servings

1 medium onion, chopped

½ teaspoon minced garlic

1 tablespoon olive oil

2 tablespoons dry sherry or water

1 can (15 ounces) Italian-seasoned tomato sauce

⅓ cup chopped roasted red peppers

2 teaspoons sugar

¼ cup reduced-fat sour cream

Per Serving:
Calories: 276
% of calories from fat: 13
Fat (gm): 4
Saturated fat (gm): 1
Cholesterol (mg): 3.3
Sodium (mg): 406
Protein (gm): 8.5
Carbohydrate (gm): 51.8

Exchanges:
Milk: 0.0
Vegetable: 1.0
Fruit: 0.0
Bread: 3.0
Meat: 0.0
Fat: 1.0

Salt and pepper, to taste

12 ounces penne, cooked, warm

1. Sauté onion and garlic in oil in large saucepan until softened, about 5 minutes. Stir in sherry, tomato sauce, roasted peppers, and sugar. Heat to boiling; reduce heat and simmer until slightly thickened, 10 to 15 minutes. Stir in sour cream; season to taste with salt and pepper. Serve over penne.

45-MINUTE PREPARATION TIP: Cook pasta while sauce is simmering.

ROTINI AND BEANS NIÇOISE

45 *Garbanzo or kidney beans can be substituted for any of the beans used in this dish.*

6 servings

½ cup chopped shallots or red onion

2 cups chopped Italian plum tomatoes

1 teaspoon minced garlic

2 teaspoons margarine or butter

2 cups diagonally sliced green beans, cooked

1 can (13¼ ounces), baby lima beans, rinsed, drained

1 can (15 ounces) cannellini beans, rinsed, drained

2 tablespoons drained capers

½ teaspoon dried tarragon leaves

6 cups cooked rotini or other shaped pasta, warm

Salt and pepper, to taste

Grated Parmesan cheese, as garnish

Per Serving:
Calories: 263
% of calories from fat: 8
Fat (gm): 2.3
Saturated fat (gm): 0.4
Cholesterol (mg): 0
Sodium (mg): 369
Protein (gm): 11.8
Carbohydrate (gm): 50.3

Exchanges:
Milk: 0.0
Vegetable: 0.0
Fruit: 0.0
Bread: 3.0
Meat: 1.0
Fat: 0.0

1. Sauté shallots, tomatoes, and garlic in margarine in large skillet 2 to 3 minutes; cook, covered, over medium heat until tomatoes are wilted, 3 to 5 minutes. Stir in fresh and canned beans, capers, and tarragon; cook, covered, over medium heat until hot, about 5 minutes. Stir in rotini and season to taste with salt and pepper; sprinkle with Parmesan cheese.

45-MINUTE PREPARATION TIP: Begin cooking pasta and green beans before preparing the rest of the recipe.

PASTA FROM PESCIA

45 *A hearty dish from the Tuscany region of Italy—any root vegetable you enjoy can be used in place of the potatoes.*

4 entrée servings

3 cups thinly sliced cabbage

8 small new potatoes, cooked, halved

1½ cups halved Brussels sprouts

2 medium carrots, diagonally sliced

2 cloves garlic, minced

½ teaspoon dried sage leaves

⅓ cup reduced-sodium vegetable broth

2 tablespoons grated Parmesan cheese

Salt and pepper, to taste

8 ounces rigatoni or ziti, cooked, warm

Per Serving:
Calories: 486
% of calories from fat: 5
Fat (gm): 2.5
Saturated fat (gm): 0.9
Cholesterol (mg): 2.5
Sodium (mg): 144
Protein (gm): 16.9
Carbohydrate (gm): 102.3

Exchanges:
Milk: 0.0
Vegetable: 3.0
Fruit: 0.0
Bread: 6.0
Meat: 0.0
Fat: 0.0

1. Heat cabbage, potatoes, Brussels sprouts, carrots, garlic, sage, and broth to boiling in large skillet. Reduce heat and simmer, covered, until cabbage is wilted, about 5 minutes. Cook, uncovered, until liquid is gone and cabbage is lightly browned, about 5 minutes. Stir in cheese; season to taste with salt and pepper. Toss with pasta.

45-MINUTE PREPARATION TIP: Begin cooking the rigatoni before preparing the rest of the recipe.

CREOLE PASTA

45 *Creole flavors accent this substantial sauce. If you enjoy okra, it would be an excellent addition.*

8 servings (about ½ cup each)

1½ cups sliced green bell peppers

⅔ cup each: sliced carrots, onion, celery

3 cloves garlic, minced

2 tablespoons olive oil

1 can (14½ ounces) reduced-sodium chicken broth

1 can (8 ounces) reduced-sodium tomato sauce

1 medium tomato, chopped

1 teaspoon each: dried basil and oregano leaves, paprika

½ teaspoon each: dried thyme leaves, gumbo file powder, salt

1 bay leaf

¼ teaspoon cayenne pepper

16 ounces rigatoni, cooked, warm

Per Serving:
Calories: 285
% of calories from fat: 14
Fat (gm): 4.6
Saturated fat (gm): 0.6
Cholesterol (mg): 0
Sodium (mg): 204
Protein (gm): 9.8
Carbohydrate (gm): 50.9

Exchanges:
Milk: 0.0
Vegetable: 1.0
Fruit: 0.0
Bread: 3.0
Meat: 0.0
Fat: 1.0

1. Sauté bell peppers, carrots, onion, celery, and garlic in oil until peppers are tender, 8 to 10 minutes. Stir in remaining ingredients, except rigatoni; heat to boiling. Reduce heat and simmer, uncovered, until vegetables are tender and sauce is thickened to desired consistency, about 20 minutes; discard bay leaf. Serve with rigatoni.

45-MINUTE PREPARATION TIP: Cook pasta while sauce is simmering.

BUTTER BEANS, MOSTACCIOLI, AND HAM

45 *This extra-easy recipe has a subtle anchovy flavor. Don't like anchovies? Then leave them out!*

4 entrée servings

4 ounces lean reduced-sodium ham, diced

1 small mild chili pepper, chopped

2 teaspoons garlic

1½ cups frozen, thawed small butter beans

⅓ cup water

½ cup sliced green onions

½ can (2-ounce size) anchovies, rinsed, drained, mashed

¼ cup (1 ounce) grated Romano cheese

8 ounces mostaccioli, cooked, warm

Per Serving:
Calories: 390
% of calories from fat: 12
Fat (gm): 5
Saturated fat (gm): 1.7
Cholesterol (mg): 27.6
Sodium (mg): 1169
Protein (gm): 24.7
Carbohydrate (gm): 60.9

Exchanges:
Milk: 0.0
Vegetable: 0.0
Fruit: 0.0
Bread: 4.0
Meat: 2.0
Fat: 0.0

1. Sauté ham, chili pepper and garlic in lightly greased medium skillet until lightly browned, about 5 minutes. Add beans and water and heat to boiling. Reduce heat and simmer until tender,

3 to 4 minutes. Combine ham mixture with remaining ingredients and toss.

45-MINUTE PREPARATION TIP: Begin cooking mostaccioli before preparing the rest of the recipe.

PEASANT-STYLE PASTA WITH BEANS, TOMATOES, AND SAGE

45 | *Hearty and chunky, with 2 types of beans, this meal is so easy to make!*

8 servings (about ½ cup each)

1 can (15 ounces) each: red kidney beans, Great Northern or cannellini beans, rinsed, drained

½ cup each: chopped onion, celery

2 cloves garlic, minced

1 can (16 ounces) plum tomatoes, drained, chopped

2 cups reduced-sodium chicken broth

1 teaspoon dried sage leaves

¼ teaspoon salt

⅛ teaspoon pepper

16 ounces mostaccioli, cooked, warm

Per Serving:
Calories: 317
% of calories from fat: 4
Fat (gm): 1.5
Saturated fat (gm): 0.1
Cholesterol (mg): 0
Sodium (mg): 495
Protein (gm): 13.3
Carbohydrate (gm): 61.9

Exchanges:
Milk: 0.0
Vegetable: 0.0
Fruit: 0.0
Bread: 4.0
Meat: 0.0
Fat: 0.0

1. Heat all ingredients, except mostaccioli, to boiling in large saucepan. Reduce heat and simmer, covered, 5 minutes; simmer, uncovered, until mixture is desired sauce consistency, about 20 minutes. Serve over pasta.

45-MINUTE PREPARATION TIP: Cook pasta while sauce is simmering.

PASTA SANTA FE

45 *Picante flavors of the Southwest merge with pasta in this entrée.*

4 entrée servings

1 medium onion, sliced

3 cloves garlic, minced

2 tablespoons canola oil

2 each: sliced medium zucchini, poblano chilies, tomatoes

1 cup whole-kernel corn

2 tablespoons chili powder

1 teaspoon dried oregano leaves

½ teaspoon ground cumin

2 tablespoons chopped cilantro

Salt and pepper, to taste

8 ounces trio maliano (combination of corkscrews, shells, and rigatoni) pasta, cooked, warm

Per Serving:
Calories: 350
% of calories from fat: 24
Fat (gm): 9.6
Saturated fat (gm): 1.2
Cholesterol (mg): 0
Sodium (mg): 327
Protein (gm): 11.6
Carbohydrate (gm): 58

Exchanges:
Milk: 0.0
Vegetable: 2.0
Fruit: 0.0
Bread: 3.0
Meat: 0.0
Fat: 2.0

1. Sauté onion and garlic in oil in large skillet until tender, about 5 minutes. Add remaining vegetables, chili powder, oregano, and cumin. Cook, covered, over medium heat until vegetables are crisp-tender, about 10 minutes. Stir in cilantro; season to taste with salt and pepper. Toss with pasta.

45-MINUTE PREPARATION TIP: Begin cooking the pasta before preparing the rest of the recipe.

CHICKEN TORTELLINI WITH SHERRIED VEGETABLE SAUCE

45 *Dry sherry and thyme accent the richly textured and seasoned sauce.*

6 entrée servings

1 cup each: thinly sliced leeks, chopped mushrooms

⅓ cup each: chopped onion, shallots

½ cup dry sherry or reduced-sodium chicken broth

2 cups reduced-sodium chicken broth

1 cup chopped tomatoes

1 teaspoon dried thyme leaves

2 bay leaves

Salt and pepper, to taste

2 packages (9 ounces each) fresh chicken tortellini, cooked, warm

4 tablespoons capers, optional

Per Serving:
Calories: 334
% of calories from fat: 16
Fat (gm): 6.2
Saturated fat (gm): 3.0
Cholesterol (mg): 40.4
Sodium (mg): 438
Protein (gm): 17.4
Carbohydrate (gm): 51.6

Exchanges:
Milk: 0.0
Vegetable: 2.0
Fruit: 0.0
Bread: 3.0
Meat: 0.0
Fat: 1.0

1. Sauté leeks, mushrooms, onion, and shallots in lightly greased medium saucepan until very soft, 7 to 10 minutes. Add sherry; cook over high heat until almost absorbed, 2 to 3 minutes. Add broth, tomatoes, and herbs; heat to boiling. Reduce heat and simmer, uncovered, until tomato is very soft, about 15 minutes; discard bay leaves.

2. Process mixture in food processor or blender until smooth. Return to saucepan; cook over medium heat until hot, 2 to 3 minutes. Season to taste with salt and pepper. Spoon over tortellini; sprinkle with capers.

45-MINUTE PREPARATION TIP: Begin cooking tortellini while sauce is simmering.

TORTELLINI WITH TUNA

45 *A great "carry dish" for that next picnic or family reunion!*

8 servings

12 ounces cheese tortellini, cooked, room temperature
1 cup fresh or frozen, thawed peas
½ cup each: sliced green onions, chopped green bell pepper, parsley
1 can (14 ounces) artichoke hearts, drained, quartered
1 can (6 ounces) solid white tuna in water, drained
¼ cup chopped fresh or 2 teaspoons dried basil
Tomato Vinaigrette (recipe follows)
Salt and pepper, to taste

Per Serving:
Calories: 246
% of calories from fat: 27
Fat (gm): 7.3
Saturated fat (gm): 1.9
Cholesterol (mg): 31.5
Sodium (mg): 430
Protein (gm): 15.5
Carbohydrate (gm): 29.5

Exchanges:
Milk: 0.0
Vegetable: 3.0
Fruit: 0.0
Bread: 1.0
Meat: 1.0
Fat: 1.0

1. Toss all ingredients, except salt and pepper, in salad bowl; season to taste with salt and pepper.

Tomato Vinaigrette
Makes about 1 cup

2 small tomatoes, quartered
2 tablespoons each: white wine vinegar, extra-virgin olive oil
2 teaspoons Dijon mustard
1 teaspoon each: chopped garlic, dried oregano and basil leaves
¼ cup (1 ounce) grated fat-free Parmesan cheese

1. Process all ingredients in blender until smooth.

45-MINUTE PREPARATION TIP: Cook tortellini and rinse in cold water before preparing the rest of the recipe.

CURRIED TORTELLINI WITH BEANS AND SQUASH

45 *Coconut milk adds a subtle Asian flavor to this colorful pasta combination.*

6 entrée servings

1⅓ cups coarsely chopped onions

⅔ cup red bell pepper

2 teaspoons minced garlic

1 teaspoon curry powder

1 tablespoon olive oil

2 cups each: diagonally sliced green beans, cubed
  butternut or acorn squash

¼ cup water

1 cup reduced-fat coconut milk

2 packages (9 ounces each) mushroom or herb
  tortellini, cooked, warm

Salt and pepper, to taste

3 tablespoons chopped cilantro

Per Serving:
Calories: 269
% of calories from fat: 25
Fat (gm): 8.3
Saturated fat (gm): 3
Cholesterol (mg): 30
Sodium (mg): 220
Protein (gm): 11.4
Carbohydrate (gm): 44.1

Exchanges:
Milk: 0.0
Vegetable: 2.0
Fruit: 0.0
Bread: 2.0
Meat: 0.0
Fat: 1.5

1. Sauté onions, bell pepper, garlic, and curry powder in oil in large skillet until onions are tender, 3 to 4 minutes. Add green beans, squash, and water; heat to boiling. Reduce heat and simmer, covered, until vegetables are tender, 6 to 8 minutes. Stir in coconut milk and tortellini; cook until hot, 2 to 3 minutes. Season to taste with salt and pepper; sprinkle with cilantro.

45-MINUTE PREPARATION TIP: Begin cooking the tortellini before preparing the rest of the recipe.

CHEESE RAVIOLI WITH VEGETABLES

45 *This pasta dish is packed with fresh vegetables!*

6 servings

1 quart reduced-sodium vegetable broth

1½ cups chopped yellow summer squash

2 carrots, sliced

2 cups torn kale or escarole

4 plum tomatoes, coarsely chopped

2 packages (9 ounces each) fresh cheese
   ravioli, cooked
1 teaspoon dried basil leaves
⅛ teaspoon crushed red pepper
Salt, to taste

Per Serving:
Calories: 229
% of calories from fat: 21
Fat (gm): 5.3
Saturated fat (gm): 3
Cholesterol (mg): 29
Sodium (mg): 580
Protein (gm): 11.7
Carbohydrate (gm): 34.1

1. Heat broth to boiling in large saucepan; add squash and carrots. Reduce heat and simmer, covered, until vegetables are tender, about 10 minutes. Add remaining ingredients, except salt; simmer 5 minutes. Season to taste with salt.

Exchanges:
Milk: 0.0
Vegetable: 1.0
Fruit: 0.0
Bread: 2.0
Meat: 1.0
Fat: 0.0

45-MINUTE PREPARATION TIP: Begin cooking the ravioli before preparing the rest of the recipe.

20-MINUTE RAVIOLI

45 *Use your favorite kind of fresh ravioli in this quick, nutritious dish.*

4 entrée servings

¾ cup chopped onion
2 teaspoons minced garlic
1 tablespoon olive oil
¾ cup canned kidney beans, rinsed, drained
1 package (9 ounces) sun-dried tomato ravioli,
   cooked, warm
1 large tomato, coarsely chopped
½ teaspoon dried thyme leaves
Salt and pepper, to taste

Per Serving:
Calories: 234
% of calories from fat: 35
Fat (gm): 9.4
Saturated fat (gm): 3.8
Cholesterol (mg): 32.8
Sodium (mg): 320
Protein (gm): 9.5
Carbohydrate (gm): 29.1

Exchanges:
Milk: 0.0
Vegetable: 0.0
Fruit: 0.0
Bread: 2.0
Meat: 1.0
Fat: 1.0

1. Sauté onion and garlic in oil in large skillet until tender, about 5 minutes. Stir in beans, ravioli, tomato, and thyme; cook, covered, over medium heat until hot, about 5 minutes. Season to taste with salt and pepper.

45-MINUTE PREPARATION TIP: Begin cooking the ravioli before preparing the rest of the recipe.

SHRIMP AND ARTICHOKE RAVIOLI WITH TARRAGON SAUCE

Fresh Tomato and Herb Sauce (see p. 177) would also be a great sauce selection for these ravioli.

4 servings (4 ravioli each)

8 ounces finely chopped, peeled, deveined shrimp

1 can (14 ounces) artichoke hearts, drained, finely chopped

1 clove garlic, minced

¼ teaspoon ground nutmeg

3 tablespoons water

32 wonton wrappers

Tarragon Sauce (recipe follows)

Per Serving:
Calories: 289
% of calories from fat: 5
Fat (gm): 1.5
Saturated fat (gm): 0.3
Cholesterol (mg): 92.4
Sodium (mg): 923
Protein (gm): 20.6
Carbohydrate (gm): 45.2

Exchanges:
Milk: 0.0
Vegetable: 0.0
Fruit: 0.0
Bread: 3.0
Meat: 1.0
Fat: 0.0

1. Cook shrimp, artichoke hearts, garlic, nutmeg, and water in lightly greased large skillet over medium heat until shrimp are cooked and pink, about 5 minutes. Spoon about 2 teaspoons shrimp mixture on wonton wrapper; brush edges of wrapper with water. Top with second wonton wrapper and press edges together to seal. Repeat with remaining wonton wrappers and shrimp mixture.

2. Add 6 ravioli to 2 quarts boiling water in large saucepan; reduce heat and simmer, uncovered, until ravioli float to the surface and are al dente, 3 to 4 minutes. Remove with slotted spoon. Repeat with remaining ravioli. Serve with Tarragon Sauce.

Tarragon Sauce

Makes about 1 cup

2 medium shallots or green onions, finely chopped

1 tablespoon finely chopped fresh or ½ teaspoon dried tarragon leaves

1½ cups reduced-sodium chicken broth, divided

1 tablespoon flour

¼ teaspoon salt

⅛ teaspoon white pepper

1. Heat shallots, tarragon, and ½ cup chicken broth to boiling in small saucepan; reduce heat and simmer, uncovered, until mixture is reduced to ¼ cup. Whisk in combined remaining ingredients; heat to boiling, whisking until thickened, about 1 minute (sauce will be thin).

CHICKEN AND SWEET POTATO RAVIOLI WITH CURRY SAUCE

A light curry-flavored sauce make a delicate accompaniment to this unusual ravioli.

4 entrée servings (4 each)

8 ounces boneless, skinless chicken breast, cooked, finely shredded

1 cup mashed, cooked, sweet potatoes

2 small cloves garlic, minced

½–¾ teaspoon ground ginger

Salt and pepper, to taste

32 wonton wrappers

Curry Sauce (recipe follows)

Per Serving:
Calories: 383
% of calories from fat: 13
Fat (gm): 5.5
Saturated fat (gm): 1.1
Cholesterol (mg): 37.2
Sodium (mg): 587
Protein (gm): 19.8
Carbohydrate (gm): 62.4

Exchanges:
Milk: 0.0
Vegetable: 0.5
Fruit: 0.0
Bread: 4.0
Meat: 1.5
Fat: 0.0

1. Mix chicken, sweet potatoes, garlic, and ginger; season to taste with salt and pepper. Spoon about 1 tablespoon mixture onto wonton wrapper; brush edges of wrapper with water. Top with second wonton wrapper and press edges together to seal. Repeat with remaining wonton wrappers and potato mixture.

2. Add 6 ravioli to 2 quarts boiling water in large saucepan; reduce heat and simmer, uncovered, until ravioli float to the surface and are al dente, 3 to 4 minutes. Remove with slotted spoon. Repeat with remaining ravioli. Serve with Curry Sauce.

Curry Sauce

Makes about 4 servings (about ½ cup each)

¼ cup finely chopped onion
4 cloves garlic, minced
2 tablespoons flour
2 teaspoons curry powder
¼ teaspoon cayenne pepper
2 cups reduced-sodium chicken broth
1 tablespoon cornstarch
¼ cup dry white wine or water
Salt and pepper, to taste

1. Sauté onion and garlic in lightly greased medium saucepan 2 to 3 minutes; stir in flour, curry powder, and cayenne pepper and cook 1 minute. Mix in broth and heat to boiling; stir in combined cornstarch and wine and boil, stirring until thickened, about 1 minute. Season to taste with salt and pepper.

TURKEY AND HERBED CHEESE RAVIOLI WITH WILD MUSHROOM SAUCE

Italian-style turkey sausage can be substituted nicely in these ravioli.

4 entrée servings (4 each)

8 ounces ground turkey
1 small onion, minced
2 cloves garlic, minced
1 cup reduced-fat ricotta cheese
1 teaspoon dried rosemary leaves
32 wonton wrappers
Wild Mushroom Sauce (see p. 361)

Per Serving:
Calories: 360
% of calories from fat: 18
Fat (gm): 7.2
Saturated fat (gm): 1.4
Cholesterol (mg): 37
Sodium (mg): 593
Protein (gm): 22
Carbohydrate (gm): 53

Exchanges:
Milk: 0.0
Vegetable: 1.5
Fruit: 0.0
Bread: 3.0
Meat: 1.5
Fat: 0.5

1. Cook turkey in lightly greased small skillet over medium heat until browned, about 5 minutes. Add onion and garlic to skillet and sauté until onion is tender, about 5 minutes. Remove from heat; mix in ricotta cheese and rosemary. Spoon about 1 tablespoon cheese mixture on wonton wrapper; brush edges of wrapper with water. Top with a second wonton wrapper and press edges together to seal. Repeat with remaining wonton wrappers and cheese mixture.

2. Add 6 ravioli to 2 quarts boiling water in large saucepan; reduce heat and simmer, uncovered, until ravioli float to the surface and are al dente, 3 to 4 minutes. Remove with slotted spoon. Repeat with remaining ravioli. Serve with Wild Mushroom Sauce.

Wild Mushroom Sauce

Makes 8 servings (about ⅓ cup each)

2 cups chopped or sliced wild mushrooms (portobello, shiitake, cremini, etc.)
¼ cup finely chopped shallots or green onions
2 cloves garlic, minced
⅓ cup dry sherry or water
2–3 tablespoons lemon juice
½ teaspoon dried thyme leaves
2 cups reduced-sodium vegetable broth
2 tablespoons cornstarch
Salt and pepper, to taste

1. Sauté mushrooms, shallots, and garlic in lightly greased medium saucepan until tender, 5 to 8 minutes. Stir in sherry, lemon juice, and thyme; heat to boiling. Reduce heat and simmer, uncovered, until mushrooms are tender and liquid is gone, about 5 minutes. Stir in combined broth and cornstarch; heat to boiling. Boil, stirring, until thickened, about 1 minute. Season to taste with salt and pepper.

MUSHROOM RAVIOLI WITH RED PEPPER SALSA

Colorful Red Pepper Salsa is a perfect complement to the mushroom-filled pasta.

4 servings (6 ravioli each)

2 cups finely chopped mushrooms
¼ cup chopped shallots or green onions
2 cloves garlic, minced
¼ teaspoon each: salt, pepper
48 wonton wrappers
Red Pepper Salsa (recipe follows)

Per Serving:
Calories: 364
% of calories from fat: 20
Fat (gm): 8
Saturated fat (gm): 1.4
Cholesterol (mg): 67.6
Sodium (mg): 430
Protein (gm): 12
Carbohydrate (gm): 62

Exchanges:
Milk: 0.0
Vegetable: 2.0
Fruit: 0.0
Bread: 3.0
Meat: 0.0
Fat: 2.0

1. Sauté mushrooms, shallots, and garlic in lightly greased skillet until tender and liquid is evaporated, about 8 minutes; stir in salt and pepper. Spoon about 2 teaspoons mushroom mixture in center of 1 wonton wrapper; brush edges of wrapper with water. Top with a second wonton wrapper, and press edges together to seal. Repeat with remaining wonton wrappers and mushroom mixture.

2. Add 6 ravioli to 2 quarts boiling water in large saucepan; reduce heat and simmer, uncovered, until ravioli float to the surface and are al dente, 3 to 4 minutes. Remove with slotted spoon. Repeat with remaining ravioli. Serve with Red Pepper Salsa.

Red Pepper Salsa

Makes about 2 cups

2 each: finely chopped medium tomatoes, large red bell peppers
2 tablespoons each: finely chopped or 1 tablespoon dried basil and cilantro leaves
4 teaspoons each: olive oil, red wine vinegar, minced garlic
½–1 teaspoon minced jalapeño chili
½ teaspoon each: salt, pepper

1. Mix all ingredients; refrigerate 3 to 4 hours for flavors to blend.

SPINACH GNOCCHI AND CHICKEN PRIMAVERA

Gnocchi, Italian for dumplings, are often made from potatoes. This spinach version is delicious.

6 servings

½ cup chopped onion

2 cloves garlic, minced

3 packages (10 ounces each) frozen chopped spinach, thawed, well drained

⅔ cup plus ¼ cup all-purpose flour, divided

1 cup reduced-fat ricotta cheese

½ cup (2 ounces) grated Parmesan cheese

1 egg

¼ teaspoon ground nutmeg

½ teaspoon each: salt, pepper

1¼ pounds boneless, skinless chicken breasts, baked, sliced, warm

Primavera Sauce (recipe follows)

Per Serving:
Calories: 464
% of calories from fat: 30
Fat (gm): 15.8
Saturated fat (gm): 5.5
Cholesterol (mg): 105.2
Sodium (mg): 664
Protein (gm): 40
Carbohydrate (gm): 41.6

Exchanges:
Milk: 0.0
Vegetable: 4.0
Fruit: 0.0
Bread: 1.5
Meat: 4.0
Fat: 1.0

1. Sauté onion and garlic in lightly greased skillet until tender, about 5 minutes. Stir in spinach; cook over medium heat until mixture is quite dry, about 8 minutes, stirring frequently. Stir in ⅔ cup flour, cheeses, egg, nutmeg, salt, and pepper; cool.

2. Roll spinach mixture into 18 balls, using about 2 tablespoons for each; roll lightly in remaining ¼ cup flour.

3. Add gnocchi to 3 quarts boiling water in large saucepan; reduce heat and simmer, uncovered, until gnocchi float to the surface, about 10 minutes. Arrange on serving platter with chicken; spoon Primavera Sauce over.

Primavera Sauce

Makes about 3 cups

3 tablespoons margarine or butter

¼ cup all-purpose flour

2 cups 2% reduced-fat milk

¼ cup dry white wine or reduced-sodium chicken broth

2 cups each: broccoli and cauliflower florets, cooked crisp-tender

1 cup diagonally sliced carrots, cooked crisp-tender

1 medium bell pepper, sliced

¼ cup (1 ounce) grated Parmesan cheese

¼ teaspoon each: ground nutmeg, salt, pepper

1. Melt margarine in large saucepan; add flour and stir over medium heat 1 minute. Stir in milk and wine; heat to boiling. Boil, stirring until thickened, about 1 minute. Stir in vegetables and cook over medium heat until hot, 2 to 3 minutes. Remove from heat stir in remaining ingredients.

QUICK GNOCCHI CHOWDER WITH SMOKED TURKEY

45 *Gnocchi are often topped with butter and Parmesan cheese and served as a side dish. Here, they're the main attraction in a chowder!*

4 servings

1 cup reduced-sodium fat-free chicken broth

1 can (15 ounces) reduced-sodium crushed tomatoes, undrained

10 ounces smoked turkey breast, cubed

1 package (12 ounces) potato gnocchi

1 teaspoon poultry seasoning

2 cups each: broccoli and cauliflower florets

½ cup chopped fresh basil leaves

¼ cup (1 ounce) shredded provolone cheese

Salt and pepper, to taste

Per Serving:
Calories: 221
% of calories from fat: 17
Fat (gm): 4.2
Saturated fat (gm): 2.1
Cholesterol (mg): 24.3
Sodium (mg): 7Protein (gm): 16.8
Carbohydrate (gm): 30

Exchanges:
Milk: 0.0
Vegetable: 1.0
Fruit: 0.0
Bread: 1.5
Meat: 2.0
Fat: 0.0

1. Heat chicken broth, tomatoes and liquid, turkey, gnocchi, and poultry seasoning to boiling in large saucepan; reduce heat and simmer, covered, 5 minutes. Stir in broccoli and cauliflower; simmer until tender, 5 to 8 minutes. Add basil and cheese, stirring until cheese is melted. Season to taste with salt and pepper.

RICOTTA-STUFFED SHELLS WITH SPINACH PESTO

Spinach Pesto can be made up to 1 week in advance and refrigerated; serve at room temperature.

4 servings (6 each)

½ cup finely chopped onion

4–6 cloves garlic, minced

1 teaspoon dried basil leaves

1 cup chopped fresh spinach

1½ cups low-fat ricotta cheese

½ teaspoon each: ground nutmeg, salt, pepper

24 jumbo pasta shells, cooked

Spinach Pesto (see p. 366)

Per Serving:
Calories: 356
% of calories from fat: 24
Fat (gm): 9.4
Saturated fat (gm): 1.6
Cholesterol (mg): 14.4
Sodium (mg): 432
Protein (gm): 19
Carbohydrate (gm): 49.2

Exchanges:
Milk: 0.0
Vegetable: 2.0
Fruit: 0.0
Bread: 3.0
Meat: 1.0
Fat: 1.0

1. Sauté onion, garlic, and basil in lightly greased skillet until onions are tender, 3 to 4 minutes. Add spinach and cook over medium heat until wilted, about 5 minutes. Stir in cheese, nutmeg, salt, and pepper. Stuff mixture into shells; place in baking pan. Bake, covered, at 350 degrees until hot through, about 20 minutes. Serve with Spinach Pesto.

Spinach Pesto

Makes about ½ cup

2 cups loosely packed spinach

⅓ cup loosely packed basil leaves

2–3 cloves garlic

4 tablespoons (1 ounce) grated Parmesan cheese

4 teaspoons olive oil

2–4 teaspoons lemon juice

Salt and pepper, to taste

1. Process all ingredients, except lemon juice, salt, and pepper, in food processor until almost smooth. Season to taste with lemon juice, salt, and pepper. Serve at room temperature.

45-MINUTE PREPARATION TIP: Begin cooking the pasta shells before preparing the rest of the recipe.

ARTICHOKE TORTELLINI BAKE

Refrigerated fresh tortellini and ravioli are convenient to have on hand for speedy meals—use any favorite in this dish.

4 entrée servings

2 cups sliced mushrooms

1 small onion, sliced

1 teaspoon minced garlic

2 tablespoons flour

1 cup fat-free milk

Salt and cayenne pepper, to taste

1 can (14 ounces) artichoke hearts, drained

1 package (9 ounces) mozzarella-garlic tortellini, cooked, warm

½ cup (2 ounces) shredded reduced-fat Italian 6-cheese blend

1–2 tablespoons seasoned dry bread crumbs

Per Serving:
Calories: 267
% of calories from fat: 21
Fat (gm): 6.4
Saturated fat (gm): 3.4
Cholesterol (mg): 29.1
Sodium (mg): 523
Protein (gm): 16.9
Carbohydrate (gm): 37.4

Exchanges:
Milk: 0.0
Vegetable: 1.0
Fruit: 0.0
Bread: 2.0
Meat: 1.0
Fat: 0.5

1. Sauté mushrooms, onion, and garlic in lightly greased large saucepan until tender, about 5 minutes. Stir in flour; cook 1 to 2 minutes. Stir in milk and heat to boiling, stirring until thickened,

1 to 2 minutes. Season to taste with salt and cayenne pepper. Stir in artichokes, tortellini, and cheese. Spoon into greased 1½-quart casserole; sprinkle with bread crumbs. Bake, uncovered, at 375 degrees until bubbly, about 15 minutes.

45-MINUTE PREPARATION TIP: Begin cooking the tortellini before preparing the rest of the recipe.

NOODLES FLORENTINE

Cut into generous squares and serve with a vegetable salad and warm multigrain bread.

4 servings

¾ cup each: finely chopped red onion, red bell pepper

2 cloves garlic, minced

1 package (10 ounces each) frozen chopped spinach, thawed, drained

2 cups cooked spinach noodles

3 eggs, lightly beaten

1 cup fresh whole wheat bread crumbs

2 teaspoons sugar

½ teaspoon each: ground nutmeg, salt, pepper

½ cup (2 ounces) shredded reduced-fat Swiss cheese

Per Serving:
Calories: 359
% of calories from fat: 20
Fat (gm): 8.6
Saturated fat (gm): 2.7
Cholesterol (mg): 242.8
Sodium (mg): 414
Protein (gm): 20.3
Carbohydrate (gm): 48.7

Exchanges:
Milk: 0.0
Vegetable: 1.0
Fruit: 0.0
Bread: 3.0
Meat: 2.0
Fat: 0.0

1. Sauté onion, bell pepper, and garlic in lightly greased medium skillet until tender, about 4 minutes; stir in spinach and remove from heat. Mix in remaining ingredients, except cheese, and spoon into greased 11 x 7-inch baking dish. Bake, uncovered, at 325 degrees 30 minutes. Sprinkle with cheese; bake until sharp knife inserted near center comes out clean, about 10 minutes. Cool on wire rack 5 minutes.

45-MINUTE PREPARATION TIP: Begin cooking noodles before preparing the rest of the recipe.

VEGGIE KUGEL

45

This kugel, with lots of veggies, is high in protein and low in fat.

6 servings

¾ cup each: chopped red bell pepper, onion

2 tablespoons margarine or butter

2 cups each: halved Brussels sprouts, cubed peeled sweet potatoes, cooked

¾ teaspoon each: dried thyme, marjoram leaves

1 can (12 ounces) evaporated fat-free milk

2 tablespoons flour

1 package (10 ounces each) frozen chopped spinach, thawed, well drained

12 ounces no-yolk noodles, cooked

3 eggs, lightly beaten

½ teaspoon each: salt, pepper

Per Serving:
Calories: 432
% of calories from fat: 21
Fat (gm): 10.3
Saturated fat (gm): 2.7
Cholesterol (mg): 217
Sodium (mg): 463
Protein (gm): 20.7
Carbohydrate (gm): 64.7

Exchanges:
Milk: 0.0
Vegetable: 1.0
Fruit: 0.0
Bread: 4.0
Meat: 1.0
Fat: 1.5

1. Sauté bell pepper and onion in margarine in large skillet until tender, about 5 minutes; add Brussels sprouts, sweet potatoes, and herbs. Stir in combined evaporated milk and flour; heat to boiling, stirring until thickened, about 1 minute. Cool; mix in remaining ingredients. Spoon into greased 13 x 9-inch baking dish. Bake, uncovered, at 350 degrees 35 minutes, or until sharp knife inserted near center comes out clean. Cool on wire rack 5 minutes.

45-MINUTE PREPARATION TIP: Begin cooking noodles before preparing the rest of the recipe.

SQUASH AND MUSHROOM LASAGNE

A white sauce and tomato sauce are combined in this delicate lasagne.

8 servings

1 cup sliced onion

1 tablespoon minced garlic

1 pound portobello or cremini mushrooms, sliced

½ cup dry white wine or vegetable broth

Salt and pepper, to taste

¼ cup finely chopped shallots or green onions

2 teaspoons margarine or butter

¾ teaspoon each: dried rosemary and thyme leaves

¼ cup all-purpose flour

2 cups each: fat-free milk, prepared reduced-sodium spaghetti sauce

4 ounces fat-free cream cheese, cubed

¾ cup (3 ounces) grated fat-free Parmesan cheese, divided

12 lasagne noodles (10 ounces), cooked

1 pound acorn or butternut squash, peeled, thinly sliced

Per Serving:
Calories: 306
% of calories from fat: 14
Fat (gm): 4.8
Saturated fat (gm): 1
Cholesterol (mg): 4
Sodium (mg): 226
Protein (gm): 15
Carbohydrate (gm): 49.6

Exchanges:
Milk: 0.0
Vegetable: 1.0
Fruit: 0.0
Bread: 3.0
Meat: 1.0
Fat: 0.5

1. Sauté onion and garlic in lightly greased large skillet 3 to 4 minutes; add mushrooms and sauté 5 minutes. Add wine and heat to boiling; reduce heat to medium and cook until mixture is dry, about 5 minutes. Season to taste with salt and pepper.

2. Sauté shallots and herbs in margarine in medium saucepan until tender, 2 to 3 minutes. Whisk in combined flour and milk and heat to boiling, whisking until thickened, about 1 minute. Mix in spaghetti sauce, cream cheese, and ½ cup Parmesan cheese; cook, stirring until sauce is hot and cream cheese melted, about 5 minutes. Season to taste with salt and pepper.

3. Stir 1 cup sauce into mushroom mixture. Spread about ¾ cup remaining sauce in bottom of 13 x 9-inch baking pan; arrange 4 noodles in pan, overlapping edges. Spoon ½ of mushroom mixture and squash slices over noodles and spread with ¾ cup sauce. Repeat layers; top with layer of remaining 4 noodles and ¾ cup sauce. Sprinkle with remaining ¼ cup Parmesan cheese. Bake at 350 degrees, loosely covered, until noodles and squash are tender, 50 to 60 minutes. Let stand 10 minutes before serving.

ROASTED RED PEPPER AND SPINACH LASAGNE

For convenience, the recipe uses jarred roasted red peppers, but you can roast your own using the method in Roasted Red Pepper Sauce (see p. 50).

8 entrée servings

1 cup chopped onion

2 teaspoons minced garlic

¾ teaspoon each: dried marjoram and oregano leaves

3 cups fat-free milk, divided

⅓ cup all-purpose flour

1 cup (4 ounces) grated fat-free Parmesan cheese

4 ounces fat-free cream cheese, cubed

⅔ cup finely chopped parsley

Salt and pepper, to taste

2 packages (10 ounces each) frozen, thawed, chopped
    spinach, very well drained

⅔ cup fat-free ricotta cheese

12 lasagne noodles (10 ounces), cooked

1 jar (15 ounces) roasted red peppers, drained, cut
    into 1-inch slices

1 cup (4 ounces) reduced-fat mozzarella cheese

Per Serving:
Calories: 261
% of calories from fat: 13
Fat (gm): 3.8
Saturated fat (gm): 1.7
Cholesterol (mg): 9.1
Sodium (mg): 386
Protein (gm): 21.4
Carbohydrate (gm): 36.8

Exchanges:
Milk: 0.5
Vegetable: 2.0
Fruit: 0.0
Bread: 1.5
Meat: 1.0
Fat: 0.0

1. Sauté onion, garlic, and herbs in lightly greased large saucepan until tender, 5 to 8 minutes; add 2 cups milk and heat to boiling. Whisk in combined remaining 1 cup milk and flour and heat to boiling, whisking until thickened, about 1 minute. Remove from heat; mix in Parmesan and cream cheese, and parsley, stirring until cream cheese is melted. Season with salt and pepper. Mix spinach and ricotta cheese; season to taste with salt and pepper.

2. Spread ¾ cup sauce in bottom of 13 x 9-inch baking pan. Arrange 4 noodles in pan, overlapping edges. Top with ½ of the spinach mixture and red pepper slices; spread with generous 1 cup sauce. Repeat layers; top with remaining 4 noodles and spread with remaining 1¼ cups sauce. Sprinkle with mozzarella cheese. Bake at 350 degrees, loosely covered, until noodles are tender, 50 to 60 minutes. Let stand 10 minutes before serving.

ARTICHOKE LASAGNE

The lasagne can be assembled up to a day in advance and refrigerated, covered. Increase baking time by 15 to 20 minutes.

8 entrée servings

1½ cups each: sliced shiitake mushrooms, chopped onions

1 cup chopped red bell pepper

2 teaspoons minced garlic

8 cups loosely packed baby spinach

2 packages (9 ounces each) frozen, thawed, artichoke hearts, quartered

Salt and pepper, to taste

3 cups fat-free milk, divided

¼ cup plus 2 tablespoons flour

1 cup (4 ounces) grated fat-free Parmesan cheese

4 ounces fat-free cream cheese, cubed

⅔ cup finely chopped parsley

1 teaspoon each: dried thyme leaves, lemon juice

12 lasagne noodles (10 ounces), cooked

1 cup (4 ounces) shredded reduced-fat mozzarella cheese

Per Serving:
Calories: 278
% of calories from fat: 7
Fat (gm): 2.1
Saturated fat (gm): 0.2
Cholesterol (mg): 1.5
Sodium (mg): 438
Protein (gm): 22.5
Carbohydrate (gm): 46.4

Exchanges:
Milk: 0.0
Vegetable: 3.0
Fruit: 0.0
Bread: 2.0
Meat: 1.0
Fat: 0.0

1. Sauté mushrooms, onions, bell pepper, and garlic in lightly greased large skillet 3 minutes; add spinach and artichoke hearts. Cook, covered, over medium heat until spinach is wilted, about 5 minutes; cook, uncovered, until mixture is dry. Remove from heat; season to taste with salt and pepper.

2. Heat 2 cups milk to boiling in large saucepan. Whisk in combined remaining 1 cup milk and flour and heat to boiling, whisking, until thickened, about 1 minute. Remove from heat; mix in Parmesan and cream cheese, parsley, thyme, and lemon juice, stirring until cream cheese is melted. Season to taste with salt and pepper.

3. Spread 1 cup sauce in bottom of 13 x 9-inch baking pan; arrange 4 noodles in pan, overlapping edges. Spoon ½ of the artichoke mixture over noodles and spread with 1 cup sauce. Repeat layers; top with remaining 4 noodles and spread with 1 cup sauce. Sprinkle with mozzarella cheese. Bake at 350 degrees, loosely covered, until noodles are al dente, 50 to 60 minutes. Let stand 10 minutes before cutting.

LAZY LASAGNE

45 ♦ *One of the quickest, easiest lasagne recipes ever, thanks to no-boil lasagne noodles.*

4 entrée servings

6 no-boil lasagne noodles (4 ounces)

1 can (15 ounces) cannellini or other white beans, rinsed, drained, slightly mashed

1 cup reduced-fat cottage cheese

1 cup (4 ounces) shredded Italian 6-cheese blend, divided

1 can (14½ ounces) reduced-sodium diced tomatoes

1 tablespoon minced roasted garlic

Per Serving:
Calories: 347
% of calories from fat: 23
Fat (gm): 9.2
Saturated fat (gm): 4.7
Cholesterol (mg): 24.8
Sodium (mg): 575
Protein (gm): 24
Carbohydrate (gm): 42.3

Exchanges:
Milk: 0.0
Vegetable: 2.0
Fruit: 0.0
Bread: 2.0
Meat: 2.0
Fat: 1.0

1. Place 2 lasagne noodles in lightly greased 8-inch square baking pan. Top with ½ the beans and cottage cheese, and ⅓ cup shredded cheese. Repeat layers, ending with 2 lasagne noodles. Spoon combined diced tomatoes and roasted garlic over top of lasagne. Bake, covered, at 375 degrees until noodles are tender, about 30 minutes. Uncover and sprinkle with remaining ⅓ cup cheese; let stand 5 to 10 minutes before serving.

MEXI-CAN LASAGNE

45 ♦ *This simple South-of-the-Border lasagne is one you'll say "ole" to!*

4 entrée servings

6 no-boil lasagne noodles

1 can (15 ounces) low-fat refried beans

1 can (11 ounces) nacho cheese soup

⅓ cup fat-free milk

1 tablespoon minced jalapeño chili

1 teaspoon ground cumin

1 cup frozen or canned, drained, whole-kernel corn

1 can (14½ ounces) reduced-sodium stewed tomatoes

2 teaspoons chili powder

Per Serving:
Calories: 393
% of calories from fat: 24
Fat (gm): 11.3
Saturated fat (gm): 4.5
Cholesterol (mg): 20.2
Sodium (mg): 686
Protein (gm): 20.8
Carbohydrate (gm): 58.6

Exchanges:
Milk: 0.0
Vegetable: 2.0
Fruit: 0.0
Bread: 3.0
Meat: 2.0
Fat: 0.5

½ teaspoon dried oregano leaves

½–¾ cup (2–3 ounces) shredded reduced-fat
  Monterey Jack or Cheddar cheese

1. Place 2 lasagne noodles in lightly greased 8-inch square baking
pan; top with ½ the refried beans. Mix cheese soup, milk, jalapeño
chili, and cumin; spoon ½ the mixture over the beans and sprinkle
with ½ the corn. Repeat layers, ending with 2 noodles. Combine
tomatoes, chili powder, and oregano in small bowl; spoon over the
top. Bake, covered, at 375 degrees until noodles are tender, about
30 minutes. Uncover and sprinkle with shredded cheese; let stand
5 to 10 minutes before serving.

PASTA, WHITE BEAN, AND RED CABBAGE SALAD

45 *The salad can be made in advance; stir in the cabbage just before serving
for fresh color.*

6 entrée servings

6 ounces rotini (corkscrews), cooked,
  room temperature
1 cup each: rinsed, drained, canned Great Northern
  beans, sliced red cabbage
¼ cup each: chopped onion, green bell pepper
Caraway Dressing (recipe follows)

1. Combine all ingredients in salad bowl and toss.

Per Serving:
Calories: 185
% of calories from fat: 5
Fat (gm): 1.1
Saturated fat (gm): 0.2
Cholesterol (mg): 0
Sodium (mg): 268
Protein (gm): 8.7
Carbohydrate (gm): 35.9

Exchanges:
Milk: 0.0
Vegetable: 1.5
Fruit: 0.0
Bread: 2.0
Meat: 0.0
Fat: 0.0

Caraway Dressing
Makes about 1 cup

½ cup each: fat-free mayonnaise, fat-free sour cream
2 teaspoons lemon juice
1 teaspoon each: minced garlic, crushed caraway seeds
¼ teaspoon each: salt, pepper

1. Mix all ingredients.

45-MINUTE PREPARATION TIP: Begin cooking rotini before
preparing the rest of the recipe; rinse rotini in cold water to
cool quickly.

LIGHT SUMMER PASTA SALAD

45 *The fragrant aroma and flavor of fresh herbs accent summer's finest tomatoes in this salad.*

8 entrée servings

8 ounces spaghetti, cooked, room temperature

1 pound plum tomatoes, chopped

¾ cup (3 ounces) cubed reduced-fat mozzarella cheese (¼-inch)

¼ cup packed basil leaves, chopped

Garlic Vinaigrette (recipe follows)

1. Combine all ingredients in salad bowl and toss.

Per Serving:
Calories: 150
% of calories from fat: 30
Fat (gm): 5.7
Saturated fat (gm): 0.5
Cholesterol (mg): 3.8
Sodium (mg): 176
Protein (gm): 7.4
Carbohydrate (gm): 19.7

Exchanges:
Milk: 0.0
Vegetable: 1.0
Fruit: 0.0
Bread: 1.0
Meat: 0.0
Fat: 1.0

Garlic Vinaigrette
Makes about ⅓ cup

3 tablespoons red wine vinegar

2 tablespoons olive oil

3 cloves garlic, minced

⅛ teaspoon each salt, pepper

1. Mix all ingredients.

45-MINUTE PREPARATION TIP: Cook spaghetti and rinse in cold water before preparing the rest of the recipe.

BEEF AND PASTA SALAD VINAIGRETTE

45 *Any lean beef or pork can be substituted for the flank steak.*

4 servings

12 ounces beef flank steak, broiled or grilled to medium doneness

2 medium tomatoes, cut into wedges

¾ cup each: sliced zucchini, green bell pepper

½ cup each: sliced carrot, red onion

3 cups rotini (corkscrews), cooked, room temperature

Mixed Herb Vinaigrette (recipe follows)

Lettuce leaves, as garnish

1. Slice flank steak into very thin slices, cutting diagonally across the grain. Combine flank steak and remaining ingredients, except lettuce, and toss. Serve on lettuce-lined plates.

Mixed Herb Vinaigrette

Makes about ⅔ cup

⅓ cup each: red wine vinegar, reduced-sodium beef broth or water

1 tablespoon olive oil

2 teaspoons each: sugar, Dijon mustard, minced garlic

1 teaspoon crushed mustard seeds

1 tablespoon each: finely chopped fresh or

½ teaspoon dried marjoram, tarragon, and thyme leaves

½ teaspoon each: salt, pepper

1. Mix all ingredients.

Per Serving:
Calories: 469
% of calories from fat: 27
Fat (gm): 14
Saturated fat (gm): 4.5
Cholesterol (mg): 57
Sodium (mg): 391
Protein (gm): 32.9
Carbohydrate (gm): 52.1

Exchanges:
Milk: 0.0
Vegetable: 2.0
Fruit: 0.0
Bread: 2.5
Meat: 0.0
Fat: 1.5

CHILI-DRESSED TUNA SALAD WITH RADIATORE

45 *A fun pasta, radiatore look like the tiny radiators for which they are named! Other shaped pastas can be also be used.*

4 entrée servings

Chili Dressing (recipe follows)

3 cups (8 ounces) radiatore, cooked, room temperature

1 can (9¼ ounces) white tuna in water, drained, flaked

2 medium tomatoes, cut into wedges

½ medium avocado, cubed

2 tablespoons finely chopped cilantro

4 cups torn salad greens

Per Serving:
Calories: 388
% of calories from fat: 30
Fat (gm): 12.9
Saturated fat (gm): 1.9
Cholesterol (mg): 18.7
Sodium (mg): 238
Protein (gm): 25.5
Carbohydrate (gm): 43.2

Exchanges:
Milk: 0.0
Vegetable: 2.0
Fruit: 0.0
Bread: 2.5
Meat: 2.0
Fat: 1.0

1. Pour dressing over pasta in medium bowl and toss. Add remaining ingredients, except salad greens and toss; serve over greens.

Chili Dressing
Makes about ¼ cup

3 tablespoons lemon juice
2 tablespoons olive oil
½ teaspoon chili powder
¼ teaspoon crushed red pepper

1. Mix all ingredients.

45-MINUTE PREPARATION TIP: Begin cooking radiatore before preparing the rest of the recipe. Rinse in cold water to cool.

PASTA NIÇOISE

45 *A pasta salad with the flavors of the traditional salad Niçoise. The salad can be made several hours in advance and refrigerated.*

4 servings

3 cups cooked small pasta shells, room temperature
12–16 Greek olives, pitted, sliced
2 cups fresh green beans, cooked
¼ cup sliced green onions
1 tomato, chopped
1 can (6 ounces) solid white tuna in water, drained
Niçoise Dressing (see p. 377)
Salt and pepper, to taste

Per Serving:
Calories: 251
% of calories from fat: 25
Fat (gm): 7.2
Saturated fat (gm): 1.1
Cholesterol (mg): 17.9
Sodium (mg): 289
Protein (gm): 15.8
Carbohydrate (gm): 32.4

Exchanges:
Milk: 0.0
Vegetable: 0.0
Fruit: 0.0
Bread: 2.0
Meat: 1.0
Fat: 1.0

1. Toss all ingredients, except salt and pepper, in salad bowl; season to taste with salt and pepper.

Niçoise Dressing
Makes about ¾ cup

½ cup loosely packed parsley
¼ cup each: tarragon wine vinegar, water
1 large clove garlic
1–2 tablespoons olive oil
½ teaspoon Dijon mustard
1 teaspoon dried oregano leaves

1. Process all ingredients in blender until smooth.

45-MINUTE PREPARATION TIP: Begin cooking pasta and green beans before preparing the rest of the recipe. Rinse in cold water.

RICE NOODLE SALAD

45 *If you enjoy the flavor of sesame, substitute 1 tablespoon Asian sesame oil for 1 tablespoon of olive oil in the vinaigrette.*

4 entrée servings

1 package (7 ounces) rice noodles
1½ cups thinly sliced Chinese cabbage
2 cups snow peas, trimmed, cooked until crisp-tender
¾ cup each: sliced red and yellow bell pepper
1 cup each: sliced mushrooms and canned, drained
  lychee fruit, or pineapple chunks
½ cup fresh or canned bean sprouts, drained
Citrus Vinaigrette (see p. 378)

Per Serving:
Calories: 246
% of calories from fat: 26
Fat (gm): 7.5
Saturated fat (gm): 1
Cholesterol (mg): 0
Sodium (mg): 197
Protein (gm): 6.6
Carbohydrate (gm): 40.9

Exchanges:
Milk: 0.0
Vegetable: 2.0
Fruit: 0.0
Bread: 2.0
Meat: 0.0
Fat: 1.0

1. Place noodles in bowl; pour cold water over to cover. Let stand until noodles separate and are soft, about 5 minutes. Stir noodles into boiling water in large saucepan; reduce heat and simmer, uncovered, until tender, about 5 minutes. Drain and cool. Combine noodles, Chinese cabbage, snow peas, bell peppers, mushrooms, lychee fruit, and bean sprouts in large bowl; toss with Citrus Vinaigrette.

Citrus Vinaigrette

Makes about ⅓ cup

⅓ cup orange juice
2 tablespoons olive oil
2 cloves garlic, minced
½ teaspoon five-spice powder
¼ teaspoon each: salt and pepper

1. Mix all ingredients.

ASIAN NOODLE SALAD

45 *Enjoy the wonderful blend of flavors in this salad. Thin spaghetti or linguine can be substituted for the fresh Chinese egg noodles.*

4 entrée servings (about 1¼ cups each)

8 ounces fresh Chinese egg noodles, cooked
Yogurt Dressing (recipe follows)
1 cup each: shredded carrot, seeded, cubed cucumber
½ cup chopped red bell pepper
¼ cup each: sliced green onions, chopped cilantro

Per Serving:
Calories: 388
% of calories from fat: 17
Fat (gm): 7.7
Saturated fat (gm): 1.5
Cholesterol (mg): 1
Sodium (mg): 242
Protein (gm): 14.3
Carbohydrate (gm): 67.3

1. Combine all ingredients and toss.

Exchanges:
Milk: 0.0
Vegetable: 3.0
Fruit: 0.0
Bread: 3.5
Meat: 0.0
Fat: 1.5

Yogurt Dressing

Makes about 1½ cups

1 cup fat-free plain yogurt
¼ cup reduced-fat peanut butter
2 tablespoons rice wine vinegar
1 tablespoon each: reduced-sodium tamari soy sauce,
    sugar, minced gingerroot
1 teaspoon Asian sesame oil
½ teaspoon each: 5-spice powder, minced garlic, cayenne pepper

1. Mix all ingredients.

45-MINUTE PREPARATION TIP: Begin cooking the noodles and making the Yogurt Dressing before preparing the rest of the recipe.

ANGEL HAIR AND GOAT CHEESE SALAD

45 *Goat cheese adds a creamy texture and piquant accent to this flavorful pasta dish.*

6 entrée servings (about 1½ cups each)

2 cups each: halved snow peas, sliced mushrooms
3 medium carrots, julienned
4 large plum tomatoes, sliced
2 teaspoons dried oregano leaves
1 teaspoon dried tarragon leaves
½ cup each: reduced-sodium vegetable broth,
   fat-free milk
2 teaspoons tomato paste
¼ teaspoon each: salt, pepper
12 ounces capellini (angel hair) or thin spaghetti
   cooked, warm
3 ounces goat cheese or reduced-fat cream cheese

Per Serving:
Calories: 328
% of calories from fat: 13
Fat (gm): 4.7
Saturated fat (gm): 2.3
Cholesterol (mg): 6.8
Sodium (mg): 197
Protein (gm): 13.9
Carbohydrate (gm): 58.5

Exchanges:
Milk: 0.0
Vegetable: 2.0
Fruit: 0.0
Bread: 3.0
Meat: 0.0
Fat: 1.0

1. Sauté vegetables and herbs in lightly greased large skillet until snow peas are crisp-tender, 6 to 8 minutes. Stir in broth, milk, and tomato paste; heat to boiling. Reduce heat and simmer, uncovered, until thickened to sauce consistency, about 10 minutes, stirring occasionally. Stir in salt and pepper. Toss with pasta and goat cheese.

45-MINUTE PREPARATION TIP: Begin cooking the capellini before preparing the rest of the recipe.

NINE

Rice, Grains,
and
Beans

TWO-BEAN MINESTRONE

Cannellini beans and chickpeas provide protein, fiber, and folate in this healthful soup.

8 entrée servings

2 cloves garlic, minced

½ cup each: chopped onion, sliced carrots, celery

1 tablespoon dried Italian seasoning

2 tablespoons olive oil

1½ cups each: sliced zucchini, cabbage

1 cup each: cubed peeled potatoes, sliced leek (white part only)

1 can (14 ounces) plum tomatoes, undrained, chopped

1½ quarts water

½ cup dry red wine

1 can (15 ounces) each: rinsed, drained cannellini or Great Northern beans and chickpeas

½ cup uncooked small elbow macaroni, chopped parsley

2 tablespoons grated Parmesan cheese

Salt and pepper, to taste

Per Serving:
Calories: 267
% of calories from fat: 17
Fat (gm): 5.3
Saturated fat (gm): 0.9
Cholesterol (mg): 1.3
Sodium (mg): 331
Protein (gm): 9
Carbohydrate (gm): 43.1

Exchanges:
Milk: 0.0
Vegetable: 2.0
Fruit: 0.0
Bread: 2.0
Meat: 0.0
Fat: 1.5

1. Sauté garlic, onion, carrots, celery, and Italian seasoning in olive oil in large saucepan until onion is tender, about 5 minutes. Add fresh vegetables, tomatoes with liquid, water, and wine; heat to boiling. Reduce heat and simmer, covered, until vegetables are almost tender, about 10 minutes. Heat to boiling; stir in beans, macaroni, and parsley; reduce heat and simmer, uncovered, until macaroni is al dente, 8 to 10 minutes. Stir in Parmesan cheese; season to taste with salt and pepper.

TUSCAN BEAN SOUP

A hearty well-seasoned bean soup that is sure to please.

8 entrée servings (about 1½ cups each)

1 cup chopped onion

½ cup each: chopped celery, green bell pepper

2 teaspoons minced roasted garlic

2 tablespoons olive oil

1 tablespoon flour

1½ teaspoons dried Italian seasoning

2 bay leaves

7 cups reduced-sodium fat-free beef broth

2 cans (15 ounces each) cannellini or Great Northern beans, rinsed, drained

2 tablespoons reduced-sodium tomato paste

½ cup quick-cooking barley

1 cup each: cubed unpeeled potato, sliced carrots, packed baby spinach leaves

Salt and pepper, to taste

Per Serving:
Calories: 233
% of calories from fat: 18
Fat (gm): 5.6
Saturated fat (gm): 0.7
Cholesterol (mg): 0
Sodium (mg): 245
Protein (gm): 10.7
Carbohydrate (gm): 40.8

Exchanges:
Milk: 0.0
Vegetable: 2.0
Fruit: 0.0
Bread: 2.0
Meat: 0.0
Fat: 1.0

1. Sauté onion, celery, bell pepper, and garlic in oil in Dutch oven until tender, about 5 minutes. Add flour and herbs; cook 1 minute. Add broth, beans, and tomato paste and heat to boiling; reduce heat and simmer, covered, 15 minutes. Add barley, potatoes, carrots, and spinach; simmer until potatoes are tender, about 10 minutes. Discard bay leaves. Season to taste with salt and pepper.

CURRIED BEAN SOUP

45 *Use any white bean, such as cannellini, navy, soy, lima, or garbanzo in this creamy, rich soup.*

6 entrée servings (about 1¼ cups each)

1 cup each: chopped onion, sliced leek
  (white part only)
1 tablespoon each: minced garlic, curry powder
2 tablespoons olive oil
2 cans (15½ ounces each) Great Northern beans,
  rinsed, drained
3½ cups reduced-sodium vegetable broth
½ cup fat-free half-and-half or fat-free milk
Salt and pepper, to taste
6 tablespoons fat-free sour cream or plain yogurt
3 tablespoons each: chopped cilantro, red bell pepper

Per Serving:
Calories: 263
% of calories from fat: 16
Fat (gm): 4.9
Saturated fat (gm): 1
Cholesterol (mg): 0
Sodium (mg): 393
Protein (gm): 13.7
Carbohydrate (gm): 42.5

Exchanges:
Milk: 0.0
Vegetable: 1.5
Fruit: 0.0
Bread: 2.5
Meat: 0.5
Fat: 0.5

1. Sauté onion, leek, garlic, and curry powder in oil in large saucepan until onion is tender, 5 to 8 minutes. Add beans and broth and heat to boiling. Reduce heat and simmer, covered, 5 minutes. Process mixture in food processor or blender until smooth; return to saucepan. Stir in half-and-half; cook over medium heat 2 to 3 minutes. Season to taste with salt and pepper. Top each bowl of soup with a tablespoon of sour cream; sprinkle with cilantro and bell pepper.

NAVY BEAN SOUP WITH HAM

A quick-soak method is used for the beans. If you prefer soaking the beans overnight, omit step 1 and proceed with step 2 in the recipe, using the soaked beans.

6 entrée servings (about 1¾ cups each)

8 ounces dried navy or Great Northern beans
Water
1½ cups cubed lean smoked ham
⅔ cup each: chopped onion, carrot, celery
2 cloves garlic, minced

1 tablespoon each: canola oil, flour

4 cups reduced-sodium chicken broth

1 cup water

¼ teaspoon dried thyme leaves

1 bay leaf

Salt and pepper, to taste

Per Serving:
Calories: 223
% of calories from fat: 16
Fat (gm): 4.0
Saturated fat (gm): 0.9
Cholesterol (mg): 21.6
Sodium (mg): 639
Protein (gm): 20.1
Carbohydrate (gm): 29.5

Exchanges:
Milk: 0.0
Vegetable: 0.0
Fruit: 0.0
Bread: 2.0
Meat: 2.0
Fat: 0.0

1. Cover beans with 2 inches of water in large saucepan; heat to boiling; boil, uncovered, 2 minutes. Remove from heat and let stand, covered, 1 hour; drain.

2. Sauté ham, onion, carrot, celery, and garlic in oil in large saucepan until vegetables are tender, 5 to 8 minutes. Stir in flour; cook 1 minute. Add beans, broth, water, and herbs to saucepan; heat to boiling. Reduce heat and simmer, covered, until beans are tender, 1 to 1¼ hours. Discard bay leaf; season to taste with salt and pepper.

TWO-BEAN AND PASTA SOUP

This substantial soup thickens upon standing; thin with additional broth or water, if necessary.

6 entrée servings (about 2 cups each)

1½ cups cubed carrots

½ cup each: chopped green bell pepper, sliced green onions

3 cloves garlic, minced

2 teaspoons each: dried basil and oregano leaves

2 cans (15 ounces each) reduced-sodium chicken broth

1 cup water

1 can (16 ounces) reduced-sodium stewed tomatoes

1 can (15 ounces) each: cannellini and pinto beans, rinsed, drained

1½ cups uncooked rigatoni

2–3 teaspoons lemon juice

Salt and pepper, to taste

Per Serving:
Calories: 225
% of calories from fat: 7
Fat (gm): 2
Saturated fat (gm): 0
Cholesterol (mg): 0
Sodium (mg): 522
Protein (gm): 13.6
Carbohydrate (gm): 45.7

Exchanges:
Milk: 0.0
Vegetable: 2.0
Fruit: 0.0
Bread: 2.5
Meat: 0.0
Fat: 0.0

1. Sauté carrots, bell pepper, green onions, garlic and herbs in lightly greased large saucepan until vegetables are tender, about 7 minutes. Add broth, water, tomatoes, and beans to saucepan; heat to boiling. Reduce heat and simmer, covered, 10 minutes. Heat soup to boiling and add pasta; reduce heat and simmer, uncovered, until pasta is al dente, 12 to 15 minutes. Season with lemon juice, salt, and pepper.

CHICK PEA AND PASTA SOUP

45 *You can use any fresh vegetables you want for the zucchini and celery in this soup – carrots, cauliflower or broccoli florets, mushrooms, peas, and green beans are possible choices.*

4 entrée servings (about 1¾ cups each)

¾ cup each: chopped onion, cubed zucchini, sliced celery

3–4 cloves garlic, minced

1 teaspoon each: dried rosemary and thyme leaves

⅛ teaspoon crushed red pepper

1 can (15 ounces) each: reduced-sodium chicken broth, reduced-sodium stewed tomatoes, chick peas, rinsed, drained

1 cup uncooked farfalle (bow ties)

Salt, to taste

2–3 teaspoons lemon juice

Per Serving:
Calories: 322
% of calories from fat: 10
Fat (gm): 3.7
Saturated fat (gm): 0.5
Cholesterol (mg): 0
Sodium (mg): 514
Protein (gm): 11.5
Carbohydrate (gm): 56.4

Exchanges:
Milk: 0.0
Vegetable: 3.0
Fruit: 0.0
Bread: 3.0
Meat: 0.0
Fat: 0.5

1. Sauté onion, zucchini, celery, garlic, herbs, and red pepper in lightly greased large saucepan until onion is tender, about 5 minutes; add broth, tomatoes with liquid, and chick peas and heat to boiling. Reduce heat and simmer, covered, 10 minutes. Heat soup to boiling and add pasta; reduce heat and simmer, uncovered, until pasta is al dente, about 8 minutes; season to taste with salt and lemon juice.

BLACK AND WHITE BEAN CHILI

A colorful soup, rich in flavor.

4 entrée servings (about 1¼ cups each)

12 ounces very lean ground beef

1 cup chopped onion

½ cup chopped green bell pepper

2 teaspoons each: minced jalapeno chili, garlic

2 cans (16 ounces each) reduced-sodium whole tomatoes, undrained, coarsely chopped

1 can (15 ounces) each: Great Northern and black beans, rinsed, drained

¼ cup sun-dried tomatoes (not in oil), softened, chopped

2–3 tablespoons chili powder

1–1½ teaspoons each: ground cumin, dried oregano leaves

1 bay leaf

Salt and pepper, to taste

¼ cup chopped cilantro

Per Serving:
Calories: 305
% of calories from fat: 12
Fat (gm): 4.9
Saturated fat (gm): 1.2
Cholesterol (mg): 41.2
Sodium (mg): 770
Protein (gm): 28.9
Carbohydrate (gm): 52.4

Exchanges:
Milk: 0.0
Vegetable: 2.0
Fruit: 0.0
Bread: 2.0
Meat: 2.0
Fat: 0.0

1. Cook ground beef, onion, bell pepper, jalapeño chili, and garlic in lightly greased large saucepan until beef is browned and vegetables are tender, 8 to 10 minutes. Stir in remaining ingredients, except salt, pepper, and cilantro; heat to boiling. Reduce heat and simmer, covered, 30 minutes. Discard bay leaf; season to taste with salt and pepper. Stir in cilantro.

SPICED BEAN CHILI WITH FUSILLI

45 *Use your favorite beans and any shaped pasta in this versatile chili.*

8 entrée servings (about 1¼ cups each)

1 pound lean ground beef
2 cups chopped onions
1 cup sliced cremini or white mushrooms
½ cup sliced celery
2 cans (14½ ounces each) diced tomatoes with
    roasted garlic, undrained
1 can (15 ounces) each: garbanzo and dark red
    kidney beans, rinsed, drained
½ cup dry white wine or water
1–2 tablespoons each: chili powder, ground cumin
½ teaspoon each: dried oregano and thyme leaves
8 ounces fusilli, cooked
Salt and pepper, to taste
3–4 tablespoons sliced green or ripe olives

Per Serving:
Calories: 367
% of calories from fat: 26
Fat (gm): 10.6
Saturated fat (gm): 3.2
Cholesterol (mg): 35.2
Sodium (mg): 759
Protein (gm): 21.3
Carbohydrate (gm): 47.3

Exchanges:
Milk: 0.0
Vegetable: 1.0
Fruit: 0.0
Bread: 3.0
Meat: 1.0
Fat: 1.5

1. Sauté ground beef, onions, mushrooms, and celery in lightly greased large saucepan until beef is browned, 8 to 10 minutes. Add tomatoes with liquid, beans, wine, and herbs to saucepan; heat to boiling. Reduce heat and simmer, covered, 10 minutes. Add pasta and cook until hot, 2 to 3 minutes. Season to taste with salt and pepper; sprinkle with olives.

BLACK BEANS AND RICE

45 *If fresh epazote is available, add a sprig or two while the rice is cooking.*

6 side-dish servings (about ⅔ cup each)

¼ cup each: chopped onion, sliced green onions
4 cloves garlic, minced
1 cup long-grain rice
2½ cups reduced-sodium vegetable broth
1 can (15 ounces) black beans, rinsed, drained
2 tablespoons finely chopped cilantro
Salt and pepper, to taste

1. Sauté onion, green onions, and garlic in lightly greased medium saucepan until tender, about 5 minutes. Add rice and stir over medium heat until lightly browned, 2 to 3 minutes, stirring frequently. Add broth and heat to boiling; reduce heat and simmer, covered, until rice is tender, 20 to 25 minutes, adding beans during last 5 minutes. Stir in cilantro; season to taste with salt and pepper.

Per Serving:
Calories: 171
% of calories from fat: 2
Fat (gm): 0.4
Saturated fat (gm): 0.1
Cholesterol (mg): 0.0
Sodium (mg): 462
Protein (gm): 6
Carbohydrate (gm): 38

Exchanges:
Milk: 0.0
Vegetable: 0.0
Fruit: 0.0
Bread: 2.5
Meat: 0.0
Fat: 0.0

THREE-BEAN STEW WITH POLENTA

45 *Use any kind of canned or cooked dried beans; one 15-ounce can of drained beans yields 1½ cups.*

4 entrée servings (about 1–1½ cups each)

1 cup chopped onion
½ cup chopped red bell pepper
1 teaspoon minced roasted garlic
1 tablespoon flour
1 can (15 ounces) each: black-eyed peas, black beans and red beans, rinsed, drained
1 can (16 ounces) reduced-sodium diced tomatoes, undrained
1½ teaspoons dried Italian seasoning
¾ cup reduced-sodium vegetable broth
Salt and pepper, to taste
Polenta (see p. 425)

Per Serving:
Calories: 299
% of calories from fat: 14
Fat (gm): 5.3
Saturated fat (gm): 0.6
Cholesterol (mg): 0
Sodium (mg): 587
Protein (gm): 17.5
Carbohydrate (gm): 56

Exchanges:
Milk: 0.0
Vegetable: 2.0
Fruit: 0.0
Bread: 3.0
Meat: 0.5
Fat: 0.0

1. Sauté onion, bell pepper, and garlic in lightly greased large saucepan until tender, about 5 minutes; stir in flour and cook 1 minute. Add remaining ingredients, except salt, pepper and polenta to saucepan; heat to boiling. Reduce heat and simmer, covered, 10 minutes. Season to taste with salt and pepper. Serve stew over Polenta.

WINTER BEAN AND VEGETABLE STEW

45 *Serve this satisfying stew with Multigrain Batter Bread (see p. 554).*

6 entrée servings (about 1⅓ cups each)

1 cup each: chopped onion, cubed peeled Idaho
   potato and sweet potato
½ cup each: sliced carrot, parsnip, chopped green
   bell pepper
2 cloves garlic, minced
2 tablespoons olive oil
1 tablespoon flour
1½ cups reduced-sodium vegetable broth
1 can (15 ounces) black beans, rinsed, drained
1 can (13¼ ounces) baby lima beans, rinsed, drained
1 large tomato, cut into wedges
¾ teaspoon dried sage leaves
Salt and pepper, to taste

Per Serving:
Calories: 238
% of calories from fat: 20
Fat (gm): 5.7
Saturated fat (gm): 0.7
Cholesterol (mg): 0
Sodium (mg): 399
Protein (gm): 10.8
Carbohydrate (gm): 42.4

Exchanges:
Milk: 0.0
Vegetable: 2.0
Fruit: 0.0
Bread: 2.0
Meat: 0.0
Fat: 1.0

1. Sauté vegetables and garlic in oil in large saucepan 5 minutes;
stir in flour and cook 1 minute. Add remaining ingredients, except
salt and pepper, and heat to boiling. Reduce heat and simmer,
covered, until vegetables are tender, 15 to 20 minutes; season to
taste with salt and pepper.

EGGPLANT AND BEAN CURRY STEW

The aromatic curry seasoning is made with onion, garlic, and herbs.

4 entrée servings (about 1 cup each)

2 medium red potatoes, peeled, cubed (¾-inch)
1 small eggplant, cubed (¾-inch)
¼ cup chopped onion
1 teaspoon each: minced garlic, ground coriander
½ teaspoon ground cumin
¼ teaspoon ground turmeric
1 tablespoon olive oil

1 can (16 ounces) reduced-sodium whole tomatoes, undrained, coarsely chopped

1 can (15 ounces) garbanzo beans, rinsed, drained

½ cup water

⅛–¼ teaspoon crushed red pepper

Salt, to taste

¼ cup finely chopped cilantro

Per Serving:
Calories: 242
% of calories from fat: 21
Fat (gm): 6
Saturated fat (gm): 0.8
Cholesterol (mg): 0
Sodium (mg): 446
Protein (gm): 8.2
Carbohydrate (gm): 41.8

Exchanges:
Milk: 0.0
Vegetable: 2.0
Fruit: 0.0
Bread: 2.0
Meat: 0.0
Fat: 1.0

1. Sauté potatoes, eggplant, onion, garlic, and herbs in oil in large saucepan until potatoes are lightly browned, 5 to 8 minutes. Add remaining ingredients, except salt and cilantro; heat to boiling. Reduce heat and simmer, covered, until eggplant is tender, 20 to 25 minutes. Season to taste with salt; stir in cilantro.

SOUTHERN STEWED BLACK EYES, CHICKPEAS, AND HAM

45 *A hearty stew that can be made in 20 minutes with pantry staples. Serve with warm biscuits or corn bread.*

6 entrée servings (about 1¼ cups each)

10 ounces reduced-sodium ham, cubed

½ cup chopped onion

2 cloves garlic, minced

1 tablespoon olive oil

2 cups halved small okra

1 can (16 ounces) reduced-sodium stewed tomatoes, undrained

1 can (15½ ounces) chickpeas, rinsed, drained

2 cans (15 ounces each) black-eyed peas, rinsed, drained

½ package (10-ounce size) frozen spinach partially thawed

1 teaspoon each: dried marjoram and thyme leaves

¼ teaspoon hot pepper sauce

Salt and pepper, to taste

Per Serving:
Calories: 282
% of calories from fat: 16
Fat (gm): 5.2
Saturated fat (gm): 1
Cholesterol (mg): 21.9
Sodium (mg): 776
Protein (gm): 18.9
Carbohydrate (gm): 42.8

Exchanges:
Milk: 0.0
Vegetable: 3.0
Fruit: 0.0
Bread: 2.0
Meat: 1.0
Fat: 0.0

1. Sauté ham, onion, and garlic in oil in large saucepan until onion is tender, 5 to 8 minutes. Stir in remaining ingredients, except salt and pepper; heat to boiling. Reduce heat and simmer, covered, until okra is tender, about 10 minutes. Season to taste with salt and pepper.

ASIAN BLACK-EYED PEAS AND GREENS

45 *Asian foods and flavors combine in this sesame-accented dish. For an entrée, add cooked shrimp or chicken with the black-eyed peas in Step 2.*

12 side-dish servings (about ½ cup each)

8 ounces snow peas, diagonally halved

⅓ cup each: chopped onion, red or green bell pepper

1 jalapeno chili, finely chopped

1 tablespoon each: finely chopped gingerroot, garlic, Asian sesame oil

3 cups thinly sliced bok choy or Chinese cabbage

2 cans (15 ounces each)black-eyed peas, rinsed, drained

1–2 tablespoons reduced-sodium tamari soy sauce

1–2 teaspoons hoisin sauce

1 package (16 ounces) Chinese-style egg noodles, cooked

2 teaspoons sesame seeds, toasted

Per Serving:
Calories: 322
% of calories from fat: 6
Fat (gm): 2.3
Saturated fat (gm): 1.1
Cholesterol (mg): 0
Sodium (mg): 385
Protein (gm): 12.4
Carbohydrate (gm): 63.9

Exchanges:
Milk: 0.0
Vegetable: 2.0
Fruit: 0.0
Bread: 3.5
Meat: 0.5
Fat: 0.0

1. Stir-fry snow peas, onion, bell pepper, jalapeno chili, gingerroot, and garlic in sesame oil in wok or large skillet, 5 to 8 minutes. Stir in bok choy; cook, covered, over medium heat until wilted, 2 to 3 minutes. Add black-eyed peas, soy sauce, and hoisin sauce; cook until hot, about 5 minutes. Serve over noodles; sprinkle with sesame seeds.

SEASONED MASHED BLACK BEANS

45 *Black beans at their flavorful best—quick and easy too!*

6 side-dish servings (about ⅔ cup each)

2 medium onions, chopped
4 cloves garlic, minced
1–2 small jalapeño chilies, minced
2 cans (15 ounces each) black beans, rinsed, drained
2 cups reduced-sodium vegetable broth
¾–1 teaspoon dried cumin
⅓ cup chopped cilantro
Salt and pepper, to taste

Per Serving:
Calories: 109
% of calories from fat: 2
Fat (gm): 0.3
Saturated fat (gm): 0.0
Cholesterol (mg): 0.0
Sodium (mg): 691
Protein (gm): 6.5
Carbohydrate (gm): 25

Exchanges:
Milk: 0.0
Vegetable: 0.0;
Fruit: 0.0
Bread: 1.5
Meat: 0.0
Fat: 0.0

1. Sauté onions, garlic, and jalapeño chili in lightly greased large skillet until tender, about 5 minutes. Add beans and broth and cook over medium heat, coarsely mashing beans with fork. Stir in cumin and cilantro. Season to taste with salt and pepper.

REFRIED BEANS

Two cans (15 ounces each) pinto beans, rinsed and drained, can be substituted for the dried beans. Omit step 1 in recipe, and use 2 cups reduced-sodium vegetable broth in place of the cooking liquid.

6 side-dish servings (about ½ cup each)

1¼ cups dried pinto beans
Water
1 medium onion, coarsely chopped
Salt and pepper, to taste

Per Serving:
Calories: 106
% of calories from fat: 3
Fat (gm): 0.4
Saturated fat (gm): 0.1
Cholesterol (mg): 0
Sodium (mg): 2
Protein (gm): 6.1
Carbohydrate (gm): 20

Exchanges:
Milk: 0.0
Vegetable: 0.0
Fruit: 0.0
Bread: 1.5
Meat: 0.0
Fat: 0.0

1. Cover beans with 2 inches of water in a large saucepan; heat to boiling and boil, uncovered, 2 minutes. Remove from heat; let stand, covered, 1 hour. Drain beans; cover with 2 inches of water and heat to boiling. Reduce heat and simmer, covered, until beans are tender, 1½ to 2 hours. Drain, reserving 2 cups liquid.

2. Sauté onion in lightly greased large skillet until tender, 3 to 5 minutes. Add 1 cup beans and 1 cup reserved liquid to skillet. Cook over high heat, mashing beans with end of meat mallet or potato masher until almost smooth. Add half the remaining beans and liquid; continue cooking and mashing beans. Repeat with remaining beans and liquid. Season to taste with salt and pepper.

MEXI-BEANS AND GREENS

Four cans (15 ounces each) pinto beans, rinsed and drained, can be substituted for the dried beans; omit step 1 in recipe.

8 entrée servings (about 1¼ cups each)

2 cups dried pinto beans

1 each: chopped onion, poblano chili, red bell pepper

2 teaspoons each: minced garlic, serrano chilies, finely chopped gingerroot

2 tablespoons olive oil

3 cups water

2–3 teaspoons each: chili powder, dried oregano leaves

1 teaspoon ground cumin

¼–½ teaspoon cayenne pepper

1 can (15 ounces) diced tomatoes, undrained

2 cups coarsely chopped turnip or mustard greens

Salt, to taste

¼ cup chopped cilantro

Per Serving:
Calories: 361
% of calories from fat: 12
Fat (gm): 4.7
Saturated fat (gm): 0.7
Cholesterol (mg): 0
Sodium (mg): 103
Protein (gm): 14.4
Carbohydrate (gm): 66.7

Exchanges:
Milk: 0.0
Vegetable: 2.0
Fruit: 0.0
Bread: 3.5
Meat: 0.5
Fat: 0.5

1. Cover beans with 2 inches water in large saucepan; heat to boiling and boil, uncovered, 2 minutes. Remove from heat and let stand, covered, 1 hour; drain.

2. Sauté onion, poblano chili, bell pepper, garlic, serrano chilies, and gingerroot in oil in large saucepan until tender, 8 to 10 minutes. Add beans, water, and seasonings; heat to boiling. Reduce heat and simmer, covered, until beans are tender, 1 to 1¼ hours. Stir in tomatoes with liquid and greens; simmer, uncovered, 15 minutes. Season to taste with salt; stir in cilantro.

BLACK BEAN AND OKRA GUMBO

45 *The gumbo is delicious served over warm Country-Style Corn Bread (see p. 426).*

8 entrée servings (about 1 cup each)

8–12 ounces reduced-sodium smoked turkey
  sausage, sliced

2 cups small mushrooms

1 cup each: chopped onion, sliced carrots

¾ cup each: chopped red and green bell peppers

1 tablespoon olive oil

2 cups vegetable broth

1 can (16 ounces) tomatoes with chilies, undrained

2 cans (15 ounces each) black beans, rinsed, drained

2 cups cut okra

1 tablespoon chili powder

1 teaspoon gumbo file

Salt and pepper, to taste

Per Serving:
Calories: 376
% of calories from fat: 8
Fat (gm): 2.9
Saturated fat (gm): 0.7
Cholesterol (mg): 18.3
Sodium (mg): 832
Protein (gm): 16.7
Carbohydrate (gm): 18.3

Exchanges:
Milk: 0.0
Vegetable: 2.0
Fruit: 0.0
Bread: 4.0
Meat: 1.0
Fat: 0.0

1. Sauté sausage, mushrooms, onion, carrots, and bell peppers in oil in Dutch oven or large saucepan until sausage is lightly browned, 5 to 8 minutes. Add remaining ingredients, except salt and pepper; heat to boiling. Reduce heat and simmer, covered, until vegetables are tender, about 10 minutes. Simmer, uncovered, until thickened to desired consistency, 5 to 10 minutes. Season to taste with salt and pepper.

HOPPING JOHN

Be sure to eat your portion of Hopping John before noon on January 1 to guarantee a new year of good luck!

6 entrée servings (about 1 cup each)

1½ cups chopped onions

½ cup chopped celery

3 cloves garlic, minced

1 cup long-grain white rice

3 cups reduced-sodium vegetable broth

1 teaspoon dried oregano leaves

1 bay leaf

2 cans (15 ounces each) black-eyed peas, rinsed, drained

2–3 dashes each: red pepper sauce, liquid smoke (optional)

Salt and pepper, to taste

Per Serving:
Calories: 306
% of calories from fat: 21
Fat (gm): 7
Saturated fat (gm): 1
Cholesterol (mg): 0
Sodium (mg): 447
Protein (gm): 9.6
Carbohydrate (gm): 50.7

Exchanges:
Milk: 0.0
Vegetable: 1.0
Fruit: 0.0
Bread: 3.0
Meat: 0.5
Fat: 1.0

1. Sauté onions, celery, and garlic in lightly greased large saucepan until tender, 5 to 8 minutes. Add rice, broth, oregano, and bay leaf; heat to boiling. Reduce heat and simmer, covered, until rice is tender, about 25 minutes, stirring in black-eyed peas, red pepper sauce, and liquid smoke during last 5 minutes. Discard bay leaf; season to taste with salt and pepper.

ITALIAN-STYLE BEANS AND VEGETABLES WITH POLENTA

This colorful mélange can also be served over pasta, rice, or squares of warm corn bread.

6 entrée servings (about 1¼ cups each)

12 ounces Italian-style turkey sausage, casing removed

1½ cups each: chopped onions, portobello mushrooms

4 cloves garlic, minced

2 tablespoons olive oil

2 cups broccoli florets

1 cup sliced yellow summer squash

1 can (15 ounces) each: garbanzo and red kidney beans, rinsed, drained

1 can (14½ ounces) reduced-sodium whole tomatoes, undrained, coarsely chopped

2 teaspoons dried Italian seasoning

¼–½ teaspoon crushed red pepper

Salt and pepper, to taste

Herbed Polenta (see p. 426)

Per Serving:
Calories: 304
% of calories from fat: 21
Fat (gm): 7.7
Saturated fat (gm): 1
Cholesterol (mg): 0
Sodium (mg): 641
Protein (gm): 13.3
Carbohydrate (gm): 50.2

Exchanges:
Milk: 0.0
Vegetable: 2.0
Fruit: 0.0
Bread: 2.5
Meat: 0.5
Fat: 1.0

1. Sauté sausage, onions, mushrooms, and garlic in oil in large saucepan until browned, about 10 minutes. Stir in remaining ingredients, except salt, pepper, and Polenta; heat to boiling. Reduce heat and simmer, covered, until broccoli is tender, about 10 minutes; season to taste with salt and pepper. Serve over polenta.

ONE-STEP CASSOULET

45

This version of the French classic includes the traditional beans and meats of the original, but cuts out much of the fat and sodium.

8 entrée servings (about ½ cup each)

1 pound lean pork loin, fat trimmed, cubed (1-inch)

8 ounces lean lamb, cubed (1-inch)

4 ounces smoked turkey sausage, thickly sliced (1-inch)

3 slices low-sodium bacon, coarsely chopped

3 cans (15½ ounces each) Great Northern beans, rinsed, drained

2 cans (14½ ounces each) reduced-sodium diced tomatoes, undrained

2 cans (6 ounces each) reduced-sodium tomato paste

4 shallots or pearl onions, halved

2 teaspoons minced garlic

1 rib celery, sliced

1 bay leaf

1 teaspoon each: dried sage and thyme leaves

½ teaspoon each: salt, pepper

1 cup unseasoned dry bread crumbs

Per Serving:
Calories: 370
% of calories from fat: 23
Fat (gm): 10.4
Saturated fat (gm): 3.5
Cholesterol (mg): 57.1
Sodium (mg): 793
Protein (gm): 32.6
Carbohydrate (gm): 45.1

Exchanges:
Milk: 0.0
Vegetable: 0.0
Fruit: 0.0
Bread: 3.0
Meat: 3.0
Fat: 0.0

1. Combine all ingredients, except bread crumbs in Dutch oven; sprinkle with bread crumbs. Bake, covered, at 325 degrees until meats are tender, about 1 hour; bake, uncovered, until sauce is thickened, about 15 minutes. Discard bay leaf.

BOURBON STREET RED BEANS AND RICE

45 | *The New Orleans favorite, at its healthy, low-fat best!*

6 entrée servings (about ¾ cup each)

5 ounces reduced-fat smoked sausage, sliced
1 cup each: chopped onion, green bell peppers, celery
½–1 jalapeño chili, finely chopped
1 tablespoon olive oil
2 cans (15 ounces each) red beans, rinsed, drained
¾ cup reduced-sodium vegetable or chicken broth
1 teaspoon each: dried thyme and oregano leaves
½ teaspoon each: dried sage leaves, ground cumin
¼ teaspoon each: red pepper sauce, cayenne pepper
4–6 drops liquid smoke (optional)
Salt, to taste
4 cups cooked rice, warm

Per Serving:
Calories: 305
% of calories from fat: 12
Fat (gm): 4.1
Saturated fat (gm): 0.8
Cholesterol (mg): 11
Sodium (mg): 521
Protein (gm): 14
Carbohydrate (gm): 60

Exchanges:
Milk: 0.0
Vegetable: 2.0
Fruit: 0.0
Bread: 2.5
Meat: 0.5
Fat: 0.5

1. Sauté sausage, onion, bell peppers, celery, and jalapeno chili in oil in large saucepan 8 minutes. Add remaining ingredients, except liquid smoke, salt, and rice; cook, covered, over medium heat 10 minutes. Cook, uncovered, until thickened, 5 to 10 minutes. Season to taste with liquid smoke, salt, and rice; serve over rice in shallow bowls.

SANTA FE BAKED BEANS

45

These baked beans boast flavors of the great Southwest.

4 entrée servings (about 1¼ cups each)

1 cup chopped onion
½ cup chopped poblano chili or green bell pepper
½–1 serrano or jalapeño chili, finely chopped
1 tablespoon olive oil
2 cans (15 ounces each) pinto beans, rinsed, drained
2 cups whole kernel corn
6 sun-dried tomatoes (not in oil), softened, sliced
2–3 tablespoons honey
½ teaspoon each: ground cumin, dried thyme leaves
3 bay leaves
Salt and pepper, to taste
½ cup (2 ounces) crumbled Mexican white or
    farmer's cheese
¼ cup finely chopped cilantro

Per Serving:
Calories: 167
% of calories from fat: 21
Fat (gm): 4.1
Saturated fat (gm): 1.4
Cholesterol (mg): 5.4
Sodium (mg): 432
Protein (gm): 7.4
Carbohydrate (gm): 27.9

Exchanges:
Milk: 0.0
Vegetable: 1.0
Fruit: 0.0
Bread: 1.5
Meat: 0.0
Fat: 1.0

1. Sauté onion and chilies in oil in small skillet until tender, about 5 minutes. Combine with remaining ingredients, except salt, pepper, cheese, and cilantro, in 1½-quart casserole; season to taste with salt and pepper. Bake, covered, at 350 degrees until hot, about 30 minutes; sprinkle with cheese and bake, uncovered, until cheese is melted, about 15 minutes. Discard bay leaves. Sprinkle with cilantro.

JUST PEACHY BEAN POT

Peaches and nectar, dried fruit, and mango chutney add special flavor to this bean combo.

6 entrée servings (about 1⅓ cups each)

1 cup chopped onion

1 clove garlic, minced

1–1½ teaspoons curry powder

½ teaspoon each: ground allspice, crushed red pepper

1 tablespoon margarine or butter

2 cans (15 ounces each) red kidney beans, rinsed, drained

1 can (15 ounces) navy beans, rinsed, drained

1½ cups diced peaches

½ cup each: coarsely chopped mixed dried fruit, mango chutney, peach nectar

2 tablespoons cider vinegar

Salt and pepper, to taste

Per Serving:
Calories: 332
% of calories from fat: 8
Fat (gm): 3.4
Saturated fat (gm): 0.5
Cholesterol (mg): 0
Sodium (mg): 621
Protein (gm): 17.5
Carbohydrate (gm): 68.8

Exchanges:
Milk: 0.0
Vegetable: 0.0
Fruit: 1.5
Bread: 3.0
Meat: 0.5
Fat: 0.0

1. Sauté onion, garlic, herbs, and red pepper in margarine in small skillet until tender, about 5 minutes. Mix with remaining ingredients, except salt and pepper, in 2½-quart casserole; season to taste with salt and pepper. Bake, covered, at 350 degrees 30 minutes; bake, uncovered, if thicker consistency is desired, about 15 minutes.

FRIED LENTILS

Fried lentils, or "dal," are a staple of Indian cooking. Normally cooked in a large quantity of browned clarified butter, or "ghee," we've substituted a small amount of olive oil to keep the dish low in fat.

8 side-dish servings (about ½ cup each)

1½ cups dried red lentils

1 cup chopped onion

1 teaspoon each: ground turmeric, crushed cumin seeds

¼ teaspoon crushed red pepper

2 tablespoons olive oil

½ cup chopped cilantro

Salt, to taste

2 teaspoons grated lemon zest

Per Serving:
Calories: 171
% of calories from fat: 20
Fat (gm): 4
Saturated fat (gm): 0.5
Cholesterol (mg): 0
Sodium (mg): 4.4
Protein (gm): 10.5
Carbohydrate (gm): 24.6

Exchanges:
Milk: 0.0
Vegetable: 1.0
Fruit: 0.0
Bread: 1.5
Meat: 0.0
Fat: 1.0

1. Cook lentils in 2 inches simmering water, covered, until very soft, 30 to 40 minutes; drain. Sauté onion and seasonings in oil in large skillet until onion is tender, 5 to 8 minutes; reserve ¼ cup mixture. Add lentils to skillet; cook over low heat, stirring frequently, until mixture is thickened, about 10 minutes. Stir in cilantro; season to taste with salt. Sprinkle with reserved ¼ cup onion mixture and lemon zest.

WHEAT BERRY AND LENTIL STEW WITH DUMPLINGS

Use vegetable shortening that is trans-fat free for the dumplings.

8 entrée servings (about 1⅛ cups each)

1 cup wheat berries

2 medium onions, chopped

½ cup each: chopped celery, sliced carrots

4 cloves garlic, minced

1 teaspoon dried savory leaves

3 cups reduced-sodium vegetable broth

2 pounds russet potatoes, unpeeled, cubed

1½ cups cooked lentils

Salt and pepper, to taste

Herb Dumplings (recipe follows)

Per Serving:
Calories: 414
% of calories from fat: 10
Fat (gm): 4.7
Saturated fat (gm): 0.6
Cholesterol (mg): 0.3
Sodium (mg): 259
Protein (gm): 16.8
Carbohydrate (gm): 78.6

Exchanges:
Milk: 0.0
Vegetable: 1.0
Fruit: 0.0
Bread: 5.0
Meat: 0.0
Fat: 0.5

1. Cover wheat berries with 2 to 3 inches water in saucepan; let overnight. Heat to boiling; reduce heat and simmer, covered, until wheat berries are tender, 45 to 55 minutes. Drain.

2. Sauté onions, celery, carrots, garlic, and savory in lightly greased large saucepan until onions are tender, about 5 minutes. Add broth and potatoes and heat to boiling; reduce heat and simmer, covered, until vegetables are tender, 10 to 15 minutes. Stir in wheat berries and lentils; cook until hot, about 5 minutes. Season to taste with salt and pepper.

3. Spoon dumpling dough on top of stew; cook, uncovered, 5 minutes. Cook, covered, until dumplings are dry, 5 to 10 minutes.

Herb Dumplings

½ cup each: all-purpose flour, yellow cornmeal
1½ teaspoons baking powder
½ teaspoon each: dried sage and thyme leaves, salt
2 tablespoons vegetable shortening
½ cup fat-free milk

1. Combine flour, cornmeal, baking powder, herbs, and salt in bowl. Cut in shortening with pastry blender until mixture resembles coarse crumbs. Stir in milk to make a soft dough.

WHEAT BERRY AND GARDEN TOMATO SALAD

The texture of wheat berries is a perfect complement to crisp cucumbers and sun-ripened tomatoes. Kamut is an excellent grain to substitute for the wheat berries.

4 side-dish servings (about ¾ cup each)

3 cups cooked wheat berries
4 cups coarsely chopped ripe tomatoes
1½ cups cubed, seeded cucumber
⅓ cup each: sliced green onions, chopped parsley
½ cup (2 ounces) crumbled reduced-fat feta cheese
Roasted Garlic Vinaigrette (recipe follows)
Salt and pepper, to taste

1. Combine all ingredients, except salt and pepper, and toss; season to taste with salt and pepper.

Per Serving:
Calories: 281
% of calories from fat: 30
Fat (gm): 10
Saturated fat (gm): 2.4
Cholesterol (mg): 5.1
Sodium (mg): 221
Protein (gm): 9.4
Carbohydrate (gm): 42.7

Exchanges:
Milk: 0.0
Vegetable: 2.0
Fruit: 0.0
Bread: 2.0
Meat: 0.0
Fat: 2.0

Roasted Garlic Vinaigrette
Makes about ⅓ cup

2–4 tablespoons olive oil
¼ cup balsamic vinegar
2 teaspoons minced roasted garlic
1 teaspoon each: dried mint and oregano leaves

1. Mix all ingredients.

SWEET BULGUR PILAF

45 *A pilaf with sweet accents of yellow squash, raisins, and pie spice.*

4 entrée servings (about 1 cup each)

⅔ cup each: chopped onion, sliced green onions
1 large clove garlic, minced
1 cup bulgur
2¼ cups reduced-sodium vegetable broth
½–¾ teaspoon ground cinnamon
2 cups cubed, peeled butternut or acorn squash
¼ cup each: currants or raisins, toasted pine nuts
Salt and pepper, to taste

Per Serving:
Calories: 263
% of calories from fat: 19
Fat (gm): 6.2
Saturated fat (gm): 1
Cholesterol (mg): 0
Sodium (mg): 44
Protein (gm): 8.7
Carbohydrate (gm): 46.1

Exchanges:
Milk: 0.0
Vegetable: 0.0
Fruit: 0.0
Bread: 3.0
Meat: 0.0
Fat: 1.0

1. Sauté onion, green onions, garlic, and bulgur in lightly greased large saucepan until onions are tender, 5 to 6 minutes. Stir in broth and cinnamon and heat to boiling; reduce heat and simmer, covered, 10 minutes. Stir in squash and currants; simmer, covered, until squash is tender, about 15 minutes. Stir in pine nuts; season to taste with salt and pepper.

BULGUR AND BARLEY WITH LEMON GREENS

Grains and greens are cooked together, then combined with tomatoes and toasted nuts.

8 side-dish servings (about ½ cup each)

¾ cup barley

Vegetable cooking spray

2½ cups reduced-sodium vegetable broth

¼ cup bulgur

½ teaspoon dried thyme leaves

6 ounces thinly sliced turnip greens, kale, or spinach

½ cup thinly sliced green onions

1 large tomato, coarsely chopped

¼–½ cup coarsely chopped walnuts, toasted

1–2 tablespoons lemon juice

Salt and pepper, to taste

Per Serving:
Calories: 129
% of calories from fat: 20
Fat (gm): 3
Saturated fat (gm): 0.3
Cholesterol (mg): 0
Sodium (mg): 33
Protein (gm): 4.3
Carbohydrate (gm): 20.9

Exchanges:
Milk: 0.0
Vegetable: 0.5
Fruit: 0.0
Bread: 1.0
Meat: 0.0
Fat: 0.5

1. Add barley to lightly greased large saucepan; spray lightly with cooking spray. Cook over medium heat, stirring occasionally, until barley is golden, 5 to 8 minutes. Add broth and heat to boiling; reduce heat and simmer, covered, 40 minutes. Stir in bulgur and thyme; simmer, covered, until barley and bulgur are tender, about 15 minutes. Stir in greens and green onions; cook, covered, until liquid is absorbed, about 10 minutes. Stir in tomato and walnuts; cook 5 minutes longer. Season to taste with lemon juice, salt, and pepper.

BARLEY WITH PEPPERS AND POTATOES

Enjoy this delicious variation of the Mexican "rajas con papas." If poblano chilies are not available, substitute green bell peppers and 1 to 2 teaspoons minced jalapeño chilies.

6 side-dish servings (about ½ cup each)

3 large poblano chilies, sliced

1 medium onion, chopped

1 tablespoon olive or canola oil

3 cups cooked cubed unpeeled potatoes

2 cups cooked barley

2 tablespoons finely chopped cilantro leaves

½ teaspoon dried cumin

Salt and cayenne pepper, to taste

Per Serving:
Calories: 313
% of calories from fat: 13
Fat (gm): 5
Saturated fat (gm): 0.6
Cholesterol (mg): 0.0
Sodium (mg): 20
Protein (gm): 8
Carbohydrate (gm): 64

1. Sauté chilies and onion in oil in large skillet until crisp-tender, about 5 minutes. Add potatoes; sauté until browned, 5 to 8 minutes. Add barley and cook over medium heat until hot, 3 to 4 minutes. Stir in cilantro and cumin; season to taste with salt and cayenne pepper.

Exchanges:
Milk: 0.0
Vegetable: 0.0
Fruit: 0.0
Bread: 4.0
Meat: 0.0
Fat: 1.0

TABBOULEH

45

Always a favorite—this version includes finely chopped mint as well as parsley.

8 side-dish servings (about ½ cup each)

¾ cup bulgur

1½ cups coarsely chopped seeded tomatoes

¾ cup each: thinly sliced green onions, chopped parsley

¼ cup finely chopped mint

⅓–⅔ cup fat-free plain yogurt

¼–⅓ cup lemon juice

1½–2 tablespoons olive oil

Salt and pepper, to taste

Per Serving:
Calories: 176
% of calories from fat: 28
Fat (gm): 5.9
Saturated fat (gm): 0.8
Cholesterol (mg): 0.3
Sodium (mg): 34
Protein (gm): 5.7
Carbohydrate (gm): 28.2

Exchanges:
Milk: 0.0
Vegetable: 1.0
Fruit: 0.0
Bread: 1.5
Meat: 0.0
Fat: 1.0

1. Pour boiling water over bulgur to cover; let stand 15 minutes or until bulgur is tender but slightly chewy; drain. Mix bulgur and remaining ingredients, except salt and pepper; season to taste with salt and pepper. Refrigerate 1 to 2 hours for flavors to blend.

MUSHROOM AND ASPARAGUS PILAF

The dried Chinese black mushrooms impart a hearty, woodsy flavor to the pilaf.

8 entrée servings (about 1¼ cups each)

3⅓ cups reduced-sodium vegetable broth

1 cup dried Chinese mushrooms

1½ cups chopped onions

2 teaspoons each: minced garlic, bouquet garni

1½ pounds cut asparagus (1½-inch)

¼ cup dry sherry or water

2 packages (6 ounces each) tabbouleh wheat salad mix (discard seasoning packet)

¼ teaspoon hot pepper sauce

Salt and pepper, to taste

4 green onions, thinly sliced

¼ cup toasted pecan halves

Per Serving:
Calories: 248
% of calories from fat: 12
Fat (gm): 3.4
Saturated fat (gm): 0.3
Cholesterol (mg): 0
Sodium (mg): 537
Protein (gm): 7.5
Carbohydrate (gm): 45.8

Exchanges:
Milk: 0.0
Vegetable: 3.0
Fruit: 0.0
Bread: 2.0
Meat: 0.0
Fat: 0.5

1. Heat broth to boiling; pour over mushrooms in bowl and let stand until mushrooms are softened, about 10 minutes. Drain, reserving broth. Slice mushrooms, discarding tough stems.

2. Sauté mushrooms, onions, garlic, and bouquet garni in lightly greased large skillet until onions are tender, about 5 minutes. Add asparagus; sauté 5 minutes. Add sherry and reserved broth; heat to boiling. Stir in wheat salad mix; reduce heat and simmer, covered, until broth is absorbed and pilaf is tender, 3 to 5 minutes. Stir in hot pepper sauce; season to taste with salt and pepper. Sprinkle with green onions and pecans.

QUINOA WITH ROASTED EGGPLANT AND SQUASH

45 *Grain recipes are versatile, as almost any grain can be used in them. Couscous, millet, or kasha would work well in this recipe.*

4 entrée servings (about 1½ cups each)

1 small butternut squash, peeled, seeded, cubed

1 medium eggplant, unpeeled, cubed

2 medium onions, cut into wedges

2 large red or green bell peppers, thickly sliced

Vegetable cooking spray

1½ teaspoons dried Italian seasoning

2 cups reduced-sodium vegetable broth

1 cup quinoa

Salt and pepper, to taste

Per Serving:
Calories: 261
% of calories from fat: 10
Fat (gm): 3
Saturated fat (gm): 0.4
Cholesterol (mg): 0
Sodium (mg): 58
Protein (gm): 8.4
Carbohydrate (gm): 53.6

Exchanges:
Milk: 0.0
Vegetable: 2.0
Fruit: 0.0
Bread: 3.0
Meat: 0.0
Fat: 0.0

1. Arrange vegetables in single layer in a lightly greased aluminum foil-lined jelly roll pan. Spray vegetables with cooking spray; sprinkle with herbs. Roast at 450 degrees until vegetables are tender, about 30 minutes.

2. While vegetables are roasting, heat broth to boiling in medium saucepan; add quinoa. Reduce heat and simmer, covered, until quinoa is tender and broth absorbed, about 15 minutes. Combine quinoa and vegetables; season to taste with salt and pepper.

KASHA WITH GREEN VEGGIES

Traditionally, kasha is mixed with raw egg and cooked in a skillet until dry to keep the grains separate while cooking.

6 entrée servings

1½ cups kasha

1 egg, beaten

1 large green bell pepper, chopped

½ cup sliced green onions

2 cloves garlic, minced

1 tablespoon olive oil

4 cups reduced-sodium vegetable broth

½ teaspoon each: dried marjoram and thyme leaves

8 ounces broccoli rabe, cut into 1-inch pieces

½ cup frozen baby lima beans

Salt and pepper, to taste

Per Serving:
Calories: 217
% of calories from fat: 18
Fat (gm): 4.7
Saturated fat (gm): 0.9
Cholesterol (mg): 35.5
Sodium (mg): 40
Protein (gm): 8.6
Carbohydrate (gm): 38.8

Exchanges:
Milk: 0.0
Vegetable: 1.0
Fruit: 0.0
Bread: 2.0
Meat: 0.0
Fat: 1.0

1. Mix kasha and egg in bowl; cook over medium heat in large lightly greased large skillet until kasha is dry and grains are separated, about 5 minutes.

2. Sauté bell pepper, green onions, and garlic in oil in large saucepan until tender, about 5 minutes. Add kasha, broth, and herbs; heat to boiling. Reduce heat and simmer, covered, 20 minutes; add broccoli rabe and lima beans and simmer until kasha and broccoli rabe are tender and liquid absorbed, about 10 minutes. Season to taste with salt and pepper.

CURRIED COUSCOUS WITH VEGETABLES

45 *Couscous, a staple in Mediterranean countries, is fast and easy to cook. Serve with a selection of condiments so the dish can be enjoyed with a variety of flavor accents.*

4 entrée servings (about 1½ cups each)

8 ounces fresh or thawed, frozen whole okra

1 medium onion, chopped

2 cloves garlic, chopped

1 cup each: whole kernel corn, sliced
mushrooms, carrots

1½ teaspoons curry powder

1 cup reduced-sodium vegetable broth

⅔ cup couscous

1 medium tomato, chopped

Salt and pepper, to taste

Condiments: chopped cucumber, peanuts,
raisins, plain reduced-fat yogurt (not included
in nutritional data)

Per Serving:
Calories: 304
% of calories from fat: 11
Fat (gm): 3.9
Saturated fat (gm): 0.6
Cholesterol (mg): 0.5
Sodium (mg): 55
Protein (gm): 9.5
Carbohydrate (gm): 60.1

Exchanges:
Milk: 0.0
Vegetable: 3.0
Fruit: 1.0
Bread: 2.0
Meat: 0.0
Fat: 0.5

1. Sauté okra, onion, and garlic in lightly greased large saucepan until onion is tender, about 5 minutes. Stir in corn, mushrooms, carrots, curry powder, and broth; heat to boiling. Reduce heat and simmer, covered, until vegetables are tender, 8 to 10 minutes. Stir in couscous and tomato; remove from heat and let stand, covered, until couscous is tender and broth absorbed, about 5 minutes. Season to taste with salt and pepper. Serve with condiments.

SUN-DRIED TOMATO COUSCOUS WITH CHICKEN AND MUSHROOMS

45

Packaged couscous is available in many flavor varieties.

4 entrée servings

1 package (6 ounces) sun-dried tomato couscous

4 boneless, skinless chicken breast halves

1 pound mushrooms, halved

1 tablespoon olive oil

1½ cups water

Per Serving:
Calories: 362
% of calories from fat: 20
Fat (gm): 8.3
Saturated fat (gm): 1.3
Cholesterol (mg): 71.5
Sodium (mg): 525
Protein (gm): 34.6
Carbohydrate (gm): 39.3

Exchanges:
Milk: 0.0
Vegetable: 2.0
Fruit: 0.0
Bread: 2.0
Meat: 3.0
Fat: 0.0

1. Combine couscous and seasoning packet in 11 x 7-inch baking dish. Arrange chicken on couscous and top with mushrooms. Drizzle with olive oil; pour water over. Bake, covered, at 350 degrees until chicken is cooked, about 35 minutes.

FRUIT PILAF

45 *An easy pilaf, with dried fruit and nuts, that is simply good.*

4 entrée servings (about 1 cup each)

½ cup sliced green onions

¼ cup thinly sliced celery

1 tablespoon margarine or butter

⅔ cup brown rice

⅓ cup wild rice

2½ cups reduced-sodium vegetable broth

½ teaspoon each: dried marjoram and thyme leaves

1 large apple, peeled, cubed

⅓ cup each: chopped dried apricots, dried pears

4–6 tablespoons pecan or walnut halves, toasted

Salt and pepper, to taste

Per Serving:
Calories: 353
% of calories from fat: 23
Fat (gm): 9.2
Saturated fat (gm): 1.2
Cholesterol (mg): 0
Sodium (mg): 80
Protein (gm): 6.4
Carbohydrate (gm): 60.9

Exchanges:
Milk: 0.0
Vegetable: 0.0
Fruit: 1.5
Bread: 2.5
Meat: 0.0
Fat: 2.0

1. Sauté green onions and celery in margarine in large saucepan until celery is tender, about 5 minutes. Add rices and cook 2 minutes longer. Stir in broth and herbs and heat to boiling; reduce heat and simmer, covered, 45 minutes. Stir in fruits; simmer, covered, until rice is tender and broth absorbed, about 10 minutes. Stir in pecans; season to taste with salt and pepper.

ASIAN PILAF

A combination of brown rice, millet, and Asian ingredients make this pilaf a favorite.

4 entrée servings (about 1¼ cups each)

⅓ cup each: chopped onion, celery

2–3 teaspoons finely chopped gingerroot, garlic

1 tablespoon Asian sesame oil

½ cup each: brown rice, millet

2½ cups reduced-sodium vegetable broth

1½ cups halved snow peas

½ can (6-ounce size) water chestnuts, drained, sliced

½ cup thinly sliced green onions

2–3 tablespoons reduced-sodium tamari soy sauce

Salt and pepper, to taste

Per Serving:
Calories: 273
% of calories from fat: 18
Fat (gm): 5.4
Saturated fat (gm): 0.8
Cholesterol (mg): 0
Sodium (mg): 387
Protein (gm): 8.2
Carbohydrate (gm): 47.9

Exchanges:
Milk: 0.0
Vegetable: 1.0
Fruit: 0.0
Bread: 3.0
Meat: 0.0
Fat: 0.5

1. Sauté onion, celery, gingerroot, and garlic in sesame oil in large saucepan until onion is tender, about 10 minutes. Add rice and millet and cook 2 minutes longer; add broth and heat to boiling. Reduce heat and simmer, covered, 15 minutes. Stir in snow peas, water chestnuts, and green onions; simmer, covered, until grains and snow peas are tender and broth absorbed, about 10 minutes. Season to taste with soy sauce, salt, and pepper.

SPICY RICE

An aromatic dish of east Indian origins that will complement many meals.

8 side-dish servings (about ½ cup each)

Per Serving:
Calories: 166
% of calories from fat: 19
Fat (gm): 3.6
Saturated fat (gm): 0.5
Cholesterol (mg): 1.2
Sodium (mg): 54
Protein (gm): 4.4
Carbohydrate (gm): 27.9

Exchanges:
Milk: 0.0
Vegetable: 1.0
Fruit: 0.0
Bread: 1.5
Meat: 0.0
Fat: 0.5

1 medium onion, sliced

1 clove garlic, minced

1 tablespoon olive oil

1 cup basmati rice

½ cup reduced-fat plain yogurt

1–2 cardamom pods, crushed

¼ teaspoon each: ground turmeric, ginger

⅛ teaspoon crushed red pepper

2 cups reduced-sodium vegetable broth

Salt and pepper, to taste

1 small tomato, cut into 8 wedges

1 tablespoon finely chopped cilantro

1. Sauté onion and garlic in oil in large saucepan until tender, about 8 minutes. Add rice; stir over medium heat 2 to 3 minutes. Stir in yogurt, spices, and crushed red pepper; cook over medium heat 5 minutes, stirring frequently. Add broth and heat to boiling; reduce heat and simmer, covered, until rice is tender, about 25 minutes. Season to taste with salt and pepper. Garnish with tomato wedges; sprinkle with cilantro.

YELLOW SALSA RICE

45 *Ground turmeric contributes subtle flavor and an attractive yellow color to the rice.*

6 side-dish servings (about ⅔ cup each)

1 can (14½ ounces) reduced-sodium vegetable broth
½ teaspoon ground turmeric
1 cup long-grain rice
¼ cup prepared medium or hot salsa
1 medium tomato, chopped
Salt and pepper, to taste
Chopped cilantro, as garnish

Per Serving:
Calories: 130
% of calories from fat: 2
Fat (gm): 0.3
Saturated fat (gm): 0.1
Cholesterol (mg): 0
Sodium (mg): 103
Protein (gm): 2.7
Carbohydrate (gm): 28.4

Exchanges:
Milk: 0.0
Vegetable: 1.0
Fruit: 0.0
Bread: 1.5
Meat: 0.0
Fat: 0.0

1. Heat broth and turmeric to boiling in medium saucepan; stir in rice and salsa. Reduce heat and simmer, covered, until rice is tender and liquid absorbed, 20 to 25 minutes; stir in tomato during last 5 minutes. Season to taste with salt and pepper; sprinkle with cilantro.

ORANGE CILANTRO RICE

45 *A perfect accompaniment to grilled or roasted tofu, tempeh, or vegetables.*

6 side-dish servings (about ⅔ cup each)

½ cup sliced green onions
1 cup long-grain rice
Grated zest of 1 small orange
2¼ cups water
2 tablespoons finely chopped cilantro
Salt and pepper, to taste

Per Serving:
Calories: 118
% of calories from fat: 1
Fat (gm): 0.2
Saturated fat (gm): 0
Cholesterol (mg): 0
Sodium (mg): 2
Protein (gm): 2.3
Carbohydrate (gm): 26

Exchanges:
Milk: 0.0
Vegetable: 0.0
Fruit: 0.0
Bread: 1.5
Meat: 0.0
Fat: 0.0

1. Sauté onions in lightly greased medium saucepan until tender, 3 to 5 minutes. Add rice and orange zest; stir over medium heat until rice is lightly browned, 2 to 3 minutes. Add water and heat to boiling; reduce heat and simmer, covered, until rice is tender, 20 to 25 minutes. Stir in cilantro; season to taste with salt and pepper.

MEXICAN RED RICE

45 *The tomatoes are pureed in the traditional version of this recipe. We've chosen to chop the tomato for more appealing texture and appearance.*

6 side-dish servings (about ⅔ cup each)

1 large tomato, chopped

½ cup chopped onion, carrot

1 clove garlic, minced

½ teaspoon each: dried oregano leaves, ground cumin

1 cup long-grain rice

1 can (14½ ounces) reduced-sodium vegetable broth

⅓ cup water

½ cup frozen peas

Salt and pepper, to taste

Per Serving:
Calories: 149
% of calories from fat: 2
Fat (gm): 0.4
Saturated fat (gm): 0.1
Cholesterol (mg): 0
Sodium (mg): 45
Protein (gm): 3.7
Carbohydrate (gm): 32.5

Exchanges:
Milk: 0.0
Vegetable: 0.0
Fruit: 0.0
Bread: 2.0
Meat: 0.0
Fat: 0.0

1. Sauté tomato, onion, carrot, garlic, and herbs in lightly greased large saucepan until onion is tender, 3 to 5 minutes. Add rice; stir over medium heat 2 to 3 minutes, stirring frequently. Add broth and water and heat to boiling; reduce heat and simmer, covered, until rice is tender, about 25 minutes, adding peas during last 5 minutes. Season to taste with salt and pepper.

ITALIAN RICE SALAD

45 *This hearty rice salad can also be served as a side dish or as part of a salad buffet.*

4 entrée servings

1 cup each: cooked long-grain rice, shredded cabbage, cubed red or yellow bell pepper

4 ounces Italian-style turkey sausage, cooked, crumbled

8–12 large black olives, pitted, sliced

¼ cup minced chives or thinly sliced green onions

½–¾ cup fat-free Italian salad dressing

Salt and pepper, to taste

Per Serving:
Calories: 250
% of calories from fat: 16
Fat (gm): 4.6
Saturated fat (gm): 1.1
Cholesterol (mg): 15.2
Sodium (mg): 675
Protein (gm): 9
Carbohydrate (gm): 42.9

Exchanges:
Milk: 0.0
Vegetable: 0.0
Fruit: 0.0
Bread: 2.5
Meat: 1.0
Fat: 0.5

1. Combine all ingredients, except salt, and pepper, in bowl; season to taste with salt and pepper.

WILD RICE SOUFFLÉ

When you're in the mood for something new and different, try this great soufflé!

4 entrée servings

⅓ cup wild rice

1 cup each: reduced-sodium vegetable broth, fat-free milk

¼ cup all-purpose flour

½ cup (2 ounces) shredded reduced-fat Cheddar cheese

¼ cup thinly sliced green onions

¼–½ teaspoon each: paprika, dried savory and thyme leaves

White pepper, to taste

3 egg yolks

3 egg whites, beaten to stiff peaks

Per Serving:
Calories: 210
% of calories from fat: 28
Fat (gm): 6.5
Saturated fat (gm): 2.4
Cholesterol (mg): 168.3
Sodium (mg): 288
Protein (gm): 13
Carbohydrate (gm): 23

Exchanges:
Milk: 0.0
Vegetable: 0.0
Fruit: 0.0
Bread: 1.5
Meat: 1.5
Fat: 0.5

1. Heat rice and broth to boiling in small saucepan; reduce heat and simmer, covered, until rice is tender and broth absorbed, 45 to 55 minutes.

2. Mix milk and flour in medium saucepan; heat to boiling. Boil, whisking until thickened, about 1 minute. Remove from heat; add cheese and stir until melted (sauce will be very thick). Stir in green onions, paprika, and herbs. Season to taste with white pepper.

3. Beat egg yolks in small bowl until thick and lemon colored, about 5 minutes; mix into cheese mixture. Fold in egg whites; fold in rice. Spoon into greased 1-quart soufflé dish. Bake at 350 degrees until knife inserted halfway between center and edge comes out clean, 45 to 55 minutes.

THAI FRIED RICE

45 *Although coconut ginger rice is delicious in this recipe, any leftover rice can be used, making this speedy dish even faster!*

2 entrée servings

1 package (16 ounces) frozen vegetable stir-fry
  blend with sugar snap peas

6 green onions, sliced

4 ounces pork tenderloin, finely chopped

½–1 teaspoon hot chili sesame oil

2 eggs, lightly beaten

1 package (6.4 ounces) Thai coconut ginger rice,
  cooked, warm

2–3 tablespoons Thai peanut sauce (see Note)

1–2 tablespoons reduced-sodium tamari soy sauce

Per Serving:
Calories: 407
% of calories from fat: 25
Fat (gm): 11.2
Saturated fat (gm): 3
Cholesterol (mg): 244.8
Sodium (mg): 777
Protein (gm): 27
Carbohydrate (gm): 47

Exchanges:
Milk: 0.0
Vegetable: 3.0
Fruit: 0.0
Bread: 2.0
Meat: 3.0
Fat: 0.5

1. Stir-fry frozen vegetables, green onions, and pork in sesame oil in large skillet until tender, 3 to 4 minutes; move vegetables to side of skillet. Add eggs; cook over medium heat until set, stirring occasionally, about 2 minutes. Break up eggs with spatula and mix with vegetables and pork; stir in rice and peanut and tamari sauces.

NOTE: If you cannot find Thai peanut sauce in your supermarket, mix 1 to 2 tablespoons reduced-fat peanut butter, 2 to 3 teaspoons reduced-sodium tamari soy sauce, and ½ to 1 teaspoon minced gingerroot.

45-MINUTE PREPARATION TIP: Begin cooking the rice before preparing the rest of the recipe.

ALL-SEASON RISOTTO

A blending of summer and winter squash provides color and flavor to this creamy risotto dish.

6 entrée servings (about 1⅓ cups each)

2 cups each: peeled, cubed acorn or butternut squash
1 cup each: sliced zucchini, cremini mushrooms, chopped red bell pepper, quartered plum tomatoes
2 teaspoons dried oregano leaves
2 tablespoons olive oil, divided
1 cup chopped onion
2 cloves garlic, minced
1½ cups arborio rice
1½ quarts reduced-sodium vegetable broth
2 cups water
¼ cup (1 ounce) grated fat-free Parmesan cheese
1 can (15½ ounces) black beans, rinsed, drained
½ cup frozen peas, thawed
Salt and pepper, to taste

Per Serving:
Calories: 391
% of calories from fat: 13
Fat (gm): 6.2
Saturated fat (gm): 0.8
Cholesterol (mg): 0
Sodium (mg): 328
Protein (gm): 14.7
Carbohydrate (gm): 75.9

Exchanges:
Milk: 0.0
Vegetable: 2.0
Fruit: 0.0
Bread: 4.0
Meat: 0.0
Fat: 1.0

1. Sauté squash, zucchini, mushrooms, bell pepper, tomatoes, and oregano in 1 tablespoon oil in large skillet until tender, about 8 minutes; reserve. Sauté onion and garlic in remaining 1 tablespoon oil in large saucepan until tender, 3 to 4 minutes. Add rice; stir over medium heat until rice is beginning to brown, 2 to 3 minutes.

2. Heat broth and water to simmering in medium saucepan; reduce heat to low to keep broth hot. Add broth to rice mixture, ½ cup at a time, stirring over medium heat until broth is absorbed before adding next ½ cup. Continue process until rice is al dente and mixture is creamy, 20 to 25 minutes. Stir in cheese, beans, peas, and reserved vegetables; cook 2 to 3 minutes. Season to taste with salt and pepper.

SUMMER SQUASH RISOTTO

A perfect risotto for summer, when squash and tomatoes are fresh from the garden.

4 entrée servings (about 1 cup each)

1 cup each: sliced zucchini, summer yellow squash, chopped onion
3 cloves garlic, minced
1 tablespoon olive oil
8 Italian plum tomatoes, quartered
1½ teaspoons dried oregano leaves
1½ cups arborio rice
1½ quarts reduced-sodium vegetable broth
¼ cup (1 ounce) grated Romano cheese
Salt and pepper, to taste

Per Serving:
Calories: 423
% of calories from fat: 15
Fat (gm): 7.4
Saturated fat (gm): 2
Cholesterol (mg): 7.2
Sodium (mg): 128
Protein (gm): 11.1
Carbohydrate (gm): 79.5

Exchanges:
Milk: 0.0
Vegetable: 3.0
Fruit: 0.0
Bread: 4.0
Meat: 0.0
Fat: 1.5

1. Sauté zucchini, yellow squash, onion, and garlic in oil in lightly greased large saucepan until squashes are crisp-tender, 6 to 8 minutes. Add tomatoes and oregano; cook until tomatoes are soft, about 3 minutes. Add rice; stir over medium heat 2 to 3 minutes.

2. Heat broth to boiling in small saucepan; reduce heat to low to keep broth hot. Add broth to rice mixture, ½ cup at a time, stirring over medium heat until broth is absorbed before adding another ½ cup. Continue process until rice is al dente and mixture is creamy, 20 to 25 minutes; add zucchini mixture during last 5 minutes of cooking time. Stir in cheese; season to taste with salt and pepper.

WINTER VEGETABLE RISOTTO

Arborio rice is a short-grain rice grown in the Arborio region of Italy. It's especially suited for making risotto, as it cooks to a wonderful creaminess.

4 entrée servings (about 1¼ cups each)

1 small onion, chopped
3 cloves garlic, minced
1 cup sliced cremini or white mushrooms
1 teaspoon each: dried rosemary and thyme leaves
1½ cups arborio rice
6 cups reduced-sodium vegetable broth
1 cup each: halved Brussels sprouts, cubed, peeled
  sweet potato, cooked until crisp-tender
¼ cup (1 ounce) grated Parmesan cheese
Salt and pepper, to taste

Per Serving:
Calories: 384
% of calories from fat: 8
Fat (gm): 3.3
Saturated fat (gm): 1.4
Cholesterol (mg): 4.9
Sodium (mg): 153
Protein (gm): 11
Carbohydrate (gm): 77.3

Exchanges:
Milk: 0.0
Vegetable: 3.0
Fruit: 0.0
Bread: 4.0
Meat: 0.0
Fat: 0.5

1. Sauté onion and garlic in lightly greased large saucepan until tender, about 5 minutes. Add mushrooms and herbs; cook until mushrooms are tender, 5 to 7 minutes. Add rice; stir over medium heat until rice begins to brown, 2 to 3 minutes.

2. Heat broth just to boiling in medium saucepan; reduce heat to low to keep broth hot. Add broth to rice mixture, ½ cup at a time, stirring over medium heat until broth is absorbed before adding next ½ cup. Continue process until rice is al dente and mixture is creamy, 20 to 25 minutes; add Brussels sprouts and sweet potato during last 10 minutes of cooking time. Stir in cheese; season to taste with salt and pepper.

PORCINI RISOTTO

Use dried shiitake (Chinese black mushrooms) if porcini are not available.

4 entrée servings (about 1 cup each)

1 cup boiling water
¼–½ ounce dried porcini mushrooms
1 small onion, chopped
3 cloves garlic, minced

1 small tomato, seeded, chopped

1 teaspoon dried sage leaves

1½ cups arborio rice

1½ quarts reduced-sodium vegetable broth

¼ cup (1 ounce) grated Parmesan cheese, toasted pine nuts

Salt and pepper, to taste

Per Serving:
Calories: 389
% of calories from fat: 14
Fat (gm): 6.1
Saturated fat (gm): 1.9
Cholesterol (mg): 4.9
Sodium (mg): 135
Protein (gm): 10.2
Carbohydrate (gm): 68

Exchanges:
Milk: 0.0
Vegetable: 2.0
Fruit: 0.0
Bread: 4.0
Meat: 0.0
Fat: 1.0

1. Pour boiling water over mushrooms in bowl; let stand until mushrooms are soft, about 15 minutes; drain, reserving liquid. Slice mushrooms, discarding tough stems.

2. Sauté mushrooms, onion, and garlic in lightly greased large saucepan until tender, about 5 minutes; add tomato and sage and cook 2 minutes. Add rice; stir over medium heat 2 to 3 minutes.

3. Heat broth and reserved porcini liquid to boiling in medium saucepan; reduce heat to low to keep broth hot. Add broth to rice mixture, ½ cup at a time, stirring over medium heat until broth is absorbed before adding another ½ cup. Continue process until rice is al dente and mixture is creamy, 20 to 25 minutes; stir in cheese and pine nuts. Season to taste with salt and pepper.

SHRIMP AND MUSHROOM RISOTTO

White wine can be substituted for ½ cup of the broth in the recipe.

6 entrée servings (about ¾ cup each)

2 cups sliced mushrooms

1 small onion, chopped

3 cloves garlic, minced

1 teaspoon dried thyme leaves

1½ cups arborio rice

1½ quarts reduced-sodium chicken broth

8 ounces peeled, deveined shrimp

2 tablespoons grated Parmesan cheese

Salt and pepper, to taste

Per Serving:
Calories: 252
% of calories from fat: 8
Fat (gm): 2.1
Saturated fat (gm): 0.6
Cholesterol (mg): 59.6
Sodium (mg): 172
Protein (gm): 13.4
Carbohydrate (gm): 43.4

Exchanges:
Milk: 0.0
Vegetable: 0.5
Fruit: 0.0
Bread: 2.5
Meat: 0.5
Fat: 0.0

1. Sauté mushrooms, onion, garlic, and thyme in lightly greased large saucepan until tender, about 10 minutes. Add rice; stir over medium heat 2 to 3 minutes.

2. Heat chicken broth just to boiling in medium saucepan; reduce heat to low to keep broth hot. Add broth to rice mixture, ½ cup at a time, stirring until broth is absorbed before adding next ½ cup. Continue process until rice is al dente and mixture is creamy, 20 to 25 minutes; add shrimp during last 10 minutes. Stir in cheese; season to taste with salt and pepper.

SAUSAGE AND BROCCOLI RISOTTO

This risotto is enhanced with the addition of homemade Italian-style sausage, made with ground turkey and abundantly seasoned with spices and herbs.

6 entrée servings (about 1½ cups each)

12 ounces ground turkey

1 teaspoon each: crushed fennel seeds, dried sage and thyme leaves

½ teaspoon each: dried oregano leaves, salt

¼ teaspoon each: ground allspice, mace

1 small onion, chopped

2 cloves garlic, minced

1½ cups arborio rice

1½ quarts reduced-sodium chicken broth

2 cups broccoli florets, cooked

½ cup raisins

2 tablespoons grated Parmesan cheese

Salt and pepper, to taste

Per Serving:
Calories: 322
% of calories from fat: 16
Fat (gm): 5.6
Saturated fat (gm): 1.3
Cholesterol (mg): 21.1
Sodium (mg): 101
Protein (gm): 14.6
Carbohydrate (gm): 53.4

Exchanges:
Milk: 0.0
Vegetable: 1.0
Fruit: 0.5
Bread: 2.5
Meat: 1.0
Fat: 0.5

1. Mix ground turkey, herbs, ½ teaspoon salt, and spices; refrigerate 1 to 2 hours. Cook turkey mixture in lightly greased large saucepan until browned; remove from pan. Add onion and garlic to sauce-pan; sauté until tender, about 5 minutes. Add rice; stir over medium heat until rice begins to brown, 2 to 3 minutes.

2. Heat chicken broth to boiling in medium saucepan; reduce heat to low to keep broth hot. Add broth to rice mixture, ½ cup at a time, stirring until broth is absorbed before adding another ½ cup. Continue process until rice is al dente, 20 to 25 minutes; add turkey mixture, broccoli, and raisins during last 10 minutes. Stir in cheese; season to taste with salt and pepper.

RISI BISI

Opinions vary as to whether Risi Bisi is a risotto or a thick soup. If you agree with the latter definition, use an additional ½ to 1 cup of broth to make the mixture a thick-soup consistency.

4 entrée servings (about 1 cup each)

1 small onion, chopped

3 cloves garlic, minced

1½ cups arborio rice

2 teaspoons dried basil leaves

1½ quarts reduced-sodium vegetable broth

8 ounces frozen tiny peas

¼ cup (1 ounce) grated Parmesan cheese

Salt and pepper, to taste

Per Serving:
Calories: 407
% of calories from fat: 6
Fat (gm): 2.5
Saturated fat (gm): 1.3
Cholesterol (mg):
4.9Sodium (mg): 291
Protein (gm): 12.2
Carbohydrate (gm): 82.1

Exchanges:
Milk: 0.0
Vegetable: 1.0
Fruit: 0.0
Bread: 5.0
Meat: 0.0
Fat: 0.5

1. Sauté onion and garlic in lightly greased large saucepan until tender, about 5 minutes. Add rice and basil; stir over medium heat 2 to 3 minutes.

2. Heat broth to boiling in medium saucepan; reduce heat to low to keep broth hot. Add broth to rice mixture, ½ cup at a time, stirring over medium heat until broth is absorbed before adding another ½ cup. Continue process until rice is al dente and mixture is creamy, 20 to 25 minutes; stir in peas during last 10 minutes of cooking time. Stir in Parmesan cheese; season to taste with salt and pepper.

QUICK AND EASY CHEESE RISOTTO

45 *This two-cheese risotto is quickly prepared with a simplified method that requires little stirring.*

4 entrée servings (about 1 cup each)

½ cup finely chopped onion

1 cup arborio rice

2½ cups vegetable broth

½ cup dry white wine

1 cup (4 ounces) shredded Parmesan cheese

¼–½ cup (1 to 2 ounces) crumbled blue cheese

2–3 tablespoons chopped chives or parsley

Salt and pepper, to taste

Per Serving:
Calories: 345
% of calories from fat: 22
Fat (gm): 8.3
Saturated fat (gm): 5.2
Cholesterol (mg): 21.1
Sodium (mg): 525
Protein (gm): 13.9
Carbohydrate (gm): 47.3

Exchanges:
Milk: 0.0
Vegetable: 0.0
Fruit: 0.0
Bread: 3.0
Meat: 1.0
Fat: 1.5

1. Sauté onion and rice in lightly greased large saucepan 1 to 2 minutes. Add vegetable broth and wine and heat to boiling. Reduce heat and simmer, covered, until rice is al dente and liquid absorbed, 20 to 25 minutes, stirring occasionally. Stir in cheeses and chives. Season to taste with salt and pepper.

MICROWAVE RISOTTO

45 *This is the easiest possible way to make risotto. Use of the microwave eliminates the constant stirring usually required for this dish.*

4 entrée servings

1 cup arborio rice

3⅓ cups reduced-sodium fat-free chicken broth, divided

⅓ cup grated Parmesan cheese

Salt and pepper, to taste

Per Serving:
Calories: 235
% of calories from fat: 9
Fat (gm): 2.3
Saturated fat (gm): 1.3
Cholesterol (mg): 2.5
Sodium (mg): 266
Protein (gm): 11
Carbohydrate (gm): 39.9

Exchanges:
Milk: 0.0
Vegetable: 0.0
Fruit: 0.0
Bread: 2.5
Meat: 1.0
Fat: 0.0

1. Combine rice and ¼ cup broth in 3-quart glass casserole. Microwave, uncovered, on high power 60 seconds; stir. Add remaining broth; microwave on high power, covered, until rice is al dente, 20 to 25 minutes, stirring every 10 minutes. Let stand 2 to 3 minutes; stir in cheese and season to taste with salt and pepper.

CHEESE AND ARTICHOKE RISOTTO PANCAKES

Top each serving with a poached or fried egg for a hearty brunch or light supper.

4 entrée servings

½ cup chopped onion

1 cup arborio rice

2½ cups reduced-sodium vegetable broth

½ cup dry white wine

¾ cup (3 ounces) shredded Parmesan cheese

¼–½ cup (1–2 ounces) crumbled blue cheese

2 eggs, lightly beaten

6 canned artichoke hearts, coarsely chopped

¼ cup coarsely chopped roasted red pepper

Salt and pepper, to taste

Chopped parsley, as garnish

Per Serving:
Calories: 372
% of calories from fat: 31
Fat (gm): 12.4
Saturated fat (gm): 5.2
Cholesterol (mg): 122.8
Sodium (mg): 731
Protein (gm): 13.6
Carbohydrate (gm): 45.5

Exchanges:
Milk: 0.0
Vegetable: 0.0
Fruit: 0.0
Bread: 3.0
Meat: 1.0
Fat: 2.0

1. Sauté onion in lightly greased large saucepan 2 minutes; add rice and stir over medium heat 2 to 3 minutes. Add vegetable broth and wine; heat to boiling. Reduce heat and simmer, covered, until rice is tender and liquid absorbed, 20 to 25 minutes, stirring occasionally. Remove from heat and let stand 5 minutes; stir in cheeses, eggs, artichoke hearts, and red pepper. Season to taste with salt and pepper.

2. Heat two lightly greased 10-inch skillets over medium heat until hot. Spoon half the risotto mixture into each skillet, shaping into large pancakes. Cook over medium heat until lightly browned on the bottoms, 5 to 8 minutes. Invert pancakes onto plates; slide back into skillets and cook until lightly browned on the bottoms, 5 to 8 minutes. Cut pancakes in half; slide onto serving plates and sprinkle with parsley.

RISOTTO-VEGETABLE CAKES

A great way to use leftover risotto!

4 entrée servings

1 medium onion, finely chopped

2 cloves garlic, minced

1 teaspoon dried oregano leaves

1 cup arborio rice

3 cups reduced-sodium vegetable broth

¼ cup (1 ounce) each: shredded reduced-fat Cheddar cheese, grated fat-free Parmesan cheese

Salt and pepper, to taste

½ cup each: chopped zucchini, carrots, red bell pepper, celery

1 egg, lightly beaten

⅔ cup Italian-seasoned dry bread crumbs

8 beefsteak tomatoes, thickly sliced

Per Serving:
Calories: 409
% of calories from fat: 12
Fat (gm): 5
Saturated fat (gm): 2
Cholesterol (mg): 59
Sodium (mg): 1142
Protein (gm): 16
Carbohydrate (gm): 77

Exchanges:
Milk: 0.0
Vegetable: 3.0
Fruit: 0.0
Bread: 4.0
Meat: 0.0
Fat: 1.0

1. Sauté onion, garlic, and oregano in lightly greased large saucepan until tender, about 3 minutes. Add rice; stir over medium heat 2 to 3 minutes.

2. Heat broth to simmering in medium saucepan; reduce heat to low to keep broth warm. Add broth to rice mixture, ½ cup at a time, stirring over medium heat until broth is absorbed before adding next ½ cup. Continue process until rice is al dente and mixture is creamy, 20 to 25 minutes; remove from heat and stir in cheeses. Season to taste with salt and pepper; cool.

3. Sauté vegetables in lightly greased large skillet until tender, 5 to 8 minutes. Stir into rice mixture; stir in egg and bread crumbs. Form mixture into 8 patties, about ¾-inch thick. Broil 6 inches from heat source, until browned, 2 to 4 minutes each side. Top each patty with tomato slice and sprinkle lightly with salt and pepper; broil until tomatoes are browned, 2 to 3 minutes.

POLENTA

45 *This basic recipe can be modified to your taste—note the variations below.*

6 side-dish servings (about ½ cup each)

3 cups water
¾ cup yellow cornmeal
Salt and pepper, to taste

Per Serving:
Calories: 63
% of calories from fat: 4
Fat (gm): 0.3
Saturated fat (gm): 0.0
Cholesterol (mg): 0.0
Sodium (mg): 0.5
Protein (gm): 1.5
Carbohydrate (gm): 13

Exchanges:
Milk: 0.0;
Vegetable: 0.0
Fruit: 0.0
Bread: 1.0
Meat: 0.0
Fat: 0.0

1. Heat water to boiling in large saucepan; gradually stir in cornmeal. Cook over medium to medium-low heat, stirring until polenta thickens enough to hold its shape but is still soft, 5 to 8 minutes.

VARIATIONS

Blue Cheese Polenta — Make recipe above, stirring ½ cup (2 ounces) crumbled blue cheese, or other blue veined cheese, into the cooked polenta.

Goat Cheese Polenta — Make recipe above, stirring ¼ to ½ cup (1 to 2 ounces) crumbled goat cheese into the cooked polenta.

Garlic Polenta — Sauté ¼ cup finely chopped onion and 4 to 6 cloves minced garlic in 1 tablespoon olive oil in large saucepan; add water, as above, and complete recipe.

HERBED POLENTA

Gently seasoned with onions, garlic, and basil, the polenta can be served immediately after cooking, or cooled in a pan as the recipe directs.

4 to 6 side-dish servings

2 green onions, sliced
1 clove garlic, minced
1 teaspoon dried basil leaves
2½ cups reduced-sodium vegetable or chicken broth
¾ cup yellow cornmeal
½ teaspoon salt

Per Serving:
Calories: 124
% of calories from fat: 9
Fat (gm): 1.3
Saturated fat (gm): 0.2
Cholesterol (mg): 0
Sodium (mg): 309
Protein (gm): 2.5
Carbohydrate (gm): 22.4

Exchanges:
Milk: 0.0
Vegetable: 0.0
Fruit: 0.0
Bread: 1.5
Meat: 0.0
Fat: 0.5

1. Sauté onions, garlic, and basil in lightly greased large saucepan until tender, about 5 minutes. Add broth and heat to boiling; gradually stir in cornmeal and salt. Cook over low heat, stirring until thickened, about 10 minutes. Pour polenta into greased 8-inch cake pan; cool. Refrigerate, lightly covered, until polenta is firm, 3 to 4 hours.

2. Cut polenta into wedges; cook in lightly greased large skillet over medium heat until browned, 3 to 4 minutes on each side.

COUNTRY-STYLE CORN BREAD

9 servings

1¾ cups self-rising white cornmeal
¼ cup all-purpose flour
1 egg
2 teaspoons corn oil
1½ cups low-fat buttermilk

Per Serving:
Calories: 142
% of calories from fat: 16
Fat (gm): 2.4
Saturated fat (gm): 0.6
Cholesterol (mg): 25
Sodium (mg): 412
Protein (gm): 4.7
Carbohydrate (gm): 24.7

Exchanges:
Milk: 0.0
Vegetable: 0.0
Fruit: 0.0
Bread: 1.5
Meat: 0.0
Fat: 0.5

1. Combine all ingredients and pour into greased 8 x 8-inch baking pan. Bake at 400 degrees until golden, 20 to 25 minutes.

BEST BREAKFAST CEREAL

Delicious and nutritious! This cereal is even more delicious made with slow-cooking steel-cut oats.

6 entrée servings (about ⅔ cup each)

3 cups water

Pinch salt

1½ cups each: quick-cooking oats, cooked wheat berries

¼ cup chopped toasted pecans or walnuts

½ cup dried fruit bits or raisins

¼ cup packed dark brown sugar

1 cup fat-free milk

Per Serving:
Calories: 313
% of calories from fat: 13
Fat (gm): 4.9
Saturated fat (gm): 0.6
Cholesterol (mg): 0.7
Sodium (mg): 55
Protein (gm): 9.7
Carbohydrate (gm): 61.4

Exchanges:
Milk: 0.0
Vegetable: 0.0
Fruit: 0.5
Bread: 3.5
Meat: 0.0
Fat: 0.5

1. Heat water and salt to boiling in medium saucepan; stir in oats, wheat berries, pecans, and dried fruit. Reduce heat and simmer, uncovered, to desired consistency, about 5 minutes. Serve with brown sugar and milk.

TEN

Casseroles

ARTICHOKE AND STUFFING CASSEROLE

45

Enjoy the flavor of stuffed artichokes, with very little work!

4 side-dish servings

1 large onion, chopped

½ teaspoon each: chopped garlic, dried
   oregano leaves

1 tablespoon olive oil

1 can (14 ounces) artichoke hearts, drained, sliced

2 cups seasoned stuffing cubes

¾ cup reduced-sodium fat-free chicken broth

Salt and pepper, to taste

Per Serving:
Calories: 175
% of calories from fat: 22
Fat (gm): 4.4
Saturated fat (gm): 0.5
Cholesterol (mg): 0
Sodium (mg): 738
Protein (gm): 5.9
Carbohydrate (gm): 29.1

Exchanges:
Milk: 0.0
Vegetable: 0.0
Fruit: 0.0
Bread: 2.0
Meat: 0.0
Fat: 1.0

1. Sauté onion, garlic, and oregano in oil in medium skillet until tender, about 5 minutes. Combine all ingredients, except salt, and pepper, in 2-quart glass casserole; season to taste with salt and pepper. Bake, covered, at 350 degrees until hot, about 30 minutes.

ASPARAGUS POLENTA BAKE

45

This dish can be prepared a day in advance and refrigerated; increase baking time 5 to 10 minutes.

6 side-dish servings

6 ounces portobello mushrooms, thinly sliced

8 ounces asparagus, cut (1-inch)

1–2 teaspoons olive oil

1 package (16 ounces) prepared Italian-herb polenta

1 cup water

1 ounce sun-dried tomatoes (not in oil),
   softened, sliced

¼–½ cup (1–2 ounces) shredded Parmesan cheese

Per Serving:
Calories: 110
% of calories from fat: 18
Fat (gm): 2.2
Saturated fat (gm): 1
Cholesterol (mg): 4.2
Sodium (mg): 94
Protein (gm): 5.4
Carbohydrate (gm): 16.7

Exchanges:
Milk: 0.0
Vegetable: 2.0
Fruit: 0.0
Bread: 0.5
Meat: 0.0
Fat: 0.5

1. Sauté mushrooms and asparagus in oil in large skillet until asparagus is crisp-tender, about 5 minutes. Mash polenta with water in medium saucepan; cook over medium heat, whisking until smooth and hot, about 5 minutes. Stir in mushroom mixture and sun-dried tomatoes. Spoon into 4 ramekins or a shallow casserole or quiche dish; sprinkle with Parmesan cheese. Bake at 425 degrees until cheese is browned, about 20 minutes.

VEGGIE CASSEROLE

45

In this version of a family favorite, savory, herb-seasoned vegetables are topped with toasted bread crumbs and baked. A perfect pot-luck side dish!

6 side-dish servings

1 cup each: sliced leek (white part only), red or green bell pepper

2 teaspoons minced garlic

3 tablespoons flour

1½ teaspoons bouquet garni

2 cups reduced-sodium vegetable broth

1 cup each: cubed, peeled potatoes, sliced yellow summer squash, halved green beans

½ cup each: cauliflower florets, frozen peas

Salt and pepper, to taste

¾ cup fresh bread crumbs

2 tablespoons margarine or butter, melted

Per Serving:
Calories: 158
% of calories from fat: 24
Fat (gm): 4.3
Saturated fat (gm): 0.9
Cholesterol (mg): 0
Sodium (mg): 129
Protein (gm): 4.3
Carbohydrate (gm): 26.4

Exchanges:
Milk: 0.0
Vegetable: 2.0
Fruit: 0.0
Bread: 1.0
Meat: 0.0
Fat: 1.0

1. Sauté leek, bell pepper, and garlic in lightly greased large saucepan 5 minutes; stir in flour and bouquet garni and cook 1 minute. Add broth and remaining vegetables; heat to boiling. Reduce heat and simmer, covered, until vegetables are tender, about 10 minutes. Season to taste with salt and pepper. Pour mixture into 1½-quart casserole; top with combined bread crumbs and margarine. Bake at 350 degrees until crumbs are browned, about 10 minutes.

VEGETABLE AND MIXED RICE CASSEROLE

45

Vary the vegetables according to season or preference.

8 side-dish servings (about ¾ cup each)

1½ cups sliced shiitake or cremini mushrooms
1 cup sliced zucchini
½ cup each: chopped onion, green and red bell pepper
1 teaspoon dried thyme leaves
1 package (6 ounces) brown and wild rice mix,
   cooked with spice packet
1 can (15 ounces) pinto beans, rinsed, drained
1 cup each: whole kernel corn, fat-free sour
   cream, shredded reduced-fat Cheddar cheese
   (4 ounces), divided
Salt and pepper, to taste

Per Serving:
Calories: 203
% of calories from fat: 15
Fat (gm): 3.5
Saturated fat (gm): 1.9
Cholesterol (mg): 10.1
Sodium (mg): 141
Protein (gm): 10.5
Carbohydrate (gm): 33.7

Exchanges:
Milk: 0.0
Vegetable: 1.0
Fruit: 0.0
Bread: 2.0
Meat: 0.0
Fat: 0.5

1. Sauté mushrooms, zucchini, onion, bell peppers, and thyme in lightly greased medium skillet until vegetables are tender, 8 to 10 minutes. Combine vegetables with rice, beans, corn, sour cream, and ½ cup cheese in 2-quart casserole. Season to taste with salt and pepper; sprinkle with remaining ½ cup cheese. Bake, uncovered, at 350 degrees until hot, 30 to 40 minutes.

WILD RICE, CHEESE, AND VEGETABLE CASSEROLE

Delicious, with a generous amount of melted cheese. The vegetables can vary according to season and availability.

4 entrée servings

1 package (6¼ ounces) wild and white rice mix,
   cooked without spice packet
1½ cups each: cut asparagus spears and halved small
   Brussels sprouts, cooked crisp-tender
3 ounces fat-free cream cheese, cubed
¾ cup (3 ounces) shredded fat-free mozzarella cheese
3–4 ounces goat cheese, crumbled
Salt and pepper, to taste

Per Serving:
Calories: 307
% of calories from fat: 21
Fat (gm): 7.2
Saturated fat (gm): 4.3
Cholesterol (mg): 9.7
Sodium (mg): 200
Protein (gm): 21.7
Carbohydrate (gm): 39

Exchanges:
Milk: 0.0
Vegetable: 2.0
Fruit: 0.0
Bread: 2.0
Meat: 1.5
Fat: 0.5

1. Mix rice, vegetables, and cheeses; season to taste with salt and pepper. Spoon into 1½-quart casserole. Bake, covered, at 350 degrees until casserole is hot and cheese is melted, about 30 minutes.

SALMON, SNOW PEA, AND NEW POTATO CASSEROLE

45

Easy, colorful, delicious!

4 entrée servings

4 salmon fillets (about 4 ounces each)

2 tablespoons margarine or butter, room temperature

Salt and pepper, to taste

1 tablespoon dried tarragon leaves

1 small lemon, thinly sliced

8 ounces snow peas

6 small new potatoes, peeled, quartered

⅓ cup apple cider

Per Serving:
Calories: 404
% of calories from fat: 22
Fat (gm): 10.1
Saturated fat (gm): 1.9
Cholesterol (mg): 57.1
Sodium (mg): 156
Protein (gm): 28.1
Carbohydrate (gm): 53

Exchanges:
Milk: 0.0
Vegetable: 2.0
Fruit: 0.0
Bread: 3.0
Meat: 2.0
Fat: 1.0

1. Place salmon in greased 13 x 9-inch baking dish; spread each fillet with margarine. Sprinkle lightly with salt, pepper, and tarragon; cover with lemon slices. Arrange snow peas and potatoes around fish; sprinkle with salt and pepper. Pour cider over. Bake, covered, at 350 degrees until fish flakes with fork and potatoes are tender, 20 to 30 minutes.

ONE-DISH CHICKEN AND RICE

45

Just mix and bake—perfect for a quick dinner.

4 entrée servings

1 can (10½ ounces) reduced-fat cream of
   mushroom soup
¾ cup each: fat-free milk, long-grain rice
1 package (10 ounces) frozen cut green beans
½ teaspoon dried tarragon leaves
Salt and pepper, to taste
Paprika
2 boneless, skinless chicken breast halves
   (4 ounces each)

Per Serving:
Calories: 342
% of calories from fat: 14
Fat (gm): 5.5
Saturated fat (gm): 1.3
Cholesterol (mg): 72.9
Sodium (mg): 675
Protein (gm): 31
Carbohydrate (gm): 41

Exchanges:
Milk: 0.0
Vegetable: 2.0
Fruit: 0.0
Bread: 2.0
Meat: 3.0
Fat: 0.0

1. Combine soup, milk, rice, beans, and tarragon in 2-quart baking
dish; season to taste with salt and pepper. Arrange chicken over
rice; sprinkle with salt, pepper, and paprika. Bake, covered, at 375
degrees until chicken is cooked, about 45 minutes.

CHICKEN, VEGETABLE, AND GOAT CHEESE CASSEROLE

Delicious, with a generous amount of melted cheese.

4 entrée servings

1½ cups cut asparagus (1½-inch)
1 package (9 ounces) frozen artichoke hearts
1 package (6¼ ounces) fast-cooking long-grain
   and wild rice
12 ounces cooked chicken breast, cubed
3 ounces fat-free cream cheese, cubed
¾ cup (3 ounces) shredded reduced-fat
   mozzarella cheese
3–4 ounces reduced-fat goat cheese, crumbled
Salt and pepper, to taste

Per Serving:
Calories: 445
% of calories from fat: 20
Fat (gm): 10
Saturated fat (gm): 4.8
Cholesterol (mg): 84.1
Sodium (mg): 804
Protein (gm): 44.2
Carbohydrate (gm): 45.1

Exchanges:
Milk: 0.0
Vegetable: 3.0
Fruit: 0.0
Bread: 2.0
Meat: 4.0
Fat: 0.0

1. Cook asparagus and artichoke hearts in boiling water to cover, 4 minutes. Drain. Cook rice according to package directions, using ½ the spice packet. Combine all ingredients, except salt and pepper in 1½-quart casserole; season to taste with salt and pepper. Bake, covered, at 375 degrees until casserole is hot and cheese melted, 20 to 30 minutes.

AUTUMN POT PIE

45

Choose ingredients from your garden or produce market for this savory pie.

6 entrée servings

16 ounces pork tenderloin, cubed

½ cup each: chopped onion, sliced celery, red bell pepper

2 cloves garlic, minced

½ teaspoon each: dried sage and thyme leaves

3 tablespoons flour

2 cups reduced-sodium vegetable broth

1 cup each: cubed peeled sweet potato and turnip, unpeeled russet potato, halved Brussels sprouts

½ cup each: lima beans, halved small mushrooms

Salt and pepper, to taste

9-inch purchased pie pastry

Per Serving:
Calories: 362
% of calories from fat: 30
Fat (gm): 11.7
Saturated fat (gm): 4.8
Cholesterol (mg): 55.4
Sodium (mg): 265
Protein (gm): 20
Carbohydrate (gm): 42.5

Exchanges:
Milk: 0.0
Vegetable: 0.0
Fruit: 0.0
Bread: 3.0
Meat: 2.0
Fat: 1.0

1. Sauté pork in lightly greased large saucepan until browned, about 5 minutes; add onion, celery, bell pepper, garlic, and herbs to saucepan and sauté until vegetables are tender, about 5 minutes. Stir in flour; cook 1 minute. Add broth and remaining vegetables; heat to boiling. Reduce heat and simmer, covered, until vegetables are tender, about 10 minutes; season to taste with salt and pepper. Spoon into 1½-quart casserole.

2. Roll pastry on floured surface into circle 1 inch larger than top of casserole; place on top of casserole and flute edge. Bake at 425 degrees until pastry is browned, about 20 minutes.

BEEF AND NOODLE BAKE

An old-fashioned cold weather meal, quick to fix and hearty.

6 entrée servings

1½ pounds lean ground beef

1 cup each: chopped onion, green bell pepper, whole kernel corn

1 can (14½ ounces) reduced-sodium diced tomatoes, undrained

½ teaspoon pepper

12 ounces thin egg noodles, cooked

¼ cup seasoned dry bread crumbs

Per Serving:
Calories: 495
% of calories from fat: 30
Fat (gm): 16.5
Saturated fat (gm): 6
Cholesterol (mg): 119.4
Sodium (mg): 118
Protein (gm): 31.3
Carbohydrate (gm): 55.6

Exchanges:
Milk: 0.0
Vegetable: 2.0
Fruit: 0.0
Bread: 3.0
Meat: 3.0
Fat: 1.5

1. Cook ground beef, onion, and bell pepper over medium heat in lightly greased large skillet until beef is browned, about 10 minutes. Combine all ingredients, except bread crumbs, in 2½-quart casserole; sprinkle with bread crumbs. Bake, uncovered, at 350 degrees until hot, about 30 minutes.

BEEF STROGANOFF CASSEROLE

Add the sour cream to this casserole near the end of baking time to avoid curdling.

6 entrée servings

12 ounces uncooked wide egg noodles

1½ pounds boneless beef round or sirloin steak, cut into strips (1-inch)

½ cup all-purpose flour

1 pound mushrooms, coarsely chopped

2 tablespoons finely chopped onion

1 tablespoon paprika

½ teaspoon ground nutmeg

1 can (13¾ ounces) reduced-sodium fat-free beef broth

1 container (8 ounces) fat-free sour cream

Salt and pepper, to taste

Per Serving:
Calories: 409
% of calories from fat: 14
Fat (gm): 6.4
Saturated fat (gm): 1.9
Cholesterol (mg): 103.6
Sodium (mg): 132
Protein (gm): 33.7
Carbohydrate (gm): 52.4

Exchanges:
Milk: 0.0
Vegetable: 1.0
Fruit: 0.0
Bread: 3.0
Meat: 3.0
Fat: 0.0

1. Place uncooked noodles in 2½-quart casserole. Coat beef with flour; arrange on top of noodles. Top with combined mushrooms, onion, paprika, and nutmeg. Pour beef broth over. Bake, covered, at 325 degrees 1 hour; stir in sour cream and bake, uncovered, 15 minutes. Season to taste with salt and pepper.

SPICY BEEF AND ASPARAGUS WITH RICE NOODLES

45

Using frozen stir-fry vegetables saves kitchen prep time!

6 entrée servings

8 ounces rice noodles

1 pound boneless beef round steak, cut into strips (1½ x ½-inch)

12 ounces fresh asparagus, sliced (1-inch)

1 package (16 ounces) frozen stir-fry vegetables, thawed, drained

¾ cup reduced-sodium beef broth

2 tablespoons flour

1 tablespoon each: reduced-sodium soy sauce, catsup

1 teaspoon minced garlic

¼ teaspoon pepper

3–4 drops hot pepper sauce

Per Serving:
Calories: 291
% of calories from fat: 11
Fat (gm): 3.5
Saturated fat (gm): 1.2
Cholesterol (mg): 37.3
Sodium (mg): 274
Protein (gm): 25.8
Carbohydrate (gm): 38

Exchanges:
Milk: 0.0
Vegetable: 2.0
Fruit: 0.0
Bread: 2.0
Meat: 2.0
Fat: 0.0

1. Soak rice noodles in cold water to cover in bowl 10 minutes; drain. Combine noodles, beef, asparagus, and stir-fry vegetables in 2½-quart casserole. Whisk beef broth and remaining ingredients and pour over casserole. Bake, covered, at 350 degrees until beef is tender, about 45 minutes.

CHILIQUILES

Leftovers, Mexican style! Chiliquiles is a family-style casserole dish usually made with stale tortillas and leftover cooked meats. Vary this casserole with ingredients you have on hand!

8 entrée servings

8 corn or flour tortillas (6-inch)

Vegetable cooking spray

1 medium green bell pepper, thinly sliced

½–1 teaspoon minced jalapeno chili

Enchilada Sauce (see p. 439)

1 can (15 ounces) black beans, rinsed, drained

½ cup whole-kernel corn

16 ounces cooked chicken breast, shredded

1 large tomato, thinly sliced

1–1½ cups (4–6 ounces) shredded reduced-fat
    Cheddar cheese

Medium or hot salsa

Per Serving:
Calories: 242
% of calories from fat: 20
Fat (gm): 5.7
Saturated fat (gm): 2.4
Cholesterol (mg): 53.7
Sodium (mg): 372
Protein (gm): 24.6
Carbohydrate (gm): 26.1

Exchanges:
Milk: 0.0
Vegetable: 0.0
Fruit: 0.0
Bread: 2.0
Meat: 2.0
Fat: 0.0

1. Spray both sides of tortillas lightly with cooking spray; cook in small skillet over medium-high heat until lightly browned, 30 to 60 seconds per side. Cool slightly; cut into ½-inch strips. Sauté bell pepper and jalapeno chili in lightly greased medium skillet 2 to 3 minutes; stir in Enchilada Sauce and cook until hot.

2. Arrange ⅓ of the tortilla strips in bottom of 2-quart casserole; top with ⅓ each of the black beans, corn, chicken, tomato slices, cheese, and Enchilada Sauce mixture. Repeat layers 2 times. Bake, uncovered, at 350 degrees until hot, about 30 minutes, sprinkling with cheese during last 10 minute of baking time. Serve hot with salsa.

ENCHILADA STACK

A Mexican fiesta of flavors!

4 entrée servings

12 ounces boneless pork tenderloin, cubed (1-inch)
½ cup each: chopped onion, tomato
1 can (15 ounces) pinto beans, rinsed, drained
1 can (4 ounces) chopped green chilies, drained
1½ teaspoons ground cumin
¼ teaspoon pepper
5 corn tortillas
Enchilada Sauce (recipe follows)
½ cup each: shredded reduced-fat Cheddar cheese
(2 ounces), fat-free sour cream

Per Serving:
Calories: 379
% of calories from fat: 16
Fat (gm): 7.2
Saturated fat (gm): 2.2
Cholesterol (mg): 56.7
Sodium (mg): 793
Protein (gm): 33.1
Carbohydrate (gm): 49.4

Exchanges:
Milk: 0.0
Vegetable: 2.0
Fruit: 0.0
Bread: 2.5
Meat: 2.5
Fat: 0.0

1. Cook pork in 2 inches simmering water in medium saucepan, covered, until cooked, about 10 minutes; drain. Shred finely. Sauté onion in lightly greased medium skillet until tender, 3 to 4 minutes. Add shredded pork, tomato, beans, chilies, cumin, and pepper; cook over medium heat until hot, 3 to 4 minutes.

2. Place 1 tortilla in bottom of 1-quart soufflé dish or casserole; top with ¼ of the pork mixture and ½ cup Enchilada Sauce. Repeat layers three times; sprinkle with cheese. Bake, covered, at 350 degrees until hot, 25 to 30 minutes; let stand 5 minutes. Cut into 4 wedges; serve with sour cream.

Enchilada Sauce

Makes about 2 cups

1 ancho chili, stem, seeds, and veins discarded
1½ cups chopped tomato
¾ cup each: chopped red bell pepper, onion
2 cloves garlic, minced
½ teaspoon dried marjoram leaves
⅛ teaspoon ground allspice
1 bay leaf
Salt, to taste

1. Cover ancho chili with boiling water in small bowl; let stand until softened, 10 to 15 minutes; drain. Process all ingredients, except bay leaf and salt in food processor or blender until almost smooth. Simmer sauce and bay leaf in greased small skillet until thickened to a medium sauce consistency; discard bay leaf and season with salt.

TAMALE PIE

Enjoy the flavor and goodness of tamales the easy way with this delicious casserole.

4 entrée servings

1 pound lean ground beef

1 medium onion, chopped

1 clove garlic, minced

1 can (15 ounces) reduced-sodium tomato sauce

1 can (4 ounces) diced green chilies, drained

1 cup each: whole kernel corn, shredded fat-free Cheddar cheese (4 ounces)

2 teaspoons each: chili powder, ground cumin

2 cups water

1 cup yellow cornmeal

3–4 drops hot pepper sauce

Per Serving:
Calories: 493
% of calories from fat: 28
Fat (gm): 15.5
Saturated fat (gm): 5.7
Cholesterol (mg): 70.4
Sodium (mg): 423
Protein (gm): 37.3
Carbohydrate (gm): 52.6

Exchanges:
Milk: 0.0
Vegetable: 3.0
Fruit: 0.0
Bread: 3.0
Meat: 3.0
Fat: 1.0

1. Sauté ground beef, onion, and garlic in large skillet until beef is browned, about 8 minutes; stir in remaining ingredients, except water, cornmeal, and hot pepper sauce. Spread mixture on bottom of greased 2-quart baking dish.

2. Heat water to boiling in large saucepan; gradually stir in cornmeal; Reduce heat and simmer until thickened, about 5 minutes, stirring frequently. Stir in hot pepper sauce; pour over meat mixture in casserole. Bake, uncovered, at 375 degrees until hot and browned, about 20 minutes.

TORTA RUSTICA

An Italian pizza in a deep-dish pie.

8 entrée servings

1½ cups chopped onions

1½ teaspoons minced roasted garlic

8 ounces Italian-style turkey sausage, casing removed

1 can (16 ounces) reduced-sodium diced tomatoes, undrained

3 cups each: sliced zucchini, mushrooms

Salt and pepper, to taste

1 package (16 ounces) hot roll mix

1 cup very hot water (120 degrees)

1 egg

1–1½ cups (4–6 ounces) shredded reduced-fat mozzarella cheese

2 tablespoons fat-free milk

Per Serving:
Calories: 457
% of calories from fat: 23
Fat (gm): 11.5
Saturated fat (gm): 4.2
Cholesterol (mg): 65.8
Sodium (mg): 760
Protein (gm): 23.5
Carbohydrate (gm): 63.7

Exchanges:
Milk: 0.0
Vegetable: 1.0
Fruit: 0.0
Bread: 4.0
Meat: 2.0
Fat: 1.0

1. Sauté onions, garlic, and sausage in lightly greased large skillet until sausage is browned, about 5 minutes; stir in tomatoes with liquid, zucchini, and mushrooms; heat to boiling. Reduce heat and simmer, covered, 5 minutes. Simmer, uncovered, until sauce is thickened, about 10 minutes. Season to taste with salt and pepper.

2. Make hot roll mix according to package directions, using hot water and egg. Roll ⅔ of the dough on floured surface to fit 2-quart casserole or soufflé dish. Ease dough into casserole, allowing dough to extend 1 inch over edge. Spoon half the vegetable mixture into casserole; sprinkle with half the cheese. Top with remaining vegetable mixture and cheese.

3. Roll remaining dough into circle to fit top of casserole. Bring outside edges of dough together and crimp. Cut 1 or 2 slits in top of dough with sharp knife. Brush top of dough with milk. Bake at 400 degrees until crust is browned, about 30 minutes. Let stand 10 minutes before serving.

MACARONI CASSEROLE

All the flavors of lasagne, but made with macaroni. The casserole can also be cooked in the microwave; cook covered, on high power for about 10 minutes or until bubbly.

6 entrée servings

1 carton (15 ounces) reduced-fat ricotta cheese

2 cups (8 ounces) shredded reduced-fat mozzarella, divided

½ cup (2 ounces) grated Parmesan cheese, divided

2 cans (15 ounces each) reduced-sodium tomato sauce

1 bag (16 ounces) frozen stir-fry pepper blend, slightly thawed

1 teaspoon minced garlic

1 tablespoon dried Italian seasoning

Salt and pepper, to taste

10 ounces macaroni, cooked

Per Serving:
Calories: 467
% of calories from fat: 25
Fat (gm): 12.8
Saturated fat (gm): 7.4
Cholesterol (mg): 41.4
Sodium (mg): 641
Protein (gm): 32.9
Carbohydrate (gm): 55

Exchanges:
Milk: 0.0
Vegetable: 3.0
Fruit: 0.0
Bread: 3.0
Meat: 2.0
Fat: 1.5

1. Combine ricotta cheese, 1½ cups mozzarella cheese and ¼ cup Parmesan cheese in bowl. Combine tomato sauce, pepper blend, garlic, and Italian seasoning; season to taste with salt and pepper. Spoon ½ of the macaroni into a 3-quart casserole; spoon half the cheese mixture over macaroni and top with ½ of the sauce mixture. Repeat layers. Bake, uncovered, at 375 degrees until hot and bubbly, about 30 minutes, sprinkling top of casserole with remaining ¼ cup Parmesan and ¼ cup mozzarella cheese during last 10 minutes of baking time.

45-MINUTE PREPARATION TIP: Begin cooking macaroni before preparing the rest of the recipe.

SPAGHETTI AND EGGPLANT PARMESAN

Baked in a springform pan, the presentation of this dish is unusual and very attractive.

8 entrée servings

1 large eggplant (about 3 pounds), unpeeled, sliced (¼ inch)

1 tablespoon olive oil

1 small onion, finely chopped

3 cloves garlic, minced

2 cans (8 ounces each) reduced-sodium tomato sauce

8 medium plum tomatoes, chopped

⅛ teaspoon crushed red pepper

3 tablespoons finely chopped fresh or 2 teaspoons dried basil leaves

Salt, to taste

12 ounces spaghetti, cooked

¼ cup (1 ounce) grated Parmesan cheese

¼ cup unseasoned dry bread crumbs

Per Serving:
Calories: 279
% of calories from fat: 13
Fat (gm): 4.1
Saturated fat (gm): 1.1
Cholesterol (mg): 2.5
Sodium (mg): 104
Protein (gm): 10.1
Carbohydrate (gm): 52.5

Exchanges:
Milk: 0.0
Vegetable: 2.0
Fruit: 0.0
Bread: 2.5
Meat: 0.0
Fat: 1.0

1. Cook eggplant slices in oil large skillet until browned, 3 to 4 minutes on each side; remove from skillet. Add onion and garlic to skillet; sauté until tender, 3 to 5 minutes. Add tomato sauce, tomatoes, red pepper, and basil; heat to boiling. Reduce heat and simmer, uncovered, until mixture is medium sauce consistency, about 15 minutes. Season to taste with salt. Toss sauce with spaghetti and Parmesan cheese.

2. Coat greased 9-inch springform pan with bread crumbs. Line bottom and side of pan with ¾ of the eggplant slices, overlapping slices and allowing those on sides to extend 1 to 1½ inches above top of pan. Spoon spaghetti mixture into pan, pressing firmly. Fold eggplant slices at top of pan over spaghetti mixture. Overlap remaining eggplant slices on top, pressing firmly into place. Bake, uncovered, until hot, about 30 minutes. Let stand 10 minutes; loosen side of pan with sharp knife and remove side of pan. Cut into wedges.

BAKED FUSILLI AND CHEESE PRIMAVERA

Asparagus spears, broccoli florets, sliced zucchini, carrots, and mushrooms are other vegetable choices for this cheesy casserole.

6 entrée servings

1 cup sliced cremini or white mushrooms
¾ cup each: chopped onion, red or green bell pepper
1 teaspoon minced garlic
2 tablespoons margarine or butter
3 cups fat-free milk
⅓ cup all-purpose flour
3 ounces light pasteurized processed cheese, cubed
½ cup (2 ounces) shredded reduced-fat sharp Cheddar cheese
1 teaspoon Dijon mustard
10 ounces fusilli or rotini, cooked
¾ cup frozen peas
Salt and pepper, to taste
2 tablespoons unseasoned dry bread crumbs

Per Serving:
Calories: 369
% of calories from fat: 19
Fat (gm): 7.9
Saturated fat (gm): 2.9
Cholesterol (mg): 14
Sodium (mg): 231
Protein (gm): 19.6
Carbohydrate (gm): 54.1

Exchanges:
Milk: 0.0
Vegetable: 2.0
Fruit: 0.0
Bread: 3.0
Meat: 1.0
Fat: 1.0

1. Sauté mushrooms, onion, bell pepper, and garlic in margarine in large saucepan until tender, 5 to 8 minutes. Stir in combined milk and flour and heat to boiling; boil, stirring until thickened, about 1 minute. Reduce heat to low; add cheeses and mustard, stirring until melted. Combine sauce, fusilli, and peas in 2-quart casserole; season to taste with salt and pepper and sprinkle with bread crumbs. Bake, uncovered, at 375 degrees until hot, 20 to 25 minutes.

VEGETARIAN TETRAZZINI

45

Any combination of vegetables or pasta can be used in this versatile dish.

8 entrée servings

8 ounces mushrooms, sliced

1 cup each: sliced zucchini, red bell pepper, broccoli florets

½ cup chopped onion

1–2 tablespoons margarine or butter

1¾ cups reduced-sodium vegetable broth

1 cup fat-free milk

½ cup dry white wine or fat-free milk

2 tablespoons flour

1 pound thin or regular spaghetti, cooked

¼ cup (1 ounce) grated Parmesan cheese

¼ teaspoon each ground nutmeg, salt and pepper

Per Serving:
Calories: 344
% of calories from fat: 11
Fat (gm): 4.1
Saturated fat (gm): 1.2
Cholesterol (mg): 3
Sodium (mg): 176
Protein (gm): 12.9
Carbohydrate (gm): 60.3

Exchanges:
Milk: 0.0
Vegetable: 2.0
Fruit: 0.0
Bread: 3.5
Meat: 0.0
Fat: 1.0

1. Sauté vegetables in margarine in large saucepan until tender, 8 to 10 minutes. Add broth and milk and heat to boiling. Stir in combined wine and flour; boil, stirring until thickened, about 1 minute (sauce will be very thin). Mix with remaining ingredients in 2-quart casserole or baking dish. Bake, uncovered, at 350 degrees until hot and lightly browned, 30 to 40 minutes.

FETTUCCINE FLORENTINE TIMBALE

45

An impressive side dish for entertaining or special family meals. The casserole can be assembled several hours in advance and refrigerated.

10 side-dish servings

3 tablespoons unseasoned dry bread crumbs

1 package (1.8 ounces) white sauce mix

2¼ cups fat-free milk

1½ cups (6 ounces) shredded reduced-fat Italian 6-cheese blend, divided

12 ounces spinach fettuccine, cooked

1 package (10 ounces) frozen chopped spinach, thawed, well drained

1 cup fat-free cottage cheese

½ cup roasted red peppers, drained

1. Coat side and bottom of greased 9-inch spring-form pan with bread crumbs. Make white sauce mix in large saucepan according to package directions, using milk; stir in ½ cup shredded cheese and fettuccine; spoon ½ the mixture into prepared pan. Top with combined spinach, ½ cup shredded cheese and cottage cheese; top with red peppers and remaining pasta mixture. Bake, uncovered, at 350 degrees until golden, 55 to 60 minutes, sprinkling with remaining ½ cup shredded cheese during last 10 minutes of baking time. Let stand 10 minutes; loosen side of pan with sharp knife and remove. Cut into wedges.

Per Serving:
Calories: 190
% of calories from fat: 14
Fat (gm): 2.9
Saturated fat (gm): 1.2
Cholesterol (mg): 43.1
Sodium (mg): 399
Protein (gm): 14.4
Carbohydrate (gm): 26.4

Exchanges:
Milk: 0.0
Vegetable: 1.0
Fruit: 0.0
Bread: 1.5
Meat: 1.0
Fat: 0.0

CHICKEN-STUFFED SHELLS WITH WHITE SAUCE

Fennel, rosemary, and nutmeg are delicious flavor accents in the filling.

6 entrée servings

1 pound boneless, skinless chicken breast, cubed (1-inch)
1 cup fat-free milk
1 egg white
3 cloves garlic, minced
1½–2 tablespoons fennel seeds, crushed
1 teaspoon dried rosemary leaves
¼ teaspoon each: ground nutmeg, salt, pepper
3–4 dashes hot pepper sauce
30 jumbo shells (9 ounces), cooked al dente
White Sauce (recipe follows)

Per Serving:
Calories: 321
% of calories from fat: 18
Fat (gm): 6.5
Saturated fat (gm): 2
Cholesterol (mg): 43.8
Sodium (mg): 302
Protein (gm): 27
Carbohydrate (gm): 37.4

Exchanges:
Milk: 0.5
Vegetable: 0.0
Fruit: 0.0
Bread: 2.0
Meat: 2.5
Fat: 0.0

1. Process chicken breast in the food processor until very finely chopped. Add remaining ingredients, except pasta, and White Sauce; process just until blended. Spoon mixture into shells and arrange in greased baking dish; spoon White Sauce over shells. Bake, loosely covered, at 350 degrees until chicken filling is cooked, 30 to 35 minutes.

White Sauce

Makes about 2 cups

1 tablespoon margarine or butter
2 tablespoons flour
2 cups fat-free milk
¼ cup (1 ounce) grated Parmesan cheese
⅛ teaspoon ground white pepper

1. Melt margarine in medium saucepan; stir in flour. Cook over medium heat, stirring constantly, 1 to 2 minutes. Whisk in milk and heat to boiling; boil, whisking until thickened, about 1 minute (sauce will be very thin). Remove from heat; stir in cheese and pepper.

CHICKEN-VEGETABLE MANICOTTI WITH CREAMED SPINACH SAUCE

Tomato Sauce with Mushrooms and Sherry (see p. 449) is also an excellent accompaniment for the manicotti.

6 entrée servings

½ cup chopped onion
3 cloves garlic, minced
2 cups loosely packed chopped spinach leaves
½ cup each: chopped zucchini, yellow summer squash
1 teaspoon each: dried basil and oregano leaves
8 ounces boneless, skinless chicken, cooked, finely shredded
¾ cup fat-free ricotta cheese
Salt and pepper, to taste
1 package (8 ounces) manicotti shells, cooked al dente
Creamed Spinach Sauce (recipe follows)

Per Serving:
Calories: 340
% of calories from fat: 24
Fat (gm): 2.7
Saturated fat (gm): 2.5
Cholesterol (mg): 31
Sodium (mg): 427
Protein (gm): 23
Carbohydrate (gm): 435

Exchanges:
Milk: 0.5
Vegetable: 2.0
Fruit: 0.0
Bread: 2.0
Meat: 1.0
Fat: 1.5

1. Sauté onion and garlic in lightly greased large skillet until tender, about 3 minutes. Add vegetables and herbs; sauté until tender, 5 to 8 minutes. Stir in chicken and cheese; season to taste with salt and pepper. Spoon about 3 tablespoons mixture into each manicotti;

arrange in baking pan and spoon Creamed Spinach Sauce over. Bake at 350 degrees, loosely covered, until manicotti are hot and sauce is bubbly, 35 to 40 minutes.

Creamed Spinach Sauce
Makes about 3 cups

2 cloves garlic, minced
2 tablespoons margarine or butter
¼ cup all-purpose flour
3 cups 2% reduced-fat milk
1½ pounds fresh spinach, chopped
2 teaspoons dried basil leaves
¼ teaspoon ground nutmeg
4–6 dashes hot pepper sauce
Salt, to taste

1. Sauté garlic in margarine in large saucepan 1 to 2 minutes. Stir in flour and cook over medium heat 1 minute. Whisk in milk; heat to boiling, whisking until thickened, about 1 minute. Stir in remaining ingredients, except salt; cook over medium heat until spinach is cooked, 5 to 7 minutes. Season to taste with salt.

MUSHROOM-BROCCOLI MANICOTTI

Any pasta that's going to be filled and baked should be cooked just until al dente so the baked pasta is not overcooked.

6 entrée servings

4 shallots or green onions, chopped
2 cloves garlic, minced
1½ teaspoons each: dried basil and marjoram leaves
2 cups each: sliced mushrooms, chopped
  cooked broccoli
1 cup reduced-fat ricotta cheese
¼ teaspoon each: salt, pepper
1 package (8 ounces) manicotti, cooked al dente
Tomato Sauce with Mushrooms and Sherry
  (recipe follows)

Per Serving:
Calories: 263
% of calories from fat: 17
Fat (gm): 5.2
Saturated fat (gm): 0.5
Cholesterol (mg): 5.3
Sodium (mg): 443
Protein (gm): 12.8
Carbohydrate (gm): 42.3

Exchanges:
Milk: 0.0
Vegetable: 2.5
Fruit: 0.0
Bread: 2.0
Meat: 0.0
Fat: 1.0

1. Cook shallots, garlic, herbs, and mushrooms in lightly greased large skillet over medium heat, covered, until mushrooms release juices, 3 to 5 minutes. Cook, uncovered, over medium to medium-high heat, until liquid is gone, about 10 minutes. Stir in broccoli, cheese, salt, and pepper.

2. Spoon about 3 tablespoons vegetable-cheese mixture into each manicotti; arrange in baking pan and spoon Tomato Sauce with Mushrooms and Sherry over. Bake at 350 degrees, loosely covered, until manicotti are hot and sauce is bubbly, 30 to 35 minutes.

Tomato Sauce with Mushrooms and Sherry
Makes about 3 cups

1 small onion, finely chopped
2 cloves garlic, minced
1 tablespoon olive oil
4 cups sliced mushrooms
3 tablespoons dry sherry or water
1 can (28 ounces) crushed tomatoes, undrained
½ teaspoon each: dried rosemary and oregano leaves
1 teaspoon sugar
¼ teaspoon each: salt, pepper

1. Sauté onion and garlic in oil in medium saucepan 2 to 3 minutes. Add mushrooms and sherry; cook, covered, over medium-high heat until mushrooms are wilted and release liquid, about 5 minutes. Cook, uncovered, over medium heat, stirring occasionally, until mushrooms are browned, 10 to 15 minutes. Stir in remaining ingredients; heat to boiling. Reduce heat and simmer, covered, 10 to 15 minutes.

SPINACH TORTELLINI WITH MUSHROOMS

Try a flavored spaghetti sauce, such as roasted garlic, garden vegetable, or olive.

6 entrée servings

2 packages (9 ounces each) fresh spinach tortellini
8 ounces small whole mushrooms
1 cup each: chopped red bell pepper, frozen peas
¾ cup (3 ounces) shredded reduced-fat mozzarella cheese
1 jar (28 ounces) prepared spaghetti sauce

1. Combine all ingredients in 2½-quart casserole. Bake, covered, at 350 degrees until hot, about 30 minutes.

Per Serving:
Calories: 260
% of calories from fat: 30
Fat (gm): 8.7
Saturated fat (gm): 2.3
Cholesterol (mg): 4.2
Sodium (mg): 390
Protein (gm): 12.6
Carbohydrate (gm): 33.6

Exchanges:
Milk: 0.0
Vegetable: 0.0
Fruit: 0.0
Bread: 2.0
Meat: 1.0
Fat: 1.0

VEGGIE LASAGNE WITH EGGPLANT SAUCE

The hearty Eggplant Sauce is also delicious served over shaped pasta or any flavor tortellini.

8 entrée servings

1 cup each: sliced onion, zucchini, red bell pepper, mushrooms
3 cloves garlic, minced
2 cups fat-free ricotta cheese
¼ cup (1 ounce) grated Parmesan cheese
Eggplant Sauce (recipe follows)
12 lasagne noodles (10 ounces), cooked
2 medium sweet potatoes, cooked, sliced
2 cups (8 ounces) shredded reduced-fat mozzarella cheese, divided

Per Serving:
Calories: 375
% of calories from fat: 24
Fat (gm): 10.4
Saturated fat (gm): 4.2
Cholesterol (mg): 2.3
Sodium (mg): 685
Protein (gm): 2.4
Carbohydrate (gm): 47

Exchanges:
Milk: 0.0
Vegetable: 3.0
Fruit: 0.0
Bread: 2.0
Meat: 2.5
Fat: 0.5

1. Sauté onion, zucchini, bell pepper, mushrooms, and garlic in lightly greased large skillet until tender, about 10 minutes. Mix ricotta and Parmesan cheese. Spread about ½ cup Eggplant Sauce in bottom of 13 x 9-inch baking pan; top with 4 lasagne noodles, overlapping slightly. Top with ⅓ each ricotta cheese mixture, sweet potatoes, sautéed vegetables, and Eggplant Sauce; sprinkle with ⅓ of the mozzarella cheese. Repeat layers 2 times. Bake, loosely covered, at 350 degrees until sauce is bubbly, about 1 hour. Let stand 10 minutes before cutting.

Eggplant Sauce
Makes about 6 cups

1 pound eggplant, unpeeled, cubed (1-inch)
1 cup chopped onion
½ cup chopped green bell pepper
6 cloves garlic, minced
2 tablespoons olive oil
3 cups chopped tomatoes
1 can (28 ounces) crushed tomatoes, undrained
½ cup dry red wine or water
2 tablespoons drained capers
1 teaspoon each: dried tarragon and thyme leaves
2 teaspoons sugar
½ teaspoon each: salt, pepper

1. Sauté eggplant, onion, bell pepper, and garlic in oil in large saucepan until onion is tender, about 5 minutes. Add remaining ingredients and heat to boiling. Reduce heat and simmer, covered, until eggplant is tender, about 15 minutes. Simmer, uncovered, until desired sauce consistency, about 10 minutes more.

SAUSAGE LASAGNE

A low-fat rendering of the traditional lasagne we all love.

8 entrée servings

2 cups fat-free ricotta cheese

¼ cup (1 ounce) grated Parmesan cheese

3 cups (12 ounces) shredded reduced-fat
mozzarella cheese

Tomato Sauce with Italian Sausage (recipe follows)

12 lasagne noodles (10 ounces), cooked

Per Serving:
Calories: 375
% of calories from fat: 30
Fat (gm): 12.9
Saturated fat (gm): 6
Cholesterol (mg): 47.3
Sodium (mg): 679
Protein (gm): 31.3
Carbohydrate (gm): 33.9

Exchanges:
Milk: 0.0
Vegetable: 2.5
Fruit: 0.0
Bread: 1.5
Meat: 3.5
Fat: 0.5

1. Combine cheeses in bowl. Spread 1 cup sauce on bottom of 13 x 9-inch baking pan; top with 4 lasagne noodles, overlapping slightly. Spoon ⅓ of cheese mixture over noodles, spreading lightly with rubber spatula. Top with 1 cup sauce. Repeat layers 2 times. Bake, loosely covered, at 350 degrees until sauce is bubbly, about 1 hour. Let stand 10 minutes before cutting.

Tomato Sauce with Italian Sausage

Makes about 4 cups

8 ounces Italian-style turkey sausage, casing removed, crumbled

2 cups chopped onions

3 cloves garlic, minced

1 teaspoon each: dried basil, tarragon and thyme leaves

2 cans (16 ounces each) reduced-sodium whole tomatoes,
undrained, coarsely chopped

2 cans (8 ounces each) reduced-sodium tomato sauce

1 cup water

1–2 teaspoons sugar

¼ teaspoon each: salt, pepper

1. Sauté sausage, onions, garlic, and herbs in lightly greased large saucepan until lightly browned, about 5 minutes; add remaining ingredients; heat to boiling. Reduce heat and simmer, uncovered, until sauce is reduced to about 4½ cups, 15 to 20 minutes.

MEXICAN-STYLE LASAGNE

A lasagne with a difference!

8 entrée servings

Chili-Tomato Sauce (recipe follows)

12 lasagne noodles (10 ounces), cooked

2 cups (8 ounces) each: fat-free ricotta cheese, shredded reduced-fat Monterey Jack cheese

1 can (15 ounces) each: pinto beans, black beans, drained

Per Serving:
Calories: 360
% of calories from fat: 18
Fat (gm): 8
Saturated fat (gm): 3.1
Cholesterol (mg): 26.3
Sodium (mg): 748
Protein (gm): 30.7
Carbohydrate (gm): 51

Exchanges:
Milk: 0.0
Vegetable: 3.0
Fruit: 0.0
Bread: 2.0
Meat: 2.5
Fat: 0.5

1. Spread 1 cup sauce on bottom of a 13 x 9-inch baking pan; top with 4 lasagne noodles, overlapping slightly. Spoon ⅓ of the combined cheeses over noodles, spreading lightly with rubber spatula; top with ⅓ of the combined beans and 1⅓ cups Chili-Tomato Sauce. Repeat layers 2 times. Bake at 350 degrees, loosely covered, until hot and bubbly, about 1 hour. Let stand 10 minutes before cutting.

Chili-Tomato Sauce

Makes about 5 cups

2 cups chopped onions

2–3 teaspoons each: minced garlic, jalapeño chili

2 cans (14½ ounces each) low-sodium stewed tomatoes

2 cans (8 ounces each) low-sodium tomato sauce

2 tablespoons chili powder

2 teaspoons ground cumin

1 teaspoon dried oregano leaves

Salt, to taste

1. Sauté onions, garlic, and jalapeño chili in lightly greased large skillet until onions are tender, 5 to 8 minutes. Stir in remaining ingredients, except salt; heat to boiling. Reduce heat and simmer, uncovered, until sauce is reduced to 5 cups, about 20 minutes. Season to taste with salt.

SPINACH-MUSHROOM ROTOLO WITH MARINARA SAUCE

No-boil lasagne noodles can be used in this recipe. Soak them in warm water until softened, about 8 minutes, before using.

6 entrée servings

2 cups sliced mushrooms

1 package (10 ounces) fresh spinach, cleaned, chopped

2 cloves garlic, minced

1 teaspoon each: dried basil and tarragon leaves

½ package (8-ounce size) reduced-fat cream cheese, room temperature

½ cup fat-free ricotta cheese

¼ teaspoon each: salt, pepper

12 lasagne noodles, cooked, room temperature

Marinara Sauce (recipe follows)

Per Serving:
Calories: 286
% of calories from fat: 30
Fat (gm): 10.3
Saturated fat (gm): 2.7
Cholesterol (mg): 8.7
Sodium (mg): 686
Protein (gm): 12.5
Carbohydrate (gm): 38

Exchanges:
Milk: 0.0
Vegetable: 3.0
Fruit: 0.0
Bread: 1.5
Meat: 0.0
Fat: 2.0

1. Cook mushrooms, spinach, garlic, and herbs in lightly greased large skillet, covered, over medium heat until mushrooms release juices, about 5 minutes. Cook, uncovered, over medium-high heat until liquid is gone, about 5 minutes; cool. Remove from heat; stir in cheeses, salt, and pepper.

2. Spread 3 to 4 tablespoons mixture on each noodle; roll up and place, seam side down, in baking dish. Spoon Marinara Sauce over rotolo. Bake, loosely covered, at 350 degrees until rotolo are hot and sauce bubbly, 20 to 30 minutes.

Marinara Sauce

Makes about 4 cups

2 medium onions, chopped

6–8 cloves garlic, minced

2 tablespoons olive oil

2 cans (16 ounces each) plum tomatoes, drained, chopped

½ cup dry white wine or tomato juice

¼ cup tomato paste

2–3 tablespoons lemon juice

½ teaspoon salt

¼ teaspoon pepper

1. Sauté onions and garlic in oil in large saucepan until tender, about 5 minutes. Stir in tomatoes, wine, and tomato paste; heat to boiling. Reduce heat and simmer, uncovered, until a medium sauce consistency, about 20 minutes. Stir in lemon juice, salt, and pepper.

EASY EGGPLANT ROTOLO

45

Incredibly simple to prepare, thanks to no-boil lasagne noodles!

4 entrée servings

8 no-boil lasagne noodles

4 cups frozen stir-fry pepper blend

2 teaspoons minced garlic

1 tablespoon olive oil

1 small eggplant (about 1 pound), unpeeled, cubed

1–2 teaspoons dried Italian seasoning

2 cups fat-free ricotta cheese

Salt and pepper, to taste

2 cans (16 ounces each) reduced-sodium spaghetti sauce

¼ cup (1 ounce) grated Parmesan cheese

Per Serving:
Calories: 512
% of calories from fat: 29
Fat (gm): 16.3
Saturated fat (gm): 3.8
Cholesterol (mg): 11.4
Sodium (mg): 370
Protein (gm): 28.8
Carbohydrate (gm): 60.8

Exchanges:
Milk: 0.0
Vegetable: 3.0
Fruit: 0.0
Bread: 3.0
Meat: 2.0
Fat: 2.0

1. Arrange noodles in shallow baking dish or pan and cover with warm water; let stand until noodles are softened, about 8 minutes. Drain well.

2. Sauté pepper blend and garlic in oil in large skillet 3 to 4 minutes. Add eggplant and Italian seasoning and cook, covered, until eggplant is tender, about 10 minutes, stirring occasionally. Remove from heat and stir in ricotta cheese; season to taste with salt and pepper.

3. Spread ½ cup cheese mixture on each noodle and roll up. Arrange rotolo, seam sides down, in 13 x 9-inch baking pan. Spoon spaghetti sauce over and sprinkle with Parmesan cheese. Bake, loosely covered at 350 degrees until rotolo are hot and sauce bubbly, about 20 minutes.

CHICKEN AND CHEESE ROTOLO WITH MANY-CLOVES GARLIC SAUCE

Some people prefer cutting lasagne noodles into halves before filling, as they are easier to handle in eating. If cut, spread each noodle half with 1½ to 2 tablespoons cheese mixture.

6 entrée servings

1 pound boneless, skinless chicken breast, cooked, shredded

1¼ cups reduced-fat ricotta cheese

3–4 cloves garlic, minced

½ teaspoon each: dried marjoram and thyme leaves, salt

¼ teaspoon pepper

12 lasagne noodles (10 ounces), cooked, room temperature

Many-Cloves Garlic Sauce (see p. 17)

Per Serving:
Calories: 295
% of calories from fat: 28
Fat (gm): 9.4
Saturated fat (gm): 1.1
Cholesterol (mg): 45.1
Sodium (mg): 315
Protein (gm): 23.3
Carbohydrate (gm): 28.1

Exchanges:
Milk: 0.0
Vegetable: 1.0
Fruit: 0.0
Bread: 1.5
Meat: 2.5
Fat: 0.5

1. Mix chicken, cheese, garlic, herbs, salt, and pepper. Spread 3 to 4 tablespoons mixture evenly on each noodle; roll up and place, seam sides down, in baking dish. Spoon Many-Cloves Garlic Sauce over rotolo. Bake, loosely covered, at 350 degrees until rotolo are hot and sauce bubbly, 20 to 30 minutes.

CHICKEN AND NOODLES

45

A comfort food you may remember as a kid. It's still delicious!

4 entrée servings

3 tablespoons margarine or butter

¼ cup all-purpose flour

¼ teaspoon each: dried sage and marjoram leaves

2 cups reduced-sodium chicken broth

1 package (10 ounces) frozen mixed vegetables

1 pound boneless, skinless chicken breast, cubed

8 ounces thin egg noodles, cooked

3 tablespoons diced pimientos

Per Serving:
Calories: 507
% of calories from fat: 25
Fat (gm): 13.9
Saturated fat (gm): 3
Cholesterol (mg): 118.2
Sodium (mg): 273
Protein (gm): 38.6
Carbohydrate (gm): 55.5

Exchanges:
Milk: 0.0
Vegetable: 3.0
Fruit: 0.0
Bread: 3.0
Meat: 3.0
Fat: 1.0

¼ teaspoon black pepper

¼ cup unseasoned dry bread crumbs

1. Melt margarine in large saucepan over medium heat; whisk in flour and herbs; cook 1 minute. Whisk in broth and heat to boiling, whisking until thickened, about 1 minute. Combine with remaining ingredients, except bread crumbs, in 2-quart casserole; sprinkle with bread crumbs. Bake, uncovered, at 350 degrees until hot and browned, about 30 minutes.

CAPER CHICKEN WITH TOMATO-BASIL LINGUINE

If you cannot find tomato-basil linguine, any other flavor or plain linguine can be used.

4 entrée servings

8 ounces uncooked tomato-basil linguine

1 pound boneless, skinless chicken breast, cut into strips (1 x ½-inch)

8 ounces mushrooms, sliced

1 package (10 ounces) frozen cut broccoli, thawed

1 can (8 ounces) sliced water chestnuts, drained

1 can (13¾ ounces) reduced-sodium fat-free chicken broth

2 tablespoons cornstarch

3 tablespoons lemon juice

¼ cup diced pimientos

2 tablespoons drained capers

Salt and pepper, to taste

Per Serving:
Calories: 382
% of calories from fat: 11
Fat (gm): 4.7
Saturated fat (gm): 0.9
Cholesterol (mg): 69
Sodium (mg): 415
Protein (gm): 37.3
Carbohydrate (gm): 49.8

Exchanges:
Milk: 0.0
Vegetable: 1.0
Fruit: 0.0
Bread: 3.0
Meat: 3.0
Fat: 0.0

1. Arrange linguine in greased 12 x 8-inch baking dish; top with chicken and combined vegetables. Combine broth and cornstarch in medium saucepan; heat to boiling, whisking until thickened, about 1 minute. Stir in lemon juice, pimientos, and capers; season to taste with salt and pepper and pour over casserole. Bake, covered, at 350 degrees until linguine and chicken are cooked, about 40 minutes.

TURKEY BOW-TIE PASTA AU GRATIN

45

The flavors of a favorite pasta salad are recreated in this cold-weather casserole.

8 entrée servings

16 ounces bow-tie pasta (farfalle), cooked

1 pound cooked turkey breast, cubed

1 package (10 ounces) frozen cut broccoli, thawed, well drained

1 rib celery, chopped

½ cup each: reduced-sodium fat-free chicken broth, fat-free sour cream

1 tablespoon dried dill weed

¼ teaspoon pepper

1 cup (4 ounces) shredded reduced-fat mozzarella cheese

¼ cup unseasoned dry bread crumbs

Per Serving:
Calories: 396
% of calories from fat: 18
Fat (gm): 7.6
Saturated fat (gm): 2.6
Cholesterol (mg): 111.8
Sodium (mg): 217
Protein (gm): 32.6
Carbohydrate (gm): 46.4

Exchanges:
Milk: 0.0
Vegetable: 2.0
Fruit: 0.0
Bread: 2.0
Meat: 3.0
Fat: 0.0

1. Toss pasta, turkey, broccoli, and celery in 2½-quart casserole; mix in combined broth, sour cream, dill, and pepper. Sprinkle with cheese and bread crumbs. Bake, covered, at 350 degrees 20 minutes; uncover and bake until hot and browned, about 15 minutes longer.

TURKEY TETRAZZINI

45

This dish was named for the famous Italian opera singer, Lucia Tetrazzini, who claimed it as her favorite.

8 entrée servings

8 ounces mushrooms, sliced

2 tablespoons each: margarine or butter, flour

1 can (14½ ounces) reduced-sodium chicken broth

1½ cups fat-free milk

16 ounces thin spaghetti, cooked

12 ounces cooked boneless, skinless turkey or chicken breast, cubed

¼ cup (1 ounce) grated Parmesan cheese

¼ teaspoon each: ground nutmeg, salt, pepper

Per Serving:
Calories: 370
% of calories from fat: 16
Fat (gm): 6.5
Saturated fat (gm): 1.7
Cholesterol (mg): 35.7
Sodium (mg): 218
Protein (gm): 23.6
Carbohydrate (gm): 50.3

Exchanges:
Milk: 0.0
Vegetable: 1.0
Fruit: 0.0
Bread: 3.0
Meat: 2.0
Fat: 0.5

1. Sauté mushrooms in margarine in large saucepan until tender, about 5 minutes. Stir in flour; cook 1 minute. Stir in chicken broth and milk and heat to boiling, stirring until thickened, about 1 minute (sauce will be very thin). Combine with remaining ingredients in 2-quart casserole or baking dish; bake, uncovered, at 350 degrees until hot and lightly browned, about 30 minutes.

ELEVEN

Vegetable Side Dishes

BRAISED WHOLE ARTICHOKES

The artichokes are cooked slowly until the bottoms are browned and crusty—the resulting flavor is marvelous!

4 servings

4 medium artichokes, stems removed
Salt
2–4 teaspoons extra-virgin olive oil

Per Serving:
Calories: 80
% of calories from fat: 24
Fat (gm): 2.4
Saturated fat (gm): 0.3
Cholesterol (mg): 0
Sodium (mg): 114
Protein (gm): 4.2
Carbohydrate (gm): 13.4

Exchanges:
Milk: 0.0
Vegetable: 2.0
Fruit: 0.0
Bread: 0.0
Meat: 0.0
Fat: 0.5

1. Cut 1 inch from tops of artichokes and discard. Place artichokes in medium saucepan and sprinkle lightly with salt; add 1 inch water to pan. Heat to boiling; reduce heat and simmer, covered, until artichokes are tender, about 30 minutes (bottom leaves will pull out easily). Drain. Holding artichokes with a towel, brush bottoms with olive oil; return to saucepan. Cook, uncovered, over medium to medium-low heat until bottoms of artichokes are deeply browned, 10 to 15 minutes.

ARTICHOKES WITH MOCK HOLLANDAISE SAUCE

45

The Mock Hollandaise Sauce is excellent served over steamed asparagus spears, broccoli, or cauliflower. Also see p. 297 for delicious Eggs Benedict.

4–6 servings

4–6 whole artichokes, stems removed
Mock Hollandaise Sauce (see p. 175)

Per Serving:
Calories: 114
% of calories from fat: 2
Fat (gm): 0.3
Saturated fat (gm): 0.1
Cholesterol (mg): 0.2
Sodium (mg): 396
Protein (gm): 11.9
Carbohydrate (gm): 17.5

Exchanges:
Milk: 0.5
Vegetable: 2.0
Fruit: 0.0
Bread: 0.0
Meat: 0.5
Fat: 0.0

1. Cut 1 inch from tops of artichokes and discard. Place artichokes in medium saucepan and sprinkle lightly with salt; add 1 inch water to pan. Heat to boiling; reduce heat and simmer, covered, until artichokes are tender, about 30 minutes (bottom leaves will pull out easily). Serve with Mock Hollandaise Sauce.

45-MINUTE PREPARATION TIP: Make Mock Hollandaise Sauce while artichokes are cooking.

ASPARAGUS WITH LEMON-WINE SAUCE

45 *This rich sauce is also delicious served with crisp-tender broccoli, cauliflower, green beans, or Brussels sprouts.*

4 servings

2 tablespoons minced shallots or green onions
¼ cup dry white wine or water
¾ cup fat-free half-and-half or milk
1 tablespoon flour
½ teaspoon each: dried thyme and marjoram leaves
1 tablespoon lemon juice
Salt and white pepper, to taste
1 pound asparagus spears, cooked crisp-tender, warm

Per Serving:
Calories: 85
% of calories from fat: 4
Fat (gm): 0.4
Saturated fat (gm): 0.1
Cholesterol (mg): 0
Sodium (mg): 59
Protein (gm): 4.8
Carbohydrate (gm): 13.4

Exchanges:
Milk: 0.0
Vegetable: 2.0
Fruit: 0.0
Bread: 0.5
Meat: 0.0
Fat: 0.0

1. Sauté shallots in lightly greased small saucepan until tender, 2 to 3 minutes. Add wine and heat to boiling; reduce heat and simmer, uncovered, until wine is evaporated, 3 to 4 minutes. Stir in combined half-and-half, flour, and herbs; heat to boiling. Boil, stirring until thickened, about 1 minute. Stir in lemon juice; season to taste with salt and pepper. Spoon over asparagus.

ASPARAGUS WITH PEANUT SAUCE

45 *Asian flavors are the perfect complement to spring's freshest asparagus— serve warm or chilled.*

6 servings

2 tablespoons reduced-fat peanut butter
¼ cup sugar
2–3 tablespoons reduced-sodium tamari soy sauce
3–4 teaspoons rice wine (sake), dry sherry, or water
1 teaspoon grated gingerroot
1½ pounds asparagus spears, cooked crisp-tender

Per Serving:
Calories: 95
% of calories from fat: 21
Fat (gm): 2.3
Saturated fat (gm): 0.5
Cholesterol (mg): 0
Sodium (mg): 246
Protein (gm): 4.8
Carbohydrate (gm): 15

Exchanges:
Milk: 0.0
Vegetable: 3.0
Fruit: 0.0
Bread: 0.0
Meat: 0.0
Fat: 0.5

1. Mix peanut butter, sugar, soy sauce, rice wine, and gingerroot until smooth. Serve with asparagus.

ASPARAGUS AND WHITE BEANS, ITALIAN-STYLE

45 *A lovely accompaniment to grilled or roasted meat, this dish will also serve 4 as a meatless main course.*

8 servings

1 pound asparagus, cut (2-inch pieces)

2 teaspoons each: minced garlic, olive oil

2 cups chopped Italian plum tomatoes

1 can (15 ounces) cannellini or Great Northern, beans, rinsed, drained

¾ cup reduced-sodium vegetable broth

1 teaspoon dried rosemary leaves

Salt and pepper, to taste

8 ounces linguine or thin spaghetti, cooked, warm

¼–½ cup (1–2 ounces) shredded Parmesan cheese

Per Serving:
Calories: 169
% of calories from fat: 16
Fat (gm): 3.1
Saturated fat (gm): 0.7
Cholesterol (mg): 2
Sodium (mg): 229
Protein (gm): 7.9
Carbohydrate (gm): 29.4

Exchanges:
Milk: 0.0
Vegetable: 1.0
Fruit: 0.0
Bread: 1.0
Meat: 0.0
Fat: 0.5

1. Sauté asparagus and garlic in oil in large skillet until crisp-tender, 3 to 4 minutes. Stir in tomatoes, beans, broth, and rosemary; cook over medium heat until hot, 2 to 3 minutes. Season to taste with salt and pepper; toss with linguine and cheese.

GREEN BEAN CASSEROLE

45

Reduced-fat cream of mushroom soup and fat-free sour cream make this old favorite possible in a healthy, low-fat form. We've used fresh green beans, but canned or frozen may be used.

6 servings

1 can (10¾ ounces) reduced-fat cream of mushroom soup

½ cup fat-free sour cream

¼ cup fat-free milk

1¼ pounds cut green beans (1½-inch), cooked crisp-tender

½ cup canned French-fried onions

Per Serving:
Calories: 81
% of calories from fat: 31
Fat (gm): 2.9
Saturated fat (gm): 0.8
Cholesterol (mg): 1.3
Sodium (mg): 172
Protein (gm): 3
Carbohydrate (gm): 11.6

Exchanges:
Milk: 0.0
Vegetable: 2.0
Fruit: 0.0
Bread: 0.0
Meat: 0.0
Fat: 0.5

1. Mix soup, sour cream, milk, and beans in 2-quart casserole. Bake, uncovered, at 350 degrees until mixture is hot, 30 to 40 minutes; sprinkle with onions during last 10 minutes of baking time.

GREEK-STYLE GREEN BEANS

45 *Fresh green beans are long simmered with tomatoes, herbs, and garlic in traditional Greek style.*

4–6 servings

½ cup chopped onion

4 cloves garlic, minced

¾ teaspoon each: dried oregano and basil leaves

1 tablespoon olive oil

1 can (28 ounces) reduced-sodium tomatoes, undrained, coarsely chopped

1 pound green beans

Salt and pepper, to taste

Per Serving:
Calories: 123
% of calories from fat: 28
Fat (gm): 4.3
Saturated fat (gm): 0.6
Cholesterol (mg): 0
Sodium (mg): 30
Protein (gm): 4.5
Carbohydrate (gm): 20.5

Exchanges:
Milk: 0.0
Vegetable: 4.0
Fruit: 0.0
Bread: 0.0
Meat: 0.0
Fat: 0.5

1. Sauté onion, garlic, and herbs in oil in large skillet until onion is tender, 3 to 4 minutes. Add tomatoes with liquid and green beans and heat to boiling; reduce heat and simmer, covered, until beans are very tender, about 30 minutes. Season to taste with salt and pepper.

ORIENTAL GREEN BEANS

45 *This dish would complement any grilled or roasted meat or poultry.*

4 servings

¼ cup each: chopped onion, red bell pepper

2 teaspoons each: finely chopped gingerroot, garlic

2 cups halved green beans

1 cup rinsed, drained canned adzuki or black beans

½ cup sliced water chestnuts

1 tablespoon rice wine vinegar

1–2 teaspoons reduced-sodium tamari soy sauce

Salt and pepper, to taste

Per Serving:
Calories: 109
% of calories from fat: 2
Fat (gm): 0.2
Saturated fat (gm): 0
Cholesterol (mg): 0
Sodium (mg): 64
Protein (gm): 5.8
Carbohydrate (gm): 22.5

Exchanges:
Milk: 0.0
Vegetable: 1.5
Fruit: 0.0
Bread: 1.0
Meat: 0.0
Fat: 0.0

1. Stir-fry onion, bell pepper, gingerroot, and garlic in lightly greased wok or large skillet 2 minutes; add green beans and stir-fry until beans are crisp-tender, 5 to 8 minutes. Add adzuki beans, water chestnuts, vinegar, and soy sauce; stir-fry until hot, about 2 minutes. Season to taste with salt and pepper.

EL PASO SUCCOTASH

45 *Delicious served over rice or with warm corn bread.*

4 servings

½ cup each: chopped onion, poblano chili or
   green bell pepper

1 teaspoon each: minced jalapeño chili, garlic,
   ground cumin

2 teaspoons chili powder

1 tablespoon each: margarine or butter, flour

1 cup fat-free milk

1 can (15 ounces) each: rinsed, drained lima beans
   and black-eyed peas,

1 cup whole-kernel corn

Salt and pepper, to taste

1 medium tomato, chopped

Per Serving:
Calories: 280
% of calories from fat: 12
Fat (gm): 3.9
Saturated fat (gm): 0.8
Cholesterol (mg): 1.2
Sodium (mg): 484
Protein (gm): 15.2
Carbohydrate (gm): 48.8

Exchanges:
Milk: 0.0
Vegetable: 0.0
Fruit: 0.0
Bread: 3.0
Meat: 1.0
Fat: 0.0

2 tablespoons chopped cilantro

2–3 teaspoons lime juice

1. Sauté onion, chilies, garlic, cumin, and chili powder in margarine in large saucepan until tender, about 5 minutes. Stir in flour and cook 1 minute. Stir in milk; heat to boiling, stirring until thickened, about 1 minute. Stir in beans, black-eyed peas, and corn; cook over medium heat 2 to 3 minutes. Season to taste with salt and pepper. Stir in remaining ingredients.

NEW ENGLAND BAKED BEANS

45

Long-baked and savory, these beans are the best! Bacon replaces the higher-fat salt pork traditionally used.

8 to 10 servings

8 ounces dried navy or Great Northern beans

4 slices diced bacon, fried crisp, drained

¾ cup chopped onion

1 clove garlic

3 tablespoons each: tomato paste, dark molasses, packed light brown sugar

½ teaspoon dry mustard, salt

¼ teaspoon dried thyme leaves

Per Serving:
Calories: 161
% of calories from fat: 11
Fat (gm): 2.1
Saturated fat (gm): 0.7
Cholesterol (mg): 2.7
Sodium (mg): 246
Protein (gm): 7.8
Carbohydrate (gm): 29.1

Exchanges:
Milk: 0.0
Vegetable: 0.0
Fruit: 0.0
Bread: 2.0
Meat: 0.0
Fat: 0.5

1. Cover beans with 2 inches of water in large saucepan; heat to boiling and boil, uncovered, 2 minutes. Remove from heat and let stand, covered, 1 hour.

2. Add more water to beans to cover, if necessary. Heat to boiling; reduce heat and simmer, covered, until beans are tender, about 1¼ hours. Drain; reserve liquid. Mix beans and remaining ingredients in 1½-quart casserole, adding enough reserved cooking liquid to cover beans. Bake, covered, at 325 degrees, stirring occasionally, 3 hours. Bake, uncovered, until beans are desired consistency, 30 to 60 minutes.

HONEY GLAZED ROASTED BEETS

45

Roasting maximizes the sweet flavor of beets.

6 servings

1½ pounds medium beets

Vegetable cooking spray

2 medium red onions, cut into wedges

¼ cup currants or raisins

3–4 tablespoons toasted walnuts

¼ cup honey

2–3 tablespoons red wine vinegar

1 tablespoon canola oil

4 cloves garlic, minced

Salt and pepper, to taste

Per Serving:
Calories: 94
% of calories from fat: 18
Fat (gm): 1.9
Saturated fat (gm): 0.4
Cholesterol (mg): 0
Sodium (mg): 70
Protein (gm): 1.1
Carbohydrate (gm): 19.3

Exchanges:
Milk: 0.0
Vegetable: 2.0
Fruit: 0.0
Bread: 0.5
Meat: 0.0
Fat: 0.0

1. Arrange beets and onions in single layer on greased foil-lined jelly roll pan; spray with cooking spray. Roast at 425 degrees until beets are tender, about 40 minutes. Peel beets and cut into 1-inch pieces. Combine beets, onions, currants, and walnuts; heat combined remaining ingredients, except salt and pepper, pour over vegetables and toss. Season to taste with salt and pepper.

HARVARD BEETS

Sweet and tart, the sauce can also be served over cooked carrots or pearl onions. Vary the amount of vinegar for the right amount of tartness.

4 servings

3 tablespoons sugar

1½ tablespoons cornstarch

¾ cup water

3–4 tablespoons cider vinegar

2 teaspoons margarine or butter

Salt and white pepper, to taste

1 pound medium beets, cooked, sliced, warm

Per Serving:
Calories: 94
% of calories from fat: 18
Fat (gm): 1.9
Saturated fat (gm): 0.4
Cholesterol (mg): 0
Sodium (mg): 70
Protein (gm): 1.1
Carbohydrate (gm): 19.3

Exchanges:
Milk: 0.0
Vegetable: 2.0
Fruit: 0.0
Bread: 0.5
Meat: 0.0
Fat: 0.0

1. Mix sugar and cornstarch in small saucepan; whisk in water and vinegar. Heat to boiling, whisking until thickened, about 1 minute. Whisk in margarine; season to taste with salt and pepper. Pour sauce over beets and toss.

BEETS DIJON

The easiest way to peel beets is to cook them with the skins on; after cooking, the skins slip off easily!

4 servings

⅓ cup finely chopped onion

2 cloves garlic, minced

⅓ cup fat-free sour cream

2 tablespoons Dijon mustard

2–3 teaspoons lemon juice

Salt and white pepper, to taste

1½ pounds medium beets, cooked, cubed or sliced, warm

Per Serving:
Calories: 71
% of calories from fat: 7
Fat (gm): 0.6
Saturated fat (gm): 0.1
Cholesterol (mg): 0
Sodium (mg): 185
Protein (gm): 3.5
Carbohydrate (gm): 13.8

Exchanges:
Milk: 0.0
Vegetable: 3.0
Fruit: 0.0
Bread: 0.0
Meat: 0.0
Fat: 0.0

1. Sauté onion and garlic in lightly greased small saucepan until tender, 3 to 4 minutes. Stir in sour cream, mustard, and lemon juice; heat over low heat until hot, 2 to 3 minutes. Season to taste with salt and pepper; spoon over beets.

45-MINUTE PREPARATION TIP: Cook beets before making sour cream sauce.

HERB-CRUMBED BROCCOLI

45 *Herb-seasoned bread crumbs and pecans offer new flavor and texture contrast in this favorite broccoli dish.*

6 servings

2–4 tablespoons chopped pecans

¼ cup unseasoned dry bread crumbs

½ teaspoon each: dried marjoram and chervil leaves

1½ pounds broccoli, cut into florets and stalks sliced, cooked

Salt and pepper, to taste

1. Cook pecans, bread crumbs, and herbs in lightly greased small skillet over medium heat until toasted, 2 to 3 minutes, stirring frequently. Season broccoli to taste with salt and pepper; spoon crumb mixture over.

Per Serving:
Calories: 61
% of calories from fat: 28
Fat (gm): 2.1
Saturated fat (gm): 0.2
Cholesterol (mg): 0
Sodium (mg): 64
Protein (gm): 3.7
Carbohydrate (gm): 8.7

Exchanges:
Milk: 0.0
Vegetable: 1.5
Fruit: 0.0
Bread: 0.0
Meat: 0.0
Fat: 0.5

BROCCOLI RABE SAUTÉED WITH GARLIC

45 *This simple flavorful vegetable recipe can also be made with broccoli, green beans, or asparagus.*

4–6 servings

1 pound broccoli rabe, cooked crisp-tender

4 cloves garlic, minced

Salt and pepper, to taste

1. Sauté broccoli rabe and garlic in lightly greased large skillet until broccoli rabe is beginning to brown, 4 to 5 minutes. Season to taste with salt and pepper.

Per Serving:
Calories: 32
% of calories from fat: 8
Fat (gm): 0.4
Saturated fat (gm): 0.1
Cholesterol (mg): 0
Sodium (mg): 25
Protein (gm): 3.1
Carbohydrate (gm): 5.9

Exchanges:
Milk: 0.0
Vegetable: 1.0
Fruit: 0.0
Bread: 0.0
Meat: 0.0
Fat: 0.0

SUGAR-GLAZED BRUSSELS SPROUTS AND PEARL ONIONS

45 *Large Brussels sprouts can be halved for faster cooking. The pearl onions can be fresh, frozen, or canned.*

4–6 servings

1 tablespoon margarine
¼ cup sugar
8 ounces each: small Brussels sprouts, pearl
  onions, cooked until crisp-tender, warm
Salt and white pepper, to taste

Per Serving:
Calories: 107
% of calories from fat: 25
Fat (gm): 3.2
Saturated fat (gm): 0.6
Cholesterol (mg): 0
Sodium (mg): 48
Protein (gm): 2.3
Carbohydrate (gm): 19.7

Exchanges:
Milk: 0.0
Vegetable: 2.0
Fruit: 0.0
Bread: 0.5
Meat: 0.0
Fat: 0.5

1. Heat margarine in medium skillet until melted; stir in sugar and cook over medium heat until mixture is bubbly. Add vegetables and toss to coat. Season to taste with salt and white pepper.

WINE-BRAISED CABBAGE

45 *You'll enjoy the combination of aromatic anise and caraway seeds in this cabbage dish.*

4–6 servings

¾ cup chopped onion
½ cup chopped green bell pepper
3 cloves garlic, minced
½ teaspoon each: crushed caraway and anise seeds
1 medium head cabbage, thinly sliced
½ cup each: canned reduced-sodium vegetable broth,
  dry white wine
2 slices diced bacon, cooked crisp, drained
Salt and pepper, to taste

Per Serving:
Calories: 118
% of calories from fat: 10
Fat (gm): 1.5
Saturated fat (gm): 0.1
Cholesterol (mg): 0
Sodium (mg): 148
Protein (gm): 6.4
Carbohydrate (gm): 19.3

Exchanges:
Milk: 0.0
Vegetable: 3.0
Fruit: 0.0
Bread: 0.5
Meat: 0.0
Fat: 0.0

1. Sauté onion, green pepper, garlic, caraway, and anise seeds in lightly greased large saucepan 3 to 4 minutes. Add cabbage, vegetable broth, and wine; heat to boiling. Reduce heat and simmer, covered, until cabbage is wilted, about 5 minutes. Simmer, uncovered, until cabbage is tender, 10 to 15 minutes. Stir in bacon; season to taste with salt and pepper.

GINGERED CARROT PUREE

This intensely flavored puree has a velvety texture.

6 servings

2 pounds carrots, sliced, cooked
2 cups cubed, peeled Idaho potato, cooked
1–2 tablespoons margarine or butter
¼–½ cup fat-free half-and-half or fat-free milk, warm
½ teaspoon ground ginger
Salt and pepper, to taste

Per Serving:
Calories: 122
% of calories from fat: 16
Fat (gm): 2.2
Saturated fat (gm): 0.4
Cholesterol (mg): 0
Sodium (mg): 132
Protein (gm): 2.4
Carbohydrate (gm): 24.1

Exchanges:
Milk: 0.0
Vegetable: 2.5
Fruit: 0.0
Bread: 0.5
Meat: 0.0
Fat: 0.5

1. Process carrots and potato in food processor until smooth; transfer to large skillet and cook over medium to medium-low heat, stirring until mixture is the consistency of thick mashed potatoes (do not brown), about 15 minutes. Beat margarine and enough half-and-half into mixture to make a creamy consistency. Stir in ground ginger; season to taste with salt and pepper.

VARIATIONS

Cauliflower-Fennel Puree — Make recipe as above, substituting cauliflower for the carrots, deleting the ground nutmeg, and adding 1–1½ teaspoons crushed fennel or caraway seeds.

Celery Root Puree — Make recipe as above substituting celery root for the carrots.

Fennel Puree — Make recipe as above, substituting fennel bulbs for the carrots and deleting the nutmeg. Add ½ cup cooked onion to the fennel and potatoes when pureeing.

ORANGE-GLAZED BABY CARROTS

45 *The sweet-spiced orange glaze is also delicious over sweet potatoes or beets.*

4 servings

¾ cup orange juice

½ cup packed light brown sugar

2 tablespoons cornstarch

½ teaspoon ground cinnamon

¼ teaspoon each: ground allspice, mace

1 tablespoon margarine or butter

Salt and white pepper, to taste

1 pound baby carrots, cooked crisp-tender, warm

Per Serving:
Calories: 191
% of calories from fat: 13
Fat (gm): 3
Saturated fat (gm): 0.6
Cholesterol (mg): 0
Sodium (mg): 145
Protein (gm): 1.8
Carbohydrate (gm): 42.4

Exchanges:
Milk: 0.0
Vegetable: 2.0
Fruit: 2.0
Bread: 0.0
Meat: 0.0
Fat: 0.5

1. Mix orange juice, brown sugar, cornstarch, and spices in small saucepan; heat to boiling. Boil, stirring until thickened, about 1 minute. Stir in margarine; season to taste with salt and pepper. Stir into carrots.

45-MINUTE PREPARATION TIP: Begin cooking carrots before preparing the rest of the recipe.

CARROT PUDDING

45

This recipe is served as a dessert in Mexico—we think it makes an excellent side dish!

8 servings

2 pounds carrots, cooked, mashed

½ cup sugar

1½ tablespoons margarine or butter, melted

½ cup all-purpose flour

1½ teaspoons baking powder

½ teaspoon each: ground cinnamon, salt

½ cup each: raisins, shredded fat-free Cheddar cheese

4 egg whites, beaten to stiff peaks

¼ cup sliced almonds

Per Serving:
Calories: 191
% of calories from fat: 11
Fat (gm): 2.5
Saturated fat (gm): 0.5
Cholesterol (mg): 1.3
Sodium (mg): 339
Protein (gm): 6.3
Carbohydrate (gm): 37.9

Exchanges:
Milk: 0.0
Vegetable: 1.5
Fruit: 0.5
Bread: 1.5
Meat: 0.0
Fat: 0.5

1. Mix carrots, sugar, and margarine in bowl; mix in combined flour, baking powder, cinnamon, and salt. Mix in raisins and cheese; fold in beaten egg whites. Spoon mixture into greased 8-inch-square baking pan; sprinkle with almonds. Bake at 475 degrees 10 minutes; reduce temperature to 350 degrees and bake until browned and set, 50 to 60 minutes. Cut into squares; serve warm.

CAULIFLOWER WITH CREAMY CHEESE SAUCE

45 *For flavor variations, make the cheese sauce with other reduced-fat cheeses, such as Havarti, Gruyère, American, or blue.*

6 servings

1 large head cauliflower (about 2 pounds), sliced
Creamy Cheese Sauce (recipe follows)
Paprika, as garnish

Per Serving:
Calories: 102
% of calories from fat: 31
Fat (gm): 3.6
Saturated fat (gm): 1.5
Cholesterol (mg): 5.7
Sodium (mg): 194
Protein (gm): 6.5
Carbohydrate (gm): 11.7

1. Cook cauliflower in 2 inches simmering water in medium saucepan, covered, until tender, 20 to 25 minutes; drain. Spoon Creamy Cheese Sauce over and sprinkle with paprika.

Exchanges:
Milk: 0.0
Vegetable: 2.0
Fruit: 0.0
Bread: 0.0
Meat: 0.5
Fat: 0.5

Creamy Cheese Sauce
Makes about 1¼ cups

2 tablespoons minced onion
1 tablespoon margarine or butter
2 tablespoons flour
1 cup fat-free milk
½ cup (2 ounces) cubed reduced-fat pasteurized processed cheese
¼ teaspoon dry mustard
2–3 drops red pepper sauce
Salt and white pepper, to taste

1. Sauté onion in margarine in small saucepan 2 to 3 minutes. Stir in flour; cook 1 minute. Whisk in milk and heat to boiling; boil, stirring until thickened, about 1 minute. Reduce heat to low; add cheese, dry mustard, and pepper sauce, whisking until cheese is melted. Season to taste with salt and white pepper.

CORN PUDDING

Use fresh corn cut from the cob for best flavor, though frozen or canned can be used for convenience.

6 servings

2 tablespoons unseasoned dry bread crumbs

2 cups whole-kernel corn

½ cup fat-free milk

3 tablespoons flour

1½ tablespoons margarine or butter,
  room temperature

2 eggs, lightly beaten

1 teaspoon sugar

½ teaspoon each: dried thyme leaves, salt

⅛ teaspoon pepper

Per Serving:
Calories: 122
% of calories from fat: 28
Fat (gm): 3.9
Saturated fat (gm): 0.9
Cholesterol (mg): 35.8
Sodium (mg): 272
Protein (gm): 5.3
Carbohydrate (gm): 17.9

Exchanges:
Milk: 0.0
Vegetable: 0.0
Fruit: 0.0
Bread: 1.0
Meat: 0.5
Fat: 0.5

1. Coat lightly greased 1-quart casserole or soufflé dish with bread crumbs. Process corn, milk, and flour in food processor or blender until a coarse puree. Stir in combined remaining ingredients and pour into prepared casserole. Bake, uncovered, at 350 degrees until pudding is set and beginning to brown, about 35 minutes.

SUCCOTASH

45 *Fat-free half-and-half contributes richness without the fat calories in this old-fashioned favorite. Fresh crisp-tender cooked green beans can be substituted for the baby lima beans.*

4 servings

1 small onion, chopped

1 tablespoon margarine or butter

2 cups each: frozen baby lima beans,
  whole-kernel corn

½ cup each: reduced-sodium vegetable broth,
  fat-free half-and-half or fat-free milk

Salt and pepper, to taste

Per Serving:
Calories: 146
% of calories from fat: 13
Fat (gm): 2.1
Saturated fat (gm): 0.4
Cholesterol (mg): 0
Sodium (mg): 69
Protein (gm): 6.6
Carbohydrate (gm): 26.7

Exchanges:
Milk: 0.0
Vegetable: 0.0
Fruit: 0.0
Bread: 1.5
Meat: 0.0
Fat: 0.5

1. Sauté onion in margarine in medium saucepan until tender, 3 to 4 minutes. Stir in lima beans, corn, broth, and half-and-half; heat to boiling. Reduce heat and simmer, covered, until vegetables are tender, about 5 minutes. Season to taste with salt and pepper.

FRIED CORN

45 *Use fresh corn, if you can!*

6 servings

3 cups whole-kernel corn

¾ cup each: sliced green and red bell pepper

3 cloves garlic, minced

¼ cup water

Salt and pepper, to taste

Per Serving:
Calories: 85
% of calories from fat: 2
Fat (gm): 0.2
Saturated fat (gm): 0
Cholesterol (mg): 0
Sodium (mg): 5
Protein (gm): 3.3
Carbohydrate (gm): 21

Exchanges:
Milk: 0.0
Vegetable: 1.0
Fruit: 0.0
Bread: 1.0
Meat: 0.0
Fat: 0.0

1. Combine corn, bell peppers, and garlic in lightly greased large skillet; cook, covered, over medium heat until vegetables are tender and browned, about 25 minutes, stirring occasionally. Add water and cook, covered, over low heat until water is absorbed, about 15 minutes. Season to taste with salt and pepper.

TEX-MEX SWEET CORN

45 *Flavors of the Southwest make corn-on-the-cob better than ever!*

6 servings

2–3 tablespoons margarine or butter

½ teaspoon each: chili and garlic powder, ground cumin, dried oregano leaves

⅛ teaspoon cayenne pepper

6 ears corn, cooked, warm

Salt, to taste

Chopped cilantro, as garnish

Per Serving:
Calories: 153
% of calories from fat: 25
Fat (gm): 4.8
Saturated fat (gm): 0.9
Cholesterol (mg): 0
Sodium (mg): 52
Protein (gm): 4.1
Carbohydrate (gm): 28.5

Exchanges:
Milk: 0.0
Vegetable: 0.0
Fruit: 0.0
Bread: 1.5
Meat: 0.0
Fat: 1.0

1. Heat margarine, herbs, and cayenne pepper in small saucepan over medium heat until butter is melted. Brush on corn; sprinkle lightly with salt and cilantro.

SEASONED EGGPLANT SAUTÉ

45 *Simply delicious and easy to make!*

4 servings

1½ pounds eggplant, unpeeled, cubed
1 cup chopped onion
½ cup chopped red bell pepper
6 cloves garlic, minced
¾ teaspoon each: dried oregano and thyme leaves
¼ teaspoon crushed red pepper
½ cup reduced-sodium vegetable broth
Salt and pepper, to taste

Per Serving:
Calories: 83
% of calories from fat: 6
Fat (gm): 0.6
Saturated fat (gm): 0.1
Cholesterol (mg): 0
Sodium (mg): 18
Protein (gm): 2.8
Carbohydrate (gm): 19.3

Exchanges:
Milk: 0.0
Vegetable: 3.0
Fruit: 0.0
Bread: 0.0
Meat: 0.0
Fat: 0.0

1. Sauté vegetables, herbs, and red pepper in lightly greased large skillet 5 minutes. Add broth and heat to boiling; reduce heat and simmer, covered, until vegetables are tender and broth absorbed, 15 to 20 minutes. Season to taste with salt and pepper.

EGGPLANT AND VEGETABLE SAUTÉ

45 *Minced roasted garlic is available in jars in your produce section; substitute fresh minced garlic if desired.*

6 servings

1 large eggplant (about 1¼ pounds), unpeeled, cubed
3 cups frozen stir-fry pepper blend
4 teaspoons minced roasted garlic
½ teaspoon each: dried rosemary and thyme leaves
2 teaspoons olive oil
1 can (15 ounces) cannellini or Great Northern beans, rinsed, drained
Salt and pepper, to taste

Per Serving:
Calories: 109
% of calories from fat: 16
Fat (gm): 2
Saturated fat (gm): 0.3
Cholesterol (mg): 0
Sodium (mg): 114
Protein (gm): 4.1
Carbohydrate (gm): 19.1

Exchanges:
Milk: 0.0
Vegetable: 2.0
Fruit: 0.0
Bread: 1.0
Meat: 0.0
Fat: 0.5

1. Cook eggplant, pepper blend, garlic, and herbs in oil in large saucepan over medium heat, covered, until vegetables are tender, 8 to 10 minutes; stir in beans and cook until hot, about 2 minutes. Season to taste with salt and pepper.

EGGPLANT AND TOMATO CASSEROLE

45

Assemble the casserole up to a day in advance, then bake before serving— perfect potluck fare!

8 servings

1 large eggplant (about 1½ pounds), peeled, cubed (1-inch)
½ cup each: seasoned dry bread crumbs, chopped onion
3 cloves garlic, minced
2 teaspoons dried Italian seasoning
Salt and pepper, to taste
2 eggs, lightly beaten
3 medium tomatoes, sliced
¼ cup grated fat-free Parmesan cheese

Per Serving:
Calories: 98
% of calories from fat: 16
Fat (gm): 1.9
Saturated fat (gm): 0.5
Cholesterol (mg): 53.3
Sodium (mg): 245
Protein (gm): 5.1
Carbohydrate (gm): 16.9

Exchanges:
Milk: 0.0
Vegetable: 2.0
Fruit: 0.0
Bread: 0.5
Meat: 0.0
Fat: 0.5

1. Cook eggplant in 2 inches simmering water in medium saucepan, covered, until tender, 5 to 8 minutes; drain. Mash eggplant with fork; mix in bread crumbs, onion, garlic, and Italian seasoning. Season to taste with salt and pepper; mix in eggs. Spoon into greased 11 x 7-inch baking dish; arrange tomatoes over top and sprinkle with cheese. Bake, uncovered, at 350 degrees until hot, about 20 minutes.

LEMON-SPIKED GARLIC GREENS

45 *Kale, collard, turnip, or beet greens make excellent choices for this quick and easy healthful dish.*

4 servings

¼ cup each: finely chopped onion, red bell pepper

4 cloves garlic, minced

1½ pounds greens, coarsely chopped

½ cup water

1–2 tablespoons lemon juice

Salt and pepper, to taste

1 hard-cooked egg, chopped

Per Serving:
Calories: 58
% of calories from fat: 23
Fat (gm): 1.7
Saturated fat (gm): 0.4
Cholesterol (mg): 53.3
Sodium (mg): 43
Protein (gm): 5.9
Carbohydrate (gm): 7

Exchanges:
Milk: 0.0
Vegetable: 2.0
Fruit: 0.0
Bread: 0.0
Meat: 0.0
Fat: 0.0

1. Sauté onion, bell pepper, and garlic in lightly greased large saucepan until tender, 3 to 4 minutes. Add greens and water; heat to boiling. Reduce heat and simmer, covered, until greens are wilted, 4 to 5 minutes; drain. Season to taste with lemon juice, salt, and pepper; sprinkle with egg.

BRAISED KALE

45 *Packed with vitamins and minerals, kale and other dark leafy greens offer great nutrition. Try other greens such as beet, turnip, or mustard with this recipe too.*

4 servings

1 medium leek (white part only), sliced

2–3 teaspoons olive oil

1 pound kale, torn into pieces

½ cup reduced-sodium chicken broth

½ cup fat-free sour cream

1 teaspoon Dijon mustard

1–2 tablespoons crumbled cooked bacon

Salt and pepper, to taste

Per Serving:
Calories: 109
% of calories from fat: 27
Fat (gm): 3.5
Saturated fat (gm): 0.5
Cholesterol (mg): 0
Sodium (mg): 232
Protein (gm): 5.7
Carbohydrate (gm): 15.8

Exchanges:
Milk: 0.0
Vegetable: 3.0
Fruit: 0.0
Bread: 0.0
Meat: 0.0
Fat: 0.5

1. Sauté leek in oil in large saucepan until tender, 3 to 4 minutes. Add kale and chicken broth; heat to boiling. Reduce heat and simmer, covered, until kale is wilted, about 5 minutes; cook uncovered until greens are almost dry. Stir in sour cream, mustard, and bacon; cook over low heat 2 to 3 minutes. Season to taste with salt and pepper.

SAUTÉED LEEKS AND PEPPERS

45 *A colorful side dish that will brighten any meal!*

6 servings

3 medium leeks (white parts only), sliced (½-inch)
½ cup each: sliced yellow, red, and green bell pepper
½ teaspoon dried bouquet garni
Salt and pepper, to taste

Per Serving:
Calories: 63
% of calories from fat: 5
Fat (gm): 0.4
Saturated fat (gm): 0
Cholesterol (mg): 0
Sodium (mg): 13
Protein (gm): 2
Carbohydrate (gm): 14.6

Exchanges:
Milk: 0.0
Vegetable: 2.5
Fruit: 0.0
Bread: 0.0
Meat: 0.0
Fat: 0.0

1. Cook vegetables and bouquet garni in lightly greased large skillet, covered, over medium heat until softened, 2 to 3 minutes. Cook, uncovered, until vegetables are tender and beginning to brown, about 5 minutes. Season to taste with salt and pepper.

MUSHROOMS WITH SOUR CREAM

45 *Cooking the mushrooms very slowly until deeply browned intensifies their flavor. Especially delicious served with pierogi, ravioli, or grilled eggplant slices.*

4 servings

12 ounces shiitake or cremini mushrooms, stems discarded, sliced
¼ cup finely chopped onion
1 teaspoon minced garlic
¼ cup dry white wine or reduced-sodium vegetable broth
¼ teaspoon dried thyme leaves
½ cup fat-free sour cream
Salt and cayenne pepper, to taste

1. Sauté mushrooms, onion, and garlic in lightly greased large skillet 3 to 4 minutes. Add wine and thyme; heat to boiling. Reduce heat and simmer, covered, until mushrooms are tender, 8 to 10 minutes. Cook, uncovered, on low heat until mushrooms are dry and well browned, about 20 to 25 minutes. Stir in sour cream; season to taste with salt and pepper.

Per Serving:
Calories: 80
% of calories from fat: 2
Fat (gm): 0.2
Saturated fat (gm): 0.1
Cholesterol (mg): 0
Sodium (mg): 24
Protein (gm): 3.5
Carbohydrate (gm): 16.5

Exchanges:
Milk: 0.0
Vegetable: 2.0
Fruit: 0.0
Bread: 0.5
Meat: 0.0
Fat: 0.0

GULFPORT OKRA

45 *Select small okra for best flavor and tenderness.*

6 servings

1½ pounds fresh or frozen thawed, okra
Garlic powder, to taste
Salt and pepper, to taste

1. Cook okra in boiling water 1 to 2 minutes; drain. Cook okra in lightly greased large skillet over medium heat until well browned, about 10 minutes, stirring occasionally. Sprinkle generously with garlic powder; season to taste with salt and pepper.

Per Serving:
Calories: 37
% of calories from fat: 4
Fat (gm): 0.2
Saturated fat (gm): 0.1
Cholesterol (mg): 0
Sodium (mg): 6
Protein (gm): 2.1
Carbohydrate (gm): 8.2

Exchanges:
Milk: 0.0
Vegetable: 1.5
Fruit: 0.0
Bread: 0.0
Meat: 0.0
Fat: 0.0

QUARTET OF ONIONS

45 *Cooked slowly until caramelized, the onion mixture is scented with mint and sage.*

6 servings

2 pounds sweet onions, sliced

1 small leek (white part only), thinly sliced

½ cup each: chopped shallots, sliced green onions, reduced sodium vegetable broth

1–1½ teaspoons dried mint leaves

¼ teaspoon dried sage leaves

Salt and white pepper, to taste

Per Serving:
Calories: 90
% of calories from fat: 4
Fat (gm): 0.4
Saturated fat (gm): 0.1
Cholesterol (mg): 0
Sodium (mg): 16
Protein (gm): 2.7
Carbohydrate (gm): 20.1

Exchanges:
Milk: 0.0
Vegetable: 4.0
Fruit: 0.0
Bread: 0.0
Meat: 0.0
Fat: 0.0

1. Sauté onions, leek, shallots, and green onions in lightly greased large skillet 3 to 4 minutes. Stir in broth and herbs and heat to boiling; reduce heat and simmer, covered, 5 minutes. Cook, uncovered, over medium-low heat until onion mixture is golden, about 15 minutes. Season to taste with salt and white pepper.

TINY PEAS AND PEARL ONIONS

45 *The refreshing flavors of mint and dill give this dish a Mediterranean accent.*

6 servings

½ package (16-ounce size) frozen pearl onions

½ cup water

1 package (8 ounces) frozen tiny peas

2–3 teaspoons margarine or butter

½ teaspoon each: dried mint leaves, dill weed

Salt and pepper, to taste

Per Serving:
Calories: 63
% of calories from fat: 20
Fat (gm): 1.4
Saturated fat (gm): 0.3
Cholesterol (mg): 0
Sodium (mg): 57
Protein (gm): 2.5
Carbohydrate (gm): 10.4

Exchanges:
Milk: 0.0
Vegetable: 0.0
Fruit: 0.0
Bread: 1.0
Meat: 0.0
Fat: 0.0

1. Heat onions and water to boiling in medium saucepan; reduce heat and simmer until tender, 8 to 10 minutes, adding peas during the last 5 minutes. Drain. Add margarine and herbs, stirring until melted. Season to taste with salt and pepper.

FRUIT-STUFFED VIDALIA ONIONS

The onions can be poached and filled with fruit up to 1 day in advance; increase baking time 10 to 15 minutes.

4 servings

2 large Vidalia onions, cut crosswise into halves

½ cup each: water, dry white wine

4 each: whole peppercorns, allspice

1 teaspoon mustard seeds

2 bay leaves

Salt, to taste

1 small apple, unpeeled, finely chopped

¼ cup each: chopped dried fruit, golden raisins

2–3 teaspoons sugar

Per Serving:
Calories: 142
% of calories from fat: 4
Fat (gm): 0.6
Saturated fat (gm): 0.1
Cholesterol (mg): 0
Sodium (mg): 7
Protein (gm): 1.9
Carbohydrate (gm): 30.5

Exchanges:
Milk: 0.0
Vegetable: 2.0
Fruit: 1.5
Bread: 0.0
Meat: 0.0
Fat: 0.0

1. Cut small slices off bottoms of onion halves so onions can stand securely. Remove centers of onions, leaving scant ¾-inch shells; chop onion centers and reserve. Stand onions in medium skillet; add water, wine, and seasonings; heat to boiling. Reduce heat and simmer, covered, until crisp-tender, about 10 minutes. Remove onions with slotted spoon and transfer to baking pan; sprinkle lightly with salt. Reserve ¼ cup cooking liquid.

2. Sauté reserved onion centers and apple in lightly greased small skillet until tender, about 5 minutes. Stir in reserved ¼ cup cooking liquid, dried fruit, raisins, and sugar; cook over medium-low heat until liquid is absorbed. Spoon into onion halves. Bake, covered, at 375 degrees until onions are tender, 20 to 30 minutes.

SAUTÉED SUMMER SQUASH WITH SNOW PEAS

45 *The vegetables are best when crisp-tender, so don't overcook! Zucchini or chayote squash may also be used in the recipe.*

4 servings

2 each: sliced green onions, minced garlic cloves

1½ cups yellow summer squash

2 ounces snow peas

1 tablespoon finely chopped fresh or 1 teaspoon dried tarragon or basil leaves

Salt and white pepper, to taste

Per Serving:
Calories: 27
% of calories from fat: 10
Fat (gm): 0.3
Saturated fat (gm): 0.1
Cholesterol (mg): 0
Sodium (mg): 2
Protein (gm): 1.4
Carbohydrate (gm): 5.7

Exchanges:
Milk: 0.0
Vegetable: 1.0
Fruit: 0.0
Bread: 0.0
Meat: 0.0
Fat: 0.0

1. Sauté green onions and garlic in lightly greased large skillet 2 to 3 minutes. Add squash, snow peas, and tarragon and cook over medium heat until vegetables are crisp-tender, about 5 minutes. Season to taste with salt and pepper.

BRAISED PARSNIPS AND WINTER VEGETABLES

45 *Idaho or sweet potatoes, winter squash, or Brussels sprouts would be flavorful additions to this colorful vegetable dish.*

6 servings

1 cup each: sliced parsnips, carrots, cubed celery root or celery, shredded red or green cabbage

¼ cup minced onion

2 teaspoons minced garlic

½ cup dry red wine or vegetable broth

2 tablespoons light brown sugar

1 teaspoon balsamic or red wine vinegar

¾ teaspoon each: dried sage and thyme leaves

Salt and pepper, to taste

Per Serving:
Calories: 92
% of calories from fat: 3
Fat (gm): 0.3
Saturated fat (gm): 0.1
Cholesterol (mg): 0
Sodium (mg): 47
Protein (gm): 1.5
Carbohydrate (gm): 19.3

Exchanges:
Milk: 0.0
Vegetable: 2.0
Fruit: 0.0
Bread: 0.5
Meat: 0.0
Fat: 0.0

1. Sauté vegetables in lightly greased large skillet until beginning to brown, 8 to 10 minutes; add remaining ingredients, except salt and pepper, and heat to boiling; reduce heat and simmer, covered, until vegetables are tender, 8 to 10 minutes. Season to taste with salt and pepper.

PEPERONATA

45 *Sweet bell peppers and onions are slowly cooked until tender and creamy in this Italian-inspired dish.*

8 servings

2 cups sliced onions
1 cup each: sliced green and red bell pepper
6 cloves garlic, minced
¼ cup water
Salt and pepper, to taste

Per Serving:
Calories: 29
% of calories from fat: 4
Fat (gm): 0.1
Saturated fat (gm): 0.0
Cholesterol (mg): 0.0
Sodium (mg): 2.5
Protein (gm): 1
Carbohydrate (gm): 7

Exchanges:
Milk: 0.0
Vegetable: 1.0
Fruit: 0.0
Bread: 0.0
Meat: 0.0
Fat: 0.0

1. Sauté vegetables in lightly greased medium skillet over medium heat 5 minutes, stirring occasionally. Add water and cook, covered, over medium-low heat until vegetables are very tender, 20 to 25 minutes, stirring occasionally. Season to taste with salt and pepper.

REAL MASHED POTATOES

45 *Just like grandma used to make! For a country-style variation, leave potatoes unpeeled.*

8 servings

2 pounds Idaho potatoes, peeled, quartered, cooked
½ cup fat-free sour cream
¼ cup fat-free milk, hot
2 tablespoons margarine or butter
Salt and pepper, to taste

Per Serving:
Calories: 124
% of calories from fat: 21
Fat (gm): 2.9
Saturated fat (gm): 0.6
Cholesterol (mg): 0.2
Sodium (mg): 53
Protein (gm): 3.1
Carbohydrate (gm): 22.2

Exchanges:
Milk: 0.0
Vegetable: 0.0
Fruit: 0.0
Bread: 1.5
Meat: 0.0
Fat: 0.5

1. Mash potatoes with potato masher or electric mixer, adding sour cream, milk, and margarine. Season to taste with salt and pepper. Heat in saucepan over medium heat until hot, about 5 minutes.

VARIATIONS

Garlic Mashed Potatoes — Make recipe above, cooking 10 peeled cloves of garlic with the potatoes; mash garlic with potatoes.

Horseradish Mashed Potatoes — Make Real or Garlic Mashed Potatoes, beating in 2 teaspoons horseradish.

Potato Pancakes — Make any of the mashed potato recipes above; refrigerate until chilled. Mix in 1 egg, 4 chopped green onions, and ¼ cup (1 ounce) grated fat-free Parmesan cheese. Form mixture into 8 patties, using about ½ cup mixture for each. Coat patties in flour, dip in beaten egg, and coat with plain dry bread crumbs. Cook over medium heat in lightly greased large skillet until browned, 3 to 5 minutes on each side.

GREENS AND SMASHED POTATOES

45 *The potatoes are not peeled, giving this dish a rustic character.*

4 servings

¼ cup finely chopped onion

3 cloves garlic, minced

1½ cups thinly sliced greens (kale, mustard, or turnip greens)

¼ cup water

3 medium Idaho potatoes, cubed, cooked

¼ cup fat-free sour cream

2–4 tablespoons fat-free milk

1–2 tablespoons margarine or butter

Salt and pepper, to taste

Per Serving:
Calories: 141
% of calories from fat: 19
Fat (gm): 3.1
Saturated fat (gm): 0.6
Cholesterol (mg): 0.1
Sodium (mg): 60
Protein (gm): 3.8
Carbohydrate (gm): 25.4

Exchanges:
Milk: 0.0
Vegetable: 2.0
Fruit: 0.0
Bread: 1.0
Meat: 0.0
Fat: 0.5

1. Sauté onion and garlic in lightly greased medium skillet until tender, 3 to 4 minutes. Add greens and water; heat to boiling. Reduce heat and simmer, covered, until greens are tender about 5 minutes; cook, uncovered until water has evaporated and greens are almost dry.

2. Mash potatoes with potato masher or electric mixer, adding sour cream, milk, and margarine; stir into greens and cook over low heat until hot, about 5 minutes. Season to taste with salt and pepper.

45-MINUTE PREPARATION TIP: Begin cooking potatoes before preparing the rest of the recipe.

ROOT VEGGIES AND MASHED POTATOES

A selection of winter root vegetables, roasted to perfection and served with garlic-spiked mashed potatoes.

8 servings

3 each: peeled, cubed medium beets, turnips

2 cups halved Brussels sprouts

1 cup baby carrots

1 leek (white part only), thickly sliced

Vegetable cooking spray

1 tablespoon caraway seeds

Salt and pepper, to taste

1½ pounds Idaho potatoes, unpeeled, cubed

4 cloves garlic, peeled

¼ cup fat-free milk, hot

2 tablespoons margarine or butter, cut into pieces

Per Serving:
Calories: 194
% of calories from fat: 15
Fat (gm): 3.5
Saturated fat (gm): 0.7
Cholesterol (mg): 0.1
Sodium (mg): 164
Protein (gm): 6.2
Carbohydrate (gm): 37.8

Exchanges:
Milk: 0.0
Vegetable: 1.0
Fruit: 0.0
Bread: 2.0
Meat: 0.0
Fat: 0.5

1. Arrange vegetables, except potatoes and garlic, in single layer on greased foil-lined jelly roll pan; spray with cooking spray and sprinkle with caraway seeds, salt and pepper. Bake at 450 degrees until vegetables are tender and lightly browned, about 25 minutes.

2. Cook potatoes and garlic in simmering water in covered sauce-pan until tender, 10 to 15 minutes; drain. Mash potatoes and garlic with potato masher or electric mixer, adding milk and margarine. Season to taste with salt and pepper. Heat in saucepan over medium heat until hot, about 5 minutes. Spoon roasted vegetables over potatoes.

CREAMY POTATO AND BEAN MASHERS

45 *Beans boost flavor and nutrition in this great dish!*

6 servings (about ⅔ cup each)

1 pound Idaho potatoes, unpeeled, quartered, cooked

1 can (15½ ounces) Great Northern or navy beans, rinsed, drained

1–2 teaspoon minced roasted garlic

2 tablespoons margarine or butter

¼–½ cup fat-free milk, hot

Salt and pepper, to taste

Per Serving:
Calories: 187
% of calories from fat: 20
Fat (gm): 4
Saturated fat (gm): 0.9
Cholesterol (mg): 0.2
Sodium (mg): 55
Protein (gm): 7
Carbohydrate (gm): 31

Exchanges:
Milk: 0.0
Vegetable: 0.0
Fruit: 0.0
Bread: 2.0
Meat: 0.0
Fat: 1.0

1. Mash potatoes, beans, garlic, and margarine using potato masher or electric mixer, adding enough milk for desired consistency; season to taste with salt and pepper. Heat in saucepan over medium heat until hot, about 5 minutes.

VARIATIONS

Cheesy Bean and Onion Mashers — Sauté 1 cup chopped onion in lightly-greased small skillet until tender, about 5 minutes. Make recipe as above, adding onion mixture.

Lima Bean and Mushroom Mashers — Sauté 1 cup quartered cremini mushrooms in lightly-greased small skillet until tender, about 5 minutes. Make recipe as above, substituting lima beans for the Great Northern beans and stirring in mushrooms.

TWICE-BAKED POTATOES WITH CHEESE

These stuffed bakers are always a favorite! The potatoes can be prepared and refrigerated 24 hours in advance; increase baking time to 20 to 25 minutes.

4 servings

2 large Idaho potatoes (8 ounces each)

¼ cup each: fat-free sour cream, fat-free milk

¾ cup (3 ounces) shredded reduced-fat sharp or mild Cheddar cheese, divided

Salt and pepper, to taste

Paprika, as garnish

Per Serving:
Calories: 177
% of calories from fat: 16
Fat (gm): 3.2
Saturated fat (gm): 1.6
Cholesterol (mg): 11.6
Sodium (mg): 314
Protein (gm): 8.4
Carbohydrate (gm): 29.2

Exchanges:
Milk: 0.0
Vegetable: 0.0
Fruit: 0.0
Bread: 2.0
Meat: 0.5
Fat: 0.0

1. Pierce potatoes with a fork; grease lightly and bake at 400 degrees until tender, about 1 hour. Cut lengthwise into halves; let stand until cool enough to handle. Scoop out potatoes, being careful to leave shells intact.

2. Mash potatoes with potato masher or electric mixer, adding sour cream, milk, and ½ cup cheese; season to taste with salt and pepper. Spoon into potato shells; sprinkle with remaining ¼ cup cheese and paprika. Bake, uncovered, at 400 degrees until hot, 15 to 20 minutes.

VEGGIE-STUFFED BAKERS

The potatoes are greased and baked for a crispy skin; for a softer skin, wrap in aluminum foil.

6 servings

2 large Idaho potatoes (8–10 ounces each)

⅓ cup fat-free sour cream or plain yogurt

¾ cup (3 ounces) shredded fat-free Cheddar cheese, divided

1 cup each: chopped onion, green bell pepper

½ cup whole-kernel corn

4 cloves garlic, minced

Salt and pepper, to taste

1 cup broccoli florets, cooked crisp-tender

Per Serving:
Calories: 160
% of calories from fat: 2
Fat (gm): 0.3
Saturated fat (gm): 0
Cholesterol (mg): 0
Sodium (mg): 119
Protein (gm): 9
Carbohydrate (gm): 32.4

Exchanges:
Milk: 0.0
Vegetable: 1.0
Fruit: 0.0
Bread: 1.5
Meat: 0.5
Fat: 0.0

1. Pierce potatoes with a fork; grease lightly and bake at 400 degrees until tender, about 1 hour. Cut lengthwise into halves; let stand until cool enough to handle. Scoop out potatoes, being careful to leave shells intact. Mash potatoes in medium bowl, adding sour cream and half the Cheddar cheese.

2. Sauté onion, bell pepper, corn, and garlic in lightly greased medium skillet until tender, about 5 minutes. Mix into potatoes; season to taste with salt and pepper. Spoon into potato shells; arrange broccoli on top and sprinkle with remaining cheese. Bake, uncovered, at 350 degrees until hot, 20 to 30 minutes.

POTATOES WITH POBLANO CHILIES

45 *In this recipe, roasted poblano chilies are combined with potatoes for a hearty side dish. Serve with fried eggs and salsa for a brunch entrée.*

4 servings (about ⅔ cup each)

4 medium poblano chilies, halved

1 medium onion, sliced

1 pound Idaho potatoes, unpeeled, cooked, cubed

Salt and pepper, to taste

Per Serving:
Calories: 147
% of calories from fat: 2
Fat (gm): 0.3
Saturated fat (gm): 0.1
Cholesterol (mg): 0
Sodium (mg): 11
Protein (gm): 3.7
Carbohydrate (gm): 34

Exchanges:
Milk: 0.0
Vegetable: 1.0
Fruit: 0.0
Bread: 1.5
Meat: 0.0
Fat: 0.0

1. Broil chilies, skin sides up, 6 inches from heat source until skin is blackened and blistered. Wrap chilies in plastic bag or paper toweling 5 minutes; peel off skin and discard. Cut chilies into strips. Sauté chilies, onion, and potatoes in lightly greased large skillet over medium heat until onion is tender and potatoes browned, about 8 minutes. Season to taste with salt and pepper.

POTATOES GRATIN

45

These potatoes taste so rich and creamy you'll never imagine they were made without heavy cream!

8 servings (about ½ cup each)

2 tablespoons margarine or butter
3 tablespoons flour
1¾ cups fat-free milk
2 ounces light pasteurized processed cheese, cubed
½ cup (2 ounces) shredded reduced-fat
   Cheddar cheese
Salt and pepper, to taste
2 pounds Idaho potatoes, peeled, sliced (¼-inch)
¼ cup thinly sliced onion
Ground nutmeg, to taste

Per Serving:
Calories: 202
% of calories from fat: 23
Fat (gm): 5.1
Saturated fat (gm): 1.7
Cholesterol (mg): 8.5
Sodium (mg): 259
Protein (gm): 7.6
Carbohydrate (gm): 31.7

Exchanges:
Milk: 0.0
Vegetable: 0.0
Fruit: 0.0
Bread: 2.0
Meat: 0.5
Fat: 0.5

1. Melt margarine in medium saucepan; stir in flour and stir over medium heat 2 minutes. Whisk in milk and heat to boiling; boil, whisking until thickened, about 1 minute. Remove from heat; add cheeses, stirring until melted. Season to taste with salt and pepper.

2. Layer ⅓ of the potatoes and onion in greased 2-quart casserole; sprinkle lightly with salt, pepper, and nutmeg. Spoon ⅔ cup sauce over. Repeat layers 2 times. Bake, covered, at 350 degrees 45 minutes; uncover and bake until potatoes are tender and browned, 20 to 30 minutes.

VARIATIONS

Scalloped Potatoes — Make sauce as above, increasing margarine to 3 tablespoons, flour to ¼ cup, and milk to 2¼ cups; delete cheeses. Assemble and bake as directed.

Scalloped Potatoes and Ham — Make Scalloped Potatoes as above, layering 12 ounces cubed lean smoked ham between potatoes.

POTATOES AND WILD MUSHROOMS AU GRATIN

This time-savvy casserole utilizes frozen and dried vegetables to speed preparation.

6 servings

½ cup each: chopped red or green bell pepper, onion, frozen tiny peas

1½ cups frozen broccoli florets

1½ ounces dried shiitake mushrooms, broken into small pieces (about 6 mushrooms)

2 cups water

1 package (4½ ounces) dried julienned potatoes

¾ cup fat-free milk

1–1½ cups (4–6 ounces) shredded reduced-fat Swiss or Cheddar cheese

Per Serving:
Calories: 199
% of calories from fat: 20
Fat (gm): 4.5
Saturated fat (gm): 2.1
Cholesterol (mg): 14.1
Sodium (mg): 572
Protein (gm): 12.5
Carbohydrate (gm): 28.7

Exchanges:
Milk: 0.0
Vegetable: 3.0
Fruit: 0.0
Bread: 1.0
Meat: 0.0
Fat: 1.0

1. Sauté bell pepper and onion in lightly greased medium saucepan until tender, about 5 minutes. Add peas, broccoli, dried mushrooms, and water; heat to boiling. Pour mixture over potato and sauce mix in 2-quart casserole; stir in milk and cheese. Bake, uncovered, at 400 degrees until golden, 20 to 30 minutes.

CRISPY FRENCH "FRIES"

Golden brown, delicious, and crisp, these potatoes look and taste like they've been deep-fried: salting the raw potatoes is the secret!

4–6 servings

1 pound Idaho potatoes, unpeeled

2 teaspoons salt

Vegetable cooking spray

Salt and pepper, to taste

Per Serving:
Calories: 166
% of calories from fat: 1
Fat (gm): 0.2
Saturated fat (gm): 0
Cholesterol (mg): 0
Sodium (mg): 12
Protein (gm): 3.5
Carbohydrate (gm): 38.6

Exchanges:
Milk: 0.0
Vegetable: 0.0
Fruit: 0.0
Bread: 2.5
Meat: 0.0
Fat: 0.0

1. Cut potatoes into sticks 3 to 4 inches long and a scant ½ inch wide. Sprinkle lightly with 2 teaspoons salt and let stand 10 minutes. Rinse in cold water and dry on paper toweling. Arrange potatoes in single layer on greased foil-lined jelly roll pan; spray with cooking spray, tossing to coat all sides. Sprinkle lightly with salt and pepper. Bake at 350 degrees until golden brown and crisp, 40 to 45 minutes, turning halfway through cooking time.

NOTE: Potatoes can be kept warm in a 200-degree oven for up to 1 hour.

VARIATIONS

Parmesan "Fries" — Make recipe as above, sprinkling potatoes lightly with grated fat-free Parmesan cheese before baking.

Steak Fries — Make recipe as above, cutting potatoes into wedges 4 inches long and 1 inch wide, and increasing baking time to 1 to 1¼ hours.

ORANGE-LIME SWEET POTATOES

45 *Sweet potatoes are gently sauced with citrus juices; use freshly squeezed juices for best flavor.*

6 servings

1 cup chopped onion
1 teaspoon minced garlic
1 pound sweet potatoes, peeled, cubed (1-inch)
1 cup orange juice
¼ cup lime juice
Salt and pepper, to taste

Per Serving:
Calories: 95
% of calories from fat: 3
Fat (gm): 0.3
Saturated fat (gm): 0.1
Cholesterol (mg): 0
Sodium (mg): 9
Protein (gm): 1.7
Carbohydrate (gm): 22.3

Exchanges:
Milk: 0.0
Vegetable: 0.0
Fruit: 0.5
Bread: 1.0
Meat: 0.0
Fat: 0.0

1. Sauté onion and garlic in lightly greased medium skillet 3 to 4 minutes. Add sweet potatoes and juices; heat to boiling. Reduce heat and simmer, covered, until potatoes are tender, about 10 minutes. Cook, uncovered, until juices are thickened, 8 to 10 minutes. Season to taste with salt and pepper.

SWEET POTATO PONE

45

More of a country-style pudding than a soufflé, this comfort food will become a favorite. Drizzle with warm maple syrup, if you like.

4 servings

1 small onion, finely chopped

1 tablespoon margarine or butter

3 tablespoons flour

1 cup fat-free milk

2 eggs

2 cups cubed sweet potatoes, cooked, coarsely mashed

2 tablespoons packed light brown sugar

¼ teaspoon each: ground cinnamon, cloves, salt

2–3 dashes white pepper

4 egg whites, beaten to stiff peaks

Per Serving:
Calories: 179
% of calories from fat: 16
Fat (gm): 3.1
Saturated fat (gm): 0.7
Cholesterol (mg): 1.0
Sodium (mg): 303
Protein (gm): 5.5
Carbohydrate (gm): 27.7

Exchanges:
Milk: 0.0
Vegetable: 0.5
Fruit: 0.0
Bread: 1.0
Meat: 0.5
Fat: 0.0

1. Sauté onion in margarine in small saucepan until tender, 3 to 5 minutes. Stir in flour; cook 1 to 2 minutes. Stir in milk and heat to boiling, stirring, until thickened, about 1 minute. Remove from heat.

2. Beat eggs in medium bowl until thick and lemon colored, 3 to 4 minutes. Slowly whisk milk mixture into eggs; mix in remaining ingredients, except egg whites. Fold in egg whites. Spoon into greased 1-quart soufflé dish or casserole. Bake, uncovered, at 375 degrees until puffed and golden and a sharp knife inserted halfway between center and edge comes out almost clean, 30 to 35 minutes.

45-MINUTE PREPARATION TIP: Begin cooking sweet potatoes before preparing the rest of the recipe.

BAKED SWEET POTATOES WITH PINEAPPLE

45

For an extra touch, sprinkle the top of the potatoes with browned sugar and sprinkle with cinnamon before baking.

8 servings

1 can (4 ounces) pineapple tidbits, undrained
4 medium sweet potatoes, peeled, quartered, cooked
1 teaspoon low-fat margarine or butter
¼ teaspoon each: ground cinnamon, allspice

Per Serving:
Calories: 67
% of calories from fat: 3
Fat (gm): 0.3
Saturated fat (gm): 0
Cholesterol (mg): 0
Sodium (mg): 14
Protein (gm): 1.1
Carbohydrate (gm): 15.2

Exchanges:
Milk: 0.0
Vegetable: 0.0
Fruit: 0.0
Bread: 1.0
Meat: 0.0
Fat: 0.0

1. Drain pineapple tidbits; reserve ½ cup juice. Mash sweet potatoes with potato masher or electric mixer, adding margarine, and enough pineapple juice for desired consistency. Mix in pineapple and spices; spoon into lightly greased 1-quart baking dish. Bake, uncoverd, at 350 degrees until lightly browned, about 30 minutes.

CREAMED SPINACH

45

Try this recipe with other dark leafy greens, such as Swiss chard or kale.

4 servings

¼ cup finely chopped onion
2 teaspoons margarine or butter
2 tablespoons flour
1 cup fat-free milk or fat-free half-and-half
2 packages (10 ounces each) fresh spinach, cooked, drained
¼ cup fat-free sour cream
Ground nutmeg, to taste
Salt and pepper, to taste

Per Serving:
Calories: 92
% of calories from fat: 20
Fat (gm): 2.2
Saturated fat (gm): 0.5
Cholesterol (mg): 1
Sodium (mg): 145
Protein (gm): 6.6
Carbohydrate (gm): 13.3

Exchanges:
Milk: 0.0
Vegetable: 2.5
Fruit: 0.0
Bread: 0.0
Meat: 0.0
Fat: 0.5

1. Sauté onion in margarine in small saucepan until tender, 3 to 5 minutes. Stir in flour; cook 1 minute. Whisk in milk and heat to boiling; boil, whisking until thickened, about 1 minute. Reduce heat to medium; stir in spinach and sour cream. Cook until hot, 2 to 3 minutes; season to taste with nutmeg, salt, and pepper.

VARIATION

Spinach au Gratin — Prepare recipe as directed above, reserving ⅓ cup sauce; mix spinach and remaining sauce and spoon into a small casserole. Spread reserved sauce over spinach; sprinkle with ¼ cup (1 ounce) grated Parmesan or Cheddar cheese. Bake, uncovered, at 375 degrees until cheese is melted, 5 to 8 minutes.

CHAYOTE WITH PEPITAS

45 *To toast the "pepitas" (Mexican pumpkin seeds), cook over medium heat in a lightly greased skillet. They will begin to pop and jump in the skillet, signaling that they are toasted!*

4 servings

½ cup finely chopped onion
2 cloves garlic, minced
1 chayote squash, peeled, pitted, cubed
4 teaspoons pepitas, toasted
Salt and pepper, to taste

Per Serving:
Calories: 35
% of calories from fat: 16
Fat (gm): 0.7
Saturated fat (gm): 0.1
Cholesterol (mg): 0
Sodium (mg): 2
Protein (gm): 1.1
Carbohydrate (gm): 7

Exchanges:
Milk: 0.0
Vegetable: 1.5
Fruit: 0.0
Bread: 0.0
Meat: 0.0
Fat: 0.0

1. Sauté onion and garlic in lightly greased large skillet until tender, 3 to 5 minutes. Add squash and cook over medium heat until squash is crisp-tender, about 20 minutes, stirring occasionally. Stir in pepitas; season to taste with salt and pepper.

PARMESAN-HERB SPAGHETTI SQUASH

45 *Italian seasoning and Parmesan cheese compliment the delicate flavor of the squash.*

4 servings

1 spaghetti squash (2½–3 pounds), halved lengthwise, seeded
2 tablespoons sliced green onions
1 teaspoon each: minced garlic, dried Italian seasoning
1–2 tablespoons margarine or butter

¼ cup reduced-sodium vegetable broth or water

½ cup (2 ounces) fat-free Parmesan cheese

Salt and pepper, to taste

Per Serving:
Calories: 99
% of calories from fat: 29
Fat (gm): 3.6
Saturated fat (gm): 0.7
Cholesterol (mg): 0
Sodium (mg): 102
Protein (gm): 5.1
Carbohydrate (gm): 14.3

1. Place squash, cut sides down, in baking pan; add ½ inch hot water. Bake, covered, at 450 degrees until tender, about 30 minutes. Fluff strands of squash with tines of fork, leaving squash in shells.

Exchanges:
Milk: 0.0
Vegetable: 2.0
Fruit: 0.0
Bread: 0.0
Meat: 0.5
Fat: 0.5

2. Sauté green onions, garlic, and Italian seasoning in margarine in small saucepan until tender, 3 to 4 minutes. Stir in broth; cook until hot, about 2 minutes. Spoon half the mixture into each squash half and toss; sprinkle with Parmesan cheese and toss. Season to taste with salt and pepper.

FRIED TOMATOES

45 *Either green or red tomatoes can be used in this recipe—try both!*

4 servings

4 medium green or red tomatoes, sliced (¼-inch)

¼ cup all-purpose flour

Salt and pepper, to taste

Per Serving:
Calories: 58
% of calories from fat: 5
Fat (gm): 0.3
Saturated fat (gm): 0
Cholesterol (mg): 0
Sodium (mg): 16
Protein (gm): 2.3
Carbohydrate (gm): 12.2

1. Coat tomato slices lightly with flour; cook over medium heat in lightly greased large skillet until browned, 2 to 3 minutes on each side. Sprinkle lightly with salt and pepper.

Exchanges:
Milk: 0.0
Vegetable: 1.0
Fruit: 0.0
Bread: 0.5
Meat: 0.0
Fat: 0.0

VARIATIONS

Sugar-Glazed Fried Tomatoes — Make recipe as above, but do not coat with flour. After tomatoes are browned, sprinkle lightly with sugar and cook until caramelized, about 1 minute on each side. Do not season with salt and pepper.

Cornmeal-Fried Tomatoes — Make recipe as above, substituting yellow cornmeal for the flour.

HERBED TOMATO HALVES

Select ripe, yet firm, tomatoes, and vary the herbs to complement the main dish you're serving.

4 servings

4 medium tomatoes, halved

¼ cup (1 ounce) grated fat-free Parmesan cheese

1 tablespoon unseasoned dry bread crumbs

½ teaspoon each: dried basil, marjoram, and thyme leaves

⅛–¼ teaspoon garlic powder

2–3 pinches pepper

Per Serving:
Calories: 45
% of calories from fat: 9
Fat (gm): 0.5
Saturated fat (gm): 0.1
Cholesterol (mg): 0
Sodium (mg): 60
Protein (gm): 2.8
Carbohydrate (gm): 8.8

Exchanges:
Milk: 0.0
Vegetable: 2.0
Fruit: 0.0
Bread: 0.0
Meat: 0.0
Fat: 0.0

1. Place tomatoes, cut sides up, in baking pan; sprinkle with combined remaining ingredients. Bake at 375 degrees until tomatoes are hot and topping is browned, 15 to 20 minutes.

GREENS-STUFFED BAKED TOMATOES

We've used turnip greens, but any other dark leafy greens, such as kale, mustard greens, or spinach, may be substituted.

6 servings

6 medium tomatoes

10 ounces fresh or frozen turnip greens, cooked, coarsely chopped

½ teaspoon each: dried chervil and marjoram leaves

Salt and pepper, to taste

1 tablespoon each: grated fat-free Parmesan cheese, unseasoned dry bread crumbs

Per Serving:
Calories: 42
% of calories from fat: 11
Fat (gm): 0.6
Saturated fat (gm): 0.1
Cholesterol (mg): 0
Sodium (mg): 42
Protein (gm): 2.1
Carbohydrate (gm): 9

Exchanges:
Milk: 0.0
Vegetable: 2.0
Fruit: 0.0
Bread: 0.0
Meat: 0.0
Fat: 0.0

1. Cut thin slice from tops of tomatoes; scoop pulp from tomatoes, discarding seeds. Chop pulp and mix with turnip greens and herbs; season to taste with salt and pepper. Spoon into tomatoes and sprinkle with combined cheese and bread crumbs. Place in baking pan and bake at 350 degrees until tender, about 20 minutes.

TOMATO PUDDING

45

Dry stuffing cubes can be substituted for the croutons. Two cups coarsely chopped fresh tomatoes can be substituted for the canned tomatoes; simmer until tomatoes wilt and release juices, 5 to 8 minutes.

4 servings

½ cup each: thinly sliced celery, chopped onion, green bell pepper

1 can (16 ounces) reduced-sodium diced tomatoes, undrained

½ teaspoon each: celery seeds, dried marjoram leaves

1 tablespoon light brown sugar

Salt and pepper, to taste

1½ cups (½ recipe) Sourdough Croutons (see p. 532)

Per Serving:
Calories: 85
% of calories from fat: 9
Fat (gm): 0.9
Saturated fat (gm): 0.1
Cholesterol (mg): 0
Sodium (mg): 88
Protein (gm): 2.6
Carbohydrate (gm): 17.9

Exchanges:
Milk: 0.0
Vegetable: 2.0
Fruit: 0.0
Bread: 0.5
Meat: 0.0
Fat: 0.0

1. Sauté celery, onion, and bell pepper in lightly greased medium skillet until tender, about 8 minutes. Add tomatoes with liquid, celery seeds, marjoram, and brown sugar; season to taste with salt and pepper. Spoon into 1-quart soufflé dish or casserole. Stir in Sourdough Croutons, leaving some of the croutons on top. Bake, uncovered, at 375 degrees until hot, about 20 minutes.

45-MINUTE PREPARATION TIP: Make Sourdough Croutons before preparing the rest of the recipe.

ZUCCHINI FROM PUEBLA

45

If the Mexican white cheese "queso blanco" is not available, farmer's cheese or feta cheese can be easily substituted.

6 servings (about ½ cup each)

1 cup chopped onion

2 pounds zucchini, diagonally sliced (¼-inch)

4 roasted red bell peppers, sliced

½ cup reduced-sodium vegetable broth

½–1 teaspoon ground cumin

Salt and pepper, to taste

2 tablespoons crumbled Mexican white cheese

1. Sauté onion in lightly greased large skillet until tender, 5 to 8 minutes. Add zucchini, roasted peppers, broth, and cumin. Heat to boiling. Reduce heat and simmer, covered, until zucchini is crisp-tender, 5 to 8 minutes. Season to taste with salt and pepper; sprinkle with cheese.

Per Serving:
Calories: 62
% of calories from fat: 14
Fat (gm): 1
Saturated fat (gm): 0.1
Cholesterol (mg): 2.6
Sodium (mg): 32
Protein (gm): 2.9
Carbohydrate (gm): 11.8

Exchanges:
Milk: 0.0
Vegetable: 2.0
Fruit: 0.0
Bread: 0.0
Meat: 0.0
Fat: 0.0

ZUCCHINI FANS PROVENÇAL

Zucchini are thinly sliced, then spread out to form "fans."

4 servings

2 medium sweet onions, thinly sliced

6 cloves garlic, minced

4 small zucchini, halved lengthwise

3 medium tomatoes, thinly sliced

½ cup dry white wine or reduced-sodium vegetable broth

Salt and pepper, to taste

1½ teaspoons dried Italian seasoning

Per Serving:
Calories: 89
% of calories from fat: 6
Fat (gm): 0.6
Saturated fat (gm): 0.1
Cholesterol (mg): 0
Sodium (mg): 16
Protein (gm): 3.4
Carbohydrate (gm): 15.3

Exchanges:
Milk: 0.0
Vegetable: 3.0
Fruit: 0.0
Bread: 0.0
Meat: 0.0
Fat: 0.0

1. Separate onions into rings; arrange half the onions and garlic in bottom of 11 x 7-inch baking pan. Cut zucchini halves lengthwise into scant ¼-inch slices, cutting to, but not through, small ends. Alternate zucchini and tomato slices in rows over onions, spreading zucchini slices into "fans." Arrange remaining onions and garlic on top; pour wine over. Sprinkle lightly with salt, pepper and Italian seasoning. Bake, covered, at 350 degrees until zucchini is tender, about 25 minutes.

TWELVE

Salads
and
Dressings

FROZEN FRUIT SALAD

45 *An old-fashioned favorite—simple, tasty, and refreshing!*

8 servings

8 ounces fat-free cream cheese, room temperature

1 cup fat-free sour cream

⅓ cup sugar

1 tablespoon grated lemon zest

Pinch salt

5 cups assorted fresh, frozen, or drained, canned fruit

Lettuce leaves

Per Serving:
Calories: 77
% of calories from fat: 1
Fat (gm): 0.1
Saturated fat (gm): 0
Cholesterol (mg): 0
Sodium (mg): 5
Protein (gm): 1.4
Carbohydrate (gm): 18.7

Exchanges:
Milk: 0.0
Vegetable: 0.0
Fruit: 1.0
Bread: 0.0
Meat: 0.0
Fat: 0.0

1. Beat cream cheese, sour cream, sugar, lemon zest, and salt in large bowl until smooth. Mix in fruit. Spread in 11 x 7-inch baking dish and freeze until firm, 8 hours or overnight. Before serving, let stand at room temperature until soft enough to cut, 10 to 15 minutes. Cut into squares; serve on lettuce-lined plates.

PERFECTION SALAD

45 *For quick and easy preparation, packaged coleslaw mix can be used.*

12 servings

1 package (0.6 ounces) sugar-free lemon, lime, or orange-flavor gelatin

¼ teaspoon salt

1 can (8 ounces) unsweetened crushed pineapple in juice, drained, juice reserved

1½ cups thinly sliced or shredded cabbage

½ cup each: chopped celery, shredded carrot

¼ cup chopped red or green bell pepper

¼–½ cup sliced pimiento-stuffed olives

Lettuce leaves

¾ cup fat-free mayonnaise

Per Serving:
Calories: 36
% of calories from fat: 11
Fat (gm): 0.4
Saturated fat (gm): 0.1
Cholesterol (mg): 0
Sodium (mg): 265
Protein (gm): 1.1
Carbohydrate (gm): 6.9

Exchanges:
Milk: 0.0
Vegetable: 1.0
Fruit: 0.0
Bread: 0.0
Meat: 0.0
Fat: 0.0

1. Prepare gelatin according to package directions, adding salt and using reserved pineapple juice as part of the liquid. Mix in remaining ingredients, except lettuce and mayonnaise. Pour into ungreased 12 x 8-inch baking dish. Refrigerate until firm, 4 to 5 hours.

2. Cut salad into squares; arrange on lettuce-lined plates. Top each serving with a dollop of mayonnaise.

WALDORF SALAD

45 *This colorful version of waldorf uses both red and green apples. Add miniature marshmallows, if your family insists!*

4 servings

2 cups unpeeled, cubed red and green apples

1 cup sliced celery

¼ cup each: chopped, toasted walnuts, raisins, fat-free mayonnaise, sour cream

2–3 teaspoons lemon juice

1–2 tablespoons honey

1. Combine apples, celery, walnuts, and raisins in bowl. Mix in combined remaining ingredients.

Per Serving:
Calories: 149
% of calories from fat: 26
Fat (gm): 4.7
Saturated fat (gm): 0.3
Cholesterol (mg): 0
Sodium (mg): 227
Protein (gm): 3.5
Carbohydrate (gm): 26.5

Exchanges:
Milk: 0.0
Vegetable: 0.5
Fruit: 1.5
Bread: 0.0
Meat: 0.0
Fat: 1.0

BEAN, TOMATO, AND BREAD SALAD

45 *Use summer ripe tomatoes for best flavor. Any favorite bean can be used.*

8 servings

3 cups cubed sourdough bread (½-inch)

Olive oil cooking spray

2 large tomatoes, cubed

½ small red onion, thinly sliced

2 cans (15 ounces each) navy or Great Northern, beans, rinsed, drained

1 cup chopped roasted red peppers

Parmesan Vinaigrette (recipe follows)

Salt and pepper, to taste

Per Serving:
Calories: 199
% of calories from fat: 19
Fat (gm): 4.2
Saturated fat (gm): 0.7
Cholesterol (mg): 0
Sodium (mg): 454
Protein (gm): 9.8
Carbohydrate (gm): 30.4

Exchanges:
Milk: 0.0
Vegetable: 0.0
Fruit: 0.0
Bread: 2.0
Meat: 0.0
Fat: 1.0

1. Spray bread cubes generously with cooking spray; arrange in single layer on jelly roll pan. Bake at 350 degrees until golden, 10 to 15 minutes, stirring occasionally. Cool.

2. Combine tomatoes, onion, beans, and roasted red peppers in salad bowl; pour Parmesan Vinaigrette over and toss. Season to taste with salt and pepper. Let stand 15 to 30 minutes; add bread cubes toss. Serve immediately.

Parmesan Vinaigrette

Makes about ½ cup

2–4 tablespoons each: olive oil, red wine vinegar

2 tablespoons each: grated fat-free Parmesan cheese, chopped fresh or
   1½ teaspoons dried basil and oregano leaves

1 teaspoon minced garlic

1. Mix all ingredients.

BEAN AND PASTA SALAD
WITH WHITE BEAN DRESSING

Pureed beans, fat-free sour cream, and seasonings combine to make a rich, delicious salad dressing—use on green salads too!

10 servings

4 ounces tri-color rotini, cooked, room temperature

1 can (14¼ ounces) baby lima beans, rinsed, drained

½ can (15-ounce size) Great Northern beans,
   rinsed, drained

½ package (9-ounce size) frozen artichoke hearts,
   cooked, halved

2 cups cut green beans, cooked

¼ cup each: sliced red bell pepper, pitted black olives

½ cup (2 ounces) julienned reduced-fat brick cheese

White Bean Dressing (recipe follows)

Per Serving:
Calories: 188
% of calories from fat: 19
Fat (gm): 4.0
Saturated fat (gm): 0.8
Cholesterol (mg): 3.1
Sodium (mg): 313
Protein (gm): 9.7
Carbohydrate (gm): 30.1

Exchanges:
Milk: 0.0
Vegetable: 1.0
Fruit: 0.0
Bread: 1.5
Meat: 0.5
Fat: 0.5

1. Combine all ingredients in bowl and toss.

White Bean Dressing
Makes about 1½ cups

½ can (15-ounce size) Great Northern beans, rinsed, drained
½ cup fat-free sour cream
1 tablespoon olive oil
2–3 tablespoons red wine vinegar
2 cloves garlic
1 teaspoon dried oregano leaves
2 tablespoons sliced green onions
Salt and pepper, to taste

1. Process all ingredients, except green onions, salt, and pepper in food processor or blender until smooth. Stir in green onions; season to taste with salt and pepper. Refrigerate several hours for flavors to blend.

BROCCOLI SALAD WITH SOUR CREAM-MAYONNAISE DRESSING

45 *Serve this nutrient-packed salad on a bed of salad greens or in scooped-out tomato halves.*

12 servings

4½ cups broccoli florets and sliced stalks
1½ cups each: sliced zucchini, mushrooms, chopped green bell peppers
12 cherry tomatoes, halved
3 green onions, sliced
⅓ cup dark raisins
Sour Cream-Mayonnaise Dressing (recipe follows)

1. Combine all ingredients in bowl and toss.

Per Serving:
Calories: 55
% of calories from fat: 13
Fat (gm): 0.9
Saturated fat (gm): 0.4
Cholesterol (mg): 1.4
Sodium (mg): 101
Protein (gm): 2.8
Carbohydrate (gm): 10.3

Exchanges:
Milk: 0.0
Vegetable: 2.0
Fruit: 0.0
Bread: 0.0
Meat: 0.0
Fat: 0.0

Sour Cream-Mayonnaise Dressing
Makes about 1¼ cups

⅓ cup each: fat-free sour cream, fat-free mayonnaise
3 cloves garlic, minced
3 tablespoons each: fat-free milk, crumbled blue cheese

1. Mix all ingredients.

CARROT-RAISIN SALAD

45 *Always a popular salad—a small can of drained pineapple tidbits can be added.*

6 servings

2½ cups shredded carrots
¾ cup chopped celery
⅓ cup each: raisins, coarsely chopped walnuts
¾ cup fat-free mayonnaise
½ teaspoon Dijon mustard
1–2 teaspoons sugar
⅛ teaspoon salt

Per Serving:
Calories: 115
% of calories from fat: 30
Fat (gm): 4.1
Saturated fat (gm): 0.3
Cholesterol (mg): 0
Sodium (mg): 460
Protein (gm): 2.6
Carbohydrate (gm): 19.2

Exchanges:
Milk: 0.0
Vegetable: 2.0
Fruit: 0.5
Bread: 0.0
Meat: 0.0
Fat: 1.0

1. Combine carrots, celery, raisins, and walnuts in bowl; mix in combined remaining ingredients.

CACTUS SALAD

45 *The tender cactus paddles called "nopales" are readily available in large supermarkets today. Be sure all the thorns have been removed; if not, they can be pulled out easily with tweezers.*

6 servings

2 quarts boiling water
1½ pounds cactus paddles, cut into ½-inch pieces
1 tablespoon salt
¼ teaspoon baking soda
1½ cups halved cherry tomatoes

½ cup thinly sliced red onion
Lime Dressing (recipe follows)

1. Heat water to boiling in large saucepan; add cactus, salt, and baking soda. Reduce heat and simmer, uncovered, until cactus is crisp-tender, about 20 minutes. Rinse in cold water; drain. Toss cactus and remaining ingredients in salad bowl.

Lime Dressing

Makes about ¼ cup

2 tablespoons lime juice
1–2 tablespoons olive or canola oil
1 tablespoon water
1 teaspoon cider vinegar
2 teaspoons sugar
½ teaspoon dried oregano leaves

1. Combine all ingredients.

Per Serving:
Calories: 78
% of calories from fat: 28
Fat (gm): 2.5
Saturated fat (gm): 0.3
Cholesterol (mg): 0
Sodium (mg): 131
Protein (gm): 2.4
Carbohydrate (gm): 12.5

Exchanges:
Milk: 0.0
Vegetable: 2.0
Fruit: 0.0
Bread: 0.0
Meat: 0.0
Fat: 0.5

JICAMA SALAD

45 *Jicama adds a marvelous crispness to salads, complementing both fruits and vegetables.*

6 servings

12 ounces jicama, peeled, cut into strips
  (1½- x ½-inch)
½ cup sliced zucchini
1 small orange, peeled, cut into segments
2–3 thin slices red onion
Cilantro Lime Dressing (recipe follows)
Salt and pepper, to taste

1. Combine all ingredients, except salt and pepper, in salad bowl and toss. Season to taste with salt and pepper.

Per Serving:
Calories: 77
% of calories from fat: 27
Fat (gm): 2.4
Saturated fat (gm): 0.3
Cholesterol (mg): 0
Sodium (mg): 1
Protein (gm): 1.3
Carbohydrate (gm): 13.5

Exchanges:
Milk: 0.0
Vegetable: 1.0
Fruit: 0.5
Bread: 0.0
Meat: 0.0
Fat: 0.5

Cilantro Lime Dressing
Makes about ¼ cup

2 tablespoons each: lime juice, chopped cilantro
1 tablespoon orange juice
1–2 tablespoons olive or canola oil
2 teaspoons sugar

1. Combine all ingredients.

VEGETABLE SALAD WITH 2 BEANS

45 *Enjoy the fresh flavors of cilantro and orange and the accent of jalapeño chili in this great salad.*

8 servings

1 package (10 ounces) frozen baby lima
  beans, cooked
1 can (15 ounces) garbanzo beans, rinsed, drained
1 large Idaho potato, peeled, cooked, cubed
1 cup each: peeled, seeded, chopped cucumber,
  sliced zucchini
½ cup chopped green pepper
¼ cup chopped cilantro
Citrus Vinaigrette (recipe follows)

Per Serving:
Calories: 170
% of calories from fat: 24
Fat (gm): 4.7
Saturated fat (gm): 0.7
Cholesterol (mg): 0
Sodium (mg): 232
Protein (gm): 6.3
Carbohydrate (gm): 27.4

Exchanges:
Milk: 0.0
Vegetable: 1.0
Fruit: 0.0
Bread: 1.5
Meat: 0.0
Fat: 1.0

1. Combine all ingredients in salad bowl and toss.

Citrus Vinaigrette
Makes about ⅔ cup

¼ cup each: orange juice, lime juice
2 tablespoons olive oil
1 teaspoon each: dried cumin, minced jalapeño chili
¼ teaspoon each: paprika, salt, cayenne pepper

1. Mix all ingredients.

10-LAYER SALAD

Or make this salad as many layers as you want! Add a layer of cubed chicken breast or lean smoked ham for an entrée salad, using 3 ounces of cooked meat per person.

8 servings

2 cups thinly sliced romaine lettuce
1 cup each: sliced red cabbage, mushrooms, carrots, green bell pepper, halved cherry tomatoes, small broccoli or cauliflower florets
½ cup each: sliced cucumber, red onion
Herbed Sour Cream Dressing (recipe follows)
Finely chopped parsley, as garnish

Per Serving:
Calories: 68
% of calories from fat: 4
Fat (gm): 0.4
Saturated fat (gm): 0.1
Cholesterol (mg): 0
Sodium (mg): 380
Protein (gm): 3.3
Carbohydrate (gm): 14.8

Exchanges:
Milk: 0.0
Vegetable: 1.5
Fruit: 0.0
Bread: 0.0
Meat: 0.0
Fat: 0.0

1. Arrange lettuce in bottom of 1½-quart glass bowl; arrange remaining vegetables in layers over lettuce. Spread Herbed Sour Cream Dressing over top of salad and sprinkle with parsley. Refrigerate, loosely covered, 8 hours or overnight. Toss before serving.

Herbed Sour Cream Dressing

Makes about 1½ cups

¾ cup each: fat-free mayonnaise and sour cream
2–3 cloves garlic, minced
½ teaspoon each: dried basil and tarragon leaves
¼ teaspoon each: salt, pepper

1. Mix all ingredients.

CAESAR SALAD

45 *For food safety, real egg product is used in the salad.*

4 servings

4 thick slices French or Italian bread

1 clove garlic, halved

6 cups torn romaine lettuce

2 tablespoons each: lemon juice, no-cholesterol real egg product, grated Parmesan cheese

1 tablespoon olive oil

½ teaspoon Worcestershire sauce

2–3 anchovies, drained, chopped (optional)

⅛ teaspoon dry mustard

Dash red pepper sauce

Salt and freshly ground pepper, to taste

Per Serving:
Calories: 127
% of calories from fat: 30
Fat (gm): 4.4
Saturated fat (gm): 0.6
Cholesterol (mg): 0
Sodium (mg): 200
Protein (gm): 5.3
Carbohydrate (gm): 17.1

Exchanges:
Milk: 0.0
Vegetable: 1.0
Fruit: 0.0
Bread: 1.0
Meat: 0.0
Fat: 0.5

1. Rub both sides of bread slices with cut sides of garlic; mince remaining garlic and reserve. Cut bread into ½ to ¾-inch cubes. Bake on jelly roll pan at 425 degrees until toasted, about 5 minutes.

2. Toss lettuce with minced garlic and combined remaining ingredients, except salt and pepper, in salad bowl; season to taste with salt and pepper. Add croutons and toss.

MANGO AND BLACK BEAN SALAD

45 *Any tropical fruit, such as pineapple, kiwi, papaya, or star fruit, can be used in this refreshing salad.*

8 servings

4 large ripe mangoes, peeled, pitted, cubed

1 cup cubed pineapple

½ medium cucumber, seeded, sliced

¼ cup each: finely chopped red bell pepper, sliced green onions

1 can (15 ounces) black beans, rinsed, drained

Honey-Lime Dressing (recipe follows)

Mint sprigs, as garnish

Per Serving:
Calories: 164
% of calories from fat: 20
Fat (gm): 4.3
Saturated fat (gm): 0.6
Cholesterol (mg): 0
Sodium (mg): 169
Protein (gm): 5.2
Carbohydrate (gm): 32.7

Exchanges:
Milk: 0.0
Vegetable: 0.0
Fruit: 1.0
Bread: 1.0
Meat: 0.0
Fat: 1.0

1. Combine all ingredients, except mint, in salad bowl and toss; garnish with mint.

Honey-Lime Dressing
Makes about ⅓ cup

2 tablespoons each: olive oil, water
1 tablespoon each: honey, tarragon wine vinegar, grated lime zest
3–4 teaspoons lime juice
½ teaspoon dried mint leaves
Pinch salt

1. Mix all ingredients.

45-MINUTE PREPARATION TIP: Make Honey-Lime Dressing before preparing the rest of the recipe.

CREAMY POTATO SALAD

For the creamiest salad, toss the potatoes with the dressing while they're still slightly warm.

10 servings

1½ pounds russet potatoes, peeled, cooked,
   cubed, warm
1 cup sliced celery
½ cup sliced green onions
¼ cup each: chopped green and red bell pepper,
   sweet pickle relish
2 hard-cooked eggs, chopped
4 slices bacon, fried, well drained, crumbled
1 cup fat-free mayonnaise
½ cup fat-free sour cream
2 tablespoons cider vinegar
1 tablespoon yellow mustard
½ teaspoon celery seeds
Salt and pepper, to taste

Per Serving:
Calories: 132
% of calories from fat: 16
Fat (gm): 2.5
Saturated fat (gm): 0.8
Cholesterol (mg): 44.7
Sodium (mg): 495
Protein (gm): 4.3
Carbohydrate (gm): 24.5

Exchanges:
Milk: 1.0
Vegetable: 2.0
Fruit: 0.0
Bread: 3.0
Meat: 0.5
Fat: 0.5

1. Combine vegetables, pickle relish, eggs, and bacon in bowl. Mix in combined remaining ingredients, except salt and pepper; season to taste with salt and pepper.

GERMAN POTATO SALAD

45 *Tart and tangy in flavor, this salad is best served warm from the skillet.*

6 servings

1 cup chopped onion

1 tablespoon flour

½ cup reduced-sodium beef broth

1¼ cups cider vinegar

1 tablespoon sugar

½ teaspoon celery seeds

1½ pounds peeled potatoes, cooked, sliced, warm

Salt and pepper, to taste

2 tablespoons each: crumbled cooked bacon, chopped parsley

Per Serving:
Calories: 125
% of calories from fat: 5
Fat (gm): 0.7
Saturated fat (gm): 0.1
Cholesterol (mg): 0
Sodium (mg): 69.3
Protein (gm): 3
Carbohydrate (gm): 30.7

Exchanges:
Milk: 0.0
Vegetable: 0.0
Fruit: 0.0
Bread: 2.0
Meat: 0.0
Fat: 0.0

1. Sauté onion in lightly greased medium skillet until tender and browned, about 5 minutes. Stir in flour; cook 1 minute. Add broth, vinegar, sugar, and celery seeds and heat to boiling, stirring until thickened, about 1 minute. Add potatoes and toss. Season to taste with salt and pepper; sprinkle with bacon and parsley.

45-MINUTE PREPARATION TIP: Begin cooking the potatoes before preparing the rest of the recipe.

CARIBBEAN POTATO SALAD

45 *Sweet and white potatoes combine with a creamy cumin and lime mayonnaise dressing; olives provide a pungent accent.*

8 servings

1½ pounds each: sweet and russet potatoes, peeled, cooked, cubed (¾-inch)

¼ cup small pimiento-stuffed olives

¾ cup fat-free mayonnaise

½ cup fat-free milk

2 teaspoons lime juice

2 green onions, sliced

1 teaspoon ground cumin

Per Serving:
Calories: 167
% of calories from fat: 5
Fat (gm): 1
Saturated fat (gm): 0.2
Cholesterol (mg): 0.3
Sodium (mg): 416
Protein (gm): 3.1
Carbohydrate (gm): 37.2

Exchanges:
Milk: 0.0
Vegetable: 0.0
Fruit: 0.0
Bread: 2.5
Meat: 0.0
Fat: 0.0

⅛ teaspoon red cayenne pepper
Salt, to taste

1. Combine potatoes and olives in bowl; mix in combined remaining ingredients, except salt. Season to taste with salt. Refrigerate 2 to 3 hours for flavors to blend.

SPINACH AND MELON SALAD

45 *A colorful salad, accented with sweet Honey Dressing.*

8 servings

8 cups torn spinach
1½ cups each: watermelon, honeydew, and cantaloupe balls
⅓ cup each: thinly sliced cucumber, red onion
Honey Dressing (recipe follows)

1. Combine all ingredients in salad bowl and toss.

Honey Dressing
Makes about ½ cup

2–3 tablespoons honey
1–2 tablespoons each: red wine vinegar, olive oil
2–3 tablespoons each: orange and lime juice
1 teaspoon dried tarragon leaves
⅛ teaspoon salt

1. Mix all ingredients.

Per Serving:
Calories: 85
% of calories from fat: 36
Fat (gm): 3.6
Saturated fat (gm): 0.5
Cholesterol (mg): 0
Sodium (mg): 50
Protein (gm): 1.7
Carbohydrate (gm): 13.2

Exchanges:
Milk: 0.0
Vegetable: 0.0
Fruit: 1.0
Bread: 0.0
Meat: 0.0
Fat: 0.5

WILTED SPINACH SALAD

45 *A healthful variation of this favorite salad that includes crumbled bacon for traditional flavor.*

4 servings

1 package (10 ounces) fresh spinach
4 green onions, sliced
4 slices bacon, fried crisp, well drained, crumbled
1 hard-cooked egg, chopped
1 cup fat-free French or sweet-sour salad dressing
Salt and pepper, to taste

Per Serving:
Calories: 95
% of calories from fat: 26
Fat (gm): 2.6
Saturated fat (gm): 0.8
Cholesterol (mg): 38.2
Sodium (mg): 418
Protein (gm): 3.4
Carbohydrate (gm): 12.6

Exchanges:
Milk: 0.0
Vegetable: 1.0
Fruit: 0.0
Bread: 0.5
Meat: 0.0
Fat: 0.5

1. Combine spinach, onions, bacon, and egg in salad bowl. Heat French dressing to boiling in small saucepan; pour over salad and toss. Season to taste with salt and pepper.

MACARONI SALAD

45 *The fourth of July signals fried chicken, apple pie, and, of course, home-made macaroni salad! Add 1 cup halved summer-ripe cherry tomatoes for festive color.*

6 servings

3 cups cooked elbow macaroni, room temperature
½ cup each: frozen, thawed baby peas, chopped onion, celery, shredded carrot, red bell pepper
¼ cup sliced ripe or pimiento-stuffed olives
¾ cup fat-free mayonnaise
2 teaspoons yellow mustard
1 teaspoon sugar
Salt and pepper, to taste

Per Serving:
Calories: 152
% of calories from fat: 12
Fat (gm): 2.1
Saturated fat (gm): 0.3
Cholesterol (mg): 2.8
Sodium (mg): 357
Protein (gm): 4.5
Carbohydrate (gm): 29.8

Exchanges:
Milk: 0.0
Vegetable: 0.0
Fruit: 0.0
Bread: 2.0
Meat: 0.0
Fat: 0.0

1. Combine macaroni, vegetables, and olives in bowl. Mix in combined mayonnaise, mustard, and sugar; season to taste with salt and pepper.

45-MINUTE PREPARATION TIP: Begin cooking the macaroni before preparing the rest of the recipe; rinse macaroni in cold water to cool it quickly.

MACARONI-BLUE CHEESE SALAD

45 *A not-so-traditional macaroni salad with blue cheese pizzazz!*

8 servings

4 ounces elbow macaroni, cooked, room temperature

⅔ cup each: chopped red bell pepper, cucumber, shredded carrots

¼ cup sliced green onions

Blue Cheese Dressing (recipe follows)

1. Combine all ingredients in bowl and toss.

Per Serving:
Calories: 94
% of calories from fat: 18
Fat (gm): 1.9
Saturated fat (gm): 0.8
Cholesterol (mg): 4.5
Sodium (mg): 240
Protein (gm): 2.9
Carbohydrate (gm): 16.5

Exchanges:
Milk: 0.0
Vegetable: 0.0
Fruit: 0.0
Bread: 1.0
Meat: 0.0
Fat: 0.5

Blue Cheese Dressing

Makes about 1 cup

¾ cup fat-free mayonnaise or salad dressing

3 tablespoons crumbled blue cheese

1½ tablespoons red wine vinegar

1 teaspoon celery seeds

½ teaspoon salt

⅛ teaspoon each: cayenne and black pepper

1. Mix all ingredients.

45-MINUTE PREPARATION TIP: Begin cooking the macaroni before preparing the rest of the recipe. Rinse the macaroni in cold water to cool it quickly.

PASTA COLESLAW

45 *The addition of pasta updates a traditional cabbage slaw.*

4 servings

4 ounces fusilli (spirals) or farfalle (bow ties),
   cooked, room temperature
1 cup thinly sliced green cabbage
⅔ cup each: chopped tomato, green bell pepper
¼ cup sliced celery
Creamy Dressing (recipe follows)

Per Serving:
Calories: 139
% of calories from fat: 8
Fat (gm): 1.2
Saturated fat (gm): 0.3
Cholesterol (mg): 0.9
Sodium (mg): 156
Protein (gm): 5.4
Carbohydrate (gm): 27.3

Exchanges:
Milk: 0.0
Vegetable: 1.0
Fruit: 0.0
Bread: 1.5
Meat: 0.0
Fat: 0.0

1. Combine all ingredients in bowl and toss.

Creamy Dressing

Makes about ½ cup

¼ cup each: fat-free mayonnaise, low-fat plain yogurt
1 tablespoon lemon juice
2 cloves garlic, minced
½ teaspoon dried tarragon leaves
¼ teaspoon each: salt, pepper

1. Mix all ingredients.

45-MINUTE PREPARATION TIP: Begin cooking the fusilli before preparing the rest of the recipe; rinse fusilli in cold water to cool it quickly.

SESAME PASTA SALAD WITH SUMMER VEGETABLES

45 *The vegetables used in this salad can vary according to seasonal availability.*

6 servings

1 small eggplant
1 cup each: sliced carrots, yellow summer squash,
   cooked broccoli florets
1 medium red bell pepper, sliced

¼ cup sliced green onions

8 ounces thin spaghetti, cooked, room temperature

Sesame Dressing (recipe follows)

2 teaspoons toasted sesame seeds

Per Serving:
Calories: 220
% of calories from fat: 17.7
Fat (gm): 4.3
Saturated fat (gm): 0.6
Cholesterol (mg): 0
Sodium (mg): 136
Protein (gm): 6.7
Carbohydrate (gm): 38.8

Exchanges:
Milk: 0.0
Vegetable: 2.0
Fruit: 0.0
Bread: 2.0
Meat: 0.0
Fat: 1.0

1. Pierce eggplant 6 to 8 times with fork; roast in baking pan at 425 degrees until tender, about 30 minutes; cool. Cut eggplant in half; scoop out pulp and cut into ¾-inch pieces. Combine eggplant, vegetables, and pasta in salad bowl; toss with Sesame dressing and sprinkle with sesame seeds.

Sesame Dressing

Makes about ⅓ cup

2 tablespoons each: reduced-sodium soy sauce, sesame oil

1 teaspoon hot chili oil (optional)

1 tablespoon each: balsamic or red wine vinegar, chopped cilantro

1½ tablespoons sugar

1 clove garlic, minced

1. Mix all ingredients.

45-MINUTE PREPARATION TIP: Cook the spaghetti and cut vegetables while the eggplant is roasting.

MIXED VEGETABLES AND ORZO VINAIGRETTE

45 *The turmeric gives the salad dressing its unusual yellow color. Curry powder can be used instead to impart the same color and add a delicate curry flavor.*

8 servings

2 cups cut asparagus (1½-inch pieces), cooked crisp-tender

1½ cups thinly sliced zucchini

1 cup frozen peas, thawed

½ cup sliced carrots, cooked crisp-tender

¾ cup halved cherry tomatoes

¼ cup orzo, cooked, room temperature

Mustard-Turmeric Vinaigrette (recipe follows)

1. Combine all ingredients in salad bowl and toss.

Mustard-Turmeric Vinaigrette

Makes about ½ cup

¼ cup white wine vinegar

¼ teaspoon ground turmeric

2–3 tablespoons lemon juice

2 tablespoons olive or canola oil

2 teaspoons Dijon mustard

2 cloves garlic, minced

¼ teaspoon each: salt, pepper

Per Serving:
Calories: 142
% of calories from fat: 27
Fat (gm): 4.2
Saturated fat (gm): 0.6
Cholesterol (mg): 0
Sodium (mg): 112
Protein (gm): 5.5
Carbohydrate (gm): 20.9

Exchanges:
Milk: 0.0
Vegetable: 1.0
Fruit: 0.0
Bread: 1.0
Meat: 0.0
Fat: 1.0

1. Heat vinegar and turmeric in small saucepan over medium heat, stirring until turmeric is dissolved, 2 to 3 minutes; cool. Combine with remaining ingredients.

45-MINUTE PREPARATION TIP: Begin cooking the orzo, carrots, and asparagus before preparing the rest of the recipe.

ORZO WITH SUN-DRIED TOMATOES AND MUSHROOMS

45 *A simple salad, intensely flavored with sun-dried tomatoes, rosemary, and sherry.*

4 servings

2 sun-dried tomatoes (not in oil), softened, sliced

1½ cups sliced mushrooms

¼ cup sliced green onions

2 cloves garlic, minced

½ cup vegetable broth

2 tablespoons dry sherry (optional)

½ cup (4 ounces) orzo, cooked, room temperature

2 tablespoons chopped fresh, or 1 teaspoon dried, rosemary leaves

¼ teaspoon each: salt, pepper

Per Serving:
Calories: 135
% of calories from fat: 6
Fat (gm): 0.8
Saturated fat (gm): 0.1
Cholesterol (mg): 0
Sodium (mg): 218
Protein (gm): 5.1
Carbohydrate (gm): 27.2

Exchanges:
Milk: 0.0
Vegetable: 0.0
Fruit: 0.0
Bread: 2.0
Meat: 0.0
Fat: 0.0

1. Sauté sun-dried tomatoes, mushrooms, green onions, and garlic in lightly greased large skillet until mushrooms are tender, 5 to 7 minutes. Add broth and sherry; heat to boiling. Reduce heat and simmer, uncovered, until liquid is reduced to about ¼ cup, about 5 minutes; cool. Toss with orzo, rosemary, salt and pepper in salad bowl.

45-MINUTE PREPARATION TIP: Begin cooking the orzo before preparing the rest of the recipe.

GARDEN VEGETABLE AND PASTA SALAD

45

The eggplant can be roasted and refrigerated 1 to 2 days in advance.

6 servings

1 medium eggplant, unpeeled, cubed (¾-inch)
Vegetable cooking spray
2 cups each: cauliflower and broccoli florets, cooked crisp-tender
10 cherry tomatoes, halved
½ medium green bell pepper, sliced
8 ounces fettuccine or linguine, cooked, room temperature
Basil Vinaigrette (recipe follows)
Salt and pepper, to taste
2 ounces feta cheese, crumbled

Per Serving:
Calories: 202
% of calories from fat: 25
Fat (gm): 6
Saturated fat (gm): 1.8
Cholesterol (mg): 8.3
Sodium (mg): 282
Protein (gm): 8.5
Carbohydrate (gm): 31.5

Exchanges:
Milk: 0.0
Vegetable: 1.0
Fruit: 0.0
Bread: 1.5
Meat: 0.0
Fat: 1.0

1. Arrange eggplant on greased foil-lined jelly roll pan; spray with cooking spray. Roast at 425 degrees until tender, about 30 minutes; cool. Combine eggplant, remaining vegetables, and pasta in salad bowl; toss with Basil Vinaigrette. Season to taste with salt and pepper; sprinkle with cheese.

Basil Vinaigrette
Makes about ⅓ cup

¼ cup balsamic vinegar
1 tablespoon olive oil
3 tablespoons chopped basil leaves

1. Mix all ingredients.

45-MINUTE PREPARATION TIP: Cook the fettuccine and vegetables while the eggplant is roasting. Rinse the fettuccine in cold water to cool it quickly.

BRUSSELS SPROUTS AND GNOCCHI SALAD

Use spinach or potato gnocchi; pasta shells can be substituted, if preferred.

8 servings

8 ounces gnocchi, cooked, room temperature
8 ounces Brussels sprouts, halved, cooked
1 cup each: chopped tomato, sliced green bell pepper
¼ cup thinly sliced red onion
Sun-Dried Tomato and Goat Cheese Dressing
 (recipe follows)

Per Serving:
Calories: 172
% of calories from fat: 27
Fat (gm): 5.4
Saturated fat (gm): 0.9
Cholesterol (mg): 3.5
Sodium (mg): 179
Protein (gm): 6.3
Carbohydrate (gm): 26.3

Exchanges:
Milk: 0.0
Vegetable: 1.0
Fruit: 0.0
Bread: 1.5
Meat: 0.0
Fat: 1.0

1. Combine all ingredients bowl and toss.

Sun-Dried Tomato and Goat Cheese Dressing
Makes about ⅓ cup

2 tablespoons each: olive oil, white wine vinegar, lemon juice,
 grated Romano cheese
1 tablespoon goat cheese or cream cheese, room temperature
3 sun-dried tomatoes (not in oil), softened, finely chopped
2 cloves garlic, minced
½ teaspoon each: dried marjoram and thyme leaves
¼ teaspoon each: salt, pepper

1. Mix all ingredients.

ORIENTAL NOODLE SALAD

45 *If you enjoy the flavor of sesame oil, substitute 1 tablespoon each Asian sesame and canola oil for the olive oil.*

8 servings

2 packages (4 ounces each) rice noodles
2 cups each: halved snow peas, cooked crisp-tender, sliced red bell pepper
1 cup each: bean sprouts, sliced mushrooms, orange segments
5-Spice Salad Dressing (recipe follows)

1. Pour boiling water over noodles to cover in large bowl; let stand until noodles separate and are tender, about 10 minutes; drain. Cool. Combine noodles and remaining ingredients in salad bowl and toss.

Per Serving:
Calories: 198
% of calories from fat: 16
Fat (gm): 3.7
Saturated fat (gm): 0.5
Cholesterol (mg): 0
Sodium (mg): 72
Protein (gm): 5.9
Carbohydrate (gm): 36.9

Exchanges:
Milk: 0.0
Vegetable: 0.5
Fruit: 0.5
Bread: 2.0
Meat: 0.0
Fat: 0.5

5-Spice Salad Dressing
Makes about ½ cup

⅓ cup orange juice
1 tablespoons olive oil
2 cloves garlic, minced
½ teaspoon five-spice powder
¼ teaspoon each: salt, pepper

1. Mix all ingredients.

TOSSED GREENS WITH RICE NOODLES AND VEGETABLES

45 *Tender rice noodles and vegetables are bedded on gourmet greens.*

4 servings

½ package (4-ounce size) rice noodles

4 cups mesclun or other mixed greens

¼ cup each: chopped mint, cilantro

Warm Lime Dressing (recipe follows)

1 cup each: snow peas, cooked crisp-tender, seeded chopped cucumber, tomato

Per Serving:
Calories: 146
% of calories from fat: 10
Fat (gm): 1.7
Saturated fat (gm): 0.2
Cholesterol (mg): 0
Sodium (mg): 228
Protein (gm): 4.9
Carbohydrate (gm): 29.8

Exchanges:
Milk: 0.0
Vegetable: 3.0
Fruit: 2.0
Bread: 2.0
Meat: 0.0
Fat: 1.5

1. Pour boiling water over noodles to cover in large bowl; let stand until noodles are separate and tender, about 10 minutes; drain. Cool. Toss greens and herbs with ½ the Warm Lime Dressing and arrange on salad plates; top with rice noodles and vegetables and drizzle with remaining dressing.

Warm Lime Dressing

Makes about ¾ cup

⅓ cup each: water, lime juice

1 teaspoon cornstarch

2 tablespoons sugar

2 teaspoons minced garlic

2–3 teaspoons reduced-sodium tamari soy sauce

1 teaspoon each: Asian sesame oil, black bean sauce

½ teaspoon hot chili paste

1. Whisk all ingredients in small saucepan; heat to boiling. Boil, whisking until thickened, about 1 minute.

LENTIL SALAD WITH FETA CHEESE

Don't overcook the lentils—they need to retain their shape for this salad.

10 servings

1¼ cups dried lentils

2½ cups reduced-sodium vegetable broth

1½ cups each: coarsely chopped iceberg
    lettuce, tomatoes

½ cup each: thinly sliced celery, chopped yellow
    bell pepper, onion, cucumber

¾ cup (2 ounces) crumbled fat-free feta cheese

Balsamic Dressing (recipe follows)

Salt and pepper, to taste

Per Serving:
Calories: 169
% of calories from fat: 21
Fat (gm): 4.0
Saturated fat (gm): 1.0
Cholesterol (mg): 2.0
Sodium (mg): 110
Protein (gm): 9.8
Carbohydrate (gm): 24.8

Exchanges:
Milk: 0.0
Vegetable: 0.5
Fruit: 0.0
Bread: 1.5
Meat: 0.5
Fat: 0.0

1. Heat lentils and broth to boiling in large saucepan; reduce heat and simmer, covered, until lentils are just tender, about 20 minutes. Drain; cool. Combine lentils and remaining ingredients, except salt and pepper, in bowl and toss; season to taste with salt and pepper.

Balsamic Dressing

Makes about ⅓ cup

3 tablespoons balsamic or red wine vinegar

2 tablespoons each: olive oil, lemon juice

2 cloves garlic, minced

½ teaspoon dried thyme leaves

1. Mix all ingredients.

SPROUTED LENTIL SALAD

All kinds of dried beans and grains can be sprouted. Sprouts are delicious for salads, as garnishes on main dishes and side dishes, or to eat as snacks. Any favorite sprouted bean or grain can be used in this salad.

4 servings

Sprouted Lentils (recipe follows)
1 cup each: torn radicchio leaves, chopped tomato
½ cup each: chopped cucumber, yellow bell pepper
½–⅔ cup fat-free or reduced-fat mayonnaise
Salt and pepper, to taste

1. Combine lentils, vegetables, and mayonnaise in bowl; season to taste with salt and pepper.

Per Serving:
Calories: 43
% of calories from fat: 11
Fat (gm): 0.6
Saturated fat (gm): 0.1
Cholesterol (mg): 1.4
Sodium (mg): 131
Protein (gm): 2.2
Carbohydrate (gm): 8.8

Exchanges:
Milk: 0.0
Vegetable: 0.5
Fruit: 0.0
Bread: 0.5
Meat: 0.0
Fat: 0.0

Sprouted Lentils

Makes about 2 cups

½ cup dried lentils
Water

1. Place lentils in quart jar; add water to cover lentils by 2 to 3 inches and soak overnight. Drain. Return drained lentils to jar and cover with cheesecloth. Let stand at room temperature until lentils have sprouted, about 2 days, rinsing lentils with cold water and draining 3 to 4 times a day.

2. Refrigerate sprouted lentils. Check sprouts daily; if they appear dry, rinse, drain, and return to refrigerator.

NOTES: All grains and beans can be sprouted according to the directions for Sprouted Lentils, although they may require shorter or longer times to sprout. The various grains and beans will also yield different amounts.

Wheat berries: ½ cup dry wheat berries yield about 1½ cups sprouted wheat berries.

Chick peas: ½ cup dry chick peas yield about 1½ cups sprouted chick peas.

SPROUTS AND VEGETABLE SALAD

Use any combination of sprouted beans or grains you like in this salad.

4 servings

1 cup broccoli florets, chopped tomato

½ cup each: sprouted wheat berries, chick peas, and
lentils (see Sprouted Lentils recipe and notes p. 524)

2 green onions, sliced

½ cup fat-free blue cheese or other desired
salad dressing

¼ cup (1 ounce) crumbled blue cheese

Per Serving:
Calories: 129
% of calories from fat: 16
Fat (gm): 2.5
Saturated fat (gm): 1.4
Cholesterol (mg): 5.2
Sodium (mg): 452
Protein (gm): 5.7
Carbohydrate (gm): 23.5

Exchanges:
Milk: 0.0
Vegetable: 1.5
Fruit: 0.0
Bread: 1.0
Meat: 0.0
Fat: 0.5

1. Combine all ingredients, except blue cheese,
in bowl and toss; sprinkle with blue cheese.

WHEAT BERRY WALDORF

*Enjoy the variety of textures in this salad—substitute any grain that
you like.*

8 servings

1¼ cups wheat berries

1½ cups peeled, cored, cubed pineapple

1 cup each: fresh orange segments, cubed
unpeeled apple, thinly sliced fennel bulb

¼ cup coarsely chopped walnuts

⅓ cup fat-free mayonnaise

2½ teaspoons Dijon mustard

1½ tablespoons lemon juice

2 teaspoons sugar

¾ teaspoon crushed fennel seeds

Per Serving:
Calories: 159.2
% of calories from fat: 12
Fat (gm): 2.3
Saturated fat (gm): 0.2
Cholesterol (mg): 0
Sodium (mg): 155
Protein (gm): 3.9
Carbohydrate (gm): 32.9

Exchanges:
Milk: 0.0
Vegetable: 0.0
Fruit: 1.0
Bread: 1.5
Meat: 0.0
Fat: 0.0

1. Cover wheat berries with 2 to 3 inches water in saucepan; let
stand overnight. Heat to boiling; reduce heat and simmer, covered,
until wheat berries are tender, 50 to 60 minutes. Drain and cool.

2. Combine wheat berries, fruit, fennel, and walnuts in bowl; mix
in combined remaining ingredients.

TABBOULEH AND VEGETABLE SALAD MEDLEY

Two salads—tabbouleh dressed with Lemon-Cinnamon Vinaigrette, and a mixed vegetable salad with chunky Cucumber-Sour Cream Dressing—are lightly combined for a contrast of flavors. Or, the salads can be served side by side if you prefer.

8 servings

1 package (5¼ ounces) tabbouleh wheat salad mix (spice packet discarded)

1 cup cold water

⅓ cup each: finely chopped celery, sliced green onions

8 pitted prunes, chopped

1 tablespoon finely chopped fresh or 1 teaspoon dried basil leaves

1 clove garlic, minced

Lemon-Cinnamon Vinaigrette (recipe follows)

2 cups cauliflower florets

⅔ cup each: chopped red bell pepper, diagonally sliced carrots, halved cherry tomatoes

Cucumber-Sour Cream Dressing (recipe follows)

Salt and pepper, to taste

¼ cup (1 ounce) crumbled feta cheese

Per Serving:
Calories: 191
% of calories from fat: 28
Fat (gm): 6.3
Saturated fat (gm): 1.3
Cholesterol (mg): 3.3
Sodium (mg): 300
Protein (gm): 5.7
Carbohydrate (gm): 30.8

Exchanges:
Milk: 0.0
Vegetable: 1.5
Fruit: 0.5
Bread: 0.5
Meat: 0.0
Fat: 1.0

1. Mix tabbouleh and cold water in medium bowl; let stand until water is absorbed, about 30 minutes. Toss with celery, green onions, prunes, basil, garlic, and Lemon-Cinnamon Vinaigrette.

2. Combine cauliflower, bell pepper, carrots, and tomatoes in large bowl; spoon Cucumber-Sour Cream Dressing over and toss. Add tabbouleh salad and toss; season to taste with salt and pepper. Sprinkle with feta cheese.

Lemon-Cinnamon Vinaigrette
Makes about ½ cup

⅓ cup lemon juice
3 tablespoons olive or canola oil
¼ teaspoon dried cinnamon

1. Combine all ingredients.

Cucumber-Sour Cream Dressing
Makes about 1 cup

½ cup fat-free sour cream
¼ cup fat-free plain yogurt
1 teaspoon each: white wine vinegar, dried dill weed
½ medium cucumber, peeled, seeded, chopped

1. Combine all ingredients.

THIRTEEN

Breads, Coffee Cakes, Muffins, *and* More

EASY HERB LAVOSH

45 *Quick, easy, delicious, and versatile!*

6 servings

1 Whole Wheat Lavosh (see p. 534) or
  purchased lavosh
Vegetable or olive oil cooking spray
½–¾ teaspoon caraway seeds or other desired herbs

Per Serving:
Calories: 132
% of calories from fat: 3
Fat (gm): 0.6
Saturated fat (gm): 0.1
Cholesterol (mg): 0
Sodium (mg): 1
Protein (gm): 5
Carbohydrate (gm): 29.9

Exchanges:
Milk: 0.0
Vegetable: 0.0
Fruit: 0.0
Bread: 2.0
Meat: 0.0
Fat: 0.0

1. Spray top of lavosh lightly with cooking spray and sprinkle with herbs. Bake on a cookie sheet at 350 degrees until browned, 4 to 6 minutes (watch carefully, as lavosh can burn easily).

VARIATION

Parmesan-Thyme Lavosh — Make recipe as above, substituting dried thyme leaves for the caraway seeds and sprinkling with ¼ cup grated Parmesan cheese.

BRUSCHETTA

45 *These simple-to-make Italian garlic toasts are perfect for serving with any kind of savory appetizer spread.*

12 servings (2 each)

1 loaf French bread (8 ounces) (about 15 inches long)
Olive oil cooking spray
2 cloves garlic, halved

Per Serving:
Calories: 53
% of calories from fat: 10
Fat (gm): 0.6
Saturated fat (gm): 0.1
Cholesterol (mg): 0.0
Sodium (mg): 115
Protein (gm): 1.7
Carbohydrate (gm): 10

Exchanges:
Milk: 0.0
Vegetable: 0.0
Fruit: 0.0
Bread: 0.5
Meat: 0.0
Fat: 0.0

1. Cut bread into 24 slices; spray both sides of bread lightly with cooking spray. Broil on cookie sheet 4 inches from heat source until browned, 2 to 3 minutes on each side. Rub top sides of bread slices with cut sides of garlic.

VARIATIONS

Herb Bruschetta — Make recipe as above, sprinkling one side of bread with desired dried herb leaves, such as basil, oregano, or dried Italian seasoning before broiling.

Parmesan Bruschetta — Make recipe as above, sprinkling one side of bread with ½–2 teaspoon grated Parmesan cheese before broiling; watch carefully so cheese does not burn.

CROUSTADES

45

These crisp toast cups can be filled with just about any hot or cold, sweet or savory filling. Bake the Croustades up to a week in advance and store in an airtight container.

8 servings (2 each)

16 slices soft white or whole wheat bread
Butter-flavored cooking spray

1. Cut 2½-inch rounds out of bread slices with cookie cutter (remaining bread can be used for croutons or soft or dry bread crumbs). Press bread rounds firmly into 16 greased mini-muffin cups. Spray bread generously with cooking spray. Bake at 350 degrees until browned and crisp, 10 to 12 minutes.

Per Serving:
Calories: 67
% of calories from fat: 12
Fat (gm): 0.9
Saturated fat (gm): 0.2
Cholesterol (mg): 0
Sodium (mg): 135
Protein (gm): 2.1
Carbohydrate (gm): 12.4

Exchanges:
Milk: 0.0
Vegetable: 0.0
Fruit: 0.0
Bread: 1.0
Meat: 0.0
Fat: 0.0

GARLIC BREAD

45

Select a good quality French or Italian loaf for this aromatic bread, or use sourdough bread for a flavorful variation.

4 servings

4 thick slices French or Italian bread
Olive oil cooking spray
2 cloves garlic, halved

1. Spray both sides of bread generously with cooking spray. Broil on cookie sheet 4 inches from heat source until browned, about 1 minute on each side. Rub both sides of hot toast with cut sides of garlic.

VARIATION

Parmesan Garlic Bread — Combine 2 table-spoons grated Parmesan cheese and 4 teaspoons minced garlic. Spray bread with cooking spray as above and spread top of each slice with cheese mixture. Broil as above, or wrap loosely in foil and bake at 350 degrees until warm, about 10 minutes.

Per Serving:
Calories: 71
% of calories from fat: 10
Fat (gm): 0.8
Saturated fat (gm): 0.2
Cholesterol (mg): 0
Sodium (mg): 152
Protein (gm): 2.3
Carbohydrate (gm): 13.5

Exchanges:
Milk: 0.0
Vegetable: 0.0
Fruit: 0.0
Bread: 1.0
Meat: 0.0
Fat: 0.0

CROUTONS

Croutons can brighten a soup, add crunch to a salad, and provide a flavor accent for many dishes.

12 servings (¼ cup each)

3 cups cubed firm or day-old French or Italian bread (½–¾–inch)
Vegetable cooking spray

Per Serving:
Calories: 20
% of calories from fat: 13
Fat (gm): 0.3
Saturated fat (gm): 0.1
Cholesterol (mg): 0
Sodium (mg): 39
Protein (gm): 0.6
Carbohydrate (gm): 3.7

Exchanges:
Milk: 0.0
Vegetable: 0.0
Fruit: 0.0
Bread: 0.0
Meat: 0.0
Fat: 0.0

1. Spray bread cubes with cooking spray; arrange in single layer on jelly roll pan. Bake at 375 degrees until browned, 8 to 10 minutes, stirring occasionally. Cool; store in airtight container up to 2 weeks.

VARIATIONS

Italian-Style Croutons — Spray Italian bread cubes with vegetable cooking spray; sprinkle with combined 1 teaspoon garlic powder and 1 teaspoon dried Italian seasoning and toss. Bake as above.

Sourdough Croutons — Spray sourdough bread cubes with vegetable cooking spray; sprinkle with 2 teaspoons bouquet garni and toss. Bake as above.

Parmesan Croutons — Spray Italian bread cubes with vegetable cooking spray; sprinkle with 1 to 2 tablespoons grated Parmesan cheese and toss. Bake as above.

Rye Caraway Croutons — Spray rye bread cubes with vegetable cooking spray; sprinkle with 2 teaspoons crushed caraway seeds and toss. Bake as above.

Sesame Croutons — Spray bread cubes with vegetable cooking spray; sprinkle with 3 to 4 teaspoons sesame seeds and toss. Bake as above.

Herb Croutons — Spray multigrain or whole wheat bread cubes with vegetable cooking spray; sprinkle with 2 teaspoons dried herbs or herb combinations, and toss. Bake as above.

PITA BREADS

Also called Syrian bread or pocket breads, pitas can be eaten plain or split and filled. The breads freeze well, so make lots!

12 pitas (1 each)

1 package active dry yeast
1⅓ cups warm water (110–115 degrees)
¼ teaspoon sugar
1½ tablespoons olive oil
3–4 cups all-purpose flour, divided
1 teaspoon salt

Per Serving:
Calories: 131
% of calories from fat: 14
Fat (gm): 2
Saturated fat (gm): 0.3
Cholesterol (mg): 0
Sodium (mg): 178
Protein (gm): 3.5
Carbohydrate (gm): 24.2

Exchanges:
Milk: 0.0
Vegetable: 0.0
Fruit: 0.0
Bread: 2.0
Meat: 0.0
Fat: 0.0

1. Combine yeast, warm water, and sugar in large bowl; let stand 5 minutes. Add oil, 3 cups flour, and salt, mixing until smooth. Mix in enough remaining 1 cup flour to make smooth dough.

2. Knead dough on floured surface until smooth and elastic, about 5 minutes. Place in greased bowl; let stand, covered, in warm place until double in size, about 1 hour. Punch dough down.

3. Shape dough into 12 balls; let stand, covered, 30 minutes (dough will not double in size). Roll balls of dough on floured surface into rounds 5 to 6 inches in diameter; place 2 to 3 inches apart on greased cookie sheets; let stand 30 minutes. Bake, 1 pan at a time, at 500 degrees until pitas are puffed and brown, 3 to 5 minutes. Remove to wire racks and cool.

WHOLE WHEAT LAVOSH

A flat cracker bread that is perfect to serve with dips and spreads, or as an accompaniment to soups and salads.

8 lavosh (1 each)

½ cup fat-free milk, warm (110–115 degrees)

1 package active dry yeast

2⅓ cups whole wheat flour

½–1 cup all-purpose flour, divided

½ teaspoon salt

1 egg white, lightly beaten

1 tablespoon water

Per Serving:
Calories: 186
% of calories from fat: 4
Fat (gm): 0.8
Saturated fat (gm): 0.2
Cholesterol (mg): 0.3
Sodium (mg): 150
Protein (gm): 7.7
Carbohydrate (gm): 38.5

Exchanges:
Milk: 0.0
Vegetable: 0.0
Fruit: 0.0
Bread: 2.5
Meat: 0.0
Fat: 0.0

1. Mix milk and yeast in large bowl; let stand 5 minutes. Mix in whole wheat flour, ½ cup all-purpose flour, and salt; mix in enough remaining ½ cup all-purpose flour to make a smooth dough. Let stand, covered, 15 to 20 minutes.

2. Divide dough into 8 equal pieces. Roll each on lightly floured surface into a 3-inch round; place on greased cookie sheet. Brush combined egg white and water over top of dough. Bake at 425 degrees until crisp and browned, 5 to 8 minutes, turning over halfway through baking time. (Lavosh will become crisper upon cooling, so do not overbake.) Cool on wire rack.

SPINACH-MUSHROOM FLATBREAD

This attractive bread is made in a freeform shape and topped with spinach and Parmesan cheese. The bread can be made in advance and reheated at 300 degrees, loosely wrapped in foil, for 15 to 20 minutes.

1 loaf (12–16 servings)

2½–3½ cups all-purpose flour, divided

1½ cups whole wheat flour

2 tablespoons sugar

1½ teaspoons dried rosemary leaves, crushed

½ teaspoon each: dried thyme leaves, salt

1 package fast-rising yeast

2 cups very hot water (125–130 degrees)

¼ cup sliced onion

3 cloves garlic, minced

2 cups torn spinach leaves

1 cup sliced cremini or white mushrooms

¼ cup (2 ounces) shredded reduced-fat
mozzarella cheese

2–3 tablespoons grated fat-free Parmesan cheese

Per Serving:
Calories: 190
% of calories from fat: 5
Fat (gm): 1
Saturated fat (gm): 0.4
Cholesterol (mg): 1.3
Sodium (mg): 123
Protein (gm): 7
Carbohydrate (gm): 38.8

Exchanges:
Milk: 0.0
Vegetable: 0.0
Fruit: 0.0
Bread: 2.5
Meat: 0.0
Fat: 0.0

1. Combine 2½ cups all-purpose flour, whole wheat flour, sugar, herbs, salt, and yeast in large bowl; add water, mixing until smooth. Mix in enough remaining 1 cup all-purpose flour to make soft dough.

2. Knead dough on floured surface until smooth and elastic, about 5 minutes. Place in greased bowl; let rise, loosely covered, in warm place until double in size, 30 to 45 minutes. Punch dough down.

3. Pat dough into a round on floured surface. Pull the edges of the dough into a freeform shape, about 10 x 14 inches. Transfer dough to greased cookie sheet and let stand 20 minutes (dough will rise, but will not double in size). Bake at 350 degrees until golden, about 20 minutes.

4. While bread is baking, sauté onion and garlic in lightly greased skillet until tender, 3 to 4 minutes. Add spinach and mushrooms; cook, covered, over medium until spinach is wilted, about 5 minutes. Cook, uncovered, until mushrooms are tender, about 5 minutes. Remove from heat. Arrange spinach mixture over top of baked bread; sprinkle with cheeses. Return to oven until cheese is melted, 5 to 10 minutes. Transfer to wire rack and cool.

FOCACCIA

This delicious Italian bread is very versatile—see Leek and Onion Focaccia and Fruit Focaccia (p. 537). Focaccia can be frozen, so bake extra to have on hand.

2 focaccia (10 servings each)

4–5½ cups bread or all-purpose flour, divided

1 package (¼ ounce) fast-rising yeast

1 teaspoon each: sugar, salt

1¾ cups very hot water (125–130 degrees)

Olive oil cooking spray

¼ cup (1 ounce) grated Parmesan cheese

Per Serving:
Calories: 139
% of calories from fat: 5
Fat (gm): 0.8
Saturated fat (gm): 0.2
Cholesterol (mg): 1
Sodium (mg): 131
Protein (gm): 5.2
Carbohydrate (gm): 28.2

Exchanges:
Milk: 0.0
Vegetable: 0.0
Fruit: 0.0
Bread: 2.0
Meat: 0.0
Fat: 0.0

1. Combine 4 cups flour, yeast, sugar, and salt in large mixing bowl. Add water, mixing until smooth. Mix in enough remaining 1½ cups flour to make soft dough.

2. Knead dough on floured surface until dough is smooth and elastic, about 5 minutes. Place in greased bowl; turn greased side up and let rise, covered, in warm place until double in size, about 1 hour. Punch dough down.

3. Divide dough into halves. Roll 1 piece dough on floured surface to fit jelly roll pan, 15 x 10 inches; ease dough into greased pan. Repeat with remaining dough. Let dough rise until double in size, 45 to 60 minutes. Make ¼-inch-deep indentations with fingers to "dimple" the dough; spray lightly with cooking spray and sprinkle with Parmesan cheese. Bake at 425 degrees until browned, about 30 minutes. Cool in pans on wire racks. Serve warm or at room temperature.

FRUIT FOCACCIA

Serve as a dessert or a meal accompaniment.

8 servings

1 cup boiling water

½ cup each: dried cranberries or cherries, dried fruit bits

1 Focaccia (½ recipe) (see p. 536)

2 tablespoons granulated sugar

1 tablespoon melted margarine or butter

⅓ cup packed light brown sugar

Per Serving:
Calories: 253
% of calories from fat: 8
Fat (gm): 2.4
Saturated fat (gm): 0.6
Cholesterol (mg): 1.2
Sodium (mg): 188
Protein (gm): 6.6
Carbohydrate (gm): 52.6

Exchanges:
Milk: 0.0
Vegetable: 0.0
Fruit: 0.5
Bread: 3.0
Meat: 0.0
Fat: 0.0

1. Pour boiling water over combined dried fruit in bowl; let stand until softened, 10 to 15 minutes. Drain.

2. Make Focaccia, adding granulated sugar to the flour mixture. After first rising, spread dough in greased baking dish, 11 x 7 inches. Let rise until double in size, about 30 minutes. Make ¼-inch indentations with fingers to "dimple" dough. Spread margarine over dough; sprinkle with fruit and brown sugar. Bake at 425 degrees until browned, 20 to 25 minutes.

LEEK AND ONION FOCACCIA

This bread would make a perfect addition to a soup and salad supper.

8 servings

1 Focaccia (½ recipe; see p. 536)

½ cup each: thinly sliced leek (white part only), yellow and red onion

½ teaspoon crumbled dried sage leaves

1–2 teaspoons olive oil

Salt and pepper, to taste

1–2 tablespoons grated fat-free Parmesan cheese

Per Serving:
Calories: 193
% of calories from fat: 7
Fat (gm): 1.6
Saturated fat (gm): 0.4
Cholesterol (mg): 1.2
Sodium (mg): 171
Protein (gm): 7.1
Carbohydrate (gm): 38.4

Exchanges:
Milk: 0.0
Vegetable: 1.0
Fruit: 0.0
Bread: 2.5
Meat: 0.0
Fat: 0.0

1. Make Focaccia; after first rising, spread dough in greased jelly roll pan, 15 x 10 inches. Let stand until dough is doubled in size, about 30 minutes. Make ¼-inch indentations with fingers to "dimple" the dough. Toss leek, onion, and sage with oil and spread over dough. Sprinkle with salt, pepper, and Parmesan cheese. Bake at 425 degrees until golden, 20 to 25 minutes.

SOFT PRETZELS

To achieve their typical dense, chewy texture, pretzels are cooked in boiling water before baking.

12 pretzels (1 each)

1 package active dry yeast
½ cup warm water (110–115 degrees)
1 tablespoon sugar
1 cup fat-free milk, heated to simmering, cooled
2–4 cups all-purpose flour, divided
1 teaspoon salt
2 quarts water
1 tablespoon baking soda
1 egg, lightly beaten
1 tablespoon cold water
Toppings: poppy seeds, sesame seeds, coarse salt, herbs, dried onion flakes, etc.

Per Serving:
Calories: 152
% of calories from fat: 5
Fat (gm): 0.8
Saturated fat (gm): 0.2
Cholesterol (mg): 18.1
Sodium (mg): 509
Protein (gm): 5.2
Carbohydrate (gm): 30.2

Exchanges:
Milk: 0.0
Vegetable: 0.0
Fruit: 0.0
Bread: 2.0
Meat: 0.0
Fat: 0.0

1. Mix yeast, warm water, and sugar in large bowl; let stand 5 minutes. Add milk, 2 cups flour, and salt, beating until smooth. Mix in enough remaining 2 cups flour to make smooth dough. Knead dough on floured surface until smooth and elastic, about 5 minutes. Place in greased bowl; let rise, covered, in warm place until double in size, 45 to 60 minutes. Punch dough down.

2. Roll dough on floured surface to rectangle 16 x 12 inches. Cut dough lengthwise into 12 strips, 1 inch wide. Roll one strip dough with palms of hands into "rope," 18 to 20 inches long. Form loop, holding ends of "rope" and twisting 2 times. Bring ends of "rope" down and fasten at opposite sides of loop to form pretzel shape. Repeat with remaining dough, transferring pretzels to floured surface. Let pretzels stand, lightly covered, 30 minutes (they may not double in size).

3. Heat 2 quarts water to boiling in large saucepan; stir in baking soda. Transfer pretzels, a few at a time, into boiling water; boil until dough feels firm, about 1 minute. Remove pretzels from boiling water with slotted spoon, draining well. Place on generously greased foil-lined cookie sheets. Brush pretzels with combined egg and cold water; sprinkle with desired toppings. Bake at 400 degrees until golden, 18 to 20 minutes. Cool on wire racks.

BOLILLOS

Bolillos are the crusty, "bobbin-shaped" yeast rolls popular throughout Mexico. The dough is similar to French bread dough.

12 rolls (1 each)

1 package active dry yeast
½ teaspoon sugar
1 cup hot water (110–115 degrees)
2 tablespoons vegetable shortening, room temperature
3½–4 cups all-purpose flour
½ teaspoon salt
2 tablespoons fat-free milk

Per Serving:
Calories: 155
% of calories from fat: 15
Fat (gm): 2.5
Saturated fat (gm): 0.6
Cholesterol (mg): 0
Sodium (mg): 91
Protein (gm): 4.1
Carbohydrate (gm): 28.4

Exchanges:
Milk: 0.0
Vegetable: 0.0
Fruit: 0.0
Bread: 2.0
Meat: 0.0
Fat: 0.5

1. Mix yeast, sugar, and hot water in medium bowl; add shortening, stirring until melted. Let stand 5 minutes. Mix in 3½ cups flour and salt; mix in enough remaining ½ cup flour to make soft dough.

2. Knead dough on floured surface until smooth and elastic, about 5 minutes. Place in greased bowl; let stand, covered, in warm place until dough is double in size, 1 to 1½ hours. Punch dough down.

3. Divide dough into 12 equal pieces. Roll or pat 1 piece into an oval shape, a scant ½–inch thick. Fold ⅓ of the dough along the long edge toward the center and flatten with palm of hand; fold dough in half in same direction and flatten with palm of hand. Roll dough lightly with hand to make a rounded oval shape. Place, seam side up, on lightly greased cookie sheet. Repeat with remaining dough. Let rolls stand, loosely covered, until double in size, about 1 hour; brush with milk. Bake at 375 degrees until lightly browned, about 25 minutes.

SQUASH DINNER ROLLS

Use pumpkin, Hubbard, or acorn squash for these rolls; mashed sweet potatoes can be used also. If a loaf is preferred, bake in a greased 8 x 4-inch loaf pan until loaf is browned and sounds hollow when tapped, about 40 minutes.

24 rolls (1 each)

1½–2½ cups all-purpose flour, divided

1 cup whole wheat flour

2 packages fast-rising yeast

1–2 teaspoons salt

½ cup fat-free milk

¼ cup honey

1–2 tablespoons margarine or butter

¾ cup mashed cooked winter squash

1 egg

Per Serving:
Calories: 70
% of calories from fat: 11
Fat (gm): 0.9
Saturated fat (gm): 0.2
Cholesterol (mg): 9
Sodium (mg): 100
Protein (gm): 2.2
Carbohydrate (gm): 13.5

Exchanges:
Milk: 0.0
Vegetable: 0.0
Fruit: 0.0
Bread: 1.0
Meat: 0.0
Fat: 0.0

1. Combine 1½ cups all-purpose flour, whole wheat flour, yeast, and salt in large bowl. Heat milk, honey, and margarine in small saucepan to 125–130 degrees; add to flour mixture, mixing until smooth. Mix in squash, egg, and enough remaining 1 cup all-purpose flour to make smooth dough.

2. Knead dough on floured surface until smooth and elastic, about 5 minutes. Place in greased bowl; let stand, covered, in warm place until double in size, 30 to 45 minutes. Punch dough down.

3. Divide dough into 24 pieces; shape into round rolls and place in greased muffin tins. Bake at 375 degrees until browned, 20 to 25 minutes.

VARIATION

Raisin-Walnut Pumpkin Bread — Make recipe as above, substituting mashed cooked or canned pumpkin for the squash and adding ½ cup each raisins and chopped walnuts. Shape into loaf in 9 x 5-inch loaf pan and let rise; bake at 375 degrees until loaf is browned and sounds hollow when tapped, about 40 minutes.

POTATO BREAD

Breads made with mashed potatoes are very moist and retain freshness well. This dough can be made in advance and refrigerated up to 5 days.

2 loaves (16 servings each)

1 package active dry yeast

1½ cups warm water (110–115 degrees)

2 tablespoons sugar

3 tablespoons margarine or butter room temperature

2 eggs

1 cup mashed potatoes, lukewarm

5½–6½ cups all-purpose flour, divided

1 cup whole wheat flour

1 teaspoon salt

Fat-free milk

Per Serving:
Calories: 121
% of calories from fat: 13
Fat (gm): 1.7
Saturated fat (gm): 0.4
Cholesterol (mg): 13.4
Sodium (mg): 103
Protein (gm): 3.6
Carbohydrate (gm): 22.7

Exchanges:
Milk: 0.0
Vegetable: 0.0
Fruit: 0.0
Bread: 1.5
Meat: 0.0
Fat: 0.5

1. Mix yeast and warm water in large bowl; let stand 5 minutes. Mix in sugar, margarine, eggs, and mashed potatoes until blended; mix in 5½ cups all-purpose flour, whole wheat flour, and salt. Mix in enough remaining 1 cup all-purpose flour to make smooth dough.

2. Knead dough on floured surface until smooth and elastic, about 5 minutes. Place in greased bowl; let rise, covered, in warm place until double in size, 1 to 1½ hours. Punch dough down.

3. Divide dough into halves; shape into loaves and place in greased 9 x 5-inch loaf pans. Let stand, loosely covered, until double in size, about 45 minutes. Brush tops of loaves with milk. Bake at 375 degrees until loaves are golden and sound hollow when tapped, about 45 minutes. Remove from pans; cool on wire racks.

ROASTED RED PEPPER BREAD

Bake this loaf in a freeform long or round shape, or in a pan.
For convenience, use jarred roasted red pepper.

1 loaf (16 servings)

2¼–2¾ cups all-purpose flour, divided

¾ cup whole wheat flour

¼ cup grated fat-free Parmesan cheese

1½ teaspoons dried Italian seasoning, divided

½ teaspoon salt

1 package fast-rising active dry yeast

1¼ cups very hot water (125–130 degrees)

1 tablespoon olive oil

4 ounces reduced-fat mozzarella cheese,
   cubed (½-inch)

½ cup coarsely chopped roasted red pepper

1 egg white, beaten

Per Serving:
Calories: 119
% of calories from fat: 16
Fat (gm): 2.2
Saturated fat (gm): 0.9
Cholesterol (mg): 3.8
Sodium (mg): 133
Protein (gm): 5.6
Carbohydrate (gm): 19

Exchanges:
Milk: 0.0
Vegetable: 0.0
Fruit: 0.0
Bread: 1.5
Meat: 0.0
Fat: 0.5

1. Combine 2¼ cups all-purpose flour, whole wheat flour, Parmesan cheese, 1 teaspoon Italian seasoning, salt, and yeast in large bowl; add hot water and oil, mixing until blended. Mix in mozzarella cheese, red pepper, and enough remaining ½ cup all-purpose flour to make smooth dough.

2. Knead dough on floured surface until smooth and elastic, about 5 minutes. Place in greased bowl; let rise, covered, in warm place until double in size, about 30 minutes. Punch dough down.

3. Shape dough into loaf and place in greased 9 x 5-inch loaf pan. Let stand, covered, until double in size, about 30 minutes. Make 3 or 4 slits in top of loaf with sharp knife. Brush egg white over dough and sprinkle with remaining Italian seasoning. Bake at 375 degrees until loaf is golden and sounds hollow when tapped, 35 to 40 minutes. Remove from pan and cool on wire rack.

ENGLISH MUFFIN BREAD

This quick and easy single-rise bread has a coarse texture similar to English muffins. Delicious warm from the oven, or toasted, with Spiced Apple-Prune Jam (see p. 568).

1 loaf (16 servings)

1½–2½ cups all-purpose flour, divided

½ cup quick-cooking oats

1 package active dry yeast

¼ teaspoon baking soda

1 teaspoon salt

1¼ cups warm fat-free milk (110–115 degrees)

1 tablespoon honey

Cornmeal

Per Serving:
Calories: 79
% of calories from fat: 4
Fat (gm): 0.4
Saturated fat (gm): 0.1
Cholesterol (mg): 0.3
Sodium (mg): 163
Protein (gm): 2.9
Carbohydrate (gm): 15.9

Exchanges:
Milk: 0.0
Vegetable: 0.0
Fruit: 0.0
Bread: 1.0
Meat: 0.0
Fat: 0.0

1. Combine 1½ cups flour, oats, yeast, baking soda, and salt in large bowl. Add milk and honey, mixing until smooth. Stir in enough of remaining 1 cup flour to make a thick batter. Pour into greased, cornmeal-coated 8 x 4-inch loaf pan. Let rise, covered, in warm place until double in size, 45 to 60 minutes. Bake at 400 degrees until bread is golden and sounds hollow when tapped, 25 to 30 minutes. Remove from pan and cool on wire rack.

VARIATION

Cinnamon-Raisin Bread — Make recipe as above, adding 1 teaspoon ground cinnamon and ½ cup raisins to the batter; do not coat loaf pan with cornmeal.

SWEET POTATO BRAIDS

Canned pumpkin can be substituted for the sweet potatoes, if desired.

2 loaves (12 servings each)

2 packages active dry yeast

¼ cup warm fat-free milk (110–115 degrees)

1 cup mashed cooked sweet potatoes

1¾ cups fat-free milk

¼ cup canola oil

1 egg

3–4 cups all-purpose flour, divided

2 cups whole wheat flour

1 teaspoon salt

Per Serving:
Calories: 156
% of calories from fat: 17
Fat (gm): 2.9
Saturated fat (gm): 0.5
Cholesterol (mg): 9.2
Sodium (mg): 105
Protein (gm): 4.9
Carbohydrate (gm): 27.7

Exchanges:
Milk: 0.0
Vegetable: 0.0
Fruit: 0.0
Bread: 2.0
Meat: 0.0
Fat: 0.5

1. Mix yeast and warm milk in large bowl; let stand 5 minutes. Mix in sweet potatoes, 1¾ cups milk, oil, and egg until blended; mix in 3 cups all-purpose flour, whole wheat flour, and salt. Mix in enough remaining 1 cup all-purpose flour to make smooth dough.

2. Knead dough on floured surface until smooth and elastic, about 5 minutes. Place in greased bowl; let rise, covered, in warm place until double in size, about 1 hour. Punch dough down.

3. Divide dough into halves; divide each half into thirds. Roll pieces of dough into strips, 12 inches long. Braid 3 strips; fold ends under and place on greased cookie sheet. Repeat with remaining dough. Let rise, loosely covered, until double in size, 30 to 45 minutes. Bake at 375 degrees until breads are golden and sound hollow when tapped, 45 to 55 minutes. Transfer to wire racks and cool.

BUBBLE LOAF

Also called Bath Buns and Monkey Bread, this pull-apart loaf is easy to make, fun to eat, and perfect for potluck offerings and parties. The recipe can be halved and baked in a 6-cup fluted cake pan.

1 loaf (16 servings)

2 packages active dry yeast

1 cup fat-free milk, warm (110–115 degrees)

6 tablespoons margarine or butter room temperature

¼ cup sugar

3 eggs

4 cups all-purpose flour

½ teaspoon salt

Per Serving:
Calories: 186
% of calories from fat: 27
Fat (gm): 5.5
Saturated fat (gm): 1.2
Cholesterol (mg): 40.2
Sodium (mg): 137
Protein (gm): 5.3
Carbohydrate (gm): 28.3

Exchanges:
Milk: 0.0
Vegetable: 0.0
Fruit: 0.0
Bread: 2.0
Meat: 0.0
Fat: 1.0

1. Stir yeast into milk in bowl; let stand 2 to 3 minutes. Beat margarine and sugar until fluffy in large bowl; beat in eggs, 1 at a time. Mix in combined flour and salt alternately with milk mixture, beginning and ending with dry ingredients and beating well after each addition. Let stand, covered, in warm place until dough is double in size, about 1 hour. Punch dough down.

2. Drop dough by large spoonfuls into greased 10-inch tube pan. Let rise, covered, until dough is double in size, about 30 minutes. Bake at 350 degrees until browned, 25 to 30 minutes. Cool in pan on wire rack 10 minutes; remove from pan. Serve warm.

GRANOLA BREAD

A wonderful breakfast bread—serve with plenty of Ginger-Rhubarb Jam (see p. 568). For convenience, this bread is made with an electric mixer and has only 1 rise.

2 loaves (16 servings each)

2 packages active dry yeast

¾ cup warm water (110–115 degrees)

2 tablespoons light brown sugar

1¼ cups buttermilk

3 cups all-purpose flour

¾–1½ cups whole wheat flour, divided

2 teaspoons baking powder

1 teaspoon salt

2–3 tablespoons margarine or butter, room temperature

1½ cups low-fat granola

Buttermilk

Per Serving:
Calories: 200
% of calories from fat: 17
Fat (gm): 3.8
Saturated fat (gm): 0.6
Cholesterol (mg): 9
Sodium (mg): 131
Protein (gm): 3.1
Carbohydrate (gm): 38.9

Exchanges:
Milk: 0.0
Vegetable: 0.0
Fruit: 0.0
Bread: 2.5
Meat: 0.0
Fat: 0.5

1. Mix yeast, warm water, and brown sugar in large mixer bowl; let stand 5 minutes. Mix in buttermilk, all-purpose flour, ¾ cup whole wheat flour, baking powder, salt, and margarine on low speed until smooth. Mix in granola and enough remaining ¾ cup whole wheat flour to make a smooth dough (dough will be slightly sticky.) Knead dough on floured surface until smooth and elastic, about 5 minutes.

2. Divide dough into halves. Roll each into a rectangle 18 x 10 inches. Roll up, beginning at short ends; press ends to seal. Place loaves, seam sides down, in greased 9 x 5-inch loaf pans. Let rise, covered, in warm place until double in size, about 1 hour; brush with buttermilk. Bake at 375 degrees until loaves are golden and sound hollow when tapped, 40 to 45 minutes. Remove from pans and cool on wire racks.

CRANBERRY-NUT WHEAT LOAF

Dried cranberries and walnuts make this bread a perfect fall and winter offering.

1 loaf (16 servings)

1 package active dry yeast

¾ cup warm water (110–115 degrees)

3 tablespoons honey

2–3 tablespoons margarine or butter
  room temperature

1 egg

1–2 cups all-purpose flour, divided

1 cup whole wheat flour

1 teaspoon salt

1 cup dried cranberries

⅔ cup coarsely chopped walnuts

Fat-free milk, for glaze

Per Serving:
Calories: 153
% of calories from fat: 27
Fat (gm): 4.7
Saturated fat (gm): 0.6
Cholesterol (mg): 0
Sodium (mg): 141
Protein (gm): 4.1
Carbohydrate (gm): 24.6

Exchanges:
Milk: 0.0
Vegetable: 0.0
Fruit: 0.5
Bread: 1.0
Meat: 0.0
Fat: 1.0

1. Mix yeast, warm water, and honey in large bowl; let stand 5 minutes. Add margarine, egg, 1 cup all-purpose flour, whole wheat flour, and salt, mixing until blended. Mix in cranberries, walnuts, and enough remaining 1 cup all-purpose flour to make smooth dough.

2. Knead dough on floured surface until smooth and elastic, about 5 minutes. Place in greased bowl; let rise, covered, in warm place until double in size, 1 to 1½ hours. Punch dough down.

3. Shape into loaf and place in greased 9 x 5-inch loaf pan. Let stand, covered, until double in size, about 45 minutes. Brush top of loaf with fat-free milk. Bake at 375 degrees until loaf is golden and sounds hollow when tapped, 35 to 40 minutes. Remove from pan and cool on wire rack.

LIMA BEAN WHEAT BREAD

Any kind of pureed bean can be used in this moist, dense bread.

3 loaves (10–12 servings each)

2 packages active dry yeast

¼ cup warm water (110–115 degrees)

1 cup each: cooked dried lima beans or rinsed, drained canned lima beans, cold water

2 cups fat-free milk

4–6 tablespoons melted margarine or butter

⅓ cup sugar

4½–5½ cups all-purpose flour, divided

1½ cups whole wheat flour

1½ teaspoons salt

Fat-free milk, for glaze

Per Serving:
Calories: 125
% of calories from fat: 13
Fat (gm): 1.9
Saturated fat (gm): 0.4
Cholesterol (mg): 0.3
Sodium (mg): 133
Protein (gm): 4
Carbohydrate (gm): 23.2

Exchanges:
Milk: 0.0
Vegetable: 0.0
Fruit: 0.0
Bread: 1.5
Meat: 0.0
Fat: 0.5

1. Mix yeast and warm water in small bowl; let stand 5 minutes. Process beans and 1 cup cold water in food processor or blender until smooth. Mix bean puree, 2 cups fat-free milk, margarine, and sugar in large bowl. Mix in yeast mixture, 4½ cups all-purpose flour, whole wheat flour, and salt. Mix in enough remaining 1 cup all-purpose flour to make soft dough.

2. Knead dough on floured surface until smooth and elastic, about 5 minutes. Place in greased bowl and let rise, covered, in warm place until double in size, about 1 hour. Punch dough down.

3. Divide dough into 3 equal pieces. Shape each into oval loaf on greased cookie sheet. Let rise, loosely covered, until double in size, about 45 minutes; brush with milk. Bake at 375 degrees until loaves are golden and sound hollow when tapped, about 1 hour. Transfer to wire racks and cool.

PEASANT BREAD

Five grains and ground pecans combine in this hearty dense-textured country-style bread. Wonderful toasted, delicious with honey!

2 small loaves (8–10 servings each)

2 packages active dry yeast
½ cup warm water (110–115 degrees)
1¼ cups whole wheat flour
½ cup each: millet, cracked wheat, yellow cornmeal, bulgur wheat, quick cooking oats, ground pecans
1 teaspoon salt
1¼ cups lukewarm water
¼ cup honey
2 tablespoons canola oil
1–2 cups unbleached all-purpose flour

Per Serving:
Calories: 197
% of calories from fat: 22
Fat (gm): 5
Saturated fat (gm): 0.6
Cholesterol (mg): 0
Sodium (mg): 137
Protein (gm): 5.4
Carbohydrate (gm): 34.2

Exchanges:
Milk: 0.0
Vegetable: 0.0
Fruit: 0.0
Bread: 2.0
Meat: 0.0
Fat: 1.0

1. Mix yeast and ½ cup warm water in large bowl; let stand 5 minutes. Mix in remaining ingredients, except all-purpose flour; mix in enough all-purpose flour to make smooth dough.

2. Knead dough on floured surface until smooth and elastic, about 5 minutes (dough will be heavy and difficult to maneuver). Place in greased bowl; let rise, covered, in warm place until double in size, about 1½ hours. Punch dough down.

3. Divide dough into halves; shape into round loaves on greased baking sheet. Let stand, loosely covered, until double in size, about 1½ hours. Bake at 350 degrees until loaves are deep golden brown and sound hollow when tapped, about 40 minutes. Transfer to wire racks to cool.

HEARTY VEGETABLE-RYE BREAD

Cauliflower adds moistness and subtle flavor to this aromatic rye loaf.

1 loaf (10–12 servings)

1 package active dry yeast

⅓ cup warm water (110–115 degrees)

1 teaspoon sugar

1 cup pureed cooked cauliflower

1 tablespoon each: melted margarine or butter,
light molasses, spicy brown mustard

2–3 cups all-purpose flour, divided

1 cup rye flour

½ teaspoon salt

1½ teaspoons each: caraway and fennel seeds,
crushed, divided

1 teaspoon dried dill weed

Melted margarine or butter

Per Serving:
Calories: 177
% of calories from fat: 9
Fat (gm): 1.9
Saturated fat (gm): 0.3
Cholesterol (mg): 0
Sodium (mg): 149
Protein (gm): 5.3
Carbohydrate (gm): 34.8

Exchanges:
Milk: 0.0
Vegetable: 0.0
Fruit: 0.0
Bread: 2.0
Meat: 0.0
Fat: 0.5

1. Mix yeast, warm water, and sugar in large bowl; let stand 5 minutes. Mix in cauliflower, 1 tablespoon margarine, molasses, and mustard until blended. Mix in 2 cups all-purpose flour, rye flour, salt, 1 teaspoon each caraway and fennel seeds, and dill weed. Mix in enough remaining 1 cup all-purpose flour to make smooth dough.

2. Knead dough on floured surface until smooth and elastic, about 5 minutes. Place in greased bowl; let stand, covered, in warm place until double in size, about 1 hour. Punch dough down.

3. Shape dough into long or round loaf on greased cookie sheet. Let rise, loosely covered, until double in size, 45 to 60 minutes. Make 3 or 4 slits in top of loaf with sharp knife; brush with melted margarine and sprinkle with remaining ½ teaspoon each caraway and fennel seeds. Bake at 350 degrees until bread is golden and sounds hollow when tapped, 40 to 50 minutes. Transfer to wire rack to cool.

GREEN CHILI CORN BREAD

45

Corn bread, Southwest-style! If using mild canned chilies, consider adding a teaspoon or so of minced jalapeño chili for a piquant accent.

9 servings

¼ cup chopped red bell pepper

2 cloves garlic, minced

½ teaspoon cumin seeds, crushed

1¼ cups yellow cornmeal

¾ cup all-purpose flour

2 teaspoons baking powder

1 teaspoon sugar

½ teaspoon each: baking soda, salt

1¼ cups buttermilk

½ cup canned cream-style corn

1 can (4 ounces) chopped hot or mild green chilies,
   well drained

2 eggs

3½ tablespoons margarine or butter, melted

Per Serving:
Calories: 184
% of calories from fat: 29
Fat (gm): 6.1
Saturated fat (gm): 1.3
Cholesterol (mg): 24.9
Sodium (mg): 563
Protein (gm): 5.6
Carbohydrate (gm): 27.6

Exchanges:
Milk: 0.0
Vegetable: 0.0
Fruit: 0.0
Bread: 2.0
Meat: 0.0
Fat: 1.0

1. Sauté bell pepper, garlic, and cumin seeds in lightly greased small skillet until pepper is tender, 2 to 3 minutes.

2. Combine cornmeal, flour, baking powder, sugar, baking soda, and salt in large bowl. Mix in bell pepper mixture, buttermilk, and remaining ingredients; spread in greased 8-inch-square baking pan. Bake at 425 degrees until golden, about 30 minutes. Cool in pan on wire rack; serve warm.

BANANA BREAD

45

Brown sugar gives this banana bread a caramel flavor; the applesauce adds moistness. It's the best!

1 loaf (16 servings)

4 tablespoons margarine or butter, room temperature

¼ cup applesauce

2 eggs

2 tablespoons fat-free milk or water

¾ cup packed light brown sugar

1 cup mashed banana (2–3 medium bananas)

1¾ cups all-purpose flour

2 teaspoons baking powder

½ teaspoon baking soda

¼ teaspoon salt

¼ cup coarsely chopped walnuts or pecans

Per Serving:
Calories: 151
% of calories from fat: 28
Fat (gm): 4.8
Saturated fat (gm): 0.9
Cholesterol (mg): 26.7
Sodium (mg): 160
Protein (gm): 2.9
Carbohydrate (gm): 24.9

Exchanges:
Milk: 0.0
Vegetable: 0.0
Fruit: 0.5
Bread: 1.0
Meat: 0.0
Fat: 1.0

1. Beat margarine, applesauce, eggs, milk, and brown sugar in large mixer bowl until smooth. Add banana and mix at low speed; beat at high speed 1 to 2 minutes. Mix in combined flour, baking powder, baking soda, and salt; mix in walnuts. Pour into greased 8 x 4-inch loaf pan. Bake at 350 degrees until bread is golden and toothpick inserted in center comes out clean, 55 to 60 minutes. Cool in pan 10 minutes; remove from pan and cool on wire rack.

MINT AND CITRUS TEA BREAD

45

Finely textured and lightly scented with mint, orange, and lemon, this bread is a delicious addition to any meal.

1 loaf (12 servings)

½ cup fat-free milk

2 tablespoons each: finely chopped fresh or 2
    teaspoons dried mint leaves, grated orange zest

1 tablespoon grated lemon zest

5 tablespoons margarine, softened

¾ cup sugar

2 eggs

1½ cups all-purpose flour

½ cup whole wheat flour

1½ teaspoons baking powder

½ teaspoon salt

¼ cup orange juice

½ cup powdered sugar

Fat-free milk

Ground nutmeg, as garnish

Per Serving:
Calories: 153
% of calories from fat: 25
Fat (gm): 4.4
Saturated fat (gm): 0.9
Cholesterol (mg): 26.8
Sodium (mg): 151
Protein (gm): 2.9
Carbohydrate (gm): 26

Exchanges:
Milk: 0.0
Vegetable: 0.0
Fruit: 0.0
Bread: 1.5
Meat: 0.0
Fat: 1.0

1. Heat milk, mint, orange zest, and lemon zest in small saucepan to simmering; strain and cool. Beat margarine and sugar until smooth in medium bowl; beat in eggs. Mix in combined all-purpose and whole wheat flour, baking powder, and salt alternately with cooled milk mixture and orange juice, beginning and ending with dry ingredients. Pour batter into greased 8 x 4-inch loaf pan. Bake at 325 degrees until bread is golden and toothpick inserted in center comes out clean, about 45 minutes. Remove from pan and cool on wire rack.

2. Mix powdered sugar with enough milk to make medium glaze consistency; drizzle glaze over bread and sprinkle lightly with nutmeg.

FRUITED BRAN BREAD

45

Use any combination of dried fruit you want in this quick, healthy, no-rise batter bread.

1 loaf (16 servings)

1¼ cups all-purpose flour
½ cup whole wheat flour
2 teaspoons baking powder
½ teaspoon each: baking soda, salt
1½ cups whole bran cereal
1⅓ cups buttermilk
¾ cup packed light brown sugar
3 tablespoons margarine or butter melted
1 egg
1 cup coarsely chopped mixed dried fruit
¼–½ cup chopped walnuts

Per Serving:
Calories: 169
% of calories from fat: 20
Fat (gm): 4.2
Saturated fat (gm): 0.8
Cholesterol (mg): 14.1
Sodium (mg): 261
Protein (gm): 4.1
Carbohydrate (gm): 33.1

Exchanges:
Milk: 0.0
Vegetable: 0.0
Fruit: 0.0
Bread: 2.0
Meat: 0.0
Fat: 0.5

1. Combine flours, baking powder, baking soda, salt, and bran cereal in medium bowl. Add buttermilk, brown sugar, margarine, and egg, mixing just until dry ingredients are moistened. Gently fold in dried fruit and walnuts. Pour into greased and floured 9 x 5-inch loaf pan. Bake at 350 degrees until wooden pick inserted in center comes out clean, about 1 hour. Remove from pan; cool on wire rack before slicing.

MULTIGRAIN BATTER BREAD

Batter bread preparation is quick and easy, requiring no kneading and only one rise.

2 loaves (16 servings each)

3¼ cups all-purpose flour
1 cup whole wheat flour
¼ cup soy flour or quick-cooking oats
¾ cup quick-cooking oats
¼ cup sugar
½ teaspoon salt

2 packages fast-rising yeast

1 cup cooked brown rice

2¼ cups fat-free milk, hot (125–130 degrees)

2 tablespoons vegetable oil

Per Serving:
Calories: 97
% of calories from fat: 13
Fat (gm): 1.4
Saturated fat (gm): 0.2
Cholesterol (mg): 0.3
Sodium (mg): 43
Protein (gm): 3.5
Carbohydrate (gm): 17.9

Exchanges:
Milk: 0.0
Vegetable: 0.0
Fruit: 0.0
Bread: 1.0
Meat: 0.0
Fat: 0.5

1. Combine flours, oats, sugar, salt, and yeast in large bowl; add rice, milk, and oil, mixing until smooth. Spoon into 2 greased 8 x 4-inch bread pans; let stand, covered, until double in size, about 30 minutes. Bake at 375 degrees until loaves are browned and sound hollow when tapped, 35 to 40 minutes. Remove from pans and cool on wire racks.

APPLE HONEY KUCHEN

Use your favorite baking apple, tart or sweet, for this brunch bread.

2 kuchens (8–10 servings each)

1 package active dry yeast

¾ cup warm fat-free milk (110–115 degrees)

6 tablespoons granulated sugar, divided

4 tablespoons margarine or butter, divided

1 egg

2–3 cups all-purpose flour

¾ teaspoon salt

1 pound baking apples, peeled, sliced

½ cup raisins

¼ cup packed light brown sugar

2 tablespoons grated orange zest

¼ teaspoon ground cinnamon

⅛ teaspoon ground nutmeg

2–4 tablespoons honey

Fat-free milk

Per Serving:
Calories: 162
% of calories from fat: 19
Fat (gm): 3.4
Saturated fat (gm): 0.7
Cholesterol (mg): 13.5
Sodium (mg): 145
Protein (gm): 2.8
Carbohydrate (gm): 30.9

Exchanges:
Milk: 0.0
Vegetable: 0.0
Fruit: 0.0
Bread: 2.0
Meat: 0.0
Fat: 0.5

1. Mix yeast, milk, and 2 tablespoons granulated sugar in large bowl; let stand 5 minutes. Add 2 tablespoons margarine, egg, 2 cups flour, and salt, mixing until blended. Mix in enough remaining 1 cup flour to make smooth dough.

2. Knead dough on floured surface until smooth and elastic, about 5 minutes. Place in greased bowl; let rise, covered, in warm place until double in size, 1 to 1½ hours. Punch dough down.

3. Heat remaining 2 tablespoons margarine in large skillet until melted; add apples and raisins and cook over medium heat until apples are tender, 5 to 8 minutes. Remove from heat. Sprinkle combined brown sugar, orange zest, cinnamon, and nutmeg over apple mixture and toss.

4. Divide dough into halves. Roll each on floured surface into a 12-inch round. Arrange apple mixture on half of each round; drizzle each with 1 to 2 tablespoons honey. Brush edges of dough with milk; fold dough over filling and press edges with tines of fork to seal. Transfer to greased cookie sheets; sprinkle with remaining 4 tablespoons granulated sugar. Let rise, covered, until impression of finger remains in dough when touched, about 1 hour. Reseal edges, if necessary. Bake at 375 degrees until golden, about 20 minutes. Transfer to wire racks and cool; serve warm.

CRANBERRY COFFEECAKE

45

Quick and easy to make, this sweet-tart coffeecake can be ready to bake in less than 10 minutes.

1 coffeecake (12 servings)

1½ cups fresh or frozen, thawed, cranberries

1 cup sugar, divided

1 teaspoon grated orange zest

1½ cups all-purpose flour

2 teaspoons baking powder

½ teaspoon salt

1 egg

¼ cup each: orange juice, fat-free milk

3 tablespoons margarine or butter, room temperature

¼–½ cup chopped pecans

Per Serving:
Calories: 180
% of calories from fat: 25
Fat (gm): 5
Saturated fat (gm): 0.8
Cholesterol (mg): 17.8
Sodium (mg): 185
Protein (gm): 2.6
Carbohydrate (gm): 31.8

Exchanges:
Milk: 0.0
Vegetable: 0.0
Fruit: 0.0
Bread: 2.0
Meat: 0.0
Fat: 1.0

1. Arrange cranberries in greased 8-inch-square baking pan; sprinkle with ½ cup sugar and orange zest. Mix remaining ingredients until just moistened in medium bowl; drop by spoonfuls over cranberries, spreading batter evenly to sides of pan. Bake at 400 degrees until wooden pick inserted in center comes out clean, 25 to 30 minutes. Immediately invert onto serving plate; serve warm.

WILD RICE MUFFINS

Wild rice adds crunchy texture and a nutritional boost to these muffins.

12 muffins (1 each)

1 cup fat-free milk
4 tablespoons margarine or butter, melted
1 egg
½ cup wild rice, cooked, cooled
1 cup all-purpose flour
½ cup whole wheat flour
3 tablespoons baking powder
1 tablespoon sugar
½ teaspoon salt

Per Serving:
Calories: 136
% of calories from fat: 30
Fat (gm): 4.5
Saturated fat (gm): 0.9
Cholesterol (mg): 18.1
Sodium (mg): 494
Protein (gm): 4.6
Carbohydrate (gm): 19.4

Exchanges:
Milk: 0.0
Vegetable: 0.0
Fruit: 0.0
Bread: 1.5
Meat: 0.0
Fat: 0.5

1. Mix milk, margarine, egg, and rice in large bowl. Add combined flours, baking powder, sugar, salt, mixing just until dry ingredients are moistened.

2. Spoon batter into 12 greased muffin cups. Bake at 400 degrees until browned, 20 to 25 minutes. Remove from pans and cool on wire racks.

PUMPKIN CINNAMON-SPICE MUFFINS

45

Serve warm with a drizzle of honey!

18 muffins (1 per serving)

1½ cups all-purpose flour

½ cup whole wheat flour

¾ cup packed light brown sugar

1½ teaspoons each: baking powder

½ teaspoon each: baking soda, ground cinnamon, nutmeg, and allspice

⅛ teaspoon ground cloves

1 cup canned pumpkin

1 egg

¼ cup canola oil

⅓ cup fat-free milk

⅓ cup frozen orange juice concentrate, thawed

Per Serving:
Calories: 99
% of calories from fat: 2
Fat (gm): 0.2
Saturated fat (gm): 0.1
Cholesterol (mg): 0
Sodium (mg): 87
Protein (gm): 2.2
Carbohydrate (gm): 22.6

Exchanges:
Milk: 0.0
Vegetable: 0.0
Fruit: 0.0
Bread: 1.5
Meat: 0.0
Fat: 0.0

1. Combine flours, baking powder, brown sugar, baking power, baking soda, and spices in large bowl; add combined remaining ingredients, mixing just until dry ingredients are moistened. Spoon into 18 greased muffin cups. Bake at 400 degrees until muffins are browned and toothpick inserted in centers comes out clean, 12 to 14 minutes.

VERY BERRY MUFFINS

45

These muffins can be made any time of year, since they use frozen blueberries; of course, fresh can be substituted!

18 muffins (1 per serving)

2½ cups all-purpose flour

½ teaspoon baking soda

2 teaspoons baking powder

¼ teaspoon salt

½ cup packed light brown sugar

1½ cups low-fat buttermilk

¼ cup vegetable oil

1 egg, beaten

½ teaspoon lemon extract

1 teaspoon vanilla extract

1 package (12 ounces) frozen, unsweetened
blueberries

Per Serving:
Calories: 137
% of calories from fat: 24
Fat (gm): 3.7
Saturated fat (gm): 0.6
Cholesterol (mg): 12.5
Sodium (mg): 151
Protein (gm): 2.9
Carbohydrate (gm): 22.7

Exchanges:
Milk: 0.0
Vegetable: 0.0
Fruit: 0.0
Bread: 1.5
Meat: 0.0
Fat: 0.5

1. Combine flour, baking soda, baking powder, salt, and brown sugar in large bowl. Add combined remaining ingredients, except blueberries, mixing until dry ingredients are just moistened; fold in blueberries. Spoon batter into 18 greased muffin cups, filling ¾ full. Bake at 350 degrees until muffins are browned and toothpick inserted in centers comes out clean, 20 to 25 minutes.

CARDAMOM-PEAR MUFFINS

45

Any dried fruit can be substituted for the pears, and cinnamon can be substituted for the cardamom.

12 muffins (1 each)

1 cup fat-free milk

4 tablespoons margarine or butter, melted

1 egg

2 cups all-purpose flour

⅓ cup plus 2 tablespoons sugar, divided

3 teaspoons baking powder

½ teaspoon salt

1 cup chopped dried pears

1 teaspoon grated orange or lemon zest

½ teaspoon ground cardamom

Per Serving:
Calories: 193
% of calories from fat: 21
Fat (gm): 4.5
Saturated fat (gm): 1
Cholesterol (mg): 18.1
Sodium (mg): 232
Protein (gm): 3.7
Carbohydrate (gm): 35.4

Exchanges:
Milk: 0.0
Vegetable: 0.0
Fruit: 0.0
Bread: 2.0
Meat: 0.0
Fat: 1.0

1. Mix milk, margarine, and egg in medium bowl. Add combined flour, ⅓ cup sugar, baking powder, and salt, mixing just until dry ingredients are moistened. Gently mix in pears and orange zest.

2. Spoon batter into 12 greased muffin cups; sprinkle with remaining 2 tablespoons sugar and cardamom. Bake at 400 degrees until muffins are browned and toothpick inserted in centers of muffins comes out clean, 20 to 25 minutes. Remove from pans and cool on wire racks.

"LITTLE PANTS" BISCUITS

These Mexican-inspired sugar and cinnamon-topped breads are a cross between a biscuit and a cookie. They are usually made into "pants" shapes but can be cut into rounds or squares if you prefer.

18 biscuits (1 each)

¼ cup vegetable shortening

½ cup sugar, divided

2 cups all-purpose flour

2 teaspoons baking powder

½ teaspoon salt

½ cup plus 2 tablespoons fat-free milk, divided

½ teaspoon ground cinnamon

Per Serving:
Calories: 101
% of calories from fat: 27
Fat (gm): 3
Saturated fat (gm): 0.8
Cholesterol (mg): 0.1
Sodium (mg): 100
Protein (gm): 1.7
Carbohydrate (gm): 16.7

Exchanges:
Milk: 0.0
Vegetable: 0.0
Fruit: 0.0
Bread: 1.0
Meat: 0.0
Fat: 0.5

1. Beat shortening and 6 tablespoons sugar in medium bowl until smooth. Beat in combined flour, baking powder, and salt alternately with ½ cup milk to form soft dough.

2. Roll dough on floured surface into a rectangle, a scant ½–inch thick. Cut dough into 18 trapezoid shapes, 2½ inches on the bottom, 1½ inches on the top, and 3 inches on the sides. Cut out a small wedge of dough from the bottom, center of each piece to form "pants legs."

3. Brush biscuits with remaining 2 tablespoons milk; sprinkle with combined remaining 2 tablespoons sugar and cinnamon. Bake at 350 degrees on greased cookie sheet until browned, 15 to 20 minutes.

QUICK SELF-RISING BISCUITS

Two cups of all-purpose flour, combined with 1 tablespoon baking powder and ½ teaspoon salt, can be substituted for the self-rising flour.

18 biscuits (1 each)

1 tablespoon vegetable shortening

2 cups self-rising flour

¾–1 cup fat-free milk

1 tablespoon margarine or butter melted

1. Cut shortening into flour in medium bowl until mixture resembles coarse crumbs. Stir in enough milk to make a soft dough. Roll dough on floured surface to ½–inch thickness; cut into 18 biscuits with 2-inch cutter. Place in greased 13 x 9-inch baking pan; brush with melted margarine. Bake at 425 degrees until golden, about 15 minutes.

Per Serving:
Calories: 65
% of calories from fat: 21
Fat (gm): 1.4
Saturated fat (gm): 0.3
Cholesterol (mg): 0.2
Sodium (mg): 189
Protein (gm): 1.7
Carbohydrate (gm): 10.8

Exchanges:
Milk: 0.0
Vegetable: 0.0
Fruit: 0.0
Bread: 1.0
Meat: 0.0
Fat: 0.0

VARIATIONS

Chive Biscuits — Make biscuits as above, mixing 3 tablespoons snipped fresh or dried chives into the dough.

Parmesan Biscuits — Make biscuits as above; sprinkle with 2 tablespoons grated fat-free Parmesan cheese before baking.

SWEET POTATO BISCUITS

45 *Sweet potatoes offer moistness and a delicate sweetness to these biscuits. For a nonsweet biscuit, white potatoes can be substituted.*

18 biscuits (1 each)

¾ cup mashed, cooked sweet potatoes
3–4 tablespoons margarine or butter, melted
⅔ cup fat-free milk
2 cups all-purpose flour, divided
4 teaspoons baking powder
1 tablespoon brown sugar
½ teaspoon salt
Fat-free milk
Ground nutmeg

Per Serving:
Calories: 82
% of calories from fat: 23
Fat (gm): 2.1
Saturated fat (gm): 0.4
Cholesterol (mg): 0.1
Sodium (mg): 161
Protein (gm): 1.8
Carbohydrate (gm): 14

Exchanges:
Milk: 0.0
Vegetable: 0.0
Fruit: 0.0
Bread: 1.0
Meat: 0.0
Fat: 0.5

1. Mix sweet potatoes and margarine in medium bowl; stir in ⅔ cup milk. Mix in 1¾ cups flour, baking powder, brown sugar, and salt. Mix in remaining ¼ cup flour if dough is too sticky to handle easily.

2. Knead dough on floured surface 5 to 6 times. Roll on floured surface to ½–inch thickness; cut into 18 biscuits with 2-inch biscuit cutter and place close together on greased baking sheet. Brush biscuits lightly with milk and sprinkle with nutmeg. Bake at 425 degrees until golden, 12 to 15 minutes.

VINEGAR BISCUITS

45

Vegetable shortening contributes to the fine texture of these biscuits. Vegetable shortening with no trans-fats is now available.

12 biscuits (1 each)

¾ cup fat-free milk
¼ cup cider vinegar
3 tablespoons vegetable shortening, melted
2 cups all-purpose flour
1½ teaspoons baking soda
1 teaspoon cream of tartar
½ teaspoon salt

Per Serving:
Calories: 109
% of calories from fat: 27
Fat (gm): 3.2
Saturated fat (gm): 0.8
Cholesterol (mg): 0.3
Sodium (mg): 255
Protein (gm): 2.7
Carbohydrate (gm): 17.1

Exchanges:
Milk: 0.0
Vegetable: 0.0
Fruit: 0.0
Bread: 1.0
Meat: 0.0
Fat: 0.5

1. Mix milk, vinegar, and shortening; mix into combined flour, baking soda, cream of tartar, and salt in medium bowl. Knead dough on generously floured surface 1 to 2 minutes. Pat dough into ½–inch thickness; cut into 12 biscuits with 3-inch-round cutter. Bake on greased cookie sheet at 425 degrees until golden, 10 to 12 minutes.

BLUEBERRY PANCAKES WITH BLUEBERRY MAPLE SYRUP

45

For special occasions or just for fun, drizzle pancake batter into heart or other shapes in the skillet!

4 servings

¾ cup fat-free milk
1 egg
1 tablespoon margarine or butter, melted
¾ cup all-purpose flour

¼ cup whole wheat flour

1–2 tablespoons sugar

2 teaspoons baking powder

½ teaspoon salt

⅛ teaspoon ground nutmeg

¾ cup fresh or frozen, thawed, blueberries

Blueberry Maple Syrup (recipe follows) or light
pancake syrup, warm

Per Serving:
Calories: 308
% of calories from fat: 14
Fat (gm): 4.7
Saturated fat (gm): 1.1
Cholesterol (mg): 54
Sodium (mg): 511
Protein (gm): 6.9
Carbohydrate (gm): 60.9

Exchanges:
Milk: 0.0
Vegetable: 0.0
Fruit: 2.0
Bread: 2.0
Meat: 0.0
Fat: 1.0

1. Mix milk, egg, and margarine in medium bowl; add combined remaining ingredients, except blueberries and syrup, beating until almost smooth. Gently mix in blueberries.

2. Pour batter into lightly greased large skillet, using about ¼ cup batter for each pancake. Cook over medium heat until bubbles form in pancakes and they are browned on the bottoms, 3 to 5 minutes. Turn pancakes; cook until browned on other side, 3 to 5 minutes. Serve with Blueberry Maple Syrup.

Blueberry Maple Syrup

Makes about 1 cup

½–¾ cup maple syrup

½ cup fresh, or frozen, blueberries

1 teaspoon each: grated orange and lemon zest

1. Heat all ingredients in small saucepan over medium heat until hot, 3 to 5 minutes.

BUTTERMILK BUCKWHEAT PANCAKES

45 *Whole wheat flour can be substituted for the buckwheat flour.*

4 servings

1 cup buttermilk

1 egg

1–2 tablespoons vegetable oil

½ cup each: all-purpose flour, buckwheat flour

1 tablespoon sugar

1 teaspoon each: baking powder, orange zest

½ teaspoon each: baking soda, salt

½–1 cup maple syrup, light pancake syrup, or
    Blueberry Maple Syrup (see p. 563), warm

Per Serving:
Calories: 291
% of calories from fat: 18
Fat (gm): 5.8
Saturated fat (gm): 1.3
Cholesterol (mg): 55.5
Sodium (mg): 593
Protein (gm): 7.1
Carbohydrate (gm): 54

Exchanges:
Milk: 0.0
Vegetable: 0.0
Fruit: 1.5
Bread: 2.0
Meat: 0.0
Fat: 1.0

1. Mix buttermilk, egg, and oil in medium bowl; add combined remaining ingredients, except syrup, beating until almost smooth.

2. Pour batter into lightly greased large skillet, using about ¼ cup batter for each pancake. Cook over medium heat until bubbles form in pancakes and they are browned on the bottoms, 3 to 5 minutes. Turn pancakes; cook until browned on other side, 3 to 5 minutes. Serve with warm syrup.

CREPES

45 *Cooked crepes can be kept warm in a 200-degree oven while cooking remaining crepes. Crepes can also be made in advance and frozen; layer crepes in plastic wrap and wrap in aluminum foil. To heat, place unwrapped crepes on cookie sheet; bake at 325 degrees until hot, 5 to 8 minutes.*

4 servings (2 each)

½ cup each: all-purpose flour, fat-free milk

2 eggs

1 tablespoon melted margarine or canola oil

¼ teaspoon salt

1. Beat all ingredients in small bowl until smooth (batter will be thin). Pour scant ¼ cup batter into lightly greased 8-inch crepe pan or small skillet, tilting pan to coat bottom evenly with batter. Cook over medium heat until browned on the bottom, 2 to 3 minutes. Turn crepe and cook until browned on other side, 2 to 3 minutes. Repeat with remaining batter.

Per Serving:
Calories: 120
% of calories from fat: 33
(will decrease when filled)
Fat (gm): 4.3
Saturated fat (gm): 1
Cholesterol (mg): 53.8
Sodium (mg): 226
Protein (gm): 6
Carbohydrate (gm): 13.8

Exchanges:
Milk: 0.0
Vegetable: 0.0
Fruit: 0.0
Bread: 1.0
Meat: 0.0
Fat: 1.0

VARIATION

Dessert Crepes — Make crepes as above, adding 1 to 2 tablespoons sugar to the batter.

SWEET-STUFFED FRENCH TOAST

45 *A rich breakfast entrée with a sweet surprise inside! Serve with warm maple syrup or a drizzle of honey.*

4 servings

4 thick slices sourdough or Italian bread (1-inch)
4 tablespoons fat-free cream cheese
4 teaspoons strawberry or other flavor fruit preserves
2 eggs
¼ cup fat-free half-and-half or fat-free milk
1 teaspoon ground cinnamon
¼ teaspoon ground nutmeg
1–2 tablespoons margarine or butter
1 cup maple syrup or light pancake syrup, warm

Per Serving:
Calories: 383
% of calories from fat: 16
Fat (gm): 7
Saturated fat (gm): 2
Cholesterol (mg): 108
Sodium (mg): 334
Protein (gm): 8
Carbohydrate (gm): 74

Exchanges:
Milk: 0.0
Vegetable: 0.0
Fruit: 0.0
Bread: 5.0
Meat: 0.0
Fat: 0.5

1. Cut a pocket in the side of each bread slice; fill with each with 1 tablespoon cream cheese and 1 teaspoon preserves. Lightly beat eggs, half-and-half, and spices in shallow bowl. Dip bread in egg mixture, turning to coat both sides.

2. Cook bread slices in margarine in large skillet on medium to medium-low heat until browned, about 5 minutes on each side. Serve with warm syrup.

CINNAMON-RAISIN CREAM CHEESE

45 *A perfect spread for warm bagels, scones, or biscuits; serve at room temperature for ease in spreading.*

About 1 cup (1 tablespoon each)

4 ounces light cream cheese, room temperature
2 tablespoons chopped raisins
1 tablespoon brown sugar
¼ teaspoon ground cinnamon
2–3 teaspoons fat-free milk

1. Mix all ingredients.

Per Serving:
Calories: 37
% of calories from fat: 45
Fat (gm): 1.8
Saturated fat (gm): 1.2
Cholesterol (mg): 5.3
Sodium (mg): 54
Protein (gm): 1.2
Carbohydrate (gm): 3.8

Exchanges:
Milk: 0.0
Vegetable: 0.0
Fruit: 0.0
Bread: 0.0
Meat: 0.0
Fat: 0.5

ROSE GERANIUM JELLY

45 *Simply delicious, and perfect for gift giving.*

About 2 pints (1 tablespoon each)

1 cup boiling water
½ cup packed, torn rose geranium leaves
1 can (6 ounces) unsweetened frozen apple
   juice concentrate
1 package (1¾ ounces) powdered fruit pectin
2–3 tablespoons lemon juice
1 tablespoon white distilled vinegar
Pinch salt
3⅓ cups sugar

Per Serving:
Calories: 48
% of calories from fat: 0
Fat (gm): 0
Saturated fat (gm): 0
Cholesterol (mg): 0
Sodium (mg): 2
Protein (gm): 0
Carbohydrate (gm): 12.33

Exchanges:
Milk: 0.0
Vegetable: 0.0
Fruit: 1.0
Bread: 0.0
Meat: 0.0
Fat: 0.0

1. Pour boiling water over rose geranium leaves in small bowl; let stand until cool. Strain; discard rose geranium leaves. Combine rose geranium water and apple juice in 2-cup measure; add water to measure 2 cups. Heat juice mixture and remaining ingredients, except sugar, to boiling in large saucepan; stir in sugar and return to boiling, stirring. Boil hard 1 minute, stirring. Pour into sterilized pint jars; seal and cool. Refrigerate up to 1 month.

VARIATIONS

Apple-Mint Jelly — Make recipe as above, substituting ½ cup packed fresh or 3 tablespoons dried mint leaves for the rose geranium leaves.

Orange-Rosemary Jelly — Make recipe as above, substituting 2 tablespoons crushed fresh or 1 tablespoon dried rosemary leaves for the rose geranium leaves, and orange concentrate for the apple. Increase lemon juice to ¼ cup.

APPLE-PEAR BUTTER

45 *Serve this creamy butter on warm slices of nut bread or multigrain toast.*

About 2 pints (2 tablespoons per serving)

1 pound each: firm, ripe pears and apples, peeled, cored, chopped

1 can (12 ounces) frozen apple juice concentrate

1 tablespoon lemon juice

1 teaspoon finely grated orange zest

¼ teaspoon each: ground ginger and cinnamon

Per Serving:
Calories: 31
% of calories from fat: 3
Fat (gm): 0.1
Saturated fat (gm): 0
Cholesterol (mg): 0
Sodium (mg): 2
Protein (gm): 0.1
Carbohydrate (gm): 7.8

Exchanges:
Milk: 0.0
Vegetable: 0.0
Fruit: 0.5
Bread: 0.0
Meat: 0.0
Fat: 0.0

1. Heat all ingredients to boiling in large saucepan; reduce heat and simmer, covered, until pears and apples are tender and mixture is a jam consistency, 20 to 30 minutes. Pour into sterilized jars; cool and cover with lids. Refrigerate up to 2 weeks.

GINGER-RHUBARB JAM

45 *Cook this jam to desired consistency, as it's not made with pectin.*

About 2 pints (1 tablespoon per serving)

1½ pounds rhubarb, sliced (1-inch)
2 cups sugar
1 cup water
2 pieces gingerroot (1-inch), halved lengthwise
1 cinnamon stick
¼ teaspoon ground cardamom

Per Serving:
Calories: 27
% of calories from fat: 1
Fat (gm): 0
Saturated fat (gm): 0
Cholesterol (mg): 0
Sodium (mg): 1
Protein (gm): 0.1
Carbohydrate (gm): 6.8

Exchanges:
Milk: 0.0
Vegetable: 0.0
Fruit: 0.5
Bread: 0.0
Meat: 0.0
Fat: 0.0

1. Heat rhubarb, sugar, and water to boiling in large saucepan; reduce heat and simmer, covered, until rhubarb is tender, about 10 minutes. Strain rhubarb, returning juice to saucepan; reserve rhubarb. Add spices to juice and heat to boiling. Reduce heat and simmer rapidly, stirring occasionally, until very thick, 10 to 15 minutes. Discard cinnamon stick and gingerroot.

2. Stir rhubarb into juice mixture; simmer, if necessary for mixture to be a jam consistency, stirring to prevent sticking. Pour jam into sterilized jars; cool and cover with lids. Refrigerate up to 2 weeks.

SPICED APPLE-PRUNE JAM

45 *The perfect breakfast treat with muffins and bagels.*

About 2 pints (1 tablespoon each)

4 large Granny Smith apples, peeled, cored, sliced
1 package (12 ounces) pitted prunes, chopped
1 cup unsweetened apple juice
1½ teaspoons ground cinnamon
½ teaspoon each: ground allspice, lemon juice

Per Serving:
Calories: 20
% of calories from fat: 3
Fat (gm): 0.1
Saturated fat (gm): 0
Cholesterol (mg): 0
Sodium (mg): 0
Protein (gm): 0.2
Carbohydrate (gm): 5.2

Exchanges:
Milk: 0.0
Vegetable: 0.0
Fruit: 0.0
Bread: 0.0
Meat: 0.0
Fat: 0.0

1. Heat all ingredients to boiling in large saucepan; reduce heat and simmer, covered, 10 minutes. Simmer, uncovered, until fruit is tender and mixture is a jam consistency, about 15 minutes. Pour into jars; cool and cover with lids. Refrigerate up to 3 weeks.

FOURTEEN

Sandwiches,

Snacks,

and

Beverages

GORP, BY GOLLY!

The great snack mix for curing the munchies or for sharing with a gathering of friends.

16 servings (about ½ cup each)

3 cups low-fat granola

2 cups pretzel goldfish

½ cup sesame sticks, broken into halves

3 cups coarsely chopped mixed dried fruit

Butter-flavored cooking spray

1 teaspoon ground cinnamon

½ teaspoon ground nutmeg

Per Serving:
Calories: 172
% of calories from fat: 13
Fat (gm): 2.6
Saturated fat (gm): 0.2
Cholesterol (mg): 0
Sodium (mg): 82
Protein (gm): 2.7
Carbohydrate (gm): 37.8

Exchanges:
Milk: 0.0
Vegetable: 0.0
Fruit: 2.0
Bread: 0.5
Meat: 0.0
Fat: 0.5

1. Mix granola, pretzel goldfish, sesame sticks, and dried fruit on large jelly roll pan. Spray mixture generously with cooking spray; sprinkle with combined spices and toss. Bake at 350 degrees 15 to 20 minutes, stirring after 10 minutes; cool and store in covered container at room temperature.

HOT STUFF!

If this snack mix isn't hot enough for you, add a few sprinkles of red pepper sauce! Use 2 cups of purchased plain pita chips can be used.

16 servings (about ½ cup each)

2 cups oyster crackers

Pita Chips (see pg. 574)

½ cup dry-roasted smoked almonds

1 cup each: coarsely chopped mixed dried fruit, dried pineapple chunks

Butter-flavored cooking spray

1 teaspoon each: dried oregano leaves, garlic powder, chili powder, cayenne pepper, black pepper

Per Serving:
Calories: 120
% of calories from fat: 22
Fat (gm): 3.2
Saturated fat (gm): 0.2
Cholesterol (mg): 0
Sodium (mg): 160
Protein (gm): 3.2
Carbohydrate (gm): 21.7

Exchanges:
Milk: 0.0
Vegetable: 0.0
Fruit: 0.5
Bread: 1.0
Meat: 0.0
Fat: 0.5

1. Mix crackers, Pita Chips, almonds, and dried fruit on large jelly roll pan. Spray mixture generously with cooking spray; sprinkle with combined remaining ingredients and toss. Bake at 350 degrees 15 to 20 minutes, stirring after 10 minutes; cool and store in covered container.

CHILI BANZOS

45

These highly spiced crisp snackers are great tasting and good for you too!

8 servings (about ¼ cup each)

2 cans (15 ounces each) garbanzo beans, rinsed, drained
Olive oil cooking spray
1 tablespoon reduced-sodium Worcestershire sauce
2–3 dashes hot pepper sauce
1–2 teaspoons each: chili, garlic and onion powder
1 teaspoon paprika
½ teaspoon salt

Per Serving:
Calories: 109
% of calories from fat: 16
Fat (gm): 2.0
Saturated fat (gm): 0.3
Cholesterol (mg): 0
Sodium (mg): 440
Protein (gm): 5.1
Carbohydrate (gm): 18.5

Exchanges:
Milk: 0.0
Vegetable: 0.0
Fruit: 0.0
Bread: 1.5
Meat: 0.0
Fat: 0.0

1. Dry beans well on paper toweling and transfer to large skillet; spray generously with cooking spray. Cook over medium heat, stirring frequently, until beans begin to brown, about 10 minutes. Remove from heat; drizzle combined Worcestershire and pepper sauce over beans and toss. Sprinkle with combined remaining ingredients and toss. Transfer mixture to jelly roll pan and bake at 325 degrees until beans are very crisp on the outside, 20 to 25 minutes, stirring twice. Cool; store in airtight container.

VEGGIE CRISPS

Cut veggies as thinly as you can to ensure even cooking for crispness. And be sure they are completely dried; if slightly moist inside, spoilage can develop.

8 servings (about ½ cup each)

2 pounds assorted vegetables (sweet potatoes, russet potatoes, large radishes, butternut squash, large carrots, turnips, parsnips, rutabaga, beets), peeled, thinly sliced (¹⁄₁₆ inch)
Salt, to taste
Vegetable cooking spray

Per Serving:
Calories: 87
% of calories from fat: 1
Fat (gm): 0.2
Saturated fat (gm): 0.1
Cholesterol (mg): 0
Sodium (mg): 22
Protein (gm): 1.8
Carbohydrate (gm): 20

Exchanges:
Milk: 0.0
Vegetable: 0.5
Fruit: 0.0
Bread: 1.0
Meat: 0.0
Fat: 0.0

1. Sprinkle vegetable slices lightly and evenly with salt. Let stand 20 to 30 minutes, allowing vegetables to release moisture. Rinse well in cold water and dry completely on paper toweling.

2. To dry vegetables in the microwave, arrange slices in single layer on large greased microwave-safe plate; spray lightly with cooking spray. Microwave on high power until vegetables are dried, 5 to 7 minutes, checking and rearranging after 4 or 5 minutes and removing vegetables as they dry. The vegetables will become crisper as they cool. Store in airtight container.

3. To dry vegetables in the oven, arrange slices in single layer on greased foil-lined jelly roll pan; spray lightly with cooking spray. Bake at 275 degrees for 40 to 50 minutes, checking occasionally and removing vegetables as they dry. The vegetables will become crisper as they cool. Store in airtight container.

NOTE: Different kinds of vegetables cook in different times, so it's important to check for doneness frequently. In microwave cooking it is better to cook 1 kind of vegetable at a time.

FRUIT NUGGETS

45 *These nuggets are bite-sized and perfect for high-energy snacking or for a sweet ending to a meal.*

3 dozen

2 cups finely ground low-fat graham cracker crumbs

½ cup finely ground ginger snaps or low-fat graham cracker crumbs

½ teaspoon each: ground cinnamon, nutmeg, ginger

½ cup each: finely chopped dried apples, dried apricots, dates, golden raisins

½ cup orange juice

2–3 tablespoons honey

3 tablespoons sugar

Per Nugget:
Calories: 57
% of calories from fat: 8
Fat (gm): 0.5
Saturated fat (gm): 0.1
Cholesterol (mg): 0
Sodium (mg): 29
Protein (gm): 0.8
Carbohydrate (gm): 12.8

Exchanges:
Milk: 0.0
Vegetable: 0.0
Fruit: 0.5
Bread: 0.5
Meat: 0.0
Fat: 0.0

1. Combine all ingredients, except sugar, in bowl, stirring until mixture holds together. Roll into 36 balls, each about 1 inch in diameter. Measure 1 tablespoon sugar into large plastic bag; add 1 dozen nuggets and shake until coated. Repeat with remaining sugar and nuggets. Store in covered container at room temperature.

TOASTED ONION DIP

45 *This will bring back memories of the popular dip made with onion soup mix! Toasting the dried onion flakes is the flavor secret.*

12 servings (about 2 tablespoons each)

3–4 tablespoons dried onion flakes

1 package (8 ounces) fat-free cream cheese

⅓ cup each: reduced-fat plain yogurt, fat-free mayonnaise

2 small green onions, chopped

2 cloves garlic, minced

¼ teaspoon crushed vegetable bouillon cube

2–3 tablespoons fat-free milk

½–1 teaspoon lemon juice

2–3 drops red pepper sauce

Salt and white pepper, to taste

Dippers: assorted vegetable relishes and bread sticks

Per Serving:
Calories: 32
% of calories from fat: 4
Fat (gm): 0.1
Saturated fat (gm): 0.1
Cholesterol (mg): 0.4
Sodium (mg): 223
Protein (gm): 3.3
Carbohydrate (gm): 3.9

Exchanges:
Milk: 0.0
Vegetable: 0.0
Fruit: 0.0
Bread: 0.0
Meat: 0.5
Fat: 0.0

1. Cook onion flakes in small skillet over medium to medium-low heat until toasted, 3 to 4 minutes, stirring frequently; remove from heat. Mix cream cheese, yogurt, mayonnaise, green onions, garlic, and bouillon in medium bowl until smooth, adding enough milk to thin the mixture to the desired dipping consistency. Stir in onions; season to taste with lemon juice, pepper sauce, salt, and white pepper. Serve with dippers (not included in nutritional data).

BLACK BEAN HUMMUS

45

Tahini (ground sesame paste) and soy sauce season this unusual bean dip.

6 servings (about ¼ cup each)

1 can (15 ounces) black beans, rinsed, drained
¼ cup reduced-sodium vegetable broth or water
2–3 tablespoons tahini
3 cloves garlic
2–2½ tablespoons lemon juice
1½ tablespoons soy sauce
Salt and cayenne pepper, to taste
Pita Chips (recipe follows) or pita breads, cut into wedges

Per Serving:
Calories: 178
% of calories from fat: 17
Fat (gm): 3.5
Saturated fat (gm): 0.5
Cholesterol (mg): 0
Sodium (mg): 668
Protein (gm): 7.8
Carbohydrate (gm): 30.2

Exchanges:
Milk: 0.0
Vegetable: 0.0
Fruit: 0.0
Bread: 2.0
Meat: 0.0
Fat: 0.5

1. Process beans, broth, tahini, garlic, lemon juice, and soy sauce in food processor until smooth; season to taste with salt and cayenne pepper. Refrigerate 1 to 2 hours for flavors to blend. Serve with Pita Chips.

Pita Chips
Perfect to serve with any dip, or to eat as a snack.

6 servings (8 each)

3 whole wheat pocket breads
Butter-flavored cooking spray
3–4 teaspoons Italian seasoning or other desired herbs

1. Open breads and separate each into 2 halves; cut each half into 8 wedges. Arrange wedges, soft sides up, in single layer on jelly roll pan. Spray with cooking spray and sprinkle with Italian seasoning. Bake at 425 degrees until browned and crisp, 5 to 10 minutes.

Seasoned Pita Chips — Make recipe above, substituting 1 to 2 teaspoons chili powder, ground cumin or garlic powder for the Italian seasoning.

Parmesan Pita Chips — Make recipe above, substituting 2 to 3 tablespoons grated Parmesan cheese for the Italian Seasoning.

SLOPPY JOES

45 *Toasted buns are a must for this sweet-sour beef filling.*

4 servings

1 pound ground beef eye of round

½ cup each: chopped onion, celery, red or green bell pepper

2 cloves garlic, minced

1 cup reduced-sodium catsup

½ cup water

2 tablespoons prepared mustard

1 tablespoon cider vinegar

2 teaspoons packed light brown sugar

Salt and pepper, to taste

4 hamburger buns, toasted

Per Serving:
Calories: 385
% of calories from fat: 17
Fat (gm): 7.4
Saturated fat (gm): 2.2
Cholesterol (mg): 64
Sodium (mg): 423
Protein (gm): 32.5
Carbohydrate (gm): 48.2

Exchanges:
Milk: 0.0
Vegetable: 2.0
Fruit: 0.0
Bread: 2.0
Meat: 3.5
Fat: 0.0

1. Cook ground beef, onion, celery, bell pepper, and garlic in lightly greased medium skillet over medium heat until beef is browned and vegetables tender, about 10 minutes. Stir in remaining ingredients, except salt, pepper, and buns; heat to boiling. Reduce heat and simmer, uncovered, until mixture is thickened, about 5 minutes. Season to taste with salt and pepper. Serve in buns.

VARIATION

Baked Sloppy Potatoes — Make recipe as above, deleting buns. Spoon mixture into 4 large baked potatoes.

CHEESEBURGERS SUPREME

45 *Top these moist burgers with your choice of catsup, mustard, raw or sautéed onions, sautéed mushrooms, or chopped olives, and serve with plenty of dill pickles and Crispy French Fries (see p. 492).*

4 servings

1 pound very lean ground beef

2–4 tablespoons finely chopped onion

3 tablespoons water

½ teaspoon salt

¼ teaspoon pepper

4 slices (1 ounce each) fat-free or reduced-fat Cheddar or Swiss cheese

4 hamburger buns, toasted

Per Serving:
Calories: 326
% of calories from fat: 19
Fat (gm): 6.7
Saturated fat (gm): 2.2
Cholesterol (mg): 64
Sodium (mg): 768
Protein (gm): 39.5
Carbohydrate (gm): 24.1

Exchanges:
Milk: 0.0
Vegetable: 0.0
Fruit: 0.0
Bread: 1.5
Meat: 4.0
Fat: 0.0

1. Mix ground beef, onion, water, salt, and pepper in medium bowl just until blended. Shape mixture into four 1-inch-thick patties. Cook burgers in lightly greased skillet to desired degree of doneness, 3 to 4 minutes per side for medium. Top each burger with slice of cheese; cover skillet and cook until cheese is beginning to melt, 1 to 2 minutes. Serve in buns.

COUNTRY EGG AND GREEN ONION SANDWICH

45 *A simple, unsophisticated sandwich that is super quick to make and remarkably satisfying.*

2 servings

4 slices multigrain bread

Vegetable cooking spray

2 tablespoons chili sauce

2 large eggs, fried

Salt and pepper, to taste

2 green onions, sliced

Per Serving:
Calories: 215
% of calories from fat: 29
Fat (gm): 7.1
Saturated fat (gm): 2
Cholesterol (mg): 212
Sodium (mg): 442
Protein (gm): 11.1
Carbohydrate (gm): 26.8

Exchanges:
Milk: 0.0
Vegetable: 0.0
Fruit: 0.0
Bread: 2.0
Meat: 1.0
Fat: 0.5

1. Spray both sides of bread with cooking spray; cook bread in large skillet over medium heat until toasted. 2 to 3 minutes on each side. Spread 2 slices of bread with chili sauce; top with eggs and sprinkle with salt and pepper. Top with green onions, and remaining bread.

TUNA PAN BAGNA

45

The bread absorbs the savory dressing, thus giving this Mediterranean sandwich its name, literally, bathed bread.

4 servings

2 cans (6 ounces each) oil-packed solid white tuna

½ cup chopped roasted red bell peppers

1½ tablespoons drained capers

2 tablespoons each: balsamic or red wine vinegar, chopped fresh chives or green onions

1 loaf (12 ounces) French bread, halved horizontally

4 leaves romaine lettuce

1 tomato, sliced

2 slices red onion

2–4 pepperoncini

Per Serving:
Calories: 443
% of calories from fat: 20
Fat (gm): 9.7
Saturated fat (gm): 1.9
Cholesterol (mg): 15.3
Sodium (mg): 802
Protein .(gm): 33
Carbohydrate (gm): 52.5

Exchanges:
Milk: 0.0
Vegetable: 2.0
Fruit: 0.0
Bread: 3.0
Meat: 3.0
Fat: 0.0

1. Drain tuna, reserving 3 tablespoons oil. Combine tuna, reserved oil, bell peppers, capers, vinegar, and chives in bowl; spread over bottom half of bread. Cover with remaining ingredients and top half of bread. Wrap sandwich tightly in plastic wrap, pressing to compact sandwich. Refrigerate at least 10 minutes, or up to 8 hours.

EGGPLANT PARMESAN SANDWICHES

45 *Try crumbled feta cheese as a delicious alternative for the mozzarella.*

4 servings

4 thick slices eggplant (¾-inch)

1 egg, beaten

⅓ cup seasoned dry bread crumbs

2 tablespoons grated fat-free Parmesan cheese

4 ounces sliced fat-free mozzarella cheese

4 French rolls or hoagie buns, toasted

2 roasted small red peppers, halved

Pizza Sauce (recipe follows)

Per Serving:
Calories: 255
% of calories from fat: 13
Fat (gm): 3.6
Saturated fat (gm): 1
Cholesterol (mg): 58
Sodium (mg): 588
Protein (gm): 17
Carbohydrate (gm): 37.6

Exchanges:
Milk: 0.0
Vegetable: 0.0
Fruit: 0.0
Bread: 2.5
Meat: 1.0
Fat: 0.0

1. Dip eggplant slices in egg and coat with combined bread crumbs and Parmesan cheese. Cook in lightly greased large skillet over medium heat until tender and browned, about 5 minutes on each side. Top each eggplant slice with 1 ounce cheese; cook, covered, until cheese is melted, 2 to 3 minutes. Serve in buns with roasted red peppers and Pizza Sauce.

Pizza Sauce

4 servings (¼ cup each)

¼ cup each: chopped onion, green bell pepper

2 cloves garlic, minced

1 can (8 ounces) reduced-sodium tomato sauce

½ teaspoon each: dried basil and oregano leaves

Salt and pepper, to taste

1. Sauté onion, bell pepper, and garlic in lightly greased medium saucepan until tender, about 5 minutes. Stir in tomato sauce and herbs; heat to boiling. Reduce heat and simmer, uncovered, until sauce thickens, about 5 minutes. Season to taste with salt and pepper.

45-MINUTE PREPARATION TIP: Make Pizza Sauce before preparing the rest of the recipe.

HERBED VEGGIE BURGERS

These fabulous meatless burgers can star in any meal.

4 servings

¾ cup each: finely chopped broccoli florets, mushrooms

¼ cup finely chopped onion

2 cloves garlic, minced

2 teaspoons each: dried bouquet garni

⅔ cup cooked wild or brown rice

⅓ cup each: quick-cooking oats, coarsely chopped toasted walnuts

½ cup each: shredded fat-free Cheddar cheese (2 ounces), 1% fat cottage cheese

Salt and pepper, to taste

1 egg

3 multigrain or whole wheat buns, toasted

⅓ cup fat-free mayonnaise

Lettuce leaves

Per Serving:
Calories: 313
% of calories from fat: 26
Fat (gm): 9.5
Saturated fat (gm): 1.3
Cholesterol (mg): 1.3
Sodium (mg): 700
Protein (gm): 19.6
Carbohydrate (gm): 40

Exchanges:
Milk: 0.0
Vegetable: 0.0
Fruit: 0.0
Bread: 2.5
Meat: 2.0
Fat: 0.5

1. Sauté broccoli, mushrooms, onion, garlic, and bouquet garni in lightly greased medium skillet until tender, 8 to 10 minutes. Mix in rice, oats, walnuts, and cheeses; season to taste with salt and pepper. Mix in egg.

2. Shape mixture into 4 burgers; cook in lightly greased skillet over medium to medium-low heat until browned, 3 to 4 minutes on each side. Serve in buns with mayonnaise and lettuce.

FALAFEL BURGERS WITH TAHINI DRESSING

Enjoy these healthful meatless burgers with Eggplant Soup with Roasted Red Pepper Sauce (see p. 50).

4 servings

1½ cups cooked dried or drained, canned
  garbanzo beans, coarsely pureed

¼ cup finely chopped parsley

2 tablespoons chopped onion

2 cloves garlic, minced

1–2 tablespoons lemon juice

¼ cup all-purpose flour

1¼ teaspoons ground cumin

Salt and pepper, to taste

2 pita breads, halved

Tahini Dressing (recipe follows)

¼ cup each: chopped tomato, cucumber,
  thinly sliced green onions

Per Serving:
Calories: 291
% of calories from fat: 23
Fat (gm): 7.6
Saturated fat (gm): 0.3
Cholesterol (mg): 0.3
Sodium (mg): 194
Protein (gm): 13.2
Carbohydrate (gm): 45.0

Exchanges:
Milk: 0.0
Vegetable: 2.0
Fruit: 0.0
Bread: 2.5
Meat: 0.5
Fat: 1.0

1. Mix garbanzo beans, parsley, onion, garlic, lemon juice, flour, and cumin in bowl; season to taste with salt and pepper.

2. Shape mixture into 4 burgers and cook in lightly greased skillet until browned, 3 to 4 minutes on each side. Arrange burgers in pitas; drizzle 2 tablespoons Tahini Dressing over each burger. Spoon combined tomato, cucumber, and sliced green onions into pitas.

Tahini Dressing
Makes about 1⅓ cups

⅓ cup fat-free yogurt

2–3 tablespoons tahini (sesame seed paste)

1 small clove garlic, minced

½–1 teaspoon lemon juice

1. Mix all ingredients; refrigerate until ready to use.

45-MINUTE PREPARATION TIP: Make Tahini Dressing before preparing the rest of the recipe.

Falafel Pitas — Make recipe as above, but shape mixture into meatballs; coat lightly with unseasoned dry bread crumbs. Spray meatballs with cooking spray and bake at 375 degrees until browned, about 15 minutes. Serve in pitas.

VEGGIE BARBECUE PITAS

45 *Use your favorite barbecue sauce for these veggie snacks.*

8 servings

1 cup each: thinly sliced onion, green bell pepper, zucchini
3 cups sliced mushrooms
1 tablespoon canola oil
½ cup barbecue sauce
4 pita breads, halved, warm
1 cup (4 ounces) shredded reduced-fat Monterey Jack cheese

Per Serving:
Calories: 159
% of calories from fat: 25
Fat (gm): 4.4
Saturated fat (gm): 1.6
Cholesterol (mg): 7.5
Sodium (mg): 375
Protein (gm): 6.6
Carbohydrate (gm): 23.3

Exchanges:
Milk: 0.0
Vegetable: 2.0
Fruit: 0.0
Bread: 1.0
Meat: 0.0
Fat: 1.0

1. Sauté vegetables in oil in large skillet until tender, 8 to 10 minutes. Stir in barbecue sauce and cook until hot, 2 to 3 minutes. Spoon vegetable mixture into pitas; sprinkle with cheese.

CRAB MELT

45 *Canned tuna, cooked shrimp, or surimi (imitation crabmeat) can be used in place of the crab.*

2 servings

4 ounces cooked crabmeat, flaked
1 medium green onion, thinly sliced
2 tablespoons each: chopped red bell pepper, fat-free mayonnaise, fat-free sour cream
½ teaspoon dried dill weed
1–2 teaspoons lemon juice
Salt and pepper, to taste
2 slices each: white or whole wheat bread, fat-free American cheese

1. Mix crabmeat, green onion, red bell pepper, mayonnaise, sour cream, and dill weed in small bowl; season to taste with lemon juice, salt, and pepper. Spread on bread slices and top with cheese. Bake at 400 degrees or broil until sandwiches are hot and cheese melted.

Per Serving:
Calories: 182
% of calories from fat: 10
Fat (gm): 2
Saturated fat (gm): 0.3
Cholesterol (mg): 56.7
Sodium (mg): 786
Protein (gm): 19.9
Carbohydrate (gm): 20.4

Exchanges:
Milk: 0.0
Vegetable: 0.0
Fruit: 0.0
Bread: 1.0
Meat: 2.0
Fat: 0.0

MONTE CRISTO

45 *The sourdough bread and egg-batter coating make this grilled sandwich special. Substitute any desired lean meat and cheese for variety.*

4 servings

4 slices (3 ounces) each: lean smoked ham, turkey
    or chicken breast
4 slices (4 ounces) fat-free Cheddar cheese
8 slices sourdough or Italian bread
2 eggs, lightly beaten

Per Serving:
Calories: 248
% of calories from fat: 9
Fat (gm): 2.4
Saturated fat (gm): 0.5
Cholesterol (mg): 27.7
Sodium (mg): 756
Protein (gm): 26.8
Carbohydrate (gm): 28.9

Exchanges:
Milk: 0.0
Vegetable: 0.0
Fruit: 0.0
Bread: 2.0
Meat: 2.0
Fat: 0.0

1. Arrange meats and cheese on 4 slices of bread; top with remaining bread. Dip sandwiches in egg, coating both sides of sandwiches; cook in lightly greased large skillet over medium to medium-low heat until browned, about 5 minutes on each side.

SMOKED TURKEY AND GOAT CHEESE HOAGIES

45 *A sandwich full of flavor surprises!*

4 servings

4 cups sliced onions

2 cups sliced green bell peppers

2 teaspoons minced garlic

⅓ cup water

¼ cup raisins

1–1½ tablespoons balsamic vinegar

Salt and pepper, to taste

4 ounces fat-free cream cheese, room temperature

½ cup (2 ounces) goat cheese

4 French rolls or hoagie buns

16 spinach leaves

4 ounces thinly sliced smoked turkey breast

Per Serving:
Calories: 330
% of calories from fat: 18
Fat (gm): 6.7
Saturated fat (gm): 3.5
Cholesterol (mg): 12.3
Sodium (mg): 792
Protein (gm): 18.3
Carbohydrate (gm): 52.1

Exchanges:
Milk: 0.0
Vegetable: 3.0
Fruit: 0.0
Bread: 2.0
Meat: 2.0
Fat: 0.0

1. Cook onions, bell peppers, and garlic in lightly greased large skillet over medium to medium-low heat, covered, until softened and beginning to brown, 15 to 20 minutes. Add water, raisins, and vinegar; heat to boiling. Reduce heat and simmer, covered, until water has evaporated, 5 to 8 minutes. Season to taste with salt and pepper. Spread combined cheeses on tops and bottoms of rolls; fill with spinach, turkey, and vegetable mixture.

TURKEY AND CRANBERRY CHEESE MELT

45 *Lots of melted cheese, with cranberry and walnut accents.*

4 servings

2 ounces fat-free cream cheese, room temperature

¼ cup (1 ounce) shredded smoked Gouda or
   Swiss cheese

¼ cup chopped walnuts

8 slices whole wheat bread

8 ounces thinly sliced turkey breast

½ medium onion, thinly sliced

¼ cup whole-berry cranberry sauce

½ cup (2 ounces) shredded fat-free Cheddar cheese

Vegetable cooking spray

Per Serving:
Calories: 336
% of calories from fat: 28
Fat (gm): 10.6
Saturated fat (gm): 2.7
Cholesterol (mg): 32.9
Sodium (mg): 734
Protein (gm): 27.8
Carbohydrate (gm): 34.2

Exchanges:
Milk: 0.0
Vegetable: 0.0
Fruit: 0.5
Bread: 2.0
Meat: 3.0
Fat: 0.0

1. Mix cream and Gouda cheeses and walnuts; spread on 4 slices
bread. Top with turkey, onion, cranberry sauce, Cheddar cheese,
and remaining bread. Spray both sides of sandwiches lightly with
cooking spray; cook in large skillet over medium to medium-low
heat until browned, about 5 minutes on each side.

TURKEY AND SUN-DRIED TOMATO PESTO GRILL

45 *Cilantro Pesto (see p. 244) can also be used. Thin onion slices can be added
to the sandwich or substituted for the tomato slices.*

4 servings

8 slices sourdough bread

½ cup prepared sun-dried tomato pesto

8 slices (6 ounces) fat-free mozzarella cheese

4 ounces thinly sliced turkey breast

8 thin slices ripe tomato

Vegetable cooking spray

Per Serving:
Calories: 366
% of calories from fat: 30
Fat (gm): 12.2
Saturated fat (gm): 1.8
Cholesterol (mg): 23.5
Sodium (mg): 777
Protein (gm): 28.1
Carbohydrate (gm): 35.8

Exchanges:
Milk: 0.0
Vegetable: 1.0
Fruit: 0.0
Bread: 2.0
Meat: 3.0
Fat: 1.0

1. Spread each bread slice with 1 tablespoon
pesto. Layer 4 slices bread with cheese, turkey,
tomato, and remaining bread slices. Spray both

sides of sandwiches with cooking spray; cook in lightly greased large skillet over medium to medium-low heat until browned, about 5 minutes on each side.

CUCUMBER CHEESE MELT

45 *A great combination of flavors that will keep you coming back for more!*

4 servings

2 ounces fat-free cream cheese, room temperature
2 tablespoons crumbled blue cheese
8 slices multigrain bread
¼ cup apricot jam
16 cucumber slices
2 ounces shaved reduced-sodium ham
4 slices (4 ounces) fat-free Swiss cheese
Vegetable cooking spray

Per Serving:
Calories: 237
% of calories from fat: 9
Fat (gm): 2.7
Saturated fat (gm): 0.9
Cholesterol (mg): 10.4
Sodium (mg): 692
Protein (gm): 18.4
Carbohydrate (gm): 39.5

Exchanges:
Milk: 0.0
Vegetable: 0.0
Fruit: 0.5
Bread: 2.0
Meat: 1.0
Fat: 0.0

1. Mix cream cheese and blue cheese; spread on 4 slices of bread. Spread each with 1 tablespoon jam and top with 4 cucumber slices, ham, a slice of Swiss cheese, and remaining bread. Spray both sides of sandwiches with cooking spray; cook in large skillet over medium to medium-low heat until browned, about 5 minutes on each side.

BLUE CHEESE AND PEAR MELT

45 *Blue cheese and pears are perfect flavor companions, any way they are served.*

4 servings

8 slices honey wheat or light rye bread
4 slices (4 ounces) fat-free Swiss cheese
¼ cup mango chutney
1 medium pear, cored, sliced (¼-inch)
½ cup (2 ounces) crumbled blue cheese
Vegetable cooking spray

1. Top 4 slices bread with Swiss cheese and spread each with 1 tablespoon chutney; top with pear slices, blue cheese, and remaining bread. Spray both sides of sandwiches with cooking spray; cook in large skillet over medium to medium-low heat until browned, about 5 minutes on each side.

Per Serving:
Calories: 284
% of calories from fat: 20
Fat (gm): 6.6
Saturated fat (gm): 3.2
Cholesterol (mg): 10.5
Sodium (mg): 780
Protein (gm): 13.6
Carbohydrate (gm): 44.6

Exchanges:
Milk: 0.0
Vegetable: 0.0
Fruit: 1.0
Bread: 2.0
Meat: 1.0
Fat: 0.5

GAZPACHO PIZZA

45 | *Gazpacho, chilled and refreshing, served on a crust!*

8 slices

8 ounces fat-free cream cheese, room temperature

2 tablespoons fat-free mayonnaise

½ teaspoon dry mustard

1 tablespoon chopped chives

1 large whole wheat lavosh (16 inches)

1 cup each: chopped seeded tomato, cucumber

½ cup each: chopped onion, yellow and green bell pepper, avocado

1 teaspoon each: minced garlic, jalapeño chili

¼ cup fat-free Italian salad dressing

Per Slice:
Calories: 153
% of calories from fat: 29
Fat (gm): 5.1
Saturated fat (gm): 0.4
Cholesterol (mg): 0
Sodium (mg): 415
Protein (gm): 7.4
Carbohydrate (gm): 19.9

Exchanges:
Milk: 0.0
Vegetable: 1.5
Fruit: 0.0
Bread: 1.0
Meat: 0.0
Fat: 1.0

1. Mix cream cheese, mayonnaise, dry mustard, and chives; spread on lavosh. Combine remaining ingredients and spoon evenly onto lavosh; serve immediately.

TOMATO FILLO PIZZA

45

Use summer's ripest tomatoes for this delectable pizza.

8 slices

Olive oil cooking spray
8 sheets frozen fillo pastry, thawed
2 cups (8 ounces) shredded fat-free mozzarella cheese
½ cup thinly sliced onion
1 pound tomatoes, thinly sliced
Salt and pepper, to taste
¼ cup (1 ounce) grated Parmesan cheese
¾ teaspoon each: dried dill weed, basil leaves

Per Slice:
Calories: 79
% of calories from fat: 14
Fat (gm): 1.2
Saturated fat (gm): 0.6
Cholesterol (mg): 2.5
Sodium (mg): 270
Protein (gm): 12
Carbohydrate (gm): 5.4

Exchanges:
Milk: 0.0
Vegetable: 0.0
Fruit: 0.0
Bread: 0.5
Meat: 1.0
Fat: 0.0

1. Spray jelly roll pan with cooking spray; place sheet of fillo on pan and spray generously with spray. Repeat with remaining fillo. Sprinkle mozzarella cheese and onion over fillo; arrange tomato slices on top. Sprinkle with salt and pepper, Parmesan cheese, and herbs. Bake at 375 degrees until fillo is browned and cheese melted, about 15 minutes.

GARDEN PATCH PIZZA

45

This great snack can be prepared without the salad dressing and refrigerated up to 1 hour; drizzle with dressing just before serving.

8 slices

8 ounces fat-free cream cheese, room temperature
2 tablespoons fat-free sour cream
1 teaspoon dried Italian seasoning
1 large whole wheat lavosh (16 inches)
1 cup each: broccoli florets, chopped, seeded cucumber
2–3 marinated artichoke hearts, drained, sliced
¼ cup each: sliced carrot, sliced green onion
1–2 tablespoons sliced ripe olives
½ cup (2 ounces) shredded reduced-fat Havarti cheese
¼ cup French or other fat-free salad dressing

Per Slice:
Calories: 149
% of calories from fat: 28
Fat (gm): 4.6
Saturated fat (gm): 0.8
Cholesterol (mg): 5.1
Sodium (mg): 419
Protein (gm): 9.3
Carbohydrate (gm): 17.2

Exchanges:
Milk: 0.0
Vegetable: 2.0
Fruit: 0.0
Bread: 0.5
Meat: 0.5
Fat: 0.5

1. Mix cream cheese, sour cream, and Italian seasoning; spread on lavosh. Arrange vegetables and cheese on top and drizzle with salad dressing.

SPINACH SALAD PIZZA

45 *This salad on a pizza is made with a large, crisp lavosh. Serve with any salad dressing you like.*

8 slices

12 ounces fat-free cream cheese, room temperature

5 tablespoons fat-free sweet-sour salad dressing, divided

1 large whole wheat lavosh (16 inches)

2 cups packed torn spinach leaves

1 cup sliced mushrooms

½ cup thinly sliced red onion

2 hard-cooked eggs, sliced

2 slices bacon, cooked crisp, crumbled

Per Serving:
Calories: 178
% of calories from fat: 30
Fat (gm): 6.1
Saturated fat (gm): 1.6
Cholesterol (mg): 57.7
Sodium (mg): 450
Protein (gm): 10.6
Carbohydrate (gm): 21.4

Exchanges:
Milk: 0.0
Vegetable: 1.0
Fruit: 0.0
Bread: 1.0
Meat: 1.0
Fat: 0.5

1. Mix cream cheese and 2 tablespoons sweet-sour dressing; spread on lavosh. Top with spinach, mushrooms, onion, eggs, and bacon. Serve immediately, or refrigerate no longer than 1 hour, drizzling with remaining 3 tablespoons sweet-sour dressing before serving.

CALZONES

These Italian-style pies filled with cheese and vegetables can also be served for lunch or supper. A packaged mix makes a quick and easy dough.

16 servings

1 cup each: chopped zucchini, sliced mushrooms

½ cup each: chopped onion, green bell pepper

1 can (14½ ounces) diced tomatoes with roasted garlic, undrained

2 teaspoons Italian seasoning

1 cup fat-free ricotta cheese

2 cups (8 ounces) shredded reduced-fat mozzarella cheese

Salt and pepper, to taste

1 package (16 ounces) hot roll mix

1¼ cups hot water

1 tablespoon olive oil

Fat-free milk

Per Serving:
Calories: 185
% of calories from fat: 28
Fat (gm): 5.8
Saturated fat (gm): 1.6
Cholesterol (mg): 7.6
Sodium (mg): 379
Protein (gm): 9.4
Carbohydrate (gm): 23.6

Exchanges:
Milk: 0.0
Vegetable: 1.5
Fruit: 0.0
Bread: 1.0
Meat: 1.0
Fat: 0.5

1. Sauté zucchini, mushrooms, onion, and bell pepper in lightly greased skillet 5 minutes. Add tomatoes with liquid and Italian seasoning; simmer until vegetables are tender and excess liquid is gone, about 10 minutes. Remove from heat; stir in cheeses and season to taste with salt and pepper.

2. Make hot roll mix according to package directions for pizza, using hot water and oil. Divide dough into 8 equal pieces; roll each on floured surface into a 7-inch circle. Spoon about ½ cup vegetable mixture on each; fold in half and flute edges or seal edges with tines of fork. Brush tops of pastries with fat-free milk. Bake on cookie sheet at 375 degrees until browned, about 15 minutes. Cut calzones into halves.

SWEET FENNEL CALZONES

Fresh fennel, onion, sour cream, and melted cheese are combined in these golden calzones.

8 servings

6 cups thinly sliced fennel bulb

1½ cups chopped onion

⅔ cup chopped red bell pepper

2 cloves garlic, minced

1 cup (4 ounces) shredded fat-free mozzarella cheese

½ cup fat-free sour cream

Salt and pepper, to taste

1 package (16 ounces) hot roll mix

1¼ cups very hot water (120 degrees)

1 tablespoon olive oil

2 tablespoons fat-free milk

Per Serving:
Calories: 307
% of calories from fat: 15
Fat (gm): 5.3
Saturated fat (gm): 0.8
Cholesterol (mg): 3.4
Sodium (mg): 378
Protein (gm): 13.8
Carbohydrate (gm): 52

Exchanges:
Milk: 0.0
Vegetable: 1.5
Fruit: 0.0
Bread: 3.0
Meat: 0.5
Fat: 0.5

1. Cook fennel, onion, bell pepper, and garlic in lightly greased large skillet, covered, over medium heat until tender, about 10 minutes, stirring occasionally. Cool; stir in cheese and sour cream. Season to taste with salt and pepper.

2. Make hot roll mix according to package directions for pizza, using hot water and oil. Divide dough into 8 equal pieces; roll each piece of dough on floured surface into a 7-inch circle. Spoon about ⅔ cup fennel mixture on each; fold into halves and flute edges of dough or seal with tines of fork. Brush tops of pastries with milk. Bake on greased cookie sheet at 375 degrees until browned, about 15 minutes. Cut calzones into halves.

NACHOS

Your favorite Mexican appetizer, without the guilt. Cooked, crumbled Chorizo (see p. 140) can be added to make these nachos "grandes"!

6 servings

Baked tortilla chips

1 can (15½ ounces) pinto beans, rinsed, drained, coarsely mashed

Red Tomato Salsa (recipe follows), divided

¾ teaspoon each: chili powder, dried oregano leaves

2–3 cloves garlic, minced

¼ teaspoon salt

½ cup (2 ounces) shredded reduced-fat Cheddar or Monterey Jack cheese

1 medium tomato, chopped

½ small avocado, chopped

2 green onions, sliced

6 pitted ripe olives, sliced

¼ cup fat-free sour cream

Per Serving:
Calories: 182
% of calories from fat: 24
Fat (gm): 5.2
Saturated fat (gm): 1.2
Cholesterol (mg): 6.3
Sodium (mg): 376
Protein (gm): 7.7
Carbohydrate (gm): 28.8

Exchanges:
Milk: 0.0
Vegetable: 0.0
Fruit: 0.0
Bread: 2.0
Meat: 0.0
Fat: 1.0

1. Spread tortilla chips in single layer in jelly roll pan. Spoon combined beans, ¼ cup salsa, herbs, garlic, and salt over tortilla chips; sprinkle with cheese. Bake at 350 degrees until beans are hot and cheese melted, about 10 minutes. Sprinkle with tomato, avocado, onions, and olives; garnish with dollops of sour cream. Serve with remaining ¾ cup salsa.

Red Tomato Salsa
Makes about 1 cup

1 cup chopped tomato
3 tablespoons each: chopped onion, poblano chili or green bell pepper
¼ jalapeño chili, minced
1 clove garlic, minced
¼ cup loosely packed cilantro, chopped
Salt, to taste

1. Mix all ingredients, except salt. Season to taste with salt.

QUESADILLAS

The simplest quesadillas are made only with cheese. Our version adds the Mexican poblano chili, onion, and cilantro; Chorizo (see p. 140) would be a flavorful addition.

6 servings

½ cup each: chopped poblano chili or green
    bell pepper, finely chopped onion
1 teaspoon ground cumin
3 tablespoons chopped cilantro
1 cup (4 ounces) shredded reduced-fat Cheddar cheese
6 flour tortillas (6-inch)
Vegetable cooking spray
Green Tomato Salsa (recipe follows)
6 tablespoons fat-free sour cream

Per Serving:
Calories: 165
% of calories from fat: 26
Fat (gm): 4.8
Saturated fat (gm): 1.7
Cholesterol (mg): 10.1
Sodium (mg): 393
Protein (gm): 8.3
Carbohydrate (gm): 22.9

Exchanges:
Milk: 0.0
Vegetable: 1.5
Fruit: 0.0
Bread: 1.0
Meat: 0.5
Fat: 0.5

1. Sauté poblano chili, onion, and cumin in lightly greased large skillet until vegetables are tender, 3 to 5 minutes; stir in cilantro. Sprinkle cheese on half of each tortilla; spoon vegetable mixture over. Fold tortillas in half. Cook in lightly greased large skillet over medium to medium-low heat until browned on the bottom, 2 to 3 minutes. Spray tops of quesadillas with cooking spray; turn and cook until browned on other side. Cut into wedges; serve warm with salsa and sour cream.

Green Tomato Salsa
Makes about 1 cup

12 ounces tomatillos, husked

2 tablespoons finely chopped onion

1 clove garlic, minced

¼ small jalapeño chili, finely chopped

2 tablespoons finely chopped cilantro

½ teaspoon ground cumin

¼ teaspoon dried oregano leaves

⅛–¼ teaspoon sugar

Salt, to taste

1. Simmer tomatillos in water to cover in large saucepan until tender, 5 to 8 minutes. Cool; drain, reserving liquid. Process all ingredients, except sugar and salt, in food processor or blender until almost smooth, adding enough reserved liquid to make medium dipping consistency. Season to taste with sugar and salt.

TORTILLA WEDGES

Fun to make and eat—our Mexican version of a pizza, perhaps! Lean ground beef can replace the Chorizo, if you prefer.

12 servings

Chorizo (see p. 140)

½ cup each: chopped green bell pepper, onion

4 large flour tortillas (10-inch)

1 cup (4 ounces) each: shredded reduced-fat Monterey Jack cheese, shredded fat-free Cheddar cheese

Red Tomato Salsa (see p. 591) or prepared salsa

¾ cup fat-free sour cream

Per Serving:
Calories: 135
% of calories from fat: 24
Fat (gm): 3.7
Saturated fat (gm): 1.5
Cholesterol (mg): 24.8
Sodium (mg): 313
Protein (gm): 14.4
Carbohydrate (gm): 11.4

Exchanges:
Milk: 0.0
Vegetable: 0.5
Fruit: 0.0
Bread: 0.5
Meat: 1.5
Fat: 0.0

1. Cook Chorizo, bell pepper, and onion in lightly greased medium skillet over medium heat until onion is tender and Chorizo is browned, crumbling with fork.

2. Place tortillas on baking sheets; sprinkle evenly with Monterey Jack cheese. Sprinkle with Chorizo mixture and top with Cheddar cheese. Bake at 450 degrees until edges of tortillas are browned and cheese is melted, 6 to 8 minutes. Top with Red Tomato Salsa and sour cream. Cut each tortilla into 6 wedges.

GOAT CHEESE QUESADILLAS WITH TROPICAL SALSA

Goat cheese and tropical fruits combine for a new flavor in quesadillas.

8 servings

4 ounces fat-free cream cheese, softened

2 ounces goat cheese

½ small jalapeño chili, minced

½ teaspoon each: dried marjoram and thyme leaves

⅛ teaspoon white pepper

8 whole wheat or white flour tortillas (6-inch)

Vegetable cooking spray

Tropical Salsa (see p. 242)

Per Serving:
Calories: 186
% of calories from fat: 25
Fat (gm): 5.2
Saturated fat (gm): 2.2
Cholesterol (mg): 7.5
Sodium (mg): 285
Protein (gm): 8
Carbohydrate (gm): 26.3

Exchanges:
Milk: 0.0
Vegetable: 1.0
Fruit: 0.5
Bread: 1.0
Meat: 0.5
Fat: 0.5

1. Combine cream cheese, goat cheese, jalapeño chili, herbs, and white pepper; spread about 3 tablespoons mixture on each of 4 tortillas. Top with remaining tortillas.

2. Cook 1 quesadilla in lightly greased medium skillet on medium to medium-low heat until browned on the bottom, 2 to 3 minutes. Spray top of quesadilla with cooking spray; turn and cook until browned on other side. Repeat with remaining quesadillas. Cut into wedges; serve with Tropical Salsa.

BLACK BEAN QUESADILLAS

45 *Substitute pinto beans for the black beans if you like, and vary the amount of jalapeño chili to taste.*

12 servings

1 can (15 ounces) black beans, rinsed, drained
1 cup mild or hot chili salsa, divided
¼ cup thinly sliced green onions
3 tablespoons finely chopped cilantro
2–3 teaspoons minced jalapeño chili
12 whole wheat or white flour tortillas (6-inch)
¾ cup (3 ounces) each: shredded reduced-fat
   Monterey Jack cheese, fat-free Cheddar cheese
Butter-flavored cooking spray

Per Serving:
Calories: 169
% of calories from fat: 21
Fat (gm): 3.9
Saturated fat (gm): 1.2
Cholesterol (mg): 5.1
Sodium (mg): 427
Protein (gm): 9
Carbohydrate (gm): 24.2

Exchanges:
Milk: 0.0
Vegetable: 0.0
Fruit: 0.0
Bread: 1.5
Meat: 0.5
Fat: 0.5

1. Mash beans slightly; mix in ¼ cup salsa, green onions, cilantro, and jalapeno chili. Divide mixture on 6 tortillas, spreading almost to edges. Sprinkle with cheeses and top with remaining tortillas.

2. Cook 1 quesadilla on medium to medium-low heat in lightly greased skillet until browned on the bottom, 2 to 3 minutes. Spray top of quesadilla with cooking spray; turn and cook until browned on the bottom. Repeat with remaining quesadillas. Cut into wedges; serve warm with remaining ¾ cup salsa.

THREE-CHILI TAMALES

Ancho chilies are fresh poblano chilies that have been dried. Ancho chilies, corn husks and masa harina (corn flour) can be purchased in large super-markets or Mexican groceries.

6 servings (2 each)

2 ancho chilies, stems, seeds, and veins discarded
½ cup boiling water
1 large poblano chili, chopped
1 can (4 ounces) chopped green chilies, drained
½ teaspoon each: dried oregano and thyme leaves
Tamale Dough (recipe follows)

Salt, to taste

12 corn husks, softened in boiling water, drained

1. Crumble ancho chilies into small saucepan; pour boiling water over and let stand until softened, 15 to 20 minutes. Add poblano and green chilies and herbs; cook over medium heat until chilies are tender, 5 to 8 minutes, stirring frequently. Mix in Tamale Dough; season to taste with salt.

2. Spoon about ¼ cup tamale mixture onto center of each corn husk; fold sides of husks over filling. Tie ends of tamales with string, making "bundles." Place tamales on steamer rack in saucepan with 2 inches water. Steam, covered, 2 hours, adding more water to saucepan if necessary.

Tamale Dough
Makes about 1 cup

1 cup masa harina
¾ teaspoon baking powder
1½ tablespoons margarine or butter, softened
¼–½ teaspoon salt
1 cup reduced-sodium vegetable broth

1. Combine masa harina, baking powder, margarine, and salt in bowl; gradually stir in broth (mixture will be soft).

Per Serving:
Calories: 117
% of calories from fat: 27
Fat (gm): 3.6
Saturated fat (gm): 0.5
Cholesterol (mg): 0
Sodium (mg): 267
Protein (gm): 3.0
Carbohydrate (gm): 18.9

Exchanges:
Milk: 0.0
Vegetable: 0.5
Fruit: 0.0
Bread: 1.0
Meat: 0.0
Fat: 0.5

CHICKEN AND POBLANO TAMALES

Tamales can be tied in "bundles," as in Three Chili Tamales (see p. 594), or in "envelopes," as in this recipe.

6 servings (2 each)

½ cup each: chopped onion, poblano chili

3 cloves garlic, minced

½ teaspoon minced jalapeño chili

¾ teaspoon each: dried oregano leaves, ground cumin

12 ounces boneless, skinless chicken breast, cooked, shredded

2 tablespoons finely chopped cilantro

Tamale Dough (see p. 595)

½ cup reduced-sodium chicken broth or water

Salt, to taste

12 corn husks, softened in boiling water, drained

Per Serving:
Calories: 190
% of calories from fat: 24
Fat (gm): 5.2
Saturated fat (gm): 1.0
Cholesterol (mg): 34.4
Sodium (mg): 214
Protein (gm): 16.3
Carbohydrate (gm): 20.0

Exchanges:
Milk: 0.0
Vegetable: 1.0
Fruit: 0.0
Bread: 1.0
Meat: 1.5
Fat: 0.5

1. Sauté onion, poblano chili, garlic, jalapeño chili, oregano, and cumin in lightly greased medium skillet until vegetables are tender, about 5 minutes. Add chicken and cilantro; mix in Tamale Dough and chicken broth. Season to taste with salt.

2. Spoon about ¼ cup tamale mixture onto center of each corn husk. Fold sides of husks over filling; fold tops and bottoms of husks toward center and tie in the center with string. Place tamales on steamer rack in saucepan with 2 inches of water. Steam, covered, 2 hours, adding more water to saucepan if necessary.

BEEF PINTO BEAN TAMALES

For variation, lean pork can be substituted for the beef, and black beans for the pintos.

6 servings (2 each)

1 medium onion, chopped

3 cloves garlic, minced

¾ teaspoon dried marjoram leaves

¼ teaspoon ground allspice

½ teaspoon cayenne pepper

½ can (15-ounce size) pinto beans, rinsed, drained, coarsely mashed

12 ounces boneless beef eye of round, cubed, cooked, shredded

Tamale Dough (see p. 595)

½ cup reduced-sodium beef broth or water

Salt, to taste

12 corn husks, softened in boiling water, drained

Per Serving:
Calories: 204
% of calories from fat: 25
Fat (gm): 5.7
Saturated fat (gm): 1.3
Cholesterol (mg): 27.3
Sodium (mg): 328
Protein (gm): 15.8
Carbohydrate (gm): 23.6

Exchanges:
Milk: 0.0
Vegetable: 0.5
Fruit: 0.0
Bread: 1.0
Meat: 1.0
Fat: 0.5

1. Sauté onion, garlic, marjoram, allspice, and cayenne pepper in lightly greased medium skillet until onion is tender, about 5 minutes. Stir in beans and beef and cook 2 to 3 minutes; mix in Tamale Dough and beef broth. Season to taste with salt.

2. Spoon about ¼ cup tamale mixture onto center of each corn husk. Fold sides of husks over filling; fold top and bottom of husks toward center and tie in the center with string. Place tamales on steamer rack in saucepan with 2 inches water; steam, covered, 2 hours, adding more water to saucepan if necessary.

TACOS WITH CHORIZO AND POTATOES

In many parts of Mexico, tacos are made by pan-sautéing folded filled tortillas—a delectable alternative to the crisp taco shells we are accustomed to!

8 servings (1 each)

Chorizo (see p. 140)

1 cup each: chopped onion, cubed cooked potato, shredded fat-free Cheddar cheese (4 ounces)

2 tablespoons finely chopped cilantro

Salt and pepper, to taste

8 corn or flour tortillas (6-inch)

Vegetable cooking spray

½ cup (½ recipe) Green Tomato Salsa (see p. 592)

¼ cup fat-free sour cream

Per Serving:
Calories: 179
% of calories from fat: 13
Fat (gm): 2.5
Saturated fat (gm): 0.7
Cholesterol (mg): 27
Sodium (mg): 303
Protein (gm): 16.5
Carbohydrate (gm): 23.3

Exchanges:
Milk: 0.0
Vegetable: 1.0
Fruit: 0.0
Bread: 1.0
Meat: 1.5
Fat: 0.0

1. Cook Chorizo in lightly greased large skillet over medium heat until browned, about 5 minutes, crumbling with a fork. Add onion and potato; cook until onion is tender, 2 to 3 minutes. Remove from heat; stir in cheese and cilantro. Season to taste with salt and pepper.

2. Heat tortillas in skillet or microwave oven until soft enough to fold. Spoon about ½ cup Chorizo mixture on each tortilla and fold in half. Cook tacos in lightly greased large skillet until browned on the bottom, 1 to 2 minutes; spray with vegetable spray, turn, and cook until browned, 1 to 2 minutes. Serve with Green Tomato Salsa and sour cream.

SOFT TACOS PICADILLO

Picadillo, a favorite Mexican pork dish is seasoned with raisins, almonds, sweet spices, and jalapeno chili.

12 servings (1 each)

1½ pounds pork tenderloin, cubed (1-inch)
½ cup chopped onion
2 teaspoons each: minced garlic, jalapeno chili
1 cup chopped tomato
½ cup each: dark raisins, toasted slivered almonds
1–2 teaspoons cider vinegar
2 teaspoons ground cinnamon
½ teaspoon each: dried oregano leaves, ground cloves and allspice
Salt and pepper, to taste
12 flour or corn tortillas (6-inch)
Tomato Poblano Salsa (recipe follows)

Per Serving:
Calories: 176
% of calories from fat: 23
Fat (gm): 4.5
Saturated fat (gm): 1.0
Cholesterol (mg): 327
Sodium (mg): 151
Protein (gm): 14.6
Carbohydrate (gm): 18.9

Exchanges:
Milk: 0.0
Vegetable: 1.0
Fruit: 0.0
Bread: 1.0
Meat: 1.5
Fat: 0.0

1. Cover pork with water in medium saucepan; heat to boiling. Reduce heat and simmer, covered, until pork is tender, about 10 minutes. Drain; shred into small pieces.

2. Sauté onion, garlic, and jalapeno chili in oil in medium skillet until tender, about 5 minutes. Add pork and remaining ingredients, except salt, pepper, tortillas, and Tomato Poblano Salsa. Cook over medium heat until mixture is hot, about 5 minutes; season to taste with salt and pepper. Spoon about ⅓ cup mixture on each tortilla and roll up. Serve with Tomato Poblano Salsa.

Tomato Poblano Salsa
Makes about 1 cup

¾ cup chopped tomato
¼ cup each: chopped poblano chili, cilantro
2 tablespoons finely chopped onion
1 teaspoon finely chopped jalapeno chili
1 clove garlic, minced
Salt, to taste

1. Mix all ingredients, except salt; season to taste with salt.

MARGARITAS

45   *Mexico's favorite libation! For best flavor, use fresh lime juice.*

2 servings (about ½ cup each)

1 lime wedge
Coarse salt (optional)
½ cup tequila
¼ cup fresh lime juice
2 tablespoons orange liqueur
Ice cubes

Per Serving:
Calories: 185
% of calories from fat: 0
Fat (gm): 0
Saturated fat (gm): 0
Cholesterol (mg): 0
Sodium (mg): 1
Protein (gm): 0.2
Carbohydrate (gm): 8.6

Exchanges:
Milk: 0.0
Vegetable: 0.0
Fruit: 0.5
Bread: 0.0
Meat: 0.0
Fat: 3.5

1. Rub rims of 2 margarita or stemmed glasses with lime wedge; dip rims in salt. Pour combined tequila, lime juice, and orange liqueur over ice cubes in margarita or stemmed glasses.

VARIATION

Strawberry Margaritas — Make recipe as above, processing tequila, lime juice, orange liqueur, and 12 to 14 fresh or frozen strawberries in food processor or blender until smooth; pour over ice cubes in margarita glasses.

SANGRIA

45 *America has adopted this famous Spanish wine punch; it also can be made with the addition of sparkling water. Serve well chilled.*

6 servings (about 1 cup each)

4 cups dry red wine, chilled
2 cups orange juice, chilled
¼ cup lime juice
¾–1 cup Splenda or sugar
½ each: thinly sliced lime, orange
Ice cubes

1. Mix all ingredients, except ice in large pitcher; pour over ice cubes in tall glasses.

Per Serving:
Calories: 88
% of calories from fat: 1
Fat (gm): 0.1
Saturated fat (gm): 0
Cholesterol (mg): 0
Sodium (mg): 6
Protein (gm): 0.6
Carbohydrate (gm): 9

Exchanges:
Milk: 0.0
Vegetable: 0.0
Fruit: 0.5
Bread: 0.0
Meat: 0.0
Fat: 1.5

CRAN-ORANGE TEA

45 *A refreshing punch that is especially nice for the holidays.*

12 servings (about ¾ cup each)

6 cups boiling water
2 tea bags
4 whole cloves
3 sticks cinnamon
2 cups each: light cranberry juice, orange juice
¼ cup sugar
2 tablespoons lemon juice
Ice cubes

Per Serving:
Calories: 43
% of calories from fat: 1
Fat (gm): 0.1
Saturated fat (gm): 0
Cholesterol (mg): 0
Sodium (mg): 14
Protein (gm): 0.3
Carbohydrate (gm): 10.6

Exchanges:
Milk: 0.0
Vegetable: 0.0
Fruit: 1.0
Bread: 0.0
Meat: 0.0
Fat: 0.0

1. Pour water over tea bags, cloves, and cinnamon in large saucepan. Let stand, covered, 10 minutes; discard tea bags. Stir in remaining ingredients except ice cubes. Heat to boiling; reduce heat and simmer 10 minutes. Cool; refrigerate until chilled. Pour over ice cubes in tall glasses.

SPARKLING GREEN PUNCH

45 *Remember this punch for St. Patrick's Day and winter holidays!*

16 servings (about ½ cup each)

2 cans (6 ounces each) frozen limeade
   concentrate, thawed
1 can (6 ounces) frozen lemonade concentrate, thawed
2 cups cold water
Few drops green food color
2 bottles (28 ounces each) diet ginger ale, chilled
Ice cubes

1. Mix concentrates, water, and food color
in large pitcher; pour into punch bowl; stir in
ginger ale and ice.

Per Serving:
Calories: 59
% of calories from fat: 1
Fat (gm): 0
Saturated fat (gm): 0
Cholesterol (mg): 0
Sodium (mg): 16
Protein (gm): 0.1
Carbohydrate (gm): 15.6

Exchanges:
Milk: 0.0
Vegetable: 0.0
Fruit: 1.0
Bread: 0.0
Meat: 0.0
Fat: 0.0

EGGNOG WITH RUM

45 *A holiday favorite—thick, rich, and creamy!*

12 servings (about ½ cup each)

½ cup Splenda or sugar
2 tablespoons cornstarch
1 quart fat-free milk, divided
2 eggs, lightly beaten
1–1½ cups light rum
1 cup light whipped topping
Ground cinnamon or nutmeg, as garnish

Per Serving:
Calories: 106
% of calories from fat: 14
Fat (gm): 1.6
Saturated fat (gm): 1
Cholesterol (mg): 36.8
Sodium (mg): 57
Protein (gm): 3.8
Carbohydrate (gm): 7.6

Exchanges:
Milk: 0.5
Vegetable: 0.0
Fruit: 0.0
Bread: 0.0
Meat: 0.0
Fat: 1.5

1. Mix Splenda, cornstarch, and 3 cups milk in
medium saucepan; heat to boiling, whisking
frequently. Boil, whisking until thickened, about
1 minute. Stir about half the milk mixture into
the eggs; stir egg mixture back into saucepan.
Cook over low heat, whisking, 1 minute. Cool;
refrigerate until chilled, 3 to 4 hours.

2. Stir remaining 1 cup milk and rum into eggnog; stir in whipped
topping. Serve in small glasses or mugs; sprinkle with cinnamon.

SWEET CINNAMON COFFEE

45 *This spiced coffee is also refreshing served chilled and over ice.*

8 servings (about ½ cup each)

4 cups water
⅓–½ cup packed light brown sugar
1 small cinnamon stick
4 whole cloves
¼ cup dark roast regular grind coffee

Per Serving:
Calories: 37
% of calories from fat: 0
Fat (gm): 0
Saturated fat (gm): 0
Cholesterol (mg): 0
Sodium (mg): 6
Protein (gm): 0.1
Carbohydrate (gm): 9.4

Exchanges:
Milk: 0.0
Vegetable: 0.0
Fruit: 0.0
Bread: 0.5
Meat: 0.0
Fat: 0.0

1. Heat water, brown sugar, and spices to boiling in medium saucepan; stir in coffee. Reduce heat and simmer, covered, 2 to 3 minutes. Remove from heat and let stand 2 to 3 minutes for grounds to settle. Strain coffee; serve in small mugs.

WARM WINE PUNCH

45 *A warming beverage for all the winter holidays—also good chilled in the summer!*

12 servings (about ½ cup each)

4 cups sweet red wine
3 cups orange juice
½ cup Splenda or sugar
¼ cup lemon juice
4 whole cloves
1 whole cinnamon stick

Per Serving:
Calories: 90
% of calories from fat: 1
Fat (gm): 0.1
Saturated fat (gm): 0
Cholesterol (mg): 0
Sodium (mg): 5
Protein (gm): 0.6
Carbohydrate (gm): 9.3

Exchanges:
Milk: 0.0
Vegetable: 0.0
Fruit: 0.5
Bread: 0.0
Meat: 0.0
Fat: 1.5

1. Heat all ingredients just to simmering in large saucepan, stirring occasionally; do not boil. Serve warm.

BREAKFAST SHAKE

45 *Great for breakfast-on-the-run!*

4 servings (about ¾ cup each)

1 large banana, cut into chunks
1 cup each: orange juice, fat-free milk
¼ cup wheat germ
1 teaspoon vanilla
4 ice cubes

1. Process all ingredients in blender until smooth.

Per Serving:
Calories: 104
% of calories from fat: 7
Fat (gm): 1.8
Saturated fat (gm): 0.2
Cholesterol (mg): 1.1
Sodium (mg): 32
Protein (gm): 4.8
Carbohydrate (gm): 19.4

Exchanges:
Milk: 1.0
Vegetable: 0.0
Fruit: 1.0
Bread: 0.0
Meat: 0.0
Fat: 0.0

STRAWBERRY-BANANA SMOOTHIE

45 *Replace the strawberries with any berry or fruit that you like for a versatile menu or smoothies!*

3 servings (⅔ cup each)

1 banana
1 cup plain fat-free yogurt
1½ cups orange juice, chilled
1¼ cups fresh or frozen unsweetened strawberries
½ teaspoon vanilla extract
1 packet Splenda or 2–3 teaspoons sugar

1. Process all ingredients in blender until smooth.

Per Serving:
Calories: 155
% of calories from fat: 4
Fat (gm): 0.8
Saturated fat (gm): 0.2
Cholesterol (mg): 1.4
Sodium (mg): 60
Protein (gm): 6
Carbohydrate (gm): 32.4

Exchanges:
Milk: 0.5
Vegetable: 0.0
Fruit: 2.0
Bread: 0.0
Meat: 0.0
Fat: 0.0

TOFRUITY

45 *A great sipping snack, or double the portion for a light, yet nutritious, meal on-the-go!*

4 servings (about 1 cup each)

½ package (14-ounce size) light silken tofu, drained
1 cup cubed mango or papaya
1 cup fresh or frozen raspberries or strawberries
1–1½ cups orange juice
Honey, to taste

Per Serving:
Calories: 75
% of calories from fat: 8.6
Fat (gm): 0.8
Saturated fat (gm): 0.1
Cholesterol (mg): 0
Sodium (mg): 43.6
Protein (gm): 3.9
Carbohydrate (gm): 14.5

Exchanges:
Milk: 0.0
Vegetable: 0.0
Fruit: 1.0
Bread: 0.0
Meat: 0.5
Fat: 0.0

1. Process all ingredients, except honey, in blender or food processor until smooth, adding enough orange juice to make desired consistency; sweeten to taste with honey.

VERY BERRY SMOOTHIE

45 *Perfect for a nutritious snack or light meal when you need a pick-me-up.*

6 servings (about 1 cup each)

1½–2 cups orange juice
1 can (15 ounces) Great Northern or navy, beans, rinsed, drained
1 cup each: fresh or frozen strawberries and blueberries
1 small banana
1½ teaspoons ground cinnamon
⅛ teaspoon ground nutmeg
6–8 ice cubes
Honey, to taste

Per Serving:
Calories: 149
% of calories from fat: 3.7
Fat (gm): 0.7
Saturated fat (gm): 0.1
Cholesterol (mg): 0
Sodium (mg): 4.3
Protein (gm): 6.2
Carbohydrate (gm): 31.6

Exchanges:
Milk: 0.0
Vegetable: 0.0
Fruit: 1.0
Bread: 1.0
Meat: 0.5
Fat: 0.0

1. Process all ingredients, except honey, in blender or food processor until smooth. Sweeten to taste with honey.

POMEGRANATE PASSION

45 *Heart healthy pomegranate juice is an excellent source of antioxidants. Add a scoop or two of protein powder for a protein boost, if you like.*

4 servings (about 1 cup each)

1 cup pomegranate juice
½ cup orange juice
1½ cups halved strawberries
1 large banana, sliced
Honey, to taste

1. Process all ingredients, except honey, in blender or food processor until smooth; sweeten to taste with honey.

Per Serving:
Calories: 95
% of calories from fat: 3
Fat (gm): 0.3
Saturated fat (gm): 0.1
Cholesterol (mg): 0.0
Sodium (mg): 3.6
Protein (gm): 1
Carbohydrate (gm): 23.4

Exchanges:
Milk: 0.0
Vegetable: 0.0
Fruit: 1.5
Bread: 0.0
Meat: 0.0
Fat: 0.0

VARIATION

Blueberry Breeze — Make recipe as above, substituting blueberries for the strawberries and apple cider for the orange juice.

CANTALOUPE COOLER

45 *Use any ripe, flavorful melon in this recipe.*

4 servings (about 1 cup each)

1 quart peeled, seeded, cubed, ripe cantaloupe
½ cup orange juice
3–4 tablespoons lemon or lime juice
¼–½ cup fat-free milk
Honey, to taste

1. Process all ingredients, except honey, in blender or food processor until smooth; sweeten to taste with honey.

Per Serving:
Calories: 108
% of calories from fat: 3
Fat (gm): 0.4
Saturated fat (gm): 0.1
Cholesterol (mg): 0.3
Sodium (mg): 33
Protein (gm): 2.2
Carbohydrate (gm): 26.7

Exchanges:
Milk: 0.0
Vegetable: 0.0
Fruit: 2.0
Bread: 0.0
Meat: 0.0
Fat: 0.0

FIFTEEN

Cakes, Pies, Cookies,
and
Other Desserts

FLOURLESS CHOCOLATE CAKE

A sumptuous chocolate indulgence! Although regular cocoa can be used, Dutch process cocoa lends a special flavor.

8 servings

4 tablespoons margarine or butter, room temperature

¼ cup raspberry spreadable fruit

1 egg

7¼ teaspoons Equal® for Recipes or 24 packets Equal®

1 cup all-purpose flour

3 tablespoon Dutch process cocoa

1 teaspoon baking powder

½ teaspoon baking soda

¼ teaspoon salt

½ cup fat-free milk

Chocolate Glaze (recipe follows)

Per Serving:
Calories: 291
% of calories from fat: 47
Fat (gm): 16.2
Saturated fat (gm): 6.7
Cholesterol (mg): 36.7
Sodium (mg): 417
Protein (gm): 13.3
Carbohydrate (gm): 27.2

Exchanges:
Milk: 0.0
Vegetable: 0.0
Fruit: 0.0
Bread: 2.0
Meat: 0.0
Fat: 3.0

1. Beat margarine, spreadable fruit, egg, and Equal® for Recipes in medium bowl until smooth. Mix in combined flour, cocoa, baking powder, baking soda, and salt alternately with milk, beginning and ending with dry ingredients. Pour into greased parchment-lined 8-inch round cake pan.

2. Bake at 350 degrees until toothpick inserted in center of cake comes out clean, about 20 minutes. Cool in pan on wire rack; refrigerate, covered 8 hours or overnight.

3. Invert cake onto serving plate; discard parchment. Spread with Chocolate Glaze.

Chocolate Glaze
Makes about ½ cup

⅓ cup 2% reduced-fat milk

3 ounces unsweetened chocolate, cut into small pieces

5½ teaspoons Equal® for Recipes or 18 packets Equal® sweetener

1. Heat milk in small saucepan until very hot (do not boil). Remove pan from heat; add chocolate and Equal for Recipes, stirring until chocolate is melted. Cool to room temperature; refrigerate glaze until thickened enough to spread, about 15 minutes.

VARIATION

Chocolate Lace Cake — Make cake as above, omitting Chocolate Glaze. Place cake on serving plate. Melt 2 ounces unsweetened baking chocolate over low heat in small saucepan, stirring frequently; drizzle over top of cake in "lace" pattern. Refrigerate until chocolate has hardened, about 10 minutes. Garnish cake with dollops or rosettes of light whipped topping, raspberries, and mint sprigs.

CHOCOLATE MOUSSE TORTE

This cake is more time consuming to make, but the soufflé-like flourless cake layers, filled and frosted with rich chocolate mousse, will make any occasion special.

12 servings

5 egg yolks

⅔ cup sugar, divided

1 teaspoon almond extract

5 egg whites

¼ teaspoon cream of tartar

¼ cup Dutch process cocoa

Chocolate Mousse (recipe follows)

¼ cup sliced almonds, toasted

Per Serving:
Calories: 247
% of calories from fat: 29
Fat (gm): 8.3
Saturated fat (gm): 3.2
Cholesterol (mg): 125.3
Sodium (mg): 54
Protein (gm): 7.1
Carbohydrate (gm): 39.2

Exchanges:
Milk: 0.0
Vegetable: 0.0
Fruit: 0.0
Bread: 2.5
Meat: 0.0
Fat: 1.5

1. Beat egg yolks, ⅓ cup sugar, and almond extract in large bowl until mixture is thick and lemon colored, about 5 minutes. Using clean beaters and bowl, beat egg whites and cream of tartar to soft peaks; beat to stiff peaks, adding remaining ⅓ cup sugar gradually. Mix ¼ of the egg whites into the egg yolk mixture; fold egg yolk mixture into egg whites. Fold in cocoa. Spread batter in 3 greased and floured parchment-lined 8- or 9-inch round cake pans.

2. Bake at 350 degrees until toothpick inserted in centers of cakes come out clean, 15 to 18 minutes. Cool cakes in pans on wire racks; remove from pans. Place 1 cake layer, parchment side up, in bottom of 9-inch springform pan; discard parchment. Spread cake with ⅓ of the Chocolate Mousse; repeat layers 2 times. Sprinkle top of cake with almonds. Refrigerate 8 hours or overnight. Loosen cake from side of pan with sharp knife; remove side of pan and place cake on serving plate.

Chocolate Mousse

Makes about 4 cups

1 envelope (¼ ounce) unflavored gelatin
¼ cup cold water
1 cup sugar, divided
½ cup Dutch process cocoa
1¼ cups 1% low-fat milk
2 egg yolks
4 ounces semisweet chocolate, finely chopped
2 egg whites
⅛ teaspoon cream of tartar

1. Sprinkle gelatin over cold water in small saucepan; let stand 3 to 4 minutes. Heat over low heat until gelatin is dissolved, stirring constantly.

2. Mix ½ cup sugar and cocoa in small saucepan; whisk in milk. Heat to boiling over medium-high heat; reduce heat and simmer briskly, whisking until thickened, 3 to 4 minutes. Whisk about ½ the milk mixture into egg yolks; whisk yolk mixture back into saucepan. Whisk over low heat 1 to 2 minutes; remove from heat. Whisk in gelatin mixture and chocolate, whisking until chocolate is melted. Refrigerate until cool, but not set, about 20 minutes.

3. Beat egg whites, remaining ½ cup sugar, and cream of tartar until foamy in medium bowl; place bowl over pan of simmering water and beat at medium speed until egg whites reach 160 degrees on candy thermometer. Remove from heat and beat at high speed until very thick and cool, about 5 minutes. Mix ¼ of the egg whites into chocolate mixture; fold chocolate mixture into remaining egg whites.

COFFEE-FROSTED COCOA CAKE

45

A perfect cake for potluck dinners and picnics.

16 servings

1½ cups sugar

½ cup margarine or butter, room temperature

2 eggs

1 teaspoon vanilla

2 cups all-purpose flour

¾ cup unsweetened cocoa

2 teaspoons baking soda

1 teaspoon salt

1 cup fat-free milk

Coffee Frosting (recipe follows)

Per Serving:
Calories: 240
% of calories from fat: 27
Fat (gm): 7.6
Saturated fat (gm): 1.6
Cholesterol (mg): 26.9
Sodium (mg): 385
Protein (gm): 3.9
Carbohydrate (gm): 41.6

Exchanges:
Milk: 0.0
Vegetable: 0.0
Fruit: 0.0
Bread: 2.5
Meat: 0.0
Fat: 1.5

1. Beat sugar and margarine in large bowl until fluffy. Beat in eggs one at a time; mix in vanilla. Mix in combined flour, cocoa, baking soda, and salt alternately with milk, beginning and ending with dry ingredients. Spread batter in greased and floured 13 x 9-inch cake pan.

2. Bake at 350 degrees until toothpick inserted in center or cake comes out clean, 25 to 30 minutes. Cool in pan on wire rack. Frost with Coffee Frosting.

Coffee Frosting

Makes about ½ cup

1 tablespoon each: instant coffee granules, hot water, margarine or butter, room temperature

1 cup powdered sugar

2–3 tablespoons fat-free milk

1. Dissolve coffee in hot water in medium bowl. Beat in margarine, powdered sugar, and enough milk to make a spreadable consistency.

HOT FUDGE PUDDING CAKE

45

For the ultimate treat serve warm, topped with scoops of sugar-free ice cream or frozen yogurt.

6 servings

1 cup all-purpose flour

½ cup packed light brown sugar

6 tablespoons Dutch process cocoa, divided

1½ teaspoons baking powder

¼ teaspoon salt

½ cup fat-free milk

2 tablespoons vegetable oil

1 teaspoon vanilla

⅓ cup granulated sugar

1½ cups boiling water

Per Serving:
Calories: 259
% of calories from fat: 18
Fat (gm): 5.2
Saturated fat (gm): 0.9
Cholesterol (mg): 0.4
Sodium (mg): 240
Protein (gm): 4.1
Carbohydrate (gm): 49.1

Exchanges:
Milk: 0.0
Vegetable: 0.0
Fruit: 0.0
Bread: 3.0
Meat: 0.0
Fat: 1.0

1. Combine flour, brown sugar, 3 tablespoons cocoa, baking powder, and salt in medium bowl. Add combined milk, oil, and vanilla to flour mixture, mixing well. Spoon batter into greased 8- or 9-inch square baking pan; sprinkle with combined remaining 3 tablespoons cocoa and granulated sugar. Pour boiling water over batter; do not stir.

2. Bake at 350 degrees until cake springs back when touched, about 30 minutes. Cool on wire rack 5 to 10 minutes; serve warm.

VARIATION

Mocha Latte Pudding Cake — Make cake as above, substituting granulated sugar for the brown sugar and adding 1 tablespoon instant espresso coffee powder and ½ teaspoon ground cinnamon to flour mixture. Serve warm pudding cake with a scoop of sugar-free vanilla or chocolate ice cream and light whipped topping.

GLAZED APPLESAUCE-RAISIN CAKE

Cream cheese glaze is a perfect topping for this moist cake—or serve plain with scoops of sugar-free frozen yogurt.

12 to 16 servings

1 cup unsweetened applesauce
⅔ cup canola oil
2 eggs
1 teaspoon maple or vanilla extract
¾ cup raisins
½ cup coarsely chopped walnuts (optional)
2 cups all-purpose flour
7¼ teaspoons Equal® for Recipes or 24 packets
   Equal® sweetener
1 teaspoon baking soda
1½ teaspoons ground cinnamon
¼ teaspoon each: ground nutmeg, salt
Vanilla Cream Cheese Glaze (recipe follows)

Per Serving:
Calories: 263
% of calories from fat: 50
Fat (gm): 14.7
Saturated fat (gm): 2.9
Cholesterol (mg): 39.7
Sodium (mg): 211
Protein (gm): 6.6
Carbohydrate (gm): 26.5

Exchanges:
Milk: 0.0
Vegetable: 0.0
Fruit: 0.0
Bread: 2.0
Meat: 0.0
Fat: 2.5

1. Mix applesauce, oil, eggs, maple extract, raisins, and walnuts in large bowl. Add combined flour, Equal® for Recipes, baking soda, spices, and salt, mixing until blended. Spoon batter into greased 13 x 9-inch baking pan.

2. Bake at 350 degrees until cake is browned and toothpick inserted in center comes out clean, 18 to 20 minutes (do not overbake!). Cool on wire rack. Drizzle with Vanilla Cream Cheese Glaze.

Vanilla Cream Cheese Glaze
Makes about ½ cup

4 ounces reduced-fat cream cheese, room temperature
½ teaspoon vanilla
1 teaspoon Equal® for Recipes or 3 packets Equal® sweetener
Fat-free milk

1. Beat all ingredients in bowl until smooth, adding enough milk to make desired consistency.

BLUEBERRY CRUMB CAKE

Best served warm—top with light whipped topping or sugar-free frozen yogurt!

9 to 12 servings

4 tablespoons margarine or butter

1 egg

5½ teaspoons Equal® for Recipes or 18 packets
  Equal® sweetener

1 cup all-purpose flour

1½ teaspoons baking powder

½ teaspoon baking soda

¼ teaspoon salt

1 teaspoon ground cinnamon

½ cup reduced-fat buttermilk

½ teaspoon vanilla

Blueberry Crumb Topping (recipe follows)

Per Serving:
Calories: 196
% of calories from fat: 50
Fat (gm): 11
Saturated fat (gm): 2.3
Cholesterol (mg): 24
Sodium (mg): 358
Protein (gm): 6.5
Carbohydrate (gm): 18

Exchanges:
Milk: 0.0
Vegetable: 0.0
Fruit: 0.0
Bread: 1.0
Meat: 0.0
Fat: 2.5

1. Beat margarine, egg, and Equal® for Recipes until smooth in medium bowl. Mix in combined flour, baking powder, baking soda, salt, and cinnamon alternately with combined buttermilk and vanilla, beginning and ending with dry ingredients. Pour batter into greased and floured 8-inch square cake pan; sprinkle Blueberry Crumb Topping evenly over top.

2. Bake at 350 degrees until toothpick inserted in center of cake comes out clean, 35 to 40 minutes. Serve warm.

Blueberry Crumb Topping

⅓ cup all-purpose flour

3½ teaspoons Equal® for Recipes or 12 packets Equal® sweetener

1 teaspoon ground cinnamon

½ teaspoon maple extract

4 tablespoons cold margarine or butter, cut into pieces

1 cup fresh or frozen blueberries

1. Combine flour, Equal® for Recipes, and cinnamon in small bowl; sprinkle with maple extract. Cut in margarine until mixture resembles coarse crumbs. Add blueberries and toss.

RICH LEMON POUND CAKE

45

Savor the rich flavor of this cake, which is enhanced with the Lemon Syrup.

12 servings

¾ cup sugar

⅓ cup margarine or butter, room temperature

1 cup reduced-fat sour cream

3 egg whites

2 teaspoons lemon juice

1 tablespoon grated lemon zest

2½ cups cake flour

1 teaspoon baking soda

¼ teaspoon salt

Lemon Syrup (recipe follows)

Powdered sugar, as garnish

Per Serving:
Calories: 230
% of calories from fat: 26
Fat (gm): 6.5
Saturated fat (gm): 1
Cholesterol (mg): 6.3
Sodium (mg): 235
Protein (gm): 3.5
Carbohydrate (gm): 38.8

Exchanges:
Milk: 0.0
Vegetable: 0.0
Fruit: 0.0
Bread: 2.5
Meat: 0.0
Fat: 1.0

1. Beat sugar and margarine in large bowl until fluffy; beat in sour cream, egg whites, lemon juice, and zest until smooth. Mix in combined flour, baking soda, and salt, beating about 1 minute. Spoon into greased and floured 6-cup fluted cake pan.

2. Bake 40 to 50 minutes or until toothpick inserted in center of cake comes out clean. Cool in pan on wire rack 20 minutes. Pierce cake at 1-inch intervals with skewer or long-tined fork. Spoon warm Lemon Syrup over and let stand 30 minutes. Invert onto serving plate; sprinkle generously with powdered sugar.

Lemon Syrup
Makes about ⅔ cup

⅔ cup powdered sugar

¼ cup lemon juice

3 tablespoons water

1. Heat all ingredients to boiling in small saucepan, stirring until sugar is dissolved. Cool slightly.

LEMON PUDDING CAKE

A luscious combination of moist cake and creamy pudding—for best flavor, use fresh lemon juice.

8 servings

1¼ cups sugar, divided

½ cup all-purpose flour

⅛ teaspoon salt

1 cup reduced-fat 2% milk

⅓ cup lemon juice

2 tablespoons margarine or butter, melted

1 egg

1 tablespoon grated lemon zest

3 egg whites

⅛ teaspoon cream of tartar

Per Serving:
Calories: 208
% of calories from fat: 17
Fat (gm): 4.1
Saturated fat (gm): 1.1
Cholesterol (mg): 28.8
Sodium (mg): 114
Protein (gm): 4
Carbohydrate (gm): 39.9

Exchanges:
Milk: 0.0
Vegetable: 0.0
Fruit: 0.0
Bread: 2.5
Meat: 0.0
Fat: 0.5

1. Combine 1 cup sugar, flour, and salt in large bowl. Mix in combined milk, lemon juice, margarine, egg, and lemon zest.

2. Beat egg whites and cream of tartar to soft peaks in large bowl; beat to stiff peaks, adding remaining ¼ cup sugar gradually. Fold egg whites into cake batter (batter will be slightly lumpy and thin). Pour batter into greased 1½-quart casserole or soufflé dish. Place casserole in roasting pan on oven rack; add 1 to 2 inches boiling water to pan.

3. Bake at 350 degrees until cake is golden and springs back when touched, about 40 minutes. Cool on wire rack 15 minutes; serve warm.

ORANGE POPPY SEED CAKE

45

This citrus-fresh cake is a perfect addition to any brunch menu.

12 servings

½ cup sugar

6 tablespoons margarine or butter, room temperature

2 eggs

¾ cup fat-free sour cream

2 tablespoons frozen orange juice concentrate, thawed

2 cups cake flour

2 tablespoons poppy seeds

1 teaspoon baking powder

½ teaspoon baking soda

¼ teaspoon salt

Citrus Glaze (recipe follows)

Per Serving:
Calories: 278
% of calories from fat: 33
Fat (gm): 10
Saturated fat (gm): 3
Cholesterol (mg): 48
Sodium (mg): 277
Protein (gm): 5
Carbohydrate (gm): 42

Exchanges:
Milk: 0.0
Vegetable: 0.0
Fruit: 0.0
Bread: 2.5
Meat: 0.0
Fat: 2.0

1. Beat sugar and margarine in large bowl until fluffy. Beat in eggs, sour cream, and orange juice; add combined remaining ingredients, except Citrus Glaze, beating on medium-high speed 1 to 2 minutes. Pour into greased and floured 6-cup fluted cake pan.

2. Bake at 350 degrees until toothpick inserted in center of cake comes out clean, 40 to 50 minutes. Cool in pan on wire rack 25 to 30 minutes; invert onto wire rack and cool. Spoon Citrus Glaze over cake.

Citrus Glaze

1 cup powdered sugar

3–4 tablespoons orange juice

1. Mix sugar and enough orange juice to make glaze consistency.

PEACH MERINGUE CAKE

Meringues, light as clouds, are layered with cake and Peach Cream Filling.

12 servings

8 tablespoons margarine or butter, room temperature

½ cup sugar

4 egg yolks

1 teaspoon vanilla

1 cup all-purpose flour

2 teaspoons baking powder

¼ teaspoon salt

⅓ cup fat-free milk

Peach Cream Filling (recipe follows)

Meringue Layers (recipe follows)

Per Serving:
Calories: 263
% of calories from fat: 36
Fat (gm): 10.4
Saturated fat (gm): 3
Cholesterol (mg): 71.1
Sodium (mg): 243
Protein (gm): 3.5
Carbohydrate (gm): 38.8

Exchanges:
Milk: 0.0
Vegetable: 0.0
Fruit: 0.0
Bread: 2.5
Meat: 0.0
Fat: 2.0

1. Beat margarine and sugar in large bowl until fluffy; beat in egg yolks and vanilla. Mix in combined flour, baking powder, and salt alternately with milk, beginning and ending with dry ingredients. Spread batter in 2 greased and floured 9-inch round cake pans.

2. Bake at 350 degrees until toothpick inserted in center comes out clean, 35 to 40 minutes. Cool cakes in pans on wire rack 10 minutes; remove from pans and cool. Place 1 cake layer on serving plate; spread with ½ cup Peach Cream Filling. Top with 1 Meringue Layer and spread with ½ cup Peach Cream Filling. Repeat layers, ending with a Meringue Layer.

Peach Cream Filling

Makes about 1½ cups

1½ cups light whipped topping

2 tablespoons peach preserves

1 tablespoon powdered sugar

1. Mix all ingredients.

Meringue Layers
Makes 2

4 egg whites
⅛ teaspoon cream of tartar
1 cup sugar

1. Beat egg whites and cream of tartar to soft peaks in large bowl; beat to stiff peaks, adding sugar gradually. Spread mixture on greased and floured bottoms of 2 inverted 9-inch round cake pans, spreading to edges of pans. Bake at 350 degrees until meringues are golden and crisp, about 40 minutes. Carefully remove meringues from pan bottoms with metal spatula; cool on wire rack.

GINGERED PEAR CAKE

Serve this cake topped with sweetened sour cream and ginger; a drizzle of Citrus Glaze (see p. 617) is also delicious.

12 servings

1 cup packed light brown sugar
¼ cup margarine or butter, room temperature
1 egg
1½ cups all-purpose flour
1½ teaspoons baking soda
¼ teaspoon each: salt, ground cloves
1 teaspoon ground ginger
2 tablespoons chopped crystallized ginger
2 small pears, peeled, cored, shredded
Gingered Sour Cream Topping (recipe follows)

Per Serving:
Calories: 228
% of calories from fat: 22
Fat (gm): 5.7
Saturated fat (gm): 2.1
Cholesterol (mg): 6.7
Sodium (mg): 287
Protein (gm): 4
Carbohydrate (gm): 40.7

Exchanges:
Milk: 0.0
Vegetable: 0.0
Fruit: 0.0
Bread: 2.5
Meat: 0.0
Fat: 1.0

1. Beat brown sugar, margarine, and egg in large bowl until smooth; mix in combined flour, baking soda, salt, spices, and crystallized ginger. Gently mix in pears. Pour batter into greased and floured 6-cup fluted tube pan.

2. Bake at 350 degrees until toothpick inserted in center of cake comes out clean, 50 to 60 minutes. Cool cake in pan on wire rack 10 minutes; remove from pan and cool. Serve with Gingered Sour Cream Topping.

Gingered Sour Cream Topping
Makes 1 to 1½ cups

1–1½ cups reduced-fat sour cream
2–3 tablespoons sugar
2–4 tablespoons coarsely chopped crystallized ginger

1. Mix all ingredients.

RAISIN SAUCEPAN CAKE

A spice cake that's truly delicious!

12 servings

1 cup raisins
2 cups water
½ cup margarine or butter, room temperature
1¾ cup all-purpose flour
1 cup granulated sugar
1 teaspoon each: baking soda, salt
½ teaspoon each: ground cinnamon, nutmeg
Powdered sugar, as garnish

Per Serving:
Calories: 235
% of calories from fat: 29
Fat (gm): 7.8
Saturated fat (gm): 1.6
Cholesterol (mg): 0
Sodium (mg): 389
Protein (gm): 2.4
Carbohydrate (gm): 40.3

Exchanges:
Milk: 0.0
Vegetable: 0.0
Fruit: 0.0
Bread: 2.5
Meat: 0.0
Fat: 1.5

1. Heat raisins and water to boiling in medium saucepan; reduce heat and simmer, uncovered, 10 minutes. Add margarine, stirring until melted; cool. Add combined remaining ingredients, except powdered sugar, mixing well. Pour batter into greased 13 x 9-inch baking pan.

2. Bake at 350 degrees until cake springs back when touched, about 35 minutes. Cool on wire rack; sprinkle with powdered sugar.

CLASSIC SPONGE CAKE

45

This luscious, very low-fat cake can be combined with different fillings and frostings—or simply sprinkle with powdered sugar and serve with a medley of berries.

12 servings

3 egg yolks

1 cup sugar, divided

2 teaspoons vanilla

¼ cup water

1 cup cake flour

1 teaspoon baking powder

¼ teaspoon salt

5 egg whites

¼ teaspoon cream of tartar

Per Serving:
Calories: 122
% of calories from fat: 10
Fat (gm): 1.4
Saturated fat (gm): 0.4
Cholesterol (mg): 53.2
Sodium (mg): 114
Protein (gm): 2.9
Carbohydrate (gm): 24.3

Exchanges:
Milk: 0.0
Vegetable: 0.0
Fruit: 0.0
Bread: 1.5
Meat: 0.0
Fat: 0.0

1. Beat egg yolks in large mixing bowl, gradually adding ¾ cup sugar; beat at high speed until yolks are thick and lemon colored, about 5 minutes. Mix in vanilla and water; mix in combined flour, baking powder, and salt on low speed just until blended.

2. With clean beaters and large bowl, beat egg whites and cream of tartar to soft peaks. Beat to stiff peaks, gradually adding remaining ¼ cup sugar. Stir ¼ of the egg whites into batter; fold batter into remaining whites. Pour batter into ungreased 12-cup tube pan.

3. Bake at 350 degrees 35 minutes or until cake springs back when touched lightly. Invert pan on funnel and cool to room temperature. Loosen side of cake with small metal spatula and remove from pan.

TIP: Cake can be baked in an ungreased 10-inch springform pan. Invert on wire rack to cool.

LEMON CUSTARD SPONGE CAKE

45

A beautiful cake that will make any occasion memorable.

12 servings

3 egg yolks

¾ cup sugar, divided

1 teaspoon vanilla

3 egg whites

⅛ teaspoon cream of tartar

⅓ cup each: all-purpose flour, cornstarch

⅛ teaspoon salt

Lemon Custard (recipe follows)

2½ cups light whipped topping, divided

½ cup raspberries

Lemon zest, as garnish

Mint sprigs, as garnish

Per Serving:
Calories: 196
% of calories from fat: 25
Fat (gm): 5.4
Saturated fat (gm): 2.6
Cholesterol (mg): 71.5
Sodium (mg): 126
Protein (gm): 3.2
Carbohydrate (gm): 33

Exchanges:
Milk: 0.0
Vegetable: 0.0
Fruit: 0.0
Bread: 2.0
Meat: 0.0
Fat: 1.0

1. Beat egg yolks, ½ cup sugar, and vanilla in small bowl until thick and lemon colored, 3 to 5 minutes. Using clean beaters and bowl, beat egg whites and cream of tartar to soft peaks; beat to stiff peaks, adding remaining ¼ cup sugar gradually. Fold egg yolk mixture into egg whites. Fold in combined flour, cornstarch, and salt. Spread batter in greased and floured parchment-lined 9-inch round cake pan.

2. Bake at 350 degrees until toothpick inserted in center of cake comes out clean, about 30 minutes. Cool cake in pan 10 minutes; remove from pan and cool completely. Discard parchment.

3. Cut cake horizontally in half. Place bottom of cake on serving plate. Spread 1 cup Lemon Custard on cake and top with second layer. Spread remaining 1 cup Lemon Custard on top of cake. Spread 2 cups whipped topping on side of cake. Using a pastry bag with star tip, pipe remaining ½ cup whipped topping around edge of cake. Garnish with raspberries, lemon zest, and mint. Refrigerate until serving time.

Lemon Custard

Makes about 2 cups

⅓ cup sugar
¼ cup cornstarch
¼ teaspoon salt
1⅓ cups fat-free milk
1 egg yolk
2 tablespoons margarine or butter
2 teaspoons grated lemon zest
⅓ cup lemon juice

1. Combine sugar, cornstarch, and salt in medium saucepan; whisk in milk. Heat to boiling over medium-high heat, whisking constantly; boil, whisking, until thickened, about 1 minute. Whisk about ½ cup milk mixture into egg yolk; whisk yolk mixture back into saucepan. Cook over low heat, whisking 1 to 2 minutes. Remove from heat; stir in margarine, lemon zest, and lemon juice. Cool; refrigerate until chilled.

VARIATION

Sponge Cake with Rosemary Syrup and Blueberries — Make cake as above, omitting Lemon Custard. Cool uncut cake on wire rack 20 minutes; remove from pan and place on serving plate. To make Rosemary Syrup, heat ¾ cup each sugar and water, 2 tablespoons crushed dried rosemary leaves, and 1 tablespoon lemon juice to boiling in small saucepan. Reduce heat and simmer, uncovered, 10 minutes; strain, discarding rosemary. Pierce top of cake with long-tined fork; drizzle ½ cup warm syrup over warm cake. Mix remaining syrup with 1½ quarts blueberries and serve over cake slices.

CITRUS POPPYSEED ANGEL FOOD CAKE

45

A tall, tender cake, bursting with sweet citrus flavor!

16 servings

12 egg whites, room temperature
1 teaspoon cream of tartar
2 teaspoons lemon juice
1½ cups sugar, divided
1 cup cake flour
½ teaspoon salt
1 tablespoon finely grated lemon zest
2 tablespoons each: finely grated orange zest,
    poppy seeds
Citrus Glaze (recipe follows)

Per Serving:
Calories: 149
% of calories from fat: 3
Fat (gm): 0.5
Saturated fat (gm): 0.1
Cholesterol (mg): 0
Sodium (mg): 118
Protein (gm): 3.6
Carbohydrate (gm): 32.8

Exchanges:
Milk: 0.0
Vegetable: 0.0
Fruit: 0.0
Bread: 2.0
Meat: 0.0
Fat: 0.0

1. Beat egg whites and cream of tartar to soft peaks in large bowl. Beat in lemon juice; beat just to stiff peaks, adding ½ cup sugar gradually (do not overbeat). Sprinkle ½ cup sugar over egg whites and fold in. Combine remaining ½ cup sugar, flour, and salt; sift half the flour mixture over egg whites and fold in. Repeat with remaining flour mixture. Fold in citrus zest and poppy seeds. Pour batter into ungreased 12-cup tube pan.

2. Bake at 350 degrees until cake is golden and cracks look dry, about 40 minutes. Invert pan on funnel and cool completely. Loosen side of cake from pan with metal spatula and invert onto serving plate. Drizzle with Citrus Glaze.

Citrus Glaze

Makes about ½ cup

1 cup powdered sugar
3–4 tablespoons orange juice

1. In small bowl, combine powdered sugar and enough orange juice to make glaze consistency.

CHEESECAKE CUPCAKES

No need to frost, as these chocolate cupcakes are baked with a topping of cream cheese.

20 servings (1 each)

¾ cup each: all-purpose flour, sugar,
  reduced-fat buttermilk

⅓ cup unsweetened cocoa

¾ teaspoon baking soda

½ teaspoon salt

¼ cup shortening

1 egg

1 teaspoon vanilla

Cheesecake Topping (recipe follows)

½ cup reduced-fat semisweet chocolate morsels

Per Serving:
Calories: 136
% of calories from fat: 29
Fat (gm): 4.6
Saturated fat (gm): 2.3
Cholesterol (mg): 22.5
Sodium (mg): 186
Protein (gm): 3.4
Carbohydrate (gm): 21.7

Exchanges:
Milk: 0.0
Vegetable: 0.0
Fruit: 0.0
Bread: 1.5
Meat: 0.0
Fat: 0.5

1. Combine all ingredients, except Cheesecake Topping and chocolate morsels, in large bowl. Beat at low speed until blended; beat at high speed 3 minutes, scraping side of bowl occasionally. Pour batter into paper-lined muffin cups, filling each about ½ full. Spread about 1 tablespoon Cheesecake Topping over batter in each, covering completely. Sprinkle each with about 1 teaspoon chocolate morsels. Bake at 350 degrees until golden, about 30 minutes. Cool in pans on wire rack.

Cheesecake Topping

8 ounces fat-free cream cheese, room temperature

½ cup sugar

1 egg

1. Mix all ingredients until smooth.

BASIC PIE CRUST

45

This pastry contains a minimum of margarine yet is not difficult to handle or roll. Use your preference of artificial sweetener or sugar.

8 servings (one 8- or 9-inch pie crust)

1¼ cups all-purpose flour

1 teaspoon Equal® for Recipes or 2 tablespoons sugar

¼ teaspoon salt

3 tablespoons cold margarine or butter

4–5 tablespoons ice water

Per Serving:
Calories: 121
% of calories from fat: 33
(will decrease in pie servings)
Fat (gm): 4.4
Saturated fat (gm): 0.9
Cholesterol (mg): 0
Sodium (mg): 117
Protein (gm): 2.1
Carbohydrate (gm): 18.1

Exchanges:
Milk: 0.0
Vegetable: 0.0
Fruit: 0.0
Bread: 1.0
Meat: 0.0
Fat: 1.0

1. Combine flour, Equal® for Recipes or sugar, and salt in medium bowl. Cut in margarine with pastry blender or 2 knives until mixture resembles coarse crumbs. Sprinkle with water, 1 tablespoon at a time, mixing lightly with a fork after each addition until pastry just holds together. Flatten into a round, wrap in plastic wrap and refrigerate 30 minutes.

2. Roll pastry on lightly floured surface into circle 1½ inches larger than inverted pie pan. Wrap pastry around rolling pin and unroll into 8- or 9-inch pie or tart pan, easing it onto bottom and side of pan. Trim edge, fold under, and flute. Fill and bake as recipe directs. If recipe indicates that the crust is baked before filling, pierce bottom of crust with tines of fork and bake at 425 degrees until browned, about 15 minutes; cool on wire rack.

VARIATION

Double Pie Crust — Make recipe above, using 2 cups flour, 1½ teaspoons Equal® for Recipes (or 3 tablespoons sugar), ½ teaspoon salt, 5 tablespoons margarine and 6–7 tablespoons ice water. Roll as directed in recipe.

CORNMEAL DOUBLE PIE CRUST

45

❄

This Italian-Style crust is particularly good with fruit pies.

8 servings (one 8- or 9-inch double crust pie crust)

2 cups all-purpose flour

⅓ cup yellow cornmeal

1 teaspoon baking powder

½ teaspoon salt

5 tablespoons cold margarine or butter, cut
   into pieces

2 ounces cold fat-free cream cheese, cut into pieces

3 egg whites

Per Serving:
Calories: 209
% of calories from fat: 33
(will decrease in pie
servings)
Fat (gm): 7.6
Saturated fat (gm): 1.5
Cholesterol (mg): 0.6
Sodium (mg): 351
Protein (gm): 6.1
Carbohydrate (gm): 28.4

Exchanges:
Milk: 0.0
Vegetable: 0.0
Fruit: 0.0
Bread: 2.0
Meat: 0.0
Fat: 1.5

1. Combine flour, cornmeal, baking powder, and salt in bowl; cut in margarine and cream cheese until mixture resembles coarse crumbs. Add egg whites, mixing until dough is moist and crumbly. Flatten into a round, wrap in plastic wrap and refrigerate 30 minutes. Roll and bake as pie recipe directs.

SHORTBREAD PASTRY

45

❄

A tender, sweet pastry that is almost like a cookie.

12 servings (one 10- or 12-inch tart crust)

1⅓ cups all-purpose flour

½ cup powdered sugar

Pinch salt

5 tablespoons cold margarine or butter, cut into
   pieces

1 egg, lightly beaten

1 teaspoon vanilla

Per Serving:
Calories: 209
% of calories from fat: 33
(will decrease in pie
servings)
Fat (gm): 7.6
Saturated fat (gm): 1.5
Cholesterol (mg): 0.6
Sodium (mg): 351
Protein (gm): 6.1
Carbohydrate (gm): 28.4

Exchanges:
Milk: 0.0
Vegetable: 0.0
Fruit: 0.0
Bread: 2.0
Meat: 0.0
Fat: 1.5

1. Combine flour, sugar, and salt in medium bowl. Cut in margarine until mixture resembles coarse crumbs. Mix in combined egg and vanilla with fork, stirring just until mixture forms a dough. Form dough into a ball; flatten slightly and wrap in plastic wrap and refrigerate 1 hour. Roll and bake as recipe directs.

GRAHAM CRACKER CRUMB CRUST

45

Mix this crust right in the pie pan—quick and easy, no bowl to clean!

8 servings (one 8- or 9-inch pie crust)

1¼ cups graham cracker crumbs
2 tablespoons sugar
3 tablespoons margarine or butter, melted
1–2 tablespoon honey

1. Combine graham crumbs, sugar, and margarine in 8- or 9-inch pie pan, adding enough honey for mixture to hold together; pat mixture evenly on bottom and side of pan. Bake at 350 degrees 8 to 10 minutes or until edge of crust is lightly browned. Cool on wire rack.

Per Serving:
Calories: 131
% of calories from fat: 44
(will decrease in pie servings)
Fat (gm): 6.4
Saturated fat (gm): 0.8
Cholesterol (mg): 0
Sodium (mg): 148
Protein (gm): 1.3
Carbohydrate (gm): 17.2

Exchanges:
Milk: 0.0
Vegetable: 0.0
Fruit: 0.0
Bread: 1.0
Meat: 0.0
Fat: 1.0

CHOCOLATE COOKIE CRUMB CRUST

45

You can choose chocolate wafer crumbs or chocolate sandwich cookie crumbs.

8 servings (one 8- or 9-inch pie crust)

1¼ cups chocolate cookie crumbs
2 tablespoons sugar
3 tablespoons margarine or butter, melted
1–2 tablespoons honey

1. Combine cookie crumbs, sugar, and margarine in bottom of 8- or 9-inch pie pan; add enough honey for mixture to stick together. Press evenly on bottom and side of pie pan. Bake at 350 degrees 6 to 8 minutes. Cool on wire rack.

Per Serving:
Calories: 158
% of calories from fat: 44
(will decrease in pie servings)
Fat (gm): 8
Saturated fat (gm): 1.5
Cholesterol (mg): 0
Sodium (mg): 225
Protein (gm): 1.3
Carbohydrate (gm): 21.6

Exchanges:
Milk: 0.0
Vegetable: 0.0
Fruit: 0.0
Bread: 1.5
Meat: 0.0
Fat: 1.0

VARIATION

Chocolate Pecan Crumb Crust — Make crust as above, decreasing margarine to 1 tablespoon, increasing honey to 3 tablespoons, and adding ¼ cup ground pecans.

CINNAMON-APPLE PIE

One of the juiciest apple pies you'll ever taste! Use a tart baking apple— Granny Smith is our favorite.

8 servings

Double Pie Crust (see p. 626)

7¼ teaspoons Equal® for Recipes or 27 packets Equal® sweetener, divided

½ teaspoon ground cinnamon

2–3 pinches ground nutmeg

6 cups sliced, peeled baking apples (about 6 large)

¾ cup unsweetened apple juice

1 tablespoon cornstarch

1 teaspoon grated lemon zest

Per Serving:
Calories: 246
% of calories from fat: 28
Fat (gm): 7.8
Saturated fat (gm): 1.5
Cholesterol (mg): 0
Sodium (mg): 232
Protein (gm): 6.2
Carbohydrate (gm): 39.1

Exchanges:
Milk: 0.0
Vegetable: 0.0
Fruit: 1.0
Bread: 1.5
Meat: 0.0
Fat: 1.5

1. Make Double Pie Crust. Roll ⅔ of the pastry on lightly floured surface into circle 1½ inches larger than inverted 9-inch pie pan; ease into pan.

2. Combine 5½ teaspoons Equal® for Recipes, cinnamon, and nutmeg; sprinkle over apples in large bowl and toss. Heat combined apple juice, remaining 1¾ teaspoons Equal® for Recipes, cornstarch, and lemon zest to boiling in small saucepan, whisking until thickened, about 1 minute. Pour mixture over apples and toss; arrange in pastry.

3. Roll remaining pastry on lightly floured surface to ⅛ inch thickness and place over apples. Trim edges of pastry to within ½ inch of pan edge; fold top pastry over bottom pastry and flute. Cut decorative slits in top of pastry. Bake at 425 degrees until pastry is golden and apples are tender, 40 to 50 minutes; cover edge of pie with aluminum foil if necessary to prevent excess browning. Cool on wire rack.

APPLE-CRANBERRY STREUSEL PIE

This pie will be a delicious addition to your winter holiday dessert table.

8 servings

Basic Pie Crust (see p. 626)

1 tablespoon cornstarch

9 teaspoons Equal® for Recipes or 33 packets
Equal® sweetener

1 cup apple cider or unsweetened apple juice

1½ cups cranberries, coarsely chopped

¾ teaspoon ground cinnamon

¼ teaspoon each: ground nutmeg, salt

5 cups sliced, cored, peeled tart baking apples
(about 5 large)

Cinnamon Streusel (recipe follows)

Per Serving:
Calories: 334
% of calories from fat: 36
Fat (gm): 13.7
Saturated fat (gm): 2.7
Cholesterol (mg): 0
Sodium (mg): 372
Protein (gm): 9.4
Carbohydrate (gm): 45.2

Exchanges:
Milk: 0.0
Vegetable: 0.0
Fruit: 1.0
Bread: 2.0
Meat: 0.0
Fat: 2.5

1. Make Basic Pie Crust, using a 9-inch pie pan.

2. Combine cornstarch and Equal® for Recipes in small saucepan;
stir in apple cider and cranberries. Heat to boiling; reduce heat and
simmer, stirring until thickened, about 1 minute. Stir in spices and
salt. Toss cranberry mixture with apples; arrange in pastry and
sprinkle evenly with Cinnamon Streusel. Bake at 400 degrees until
pastry is golden and apples are tender, 50 to 60 minutes, covering
pie loosely with aluminum foil during last 20 to 30 minutes of
baking time if necessary to prevent excessive browning. Cool on
wire rack; serve warm.

Cinnamon Streusel

Makes about ½ cup

¼ cup quick-cooking oats

3 tablespoons all-purpose flour

3½ teaspoons Equal® for Recipes or 12 packets Equal® sweetener

1 teaspoon ground cinnamon

½ teaspoon ground nutmeg

4 tablespoons cold margarine or butter, cut into pieces

1. Combine oats, flour, Equal® for Recipes, cinnamon, and nutmeg in
small bowl; cut in margarine until mixture resembles coarse crumbs.

TARTE TATIN

Caramelized sugar contributes special flavor to this French-style upside-down apple tart.

8 servings

5 cups sliced, peeled Granny Smith apples (about 5 large)

¾ cup sugar, divided

¼ teaspoon ground nutmeg

1 tablespoon lemon juice

2 tablespoons margarine or butter

Basic Pie Crust (see p. 626)

Per Serving:
Calories: 279
% of calories from fat: 24
Fat (gm): 7.6
Saturated fat (gm): 1.5
Cholesterol (mg): 0
Sodium (mg): 83.1
Protein (gm): 1.4
Carbohydrate (gm): 53.8

Exchanges:
Milk: 0.0
Vegetable: 0.0
Fruit: 1.5
Bread: 2.0
Meat: 0.0
Fat: 1.0

1. Toss apples with combined ½ cup sugar and nutmeg in bowl; sprinkle with lemon juice. Heat remaining ¼ cup sugar in 10-inch oven-proof skillet over medium heat until melted and golden, about 5 minutes, stirring occasionally (watch carefully as the sugar can burn easily). Add apple mixture and margarine; cook until apples are just tender, about 5 minutes, stirring occasionally. Remove from heat; arrange apples in skillet so they are slightly mounded in the center.

2. Roll pastry into 11-inch circle; place on top of skillet, tucking edges around apples. Cut slits in pastry. Bake at 425 degrees 20 to 25 minutes or until pastry is lightly browned. Invert onto serving plate. Serve warm or at room temperature.

VARIATIONS

Caramelized Pear and Almond Tarte Tatin — Substitute pears for the apples, tossing with combined ½ cup sugar, ⅓ cup sliced almonds, 1 tablespoon flour, 1 teaspoon grated lemon zest, ½ teaspoon ground cinnamon, and ¼ teaspoon ground nutmeg. Complete recipe as above, beginning with Step 2.

Apple-Cheddar Tarte Tatin — Make recipe as above, adding ⅓ cup raisins to apples in Step 1. Prepare Basic Pie Crust, substituting vegetable shortening for the margarine, and adding ⅓ cup shredded reduced-fat or fat-free Cheddar cheese before sprinkling with water; add additional water if necessary.

BLUEBERRY PATCH PIE

Weave a lattice topping for this garden fresh pie.

8 servings

Double Pie Crust (see p. 626)

10¾ teaspoons Equal® for Recipes or 39 packets
  Equal® sweetener

¼ cup plus 2 teaspoons cornstarch, divided

⅓ cup apple juice

2 tablespoons lemon juice

6 cups fresh blueberries or 2 packages
  (16 ounces each) frozen unsweetened
  blueberries, partially thawed

Per Serving:
Calories: 266
% of calories from fat: 26
Fat (gm): 7.7
Saturated fat (gm): 1.5
Cholesterol (mg): 0
Sodium (mg): 238
Protein (gm): 8.3
Carbohydrate (gm): 42

Exchanges:
Milk: 0.0
Vegetable: 0.0
Fruit: 1.0
Bread: 2.0
Meat: 0.0
Fat: 1.5

1. Make Double Pie Crust. Roll ⅔ of the pastry on lightly floured surface into circle 1½ inches larger than inverted 9-inch pie pan. Ease pastry into pan.

2. Heat combined Equal® for Recipes, 2 teaspoons cornstarch, apple juice, and lemon juice to boiling in small saucepan, whisking until thickened, about 1 minute. Sprinkle remaining ¼ cup cornstarch over blueberries and toss; stir apple juice mixture into blueberries and spoon into pastry.

3. Roll remaining pastry on lightly floured surface to ⅛ inch thickness; cut into ½-inch strips. Lay pastry strips across top of pie and weave into lattice design. Trim ends of strips; fold edge of lower pastry over ends of strips and seal and flute edge. Bake at 425 degrees until pastry is golden and pie is bubbly, 30 to 40 minutes, covering edge of pastry with aluminum foil if necessary to prevent excessive browning. Cool on wire rack.

CHERRY LATTICE PIE

This pie will disappear so quickly that you'd better bake two!

8 servings

Double Pie Crust (see pg. 626)

3 packages (16 ounces each) frozen no-sugar-added pitted tart cherries, thawed

17 teaspoons Equal® for Recipes or 60 packets Equal® sweetener

3 tablespoons cornstarch, divided

2 tablespoons flour, divided

⅛ teaspoon ground nutmeg

6–8 drops red food color (optional)

Per Serving:
Calories: 290
% of calories from fat: 24
Fat (gm): 8.1
Saturated fat (gm): 1.6
Cholesterol (mg): 0
Sodium (mg): 233
Protein (gm): 12.2
Carbohydrate (gm): 43.9

Exchanges:
Milk: 0.0
Vegetable: 0.0
Fruit: 1.5
Bread: 2.0
Meat: 0.0
Fat: 1.5

1. Make Double Pie Crust, using 9-inch pie pan.

2. Drain cherries, reserving ¾ cup cherry juice. Mix Equal® for Recipes, 1 tablespoon cornstarch, 1 tablespoon flour, reserved cherry juice, nutmeg, and food color in small saucepan; heat to boiling, whisking until thickened, about 1 minute. Sprinkle remaining 2 tablespoons cornstarch and 1 tablespoon flour over cherries and toss; stir cherry juice mixture into cherries. Spoon cherry mixture into pastry.

3. Roll remaining pastry on lightly floured surface to ⅛ inch thickness; cut into ½-inch strips. Lay pastry strips across top of pie and weave into lattice design. Trim ends of strips; fold edge of lower pastry over ends of strips and seal and flute edge. Bake at 425 degrees until pastry is golden and pie is bubbly, 35 to 45 minutes; cover edge of pastry with aluminum foil if necessary to prevent excessive browning. Cool on wire rack.

MIXED BERRY TART

Select as many kinds of berries as you can for beautiful color and texture contrast.

8 servings

Shortbread Pastry (see p. 627)

Mock Mascarpone (recipe follows)

3–4 cups mixed berries (raspberries, blackberries, strawberries, blueberries, gooseberries, currants, etc.)

¼ cup sugar-free currant or apple jelly, melted

Powdered sugar, as garnish

Per Serving:
Calories: 264
% of calories from fat: 31
Fat (gm): 9
Saturated fat (gm): 2.3
Cholesterol (mg): 30.9
Sodium (mg): 255
Protein (gm): 8
Carbohydrate (gm): 37.9

Exchanges:
Milk: 0.0
Vegetable: 0.0
Fruit: 0.5
Bread: 2.0
Meat: 0.0
Fat: 2.0

1. Roll pastry between 2 sheets of waxed paper into 12-inch circle. Ease into 10-inch tart pan and trim; pierce bottom with fork. Bake at 425 degrees until crisp and golden brown, 10 to 15 minutes. Cool on wire rack.

2. Spread Mock Mascarpone evenly on cooled pastry; top with berries and drizzle with jelly. Dust serving plates with powdered sugar; top with tart slices.

Mock Mascarpone
Makes about 1¼ cups

8 ounces fat-free cream cheese, room temperature

3 tablespoons reduced-fat sour cream

2–3 tablespoons 2% reduced-fat milk

1. Beat cream cheese until fluffy; mix in sour cream and milk. Refrigerate several hours or up to several days.

NECTARINE AND BERRY TART

Fresh apricots or fresh or frozen, thawed peaches can be substituted for the nectarines in this summer-fresh, country-style tart.

6 servings

Basic Pie Crust (see p. 626)

5 cups sliced nectarines

1 cup each: fresh or frozen, partially thawed raspberries or blueberries

7¼ teaspoons Equal® for Recipes or 27 packets Equal® sweetener

2 teaspoons lemon juice

3 tablespoons cornstarch

1 teaspoon grated lemon zest

¼ teaspoon ground allspice

Per Serving:
Calories: 275
% of calories from fat: 27
Fat (gm): 8.5
Saturated fat (gm): 1.6
Cholesterol (mg): 0
Sodium (mg): 189
Protein (gm): 8.5
Carbohydrate (gm): 42.9

Exchanges:
Milk: 0.0
Vegetable: 0.0
Fruit: 1.0
Bread: 2.0
Meat: 0.0
Fat: 1.5

1. Make Basic Pie Crust. Roll pastry on floured surface into 12-inch circle; transfer to ungreased cookie sheet.

2. Toss fruit with Equal® for Recipes and lemon juice in large bowl; sprinkle with combined cornstarch, lemon zest, and allspice and toss. Arrange fruit on pastry, leaving 2-inch border of pastry around the edge. Fold edge of pastry over fruit, overlapping as necessary. Bake at 425 degrees until pastry is golden and fruit tender, 35 to 40 minutes. Cool on wire rack.

HEAVENLY PEACH PIE

Enjoy this pie in winter too, using frozen, thawed peaches or drained canned peaches.

8 servings

Double Pie Crust (see p. 626)

6 cups sliced pitted, peeled peaches (about 6 large)

7¼ teaspoons Equal® for Recipes or 27 packets Equal® sweetener

2 tablespoons flour

½ teaspoon ground cinnamon

2–3 pinches ground nutmeg

1. Make Double Pie Crust. Roll ⅔ of the pastry on lightly floured surface to form circle 1½ inches larger than inverted 9-inch pie pan; ease into pan.

2. Toss peaches with combined Equal® for Recipes, flour, cinnamon, and nutmeg. Arrange fruit in pastry. Roll remaining pastry on lightly floured surface to ⅛ inch thickness; cut into ½-inch strips. Lay pastry strips across top of pie and weave into lattice design. Trim ends of strips; fold edge of lower crust over ends of strips and seal and flute edge. Bake at 425 degrees until bubbly, 30 to 40 minutes, covering edge of crust with aluminum foil if necessary to prevent excessive browning. Cool on wire rack.

Per Serving:
Calories: 238
% of calories from fat: 28
Fat (gm): 7.4
Saturated fat (gm): 1.5
Cholesterol (mg): 0
Sodium (mg): 230
Protein (gm): 7.2
Carbohydrate (gm): 36.6

Exchanges:
Milk: 0.0
Vegetable: 0.0
Fruit: 1.0
Bread: 1.5
Meat: 0.0
Fat: 1.5

PINEAPPLE CRUMB TART

45

The rich crumb mixture is used both as a crust and topping in this delectable French-style tart. Substitute other canned fruit for the pineapple, if desired.

10 to 12 servings

1¼ cups all-purpose flour

5½ teaspoons Equal® for Recipes or 18 packets Equal® sweetener

4 teaspoons cornstarch

¼ teaspoon salt

10 tablespoons cold margarine or butter, cut into pieces

2 cans (8 ounces each) sliced pineapple in juice, drained

¼ cup apricot preserves, warm

Per Serving:
Calories: 207
% of calories from fat: 50
Fat (gm): 11.5
Saturated fat (gm): 2.3
Cholesterol (mg): 0
Sodium (mg): 201
Protein (gm): 3.7
Carbohydrate (gm): 22.3

Exchanges:
Milk: 0.0
Vegetable: 0.0
Fruit: 0.5
Bread: 1.0
Meat: 0.0
Fat: 2.0

1. Combine flour, Equal® for Recipes, cornstarch, and salt in medium bowl; cut in margarine until mixture resembles coarse crumbs. Reserve ½ cup crumb mixture. Pat remaining mixture evenly on bottom of ungreased 10-inch tart pan or quiche dish. Bake at 350 degrees until browned, about 15 minutes. Cool on wire rack.

2. Cut pineapple slices in half and arrange on crust; sprinkle with reserved ½ cup crumb mixture. Bake at 400 degrees until topping is browned, about 10 minutes. Cool on wire rack; drizzle with preserves.

KEY LIME PIE

A Southern dessert that's famous for its smooth creamy texture and unique cool lime taste.

8 servings

1 cup reduced-fat graham cracker crumbs

3–4 tablespoons margarine or butter, melted

4½ teaspoons Equal® for Recipes or 15 packets Equal® sweetener, divided

1 envelope unflavored gelatin

1¾ cups fat-free milk, divided

8 ounces fat-free cream cheese, room temperature

½ cup key lime or Persian lime juice

Light whipped topping, as garnish

Mint sprigs, as garnish

Per Serving:
Calories: 147
% of calories from fat: 32
Fat (gm): 5.4
Saturated fat (gm): 1.4
Cholesterol (mg): 3.2
Sodium (mg): 320
Protein (gm): 8.7
Carbohydrate (gm): 16.6

Exchanges:
Milk: 0.0
Vegetable: 0.0
Fruit: 0.0
Bread: 1.0
Meat: 1.0
Fat: 0.5

1. Combine graham cracker crumbs, margarine, and 1 teaspoon Equal® for Recipes in 7-inch springform pan; pat evenly on bottom and ½ inch up side of pan.

2. Sprinkle gelatin over ½ cup milk in small saucepan; let stand 2 to 3 minutes. Heat just to simmering, stirring; cool. Beat cream cheese until fluffy in bowl; beat in remaining 1¼ cups milk and the gelatin mixture. Mix in lime juice and remaining 3½ teaspoons Equal® for Recipes. Pour into pan; refrigerate until set, 3 to 4 hours. Remove side of pan; place pie on serving plate. Garnish with light whipped topping and mint.

DOUBLE COCONUT CREAM MERINGUE PIE

Reduced-fat coconut milk lends a subtle coconut flavor to the pie filling.

8 servings

Basic Pie Crust (see p. 626)

¾ cup sugar

⅓ cup cornstarch

⅛ teaspoon salt

2 cups fat-free milk

½ can (14-ounce size) light coconut milk

2 egg yolks

1 teaspoon vanilla

1 tablespoon margarine or butter

¼ cup plus 2 tablespoons flaked coconut, divided

3 egg whites

¼ teaspoon cream of tartar

Per Serving:
Calories: 298
% of calories from fat: 33
Fat (gm): 11
Saturated fat (gm): 2.9
Cholesterol (mg): 54.4
Sodium (mg): 248
Protein (gm): 6.5
Carbohydrate (gm): 43.2

Exchanges:
Milk: 0.0
Vegetable: 0.0
Fruit: 0.0
Bread: 3.0
Meat: 0.0
Fat: 2.0

1. Make Basic Pie Crust using a 9-inch pie pan. Bake and cool on wire rack.

2. Combine ½ cup sugar, cornstarch, and salt in medium saucepan; whisk in milk and coconut milk. Heat to boiling, whisking until thickened, about 1 minute. Whisk about ½ the milk mixture into egg yolks; whisk yolk mixture back into saucepan. Cook over medium-low heat, whisking, 1 minute. Remove from heat; stir in vanilla, margarine, and ¼ cup coconut. Pour into crust.

3. Beat egg whites and cream of tartar to soft peaks in medium bowl; beat to stiff peaks, adding remaining ¼ cup sugar gradually. Spread meringue over hot filling, sealing to edge of crust; sprinkle with 2 tablespoons coconut. Bake at 400 degrees until meringue is browned, about 5 minutes; cool on wire rack. Refrigerate until chilled, 3 to 4 hours.

VARIATION

Island Pie — Slice 1 small banana and arrange in cooled pie crust. Make pie as above, substituting 1 cup fat-free milk for the coconut milk and adding ½ teaspoon coconut extract. Substitute chopped macadamia nuts for the coconut in the filling and in the meringue.

LEMON CLOUD PIE

45

Other flavors of this wonderful dessert are easy to make—just substitute another flavor yogurt, such as strawberry, raspberry, or cherry.

8 servings

1½ cups each: light whipped topping, low-fat custard-style lemon yogurt
2 tablespoons grated lemon zest
Meringue Pie Crust (recipe follows)
Lemon slices, as garnish

Per Serving:
Calories: 170
% of calories from fat: 17
Fat (gm): 3.5
Saturated fat (gm): 0.3
Cholesterol (mg): 2
Sodium (mg): 62
Protein (gm): 3.6
Carbohydrate (gm): 35.5

Exchanges:
Milk: 0.5
Vegetable: 0.0
Fruit: 2.0
Bread: 0.0
Meat: 0.0
Fat: 0.5

1. Combine whipped topping, yogurt, and lemon zest and spoon into Meringue Pie Crust at serving time. Garnish with lemon slices.

Meringue Pie Crust

Makes one 9-inch crust

4 egg whites
½ teaspoon cream of tartar
1 cup sugar

1. Beat egg whites and cream of tartar in medium bowl to soft peaks; beat to stiff, but not dry peaks, adding sugar gradually. Spoon into ungreased 9-inch pie plate, spreading on bottom and side to form a large bowl shape. Bake at 275 degrees until crust is firm to touch and very lightly browned, about 45 minutes. Turn oven off and let crust cool in oven.

45-MINUTE PREPARATION TIP: Make Meringue Pie Crust before preparing the rest of the recipe.

PUMPKIN CHIFFON PIE

The perfect addition to any fall holiday menu.

8 servings

Basic Pie Crust (see p. 626)

2½ teaspoons Equal® for Recipes or 12 packets
  Equal® sweetener

1 envelope unflavored gelatin

1 teaspoon cornstarch

½ cup fat-free milk

2 egg yolks

2 cups canned pumpkin

1 teaspoon each: pumpkin pie spice, vanilla

⅛ teaspoon salt

1 cup light whipped topping

Light whipped topping, as garnish

Per Serving:
Calories: 196
% of calories from fat: 39
Fat (gm): 8.3
Saturated fat (gm): 2.7
Cholesterol (mg): 53.5
Sodium (mg): 191
Protein (gm): 5.5
Carbohydrate (gm): 24.1

Exchanges:
Milk: 0.0
Vegetable: 0.0
Fruit: 0.0
Bread: 2.0
Meat: 0.0
Fat: 1.5

1. Make Basic Pie Crust, using 9-inch pie pan. Ease pastry into pan; trim and flute. Bake and cool on wire rack.

2. Combine Equal® for Recipes, gelatin, cornstarch, and milk in medium saucepan; heat to boiling over medium-high heat, whisking until thickened, 2 to 3 minutes. Stir about ½ the milk mixture into the egg yolks; whisk egg mixture into saucepan. Whisk over low heat 1 to 2 minutes. Remove from heat and stir in pumpkin, pumpkin pie spice, vanilla, and salt. Cool to room temperature; refrigerate until mixture mounds when dropped from a spoon, about 20 minutes.

3. Whisk mixture gently until smooth; fold in 1 cup whipped topping and spoon into pie crust, smoothing top. Refrigerate until set, 3 to 4 hours. Garnish with dollops of whipped topping.

STRAWBERRY CREAM PIE

Celebrate spring with this colorful fresh berry pie.

8 servings

1¼ cups reduced-fat graham cracker crumbs

4–5 tablespoons margarine or butter, melted

6¼ teaspoons Equal® for Recipes or 19 packets
  Equal® sweetener, divided

8 ounces fat-free cream cheese, room temperature

1 teaspoon vanilla

1 cup boiling water

1 package (0.3 ounces) sugar-free strawberry gelatin

2 cups sliced strawberries

Light whipped topping, as garnish

Per Serving:
Calories: 165
% of calories from fat: 38
Fat (gm): 6.9
Saturated fat (gm): 1.6
Cholesterol (mg): 2.3
Sodium (mg): 330
Protein (gm): 8.9
Carbohydrate (gm): 17.1

Exchanges:
Milk: 0.0
Vegetable: 0.0
Fruit: 0.0
Bread: 1.0
Meat: 1.0
Fat: 1.0

1. Mix graham cracker crumbs, margarine, and 1 teaspoon Equal®
for Recipes in 8-inch pie pan; pat evenly on bottom and side of pan.
Bake at 350 degrees until lightly browned, 6 to 8 minutes. Cool.

2. Beat cream cheese, vanilla, and 1¾ teaspoons Equal® for Recipes
in small bowl until fluffy; spread evenly in bottom of crust.

3. Pour boiling water over gelatin and remaining 3½ teaspoons
Equal® for Recipes in bowl, whisking until gelatin is dissolved.
Refrigerate until mixture is the consistency of unbeaten egg whites,
20 to 30 minutes. Arrange half the strawberries over the cream
cheese; spoon half the gelatin mixture over strawberries. Arrange
remaining strawberries over pie and spoon remaining gelatin
mixture over. Refrigerate until pie is set and chilled, 2 to 3 hours.
Serve with light whipped topping.

VARIATIONS

Double Berry Pie — Make recipe as above, substituting 1 cup
blueberries for 1 cup strawberries. Arrange 1 cup blueberries over
cream cheese in pie crust; spoon half the gelatin mixture over
berries; top with 1 cup sliced strawberries and spoon remaining
gelatin mixture over.

Strawberry Banana Pie — Make recipe as above, substituting
sugar-free strawberry-banana gelatin for the strawberry gelatin

and 1 small sliced banana for 1 cup strawberries. Arrange banana over cream cheese; spoon half the gelatin mixture over; top with 1 cup sliced strawberries and spoon remaining gelatin mixture over.

OLD-FASHIONED CUSTARD PIE

One of the best custard pies you've ever tasted! For a richer custard, use 2% reduced-fat milk.

8 servings

Basic Pie Crust (see p. 626)

4 eggs

¼ teaspoon salt

2½ cups fat-free milk

5½ teaspoons Equal® for Recipes or 21 packets Equal® sweetener

1½ teaspoons vanilla

¼ teaspoon ground cinnamon

⅛ teaspoon ground nutmeg

Per Serving:
Calories: 199
% of calories from fat: 39
Fat (gm): 8.5
Saturated fat (gm): 2
Cholesterol (mg): 107.4
Sodium (mg): 284
Protein (gm): 10.3
Carbohydrate (gm): 19.3

Exchanges:
Milk: 0.0
Vegetable: 0.0
Fruit: 0.0
Bread: 1.5
Meat: 1.0
Fat: 1.0

1. Make Basic Pie Crust, using 9-inch pie pan.

2. Beat eggs and salt in large bowl until thick and lemon colored, about 5 minutes. Mix in milk, Equal® for Recipes, and remaining ingredients; pour into pastry. Bake at 425 degrees 15 minutes; reduce temperature to 350 degrees and bake until sharp knife inserted halfway between center and edge comes out clean, about 12 minutes. Cool on wire rack. Serve at room temperature, or refrigerate and serve chilled.

VARIATION

Coconut Custard Pie — Make recipe as above, reducing milk to 2 cups, adding ½ cup flaked coconut, and substituting 1 to 2 teaspoons coconut extract for the vanilla.

PECAN CRUNCH TART

45

We've reduced the calories and fat in this rich-tasting pecan pie.

8 servings

Basic Pie Crust (see p. 626)

2 eggs

1 cup maple syrup or pancake syrup

1 tablespoon vanilla

⅛ teaspoon salt

⅔ cup each: reduced-fat granola, coarsely
    chopped pecans

⅓ cup barley-wheat cereal (Grape-Nuts)

Per Serving:
Calories: 356
% of calories from fat: 22
Fat (gm): 8.9
Saturated fat (gm): 3.2
Cholesterol (mg): 56.2
Sodium (mg): 279
Protein (gm): 9.6
Carbohydrate (gm): 63.1

Exchanges:
Milk: 0.0
Vegetable: 0.0
Fruit: 0.0
Bread: 4.0
Meat: 0.0
Fat: 1.5

1. Make Basic Pie Crust, using 10-inch tart pan. Beat eggs, syrup, vanilla, and salt until smooth. Stir in remaining ingredients; pour into pastry. Bake at 350 degrees until set, about 35 minutes.

PUMPKIN CHEESECAKE

45

A creamy smooth cheesecake, scented with holiday flavors of pumpkin and spices.

12 to 14 servings

¾ cup each: ground reduced-fat graham crackers
    and gingersnap cookies

8¼ teaspoons Equal® for Recipes or 27 packets Equal®
    sweetener, divided

4–5 tablespoons margarine or butter, melted

16 ounces fat-free cream cheese, room temperature

8 ounces reduced-fat cream cheese, room temperature

1 cup canned pumpkin

3 eggs

2 teaspoons ground cinnamon

1 teaspoon each: ground cloves, ginger

2 tablespoons cornstarch

1 cup light whipped topping

Chopped toasted pecans, as garnish

Per Serving:
Calories: 213
% of calories from fat: 42
Fat (gm): 9.8
Saturated fat (gm): 4.3
Cholesterol (mg): 47.2
Sodium (mg): 444
Protein (gm): 12.1
Carbohydrate (gm): 18.2

Exchanges:
Milk: 0.0
Vegetable: 0.0
Fruit: 0.0
Bread: 1.0
Meat: 1.0
Fat: 2.0

1. Mix graham cracker and gingersnap crumbs, 1 teaspoon Equal® for Recipes, and margarine in bottom of 9-inch springform pan; reserve 2 tablespoons crumb mixture. Pat remaining mixture evenly on bottom and ½ inch up side of pan. Bake at 350 degrees until lightly browned, about 8 minutes. Cool on wire rack.

2. Beat cream cheese and remaining 7¼ teaspoons Equal® for Recipes until smooth in large bowl; beat in remaining ingredients, except whipped topping and pecans. Pour into springform pan. Bake at 300 degrees just until set in the center, 45 to 60 minutes; sprinkle with reserved crumbs and return to oven. Turn oven off and let cheesecake cool in oven with door ajar for 3 hours. Refrigerate 8 hours or overnight.

3. Remove side of springform pan; place cheesecake on serving plate. Spread with light whipped topping and sprinkle with pecans.

RICH CHOCOLATE CHEESECAKE

A chocolate lover's delight!

16 servings

1¼ cups graham cracker crumbs

4–5 tablespoons margarine or butter, melted

6½ teaspoons Equal® for Recipes or 21 packets Equal® sweetener, divided

16 ounces fat-free cream cheese, room temperature

8 ounces reduced-fat cream cheese, room temperature

1 cup fat-free sour cream

3 eggs

2 tablespoons cornstarch

⅓ cup Dutch process cocoa

1 teaspoon vanilla

1 cup light whipped topping

Unsweetened chocolate shavings, as garnish

Per Serving:
Calories: 182
% of calories from fat: 43
Fat (gm): 8.5
Cholesterol (mg): 3.6
Sodium (mg): 320
Protein (gm): 10
Carbohydrate (gm): 14.9

Exchanges:
Milk: 0.0
Vegetable: 0.0
Fruit: 0.0
Bread: 1.0
Meat: 1.0
Fat: 1.0

1. Mix graham cracker crumbs, margarine, and 1 teaspoon Equal® for Recipes in 9-inch springform pan; pat evenly on bottom and ½ inch up side of pan.

2. Beat cream cheese, remaining 5½ teaspoons Equal® for Recipes, and sour cream until smooth in large bowl; beat in eggs, cornstarch, cocoa, and vanilla. Pour into crust. Bake at 300 degrees just until set in the center, 45 to 50 minutes. Turn oven off and let cheesecake cool in oven with door ajar for 3 hours. Refrigerate 8 hours or overnight.

3. Remove side of pan; place cheesecake on serving plate. Spread light whipped topping over top and garnish with chocolate shavings.

ALMOND CHEESECAKE SQUARES

45

Rich in flavor and texture, yet made with fat-free cream cheese!

24 servings

24 ounces fat-free cream cheese, room temperature
1 cup fat-free sour cream
5½ teaspoons Equal® for Recipes or 18 packets
  Equal® sweetener
3 each: eggs
2 tablespoons cornstarch
½ teaspoon vanilla
¼ teaspoon almond extract
Chocolate Crumb Crust (recipe follows)
¼ cup sliced almonds

Per Serving:
Calories: 112
% of calories from fat: 34
Fat (gm): 4.1
Saturated fat (gm): 1
Cholesterol (mg): 19.9
Sodium (mg): 244
Protein (gm): 7.5
Carbohydrate (gm): 10.2

Exchanges:
Milk: 0.0
Vegetable: 0.0
Fruit: 0.0
Bread: 1.0
Meat: 0.0
Fat: 1.0

1. Beat cream cheese and sour cream until smooth in large bowl; beat in remaining ingredients, except Chocolate Crumb Crust and almonds. Pour into crust; sprinkle with almonds. Bake at 300 degrees until set, about 30 minutes. Cool on wire rack; refrigerate until chilled, 8 hours or overnight. Cut into squares.

Chocolate Crumb Crust

1½ cups ground reduced-fat graham crackers
¼ cup Dutch process cocoa
2½ teaspoons Equal® for Recipes or 8 packets Equal® sweetener
5 tablespoons margarine or butter, melted
½–¾ teaspoon chocolate extract

1. Mix graham cracker crumbs, cocoa, and Equal® for Recipes in bottom of 13 x 9-inch baking pan; mix in margarine and chocolate extract. Pat mixture evenly on bottom of pan.

CHOCOLATE CHIP COOKIES

45 *America's favorite cookie—best eaten warm!*

5 dozen cookies (1 each)

8 tablespoons margarine or butter, room temperature
1 cup packed light brown sugar
½ cup granulated sugar
1 egg
1 teaspoon vanilla
2½ cups all-purpose flour
½ teaspoon each: baking soda, salt
⅓ cup fat-free milk
½ package (12-ounce size) reduced-fat semisweet
   chocolate morsels

Per Serving:
Calories: 66
% of calories from fat: 27
Fat (gm): 2
Saturated fat (gm): 0.7
Cholesterol (mg): 3.6
Sodium (mg): 70
Protein (gm): 0.8
Carbohydrate (gm): 11.2

Exchanges:
Milk: 0.0
Vegetable: 0.0
Fruit: 0.0
Bread: 0.5
Meat: 0.0
Fat: 0.5

1. Beat margarine and sugars in medium bowl until fluffy; beat in egg and vanilla. Mix in combined flour, baking soda, and salt alternately with milk, beginning and ending with dry ingredients. Mix in chocolate morsels. Drop cookies by tablespoonfuls onto greased cookie sheets. Bake at 375 degrees until browned, about 10 minutes. Cool on wire racks.

RAISIN OATMEAL COOKIES

45 *Moist and chewy, just the way they should be!*

2½ dozen cookies (1 each)

6 tablespoons margarine or butter, room temperature
¼ cup fat-free sour cream
1 egg
1 teaspoon vanilla
1 cup packed light brown sugar

1½ cups quick-cooking oats

1 cup all-purpose flour

½ teaspoon baking soda

¼ teaspoon baking powder

1 teaspoon ground cinnamon

½ cup raisins

Per Serving:
Calories: 90
% of calories from fat: 27
Fat (gm): 2.7
Saturated fat (gm): 0.5
Cholesterol (mg): 7.1
Sodium (mg): 57
Protein (gm): 1.5
Carbohydrate (gm): 15.3

Exchanges:
Milk: 0.0
Vegetable: 0.0
Fruit: 0.0
Bread: 1.0
Meat: 0.0
Fat: 0.5

1. Mix margarine, sour cream, egg, and vanilla in large bowl; beat in brown sugar. Mix in combined remaining ingredients, except raisins; mix in raisins. Drop dough onto greased cookie sheets, using 2 tablespoons for each cookie. Bake at 350 degrees until browned, 12 to 15 minutes. Cool on wire racks.

SOFT MOLASSES COOKIES

45

Fill your home with the scent of spices when you bake these cookies.

3 dozen cookies (1 each)

¼ cup vegetable shortening

½ cup packed dark brown sugar

1 egg yolk

1¼ cups all-purpose flour

2 teaspoons baking soda

½ teaspoon each: ground cinnamon, ginger

¼ teaspoon each: ground nutmeg, salt

¼ cup light molasses

2 tablespoons water

½ cup currants or chopped raisins

Per Serving:
Calories: 53
% of calories from fat: 25
Fat (gm): 1.5
Saturated fat (gm): 0.4
Cholesterol (mg): 5.9
Sodium (mg): 89
Protein (gm): 0.6
Carbohydrate (gm): 9.3

Exchanges:
Milk: 0.0
Vegetable: 0.0
Fruit: 0.0
Bread: 0.5
Meat: 0.0
Fat: 0.0

1. Beat shortening, brown sugar, and egg yolk in medium bowl until blended. Mix in combined flour, baking soda, spices, and salt alternately with combined molasses and water, beginning and ending with dry ingredients. Mix in currants. Drop mixture by rounded teaspoons onto greased cookie sheets. Bake at 350 until lightly browned (cookies will be soft), 8 to 10 minutes. Cool on wire racks.

CHOCOLATE CRINKLES

45

These cookies have crinkled, crisp tops but are soft inside.

4½ dozen cookies (1 each)

8 tablespoons margarine or butter, room temperature
1¼ cups packed light brown sugar
⅓ cup reduced-fat sour cream
1 egg
1–2 ounces semisweet baking chocolate, melted
1 teaspoon vanilla
1¾ cups all-purpose flour
¾ cup unsweetened cocoa
1 teaspoon each: baking soda, ground cinnamon
¼ cup granulated sugar

Per Serving:
Calories: 61
% of calories from fat: 31
Fat (gm): 2.1
Saturated fat (gm): 0.6
Cholesterol (mg): 4.5
Sodium (mg): 49
Protein (gm): 0.8
Carbohydrate (gm): 9.8

Exchanges:
Milk: 0.0
Vegetable: 0.0
Fruit: 0.0
Bread: 0.5
Meat: 0.0
Fat: 0.5

1. Beat margarine and brown sugar in large bowl until fluffy. Mix in sour cream, egg, chocolate, and vanilla. Mix in combined flour, cocoa, baking soda, and cinnamon. Refrigerate, covered, 2 to 3 hours.

2. Drop dough by tablespoons into granulated sugar in pie plate; roll into balls (dough will be soft). Place cookies on greased cookie sheets; flatten with fork or bottom of glass. Bake at 350 degrees until firm to touch, 10 to 12 minutes. Cool on wire racks.

HAZELNUT MACAROONS

45

Use any favorite nuts in these moist and crunchy macaroons.

30 cookies (1 each)

4 egg whites
⅛ teaspoon cream of tartar
¼ teaspoon salt
1 cup each: sugar, sweetened flaked coconut
¼ cup finely chopped hazelnuts or pecans

Per Serving:
Calories: 44
% of calories from fat: 28
Fat (gm): 1.4
Saturated fat (gm): 0.8
Cholesterol (mg): 0
Sodium (mg): 25.6
Protein (gm): 0.7
Carbohydrate (gm): 7.6

Exchanges:
Milk: 0.0
Vegetable: 0.0
Fruit: 0.0
Bread: 0.5
Meat: 0.0
Fat: 0.5

1. Beat egg whites, cream of tartar, and salt to stiff, but not dry, peaks, adding sugar gradually. Fold in coconut and hazelnuts. Drop mixture by tablespoons onto parchment or foil-lined cookie sheets. Bake at 300 degrees until cookies begin to brown and feel crisp when touched, 20 to 25 minutes. Cool in pans on wire racks.

SHORTBREAD COOKIES

45

A crisp yet tender cookie, with a wonderful buttery flavor.

1 dozen cookies (1 each)

1 cup all-purpose flour
3½ teaspoons Equal® for Recipes or 12 packets Equal® sweetener
1 tablespoon cornstarch
⅛ teaspoon salt
8 tablespoons cold margarine or butter, cut into pieces
½–1 teaspoon each: butter extract, vanilla

Per Serving:
Calories: 113
% of calories from fat: 61
Fat (gm): 7.6
Saturated fat (gm): 1.5
Cholesterol (mg): 0
Sodium (mg): 113
Protein (gm): 2.1
Carbohydrate (gm): 8.7

Exchanges:
Milk: 0.0
Vegetable: 0.0
Fruit: 0.0
Bread: 0.5
Meat: 0.0
Fat: 1.5

1. Combine flour, Equal® for Recipes, cornstarch, and salt in medium bowl; cut in margarine until mixture resembles coarse crumbs. Sprinkle butter extract and vanilla over mixture and mix with hands briefly until dough begins to hold together. Pat dough evenly in bottom of greased 8-inch round cake pan. Lightly cut dough into 12 wedges with sharp knife, cutting about halfway through dough. Pierce each wedge 3 to 4 times with tines of fork. Bake at 325 degrees until lightly browned, 25 to 30 minutes. Cool on wire rack; cut into wedges while warm.

VARIATIONS

Almond Shortbread — Make recipe as above, substituting almond extract for the butter extract and omitting vanilla. Separate 6 whole blanched almonds into halves; press 1 half into each shortbread wedge before baking.

Chocolate Shortbread — Make recipe as above, adding ¼ cup Dutch process cocoa, increasing Equal® for Recipes to 5½ teaspoons or 18 packets, and substituting vanilla for butter extract.

CARDAMOM CUT-OUTS

Intensely flavored with cardamom, these delicate cookies are also delicious made with cinnamon. Cut into tiny 1-inch rounds for tea cookies.

5 dozen cookies (1 each)

½ cup vegetable shortening
1 cup plus 2 tablespoons sugar, divided
3 tablespoons fat-free milk
1 egg yolk
¾ teaspoon ground cardamom, divided
2 cups all-purpose flour
¼ teaspoon salt

Per Serving:
Calories: 46
% of calories from fat: 34
Fat (gm): 1.7
Saturated fat (gm): 0.4
Cholesterol (mg): 3.6
Sodium (mg): 10
Protein (gm): 0.5
Carbohydrate (gm): 7

Exchanges:
Milk: 0.0
Vegetable: 0.0
Fruit: 0.0
Bread: 0.5
Meat: 0.0
Fat: 0.0

1. Beat shortening, 1 cup sugar, milk, egg yolk, and ½ teaspoon cardamom in medium bowl until well blended; mix in flour and salt. Roll ½ the dough on floured surface to scant ¼ inch thickness; cut into rounds or decorative shapes with 2-inch cutter. Repeat with remaining dough. Bake on greased baking sheets at 375 degrees until browned, 8 to 10 minutes. Combine remaining 2 tablespoons sugar and ¼ teaspoon cardamom; sprinkle over warm cookies. Cool on wire racks.

TART LEMON DAINTIES

Enjoy the subtle lemon flavor of these tiny crisp cookies—perfect with coffee or tea.

4 dozen cookies (1 each)

4 tablespoons margarine or butter, room temperature
1 cup granulated sugar
1 egg
3 tablespoons fat-free milk
2 teaspoons lemon juice
1 teaspoon finely grated lemon zest
2 cups all-purpose flour
1 teaspoon baking powder
¼ teaspoon salt

Per Serving:
Calories: 46
% of calories from fat: 22
Fat (gm): 1.1
Saturated fat (gm): 0.2
Cholesterol (mg): 4.4
Sodium (mg): 35
Protein (gm): 0.7
Carbohydrate (gm): 8.2

Exchanges:
Milk: 0.0
Vegetable: 0.0
Fruit: 0.0
Bread: 0.5
Meat: 0.0
Fat: 0.0

1. Beat margarine, sugar, egg, milk, lemon juice, and lemon zest in bowl until blended. Mix in combined flour, baking powder, and salt. Refrigerate until chilled, 2 to 3 hours.

2. Roll ½ the dough on floured surface to ¼ inch thickness; cut into rounds or decorative shapes with 1½-inch cutter. Repeat with remaining dough. Bake on greased cookie sheets at 375 degrees until lightly browned, 7 to 8 minutes. Cool on wire racks.

ALMOND TUILES

These lacy crisp cookies can be folded, rolled, or formed into small basket shapes for ice cream or other fillings.

3 dozen cookies (1 each)

½ cup quick-cooking oats
¼ cup finely chopped blanched almonds
4 tablespoons margarine or butter, melted
½ cup light corn syrup
⅓ cup sugar
1 teaspoon almond extract
½ cup all-purpose flour
¼ teaspoon salt

Per Serving:
Calories: 49
% of calories from fat: 33
Fat (gm): 1.7
Saturated fat (gm): 0.3
Cholesterol (mg): 0
Sodium (mg): 36
Protein (gm): 0.5
Carbohydrate (gm): 7.5

Exchanges:
Milk: 0.0
Vegetable: 0.0
Fruit: 0.0
Bread: 0.5
Meat: 0.0
Fat: 0.5

1. Place oats and almonds in separate pie pans. Bake at 350 degrees until toasted, 5 to 8 minutes for the almonds and about 10 minutes for the oats. Cool.

2. Mix margarine, corn syrup, sugar, and almond extract in medium bowl; mix in combined oats, almonds, flour, and salt. Drop batter by well-rounded teaspoons, 3 inches apart, onto parchment-lined cookie sheets (4 to 6 cookies per pan). Bake at 350 degrees until golden and bubbly, 7 to 10 minutes. Let cookies cool just until firm enough to remove from pan, about 1 minute. Working quickly, remove each cookie and roll or fold over the handle of a wooden spoon, or leave flat; cool on wire racks. If cookies have cooled too much to shape, return to warm oven for about 1 minute to soften.

VARIATION

Cream-Filled Tuiles — Remove warm tuiles from cookie sheet 1 at a time and roll loosely around handle of wooden spoon; transfer to wire rack and cool. Mix 3 cups light whipped topping and ⅓ cup powdered sugar. Using pastry bag with medium plain tip, fill cookies with mixture. Drizzle cookies with 1 ounce melted semisweet chocolate.

GRANOLA LACE COOKIES

When the cookies are still warm, they can be rolled or folded over the handle of a wooden spoon, or "pinched" in the center to form bow shapes; see recipe for Almond Tuiles, p. 651, for shaping directions. Bake only 4 to 6 cookies at a time, as they must be handled quickly and carefully before cooling.

4 dozen cookies (1 each)

4 tablespoons margarine or butter, room temperature

¼ cup each: granulated sugar, packed light brown sugar

2 egg whites

1 tablespoon orange juice

¼–½ teaspoon orange extract

½ cup each: finely crushed reduced-fat granola without raisins, all-purpose flour

¼ teaspoon each: baking soda, salt

2 teaspoons finely grated orange zest

Per Serving:
Calories: 27
% of calories from fat: 33
Fat (gm): 1
Saturated fat (gm): 0.2
Cholesterol (mg): 0
Sodium (mg): 35
Protein (gm): 0.4
Carbohydrate (gm): 4.1

Exchanges:
Milk: 0.0
Vegetable: 0.0
Fruit: 0.0
Bread: 0.5
Meat: 0.0
Fat: 0.0

1. Beat all ingredients in large bowl until smooth. Drop rounded ½ teaspoons dough 3 inches apart on parchment-lined cookie sheets, making 4 to 6 cookies per pan. Bake at 400 degrees until lightly browned, about 3 minutes. Let stand until firm enough to remove from pans, about 1 minute. Cool on wire racks.

RASPBERRY-ALMOND BARS

45

A pretty bar cookie with a rich-tasting shortbread pastry.

2 dozen cookies (1 each)

2 cups all-purpose flour

3½ teaspoons Equal® for Recipes or 12 packets
Equal® sweetener

⅛ teaspoon salt

8 tablespoons cold margarine or butter, cut into
pieces

1 large egg, beaten

1 tablespoon fat-free milk or water

⅔ cup seedless raspberry preserves

1 teaspoon cornstarch

¼–⅓ cup finely chopped almonds, walnuts or
pecans, toasted

Per Serving:
Calories: 96
% of calories from fat: 45
Fat (gm): 4.6
Saturated fat (gm): 0.9
Cholesterol (mg): 8.8
Sodium (mg): 69
Protein (gm): 2.1
Carbohydrate (gm): 10.5

Exchanges:
Milk: 0.0
Vegetable: 0.0
Fruit: 0.0
Bread: 0.5
Meat: 0.0
Fat: 1.0

1. Combine flour, Equal® for Recipes, and salt in medium bowl; cut in margarine until mixture resembles coarse crumbs. Mix in egg and milk. Press mixture evenly in bottom of greased 11 x 7-inch baking dish. Bake at 400 degrees until edges of crust are browned, about 15 minutes. Cool on wire rack.

2. Mix preserves and cornstarch in small saucepan; heat to boiling, stirring until thickened, about 1 minute; cool 5 minutes. Spread mixture over cooled crust; sprinkle with almonds. Bake at 400 degrees until preserves are thick and bubbly, about 15 minutes. Cool on wire rack.

LIGHT LEMON SQUARES

45

One of America's favorite bar cookies, made without added sugar!

1 dozen cookies (1 each)

2 eggs
5½ teaspoons Equal® for Recipes or 18 packets
   Equal® sweetener
⅓ cup lemon juice
4 tablespoons margarine or butter, melted, cooled
1 tablespoon grated lemon zest
Rich Pastry (recipe follows)

Per Serving:
Calories: 138
% of calories from fat: 67
Fat (gm): 10.4
Saturated fat (gm): 2.1
Cholesterol (mg): 35.3
Sodium (mg): 146
Protein (gm): 3.9
Carbohydrate (gm): 7.5

Exchanges:
Milk: 0.0
Vegetable: 0.0
Fruit: 0.0
Bread: 0.5
Meat: 0.0
Fat: 2.0

1. Beat eggs and Equal® for Recipes; mix in lemon juice, margarine, and lemon zest. Pour mixture into baked Rich Pastry. Bake at 350 degrees until filling is set, about 15 minutes. Cool on wire rack.

Rich Pastry

¾ cup all-purpose flour
2½ teaspoons Equal® for Recipes or 8 packets Equal® sweetener
2¼ teaspoons cornstarch
⅛ teaspoon salt
6 tablespoons cold margarine or butter, cut into pieces
¾ teaspoon vanilla
1 teaspoon lemon zest

1. Combine flour, Equal® for Recipes, cornstarch, and salt in medium bowl; cut in margarine until mixture resembles coarse crumbs. Sprinkle with vanilla and lemon zest; mix with hands to form dough. Press dough evenly on bottom and ¼ inch up side of 8-inch square baking pan. Bake at 350 degrees until lightly browned, about 10 minutes. Cool on wire rack.

FUDGY BROWNIES

45

Easy to make whenever you get an urge for a chocolate treat!

1¼ dozen brownies (1 each)

6 tablespoons margarine or butter

4 ounces unsweetened chocolate

⅓ cup each: fat-free milk, apricot spreadable fruit

1 egg yolk

1 teaspoon vanilla

½ cup all-purpose flour

10¾ teaspoons Equal® for Recipes or 36 packets Equal® sweetener

½ teaspoon baking powder

⅛ teaspoon salt

3 egg whites

⅛ teaspoon cream of tartar

½ cup coarsely chopped walnuts or pecans (optional)

Per Serving:
Calories: 120
% of calories from fat: 61
Fat (gm): 8.7
Saturated fat (gm): 3.4
Cholesterol (mg): 14.3
Sodium (mg): 111
Protein (gm): 4.7
Carbohydrate (gm): 7.9

Exchanges:
Milk: 0.0
Vegetable: 0.0
Fruit: 0.0
Bread: 0.5
Meat: 0.0
Fat: 1.5

1. Heat margarine, chocolate, milk, and spreadable fruit in small saucepan, stirring frequently, until chocolate is melted. Remove from heat; stir in egg yolk and vanilla. Mix in combined flour, Equal® for Recipes, baking powder, and salt.

2. Beat egg whites and cream of tartar to stiff, but not dry, peaks in medium bowl; fold chocolate mixture into egg whites. Fold in walnuts, if using. Pour batter into greased 8-inch square baking pan. Bake at 350 degrees until brownies are firm to touch and toothpick comes out clean, 18 to 20 minutes (do not overbake). Cool on wire rack. Serve warm or at room temperature.

ANISE-ALMOND BISCOTTI

Crisp because they're baked twice, biscotti are perfect for dunking into coffee, tea, or Vin Santo, the Italian way!

60 bars (1 each)

4 tablespoons margarine or butter, room temperature

¾ cup sugar

3 eggs

2½ cups all-purpose flour

2 teaspoons crushed anise seeds

1½ teaspoons baking powder

½ teaspoon baking soda

¼ teaspoon salt

⅓ cup (1 ounce) whole blanched almonds

Per Serving:
Calories: 41
% of calories from fat: 26
Fat (gm): 1.2
Saturated fat (gm): 0.2
Cholesterol (mg): 7.1
Sodium (mg): 40
Protein (gm): 1
Carbohydrate (gm): 6.7

Exchanges:
Milk: 0.0
Vegetable: 0.0
Fruit: 0.0
Bread: 0.5
Meat: 0.0
Fat: 0.0

1. Beat margarine, sugar, and eggs until smooth. Mix in combined remaining ingredients, except almonds; mix in almonds. Shape dough on greased cookie sheets into 4 slightly flattened rolls, 1½ inches in diameter. Bake at 350 degrees until lightly browned, about 20 minutes. Cool on wire rack 10 to 15 minutes.

2. Cut rolls into ½-inch slices; arrange slices, cut sides down, on ungreased cookie sheets. Bake at 350 degrees until toasted and almost dry, 7 to 10 minutes on each side. Cool on wire racks.

PUTTING ON THE RITZ BARS

45

Never have these rice cereal treats been quite so glamorous!

2½ dozen bars (1 each)

1 package (10 ounces) marshmallows

4 tablespoons margarine or butter

3 cups rice cereal (Rice Krispies)

½ cup flaked coconut

1 cup each: dried cranberries or raisins, chopped dried mixed fruit

½–¾ cup coarsely chopped walnuts

2 ounces semisweet baking chocolate, melted

1. Heat marshmallows and margarine in large saucepan over low heat until melted, stirring frequently. Stir in remaining ingredients, except chocolate, mixing well. Press into an even layer in greased 15 x 10-inch jelly roll pan; refrigerate 1 hour. Drizzle top with chocolate; refrigerate until set, about 15 minutes. Cut into bars.

Per Serving:
Calories: 108
% of calories from fat: 30
Fat (gm): 3.7
Saturated fat (gm): 1.1
Cholesterol (mg): 0
Sodium (mg): 59
Protein (gm): 1.2
Carbohydrate (gm): 18.7

Exchanges:
Milk: 0.0
Vegetable: 0.0
Fruit: 0.0
Bread: 1.0
Meat: 0.0
Fat: 1.0

LIME MELON COMPOTES

45

A medley of melon, served with delicious Minted Lime Sauce.

6 servings (about 1 cup each)

2 cups each: cubed honeydew, cantaloupe,
    and watermelon
1 teaspoon Equal® for Recipes or 3 packets
    Equal® sweetener
Minted Lime Sauce (recipe follows)
Mint sprigs, as garnish

Per Serving:
Calories: 86
% of calories from fat: 23
Fat (gm): 2.3
Saturated fat (gm): 0.5
Cholesterol (mg): 0
Sodium (mg): 34
Protein (gm): 2.6
Carbohydrate (gm): 15.5

Exchanges:
Milk: 0.0
Vegetable: 0.0
Fruit: 1.0
Bread: 0.0
Meat: 0.0
Fat: 0.5

1. Combine melon in serving bowl; sprinkle with Equal® for Recipes and toss. Serve with Minted Lime Sauce and garnish with mint.

Minted Lime Sauce

Makes 1¼ cups

1 tablespoon cornstarch
1¾ teaspoons Equal® for Recipes or 6 packets Equal® sweetener
1 cup water
3 tablespoons lime juice
1 teaspoon dried mint leaves
1 tablespoon margarine or butter, room temperature

1. Whisk all ingredients, except margarine, in small saucepan; heat over medium-high heat to boiling, whisking until thickened, about 1 minute. Stir in margarine. Cool; refrigerate until chilled.

PEARS BELLE HÉLÈNE

Serve Almond Shortbread (see p. 649) to compliment this elegant offering.

6 servings

2 cups unsweetened apple juice
1¾ teaspoons Equal® for Recipes or 6 packets Equal® sweetener
3 large pears, peeled, cored, cut into halves
3 cups sugar-free, fat-free ice cream
Bittersweet Chocolate Sauce (recipe follows)
Mint sprigs, as garnish

Per Serving:
Calories: 235
% of calories from fat: 11
Fat (gm): 3
Saturated fat (gm): 0.8
Cholesterol (mg): 0.4
Sodium (mg): 85
Protein (gm): 9.7
Carbohydrate (gm): 45.3

Exchanges:
Milk: 0.0
Vegetable: 0.0
Fruit: 1.0
Bread: 2.0
Meat: 0.0
Fat: 0.5

1. Heat apple juice and Equal® for Recipes to simmering in large skillet; add pear halves, cut sides down. Simmer, covered, until pears are tender, 10 to 15 minutes. Remove pears with slotted spoon.

2. Flatten scoops of ice cream in 6 shallow dishes; place pears on top and drizzle with Bittersweet Chocolate Sauce. Garnish with mint.

Bittersweet Chocolate Sauce

Makes about 1 cup

½ cup fat-free milk
½ cup Dutch process cocoa
3½ teaspoons Equal® for Recipes or 12 packets Equal® sweetener
1–2 tablespoons margarine
1½ teaspoons vanilla

1. Whisk milk, cocoa, and Equal® for Recipes in small saucepan; add margarine and vanilla and whisk over medium heat just to simmering. Serve warm, or refrigerate and serve chilled.

VARIATION

Pears Melba — Make recipe as above, omitting Bittersweet Chocolate Sauce. Process 1 pint fresh or thawed frozen raspberries and ⅓ cup sugar in blender or food processor until smooth. Strain, discarding seeds. Serve over pears. Makes about 1 cup.

STEWED RHUBARB AND BERRIES

45 *A great team of flavors—serve with light whipped topping and a sprinkle of toasted chopped pecans.*

6 servings (about ⅔ cup each)

1 pound fresh or frozen rhubarb, sliced (1-inch)
¼ cup water
2 cups sliced strawberries
2½ teaspoons Equal® for Recipes or 8 packets Equal® sweetener

Per Serving:
Calories: 36
% of calories from fat: 7
Fat (gm): 0.3
Saturated fat (gm): 0.1
Cholesterol (mg): 0
Sodium (mg): 4
Protein (gm): 2.3
Carbohydrate (gm): 6.9

Exchanges:
Milk: 0.0
Vegetable: 0.0
Fruit: 0.5
Bread: 0.0
Meat: 0.0
Fat: 0.0

1. Combine rhubarb and water in medium saucepan; cook, covered, over medium heat until soft, about 10 minutes. Stir in strawberries and Equal® for Recipes; cook until hot, 1 to 2 minutes. Serve warm, or refrigerate and serve chilled.

APRICOT BAVARIAN

45

This elegant dessert is party perfect.

4 servings (about ⅔ cup each)

2½ teaspoons Equal® for Recipes or 8 packets Equal® sweetener
1 tablespoon cornstarch
1 envelope unflavored gelatin
1 cup apricot nectar
2 egg yolks
2 teaspoons finely grated lemon zest
2 cups light whipped topping
Light whipped topping, as garnish

1. Mix Equal® for Recipes, cornstarch, and gelatin in small saucepan; whisk in apricot nectar and heat to boiling, whisking until thickened, about 1 minute. Whisk about ½ of the apricot mixture into the egg yolks; whisk egg yolk mixture back into saucepan. Whisk over low heat 1 to 2 minutes. Whisk in lemon zest. Cool to room temperature. Fold 2 cups whipped topping into apricot mixture and spoon into serving bowl or individual dishes. Refrigerate until set, 3 to 4 hours. Garnish with light whipped topping.

Per Serving:
Calories: 168
% of calories from fat: 38
Fat (gm): 6.6
Saturated fat (gm): 4.8
Cholesterol (mg): 106.5
Sodium (mg): 11
Protein (gm): 3.9
Carbohydrate (gm): 20.7

Exchanges:
Milk: 0.0
Vegetable: 0.0
Fruit: 1.5
Bread: 0.0
Meat: 0.0
Fat: 1.0

VARIATION

Orange Bavarian — Make recipe as above, substituting orange juice for the apricot nectar, 1 tablespoon finely grated orange zest for the lemon zest, and adding ½ teaspoon orange extract. Garnish with light whipped topping and orange slices.

OLD-FASHIONED APPLE CRISP

Juicy apples baked with a crisp sweet-spiced topping will warm hearts in any season.

6 servings

3½ teaspoons Equal® for Recipes or 12 packets
   Equal® sweetener
1 tablespoon cornstarch
¾ cup unsweetened apple juice
1 teaspoon finely grated lemon zest
4 cups sliced peeled apples
Crispy Spiced Topping (recipe follows)

Per Serving:
Calories: 198
% of calories from fat: 41
Fat (gm): 9.3
Saturated fat (gm): 2.5
Cholesterol (mg): 0
Sodium (mg): 93
Protein (gm): 4.8
Carbohydrate (gm): 25.7

Exchanges:
Milk: 0.0
Vegetable: 0.0
Fruit: 1.0
Bread: 1.5
Meat: 0.0
Fat: 2.0

1. Combine Equal® for Recipes, cornstarch, apple juice, and lemon zest in medium saucepan; heat over medium-high heat to boiling, whisking until thickened, about 1 minute. Add apples and simmer, uncovered, until apples begin to lose their crispness, about 5 minutes.

2. Transfer mixture to 8-inch square baking pan; sprinkle with Crispy Spiced Topping. Bake at 400 degrees until topping is browned and apples are tender, about 25 minutes. Serve warm.

Crispy Spiced Topping
Makes about ¾ cup

¼ cup all-purpose flour
2½ teaspoons Equal® for Recipes or 8 packets Equal® sweetener
1 teaspoon ground cinnamon
½ teaspoon ground nutmeg
4 tablespoons cold margarine or butter, cut into pieces
¼ cup each: quick-cooking oats, flaked coconut

1. Combine flour, Equal® for Recipes, and spices in small bowl; cut in margarine until mixture resembles coarse crumbs. Stir in oats and coconut.

CINNAMON BREAD PUDDING

For best texture, use day-old firm bread, such as French, Italian, or Vienna. Or, try sourdough bread, which lends a robust flavor.

8 servings

2 cups fat-free milk
4 tablespoons margarine or butter, cut into pieces
2 eggs
3½ teaspoons Equal® for Recipes or 12 packets Equal® sweetener
1½ teaspoons ground cinnamon
⅛ teaspoon ground cloves
3 dashes ground nutmeg
¼ teaspoon salt
6 cups day-old French or Italian bread, cubed (¾-inch)

Per Serving:
Calories: 153
% of calories from fat: 43
Fat (gm): 7.2
Saturated fat (gm): 1.7
Cholesterol (mg): 27.6
Sodium (mg): 308
Protein (gm): 6.8
Carbohydrate (gm): 14.8

Exchanges:
Milk: 0.0
Vegetable: 0.0
Fruit: 0.0
Bread: 1.0
Meat: 0.5
Fat: 1.0

1. Heat milk and margarine to simmering in medium saucepan; remove from heat and stir until margarine is melted. Cool 10 minutes. Beat eggs in large bowl until foamy; mix in Equal® for Recipes, spices, and salt. Mix in milk mixture and bread.

2. Spoon mixture into ungreased 1½-quart casserole. Place casserole in roasting pan on middle oven rack; pour 1 inch hot water into pan. Bake, uncovered, at 350 degrees until pudding is set and sharp knife inserted halfway between center and edge comes out clean, 40 to 45 minutes.

BAKED CUSTARD WITH ORANGE SAUCE

45

This delicate custard is complemented with a sweet orange sauce.

6 servings (about ⅔ cup each)

1 quart fat-free milk

5 eggs, lightly beaten

5 teaspoons Equal® for Recipes or 16 packets Equal® sweetener

2 teaspoons vanilla

Orange Sauce (recipe follows)

Per Serving:
Calories: 174
% of calories from fat: 24
Fat (gm): 4.6
Saturated fat (gm): 1.5
Cholesterol (mg): 179.6
Sodium (mg): 138
Protein (gm): 14.3
Carbohydrate (gm): 17.7

Exchanges:
Milk: 1.0
Vegetable: 0.0
Fruit: 0.0
Bread: 0.5
Meat: 1.0
Fat: 0.0

1. Heat milk just to simmering in medium saucepan. Mix eggs, milk, Equal® for Recipes, and vanilla. Pour mixture through strainer into ungreased 1-quart casserole or soufflé dish.

2. Place casserole in roasting pan on middle oven rack; pour 2 inches hot water into pan. Bake, covered, at 325 degrees until custard is set and sharp knife inserted halfway between center and edge comes out clean, 1 to 1¼ hours. Remove casserole from roasting pan; cool to room temperature on wire rack. Refrigerate until chilled; serve with Orange Sauce.

Orange Sauce

Makes about 1¾ cups

¾ cup orange juice

1 tablespoon cornstarch

1 teaspoon Equal® for Recipes or 3 packets Equal® sweetener

1 cup orange segments

1. Mix orange juice and cornstarch in small saucepan; heat to boiling, whisking until thickened, 2 to 3 minutes. Stir in Equal® for Recipes and orange segments. Cool to room temperature; refrigerate until chilled.

VARIATION

Baked Chocolate Custard — Make recipe as above, increasing Equal® for Recipes to 6¼ teaspoons and adding ⅓ cup Dutch process cocoa to the milk mixture. Serve with dollops of light whipped topping.

SPICED CUSTARD

45

Pumpkin pie spice adds an extraordinary flavor to this smooth custard.

4 servings

2 cups fat-free milk

¼ cup sugar

⅛ teaspoon salt

2 eggs, beaten

½ teaspoon vanilla

2–3 teaspoons pumpkin pie spice

Per Serving:
Calories: 133
% of calories from fat: 19
Fat (gm): 2.8
Saturated fat (gm): 1
Cholesterol (mg): 108.2
Sodium (mg): 168
Protein (gm): 7.4
Carbohydrate (gm): 19.5

Exchanges:
Milk: 0.5
Vegetable: 0.0
Fruit: 0.0
Bread: 1.0
Meat: 0.5
Fat: 0.0

1. Whisk all ingredients until well blended in medium bowl; strain mixture into 1½-quart casserole. Place casserole in roasting pan on middle oven rack; add 1 inch hot water to pan. Bake, covered, at 325 degrees until knife inserted near center of custard comes out clean, about 1 hour. Remove casserole from pan; cool on wire rack. Serve warm, or refrigerate and serve chilled.

INDEX

MORE 1,001 COOKBOOKS FROM SURREY

1,001 Delicious Desserts For People With Diabetes
ISBN 978-1-57284-049-2, $19.95

Fabulous, easy-to-make desserts.

1,001 Delicious Soups & Stews, 2nd Edition
ISBN 978-1-57284-068-3, $19.95

From elegant classics to hearty one-pot meals.

1,001 Low-Fat Recipes, 3rd Edition
ISBN 978-1-57284-048-5, $19.95

1,001 More Low-Fat Recipes
ISBN 978-1-57284-031-7, $19.95

Thousands of low-fat recipes for every occasion.

1,001 Low-Fat Vegetarian Recipes, 4th Edition
ISBN 978-1-57284-083-6, $19.95

Delicious, healthy meals for everyone.

Visit agatepublishing.com for more cookbooks from Surrey.

MORE BOOKS FOR PEOPLE WITH DIABETES FROM SURREY BOOKS

1,001 Delicious Desserts For People With Diabetes
ISBN 978-1-57284-049-2, $19.95

Fabulous, easy-to-make desserts.

Diabetes Double-Quick Cookbook, 2nd Edition
ISBN 978-1-57284-039-3, $14.95

Use your microwave to bring tasty dishes to the table in 15 minutes or less.

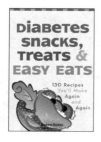

Diabetes Snacks, Treats, & Easy Eats
ISBN 978-1-57284-060-7, $12.95

One hundred and thirty recipes you'll make again and again.

Diabetes Snacks, Treats and Easy Eats for Kids
ISBN 978-1-57284-085-0, $14.95

One hundred and thirty recipes for the foods kids really like to eat.

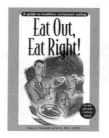

Eat Out, Eat Right! 2nd Edition
ISBN 978-1-57284-052-2, $11.95

A pocket guide to healthier restaurant eating.

METRIC GUIDELINES

With the tables below and a little common sense, you'll have no trouble making these recipes using metric measuring instruments. We have rounded off the liters, milliliters, centimeters and kilos to make conversion as simple as possible.

SOME BENCHMARKS—ALL YOU REALLY NEED TO KNOW

Water boils at 212°F

Water freezes at 32°F

325°F is the oven temperature for roasting

Your 250 mL measure replaces one 8 oz cup

Your 15 mL measure replaces one tablespoon

Your 5 mL measure replaces one teaspoon

a 20 cm x 20 cm baking pan replaces a U.S. 8" x 8"

a 22.5 x 22.5 cm baking pan replaces a U.S. 9" x 9"

a 30 cm x 20 cm baking pan replaces a U.S. 12" x 8"

a 22.5 cm pie pan replaces a 9" pie pan

a 21.25 cm x 11.25 cm loaf pan replaces an 8" x 4" loaf pan

a 1.5 liter casserole, sauce pan or soufflé dish replaces a 1 1/2 qt dish

a 3 liter casserole, sauce pan or soufflé dish replaces a 3 qt dish

5 cm is about 2 inches

1 pound is a little less than 500 gm

2 pounds is a little less than 1 kg

OVEN TEMPERATURES

175°F	80°C	350°F	180°C
200°F	100°C	375°F	190°C
225°F	110°C	400°F	200°C
250°F	120°C	425°F	220°C
275°F	140°C	450°F	240°C
300°F	150°C	500°F	260°C

FAHRENHEIT TO U.K. GAS STOVE MARKS

275°F	mark 1	400°F	mark 6
300°F	mark 2	425°F	mark 7
325°F	mark 3	450°F	mark 8
350°F	mark 4	475°F	mark 9
375°F	mark 5		

VOLUME

1/4 cup	50 mL	4 cups (1 quart)	0.95 L
1/2 cup	125 mL	1.06 quarts	1 L
1/3 cup	75 mL	4 quarts (1 gallon)	3.8 L
3/4 cup	175 mL		
1 cup	250 mL		
1 1/4 cups	300 mL	1 teaspoon	5 mL
1 1/2 cups	375 mL	1/2 teaspoon	2 mL
2 cups	500 mL	1/4 teaspoon	1 mL
2 1/2 cups	625 mL	1 tablespoon	15 mL
3 cups	750 mL	2 tablespoons	25 mL
		3 tablespoons	50 mL

WEIGHT

1 oz	25 gm	1 pound	500 grams
2 oz	50 gm	2 pounds	1 kg
1/4 pound	125 gm (4 oz.)	5 pounds	2 1/2 kg

LENGTH

1/2 inch	1 cm
1 inch	2.5 cm
4 inches	10 cm

This material was prepared with the assistance of the Canadian Home Economics Association and the American Association of Family and Consumer Services